THE WAR CHRONICLES
FROM FLINTLOCKS TO MACHINE GUNS

THE WAR CHRONICLES

FROM FLINTLOCKS TO MACHINE GUNS

A GLOBAL REFERENCE OF ALL THE MAJOR MODERN CONFLICTS

JOSEPH CUMMINS

FAIR WINDS
PRESS
BEVERLY, MASSACHUSETTS

To Dede, who never runs away from a good fight.

Text © 2009 Joseph Cummins

First published in the USA in 2009 by
Fair Winds Press, a member of
Quayside Publishing Group
100 Cummings Center
Suite 406-L
Beverly, MA 01915-6101
www.fairwindspress.com

12 11 10 09   1 2 3 4 5

ISBN-13: 978-1-59233-305-9
ISBN-10: 1-59233-305-2

Library of Congress Cataloging-in-Publication Data
Cummins, Joseph.
  The war chronicles, from flintlocks to machine guns : a global reference of all the major modern conflicts / Joseph Cummins.
      p. cm.
  Includes bibliographical references and index.
  ISBN-13: 978-1-59233-305-9
  ISBN-10: 1-59233-305-2
  1. Military history, Modern—18th century. 2. Military history, Modern—19th century.
  3. Military history, Modern—20th century. I. Title.
  D361.C86 2009
  355.0209'04—dc22
                                                                    2008055937

Cover design: John Barnett
Book design: Megan Cooney

Printed and bound in Singapore

CONTENTS

INTRODUCTION

The War Chronicles: From Flintlocks to Machine Guns, the second volume to *The War Chronicles: From Chariots to Flintlocks*, examines every major war between 1783 and 1988—from the French Revolutionary Wars to the Iran–Iraq conflict. Like the first book, this volume has a twofold intent—to allow readers to grasp the color, flavor, and essence of a war, and also to provide quick-study reference features, such as timelines, profiles of major players, and battle turning points. (Check out the "Guide to *The War Chronicles*" on p. 8 for an illustrated look at how this works.)

After two volumes and hundreds of thousands of words, I have now been schooled in war, as they say, and have thought a lot about whether war has been demonstrably more horrible in the last 200 years or so than it was in the previous 2,000, as covered in the first *War Chronicles*. One can never forget the bloody carnage of Cannae, where 50,000 Roman soldiers died in a single day, or the relentless depredations of the Mongol hordes, which took literally millions of lives in Asia and Central Europe.

But there are a few ways in which the wars of the so-called modern era are indeed more odious. One is the combination of advanced technology with killing. Of course, humankind has always sought better and more efficient ways to destroy itself, else we never would have advanced from the sling to the musket. But beginning roughly in the Crimean War and blossoming bloodily in the U.S. Civil War, the advent of exploding artillery shells, rapid fire rifles, and, eventually, the machine gun, meant that we now had a way of destroying thousands of our population per minute.

The twentieth century, of course, has seen a marriage between science and killing that is not just one of convenience, but a true love match. The awesome beauty of an atomic bomb blast, the bright candy-orange flames of napalm, and the stealthy efficiency of chemical weapons ranging from jungle defoliants to bacterial agents that create Pompeii-like scenes of people frozen instantly into death—well, it takes relish and even a kind of devotion to create such ingenious and destructive engines of war. ("You can't say that civilization don't advance," the American humorist Will Rogers wrote in 1929. "In every war, they kill you in a new way.")

I think this brings us to another reason why the wars of the past few centuries are even more terrible than those that came before. Because, really, aren't we more civilized? Haven't we advanced further into the light of reason, tolerance, and compassion? We no longer accept slavery as a normal human condition. Science has shown us ways to treat the ill, grow abundant amounts of food, and live as we never have before.

"Massacre," as the eminent historian John Keegan wrote, has "effectively been outlawed." Civilized nations are not supposed to take part in the killing of innocents. And yet, we do. Germany under Hitler performed the worst of the massacres in recent years, but all nations—the United States, Vietnam, the former Soviet Union, Israel, Iraq, and Iran—have massacred on one scale or another.

Is every chronicle of war therefore a chronicle of woe? Essentially yes. But there are rationales for war. Certain wars, like World War II, are just. Certain wars, like the U.S. Civil War, World War I, and the Israeli–Arab War of 1948, are inevitable. Wars of national determination—revolutions—are an important part of conflict in the last 200 years. France, Greece, and Mexico fought just and successful revolutions, even so innocents were hurt. And when revolutionaries such as those in China and Russia in the twentieth century turn out to be as ruthless and cruel as the states they supplanted, it is important that they be overthrown as well.

As a last saving grace, certain behavior in war, especially heroism and self-sacrifice, are noble. Florence Nightingale's nursing mission during the Crimean War was noble in the sense that it changed the public's perception of how the wounded were treated. And the actions of Union commander Joshua L. Chamberlain, whose charge stemmed the Confederate tide at Gettysburg during the U.S. Civil War, was an example of the selflessness in the face of grave danger.

Studying the history of war is our best hope for not repeating mistakes of the past, hence this volume of *The War Chronicles*, which is, I hope, both inspiring and cautionary.

—*Joseph Cummins*
OCTOBER 2008

GUIDE TO
THE WAR CHRONICLES

The War Chronicles is structured so that you can approach each war from a variety of angles and examine it at different levels of detail. Throughout, the chapters are illustrated with carefully researched images that expand upon the text and further illuminate the conflict for the modern reader.

ONE-SENTENCE
SUMMARY

QUICK-REFERENCE
PANEL LISTING
COMBATANTS,
THEATER OF WAR,
CASUALTY
NUMBERS, AND
INFLUENTIAL
INDIVIDUALS

PRÉCIS OF THE
WAR THAT
EXPLAINS ITS
HISTORICAL
SIGNIFICANCE

TIMELINE TO HELP
YOU QUICKLY GRASP
THE LENGTH AND
DEVELOPMENT OF
THE WAR—
A USEFUL TOOL FOR
KEEPING TRACK OF
EVENTS WHEN
READING THE
SECTIONS THAT
FOLLOW

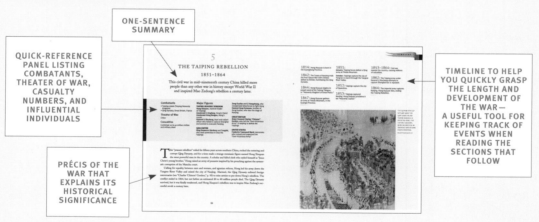

The **Opening Pages** of each chapter provide a handy overview of the war.

The **Chronicle** is the hub of the chapter. It offers a concise, chronological account of the conflict. More importantly, it directs you, through cross-references, to features that cover key aspects of the war in detail.

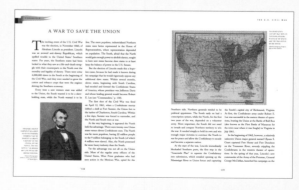

The **Turning Point** is the main feature, and a captivating read. It describes a pivotal battle in gripping detail.

The **Commanders** feature introduces the two most significant military leaders involved in the war. It explains their backgrounds, highlighting aspects of their upbringing, character, and experience that led them to a position of power and shaped their destinies— and, in turn, the world's.

The **Dossier** is a series of quirky articles that examine distinctive and often surprising aspects of the conflict. Common themes here include innovations in weaponry, unconventional combat tactics, and myths and controversies surrounding the war. But the topics range widely, allowing for features on, for instance, the use of aviation balloons in the French Revolutionary Wars, how a quarrel between two elderly British officers changed the course of the Crimean War, and why Saddam Hussein resorted to chemical weapons in his war against Iran.

1

THE FRENCH REVOLUTIONARY WARS

1792–1802

This decade-long conflict reshaped France after the
revolution and set the stage for the titanic European
power struggles of the nineteenth century.

Combatants

- France
- First Coalition (Great Britain, Austria,
  Spain, Prussia, Russia, and Holland)
- Second Coalition (Russia, Great
  Britain, Austria, Portugal, Britain,
  and the Ottoman Empire)

Theater of War

Western Europe, Italy, Spain, the
Mediterranean, Egypt

Casualties

Total military war dead for all European
countries is estimated at 580,000

Major Figures

FRANCE
General Napoleon Bonaparte, the
most brilliant commander of his era
General Charles François Dumouriez,
war minister and savior of the French
Revolutionary Army in 1792
General François Kellerman, victor at
the Battle of Valmy

PRUSSIA
King Frederick William II, ineffectual
monarch who supported the royalist
cause

General Karl Wilhelm Ferdinand,
Duke of Brunswick, losing general
at the Battle of Valmy

RUSSIA
Tsars Paul I and **Alexander I,** who
fought against the French but
capitulated early
General Alexander Suvorov, the most
famous Russian military leader of the
nineteenth century

GREAT BRITAIN
Admiral Horatio Nelson, winner of
the Battle of the Nile

C itizen soldiers dressed in rags but holding their heads up high, marching bravely off to battle a repressive foe bent on destroying their new Republic. This has long been the face that the French Revolutionary Wars has presented to history. But this ten-year-long series of battles that shaped France and Europe in the wake of the bloody French Revolution of 1789 opposes any attempts at easy definition. True, two vast coalitions consisting of every major European power and Russia were arrayed against France during the period of 1792–1802, but many heads of state thought that restoring Louis XVI and his Bourbon princes to power would be a difficult task; indeed, many prominent European thinkers thought that Louis had only brought trouble on himself by refusing to turn to a more enlightened form of monarchy. And it was France itself, seeing domestic political advantage and a chance to grab modern Belgium, that first declared war. With that said, the French Revolutionary Wars pitted a drafted army against the regular troops of old Europe and ending with France's borders being successfully redrawn—thanks in large part to a brilliant young commander named Napoleon Bonaparte.

1789: Revolutionaries seize power in France.

1791: Declaration of Pillnitz threatens France with military action if harm comes to King Louis XVI.

1792:

April: France declares war on Austria, invades the Austrian Netherlands.

June: First Coalition forms.

September: French defeat Prussians at Valmy.

November: French defeat Austrians at Jemappes.

1793:

January: King Louis XVI executed.

August: Committee of Public Safety declares *levée en masse*.

1794:

June: French defeat Austrians at Fleurus, forcing Austria to abandon Belgium.

July: Committee of Public Safety overthrown by the First Directoire.

1795:

April: French conquer the United Provinces (Netherlands), driving out British forces. Prussia makes a separate peace with France at Basel.

August: Spain leaves war.

1796:

March: Napoleon Bonaparte is appointed commander of the army of Italy.

April–November: Napoleon defeats Sardinians and Austrians in major victories in northern Italy (Rivoli, Tagliamento, Arcola) ending in his triumph over the Austrians at Arcola in November.

1797:

October: Austria signs the Treaty of Campo Formio, recognizing French territorial gains.

1798:

July: Bonaparte, at head of the army of the Orient, invades Egypt.

July: French win decisive victory over Mamluks at the Battle of the Pyramids.

August: British Admiral Horatio Nelson destroys the French fleet at Aboukir.

December: Second Coalition is formed.

1799:

January: French occupy Naples.

April–August: Austro-Russian forces recapture Switzerland and northern Italy.

November: Coup in Paris establishes First Consulate.

December: Bonaparte becomes First Consul.

1800:

June: French defeat Austrians at Battle of Marengo.

1801:

February: Austrians make peace with France with Peace of Lunéville.

September: Army of the Orient surrenders to British and Ottoman forces.

1802:

March: Great Britain signs Treaty of Amiens, ending the French Revolutionary Wars.

ARRESTATION DE LOUIS XVI À VARENNES.

LOUIS XVI s'echappa des Thuilleries la nuit du 17 Juin 1791, emmenant la Reine, ses deux Enfans, et sa soeur; Arrivé à Varennes près des frontieres, Le Conducteur de la voiture s'obstina à vouloir changer de chevaux, les signa étant rendus d'avoir couru plusieurs postes, promesses, et menaces, rien ne put l'engager à marcher. D'autres chevaux se trouvant point près à salut, s'arrêter à l'auberge. La consternation avoit attiré des spectateurs on cherche à savoir quels pouvoit être ces Voyageurs qui témoignoient tant d'empressement à continuer leur route, et qui se cachoient si soigneusement aux regards du public; Le Maire vint qui reconnut Le Roi, et lui dit qu'il ne pouvoit le laisser passer, les promesses les plus séduisantes, les prieres, les larmes de la Reine et de sa famille, rien ne put toucher l'inflexible Maire. Le Roi fut arrêté et ramené à Paris le 26.

MANY PROMINENT EUROPEAN THINKERS THOUGHT THAT FRENCH KING LOUIS XVI, SEEN HERE BEING ARRESTED WITH HIS FAMILY ON JUNE 21, 1791, HAD ONLY BROUGHT TROUBLE ON HIMSELF BY REFUSING TO TURN TO A MORE ENLIGHTENED FORM OF MONARCHY.

The Arrest of Louis XVI and his family at Varennes, 21 June, 1791 (gouache on paper), Lesueur Brothers, (18th century) / Musee de la Ville de Paris, Musee Carnavalet, Paris, France, Lauros / Giraudon / The Bridgeman Art Library

WARS OF LIBERTY

In 1789, the history of France changed forever. Burdened with the largest population in Western Europe, a faltering economy, and heavy taxation, the country saw huge masses of unemployed drift toward urban areas, where radicals stirred unrest over the repressive and unresponsive regime of King Louis XVI.

Encouraged by the successful American Revolution, the French revolted, creating a national legislative body. In September 1791, Louis

main, posturing, because almost no one felt that the Bourbon Dynasty could be restored, but in a France divided by food shortages and full of rumors of enemies, it was taken seriously.

French politicians, in the form of the National Convention, the new ruling body of France, also saw this as an opportunity to push France's borders back out to their traditional outlines, which meant heading north into the Austrian Netherlands (modern-day Belgium and Luxembourg) and

In September 1791, Louis was forced to approve a new constitution for France; a year later, the monarchy was abolished.

was forced to approve a new constitution for France; a year later, the monarchy was abolished. In January 1793, Louis XVI was beheaded. (His queen, Marie Antoinette, followed him to the guillotine in October.)

Other European countries, notably Great Britain, Austria, and Prussia, were concerned about developments in France. In August 1791, the Holy Roman Emperor Leopold II (brother of Marie Antoinette) and King Frederick William II of Prussia issued the Declaration of Pillnitz, in which they threatened unspecified consequences should anything happen to Louis XVI and Marie. The Pillnitz Declaration was, in the

west to the Rhine. In April 1792, France declared war on Austria and invaded Belgium. Alarmed, Britain, Austria, Spain, Prussia, Russia, and Holland formed what is known as the First Coalition. The disorganized French troops were easily driven back, and a mainly Prussian invasion force supported by Austrian infantry and French royalist émigrés now headed into France. The situation seemed dire for the new Republic, but the Prussians were stopped near the Belgian village of Valmy in September 1792 (see "Turning Point," p. 14) by a newly-inspired French army.

After the Prussians withdrew, the French embarked on a string of military successes that saw Revolutionary armies push south into Italy, west into Germany as far as Frankfurt, and finally north into Belgium, where the French won a victory over the Austrians at the Battle of Jemappes in November, thus occupying the whole country.

In January 1793, the execution of Louis XVI galvanized much of Europe, and the Coalition attacked with renewed energy. The allies at first pushed back the French on all fronts, regaining almost everything they had lost the previous year, but with mass conscriptions (see "The French Citizen-Soldier," p. 24), the French were able to field a huge, motivated army by the fall of 1793. In 1794, the revolutionaries won key victories, driving the Prussians across the Rhine and winning the Battle of Fleurus (see "The French Revolutionary Air Force," p. 26), which gained them back the Austrian Netherlands.

The French continued on to occupy the Dutch Netherlands, the Rhineland, and parts of Italy (the latter victories due to the successes of the charismatic young leader Napoleon Bonaparte). With Holland conquered, Spain and Prussia sued for peace in 1795. The First Coalition phase of the French Revolutionary Wars then ended in 1797 when Austria signed the Treaty of Campo Formio in October, recognizing France's territorial gains.

However, Great Britain, alone among the Coalition powers, remained in the war, depending particularly on her powerful navy, which kept France blockaded. In part to threaten British interests in India, Napoleon attacked Egypt, destroying Mamluk forces at the Battle of the Pyramids in July 1798. However, the following month the great British admiral Horatio Nelson demolished the French fleet at Aboukir in the Battle of the Nile (see "The Battle of the Nile," p. 29), thus ending Napoleon's hopes of conquering the country.

Inspired by this victory, and as other French forces struck farther south into Italy, capturing the Papal States, the Second Coalition of allied powers was formed, consisting of Russia, Britain, Austria, Portugal, Britain, and the Ottoman Empire. Russian and Austrian forces won pivotal victories in northern Italy early in 1799, but dissension between the Austrians and Russians, and growing unrest in Poland forced Russia to withdraw from the war.

The French under Napoleon (who, in a coup d'état, had become First Consul of France) defeated the Austrians at the Battle of Marengo in June 1800 and reoccupied northern Italy. The Austrians made a separate peace with France in February 1801, in the Treaty of Lunéville.

A combined British and Ottoman force finally defeated the French Army of the Orient in Egypt in September of that year. But, war-weary and fighting almost alone, the British finally signed the Treaty of Amiens in March 1802, thus ending the French Revolutionary Wars. Peace would be short-lived, however, because a newly crowned Emperor Napoleon Bonaparte would soon pit his will and army against all of Europe (see "The Napoleonic Wars," p. 30).

THE BATTLE OF VALMY: SEPTEMBER 20, 1792

A mist hugged the ground, not the light mist of spring and summer, but a thick, low mist of autumn, one that clung to the bushes and trees like lamb's wool. In the night the mist had drifted over the high plain occupied by the French, collecting in the ravines and low places, making visibility impossible. Almost no one in this ragtag Revolutionary army of some 36,000 had been able to sleep; because campfires were not allowed, the soldiers huddled together for warmth and strength.

In the dark distance, they could hear the gathering Prussian army, the hooves of crack cavalry, the thunderous tread of the formidable infantry, and the creaking supply caissons. There were 30,000 Prussians out in the Argonne Forest, in what is now modern-day Belgium, accompanied by a contingent of light Austrian troops and a regiment of Frenchmen who had remained loyal to King Louis XVI and sought to restore him to his throne.

The French soldiers on the ridge near the little village of Valmy knew that the way to Paris, one hundred miles distant, lay open to this formidable Coalition force—that in fact, the Prussians lay between them and their own homes. In the morning, the Prussians intended to crush this threat in their rear, just the way they had crushed the French armies all that fateful summer of 1792.

Then they would march on to Paris and deal, once and for all, with the Revolution.

"The Last War!"

Five months earlier, on April 20, after much debate, the French National Assembly declared war against Austria and, soon after, Prussia. This was partly in response to the Declaration of Pillnitz (see "Chronicle" on p. 12), which threatened the stability of the new French Republic, and partly because many radical French thinkers thought that now was the time to spread the word of the Revolution—and also to regain territory lost in previous wars, particularly the Austrian Netherlands (modern-day Belgium).

"This war will be the last war," declared Foreign Minister Charles François Dumouriez, meaning that after this conflict, Europe would understand the power of Revolutionary France's new way of life. The next month, Dumouriez, appointed general in charge of the French Revolutionary Army, sent troops to invade Belgium.

Dumouriez and other French politicians were soon to discover they had little cause for optimism. The French army had lost more than half of its officers as defectors to the Austrians and Prussians. The *levée en masse* of the next year (see "The French Citizen-Soldier," p. 24) was not yet in place, and so Dumouriez and his generals had to be content with a rabble of volunteers in an army that was also rife with spies for Dumouriez's political enemies back in Paris. It was, to say the least, an impossible army, poorly trained and rife with divisions.

Going up against the well-trained cadres of the Austrians and Prussians, whose skills had been honed in the Seven Years' War, the results were predictable. The first French corps, consisting of about 1,000 soldiers, crossed the frontier into Belgium in June, encountered a far smaller Austrian force at the city of Tournai, and immediately fled in panic, crying "We've been betrayed!" They didn't stop running until they were back in Lille, where they murdered their own general, whom they, in their panic, thought had betrayed them to the Austrians.

Similar scenes were played out elsewhere along France's northern border that summer—10,000 cavalry troops beat a hasty retreat after exchanging a volley with a far inferior Austrian force in France, heading southeast. Nothing lay in his way but three poorly maintained fortresses at Sedan, Longwy, and Verdun, and two small armies. One of these was commanded by a journeyman commander named General François Kellerman; the other had been leaderless since Lafayette fled.

Promenade to Paris

The pickings seemed so easy to the Prussian army that its officers gaily talked about a "promenade to Paris," a walkover of the obviously cowardly rabble who made up the French Revolutionary Army. The Prussian invasion, launched in late July, was seen as such an excursion that sightseers went along with the army, including young German poet Johann Wolfgang von Goethe, who

France was within a hairsbreadth of destruction.

Belgium, while another French division turned tail when a rumor spread through the ranks that their powder was defective. In Paris, the politicians blamed the generals in the field, old-line royalists such as the famous Marquis de Lafayette. In fact, the National Assembly declared him a traitor, and he was forced to flee for his life to Liège, where he was taken prisoner by the Austrians.

Observing all this from along the Rhine, General Karl Wilhelm Ferdinand, Duke of Brunswick and commander of the Prussian Army, saw that rapid disintegration of French forces had opened up a glorious opportunity. With his well-trained army, he could strike right at the heart of was impressed by the discipline of the Prussian regulars, although he confessed himself dismayed by some of the French aristocrats who had joined up to fight against their former fellow citizens and who put on insufferable airs.

At first, the Prussians simply rolled over the French, much as the German panzers would make mincemeat of French defenses in 1940 (see "World War II," p. 316). Fortress Longwy was lost on August 21; Verdun fell September 2.

"Moving majestically forward, with leisurely deliberation," as historian Edward Creasy wrote, the massive Prussian column placed itself between the two French armies and was preparing to destroy each in turn before striking at Paris, when General Dumouriez arrived from Paris to take control of the leaderless forces. Seeing that, as he later wrote, "France was within a hairsbreadth of destruction," he was able to gather the scattered and demoralized troops of Lafayette's former army and make a brilliant stand in the Argonne Forest, that dense swath of Belgium woodland and rocky hills that was also the scene for so much fighting in the Second World War. Forcing the Duke of Brunswick's columns ever farther south, he pushed them directly against the forces of François Kellerman, who were situated on that high plateau near Valmy, waiting in the fog.

Vive la Nation!

The French Revolutionary army, at this stage in the war, was not yet the citizen-soldiery it would become, but almost literally citizens. There were cooks, artists, shoemakers, tanners, farmers, writers, politicians, men from every walk of life. And not just men, either. The Revolution had become known for its women fighters, the most famous being Reine Chapuy, Rose Bouillon, Catherine Pocheta, and the young Fernig sisters (see The Fernig Sisters—"Very Capable of Killing," p. 28). These men and women did not have uniforms, and their weaponry ran from standard issue French muskets to fowling guns, spears, pikes, and swords.

But they had several advantages the advancing Prussians knew little about. To begin with, their subalterns—the army's class of noncommissioned officers—had not fled with the royalist officers and were there to provide backbone for these raw soldiers. True, the army had performed poorly

during the summer, but at Valmy that morning the noncoms moved quietly among the army, steadying the soldiers as the fog lifted and the white uniforms of the Prussians came into view.

Another French advantage was its artillery corps, forty cannon strong. The Duke of Brunswick outgunned the Revolutionary army by some fourteen pieces, but the French cannons were de Gribeauval 12-pounders (see "De Gribeauval and His Fabulous 12-Pounder," p. 25) with accurate sights and the ability to elevate and fire rapidly.

And—the final and decisive French advantage of the day—they were led by General François Kellerman, already fifty-seven years old, who had fought in the Seven Years' War. An object of some suspicion by radical French politicians because of his long association with the royal army, he had thus far escaped the purges that had befallen more prominent officers, mostly because of his journeyman status.

He wasn't considered a brilliant general, simply one who followed orders. That morning, however, he was inspired. Watching the Prussian cavalry move out from the main body of infantry to attempt to envelop his lines, seeing the nervousness among his troops, whom cavalry frightened particularly, he rode his horse through the French lines shouting *"Vive le nation!"* *"Vive la nation"* over and over again. Gradually, the French

THE BATTLE OF VALMY WAS ONE OF THE MOST IMPORTANT CLASHES IN WORLD HISTORY. WITHOUT THE FRENCH VICTORY THERE WOULD HAVE BEEN NO SUCCESSFUL FRENCH REVOLUTION AND NO NAPOLEONIC WARS.

Battle of Valmy, 20th September 1792, 1835 (oil on canvas) (detail of left hand side), Mauzaisse, Jean Baptiste (1784-1844) / Louvre, Paris, France / The Bridgeman Art Library

soldiers took up the chant, so that the cry could be heard by the approaching Prussians.

But of course patriotic cries meant little to the Duke of Brunswick, who simply pushed his artillery to within 1,300 yards of French defenses and opened fire with a deafening roar.

A Kind of Blood-Red Tint

Brunswick and other Coalition officers expected the French to run at the first sound of the guns, to be chased down by the cavalry and slaughtered. After all, these soldiers had not made a stand since the war began. But the unexpected happened: With an answering roar, the French artillery opened up, and the Battle of Valmy was on.

through the shelling with a young man's foolish curiosity, compared the sound of the thousands of shots fired to "the humming of tops, the gurgling of water, and the whistling of birds." As the cannonade continued, Goethe claimed that he began to see the world around him as if through "a kind of blood-red tint"—an observation that might seen fanciful, but that has been repeated by other soldiers caught in intense artillery fire.

Finally, early in the afternoon, Brunswick decided to attack, but his men immediately met a killing field of accurate cannon fire and withdrew. At this point, thinking that the Prussian fire was growing less intense, Kellerman personally led a charge against the enemy. Racing

Valmy has been called one of the strangest great battles in the history of the world. It was essentially a battle fought by cannonade, which went on for hours.

French soldiers rammed home shot after shot, sweating even on the cool day, and watched with cheers as they struck home among the massed Prussian troops. And Prussian cannonballs did their work among the French, although because of the wet ground—which caused the round shot to stick in the mud, rather than bounce murderously through the ranks—there were fewer casualties on both sides than otherwise might have been expected.

Valmy has been called one of the strangest great battles in the history of the world. It was essentially a battle fought by cannonade, which went on for hours. Goethe himself, riding

through the smoke of battle out onto an open part of the plateau, the column he led was devastated by a hidden Prussian battery; Kellerman's horse was shot out from under him, and he had to be carried back to French lines by his own men. When this happened, the Prussians massed for attack, thinking the French were finally going to break, but Kellerman, now on foot, called out to his soldiers that this was the chance they had been waiting for—to let the enemy come close and then give them the bayonet.

More cheers of *"Vive le nation"* rang across the woods, and the advancing Prussians hesitated. They would have to charge up the hill, against a

French army that seemed, for the first time, fearless and invigorated. The Duke of Brunswick paused—one of the most significant pauses in history—and decided slaughtering his fine army simply wasn't worth it.

A New Era

The casualties that day—300 French soldiers, perhaps 200 Prussians and Austrians—were insignificant in the larger scheme of things, but the victory at Valmy could not have been more momentous. That night, the weary French troops, many of whom had not even fired a shot or seen a Prussian up close, realized that the Prussians were no longer on the offensive. Indeed, after waiting ten days, the Duke of Brunswick brought his army back across the Rhine, deciding to fight another day.

There would be many other days and many other battles in the next twenty years of combat between France and the rest of Europe, but the French army proved it could defend the new liberty of its society. The day after the battle, the French Assembly declared France a Republic; four months later, King Louis XVI was executed.

A line can be drawn from the Battle of Valmy all the way to the Battle of Waterloo (see "The Napoleonic Wars," p. 30) because without the victory at Valmy there would have been no French Revolutionary conflict, no Napoleonic Wars.

The importance of some events in history takes a while to set in, but not that of Valmy. The participants knew right away that something crucial had happened. The night of the battle, the French cheered and danced around their campfires, while there was gloom in the Prussian camp. Goethe, finding himself sitting around a campfire with Prussian officers, most of whom stared in sullen silence at the crackling flames, told them: "From this place and from this day forth commences a new era in the world's history, and you can all say that you were present at its birth."

He was right, but it is doubtful the Prussians found much comfort in this.

THE YOUNG NAPOLEON:
A CHILD OF THE REVOLUTION

Although he was later to spell the end of the French Revolution when he assumed the mantle of emperor in 1804, Napoleon Bonaparte personified the egalitarian spirit of the early days of the Republic. Born in 1769 to a poor Corsican family, he did not even speak French until he was nine years old and had arrived at the Royal Military School near Troyes, to be trained as an artillery officer. Short of stature, passionate, given to fits of near-epileptic intensity when he did not get his way, Napoleon was, as one of his teachers would write: "capricious, haughty and frightfully egotistical … [yet] proud, ambitious and aspiring to everything."

Bonaparte was brilliantly talented, but it was the Revolution that made him, because this eccentric Corsican would never have risen in the ranks of the royal French army. But with thousands of officers defecting, he found his chance. Known as a fervid supporter of the Republican cause, he was assigned as a captain of artillery to the siege of the southern port city of Toulon in September 1793. Royalist forces, aided by the Spanish, held the city while the British navy patrolled threateningly offshore. The twenty-four-year-old Napoleon seized the moment, finding the perfect positions to mount his artillery, forcing the British ships to withdraw. He was then wounded with a bayonet in the thigh while leading the assault that liberated the city. Within eight weeks, he was promoted to brigadier general, and his meteoric rise began.

In 1794, Bonaparte served in Italy as chief of staff to the French army there, lost this position after Maximilien de Robespierre and his Committee of Public Safety were purged, but landed on his feet politically again due to connections with those who formed the First Directory. Always having the knack of being in the right place at the right time, Napoleon found himself, in October 1795, in charge of an artillery battery facing a mob of counter-revolutionaries and royalists on the streets of Paris. He gave the order to fire canister point blank into the crowd, killing 1,400 of them.

It was the English writer Thomas Carlyle, not Bonaparte, who coined the famously insouciant line where Napoleon claimed to have given the mob "a whiff of grapeshot." What Napoleon actually wrote to one of his brothers was equally as cool-headed: "The enemy attacked us in the Tuilleries. We killed a great many of them … As usual, I did not receive a scratch. I could not be happier."

Shortly thereafter, Napoleon was given command of the French army in Italy. It was here he engineered the lightning strikes that were to make his reputation. Napoleon believed that an army should always be on the attack and that its only goal was to completely destroy the enemy. Within three weeks, he had swept aside the Piedmontese army, captured Milan and Naples, and turned his attention to Austria.

He won the battle of Rivoli on January 14, 1797; of Tagliamento on March 16; and of Arcola on November 15–17. These were not

NAPOLEON IS SHOWN CROSSING THE ALPS IN JACQUES LOUIS DAVID'S FAMOUS PAINTING, SHORTLY AFTER BEING GIVEN COMMAND OF THE FRENCH ARMY IN ITALY, NAPOLEON ENGINEERED THE LIGHTNING STRIKES THAT WERE TO MAKE HIS REPUTATION.

Napoleon Crossing the Alps (oil on canvas), David, Jacques Louis (1748–1825) / Chateau de Versailles, France, Peter Willi / The Bridgeman Art Library

easy victories—fought over mountainous terrain, against a better-armed and trained enemy—but Napoleon triumphed. Napoleon himself led from the front—at Arcola he famously grabbed a banner and charged at the head of his men across a bridge, saving the day for the French.

Having nearly single-handedly forced the Austrians to the Treaty of Campo Formio, Napoleon returned to Paris in triumph. When he again left France at the head of the Army of the Orient in 1798—set on invading Egypt—the intimations of greatness that were always inside the young Corsican had come to the fore. One observer noted that "all bowed before the glory of his victories and the haughtiness of his demeanor. He was no longer the general of a triumphant Republic, but a conqueror on his own account…."

VICE-ADMIRAL HORATIO NELSON:
THE FLAWED BUT GOLDEN HERO

Horatio Nelson's ability to charm every-one—sailors, women (including other men's wives), and the British public—was legendary, as was his willingness to give body parts (an eye, an arm) to the cause of the British Empire.

He was a man capable of more dramatic lines in extremis than any other hero in history. When he lost his right arm at the battle of Santa Cruz de Tenerife in 1797, he refused help getting back on-board his flagship: "Leave me alone! I've got my legs left and one arm!" When he refused to follow orders and retreat at the battle of Copenhagen in 1801, he pretended it was because of the eye he had lost in combat a few years before: "You know, I have only one eye. I have the right to be blind sometimes!"

And when he lay dying on his ship at the Battle of Trafalgar in 1805, he muttered, over and over: "Thank God I have done my duty!"

Just as the Duke of Wellington was the hero of the latter part of the Napoleonic Wars (see "The Napoleonic Wars," p. 30), Horatio Nelson was the essential Coalition fighter for the French Revolutionary conflicts, the man who did more to set Bonaparte back on his heels than any other. Born in 1758, one of thirteen children of a clergy-man, Nelson had the fortune to be the nephew of Captain Maurice Suckling, who was control-ler of the navy, and who he first accompanied to sea in 1770 as an ordinary seaman. Nelson's was not a promising debut (he suffered miserably from seasickness, which would afflict him for the rest of his life), but, with Uncle Maurice's help, he rose rapidly in the ranks of the Royal Navy, becoming a captain in 1779 at the tender age of twenty. Nelson spent the next ten years in the West Indies, seeking action against the French and Spanish, before returning to England, a mar-ried man whose obligations made him leave the Navy for a few years to seek other employment.

However, as war with France approached in 1793, Nelson was given command of the 64-gun warship, HMS *Agamemnon,* and here his legend truly began. In 1794, he was blinded by stones shot from a cannon while leading an assault against Corsica. The next year he was given an even larger ship, the 74-gun HMS *Captain,* and made commodore, free to roam the Mediterranean fighting against French and Spanish forces. In February 1797, he took part in a brilliant victory against Spanish forces at the Battle of St. Vincent, sending his ships without orders to intercept the Spanish fleet. In July of the same year, he lost his arm assaulting Santa Cruz de Tenerife. By now he had caught the imagination of the British pub-lic and been made a rear admiral and knight.

Nelson was highly individual and eclectic in his tactical thinking. He relied a good deal on trusted subordinate commanders whom he en-dowed with a great deal of authority and who understood that their chief goal was to strike the enemy hard, without waiting for the entire line of British warships to form. Nelson's goal was

LORD ADMIRAL HORATIO NELSON'S ABILITY TO CHARM EVERYONE—SAILORS, WOMEN (INCLUDING OTHER MEN'S WIVES), AND THE BRITISH PUBLIC—WAS LEGENDARY.

Portrait of Nelson (1758–1805) (oil on panel), Healy, George Peter Alexander (1808–94) (after) / Chateau de Versailles, France, Giraudon / The Bridgeman Art Library

to break up and isolate segments of an opposing fleet, concentrate fire upon them, and destroy them, which is how he won the Battle of the Nile in 1799 (see "The Battle of the Nile," p. 29). After this famous victory, Nelson, stationed in Naples, became involved in a scandalous affair with Emma Hamilton, wife of British ambassador Sir William Hamilton, and was recalled to England in 1800. Astonishingly enough, back at home, Nelson left his wife and cohabited with both William and Emma, even having a child (nicely named Horatia) with the latter.

The British admiralty could no longer stand such carryings-on and sent Nelson back to sea in 1801, where he won his pivotal victory over the Danes by claiming he couldn't see a thing. And on October 21, 1805, an outnumbered British fleet led by Nelson engaged the Spanish and French fleets off Cape Trafalgar, Spain, and won a stunning victory. It was here, aboard his flagship *Victory,* that Nelson was struck by a French sniper's bullet and died, murmuring his famous last words. The English had lost a commander, but gained a hero for the ages.

The French Citizen-Soldier: *Levée En Masse*

"From this moment on until such time as all enemies have been driven from the soil of the Republic, all Frenchmen are in permanent requisition for the services of the armies. The young men shall fight; the married men shall forge arms and transport provisions; the women shall make tents and clothes and serve in the hospitals; the children shall turn linen into lint; the old men shall take to the squares in order to rouse the courage of the warriors..."

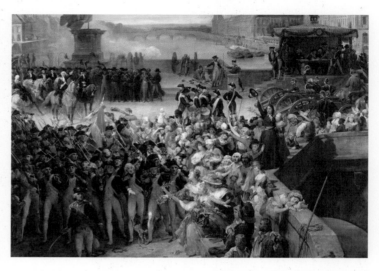

This passionate declaration, issued by the Committee of Public Safety on August 23, 1793, constituted one of the most important moments of the French Revolutionary Wars. For the first time, as the military philosopher Clausewitz later put it, there was "participation of the people in this great affair of state."

At the beginning of the Revolutionary Wars, more than half the army's officers, loyal to the king, had defected to the enemy, and the trustworthiness of those left behind was suspect. The army itself was ill-disciplined and poorly supplied. But, declaring that "the fatherland was in danger," the Committee conscripted all males between eighteen and twenty-five in what was called a *levée en masse;* appropriated as well were all material resources.

From every corner of France came not only willing men and women, but weapons, clothes, food, ammunition, and livestock. A year later, the French army had swollen to some 750,000 people, soldiers who were fairly well armed and trained. While it can't be said that such conscription was universally popular, the French achieved a great deal of success with their levy for a number of reasons. The typical draftee can be likened to a motivated volunteer fighter of the American Revolution at the time, often supplying his own arms and animals, leaving behind a family that supported him, and bringing with him men from his neighborhood or village. The very size of the levée overwhelmed the armies of the First Coalition, who had previously been on the verge of victory (see "Chronicle," p. 12).

These raw recruits were trained under the auspices of Lazare Carnot, who had been a captain of engineers, but now became a kind of human resources manager for the French, whipping this huge mass of soldiers into shape, using the small corps of young and aggressive noncommissioned officers, and officers who arose from the ranks. It was a glorious time for any French fighter with intelligence, drive, and bravery, who was willing, as Carnot urged, "to give battle on a large scale and pursue the enemy until he is destroyed." One such upstart from the ranks, a captain named Napoleon, was to shape this levée en masse into the most formidable fighting force of its era.

DECLARING THAT "THE FATHERLAND WAS IN DANGER," THE COMMITTEE OF PUBLIC SAFETY CONSCRIPTED ALL MALES BETWEEN EIGHTEEN AND TWENTY-FIVE IN WHAT WAS CALLED A *LEVÉE EN MASSE.* A YEAR LATER, THE FRENCH ARMY HAD SWOLLEN TO SOME 750,000.

The Garde Nationale de Paris Leaves to Join the Army in September 1792, c.1833–36 (oil on canvas) (detail of 34104), Cogniet, Leon (1794–1880) / Chateau de Versailles, France, Giraudon / The Bridgeman Art Library

The Coalition Soldier

The armies arrayed against the French citizen-soldiers were filled with better-trained and armed soldiers who more than held their own, but who lacked the revolutionary fervor and inspired leadership that was the hallmark of the French army.

Coalition armies entering the field were colorful affairs. The English wore scarlet, the Prussians white, the Austrians dark blue, and the Russians green. (The French started out the war in uniforms of all types, but they soon settled on blue coats with red edging and white lapels, although lack of supply often turned these uniforms into rags). The varying colors had a purpose on European battlefields: Soldiers could distinguish their fellows from the enemy in the swirling smoke that shrouded all eighteenth- and nineteenth-century conflicts. Unlike the French citizen-soldiers, most Coalition soldiers wore their hair in powdered pig-tails known as queues, which were usually greased down with candle wax.

These infantrymen were weighed down by carrying as much as seventy pounds worth of equipment, which included knapsacks stuffed with food and personal items, a smooth-bore musket and bayonet, a cartridge box with at least sixty rounds in it, and a thick, heavy blanket that was often worn rolled over the front of the chest, to protect against saber blows from cavalry. And, if the soldier had a useful vocation in civilian life (such as a cobbler or a smith), he might carry the tools of his trade along with him as well, to make repairs for his squad or company.

It was not until the Napoleonic Wars (see "The Napoleonic Wars," p. 30) that Coalition armies were led in any inspired way, but they had a reputation for toughness, particularly the Prussians and Austrians. Historians have written that French Revolutionary armies did indeed win out over the better-armed Coalition troops if they outnumbered them; but if numbers were even, or if Coalition troops had a slight edge, they were often able to beat back the French through better fire discipline and the ability to take more punishment without breaking.

De Gribeauval and His Fabulous Twelve-Pounder

Jean-Baptiste Vaquette de Gribeauval, born in 1715, was to die in 1789, before the Revolutionary Wars even began, but the artillery innovations he pioneered were crucial to the achievements of the French Revolutionary army.

De Gribeauval—tall, languid, and sophisticated—came from a well-to-do family in Amiens who, fittingly enough, had him christened on December 4, the feast day of Saint Barbara, the patron saint of artillerymen. He entered the French artillery in 1732 and for the next thirty years, during the War of the Austrian Succession and the Seven Years' War, steeped himself in artillery lore of the eighteenth century, stealing ideas from both the Austrians and the Prussians. Becoming Inspector-General of the French artillery in 1776, he began to turn the heavy artillery guns of the past into more mobile and more accurate firepieces.

Mobility came by replacing the old iron gun axles with hardwood ones and harnessing the horses in pairs rather than in single file, giving them more pulling power. De Gribeauval introduced an elevated screw mechanism (which increased rapidity of fire, because guns did not have to be re-elevated after each shot) and a "tangent sight" on the rear, which had a graduated brass measure so that gunners could aim for their targets with more precision.

De Gribeauval also made sure that his cannon were manufactured with interchangeable parts and that gun carriages were built to a standard model, so that mass production was possible. He insisted that the French Army have cannon of all types—four-pounders, eight-pounders, and twelve-pounders (based on the weight of the ball).

Napoleon's preference was famously for the heaviest caliber. A twelve-pound De Gribeauval cannon

(continued on p. 26)

25

weighed 1,200 pounds, had two notched positions for the barrel itself (the forward one for firing, the rear one, which balanced the gun better, for traveling). It was Napoleon's genius to use these relatively lightweight but powerful cannon, (which he referred to lovingly as his "daughters") as assault weapons, bringing them close to the front lines (as opposed to massing them in the rear) and using them to devastate an enemy at close range, following up quickly with an infantry charge.

The French Revolutionary Air Force

The Battle of Fleurus, fought deep in the Argonne Forest, on June 26, 1794, proved to be a pivotal French victory over the Austrians, but few people know that it also featured that first military use of an observation balloon.

The Committee of Public Safety funded a secret advisory panel to advise it on whether a hydrogen balloon could be used as a vehicle for military recon and observation. Two scientists headed this panel; they were given a special section of the Paris suburbs in which they could develop their balloon in secret. The result was *L'Entrepremant* ("the enterprising one"), a balloon designed to be tethered to the ground by strong cables, so that it was protected from buffeting winds. It was to be manned by two people, one of whom would spy on the enemy with a telescope from inside the balloon as the balloon rose to heights of 2,000 to 3,000 feet (610 to 915 m). The other man would send and receive notes from the ground (attached to cables) or semaphore flag signals to nearby troops. Special varnish applied to the balloon kept hydrogen from slowly leaking out, thus enabling it to stay in the air for a longer period of time.

A test of the *L'Entrepremant* in March 1794 found that one man with a telescope could make out details from eighteen miles (29 km) away. The Committee of Public Safety was impressed and immediately called for the creation of the world's first air force, which was named the *Compagnie d'Areonautiers*. That spring, *L'Entrepremant* was taken north with the French army to fight the Austrians in what is now Belgium; the balloon was inflated as the Austrian forces neared Fleurus. French General Georges Morlot stayed aloft in the balloon for more than ten hours, sending back reports on Austrian troop movements that essentially won the battle for the French, because the Austrians had split into five different columns to attack.

The Austrians complained that the balloon was unfair and tried to shoot it out of the sky (the French merely let the cables up until the *L'Entrepremant* was out of reach), but the French built three more balloons and used them extensively during the wars.

THE BATTLE OF FLEURUS FEATURED THE FIRST MILITARY USE OF AN OBSERVATION BALLOON THE FRENCH CALLED L'ENTREPREMANT ("THE ENTERPRISING ONE"). THE BALLOON WAS TETHERED TO THE GROUND BY STRONG CABLES AND MANNED BY TWO PEOPLE, ONE OF WHOM WOULD SPY ON THE ENEMY WITH A TELESCOPE. THE OTHER WOULD SEND AND RECEIVE NOTES FROM THE GROUND (ATTACHED TO CABLES) AND SEND FLAG SIGNALS TO NEARBY TROOPS.

Landauer Collection, Prints & Photographs Division, Library of Congress, LC-USZ62-65649

General Alexander Suvorov: "The Bayonet's a Fine Chap!"

Born in 1729, Russian general Alexander Suvorov is a soldier long overlooked in the West.

Raised in a noble family in Moscow, Suvorov served in the Seven Years' War and the Russo-Turkish War of 1768–1774. It was here, in his first incarnation as a general officer, that he began his extraordinary streak of battle victories; he remains one of the only undefeated generals in history. After destroying the Turks, he returned to Moscow to write his seminal book, *The Science of Victory,* which is known for its pithy, yet truthful, aphorisms: "Large staffs, small victories." "Attack with what comes up, with what God sends." "The bullet's an idiot, the bayonet's a fine chap."

Underlying these maxims was Suvorov's hard-hitting philosophy: train hard, move fast, travel light, attack quickly, and do your killing up close. Suvorov was named a field marshal by Empress Catherine after he put down a Polish revolt in 1794, but when she died in 1796, he fell out of favor with the new ruler, Tsar Paul I, and was forcibly retired.

However, Suvorov was far too valuable to leave on the shelf for long and, in 1799, was sent to fight in Italy as Russia joined the Second Coalition against France. There he won a stunning series of victories, driving almost every French soldier from Italy. Unfortunately, other Russian commanders lost, leaving the field marshal in a precarious position. He was forced to make an extraordinary retreat from

Italy over the Alps, with a hungry and desperate army, a successful strategic feat that has been compared with Hannibal's crossing.

Worn out from his labors, Suvorov died in Saint Petersburg the following year. He is still revered in Russia, so much so that there lingers a legend that this brave, brilliant, and compassionate man never really died but, King Arthur–like, rises up to inspire Russian soldiers in trouble.

RUSSIAN GENERAL ALEXANDER VASILIEVICH SUVOROV REMAINS ONE OF THE ONLY UNDEFEATED GENERALS IN HISTORY. HIS HARD-HITTING PHILOSOPHY WAS TO TRAIN HARD, MOVE FAST, TRAVEL LIGHT, ATTACK QUICKLY, AND KILL UP CLOSE.

Portrait of Field Marshal Generalissimo, Count Aleksandr Vasilievich Suvorov (1729–1800), 1786 (oil on canvas), Levitsky, Dmitri Grigor'evich (1735–1822) / Museum of Tropinin and His Contemporaries, Moscow, Russia / The Bridgeman Art Library

The Fernig Sisters—"Very Capable of Killing"

The French Revolution destroyed the monarchy that had ruled France for centuries, and it loosened people's ideas about the role of women in war. Just as numerous women took part in the violence of the Revolution and its aftermath (Maximilien de Robespierre had a bodyguard made up entirely of women, in part to protect him from another woman, a royalist, who was trying to assassinate him), there were brave women fighters in the French army.

Chief among these were the Fernig sisters—Félicité, twenty-two, and Théophile, seventeen. Born in Flanders, they had been raised outdoors by their huntsman father and were sharpshooters and excellent archers. When the Revolutionary Wars broke out, they fought with local militia against the Austrians, blackening their faces, wearing men's clothing, and using their knowledge of the countryside to set up night ambushes. Their exploits became known, and they were introduced to General Charles François Dumouriez, who was so impressed by Fernig sisters that he gave them horses and uniforms. The sisters fought at Valmy and Jemappes; at the latter battle, Félicité killed two Austrians who were about to bayonet a young Belgian officer to death. Both women, as a French review board later wrote, "were very capable of killing their men."

When Dumouriez ran afoul of the radical French government and defected in 1794, the loyal Fernig sisters defected with him. Although

a monument now stands to them at the site of the battle of Jemappes, the French revolutionary government at the time never forgave them, and they remained outcasts for the rest of their lives.

FRENCH HEROINES FÉLICITÉ AND THÉOPHILE FERNIG, PICTURED ABOVE, WERE ONLY A COUPLE OF THE WOMEN WHO FOUGHT WITH THE FRENCH ARMY AGAINST AUSTRIA.

The French Heroines, Félicité and Théophile de Fernig in 1792, from 'Le Petit Journal', 27th August 1894 (coloured engraving), Lix, Frédéric (1830–97) / Private Collection, Archives Charmet / The Bridgeman Art Library

The Battle of the Nile: A Rain of Body Parts

In the middle of the nighttime sea battle, there was an explosion the likes of which no sailor or soldier present had ever seen or heard. The French flagship, *L'Orient,* had disintegrated with a clap of thunder after fires set by British shells had reached its powder magazine. The concussion was so tremendous that the riggings of nearby ships shook, and many sailors thought their own vessels had exploded. (The sound could be heard miles away in Cairo.)

In the wake of the huge blast, one British observer wrote, "An awful pause and a deathlike silence for about three minutes ensued." Then the fleets of both countries were showered with body parts—legs, arms, and heads—a ghastly and bloody rain that drove some sailors crazy.

It was August 1, 1798, and the hopes of Napoleon Bonaparte in Egypt had exploded with the *L'Orient.* In May 1798, Napoleon had sailed from Toulon with a 35,000-man-strong army, intending to conquer Egypt. The French hoped that by doing so they would threaten British interests in India and set up a French base in the eastern Mediterranean. A quick victory over the Egyptian Mamluk forces by Napoleon at the Battle of the Pyramids, just three miles from Cairo, made it seem like this strategy was working, and the French entered Cairo in triumph on July 22.

But the French had bargained without Rear Admiral Horatio Nelson (see "Commanders," p. 22). The French had dodged the patrolling British Royal Navy on their way into Egypt, but Nelson, at the head of fourteen ships of the line, had discovered the thirteen-ship French fleet (led by Vice Admiral François-Paul Brueys d'Aigalliers) anchored in Aboukir Bay, east of Alexandria, off the coast of Egypt. Although the British had the slight advantage in ships, the French had the shoals near the shore to their backs and were supported by shore batteries, although these were not properly situated. And Brueys was not prepared for battle. The decks of his flagship, *L'Orient,* were covered with paint containers, because the ship was getting an overhaul, and he did not take the threat of British attack seriously enough.

The British ships made a daring evening attack, some of them even getting between the French fleet and the shore. In the end, the French fleet of thirteen had been reduced to only two ships, with perhaps 9,000 men killed, including Brueys. The British lost no ships at all. In a single night, Nelson had reclaimed the Mediterranean for the British; this stupendous victory also gave heart to the allies and contributed to the forming of the Second Coalition.

Although Napoleon continued on with his Egyptian campaign, he had no way now to resupply his army, and he eventually abandoned his soldiers and returned to France, where he helped organize the coup that made him First Consul. What was left of his army surrendered to the British and Turks in 1801.

DURING THE BATTLE OF THE NILE ON AUGUST 1, 1798, THE BRITISH, LED BY ADMIRAL HORATIO NELSON, DECIMATED THE FRENCH FLEET OF THIRTEEN, REDUCING IT TO TWO SHIPS AND KILLING AROUND 9,000 MEN, INCLUDING FRENCH VICE-ADMIRAL FRANÇOIS-PAUL BRUEYS D'AIGALLIERS.

The Battle of the Nile, 1st August 1798, engraved by Bailey for J. Jenkins's 'Naval Achievements', 1816 (colour engraving), Whitcombe, Thomas (c.1752–1824) (after) / Private Collection, The Stapleton Collection / The Bridgeman Art Library

2

THE NAPOLEONIC WARS

1803–1815

After barely a pause, Europe plunges back into war,
with France's revolutionary ideals now subsumed by
Napoleon Bonaparte's conquering ambitions.

Combatants

- France, French-occupied Spain, Italy, and small German states
- Third Coalition: Austria, Russia, Portugal, Sweden, and Britain
- Fourth Coalition: Prussia, Russia, Saxony, Sweden, and Britain
- Fifth Coalition: Britain and Austria
- Sixth Coalition: Prussia, Sweden, Austria, Britain, and small German states
- Seventh Coalition: Britain, Russia, Prussia, Sweden, Austria, and the Netherlands

Theater of War

Europe, Russia, Spain, the Atlantic, the West Indies

Casualties

Total military war dead for Europe is estimated at 2,500,000

Major Figures

FRANCE
Emperor Napoleon Bonaparte, now all-powerful ruler of France
Joseph Bonaparte, Napoleon's brother and king of Naples and Spain
Jérôme Bonaparte, Napoleon's brother and king of Westphalia

ITALY
Marshall Michel Ney, capable general who failed to aid Napoleon at the Battle of Waterloo
Marshall Louis-Nicolas Davout, Napoleon's minister of war
Marshall André Masséna, commander of French forces in Portugal

PRUSSIA
Field Marshall Gebhard von Blücher, co-victor of the Battle of Waterloo

AUSTRIA
Charles, Archduke of Austria, defeated Napoleon at the battles of Aspern-Essling and Wagram

RUSSIA
Tsar Alexander I, who was determined to resist Napoleon's invasion of his country
General Peter Bagration, able leader who fought Napoleon in Russia
General Mikhail Barclay de Tolly, who dodged Napoleon's advance into Russia

GREAT BRITAIN
Admiral Horatio Nelson, winner of the Battle of Trafalgar
Field Marshall Sir Arthur Wellesley, Duke of Wellington and winner of the Battle of Waterloo

In 1804, France voted by an overwhelming margin to make Napoleon Bonaparte emperor. Napoleon's personal ambition to conquer Europe was now overweening; thus the French Revolutionary Wars, which had barely paused after the Treaty of Amiens, now became the Napoleonic Wars. No longer were shifting coalitions of European powers struggling to contain the ambitions of a new French republic; they were fighting to stop a military genius who wanted to make France the pre-eminent country on the Continent. Before Napoleon met his Waterloo in 1815, he very nearly succeeded. By 1810, he controlled almost all of Western Europe, as well as Italy and large portions of Germany. Although in the end Napoleon lost everything, the twelve years of Napoleonic Wars reshaped Europe and caused nationalist movements to arise and change the way wars were fought.

1803:

May: War resumes between France and Great Britain.

June: In West Indies, Britain captures St. Lucia, Tobago, and Dutch Guyana.

1804:

December: Napoleon crowned emperor of France; Spain declares war on Britain after Britain attacks its shipping.

1805:

April: Britain, Russia, and Austria form the Third Coalition.

May: Napoleon crowns himself king of Italy.

October: Nelson dies winning Battle of Trafalgar; French defeat Austrians at the Battle of Ulm.

December: Napoleon defeats Austrian–Russian forces at the Battle of Austerlitz; in Treaty of Pressburg, Austria cedes territory to France.

1806:

April: Joseph Bonaparte becomes king of Naples; Britain begins its naval blockade of France.

October: Prussia, Russia, Saxony, Sweden, and Britain form the Fourth Coalition. Napoleon decimates the Prussian army at the Battle of Jena.

November: Napoleon creates "Continental System," which forbids the import of British goods to Europe.

1807:

June: Napoleon defeats Russia at the Battle of Friedland.

July: Russia and France sign the Treaty of Tilsit, ending Fourth Coalition.

November: France invades Portugal, which refuses to be part of the Continental System.

1808:

May: Napoleon invades Spain and places his brother Joseph on the throne.

August: The Peninsular War begins as the Duke of Wellington lands troops in Portugal.

1809:

April: Britain and Austria form the Fifth Coalition.

April: Napoleon defeats Austrians in Bavaria in a series of battles.

May: Austrians under Archduke Charles fight Napoleon to a draw at the Battle of Aspern-Essling.

July: Napoleon defeats Austrians under Archduke Charles at the Battle of Wagram.

October: The Treaty of Schönbrunn between France and Austria ends the fighting.

1812:

June: Prussia, Sweden, Austria, and Britain form the Sixth Coalition.

September: Napoleon enters Moscow.

October: Napoleon evacuates Moscow.

December: Napoleon abandons army, and the last elements of France leave Russia.

1813:

March: Russians enter Berlin; Prussia declares war on France.

May: Napoleon defeats combined Russian–Prussian forces at the Battle of Grossgorschen; Wellington advances through Spain.

June: The French evacuate Madrid.

October: Napoleon is defeated at the Battle of Leipzig (otherwise known as the Battle of the Nations); Wellington crosses the Pyrenees and enters France.

1814:

March: The allies enter Paris.

April: Napoleon abdicates and is exiled to Elba, Italy.

1815:

February: Napoleon escapes from Elba.

March: Napoleon enters Paris; Britain, Russia, Prussia, Sweden, Austria, and the Netherlands form the Seventh Coalition.

June: Allied forces defeat Napoleon at Waterloo; Napoleon abdicates and is exiled to the island of St. Helena in the South Atlantic.

NAPOLEON TAKES ON EUROPE

After Napoleon Bonaparte was named First Consul of France and then emperor in 1804, what had been the French Revolutionary Wars evolved into a contest pitting Napoleon's own personal drive to conquer Europe against Europe's attempts to stop him.

Following the Treaty of Amiens (1802), the French continued to seize territory, including parts of Piedmont, Italy; Switzerland; and the Netherlands, angering the British, who in turn refused to turn over Malta as mandated by the treaty and instead declared war in 1803. Napoleon's plan to invade England (see "The Invasion that

relatives as puppet kings in Spain, Italy, and the Netherlands; and defeated Coalition army after Coalition army. In 1808, he took a French army to Spain and forced the evacuation of the British army without even having to fight a major battle. The following year, however, he suffered his first defeat of the war, at the hands of the Austrians at Aspern-Essling. He won the next battle (at Wagram, in July) but only at the near-Pyrrhic cost of 34,000 French casualties.

Despite mass conscription—France had a population of 27 million at the time, compared to 11 million for the British, making it easier to

Although Napoleon owned all of Western Europe by 1810, he foolishly decided to invade Russia in 1812.

Never Was," p. 49) foundered because of the might of the British Royal Navy. France's fleet was mainly destroyed by Admiral Horatio Nelson at the Battle of Trafalgar, off Spain, in 1805. But Europe belonged to Napoleon's superb Grand Army (see "The French Soldier," p. 44). Napoleon executed a series of stunning victories, defeating Austrian armies at Ulm, Austerlitz (see "The 'Sun of Austerlitz,'" p. 47), and Jena after the first of what would be five Napoleonic War Coalitions was formed against him.

As the British navy blockaded France and seized French territory in the West Indies, Napoleon invaded Spain and Portugal; set up

recruit—Napoleon's Grand Army was gradually running out of men to replenish its ranks. Although Napoleon owned all of Western Europe by 1810, he foolishly decided to invade Russia in 1812, with famously disastrous results (see "Turning Point," p. 34).

By December of that year Napoleon, faced with unrest at home, was forced to abandon his army, which suffered perhaps 400,000 casualties in the campaign. Despite the fact that he was able to raise a large army to fight the following year, his aura of invincibility was shattered and newly confident Coalition forces closed in for the kill: General Arthur Wellesley, Lord Wellington (see

"Commanders," p. 43) won stunning victories in Portugal and Spain and entered France, while Napoleon lost the largest battle of the war at Leipzig in October 1813.

A defeated Napoleon abdicated in April 1814 and was sent into exile on the island of Elba, Italy, but, resentful of his enforced captivity, escaped in early 1815, raised an army, and marched on Paris, where he forced the newly installed King Louis XVIII to flee. The Seventh, and last, Coalition of the Napoleonic Wars was formed, and the Duke of Wellington, with a little aid from Marshall Blücher and the Prussians, destroyed Europe's nemesis once and for all at the Battle of Waterloo. Napoleon was forced once again into exile—this time to the far-flung South Atlantic island of St. Helena—where he died in 1822.

The effect of the Napoleonic Wars was widespread. A reactionary climate ensued, with the Bourbon Dynasty placed back on the throne of France, although, ironically, Napoleon's carefully scripted appeals to the nationalism of the French people had their effect on the countries that had been enemies of the French. Independence movements began in Russia, Germany, and elsewhere, including South America (after the collapse of Spain as an empire) and Greece (see "Greek War of Independence," p. 50). These nationalist movements ultimately succeeded and altered the balance of power in Europe, and the world, by the twentieth century.

PRUD'HON'S LAST PORTRAIT OF NAPOLEON IN 1810 CAPTURES A MAN AT THE HEIGHT OF HIS POWER. IN 1810 NAPOLEON HAD CONTROL OF NEARLY ALL WESTERN EUROPE, INCLUDING ITALY AND MUCH OF GERMANY.

THE INVASION OF RUSSIA: 1812

For a year or so, beginning in 1810, those around the Emperor Napoleon had found him possessed of an unnatural lassitude. The dramatic, contradictory, impossible-to-predict little man who shook his fists and threatened and yelled when things did not go his way had been replaced by a relatively easygoing and now rather overweight new father of a young son by his marriage to Marie-Louise, Archduchess of Austria, the woman he had divorced his first wife, Josephine, to marry. Napoleon doted on his son. Upon his birth, he picked the boy up and "in a fever of joy" presented him to his courtiers, proclaiming, "Now begins the finest period of my reign."

By late 1811, though, people were beginning to wonder. Napoleon had not gone back to Spain to take command, despite the fact that the bloody war there (see *"Guerra de Guerrillas,"* p. 45) had turned against the French. Was the great Napoleon tired of war and—some dared to hope—ready to see peace in Europe?

These were fond hopes indeed. Napoleon, always moody, had merely been tired of the protracted Spanish war and was waiting for a new world to conquer. And he found one. In 1812, Napoleon shook off his ennui and became as energized as anyone had ever seen him—traveling to inspect French fortifications, giving orders for new corps to be formed, and demanding that

EXPECTING TO REVEL IN THE RUSSIAN DEFEAT, NAPOLEON ENTERED MOSCOW, ONLY TO FIND THAT THE CITY WAS COMPLETELY VOID OF LIFE.

large munitions dumps be built in Poland and Germany. For those who knew Napoleon well, this manic phase meant he was going to war, a war that could only be with Russia.

"How Do You Expect to Be Able to Stop Me?"

Russia under Tsar Alexander I had been a reluctant ally of Napoleon's ever since the two countries had made peace five years earlier at Tilsit in 1807 following Napoleon's victory over a major Russian army at the Battle of Friedland in June of that year. But friendship with Napoleon was well-nigh impossible for Alexander. Napoleon's Continental System, which refused to allow barter with Great Britain, hurt Russia's trade badly. In the meantime, French encroachment in Poland, eastern Germany, and the Balkans threatened Russia's security.

In 1811, Tsar Alexander refused to comply with the Continental System and began making peace overtures to other neighbors, such as Sweden and the Ottoman Empire. When Napoleon realized this, he knew that war would surely follow. And, typically, he decided to strike first. The manic phase that many of his advisors saw in 1812 was a Napoleon in the almost-ecstatic grip of preparing for the largest invasion the world had ever known since the Mongol hordes traveled the other way in the fourteenth century. Napoleon had assembled 190,000 horses, wagons that could carry 7,000 tons of supplies daily, and an immense force of 614,000 men, compared to perhaps 220,000 Russian soldiers. He told his subordinates, "The aim of all my moves will be to concentrate an army of 400,000 men at a single point," break through Russian defenses, capture Moscow, and force Alexander in Saint Petersburg to sue for peace.

On June 24, 1812, Napoleon, at the head of a personal command group of 225,000 French soldiers, crossed the River Nieman and headed into Russian Poland. When Alexander I heard of this, he wrote a dispatch to Napoleon that began: "*Monsieur mon frère,* I learned yesterday that, in spite of the loyalty I have demonstrated in maintaining my engagements with Your Majesty, [your] troops have crossed the Russian border."

Alexander went on to beg Napoleon to reconsider his invasion. To which Napoleon replied: "I have undertaken great preparations, and my forces are three times greater than yours … How do you expect to be able to stop me?"

THIS EARLY NINE-TEENTH-CENTURY ENGRAVING DEPICTS TSAR ALEXANDER I, A RELUCTANT ALLY OF NAPOLEON'S. WHEN NAPOLEON'S CONTINENTAL SYSTEM PROVED DESTRUCTIVE TO RUSSIA'S ALREADY SUFFERING ECONOMY, ALEXANDER QUICKLY BEGAN RESHAPING CONNECTIONS WITH NEARBY COUNTRIES.

Dead Horses

The answer to that question was almost immediately clear as Napoleon advanced into the vast
plains of Russia. The Russian army did not try
to stop him, but in fact retreated before him—
as it had done against the Swedes in the Great
Northern War, as it would do 140 years later
against the Germans in World War II. Although
Napoleon should have foreseen this, he did not,
and he found himself robbed of the quick battle
and victory he desired.

The farther into Russia Napoleon went, the
farther the Russians retreated from the prongs
of his mighty army groups, and gradually weari-
ness and hunger began to tell on Napoleon's men.
Their supply lines stretched for hundreds of miles
and were easily broken up by Cossack cavalry.
The Grand Army also began to feel the toll of the
unpredictable Russian weather. Torrential rains

would fall, creating thigh-deep mud, only to be
followed by days of blazing sun that would bake
deep ruts into the rudimentary roads being used.

Horses were the first to go, their intestines
literally bursting open from eating green corn
or thatch pulled from peasants' roofs. For many
soldiers in the Grand Army, the memory of that
period was of the stench of tens of thousands of
dying horses and clouds of dust arising from the
endless plains. Soon, the men themselves began to
die, from dysentery, typhus, starvation, or simply
exhaustion. When, on July 28, Napoleon finally
crossed the Vilna River and entered the city of
Vitebsk, hoping to catch the army of the Russian
General Mikhail Barclay de Tolly, he found that
Barclay had once again withdrawn with his forces.
Napoleon raged to his advisors: "Alexander can
see perfectly well how incompetent his generals
are, and as a result he is losing his country."

But in fact, Alexander's generals were winning the war for him. Napoleon began to send peace overtures to the Tsar—written in a tone far removed from his arrogant message at the beginning of the campaign—but Alexander simply did not reply. In the meantime, the Russian retreat continued all throughout August, and now September had arrived.

Battle at Borodino

On September 7, Napoleon finally caught with the army of General Mikhail Kutuzov, who had replaced Barclay, near the little town of Borodino, some seventy-five miles southwest of Moscow. Kutuzov had approximately 106,000 men entrenched in strong positions among the hills and steep bluffs of the area, and Napoleon's commander, Marshal Louis-Nicolas Davout, recommended a flanking action to their left. Once he got past the formidable Russian guns, he told Napoleon that he could swing around and fall upon the enemy's flanks. But Napoleon—foreshadowing what would happen three years later at Waterloo—ordered a frontal attack. This was the move of an exhausted (and possibly sick) commander, because even though the French still outnumbered the Russians, they had lost thousands of men since invading and were hundreds of miles from home.

Even so, at the Emperor's command, the attack began, with Napoleon sending 100,000 of his troops straight at the lines held by Marshal Peter Bagration, one of the ablest Russian commanders. "The huge Russian redoubt belched out a veritable hell against our center," one French onlooker wrote. Many of Napoleon's faithful soldiers simply disappeared, blown to smithereens.

But after hours of fighting, which included a massive bombardment by 300 guns, the Russians, with heavy losses, including the life of General Peter Bagration, were forced to withdraw. However, Napoleon refused to allow his Old Guard reserve of troops to follow up on the victory, and the Russian army lived to fight another day.

It was a French victory, but a Pyrrhic one, with Napoleon's losses totaling an incredible 40,000 dead and wounded. The Russians lost 50,000, but, close to home, could replenish these losses. Now, even the Emperor's confidence seemed to be shaken. "These Russians let themselves be killed as if they were not men, but mere machines," he told an advisor, unable to grasp the patriotism of his opponents.

The Eerie Silence of Moscow

Still, the way now lay open to Moscow, which Napoleon entered at the head of his army on September 15. He had expected a triumphal procession through a humbled and captive city population; instead, as one historian has written, "there was no life to be seen anywhere, not a face in a window, not a child in a garden, not a horse, carriage, or wagon in the streets."

The Russians had completely evacuated Moscow, leaving the beautiful city, with its 1,200 steeples, towers, clocks, and cupolas—"more Asiatic than European in appearance," wrote one French officer—completely deserted. Nonplussed, Napoleon made his way to the Kremlin, where all that could be heard was the chiming of clocks. That night, as the army dug in around Moscow, the fires began, first in the Chinese quarter, but then spreading rapidly throughout the city.

It soon became apparent that the Russians had left behind a hidden team of arsonists, whose job it was to set fire to Moscow. Napoleon, forced to flee the city for three days while the flames raged, simply could not believe that the Russians would destroy their own beautiful capital city to deny it to the French. He wrote a note to Tsar Alexander in Saint Petersburg that shows just how out of touch with reality the Emperor was becoming. "I waged war on Your Majesty without personal animosity," Napoleon wrote. "The fine, beautiful city of Moscow no longer exists because [your commanders] have burned it. A letter of capitulation from you before or after the battle [of Borodino] could have stopped my march."

Alexander did not reply. Instead, as the Russian fall set in, he ordered his commanders to close in and encircle French troops in the burned city of Moscow.

The Death March

Napoleon's commanders expected him to evacuate Moscow. It was the only move left open to him if he wanted to save his army, but he refused, instead claiming that "I could hardly be better suited than where I am now, in Moscow, to sit out the winter."

Perhaps Napoleon was fooled by the unusually warm fall weather because October had come by now and the temperatures were practically balmy. But rumors began to spread among the French, not for the first time, that the Emperor had lost his mind. He spent most of his time holed up within the walls of the Kremlin, eating alone, keeping his own counsel. When Napoleon saw his staff officers, he seemed to be obsessed with the Tsar: "Alexander will never have had a better opportunity for a favorable peace than he does here!" he shouted one night, and people who heard him thought he had indeed lost his mind.

But Napoleon was a great survivor, and he had a survivor's instinct. Even while all of his protesting was going on, he was secretly planning to evacuate the Russian capital, although it was in part to deal with the news, which arrived from Paris, that Wellington's British army was making advances in Spain. At noon on October 19, Napoleon rode out of the gates of Moscow, heading southwest, at the head of a long column of soldiers bearing booty from the city, including statues, paintings, and Persian carpets. He had attacked Russia with 612,000 troops, 450,000 of them active combat soldiers. He now left with 102,000 men. Out of his original 1,300 pieces of artillery, he now had 533. He left about 15,000 wounded behind, as well as a rear guard detachment of 7,000 men who had orders to blow up the Kremlin, a task that was only haphazardly attempted before these men, too, retreated, leaving the grand palace intact.

The retreat back to France has fallen into legend. The first severe frost came late in October, and the first snow fell on November 4. By December, temperatures had dropped to -29°F (-34°C). Forced by Russian armies to use the same route they had taken coming into Moscow, the Grand Army found nothing but scorched earth and corpses in their path. The Russians harried them with partisan actions by Cossack cavalrymen, who isolated and slaughtered straggling units. Men froze and died standing up. Hunting packs of wolves set upon the soldiers, and some French troops, too weak to defend themselves,

IN THE RETREAT FROM MOSCOW, A BAND OF MEN UNDER MARSHAL MICHEL NEY BECAME SEPARATED FROM THE MAIN ARMY AND OPEN TO ATTACK. THEY WERE PART OF THE FEW WHO SURVIVED A CONCEN- TRATED ATTACK FROM THE RUSSIANS.

were torn apart limb from limb. A soldier remembered the state of the troops years later: "Many of them walked, leaning on sticks, their beards and hair a mass of ice …The men who fell imploring help, I fear, were not listened to."

Napoleon, having heard of an attempted coup d'état in Paris by General Claude-Francois de Malet, abandoned his troops at the village of Smorgoni, in Lithuania. With a 200-man guard, he raced for Paris on sleigh and carriage, at last arriving late one night in December, "passing at full gallop beneath the half-finished Arc de Triomphe," to arrive at his palace around midnight, much to the consternation of a sleepy guard who answered the Emperor's imperious knocking while still dressed in his nightshirt.

Although troops continued to stagger and die in the frozen wastes to the east, the campaign to conquer Russia was over. Of 612,000 French soldiers and their allies, 400,000 had died, and 100,000 had been taken prisoner. Even as Napoleon planned to rise again to destroy the Coalition armies and Russia—and he did raise an army of 300,000 men the next year—a decisive turning point had been reached in the Napoleonic Wars. Never again would Napoleon be seen as invincible. From this point on, it was only a matter of time before the Coalition forces, filled with renewed hope, would destroy the Emperor of France, once and for all.

NAPOLEON:
"SUCH FINE AND GREAT DESTINIES"

Rising from a captain of artillery to Emperor of France within a decade is no easy feat, but Napoleon made it look effortless. "I found the crown of France on the ground," he later said, "and I picked it up with my sword." This tone of careless nonchalance and supreme confidence marked Napoleon's attitude toward military matters as well as governing—but masked a fierce ambition and the instincts of a tough, pragmatic field commander.

In a sense, Napoleon needed his arrogance; his sense of god-like certitude got him out of a lot of tight spots. After becoming Emperor in 1804, all of Europe was, again, arrayed against him, yet he went on to win a string of extraordinary victories—at Ulm and Jena (in modern-day Germany) and Austerlitz (now Slavkov u Brna in the Czech Republic), where he outmaneuvered Coalition commanders as if they were befuddled children, and destroyed their armies. The allies simply could not keep up with Napoleon's brilliant tactical improvisations, the way he moved his Grand Army in dispersed, widely separated corps and then pulled them together to attack head-on or flank his enemy.

Yet Napoleon's arrogance also got him in trouble. His invasion of Russia (see "Turning Point," p. 34) was the foolish error of an overconfident man, as was his losing an entire army in Spain. He did not respect the man who would ultimately defeat him at Waterloo. The Duke of Wellington, Napoleon said, "was a sepoy general" (meaning, fit to lead only native troops, as in India). Wellington, according to Napoleon, acted only "out of fear. He had one stroke of fortune, and he knows that such fortune never comes twice."

That one stroke of fortune was the Battle of Waterloo, on June 18, 1815, but it was not luck that won the battle for Wellington. Napoleon, as Wellington later said, "did not maneuver at all." Gone were the famous slashing corps attacks, the surprise movement of armies. Instead, the weary and possibly ill—with hemorrhoids, a gastric ulcer, and cystitis, a painful bladder infection—Napoleon merely attacked headlong, in columns, and watched as his reconstituted Grand Army was turned into corpses by withering allied fire. Never having a problem abandoning his men when the moment situation turned dire—he did so in Egypt and in Russia—Napoleon fled, only to be captured by the British and exiled to St. Helena island in the far South Atlantic, which was an exile that turned out to be permanent, because he died there of a stomach ailment in 1821, at the age of fifty-two.

Napoleon goes down as one of the most brilliant military commanders in history, but also as a man, undone by his own hubris, who destroyed his country's promising future after the French Revolution. As his Moscow ambassador Armand de Caulaincourt protested before Napoleon's ill-fated attack on Russia: "I spoke to him of the reproaches he would continue to suffer for running so many risks, for putting up for lottery such fine and great destinies." But Napoleon could not hear him, and the result was disaster.

NAPOLEON IS SEEN DICTATING THE ACCOUNT OF HIS CAM-
PAIGNS AT THE FAR-FLUNG SOUTH ATLANTIC ISLAND OF
ST. HELENA IN 1816, WHERE HE WAS EXILED. HE DIED OF A
STOMACH AILMENT THERE IN 1822, AT THE AGE OF FIFTY-TWO.

St. Helena 1816: Napoleon dictating to Count Las Cases the Account of his
Campaigns (oil on canvas), Orchardson, Sir William Quiller (1832–1910) / © Lady
Lever Art Gallery, National Museums Liverpool / The Bridgeman Art Library

ARTHUR WELLESLEY, DUKE OF WELLINGTON: "THE FINGER OF PROVIDENCE WAS UPON ME"

Arthur Wesley—the family would only later change the spelling to Wellesley, a more aristocratic name that also could not be mistaken for John Wesley, a firebrand preacher of the same name—was born to Anglo-Irish nobility in County Meath, Ireland, in 1769. His parents were, as one of his brothers later put it, "frivolous and careless personages" who paid little attention to young Arthur, merely sending him off to good public schools and forgetting about him. But the famous story is that when Wellesley turned eighteen, his mother happened to spot him one night in London, across a crowded theater: "I do believe there is my ugly boy, Arthur," she exclaimed. "What can I do with him?"

The answer was to buy him a commission in the British army. After Wellesley saw short service in Ireland, he went off to India in 1796. Once in that country, Wellesley—who was indeed a bit of an "ugly boy," tall and ungainly, with such a hooked nose that his troops would later call him "Beaky"—distinguished himself in the battles against local Indian potentates in the province of Mysore and returned home, in 1803, as a major general and a knight companion of the Order of the Bath.

In 1809, Wellesley was appointed commander in chief of British forces fighting the Peninsular War (see *Guerra de Guerrillas,* p. 45) and first saw action against Napoleon's armies (although not Napoleon, who had already left Spain to fight the Austrians). There his genius as a commander came to the fore. He was primarily a defensive specialist—one reason why Napoleon despised him—who liked nothing better than to find a well-protected position, anchor his flanks against a river or some high point of land, place his troops on the rear slope of a hill or ridge, and let the enemy give battle, if they might.

These tactics—as well as the judicious use of bold strikes—won Wellesley Portugal and Spain and allowed him to invade France, thus helping bring an end to Napoleon's reign in 1814. When Napoleon escaped from Elba the following year, it was the now Duke of Wellington who commanded the Allied army that faced him in Belgium, at Waterloo. Here was the defensive specialist facing off against the offensive genius. Here were two commanders who despised each other—Wellington would later say that "Bonaparte's whole life, civil, political, military, was a fraud"—commanding in a battle that was to determine the fate of Europe.

Although Wellington was to call Waterloo "the nearest run thing," the tired Napoleon he faced was not the Napoleon of old, and Wellington's defensive strategies carried the day. While Napoleon died an early death, Wellington went on to become prime minister of Britain, one of the figures who would shape postwar Europe.

ARTHUR WELLESLEY, THE DUKE OF WELLINGTON, WOULD LEAD AN ALMOST PARALLEL LIFE TO NAPOLEON BONAPARTE. BOTH PROVED THEIR GENIUS EARLY ON; THEY HAD EGOS TO MATCH, WHICH MADE THEM PERFECT ANTAGONISTS.

Every bit as arrogant as Napoleon, in his own way—he once said, "I began to feel that the finger of Providence was upon me"—he never allowed his ego to interfere with common sense, and thus finally won out against the brilliant, passionate, but ultimately intemperate Napoleon.

The French Soldier: The Grand Army

Between 1802 and 1805, knowing that he would be fighting a lengthy war against all of Europe, Napoleon Bonaparte devoted a good deal of his time and attention to building *la Grand Armée*—the Grand Army, which saw him, over three years of hard training, transform the masses of French troops conscripted through levées into a formidable fighting machine, the best army in the world at the time.

Although not original with Napoleon, the idea of the corps was perfected in his Grand Army. He took troops from different fighting arms (infantry, artillery, cavalry) and made them into self-sufficient small armies, which marched at widely dispersed intervals from each other. This had the advantage of confusing an enemy as to Napoleon's real intentions as well as allowing him—by calling on one corps or another to make a forced march to join him (as he did at Austerlitz—see "The 'Sun of Austerlitz,'" p. 47)—to mass his troops together quickly to strike.

Napoleon also had his army live off the land as much as possible, which allowed him to move quickly and to sever vulnerable ties to supply lines, although this method did have the not inconsiderable added disadvantage of alienating civilian populations whose farms and goods were despoiled by hordes of hungry French soldiers. Still, Napoleon argued that "an army of 20,000 could exist even in a desert," although he tried to take the precaution of laying down huge munitions dumps in the projected line of march of his troops.

The Grand Army was a highly motivated army, with desertion rates between 1802 and 1810 at an astonishingly low 3 percent due mainly to the army's victories and the common soldier's complete faith in Napoleon. Napoleon's troops were well led from his marshals—men like Michel Ney, Joachim Murat, Louis Davout, and Andre Massena—right down to his noncommissioned officers, with plenty of opportunity for advancement within the ranks. And, of course— this always helps—the Grand Army was, for the first eight years of its existence, a mainly victorious army. After the debacle in Russia in 1812 (see "Turning Point," p. 34) the once-proud Grand Army began to slowly crumble.

Coalition Soldier: The British Army

The British army was made up of volunteers. Even at the height of a dozen years of war with Napoleon, no conscription system was put in place. Most of the soldiers came from the poorer segments of society. A disproportionate share of British infantrymen were young Irishmen escaping the miserable conditions of their country. They were a brave fighting force, but with the exception of certain elite units, held together by not by esprit, as in the case of the Grand Army, but by severe discipline, which included floggings and beatings. The Duke of Wellington himself resisted any notion of reforming the army as a romantic one. The men were a hardened lot who needed hard discipline and that was just the way it was. Still, Arthur Wellington's men, while not as passionate about their leader as the French soldiers were about Napoleon Bonaparte, trusted him implicitly to lead them into combat.

Their officers were generally drawn from the lesser aristocracy. There were men who were promoted through seniority—not an especially effective way of encouraging good young leaders—or through the notorious custom of purchasing promotions, which encouraged the very wealthy to rise high in the ranks of the army. Given these disadvantages, the performance of English troops under the Duke of Wellington was nothing short of astonishing, due to hard drill and training.

Wellington liked to fight from defensive positions wherever possible. His disbursement of his troops at Waterloo—hidden from sight on the reverse slope of a hill—was classic. Normally, when charged, the British infantry was trained to fire two volleys and then counterattack with the bayonet, which was an aggressive display that often routed the enemy.

The British artillery could never quite keep up with Napoleon's always superior gunnery, but it did introduced two deadly innovations—the Congreve rocket (see "The Congreve Rocket," p. 48) and shrapnel, which was developed by a Lieutenant Henry Shrapnel of the Royal Artillery and consisted of a hollow shell filled with musket balls and explosives that exploded on impact and did horrendous damage.

By the end of the war, with Great Britain's greater industrial output behind them, the British infantry were better armed and more numerous than their French counterparts, although they would never go down in legend the way the Grand Army would.

Guerra de Guerrillas: The Peninsular War

Francisco de Goya's famous painting *Execution of the Defenders of Madrid, 3 May, 1808,* captures all of the terror, blood, and passion of the Peninsular War: Surrounded by bodies, facing a French firing squad, the Spanish man at the center of the painting, wearing the white shirt of the martyr, stretches his arms wide as if to ask *Why?* before the bullets tear into his body.

In the space of little more than a decade, the French, once revolutionaries who had thrown off a tyrannical yoke, were now a force of repression. And nowhere was the repression felt more than in the Iberian Peninsula, during what became known as the Peninsular War.

The Peninsular War began in 1807 when Napoleon decided to attack Portugal for refusing to go along with his Continental System (see "Chronicle," p. 32), moving thousands of troops into Spain under the pretext of supporting this invasion. Napoleon then duped the "half-wit" Spanish monarch Charles IV into abdicating and put his own brother Joseph on the throne. The Spanish people rose in rebellion in Madrid on May 2, 1808, a rebellion brutally put down by Napoleon's chief commander, Marshal

FRANCISCO DE GOYA'S DEPICTION OF THE BRUTAL WAR IS SHOWN IN HIS PAINTING, *EXECUTION OF THE DEFENDERS OF MADRID, 3RD MAY, 1808.*

Execution of the Defenders of Madrid, 3rd May, 1808, 1814 (oil on canvas) (see also 155453 for detail), Goya y Lucientes, Francisco Jose de (1746-1828) / Prado, Madrid, Spain, / The Bridgeman Art Library

(continued on p. 46)

Joachim Murat. Hundreds of Spanish were rounded up and executed at various locations around the city, a massacre commemorated in de Goya's famous paintings, including *The Riot Against the Mameluke Mercenaries, The Second of May 1808.*

Such bloody reprisals created a national resentment against the French, and an uprising in both Spain and Portugal followed, backed by Britain, which landed an expeditionary force in August 1808 led by Lieutenant General Sir Arthur Wellesley (see "Commanders," p. 42), at which point a see-saw battle for Portugal and Spain began. Wellesley drove the French army under Napoleon's General Jean Junot out of Portugal.

Wellesley left, but then Napoleon himself returned to the Peninsula at the head of 200,000 veteran French troops and pushed the British army out of Portugal in early 1809, very nearly destroying it.

Wellesley returned that summer (after Napoleon left to fight elsewhere in Europe) and began the long, hard, slogging campaign to oust the French from the Iberian Peninsula. The campaign was ferocious, with hundreds of thousands of dead and a high toll of civilian casualties. The word "guerilla" was coined for the actions of Spanish irregular fighters against the French, because the Spanish called the Peninsular War *Guerra de Guerrillas,* or "the war of the little wars."

The Spanish guerillas, passionate about their country, outraged by atrocities against citizen populations (including nuns, monks, and priests) struck French troops hard in hit-and-run attacks. When Wellesley was finally successful in driving the French out of Portugal and Spain, it was in good measure due to the fact that the Spanish guerillas had sowed terror within the ranks of the French army there. Ironically, it would be the example of the Spanish guerilla fighters in the Peninsula that would later encourage other guerillas to rise up against Spanish rule in South America.

The Napoleonic Code: Influencing the Whole World

After Napoleon became emperor of France and took absolute rule into his own hands, he did not completely turn his back on the spirit of the Revolution. Napoleon was personally responsible for reorganizing the French civil service and tax and banking systems; he also encouraged private industrial development.

True, this was in part because these innovations helped finance and equip the French army. But the Napoleonic Code, which was issued in 1804, carried in it numerous reforms from the days when cries of *liberté, égalité, fraternité* rang up and down the avenues of Paris. In what one historian has called "one of the few documents which has influenced the

whole world," the code turned the French legal system from a medieval confusion of feudal laws recognizing the rich over everyone else into something approaching a fair and equal system of justice. The code abolished secret laws (you could be convicted and sentenced to death for something you didn't even know was a crime), set up a regulation system of laws by which all judges in the country must abide, and took such "crimes" as heresy, witchcraft, and sacrilege off the books.

Perhaps the signal accomplishment of the Napoleonic Code was to establish that all-important tenet of modern law, the fact that a person is to be considered innocent unless

proven guilty in court by openly presented evidence. This innovation kept people without means from rotting in prison, sometimes for years, before they were even bound over for trial.

It doesn't do to lionize Napoleon's libertarian leanings too much. This same man jailed political opponents, silenced the press, and, of course, flouted the Revolution by getting himself made Emperor. But the Napoleonic Code was an influential step in the direction of universal human rights, because it was adopted in numerous countries—including the Netherlands, Italy, Spain, and Portugal—during the Napoleonic Wars.

The "Sun of Austerlitz"

Later in Napoleon's career, when things were not going so well for him, he would refer longingly to "the sun of Austerlitz," the unexpectedly brilliant winter sun that shone down on a single day in Moravia when a far-outnumbered Napoleon fought a tactically brilliant battle that destroyed an Austro-Russian army and ended the threat of the Third Coalition.

After Napoleon's victory over the Austrians at Ulm in October 1805, he and his army advanced relentlessly north from Vienna in pursuit of the retreating Austrians. Knowing that the Austrians were about to join forces with a Russian force led by Tsar Alexander I and Austrian Emperor Francis I, Napoleon halted near the village of Austerlitz and carefully scouted out the ground. Positioning his 70,000-man-strong army in a valley, he seemed to be inviting himself to be outflanked by the Austro-Russian force of some 85,000 men.

And he furthered this impression, on November 27, by requesting an armistice and making it appear that his forward elements were retreating in disorder.

The military commander of the Austro-Russian forces, General Mikhail Kutuzov, correctly sensed that this was a trap, but he was overruled by Tsar Alexander and Emperor Francis, who ordered a massive flanking movement by the Allied right wing, to begin the morning of December 2. With Napoleon's scouts telling him that enemy had taken the bait, he waited until the sun of Austerlitz burned off the morning mists before sending most of his troops hurtling directly at the center of the Austro-Russian line, which had been considerably weakened by the flanking movement.

Cheering, firing, and stabbing with bayonets, the Grand Army tore through the Allied lines, gained the

Pratzen Heights in the Austro-Russian rear, turned, and began bombarding the enemy with fire, shot, and shell. In the meantime, two of Napoleon's corps, called up by forced march, engaged the flanking Austro-Russian infantry and drove them back. Within the space of a short winter's day, the Allied army simply disintegrated—2,000 French soldiers were killed and 7,000 wounded, in comparison to 27,000 Allied casualties.

As a direct result of what historians often call Napoleon's "perfect battle," the Russians were forced to march back home, and the Austrians had to sue for peace and make costly concessions, ceding great blocks of territory to the French at the Treaty of Pressburg twenty days later. Prussia, which had been on the verge of joining Austria and Russia against Napoleon, now signed a peace treaty with France, thus ending the Third Coalition.

OFTEN CALLED NAPOLEON BONAPARTE'S "PERFECT BATTLE," THE BATTLE OF AUSTERLITZ, DEPICTED HERE, DISPLAYS THE TREMENDOUS TOLL NAPOLEON'S MILITARY GENIUS TOOK ON THE AUSTRO-RUSSIAN FORCES.

Detail of 'The Battle of Austerlitz', a panoramic wallpaper design, 1827-29 (wallpaper), French School, (19th century) / Deutsches Tapetenmuseum, Kassel, Germany, © Museumslandschaft Hessen Kassel / The Bridgeman Art Library

The Congreve Rocket

Bombardments during the Napoleonic Wars were terrifying enough, especially if you were a soldier standing on an open field watching the sky in front of you fill with arching black dots that would, in a matter of seconds, turn into cannonballs, any single one of which could disembowel you and ten of your comrades. But the rocket developed by Sir William Congreve and first used against the French during the Napoleonic Wars was a very different type of missile indeed.

Congreve, son of the controller of the British Royal Armory, had been impressed by the way certain Indian princes used rockets (themselves borrowed from the Chinese) in the Mysore Wars fought in India in the late eighteenth century. And so Congreve set out to develop one that could be adapted to European warfare. He came up with what became known as the Congreve Rocket, a sturdy iron tube filled with explosions and capped with a conical nose, the whole thing weighing perhaps 30 pounds (13.5 kg). The tubes were set in metal baseplates, filled with black powder, and attached to wooden guide poles. A fuse was then lit that set off a propellant mixture. The rockets took off in a burst of flame and actually had a range of 2 miles (3 km) or so.

The Congreve rocket was not an accurate weapon, but the shrieking sound it made as it hurtled through the air, especially in conjunction with other types of artillery, was enough to set the hardiest veteran to flight. The British used it quite effectively after it became operational in 1804. Boulogne, France, was bombarded by Congreves in 1806 and suffered a fire that burned acres of the city and caused severe casualties, and

DEVELOPED BY SIR WILLIAM CONGREVE, THE CONGREVE ROCKET WAS THE BEGINNING OF ROCKETRY IN EUROPEAN WARFARE. THE SIGHT OF IT AND THE SHRIEKING SOUND IT MADE AS IT FLEW THROUGH THE SKY WAS ENOUGH TO TERRIFY ANYONE STANDING IN ITS PATH.

Chatham Barracks, a Military Punishment called the 'Triangle' and Congreve Rockets, plate 17 from 'The History of the Nations' (aquatint), Italian School, (19th century) / Private Collection, The Stapleton Collection / The Bridgeman Art Library

Copenhagen and Danzig both suffered serious destruction from hundreds of rockets launched by British artillerists. Purists such as the Duke of Wellington disliked this weapon ("I do not want to set fire to any town," he once said of the Congreves), but rockets had a powerful effect.

Congreve rockets were used by the British until the 1850s, when more sophisticated rocketry became available, but they had a second life as a distress signal for ships at sea, a life that lasted into the early twentieth century.

The Invasion that Never Was

As the Napoleonic Wars began, Napoleon was very seriously preparing for a massive invasion of England, which, had it come off, would have ended the Napoleonic Wars very quickly indeed. But—as with many planned invasions of that island country, from the Spanish Armada to the conquering Nazis—England seemed to lead a charmed life.

The first Army of England had assembled on the French Channel coast in 1798, but Napoleon's preoccupation with Egypt and the Treaty of Amiens caused it to be dismantled. However, after the outbreak of war, a new army was gathered in camps at Boulogne, Brugge, and Montreuil, growing to more than 200,000 men in the space of two years. Napoleon called for the building of a "National Flotilla" of invasion boats, 2,000 in all, to carry this massive force to England. However, planning was poor. His commanders recommended launching the invasion "under cover of one long winter's night," as one of them put it, but the channel was far too stormy for that kind of undertaking in winter. Napoleon, visiting the channel himself one stormy winter day in 1803, realized that the British warships did not abandon the channel in a storm, but remained on their posts, which meant that even if the French could launch in such weather, the British would almost certainly cut them to pieces.

This meant the invasion must be launched in plain sight, in summer, at which point Napoleon insisted that each ship be armed with a cannon to protect it from British warships. But his naval architects pointed out that such flat-bottomed, shallow-draft vessels could never support the recoil of such a gun. The problems continued to snowball—not helped by the fact that Napoleon's trusted commander of the invasion effort, Eustache Bruix, died of tuberculosis—until Napoleon ordered a large-scale test of the invasion craft, only to watch many of them sink, with attendant loss of life, in the choppy channel waters.

Napoleon hated to give up any plan, but he was finally convinced the invasion was unworkable. On August 27, 1805, Napoleon decided to use the invasion force as the core of a new Grand Army and had them break camp and march east to do battle with the Austrians. England was safe, once more.

3

THE WAR OF
GREEK INDEPENDENCE

1821–1829

The world's ancient cradle of liberty, a subject country
for 400 years, erupted in a bloody rebellion to become the
first country to throw off the yoke of the Ottoman Empire.

Combatants
- Greece, England, France, Russia
- Ottoman Empire, Egypt

Theater of War
Greece

Casualties
Estimated 25,000 Greeks dead and
20,000 dead from the Ottoman
Empire. In addition, estimated civilian
death toll as high as 105,000

Major Figures
GREECE
Rígas Feraios, Greek nationalist writer
murdered by the Turks in 1798
Alexander Ipsílántis, who led the first
armed insurrection against the Turks
Demetrius Ipsílántis, Alexander Ipsílántis's brother, who won numerous
victories in the Peloponnese
Theodore Kolokotronis, commander
in chief of the Greek forces

OTTOMAN EMPIRE
Sultan Mahmud II, who sought to
reform his army to crush Greece
Omer Vrionis, Turkish commander
at Athens

Ali Pasha, whose ambitions forced
the Turks to send an army against him

EGYPT
Muhammad Ali, pasha of Egypt
Ibrahim Pasha, Muhammad Ali's son,
whom he sent to destroy Greece

GREAT BRITAIN
Admiral Sir Edward Codrington,
whose allied forces defeated the
Turko-Egyptian fleet at Navarino
Lord George Gordon Byron, whose
efforts on behalf of the Greek cause
focused the world's attention on
its plight

It was an irony the world, and the Greeks, were well aware of: Greece, where the ideal of liberty in the Western world had been born, had been a vassal country of the powerful Ottoman Empire since the fall of Constantinople in 1453. The Ottoman Empire spanned much of the Balkans and North Africa. But in the early years of the nineteenth century, inspired by the French Revolution and worn down by years of repression, the Greeks arose, declared independence from the Ottoman Empire on January 11, 1822, and fought a bloody war against the Turks for the next seven years. Turkish outrages against Greek civilians as well as Greece's ancient reputation brought funds and soldiers from all over Europe, but it was only when Egypt entered the war and began successfully defeating the Greeks that the major European powers of Great Britain, France, and Russia stepped in on the Greek side. Their intervention was decisive, and Greece became a free country after the signing of the London Protocols in 1832.

1798: Rígas Feraios, Greek nationalist writer, is arrested by Turkish authorities and executed.

1814: The Philikí Etería, or "Society of Friends," is founded in Odessa with the purpose of rebelling against the Ottoman Empire.

1821:
March: Alexander Ipsílántis leads first armed insurrection against the Turks in Moldavia; Greek forces arise and attack Turks in four different towns in Greece.

September: Greek forces capture the Turkish fortress city of Tripolis.

1822:
January: Ali Pasha is defeated and killed by Ottoman forces.

April–July: Turks kill or enslave 70,000 Greeks on the island of Chios.

July: Greeks retake Athens from the Turks.

1823:
January: Civil war breaks out in Greece.

August: Lord George Gordon Byron arrives in Greece.

1824: Lord Byron dies at Mesolongi, Greece.

1825: Ibrahim Pasha invades Greece with Egyptian forces and ravages Peloponnesus.

1827:
July: Russia, France, and Great Britain sign the Treaty of London, calling for an immediate cease-fire and armistice in Greece.

October: Allied forces defeat the Turko-Egyptian fleet at Navarino.

1829: Greeks, fighting as regular army, defeat Turks at the Battle of Petra, the last clash of the Greek War of Independence.

1832: The Protocols of London establish an independent Greek kingdom.

A GREEK ORTHODOX PRIEST IS SHOWN HERE TEACHING CHILDREN IN SECRET, WHILE AN ARMED GUARD LOOKS ON. OTTOMAN TYRANNY HAD DECAYED A NATION THAT HAD PREVIOUSLY BEEN WORLD-RENOWNED FOR ITS LEARNING AND CULTURE.

Nicholas Cyzis, National Gallery of Art, Athens

THE NEW RISE OF GREEK LIBERTY

In the late eighteenth and early nineteenth centuries, revolutionary nationalism, born in the French Revolution, spread across Europe and found a ready home in the Greek islands, which had been a nation subservient to the Ottoman Empire for nearly 400 years. The Greeks had been subjected to capricious and onerous taxation, to second-class citizenship for their children (primary schools barely existed in a land that had once been known for its learning and culture), and to the infamous process called *devshirme*, by which the Turks forcibly inducted non-Muslim Greek youths to serve as slave-soldiers known as *janissaries*.

Although the Turks had wisely left the Greek Orthodox Church intact, allowing the Greeks to worship as of old, the Church had been co-opted by the sultans in Constantinople and preached obedience to both "divine and human laws." However, a number of Greek leaders were beginning to challenge the Ottoman state. One was Rígas Feraios, a Greek expatriate who wrote passionate articles attacking the Turks and who was arrested in Austria, handed over to Ottoman officials, and executed in 1798.

But his poetry ("Better an hour of free life/ than forty years of slavery and jail") became a rallying point for the Greeks who formed the Philikí Etería, or "Society of Friends," a Greek nationalist society, first started in the Russian port city of Odessa in 1814. The Philikí Etería drew educated Greeks to its cause, while the poorer people flocked to the *klephts* (see "The Greek Soldier," p. 62), bandits who operated in the hills and coalesced to become a guerilla army of formidable strength.

The first blow of the War of Greek Independence was struck in the spring of 1821, when Alexander Ipsílántis, head of the Philikí Etería, attacked Turkish forces in Moldavia. Ipsílántis was driven back across the Austrian frontier, where he was arrested and placed in prison, but the revolution had begun.

Taking advantage of the fact that the Turks were preoccupied in dealing with their rebellious bey Ali Pasha, Greek rebels, led by men such as Alexander Ipsílántis's brother Demetrius and by Theodore Kolokotronis, the most brilliant Greek military leader of the war, acted together in a series of land and sea attacks. They seized control of key cities and ports in the Peloponnesian Peninsula in southern Greece, where the bulk of the fighting in the Greek Revolution would occur. Greek guerilla forces scored stunning military successes, capturing the Turkish fortress city of Tripolis in September 1821 and taking back Athens, fighting in the ancient acropolis, in July 1822.

European powers such as Great Britain, France, and Russia, leery of nationalist movements and unwilling to openly provoke the Ottoman state, at first stayed out of the war, although private citizens flocked to support Greece (see "Byron and the Philhellenes," p. 64). But the Turkish atrocities on the island of Chios in the spring and summer of 1822 turned western governments, particularly Great Britain, against Turkey. Having retaken most of Greece from the Turks, the Greeks decided to try to form a constitutional government, but this turned out to be a mistake. The two legislative bodies set up, representing central Greece and the Peloponnesus, began to fight a civil war and could not consolidate their gains against the Turks. In 1824, the Ottoman Sultan Mahmud II asked for aid from Muhammad Ali, pasha of Egypt, an Ottoman vassal state with a far superior army to the decaying janissary ranks of the Turks (see "The Ottoman Soldier," p. 63).

Egypt's entry into the war changed the balance of power. Ali's son, Ibrahim Pasha, led an invasion against Greece that regained most of the Peloponnese region for the Ottomans in a scorched earth campaign of unsurpassed barbarity that saw Athens retaken in 1827. Great Britain, France, and Russia, now finally roused by the growing Egyptian power in Greece, signed the

Treaty of London in July 1827, demanding that the Egyptians withdraw and that the Ottoman Empire sign an armistice giving Greece full autonomy. When the Ottomans refused to do this, the three allied nations sent a naval force to Greece that utterly destroyed the Turko-Egyptian fleet at the Battle of Navarino on October 20, 1827 (see "Turning Point," p. 54). By the following year, the Greeks had regrouped and seized as much territory back from the Turks as possible (including Athens and Thebes) before a cease-fire was declared. The last major action of the war was the Battle of Petra in July 1829, where a newly revitalized Greek military fought victoriously against the Turks in regular army style.

The London Protocols late in 1832 established an independent Greek kingdom, although the throne was given to a Bavarian prince, who would become King Otto I. Civil strife between different factions would continue on and off in Greece for another century, but, as historian David Brewer has written, "The Greeks could rightly rejoice in what they had achieved. They had opened the first cracks in the structure of the mighty Ottoman Empire, and against the odds had become the first of its domain to win full independence as a nation state."

PATRIOT ALEXANDER IPSÍLÁNTIS WAS THE NECESSARY SPARK THAT IGNITED THE UPRISING IN GREECE.
Peter von Hess, Benaki Museum, Athens

THE BATTLE OF NAVARINO: OCTOBER 20, 1827

Navarino Bay is on the west coast of the Peloponnesian Peninsula, on the Ionian Sea. It's a beautiful and sheltered harbor, 3 miles (5 km) long, 2 miles (3 km) wide, surrounded by high, red ochre hills. It's a place of history, too. In 425 B.C., during the Peloponnesian War, the Athenians fought and won a bloody battle of triremes against the Spartans.

In those days, there were two entrances to the harbor, one to the north, in a gap where the islet of Sphacteria, which shelters the west side of the harbor, fails to meet the mainland, and a much wider one on the southern end.

But by the Greek Revolution, a sandbar had formed in that northern gap, leaving only the southern entry open. Any fleet that took possession of the harbor would have a very easy time, therefore, defending it, but at the same time could be easily bottled up there.

It was the lesson a large Turko-Egyptian fleet learned to its peril on a beautiful autumn day in 1827 during a naval battle that is unique in history, the results of which can still be seen today, should you charter a small plane and fly low over Navarino Bay. What appear to be shadows in the water turn into, on closer examination, the hulks of wooden ships, rotting in the depths of the water. These shadows represent the end of the Ottoman Empire's dreams in Greece, but the beginning of a new Grecian nation-state that persists to this day.

"Keep Peace with Your Speaking Trumpet"

By the summer of 1827, the powers of France, Great Britain, and Russia had become alarmed at the turn of events in Greece. A war that the Greek revolutionaries had been winning had now turned into a bloody battle of attrition fought mainly in the Peloponnesian Peninsula, where the Egyptian Ibrahim Pasha had embarked on a bloody campaign in 1825. Not only had his troops—sent there at the behest of his father, Mohammed Ali, vassal to the Ottoman Sultan—sent the Greek revolutionaries reeling, but Ibrahim embarked on a campaign of depopulization (the British called it "the barbarization procedure") in which Greeks were being captured and sent back to Egypt as slaves.

Public opinion was firmly on the side of the Greeks, plus great power politicians were extremely concerned as to what an Egyptian takeover of Greece would do to the balance of power in the eastern Mediterranean. Thus, on July 6, 1827, Great Britain, France, and Russia put aside their historic differences and signed the Treaty of London, which called for an immediate armistice and a negotiated peace that would leave Greece an independent country. Naturally the Turks and Egyptians, who were finally winning the war, declined to recognize this, although the Greeks were quick to accept it.

Therefore, in August of that year, the British fleet under the command of Admiral Sir Edward Codrington sailed to Navarino Bay, which had become the main base of Ibrahim Pasha's naval operations. The French and Russians soon joined them. Codrington had his orders, written in London, in which he was to "encourage" the ships of the Turko-Egyptian fleet to return to their respective home ports of Constantinople and Alexandria. But Codrington was also told to "keep the peace with your speaking trumpet, if possible; but, in case of necessity ... by cannon shot."

"The Feelings of a Brave Man"

Codrington tried the speaking trumpet first. Arraying his fleet outside Navarino Bay, he requested a meeting with Ibrahim Pasha and was granted one on September 25. Codrington and French Admiral Henri de Rigny were rowed ashore to Ibrahim's tent, which sat on a small rise overlooking the harbor and the Turko-Egyptian fleet of some eighty fighting ships.

First the principals smoked tobacco out of huge pipes with jeweled stems 10 feet (3 m) long. Then they got down to business. Codrington politely suggested that because of the Treaty of London, it was his job to stop Ibrahim from continuing to attack Greece. Ibrahim countered that his instructions were directly the opposite—that he must continue in what had heretofore been a successful war against these upstart rebels who were, after all, subjects of the Ottoman Empire.

Codrington, while tactfully stating that he was aware "what must be the feelings of a brave man under such circumstances," nevertheless firmly assured Ibrahim that if he continued in his attacks, the Allied fleet would destroy him. At this, Ibrahim replied that, in light of these new circumstances, he would have to send to both Constantinople and Alexandria for instructions. While awaiting these, he would cease actions.

Codrington and de Rigny accepted this and left their meeting at least somewhat satisfied. But in reality Ibrahim was playing for time. He did in fact cease naval actions, but his infantry ranged over the countryside, burning the olive trees of nearby Kalamáta. The resulting smoke could be seen by the allied ships, which had now been joined by the Russians. British shore parties sent by Codrington reported that the killing and capture of Greek civilians continued unabated. Upon hearing this, Codrington wrote a firm letter to Ibrahim Pasha, demanding that these land operations be stopped, but, wonder of wonders, Ibrahim was nowhere to be found, and there was no one in the Turko-Egyptian fleet vested with the authority to accept such a letter on his behalf.

In fact, Ibrahim was merely being evasive. He knew that the allies wanted him to stop the land war, but they did not have the forces to compel him to do so. He also knew that he would probably receive different orders from his two masters. The Ottoman Sultan in Constantinople would want him to fight the allied navy, while his father in Alexandria would want him to avoid confrontation, so as not to have his prized Egyptian fleet destroyed.

But evasiveness had its cost, as Ibrahim was to discover. Codrington and de Rigny decided that they must, as Codrington put it, "take measures for forcing Ibrahim's return to Egypt." And so the allied fleet entered Navarino Harbor in a display of force—hopefully not to fight, but to show the Egyptians they meant business.

Come to Give, Not Take, Orders

Late on the morning of October 20, the allied fleet entered Navarino Harbor to find the Turko-Egyptian vessels arrayed in a semi-circle, or scimitar. The allied fleet positioned itself inside the semi-circle of the Turko-Egyptian fleet, with the British in the center, the French on the right or east side of the bay, and the Russians on the west. By two o'clock, all the ships were in place and at anchor in the shallow waters.

The Egyptian admiral in actual charge of the fleet, Moharrem Bey, sent a small boat to Codrington's flagship asking him to leave the harbor, to which Codrington replied that he came to give orders, not take them. When the Egyptians received this reply, there was a tense standoff, and then the British observed that a small boat had landed a crew on a Turkish fireship, and they obviously seemed to be preparing it to attack the British.

The captain of the British ship nearest to the fireship sent a boat toward it to ask it to stop these preparations, but the fireship blew it out of the water with a single cannon shot. Suddenly shots rang out all across the azure waters of Navarino Bay, and one of the most unique naval battles in history was on.

The Battle of Navarino was the last naval engagement fought entirely between ships under sail because steam was already beginning to replace canvas in the world's navies. It was also the first naval battle fought between ships at anchor. There was no maneuvering here, no sailing in line across the enemy's line, or tacking away to safety.

Here, in a confined space, more than one hundred ships brutally pounded each other, maneuvering by swinging their ships by their anchor cables. The bay was almost immediately covered with smoke, and the flashes of guns were seen dimly through the unnatural twilit haze, while

the noise of the cannon, rolling back off the hills surrounding the bay, was so loud that men standing right next to each other had to scream to be heard.

The Egyptians had the much larger force, some ninety vessels as compared to only twenty-five for the allies, but they were at a decided disadvantage nonetheless. The allies had ten line-of-battle ships (with more than fifty guns) to only three such Turko-Egyptian vessels. The allied ships were larger and taller than their counterparts, allowing them to fire down on the enemy decks, and the English sported heavier caliber guns. As the battle raged, the allied guncrews shot their cannon not just with ball for this close-range action, but with grapeshot—iron balls in canvas bags that could tear apart an enemy vessel rigging in a moment, as well as sweep its decks in a bloody fashion.

Four brutal hours went by, with the British fire devastating the Turko-Egyptian vessels, whose crews fought bravely, firing their cannon even as the ships were sinking. Sometimes if a ship were disabled, the remaining crew would commit suicide by putting a match to the powder magazine, rather than suffer the dishonor of being taken prisoner.

By six that evening, not one Turkish or Egyptian vessel had struck its flag and surrendered. However, their firing gradually ceased.

Ottoman losses were horrendous—sixty of ninety fighting ships and an estimated 6,000 men killed and 4,000 wounded. Even with the shooting over, the Ottomans continued to blow up their disabled ships with men aboard to escape a humiliating surrender. The allies, amazingly enough, lost not a single ship, and only about 600 were killed and wounded.

"Joy and Exaltation"

Even before the smoke cleared away from Navarino Bay, church bells were ringing across the Greek countryside. With the Turko-Egyptian fleet destroyed, it was apparent to even the most unsophisticated Greek peasant that the Ottomans could not sustain their army in Greece. Wild rejoicing was the order of that night, and for the next few weeks huge bonfires were lit on the mountaintops of the Peloponnese Peninsula, bonfires that blazed with a light all Greeks understood as the light of freedom.

It would take almost two more years before hostilities would finally cease in Greece, but this, at last, was the beginning of the end. As one English politician, a firm believer in the Greek cause of liberty, wrote when he heard the news: "This day has been to me one of the happiest of my existence, and to all Greece one of joy and exaltation."

THE BATTLE OF NAVARINO WAS THE LAST NAVAL BATTLE FOUGHT BETWEEN SHIPS POWERED ENTIRELY BY SAIL.

The Battle of Navarino, 20th October 1827, 1846 (oil on canvas), Aivazovsky, Ivan Konstantinovich (1817-1900) / Marine College, St. Petersburg, Russia, / The Bridgeman Art Library

THEODORE KOLOKOTRONIS: "WE GREEKS HAVE RISEN UP AGAINST TYRANTS"

By the time the war for independence started, the man with the great mane of white hair was already considered elderly—fifty, as a matter of fact—and he wore an outmoded helmet with a huge crest atop it, looking almost like a Spartan warrior of old.

In fact, Theodore Kolokotronis bore a pretty fair resemblance to King Leonidas or one of his princes. Born in 1770 in the rugged southeastern Peloponnese, Kolokotronis was a member of a hill clan used to fighting small-scale actions against the Turks. His father and two of his uncles were all killed in these murderous skirmishes. Kolokotronis briefly saw service as a pirate, and then fought with the Russian fleet in the Russo-Turkish War of 1805, and later with the English army, against Napoleon Bonaparte's forces, in 1810.

But Kolokotronis's heart was always in the mountainous regions of the Peloponnese, where he returned just before the outbreak of the Greek Revolution, to raise a band of klephts to fight against the Turks. Because of his unusually broad military experience, Kolokotronis was named commander in chief of Greek forces in the Peloponnese and was able to provide his men with at least rudimentary military training, which stood them in good stead when he inflicted an early, and major, defeat on Turkish forces at the Battle of Valtetsi in the spring of 1821.

Kolokotronis then moved on the Turkish town of Tripolis in the central Peloponnese, a massive fortress protected by a wall 2 miles (10 km) in circumference, 6 feet (1.8 m) thick and 14 feet (14 m) high. When the Greek fighters besieging the city began to bicker among themselves, Kolokotronis mounted a huge rock and made a stirring speech, telling the men: "We have taken up arms against the Turks, and therefore it is regarded by the whole of Europe that we Greeks have risen up against tyrants … If we kill [our own people], what will the kings say?" The Greeks listened and stayed together long enough to destroy Tripolis and gain a great early victory in the war.

Kolokotronis was now in his prime, an extraordinarily colorful figure, "tall and athletic," wrote one English observer, "with a profusion of black hair and expressive features." The Greek commander did not lack for confidence. "If Wellington had given me an army of 40,000," he once wrote, "I could have governed it, but if 500 Greeks had been given to him to lead, he could not have governed them for an hour." However, those ungovernable Greeks got Kolokotronis in trouble. Taking the wrong side in the 1823 civil war, he was thrown in jail, but such were his military skills that he was released when the Egyptian army under Ibrahim Pasha invaded the Peloponnese. Kolokotronis

now turned to the guerilla war that he had learned in the hill with his klephts and managed to wear Ibrahim down through numerous vicious small-scale actions.

Kolokotronis had a gift for symbolism. When Ibrahim sent an order out to burn all the olive trees of the famous Kalamáta region, Kolokotronis's men intercepted it and brought it to him. Kolokotronis then wrote a reply that became famous throughout Greece: "We will not submit—no, not if you cut down every branch, not if you burn all our trees and houses, nor leave one stone upon the other. If only one Greek shall be left, we will still go on fighting."

Ibrahim, of course, was defeated at the Battle of Navarino, and Greece was saved. But had it not been for the actions of Kolokotronis waging war against him on the Peloponnesian peninsula, the allied fleet might have been too late to turn the tide.

IBRAHIM PASHA: "ON THE WHOLE, NOT A GOOD-LOOKING MAN"

Despite the fact that Ibrahim Pasha was described by one contemporary observer as short, pockmarked, and "as fat as a porpoise," he was both the most able and most vicious leader the Ottoman Empire possessed. Of course, it was a sign of the polyglot nature of the War of Greek Independence that Ibrahim was not Turkish at all, but Egyptian. And, in fact, he was Egyptian by adoption only.

Ibrahim was the son of the famous Muhammad Ali, pasha of Egypt, an Albanian who married a Macedonian woman and adopted Ibrahim, her son from a previous marriage. When Muhammad Ali moved to Egypt and rose in the power politics of that country to become pasha after suppressing the remnants of the Mamluks who had been broken in Napoleon Bonaparte's invasion of Egypt in 1798, Ibrahim went along with him.

Ibrahim was a warrior from a very young age, having helped his father defeat the Saudis in a war with Arabia and also invading British forces in 1816. He had also seen his father learn the art of European warfare from French advisors and had himself helped train the Egyptian army to fight in ranks. Thus Ibrahim was ready, in 1825, at the age of thirty-six, to assume command of the massive invasion force entrusted to him by his father: fifty-four battleships, countless transport vessels, (in total, the fleet counted some 400 ships) and 17,000 troops.

Muhammad Ali made the stakes clear to his son: Sultan Mahmud II wanted the Egyptians to destroy the Greeks in the Peloponnese. If Ibrahim accomplished this task, his father would give him Crete—recently subjugated by the Egyptians—as a present.

Ibrahim was more than ready. When he invaded the Peloponnese, the Greeks—who had been beating the Turks—laughed at the Egyptian troops, who wore what seemed to them to be servants' costumes of red jackets, pants, and skull caps. Ibrahim himself was unprepossessing. An English observer (displaying not a little prejudice) described him as "on the whole not a good-looking man [but] he evidently has an excellent opinion of himself, the natural consequence of being surrounded by flatterers and slaves."

But his fighting abilities could not be questioned. Ibrahim immediately took possession of Navarino Bay, the best harbor in the Peloponnese, destroying two Greek forts, and then captured the strategically important island of Sphacteria. The Greeks now realized that were fighting someone very different from the tired Turkish commanders they had previously overwhelmed. Generals such as Theodore Kolokotronis, arrested during the civil war, were granted amnesty as the Greeks frantically marshaled their forces to try to stop Ibrahim, who was now sowing a path of destruction north through the Peloponnese.

By the end of 1825, Ibrahim had taken back the fortress city of Tripolis and burned and sacked almost every major city in the Peloponnese. He wasn't just defeating armies, he was destroying

the countryside and shipping its inhabitants back to Egypt as slaves. Rumors held that he was going to deport the entire Greek population and repeople the Peloponnese with Egyptians

Whether this was true or not—certainly it would have been a very difficult plan to undertake—Ibrahim's success in defeating the Greeks militarily worked against him politically. Great Britain, alarmed at the turn of events, finally took the lead with France and Russia in signing the Treaty of London, calling for an end to hostilities. When the Ottoman Empire ignored this, England, France, and Russia sent ships to face Ibrahim's navy at Navarino Bay in 1827. Ibrahim's forces were to be defeated there (Ibrahim was not present, having wisely calculated the odds and left the scene), but more than any other commander of the war, this short, fat, not very good-looking man nearly put an end to the Greek Revolution.

The Greek Soldier: The Klephts and Armatoli

The Greek Revolution, unlike the American and French Revolutions, started out as a guerilla war and stayed that way for almost the entire eight years that it raged. Only at the very end of the war at the Battle of Petra (see "Chronicle," p. 52) did Greeks train successfully to fight as a regular army in the European style. In the early 1820s, as Greek leaders sought to build an army, they had no choice but to pick their soldiers from the ranks of two bands of tough fighting men, the *klephts* and the *armatoli*.

After the conquest of Greeks by the Ottoman Empire in the fifteenth century, Greek men faced hard choices. Many were forced to become janissaries—essentially slave-soldiers—to fight against the enemies of the Ottomans, while others were conscripted into the armies of various local beys and princes. In either event, one's personality—one's Greekness, one's Orthodox religion—was subsumed by one's masters. Therefore many rebellious Greeks over the centuries joined bands of brigands, known as klephts, which would often lead small revolts against Turkish landowners, more from a desire for plunder than anything else. To combat these, the Turks formed their own brigand armies known as armatoli.

However by the beginning of the nineteenth century, the line between armatoli and klephts had become blurred. Men would alternate between both groups as profit motives took them; gradually they began to unite based on their shared ethnic identity and hatred of the Turks. At the outbreak of the revolution, these men formed the nucleus of the Greek military, with more and more peasants swelling their ranks daily. The armatoli and klephts believed in honor and self-sacrifice above all. When wounded in the face of the oncoming enemy, they would request that their friends shoot them so that they might be spared the indignity of being taken prisoner.

And these Greek brigands were extraordinary fighters. Armed with knives, muskets, and pistols, they would wait until the enemy entered a narrow pass and then ambush from above, blazing away, before charging wildly at the Turks. When things went wrong, they refused to retreat, but rather hid behind stone walls, taking potshots and shouting insults at their enemy. In the end, it was these tough mountain fighters—bristling with so many weapons they looked like hedgehogs, according to one observer—who drove the Turks from the sacred mountains of Greece.

THE CAMP OF A KLEPHT CHIEFTAIN IS SHOWN HERE. AS TENSIONS ROSE OVER TURKISH RULE, GREEKS BEGAN FORMING THEIR OWN BRIGAND ARMIES TO FIGHT AGAINST TURKISH LANDOWNERS.

The Ottoman Soldier: Egyptian Leading the Way

For centuries, the Ottomans had kept a standing army in the form of janissaries, a term which is a combination of two words meaning "new soldiers" in Turkish. Originally, janissaries were non-Muslim slaves, often young kidnapped Christians, whom the Turks transformed into a highly disciplined fighting force, although by the 1600s, impressed young men from Greece and the Balkans formed the core of the army.

By the time of the War of Greek Independence, however, the janissaries had fallen into disarray. The once elite army was, as one historian has put it, "practically useless as a fighting force," given to idleness and corruption. A European visiting Constantinople describes these men as swaggering through the streets "their bulky sashes filled with arms; their weighty sticks rendering them objects of fear and disgust." When any attempt was made to reform this army, the janissaries revolted, causing civil strife and unrest in the Turkish capital.

Finally, in 1826, Sultan Mahmud II had had enough. He announced a reorganization of the janissaries along Egyptian lines, because the Egyptian army of Muhammad Ali was the most modern in the Middle East (see "Chronicle," p. 52). When the janissaries revolted in June of that year, Sultan Mahmud simply lined up cannons filled with grapeshot and slaughtered them inside their barracks. The janissary system was through, once and for all. What arose was an army modeled along European lines, which drilled, marched, and fought in units. A few years earlier, Muhammad's Egyptian army had invaded the Peloponnese and nearly retaken it from the Greeks using such tactics. Now, the Ottomans were ready to do the same, but it was for all intents and purposes too late. The entry of Great Britain, France, and Russia into the war and the stunning Ottoman defeat at the Battle of Navarino that fall ensured a Greek victory.

The Legend of Áyia Lávra

Every human has a myth surrounding his or her birth—what a dark and stormy night it was, how timely the intervention of the midwife!—and most countries do, too. In America, it is the midnight ride of Paul Revere, in England the signing of the Magna Carta, in France the storming of the Bastille. If certain liberties are taken in the retelling of these events, well, so much the better to capture the original spirit of liberty.

Greek, too, has its liberty myth— the tale of Bishop Georgios Yermanós, prelate of the town of Patras in the northwestern part of the Peloponnese peninsula. According to the story, Bishop Yermanós was called by the Ottoman rulers to go to Tripolis (in central Peloponnese) in March of 1821—as, in fact, were most Greek Orthodox churchmen of prominent position—as part of a fairly routine attempt by the authorities to probe the Greek bishops as to just how rebellious their congregations were.

Instead, Yermanós went to the monastery of Áyia Lávra, in the rocky hills looming above the Gulf of Corinth, and refused to go any farther. Fifteen hundred armed peasants gathered around him on March 25. He told them that when the Turks came to get him, all they had to do was shout with one voice: "Thine, O Lord, is the victory!" and the Turks would be defeated. Sure enough, according to the story, the Turks arrived to abduct Yermanós, the peasants shouted with a mighty roar, and the Turks retreated in haste and confusion. Yermanós then said Mass, gave absolution to all Greeks gathered around him, and commanded them to defend their country and their church.

In fact, the Áyia Lávra incident never happened. Bishop Yermanós was not even present there at the time. The story, according to historians, comes from French propagandist Françoise Pouqueville, consul to Greece, who supported the Greek cause and wanted to provide it with a romantic beginning when he wrote his four-volume history of the Greek Revolution. But, invented or not, the Greeks still celebrate the story of Bishop Yermanós, his miraculous salvation, and the birth of their country on March 25.

Byron and the Philhellenes

When the Greek Revolution began, most governments in Europe were careful not to take sides. They had just finished cleaning up the mess of the French Revolution and were trying to restore the old order. Plus Great Britain, France, Austria, and Russia were, at least nominally, not engaged in hostilities with the Ottoman Empire.

This did not mean, however, that the people of these nations, particularly France and Great Britain, did not take sides. Greece had, after all, given the world language, literature, art, and the very ideal of liberty. Not to go to its aid seemed criminal. In much the same way as socialists the world over would flock to Spain in the late 1930s to fight Francisco Franco's army (see "Spanish Civil War," p. 300), these lovers of Greece, or philhellenes, went to Greece to take up arms in the fight against oppression.

Prominent among them was the poet Lord George Gordon Byron, age thirty-five. He had last visited Greece in 1809 (see "Ali Pasha," p. 66) and since that time had become both famous (for his poetry) and notorious (for sexual scandals that included affairs with his half-sister Augusta and Lady Caroline Lamb, wife of a future prime minister of England). Escaping Great Britain, Byron had traveled through Europe before deciding to go to Greece in the summer of 1823, to fight for the cause and lend his considerable prestige and bank account to the revolution. (Byron took with him £9,000 to dispense to various revolutionary committees, and he was to spend a good deal more helping refit a portion of the Greek navy).

The poet's ideals were shaken a bit by the reality of circumstances on the ground in Greece. "Day and night," wrote an observer, "[fortune hunters] clung to his heels like a pack of jackals," begging for silver. And Byron himself wrote that the Greeks "are such [damned] liars. There never was such an incapacity for veracity shown since Eve lived in Paradise."

Byron ended up in Mesolongi in western Greece in early 1824. From there he planned to gather Greek rebels around him and attack the Turkish fortress at Lepanto, at the mouth of the Gulf of Corinth, but he became ill and died on April 19. (Historians are not quite sure why; the suggestions range from malarial fever to brain hemorrhage.) In death, Byron achieved far more than he could have in life for the Greeks. He was mourned deeply by the revolutionaries he befriended, and his presence in Greece at his death drew worldwide attention to the Greek cause. Byron had at last transcended the scandals of his lifetime to become a genuine national hero.

LORD GEORGE GORDON BYRON'S SCANDALS IN ENGLAND CAUSED HIM TO FLEE THE COUNTRY TEMPORARILY AND LAND IN GREECE, WHERE HIS GENEROSITY AND FRIENDSHIP MADE HIM A NATIONAL HERO.

Lord Byron after a Portrait painted by Thomas Phillips in 1814 (see 41918), 1844 (enamel), Essex, William (1784-1869) / Stapleton Collection, UK, / The Bridgeman Art Library

The Greek Fireship

When the revolution began, the Greeks—although a country with a long and storied tradition of seafaring victories, including their pivotal victory over the Persians at Salamis during the Greco-Persian wars—were at an enormous disadvantage to the Turks. Most Greek ships came from one of three islands, Hydra, Spétses, and Psara, where wealthy merchants had outfitted their vessels with guns to fight off pirate attacks. These ships were converted into men-of-war, and each island had their own private fleet, sailors, and admiral. It was a very informal arrangement with the crews of the lightly armed vessels serving only as long as they were paid, and then decamping back to their fishing villages.

The Greek Revolutionary fleet numbered perhaps twenty converted merchantmen with twenty guns, at most. The Turks, on the other hand, possessed a comparatively large and sophisticated navy, with about twenty ships totaling eighty guns or more. But, not being a sea-going people themselves, the Turks depended on the Greeks to officer and crew their vessels, and naturally, at the first shots of the revolution, most of these Greeks had deserted. That left the Turks with green crews mainly shanghaied from bars.

"The confusion on board a Turkish vessel is absolutely ridiculous," one English observer wrote. "One half of the men are ... horribly seasick, sprawling about the deck; while the other half are pulling at ropes, of which they have no knowledge."

These large, cumbersome vessels, manned by inexperienced crews, were ripe targets for the primary Greek navy weapon of the war—the fireship. Fireships were not new. They had been used as far back as the fifth century B.C. by Greeks and others. But the Greek fireships of the 1820s were far more powerful vessels of perhaps 200 tons (181,436 kg), 70 feet (21 m) long, and carrying two masts full of sail, which gave them the ability to bear quickly down on the enemy. A flimsy wooden deck covered the hold, which was full of powder kegs. Several troughs cut in the deck contained highly flammable mixtures—pitch, oil, naphtha, alcohol—and the sails and ship itself were coated with turpentine.

The captain of the fireship, as well as the insanely brave crew of perhaps twenty-five men, would steer the ship (usually at night) right at a Turkish vessel, attach it by hooks to the gunports or railings, leap into an escape boat trailing behind, and set the fireship ablaze. If all went well, a Turkish ship would be blown to smithereens. With the slightest error, however, the Greeks would be obliterated.

All in all, fireships accounted for some forty destroyed Turkish ships and sowed terror throughout the Ottoman navy.

THE GREEK FIRESHIP CONTAINED MIXTURES SUCH AS PITCH, OIL, NAPHTHA, AND ALCOHOL. THE SAILS AND SHIP ITSELF WERE COATED WITH TURPENTINE. THE CAPTAIN, AS WELL AS THE INSANELY BRAVE CREW, WOULD STEER THE SHIP (USUALLY AT NIGHT) AT A TURKISH VESSEL.

National Historical Museum, Athens

Ali Pasha: "I Talk Not of Mercy"

Although Ali Pasha was far from a supporter of the Greeks, whom he treated with sometimes barbarous cruelty, he was inadvertently instrumental in helping his subjects gain their freedom.

Ali Pasha was an Albanian, born with blood on his hands. His grandfather was a bandit who had at first fought the Turks, but then switched sides to join them. His father murdered his own brother to become governor of what is now southwestern Albania. Pasha, born in 1750, gradually built a power base in northern Greece through endless raids and the use of blackmail and extortion.

By the first decade of the nineteenth century, Ali governed a satrapy which, when combined with the territory belonging to his sons, covered most of Greece. He was, at least nominally, beholden to the Sultan in Istanbul, and he made sure to pay tribute, but in fact he governed Greece almost as an independent nation. At one point, to gain a seaport on the Albanian coast, he made a treaty with Napoleon Bonaparte, but then switched allegiance to Great Britain after the Treaty of Tilsit made Russia—enemy of the Ottoman Empire—and France allies.

Ali Pasha was the best well-known figure of the Ottoman Empire in Western Europe. Lord Byron visited Ali Pasha in 1809 and enshrined him in *Childe Harold's Pilgrimage*:

"I talk not of mercy; I talk not of fear

He neither must know who would serve the Vizier:

Since the days of our prophet the Crescent ne'er saw

A chief ever glorious like Ali Pashaw."

But Byron also recognized the that this fat, complacent-looking man was "a most remarkable tyrant, guilty of the most horrible cruelties," which included, supposedly, beating condemned prisoners to death with sledgehammers, murdering some 800 descendants of a family who had offended his mother forty years before, and drowning a young woman and seventeen of her companions because they spurned the advances of his son, Mukhtar.

Eventually, Sultan Mahmud II, made of stronger stuff than his predecessors, began scaling back Ali Pasha's powers, fearful that Ali was taking too much power for himself. When Ali Pasha reportedly attempted to assassinate a relative of his who had fled to the protection of the Ottoman authorities in Constantinople, the Sultan sent an army after him, isolated him on an island in a lake near his fortress stronghold in northwestern Greece in January 1822, and killed him when he refused to surrender. But finally destroying Ali Pasha had taken two full years of fighting and immense resources, during which the Greeks who had formerly been Ali's subjects were able to rise against a distracted Ottoman Empire.

ALI PASHA, WHILE GUILTY OF SOME BRUTAL TREATMENT OF THE GREEKS, WAS ALSO INADVERTENTLY INSTRUMENTAL IN THEIR GAINING INDEPENDENCE.

Portrait of Ali Pasha of Yannina, engraved by Robert Havell, 1822 (litho) (b/w photo), Cartwright, Joseph (c.1789-1829) (after) / Private Collection, / The Bridgeman Art Library

"Mercy Was Out of the Question": Massacre at Chios

One of the events that drew public sympathy to the Greek cause was a horrific massacre of the Greek civilian population on the island of Chios in April of 1822. Chios is a large island in the Aegean Sea, situated about 5 miles (8 km) from the Turkish coast and long known for its rich merchant traders. Situated as close as they were to the Anatolian mainland, the Chians had strong ties with the Turks, who allowed them a great deal of autonomy.

Most Chians did not want to join the Greek Revolution, but in March 1822 the island was invaded by a small Greek army from a nearby island, which besieged the local Turkish garrison, committed the sacrilege of tearing leaden tiles off the roofs of mosques to melt down into bullets, and briefly proclaimed the island a Greek revolutionary property. At this, several hundred Chians decided to join them.

But the Sultan in Constantinople could not tolerate this insult. He sent a fleet containing 15,000 soldiers to Chios. These men—many of whom had been enlisted because of the promise of rich plunder—overwhelmed the small Greek army and began massacring the civilians of Chios. One contemporary historian wrote: "Mercy was out of the question, the victors butchering indiscriminately all who came their way. Shrieks rent the air, and the streets were strewn with the dead bodies of old men, women, and children."

No one was spared, not even those in madhouses. Many Chians hid in the hills, where they were often forced to suffocate crying

children to keep them from giving away their families. Some escaped on boats that brought them to the nearby island of Psara, but these were in the minority. Out of a total population of between 100,000 and 120,000, 25,000 Chians were killed and 45,000 were taken into slavery.

While there were certainly massacres of Muslim populations by Greek fighters—prominent among them atrocities in Navarino, Monemvasia, and Tripolitsa—the killing at Chios shocked Europe, Great Britain in particular. Within a year, Great Britain had recognized the Greek cause, taking the first measures that would lead to its ultimate involvement with the revolution.

THE MASSACRE ON THE ISLAND OF CHIOS BY THE TURKS IN 1822 SHOCKED EUROPE AND ENGLAND IN PARTICULAR.
Eugène Delacroix, Louvre Museum, Paris

4

THE MEXICAN–AMERICAN WAR

1846–1848

Taking half a million square miles of territory from Mexico,
the United States assumed its present continental borders
and became the most powerful force in the Americas.

Combatants

- United States
- Mexico

Theater of War

Mexico, Texas, California

Casualties

United States: 1,700 combat dead, 11,000 dead of disease

Mexico: An estimated 6,000 combat dead and 13,000 dead of disease

Major Fighters

UNITED STATES

President James Polk, who pushed for war against Mexico
General Zachary Taylor, who defeated Mexican forces along the Rio Grande and at the Battle of Buena Vista
General Winfield Scott, who made an amphibious landing at Veracruz and marched across central Mexico to capture Mexico City
Captain John C. Frémont, who led the "Bear Flag" revolt against Mexicans in California
General Stephen Kearny, who captured Santa Fe and invaded California

MEXICO

President José Joaquín de Herrera, moderate leader who attempted to avoid war with the United States, was overthrown by Mariana Paredes y Arrillaga in a military coup to become president, but who became Mexican president again at the end of war
General Antonio López de Santa Anna, controversial general who overthrew Paredes in a military coup to become Mexican president but failed to defeat U.S. forces
General Mariano Arista, who lost a series of battles to Zachary Taylor in northern Mexico at the beginning of the war

The term "Manifest Destiny" was coined by a New York journalist in 1845 and perfectly described the mood of Americans as the country entered the 1840s. Pushing westward, most Americans felt they had a god-given right, or destiny, to expand the country's borders, not only from "sea to shining sea," as the U.S. national anthem had it, but from the Rio Grande River in the south and up to British-held Oregon territory in the north. Oregon was purchased from the British, but California and the territories belonging to Mexico (present-day California, Texas, New Mexico, Arizona, and Utah) were not so easily acquired. When Mexico refused to sell them, the United States went to war, and an overextended Mexico was no match for the aroused patriotic vigor and new manufacturing might of the United States. America's first imperialist venture—its first foreign war—made the United States the preeminent power in North and South America.

1845:

March: U.S. President John Tyler signs a resolution to annex Texas as U.S. territory; Mexico rejects Texas independence or annexation.

November: U.S. Emissary John Slidell offers Mexico $25 million to buy New Mexico and California; the Mexican government refuses.

1846:

January: U.S. President James Polk sends troops under Zachary Taylor to southern Texas at the Rio Grande.

April: Mexican troops cross the Rio Grande, attack Taylor's forces, and are repulsed.

May: United States declares war on Mexico; Taylor's army defeats Mexican troops at the battles of Palo Alto and Resaca de la Palma, driving them back across the Rio Grande.

June: Forces of Captain John C. Frémont capture Sonoma, in California, and declare Californian independence.

July: U.S. naval ships capture Monterey, the Mexican capital of California.

August: Colonel Stephen Kearny captures Santa Fe, New Mexico, a key Mexican trading post.

December: Kearny's forces defeat Mexican troops at the Battle of San Pasqual, California.

1847:

January: The United States captures Los Angeles.

February: Zachary Taylor defeats the much larger army of General Antonio López de Santa Anna at the Battle of Buena Vista.

March: U.S. General Winfield Scott makes an amphibious landing at Veracruz on the Mexican Gulf Coast, captures the city, and advances inland.

April: Scott's army defeats Mexicans at the Battle of Cerro Gordo.

August: Mexicans defeated by Scott at battles of Contreras and Churubusco.

September: Scott defeats Mexicans at Chapultepec and enters the capital, Mexico City.

October: Resistance in Mexico City ends.

1848:

February: Treaty of Guadalupe Hidalgo ends war with Mexico, ceding what are now the states of New Mexico, Texas, Arizona, Utah, and California to the United States.

GENERAL ZACHARY TAYLOR AND HIS U.S. TROOPS DEFEATED GENERAL ANTONIO LÓPEZ DE SANTA ANNA AND HIS MUCH LARGER ARMY AT THE BATTLE OF BUENA VISTA.

Battle of Buena Vista, 22nd-23rd February 1847 (colour litho), American School, (19th century) / Dallas Historical Society, Texas, USA / The Bridgeman Art Library

"A SMALL WAR"

In the 1820s and 1830s, Mexico, newly independent from Spain, needed settlers to occupy its remote northern territories, which included present-day Arizona, New Mexico, Utah and, especially, Texas. Settlers from the United States were welcome if they took an oath of allegiance to Mexico and converted to Catholicism, which thousands of Americans did. But by 1835, people living in present-day Texas (variously called "Texicans" or "Texians") had become unhappy with Mexican rule and rebelled. A series of bloody battles and border raids ensued until, in 1845, Texas declared that it was independent and U.S. President James Polk quickly convinced Congress to annex the territory.

This step, Polk said, might cause what he called "a small war" with Mexico, but what Polk had in mind made a small war worth the effort.

a large force under General Mariano Arista. The two clashed when Arista crossed the Rio Grande, and war was declared between the two nations.

From the beginning, the Mexicans had almost no chance. Although the United States' standing army at the outset of the war stood at just 5,500 officers and men, the country was wildly enthusiastic for what would become its first foreign war, and 50,000 men were soon enlisted for twelve-month terms, while the newly industrializing country turned out shoes, uniforms, flintlock muskets, and artillery (see "The U.S. Soldier," p. 78).

The Mexican army numbered about 18,000 at the beginning of the war, but there was no such national enthusiasm for the conflict, and the ranks of the Mexican army were filled with conscripts liable to desert in the face of the enemy. Too, the

President James Polk and General Winfield Scott decided on an ambitious strategy: the first ever U.S. amphibious invasion.

Believing in the United States' Manifest Destiny, Polk wanted to occupy all Mexican land north of the Rio Grande, as well as present-day New Mexico, Arizona, and California. After the Mexicans turned down Polk's offer of $25 million to purchase this territory, some 500,000 square miles of land, Polk sent General Zachary Taylor and a 4,000-man army to occupy Texas just north of the Rio Grande. The Mexicans sent

Mexican political situation was unsettled as the war started. The more moderate President José Joaquín de Herrera had been ousted in a military coup by Mariana Paredes y Arrillaga, who would in turn be ousted himself.

United States attacks on Mexican territory became three-pronged. Zachary Taylor's forces drove Arista's army down through northern Mexico, by September of 1846, winning a series of battles at Palo Alto, Resaca de Palma, and the Mexican city of Monterey. In the meantime, General Stephen Kearny led U.S. troops west, seized Santa Fe, in modern day New Mexico, and traveled overland to California, where U.S. settlers under Captain John C. Frémont had declared California independent (see "Waving the Bear Flag," p. 83) and taken the important cities of Monterey and New Mexico.

Back in Mexico, ex-president Antonio López de Santa Anna had returned from exile, overthrown President Mariana Paredes y Arrillaga in a military coup, and raised a force of 20,000 men. However, in February 1847, he was defeated by Zachary Taylor in the bloody Battle of Buena Vista. Despite this loss, as well as the loss of huge swathes of their territory, the Mexicans refused to surrender, so President James Polk and General Winfield Scott decided on an ambitious strategy: the first ever U.S. amphibious invasion. Landing 12,000 men on the beaches of Veracruz, Mexico, Winfield's forces advanced inland, taking the same route as the one taken by Hernán Cortés's conquistadors more than 300 years earlier. Fighting a series of pitched battles with the Mexicans—Cerro Gordo, Contreras, Churbusco, Molino del Rey, and Chapultepec—the Americans reached and occupied the capital of Mexico City in September (see "Turning Point," p. 72) and quelled all resistance there by October.

At this point, President Santa Anna was ousted and replaced by the more moderate President

José Joaquín de Herrera, who had been the Mexican leader when the war began. He quickly negotiated the Treaty of Guadalupe Hidalgo, which awarded what is now the southwestern United States and California to the United States, in return for $15 million.

ZACHARY "OLD ROUGH AND READY" TAYLOR RODE HIS HERO STATUS AS A SUCCESSFUL COMMANDING OFFICER FROM THE MEXICAN–AMERICAN WAR RIGHT INTO THE WHITE HOUSE IN 1848, ALTHOUGH HE FELL ILL AND DIED IN OFFICE BEFORE FINISHING HIS TERM AS PRESIDENT.

ATTACK ON MEXICO CITY: 1848

The U.S. troops crouched low as the sound of the guns died away, echoing across the expanse of Mexico City, 3 miles (5 km) distant. Fingering their rifles, they stared at the bastion on a rocky hill that rose 200 feet (61 m) above them. It had an exotic-sounding name, Chapultepec, although all that meant when translated was *hill of grasshoppers.*

The palace-fortress perched high atop the hill had once been the residence of Spanish colonial viceroys, although it was currently the home of the national military academy, whose young cadets even now manned gun positions on the hill and in the towers of the palace. Perhaps because of the Aztec name, many Americans referred to the building as "the halls of Montezuma," although in fact no Aztec ruler had ever entered it.

The palace of Chapultepec was, properly speaking, a complex, with outbuildings. A large, manicured park filled with giant cypresses, enclosed by a 12-foot-high (3.5 m) wall. Its commanding position over Mexico City made Chapultepec the key to taking the city itself, which was essentially an island approached by causeways. Attacks on the Mexican capital could be only feasibly made from the south and west. On the south, the causeways were too long and too open, allowing artillery fire to easily rain down on an invading force.

The two causeways that entered the city on the west were much shorter, but they were guarded by Chapultepec, perched atop its 700-yard (640 m) long volcanic ridge. For an entire day and night, the U.S. artillery had bombarded the palace atop the hill. Now, at eight o'clock in the morning of September 13, 1848, the big guns had fallen silent, as black smoke plumed from the palace and drifted down the hill. At a shouted order, the U.S. infantry arose and charged.

The Road to Mexico City

Since landing at Veracruz six months earlier on March 9—the largest U.S. amphibious landing to date—General Winfield Scott and his forces had made an extraordinary march through central Mexico, surprising even Scott's superiors back in Washington, who found him a bit plodding for their taste (see "Commanders," p. 76). Within a few days, a ferocious artillery barrage ordered by Scott had forced those in command of Veracruz to surrender and lay down their arms, a boon for Scott, who did not want to assault a city suffering from an epidemic of the deadly disease of yellow fever (called by the Mexicans *el vomito negro).* After the armistice was concluded, Scott took his men west on the National Highway, a 300-year-old road that had originally been built by the Spanish to follow the route of Hernán Cortés across the mountains to the Valley of Mexico and the fabled city of Tenochtitlán, now Mexico City.

The road was graded, well maintained, and the only one open to an army of some 13,000 men moving across country with all their supplies. General Antonio López de Santa Anna, president of Mexico, knew this, of course. In fact, much of the land Scott's army was traveling through belonged to him personally. Santa Anna had set

A MAP DEPICTING MEXICO AT THE TIME OF THE MEXICAN–AMERICAN WAR. THE UNITED STATES VICTORY ADDED HALF A MILLION SQUARE MILES OF MEXICAN TERRITORY TO THE CONTINENTAL UNITED STATES.

Getty Images

an ambush for the Americans at a hilly spot near the village of Cerro Gordo, but a young artillery officer named Robert E. Lee performed the unmatched feat of hauling his guns up and down a mountain to subject the Mexicans to punishing fire. They fled, leaving behind 4,000 men, who were cut off and forced to surrender mountains of supplies and ammunition and a military chest containing close to a million dollars, money that Santa Anna had raised to fund his army.

There would be several more battles along the way, in particular at Contreras and Churubusco, but always the Americans pushed the Mexicans aside and kept on going, in August descending into the Valley of Mexico, with Mexico City sitting at its center. The city was in near anarchy as different political parties fought with each other in panic while the Americans approached. Santa Anna seized total power, claiming he was the only one who could save the city, but an attempt to parlay with the Americans led nowhere. The parley had delayed Scott's advance on the city for almost two weeks, but now he was determined that nothing would get in his way.

Up Chapultepec

The U.S. forces charging up the Hill of Grasshoppers numbered about 5,000, and they scrambled up the steep slopes in two long columns, General Gideon Pillow's division from the west, General J.A. Quitman's division from the south. The Mexican defenders, commanded by General Nicolás Bravo, numbered about 850 regular troops, but he also had with him about 200 Mexican Military Academy cadets—aged thirteen to fifteen—who had refused to abandon their school and now were armed and manning positions.

Pillow led his men against the Mexican soldiers shooting from the wall that circled the parklike grounds. After fighting through a hail of bullets, they forced these soldiers to retreat, scaled the wall, and headed up the hill toward the palace, struggling through groves of cypress trees as fast-moving squads of Mexican soldiers fired and then retreated from tree to tree. Pillow was wounded in the foot, but he shouted for his men to keep going. At last, they made it to the base of the citadel, where a high wall rose. Hugging the wall close to keep from being hit by Mexican troops leaning

out windows above and shooting down, the men waited for ladders to be brought so they could climb to the ramparts.

In the meantime, Quitman's men raced up a gently sloping road that led to the gates of Chapultepec palace, led by forty handpicked U.S. Marines. Quitman, an English professor in civilian life, walked calmly among his men, a cigar in his teeth, urging them on. (He later discovered that he had lost one of his shoes early in the fight. He didn't know how, but hadn't even noticed it.) The men at last made it to the southern wall of the palace and found a weak spot that the marines widened with crowbars while frantic Mexican soldiers shot through the opening, lead pinging off the Marines' tools. At last the opening was big enough, and they forced their way inside.

In the meantime, Pillow's troops had found their ladders and swarmed over the parapet guarding the west side of the palace.

Wrapped in the Flag

For minutes that must have seemed like hours to the men inside, ferocious hand-to-hand fighting took place inside the palace. Men grunted, swung muskets, jabbed with bayonets, and slipped on blood that flowed in spreading pools across the tiled floors. Soldiers were deaf for hours after the battle because of the sound of gunshots fired in an enclosed space.

General Nicolás Bravo was captured, but not before he ordered his troops, caught between two onrushing U.S. forces, to retreat to the city down the steep slopes of the hill. Most of them did, but six cadets remained behind, fighting to the end in the high tower rooms of the palace as the Americans went in search of them. They were so young that the U.S. soldiers tried to talk them into surrendering, but they refused, kept on fighting, and were killed.

One cadet, Juan Escutia, found himself with nowhere to retreat to at the top of the castle. Wrapping himself in the citadel's Mexican flag to keep it from being captured by the Americans, he leapt to his death in the ravine below the palace, a death watched by thousands of admiring U.S. troops and celebrated to this day in Mexico.

But soon after this, the U.S. flag rose over Chapultepec, and the day belonged to Winfield Scott and his troops. The Americans had suffered 130 killed, the Mexicans 650, but the way to Mexico City was now open.

U.S. FORCES STORMED THE FORTRESS CHAPULTEPEC ("HILL OF GRASSHOPPERS") IN SEPTEMBER 1848 TO TAKE MEXICO CITY. THE PALACE-FORTRESS PERCHED HIGH ATOP THE HILL HAD ONCE BEEN THE RESIDENCE OF SPANISH COLONIAL VICEROYS.

Prints & Photographs Division, Library of Congress, LC-DIG-pga-02604

GENERAL WINFIELD SCOTT: "OLD FUSS AND FEATHERS"

General Winfield Scott looked every inch a soldier. He stood six feet, four inches (193 cm) tall, wore beautiful uniforms, walked with a strut, and was so good-looking one historian has called him "not only handsome, but magnificent." His men called him "Old Fuss and Feathers" because he could be a bit vain and pompous and liked a good military parade. But besides looking the part, Scott knew what he was doing. Born in 1786, he was a wounded hero of the War of 1812 as well as a veteran officer of two wars against American Indians.

By the time the Mexican War started, Scott was sixty years old, a savvy brigadier general with political aspirations who had twice sought and failed to get the nomination for U.S. president. President James Polk knew he had to appoint someone to take charge of the U.S. forces that would invade Veracruz and march to Mexico City. For a time Polk resisted Scott, a member of the rival Whig party, whom he also felt to be an unimaginative fighter. But Polk finally decided that Scott was a better choice, not nearly as fractious and unmanageable as Zachary Taylor, who was already fighting in Mexico.

Despite fears on the part of the Americans already in combat in Mexico that Scott preferred the parade ground to the battlefield, the new general did quite well. Insisting on working mainly with regular army forces, he detached about 13,000 men from Taylor's army in northern Mexico, made a successful amphibious landing in Veracruz, bombarded that city into submission, then marched onto Mexico City through heat, torrential downpours, difficult terrain, and numerous attacks by Mexican forces.

Scott had with him a number of brilliant young officers (see "A Good Career Opportunity," p. 82), whom he directed well in combat. He left the war with a powerful reputation that did indeed bring him to the Whig presidential nomination in 1852, although he was defeated by Franklin Pierce. He was commander in chief of Union forces as the Civil War began. Although past his prime and soon replaced, Scott devised the Anaconda Plan to beat the Confederacy into submission.

GENERAL WINFIELD SCOTT'S SHOWY AND POMPOUS PERSONALITY DID NOT ENDEAR HIM TO HIS TROOPS, BUT HE MANAGED TO GET THE JOB DONE.

GENERAL ANTONIO LÓPEZ DE SANTA ANNA: "THE NAPOLEON OF THE WEST"

The first shots of the Mexican–American War can be said to have been fired in 1836, when the settlers of Texas rebelled against Mexico in an attempt to gain their independence. The Mexican general opposing the Texans, Antonio López de Santa Anna, who was president/ dictator of his country as well, gained a reputation in the United States as a cruel and ruthless man, responsible for killing those Texan fighters who had surrendered after the Battle of the Alamo in early March, followed by the even more horrendous slaughter of a force of 300 Texans who had surrendered after the Battle of Goliad. These unarmed prisoners were simply marched out into the plains on Palm Sunday and shot and bayoneted to death.

Born in the state of Veracruz in 1794, Santa Anna joined the army at the age of sixteen and fought in Mexico's successful war against the Spanish. By 1828, he had become a general and earned fame for beating off a Spanish attempt to invade Mexico. In 1835, after reformers attempted to change the corrupt Mexican government, Santa Anna led a military coup that toppled the current president and placed himself in power.

Santa Anna personally led the forces fighting against the Texans, but was beaten and captured at the Battle of San Jacinto by General Sam Houston and his army. Santa Anna was very nearly lynched by the Texans who made him prisoner, and he signed an armistice that ended the fighting.

By the time the Mexican–American War started, Santa Anna had been in and out of power in Mexico, depending on the tumultuous politics of the country. He had even lost a leg during a battle with French invasion forces in Vera Cruz. (Ever politically savvy, he used this grievous wound to the best advantage by parading the severed limb through Mexico City and creating a large monument to it there.) Santa Anna had a flair for colorful self-promotion, calling himself the "Napoleon of the West," spending thousands of dollars on his favorite entertainment, cockfighting, and consorting with very young women.

The swirling tides of Mexican politics would bring Santa Anna in and out of the presidency of the country several more times, before he retired for good and died in 1876.

GENERAL ANTONIO LÓPEZ DE SANTA ANNA, WAS A BRUTAL MILITARIST WHO SLAUGHTERED SURRENDERING AMERICAN ARMIES IN TEXAS DURING THE BATTLE OF THE ALAMO AND THE BATTLE OF GOLIAD.

Portrait of Antonio Lopez de Santa Ana (1794-1876), c.1858 (oil on linen), L'Ouvrier, Paul (fl.1858) / © Collection of the New-York Historical Society, USA, / The Bridgeman Art Library

The U.S. Soldier

While the United States had a small standing army at the beginning of the war (see "Chronicle," p. 70), it swelled quickly as thousands of enthusiastic volunteers joined the ranks, all wanting to see action in Mexico before the war ended. To equip these men, the factories of the United States ramped into high gear. One turned out 12,000 pairs of shoes a month, another produced 49 mortars and 50,000 shells in a few months' time. The Springfield factory in Massachusetts turned out 100,000 smooth-bore flintlock muskets, which became the main weapon of the U.S. soldiers, with a range of perhaps 100 yards (91 m). The Americans also depended on their field artillery (see "The Flying Artillery," p. 79), which was better than anything the Mexicans possessed.

While enthusiastic, the U.S. volunteer soldiers, despite the efforts of the small group of regular army officers to keep them in check, could be ill-disciplined. Many of them were given to getting drunk and robbing and even killing Mexican civilians, committing excesses that General Winfield Scott claimed were enough "to make heaven weep." However, some of this behavior was in part due to the killings of U.S. soldiers by Mexican guerilla groups such as the rancheros (see "The Mexican Soldier," below).

The U.S. forces had their own form of ranchero, known as the Texas Rangers, a band of irregular horsemen that had originally protected the settlements of Texas during that territory's war with Mexico.

In the Mexican–American War, the Texas Rangers acted as guides and cavalry for the U.S. Army, but they were also a feared force, dressed in buckskin, with an avowed hatred of Mexicans, and they perpetuated numerous grisly massacres of Mexican citizens.

Only about 1,700 U.S. soldiers were killed in combat during the Mexican–American War, but seven times that number died of diseases that ranged from measles, yellow fever, typhus, and amoebic dysentery brought on by polluted water. One soldier bemoaned the fact that in this war, fought for the glory of their country, so many soldiers lives "were extinguished in the dull camp or the gloomy march."

The Mexican Soldier

Americans were mainly disdainful of the efforts of Mexican soldiers, many of whom were conscripts drafted into the war, illiterate peasants who had no idea what they were fighting for. The conscripts lived their military lives almost as if they were in their villages back home, gathering in small groups to cook and play music. (The Mexican army was full of music, everything from simple wooden flutes to brass horns. Marching north to meet the army of Zachary Taylor, General Mariano Arista's 2,000-man force had a 150-member band that played their national anthem, and bugles echoed

for minutes at a time before Mexican soldiers actually made a charge.)

Mexicans units were often followed by women, either mistresses or wives, who were known to loot battlefields before the smoke had even cleared. Sometimes the women fought alongside of their men. Women "fought like heroes," according to one American officer, in the defense of Mexico City.

The Mexicans were far more poorly armed than the Americans. Their chief weapon was the British-made, Napoleonic-era Tower musket, or Brown Bess. It was a gun meant

for volley fire because it had no front sight and was almost impossible to aim. But the Mexicans had not been trained in the art of volley fire. To make matters worse, if there was a wind when the gun was fired, flames had a tendency to flare back along the barrel. British soldiers had been trained to turn their heads aside to avoid this, but the Mexicans suffered numerous facial burns, and in the end, they mainly ended up firing the gun from the hip, rendering it even more inaccurate.

However, the Americans did respect—and fear greatly—one group of Mexican soldiers: the rancheros. Like their counterparts in the Texas Rangers, the rancheros were irregular cavalry, superb horsemen, and armed to the teeth, and many of them were part Indian. The rancheros rode behind U.S. lines, wreaking havoc. They would often seek out a lone U.S. soldier at night, lasso him, drag him across the chaparral, disembowel him, and leave him for his comrades to find. Even after the war, many of these ranchero groups would operate as banditos in northern Mexico, wielding great local power.

The Flying Artillery

By far the most effective U.S. weapon of the war was the "flying artillery," which was also known as the "horse artillery." Relatively light cannon were attached to wooden caissons and pulled by two horses (which were usually ridden by the gunners) and which could be moved quickly to any part of the battlefield where soldiers were in trouble. Once at a hot spot, they blasted at the enemy before limbering up again and finding another trouble spot.

The flying artillery was not used as battery fire against entrenchments or fortifications, but mainly as an antipersonnel weapon, firing canister shot into the enemy to break up attacks before they even started.

Flying artillery units were trained to fire a round every ten to fifteen seconds, which blew gaping holes in enemy lines at a far faster rate of fire than any Mexican unit could achieve. The Mexicans defeated by Zachary Taylor's forces at the Battle of Palo Alto calculated that they had taken

3,000 rounds of U.S. artillery, both shells and canister, as opposed to firing only 750 rounds of their own. Most of the Mexican casualties at Palo Alto and at other battles where the flying artillery had room to maneuver came from artillery fire.

THE "FLYING ARTILLERY," AS IT WAS CALLED, CONSISTED OF LIGHT CANNON PULLED BY TWO HORSES RIDDEN BY THE GUNNERS. THEY WOULD TRAVEL TO DIFFERENT PARTS OF THE BATTLEFIELD WHERE MEN NEEDED AID AND FIRE CANISTER SHOT INTO ENEMY LINES.

Prints & Photographs Division, Library of Congress, LC-USZ62-51668

The Pen and the Sword

The Mexican War, as it was usually called in the United States, was the first U.S. war popularized by a mass press. Historian Robert W. Johannson wrote, "The essential link between [the Mexican War] and the people was provided by the nation's press."

This was due to technology that produced newspapers more cheaply, a dramatic rise in literacy in the United States as primary education became the norm rather than the exception, and the consequent rise of mass circulation newspapers affordable to all. When Zachary Taylor's forces first beat the Mexicans near the Rio Grande in the spring of 1846, Americans heard about it within a week, and their patriotism was stirred to fever pitch. There was insatiable desire for news about the war, and U.S. newspapers sent war correspondents to the front, some of whom marched and even fought with U.S. soldiers. The correspondents sent their dispatches home by a mixture of ship (to New Orleans), Pony Express (one such service connected Mobile, Alabama, and Philadelphia by sixty horses), and the new telegram (which was not widespread and was expensive to use, thus it was saved for only the most important occasions). The

rise of a journalistic icon, the Associated Press, began during the Mexican War when David Hale, editor of the *New York Journal of Commerce,* proposed that six New York dailies pool their resources and information.

Prior to this, news from the front was brought only by official military or government dispatch. So the "immediate" press coverage of the Mexican War made it the first war known intimately by thousands of Americans.

THE MEXICAN–AMERICAN WAR WAS THE FIRST WAR TO RECEIVE IMMEDIATE PRESS COVERAGE. THIS NEW METHOD OF SPREADING THE NEWS WAS TAKING OFF IN DIFFERENT FORMS—BY PONY EXPRESS, SHIP, AND TELEGRAM.

© North Wind / North Wind Picture Archive

The Saint Patrick's Battalion

One of the stranger episodes of a strange and colorful war was the exploits of the Saint Patrick's Battalion. By their name, one might think they fought on the American side, but in fact, this group of soldiers, primarily Irish and German, but also Canadians, French, English, Poles, and black American slaves, battled on the side of the Mexicans.

The *Batallón de San Patricio,* as they were called, was an artillery unit that was probably the sole Mexican version of the United States' much vaunted flying artillery (see "The Flying Artillery," p. 79). Most of the men who comprised the unit had lived in Texas, and when the war started, they sided with the Mexicans for any number of reasons, which included having been held in slavery by the Americans, having little or no money, or being promised incentives of up to 320 acres (1.2 million m²) of land by the Mexicans. Many of the Irish in the group had not been allowed to practice their Catholicism freely in the United States, where many people were prejudiced against Catholics, and so they turned to Mexico, where the Church was a powerful institution. Other members of the Saint Patrick's Battalion were deserters who had been horrified by the behavior of U.S. troops in Mexico (see "The U.S. Soldier," p. 78).

To the Americans, these men were traitors, but the Mexicans considered them heroes. The battalion fought bravely throughout the war,

IN THIS NINETEENTH-CENTURY PAINT-ING, MEMBERS OF THE SAINT PATRICK'S BATTALION ARE HANGED AS AN EXAMPLE AFTER THEIR SURRENDER.

Hanging of the San Patricios following the Battle of Chapultepec. Sam Chamberlain, 19th century. San Jacinto Museum of History.

led by Lieutenant John Riley, and many of them received medals from the Mexican government. Yet, by the end of the war, because their guns had been mainly destroyed by American counterbattery fire, they became an infantry unit. During the Battle of Churubosco, as Winfield Scott advanced to Mexico City, members of the battalion killed a high number of U.S. officers. This was a sign that deserters within their ranks were shooting the men who had once made their lives miserable.

Finally the battalion was forced to surrender, and the U.S. military decided to make an example of its members. While the Battle of Chapultepec was being waged on September 13, thirty San Patricios were taken out and hanged on a nearby hill. The Mexican government still commemorates the heroism of these men, while most Americans have no idea they ever existed.

A Good Career Opportunity

The Mexican–American War turned out to be a fertile landscape for political and military figures who would later become prominent in U.S. history.

Zachary Taylor rode his hero status from the war right into the White House in 1848, although he unfortunately died in office before finishing his term. Franklin Pierce had been a regular army officer in Mexico and in 1852, became Democratic president of the United States (Pierce, a Democrat, beat his former commander, Winfield Scott, who had the nomination of the Whig party). John C. Frémont (see "Waving the Bear Flag," p. 83) ran for president in 1856, although he lost to James Buchanan. And Jefferson Davis, a hero from the war, became president of the Confederacy.

A host of famous Civil War officers were first bloodied in Mexico. Robert E. Lee, then a major, commanded troops that fought their way into Mexico City (see "Turning Point," p. 72) while Captain Ulysses S. Grant was in charge of artillery that pounded Mexican forces defending the city. Others included Braxton Bragg, Stonewall Jackson, Fitzhugh Lee, John Magruder, James Longstreet, Abner Doubleday, Joseph Hooker, George Meade, and John F. Reynolds, just to name a few. These men would, within twelve years, face each other across the battlefields of America's most costly war.

In a sense, then, the Mexican–American War became a proving ground for some of the tactics of the Civil War (see "U.S. Civil War," p. 116), including close support of troops by field artillery and the importance of moving to attack the heart of enemy country, as Winfield Scott did, and as William Tecumseh Sherman would also when he struck at Atlanta in 1864. However, advancements in weaponry during the intervening dozen years and the vast scale of the conflict proved the Civil War to be beyond anything those who fought in Mexico could have imagined.

MANY OF THE MAJOR NAMES THAT WOULD APPEAR IN THE AMERICAN CIVIL WAR, SUCH AS ULYSSES S. GRANT, SHOWN HERE, WERE FIRST TESTED IN THE MEXICAN–AMERICAN WAR.

Prints & Photographs Division, Library of Congress, LC-DIG-pga-02027

Waving the Bear Flag

John C. Frémont was one of the most fascinating figures of the Mexican–American War. Born in Georgia in 1813, he joined the U.S. Topographical Engineers, then a part of the U.S. military, received the rank of captain, and became well known for the mapping expeditions he led through the Southwest, in what was mainly Mexican territory, so much so that he earned the famous nickname "the Pathfinder."

In early 1845, Frémont and a small group of topographical engineers arrived in California and soon became involved in political unrest against the Mexican government there. Frémont was a charismatic man, handsome and darkly bearded, who was not above bending the truth in the services of his own aims. In 1846, Frémont declared himself—with no government authority whatsoever—the U.S. military commander of California. He led a small group of Californian settlers who were disgruntled with Mexican rule in a campaign against the Mexican army. With help from the forces of U.S. Naval Commodore John Sloat (and Sloat's successor Robert Stockton) Frémont's forces captured Monterey and Los Angeles and declared California American territory. When General Stephen Kearny arrived with his unit, having traveled overland from Santa Fe, he vied with Stockton for control of California. Frémont sided with Stockton and was court-martialed in a sensational trial in which public sympathy fell on the dashing Frémont.

Frémont resigned his position in the army, became a U.S. senator, and in 1856 was the first Republican candidate for president, losing to James Buchanan. During the Mexican–American War, California had been a bit of a sideshow. Orator Daniel Webster had lectured his fellow U.S. senators in a famous speech in which he claimed California was "not worth a dollar." But when gold was discovered in California early in 1848, Frémont's admirers felt he had been prescient all along in seizing control.

JOHN C. FRÉMONT JOINED FORCES WITH DISGRUNTLED AMERICANS IN CALIFORNIA AND DECLARED HIMSELF MILITARY COMMANDER THERE.

5

THE TAIPING REBELLION

1851–1864

This civil war in mid–nineteenth century China killed more people than any other war in history except World War II and inspired Mao Zedong's rebellion a century later.

Combatants
- Taiping rebels (Taiping Heavenly Kingdom)
- Qing Dynasty, Great Britain, France

Theater of War
China

Casualties
Combined 20 to 40 million civilian and military dead

Major Figures
TAIPING HEAVENLY KINGDOM
Hong Xiuquan, mystical leader of Taipings
Lieutenant Li Jingfang, Hong's friend
Lieutenant Hong Rengan, Hong's cousin
General Li Xiucheng, loyal and valiant officer who failed to capture Shanghai and wanted to evacuate Nanjing

QING EMPIRE
Qing Emperors Xianfeng and **Tongzhi,** who were powerless to stop the Taipings

Zeng Guofan and **Li Hongzhang,** who reorganized Qing forces to fight Hong
General Zeng Guoquan, brother of Zeng Guofan, who won the siege of Nanjing

GREAT BRITAIN
Major General Charles "Chinese" Gordon, who led the "Ever-Victorious Army" in helping to defeat the Taipings

UNITED STATES
Frederick Townsend Ward, mercenary who trained and organized the "Ever-Victorious Army"

This "peasant rebellion" roiled for fifteen years across southern China, rocked the tottering and corrupt Qing Dynasty, and for a time made a strange messianic figure named Hong Xiuquan the most powerful man in the country. A scholar and failed clerk who styled himself as "Jesus Christ's young brother," Hong raised an army of peasants inspired by his preaching against the systematic corruption of the Manchu court.

Calling for equality between men and women, and agrarian reform, Hong led his army down the Yangtze River Valley and seized the city of Nanjing. Alarmed, the Qing Dynasty enlisted foreign mercenaries (see "Charles 'Chinese' Gordon," p. 93) to raise armies to put down Hong's rebellion. The conflict ended in 1864, but not before an estimated 20 to 40 million people died. The Qing Dynasty survived, but it was fatally weakened, and Hong Xiuquan's rebellion was to inspire Mao Zedong's successful revolt a century later.

1814: Hong Xiuquan is born in the Guangdong Province.

1842: The Treaty of Nanjing ends the First Opium War with Chinese defeat by British, humiliating the Qing Dynasty.

1844: Hong Xiuquan begins to preach word of his Taiping Tianguo, or "Heavenly Kingdom of Great Peace."

1847: Hong Xiuquan gathers an army at Thistle Mountain, in the Guangxi Province.

1851:
January: Taiping forces defeat a Qing army at Thistle Mountain.

October: Taipings capture the city of Yong'an in march through the Yangtze River Valley.

1852: Taipings capture the city of Quanzhou.

1853: Taipings captured Nanjing. Hong Xiuquan proclaims it his "Heavenly Capital."

1853–1864: Civil war sweeps the country, causing millions of casualties.

1862: The Taiping army under General Li Xiucheng attempts to capture Shanghai but is repulsed.

1864: The Imperial army captures Nanjing. Hong Xiuquan dies, ending the Taiping Rebellion.

THE TAIPING FORCES' VICTORY OVER THE QING ARMY IN CAPTURING NANJING IS DEPICTED HERE. THE TAIPING SOLDIERS, WERE RELENTLESS IN TRAINING AND BECAME FIERCE FIGHTERS.

Harvard Yenching Library

REBELLION DRIVEN BY
A DELUSIONAL LEADER

By the 1830s, the Qing Dynasty had been ruling China for 200 years, since the Manchu conquest of the country in the seventeenth century. The Imperial Court in Beijing was sophisticated and cultivated, the tentacles of its massive bureaucracy spreading out over the countryside, but most Chinese peasants and workers lived in abject poverty. After China's humiliating defeat by Great Britain in the First Opium War in 1842, even these downtrodden people began to see the Qing rulers as corrupt and weak. When the Yellow and Yangtze rivers overflowed their banks in the 1840s, causing widespread flooding and years of starvation, the country was ripe for rebellion.

The source of the Taiping Rebellion was a highly unlikely one—a deluded failed clerk named Hong Xiuquan (see "Commanders," p. 92). Born a Hakka outsider in the southern Chinese province of Guangdong, Hong failed his civil service exam twice. Perhaps unhinged by this humiliation and influenced by the Christian missionaries who were then preaching in the country, Hong developed the delusion that he was the second son of God, Jesus Christ's younger brother—his Chinese son. In 1844, expelled by the Confucian authorities of his village, Hong set off to preach that the word of his *Taiping Tianguo,* or "Heavenly Kingdom of Great Peace."

As Hong wandered his poor and mountainous province, his message became more political. He had been sent by God to destroy the "demon devils" who ruled China, as well as to create a new way of life, a "Human Fellowship" in which men and women would be equal, and wealth would be shared.

Peasants gradually began to flock to Hong, and by 1850 he had gathered an army of 40,000 near Thistle Mountain in Guangxi Province. Finally alarmed, the Qing rulers sent an army to attack Hong there, but his highly trained and regimented cadre beat them handily in January 1851 (see "The Taiping Soldier," p. 94). After this victory, more peasants joined Hong until his army was hundreds of thousands strong.

Marching down from the Guangxi mountains, Hong and his men swept northeast through the Yangtze River Valley with the city of Nanjing and the port of Shanghai as their targets. They defeated Qing forces at Yong'an and Quanzhou and finally captured Nanjing with an army 500,000 strong in March 1853. Renaming Nanjing his "Heavenly Capital," Hong now recruited a standing army of more than 1,000,000 men and women.

The Taipings held Nanjing for eleven years, but were unable to capitalize on their victory, mainly because of Hong Xiuquan's increasing mysticism, licentiousness, and paranoia. As Taiping and Qing forces fought a series of fierce battles over central China, disease and starvation swept the country, causing untold suffering. After failing in a bid to seize Shanghai, the Taiping forces were driven back, thanks in part to the efforts of Charles "Chinese" Gordon, the charismatic British

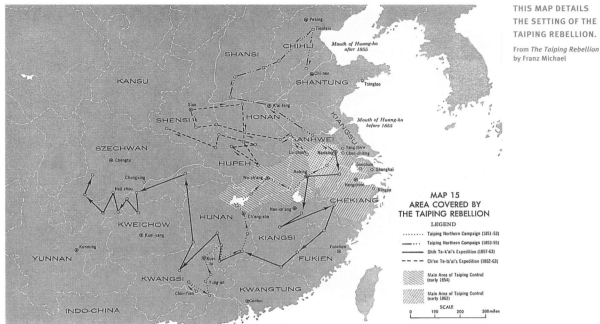

THIS MAP DETAILS
THE SETTING OF THE
TAIPING REBELLION.

From *The Taiping Rebellion*
by Franz Michael

commander of the so-called "Ever-Victorious Army," who used modern tactics and massed firepower to defeat the Taipings in battle after battle. In May 1864, the Taipings were besieged in their capital city of Nanjing by Imperial troops. Hong Xiuquan died of illness (or possibly suicide) on June 1 and the city fell a month later.

The Qing Dynasty was saved, but it was fatefully weakened. Compromised by the aid it had enlisted from foreign governments, it would fall for good in 1911. In the meantime, an estimated 20 to 40 million people died, making the Taiping Rebellion the most costly war in world history, with the exception of World War II (see "The Toll of War," p. 96). And within Hong's madness lay the seeds that would become Mao Zedong's successful revolution of the mid-twentieth century (see "Mao and Hong," p. 98).

THE SIEGE OF NANJING: OCTOBER 1863–JULY 1864

Slowly but surely, the Taiping forces were being driven back. General Li Xiucheng, commander of the rebel army that had tried and failed to take Shanghai in 1862, saw the net inexorably closing around the Heavenly Capital of Nanjing as 80,000 Qing troops, backed by foreign mercenaries and transported by shallow draft steamships owned by the French and British, took Taiping town after town, always promising mercy if the Taipings surrendered—and then slaughtering them—men, women, and children—in orgies of stabbing, shooting, and beheading.

The Qing commander, General Zeng Guoquan, was the ninth brother of Qing strategist Zeng Guofan, who had planned this attack on the vital city of Nanjing and was known with terror in the Taiping army as "General Number 9." A squat, scarred man, he gave no quarter and expected none. In October, his troops finally appeared and began to form a perimeter around Nanjing. They built a moat 10 miles (16 km) long around its southern perimeter, beginning at the Yangtze River, effectively forcing any relief for the city to come from a direction interdicted by massive amounts of Qing troops.

In mid-December, Zeng sent his men in their first assault against Nanjing's massive walls. They tunneled under them, filled the tunnels with gunpowder, and blew it up, causing sections of wall to crumble. But Taiping forces, fighting valiantly, pushed the Qings back and repaired the damage.

At this point, Li Xiucheng screwed up his courage and went to see Hong Xiuquan, Heavenly Ruler, to tell him some bad news.

"Why Should I Fear the Demon Zeng?"

Men had been beheaded merely for sneezing in this man's presence, and Li was nervous as he entered the Heavenly Palace, guarded by a cadre of foreign mercenaries, and found Hong surrounded by concubines, a pale, dangerous wraith of a man.

Bowing before Hong, Li told him that their only hope for survival was to flee. "The supply routes are cut and the gates are blocked," he told Hong, who listened impassively. "The morale of the people is not steady. The capital cannot be defended. We should give up the city and go elsewhere."

Hong stared at him and gave a chilling answer: "I have received the sacred command of God, the sacred command of the Heavenly Brother Jesus, to come down into the world to become the only true Sovereign of the myriad countries under Heaven … Why should I fear the demon Zeng?"

Li still believed that Hong was, in fact, the son of God, but he knew that this answer sealed his fate and the fate of the thousands of men, women, and children within the city's walls. Hong was out of touch with reality, unfit to command an army, and had been for some time. When the city had been captured and renamed the Heavenly Capital some eleven years before, Hong had been at the peak of his powers and had entered Nanjing in triumph, wearing yellow robes and yellow shoes, the Chinese imperial colors. But since then, Hong had steadily deteriorated.

While Hong's armies fought fruitless battles against Qing forces—battles that sapped strength and morale without achieving clear goals—he remained in Nanjing. Although issuing puritanical edicts to his people, he spent most of his time with his eighty-eight-concubine harem, within a palace protected by Irish and British mercenaries, who were a status symbol for Hong. Hong devoted a great deal of time to mystical poetry and writing down directions for the 2,000 women devoted to cleaning the palace, cooking for him, and bathing and dressing him.

It was no wonder that the reality of the situation outside the walls of Nanjing—what one historian has called "the bloody horror" of raging civil war—made no impact on the Son of Heaven.

Fierce Underground Fighting

As 1864 began, Li Xiucheng attempted to stockpile what grain he could, sortiing outside the city walls to try to capture supplies, but with little luck. By February, the last grain supplies outside the city were captured by Zeng's troops, making the town reliant upon only the rapidly dwindling rice in the granaries inside Nanjing. The corruption of Hong's relatives, whom he placed in a position of power, and who demanded large bribes for grain, caused starvation among the city's ordinary people beginning in early spring.

Well and truly trapped, General Li Xiucheng watched as the Qings captured every hill, circumvallated the city with a twin line of trenches and breastworks 300 yards (275 m) apart, and placed small forts every quarter to a half a mile (400 to 800 m), 120 in all, each manned by a Qing garrison. As people begin to starve, the Qings sent word to the city that anyone who deserted to the Qing side would be fed and treated well. People risked death to slip out of Nanjing, but when they got to Qing lines, many were executed. According to Charles Gordon, a British observer to the siege now that he had disbanded his Ever-Victorious Army, the escaping women were put in stockades where "the country people ... take as wives any who so desired."

The Qings began to build their mines, tunneling ever closer to the city walls, while Taiping forces dug countertunnels. A savage underground war broke out in the flatland near the city's walls, with Taiping forces breaking into enemy tunnels and either filling them with water or human waste or fighting hand-to-hand battles, sword and spears flashing in dark caves and recesses. One Qing tactic was to let the Taipings into their tunnels, then blow in noxious smoke with bellows, causing the rebels to die gasping and choking.

Manna

By the spring of 1864, the Qing forces had moved their breastworks to within 100 yards (91 m) of the city. The defenders, low on ammunition, could do little about this but watch. Li finally went to see Hong again, telling him: "There is no food in the whole city, and many men and women are dying. I request a directive as to what should be done to put the people's mind at ease."

Hong, still surrounded by his women and his writing instruments, but in yellow robes that had become dirty and tattered, answered him as loftily as he had before. Taking his cue from the biblical book of Exodus, in which God provided food from heaven for the escaping Israelites, he told Li Xiucheng: "Everyone in the city should eat manna. That will keep them alive."

Then he ordered: "Bring some here and after preparing it I shall partake of some first."

There was dead silence in the room. Li and Hong's women and courtiers could not begin to respond to such a strange order. Impatiently, Hong got down off his throne and went into the palace's central courtyard, where he collected weeds, lumped them into a ball, then handed them to Li, telling him: "Everyone should eat accordingly and everyone will have enough to eat."

As Li stared at him, the Son of Heaven put a small tangle of weeds into his mouth and began to chew them.

Over the next month, as the battles under and outside the city's walls became fiercer and fiercer, Hong, on his diet of weeds, grew weaker and weaker. Some historians have suggested that the weeds were poisonous, others that he was simply starving to death, still others that he may have committed suicide. In any event, the Son of

Heaven died on June 1, a day after the palace issued a decree to the haggard and starving population of Nanjing that Hong had decided to visit heaven and request of God and Jesus that they send an heavenly army down to smite the forces of General Number 9.

Li watched as Hong was buried on the palace grounds, without a coffin. After all, because he was coming back soon, why would he need one?

"Because I Did Not Understand"

At exactly noon on July 19, Zeng Guoquan gave a signal, and a huge explosion toppled a massive section of walls along the eastern side of Nanjing. Fire and smoke belched into the air as Qing forces poured into the breach. The Taipings could stop them only briefly, then turned and ran.

The battle was no longer a battle, but a slaughter. The Qings rampaged through the city, raping and murdering, while members of Hong's family sought ways to escape. Usually, burdened down by the loot they had stolen from treasuries, they were caught and executed. Hong's son and heir, the Young Monarch, managed to make his way out of the city disguised as a Qing soldier, but he was caught in the following weeks and executed.

But aside from Hong's corrupt family, none of the Taipings left in the city surrendered.

A slaughter of epic proportions took place, with Qing forces killing an estimated 80,000 to 100,000 men, women, and children while General Number 9 and his officers cantered their horses through streets literally flowing with blood. Although Taiping armies existed outside the city, the back of the rebellion was broken, and the war was soon to be over.

And what of General Li? After fighting all day, he found his way to a hilltop palace within Nanjing where he fell asleep. He was robbed during the night. The next morning, a Qing patrol captured him, and he was taken to Qing headquarters, where he gave his confession, which included recounting his conversations with the Son of Heaven. He told his captors that, with Hong gone, the Taiping rebellion was over. He begged them fruitlessly for mercy, not for himself, but for the many whose screams still echoed through the city. Then, as if awakening from a nightmare into a newer, darker nightmare, he mused as to why he never tried to stop Hong: "It is really because I did not understand. If I had understood...."

His sentence trailed off, and his confession ended there. That night, he was taken to a small courtyard in the Son of Heaven's former palace and beheaded.

HONG XIUGUAN CAPTURED THE CITY OF NANJING IN 1853, NAMING IT HIS "HEAVENLY KINGDOM." HOWEVER, THE IMPERIAL ARMY WOULD RETAKE IT IN 1864, IN AN ORGY OF SLAUGHTER.
The Art Archive / School of Oriental & African Studies / Eileen Tweedy

HONG XIUQUAN

Hong Huoxiu was born in the Guangdong Province in China in 1814. His family were peasant farmers and ethnic Hakkas—people who had emigrated to China centuries before, but who spoke a different dialect. Other Chinese looked down upon the Hakkas and refused to intermarry with them. Growing into an intelligent and quick-witted young man, Hong passed a test in his village to become an imperial clerk and then was sent to the city of Guangzhou in 1836 to take the Confucian state exam.

To Hong's mortification—and that of his entire family and village—the twenty-two year old failed the exam. The next year, he failed again. The second failure left him prostrate with shame and literally delirious. While in such a heightened state, he dreamed that he was the son of the Christian God he had heard about and that his father had tasked him with ridding China of the "demons" who were repressing its people. His new name, God told him, would be Hong Xiuquan, which means "Son of Heaven."

When Hong awoke, he insisted on being called by this name, but seven years would pass before he began his rebellion. In the meantime, he married and twice more failed to pass the civil service exam. Finally, at the urging of his friend Li Jingfang, Hong dusted off and read a tract that he had been given by a Christian missionary while in Guangzhou. Under the influence of these words, Hong decided that his dream meant that he was the second son of God—the younger brother of Jesus Christ.

Forming a small group of loyal followers who armed themselves with 20-foot (6 m) swords—to fight off demons—Hong left the village under pressure from Confucian authorities, found his way to the mountainous province of Guangxi, and slowly gathered an army of Hakka peasants. These men and women, believing that he would rid them of their Manchu oppressors, pooled their possessions, trained with rigorous discipline, and believed in Hong's Taiping Tianguo, or "Heavenly Kingdom of Great Peace."

By 1851, swollen to some 40,000 strong, the Taipings, as they became known, destroyed an army that the alarmed Qing rulers of the country had sent to defeat them. After this victory, Hong sent his army sweeping across China, heading for Nanjing. The Taiping Army would reach an almost unimaginable 1,000,000 soldiers and capture Nanjing, but their leader became increasingly unstable, extremely puritanical, and megalomaniacal.

Outside Nanjing, uncontrollable civil war swept through the countryside. Inside, Hong, paranoid and hidden, appointed his thirteen-year-old son as chief administrator, stated that he was seeing ghosts, and claimed that he was possessed by the spirit of a biblical prophet. As the Imperial army besieged Nanjing in the spring of 1864, Hong's people turned to him, begging for food. He told them: "Everyone in the city should eat manna. That will keep them alive." He himself began to eat weeds and, on June 1, died. There were rumors that Hong committed suicide, but he almost certainly perished of starvation and disease.

CHARLES "CHINESE" GORDON

Major General Charles Gordon, was born in London in 1833, son of an army officer and a shipping tycoon's daughter. He went to military school at the age of fifteen, where he showed himself bright, impertinent, brave, and willing to redress perceived wrongs done to him or others. After graduating, Gordon was commissioned into the Royal Engineers and, in 1854, served as a lieutenant in the Crimean War (see "Crimean War," p. 100), where he made a mark for himself with the cool courage with which he exposed himself to fire at the siege of Sevastopol. After the Crimean War, he was promoted to captain and became an instructor at a military school in England, but in 1860 was sent to China to fight in Great Britain's Second Opium War against the Qing Dynasty.

Gordon was fascinated by China—by the culture and religions of its people—and horrified by the excesses of the Taiping Rebellion. When a force of British troops stayed behind after the Second Opium War to protect English residents of the city of Shanghai, which was being threatened by Taiping rebels, Gordon volunteered to stay with them, attached to the staff of General William Staveley as an engineering officer.

After Frederick Ward (see "Frederick Townsend Ward," p. 99) died fighting with his Ever-Victorious Army—the first Chinese force to have any real success against the Taipings—Gordon took control and, in a series of brilliant actions, drove the Taipings away from their fortified cities near Shanghai. His relief of the siege of Chansu against overwhelming odds was the stuff his myth was made of. Attacking with a barely organized force much smaller than the Taiping army he was facing, he drove them away from the walls with massed firepower and bold tactics.

After Chansu, Gordon—soon to be nicknamed "Chinese" Gordon for his exploits—won battle after battle against the Taipings until, in 1864, he captured Chanchfu, the premier Taiping base in the Shanghai region. After that, with the Qing forces now rearmed, retrained, and advancing on all fronts against the Taipings trapped in Nanjing, Gordon disbanded his army and was awarded high honors by the Chinese. The British promoted him to lieutenant colonel.

After Gordon left China, he wandered the world as a British diplomat and soldier, serving in Russia, Egypt, and Africa. Only 5-feet-5-inches (165 cm) tall, but broad-chested and impressively mustachioed, Gordon was outspoken in his opinions and not a little eccentric. He believed the Garden of Eden was located in the Seychelles island group, and that the Earth was enclosed in a hollow box stored in the throne of God. Nonetheless, Gordon was the most famous British soldier of his era and his death—valiantly attempting fight off a Mahdist army attacking in the besieged city of Khartoum—made him a hero to future generations in Great Britain.

The Taiping Soldier: Soldiers of Heaven

In the years before the Heavenly Kingdom and the Second Son of Heaven came crumbling down to earth, the Taiping army was the finest one in China, mainly because of the intense discipline instilled in its ranks, as well as the fanatic loyalty of its soldiers.

The Taiping army, like Mao Zedong's later day peasant army, built itself from the ground up. Small units of four men and a corporal were fused into larger units of five corporals and their soldiers, led by a sergeant. Four sergeants and their troops became another unit, and so forth up to division strength units of some 13,000, which were led by generals. Each of the small units was given a different-colored, triangular-shaped flag with the name of its base camp written on it; each soldier wore that color on his or her uniform. All of these units were controlled by flags waved by their commanders, with different colored flags meaning "attack," "withdraw," etc.

Eschewing Manchu topknots, the men wore their hair long to their shoulders. Both sexes wore red jackets and blue trousers and carried muskets and swords.

Discipline in the Taiping army was, at least in the beginning, harsh. Recruits were taught that disobeying orders was like disobeying the word of God, because all orders ultimately came from Hong Xiuquan who was, of course, a god. If soldiers were caught stealing, smoking opium, or harming the general populace, they were beaten senseless or beheaded, depending on the severity of the offense.

德天

In battle, Taiping soldiers, both men and women, were fierce. They won fights by overwhelming their opponents with their numbers and with the fact that they were seemingly unafraid of death. Cannonballs would plow into their ranks, musket fire would rake them, and still they would come on, together, often singing and cheering.

But during the Son of Heaven's eleven-year-long period of deterioration in Nanjing, the army deteriorated as well. They began to pillage and destroy the countryside, thus gaining them the enmity of the very peasants upon whom they needed to depend, and the superior firepower and tactics of foreign-trained Chinese troops began to tell. In the end, Hong's once beautiful red and blue army was reduced to a tattered, starving mass fleeing before Imperial forces.

THE TAIPING REBELLION WAS LED BY THE MESSIANIC FIGURE OF HONG XIUQUAN, A FAILED CLERK WHO BELIEVED HIMSELF TO BE THE SON OF GOD, JESUS CHRIST'S YOUNGER BROTHER.
akg-images

The Qing Empire Soldier: "The Ever-Victorious Army"

At the beginning of the Taiping Rebellion, Qing Imperial forces stood little chance against the disciplined and fanatical cadres of rebels who assaulted their positions, cheering, with banners waving high. The Qings' morale had been weakened by successive defeats against Great Britain in the two Opium Wars, and the army's officers were often incompetent and corrupt. The clarion call of the Taiping way of life resonated with Imperial rank and file troops, many of whom were peasants themselves, and the Qings experienced, in the early years of the conflict, massive waves of desertion. Thousands upon thousands of soldiers crossed lines at night to throw in their lot with the Son of Heaven.

However, when Taiping forces began to threaten Shanghai, which was an important port city with a large contingent of foreigners, things began to change. The American filibuster Frederick Townsend Ward, hired by the Qing government, believed that to defeat the Taipings, with their decisive manpower advantage, Qing troops would have to be trained in the European manner, given modern weapons, and led by Europeans. He created a small fighting force—at most 5,000 men—that gained results well beyond its size. Organized into battalions of some 700 men, each commanded by a foreign mercenary but with secondary and noncom command given to Chinese, the Ever-Victorious Army—given its name by a grateful Qing government after a string of victories—was flexible in the

extreme, with each battalion functioning, if necessary, as a separate command unit.

Soldiers received Colt arms—repeating pistols and breech-loading rifles—as well as artillery, and they learned to march and maneuver as European troops did. They were also given handsome uniforms—blue, trimmed with scarlet—and wore turbans, which at first were derided by the Taipings. The laughter soon stopped, however, as Ward's troops regularly defeated much larger forces.

When Ward was killed at Cixi in September of 1862, Charles Gordon took over and led Ever-Victorious forces to even greater victories. But Gordon's more stringent, British Regular Army discipline style caused a much higher desertion rate, and the

Ever-Victorious Army was disbanded in May 1864. However, it had made a major contribution to defeating the Taipings, and it became the model for future Chinese armies trained in the European style.

THE EVER-VICTORIOUS ARMY OF THE QING EMPIRE WAS FORMED BY FREDERICK TOWNSEND WARD, WHO BELIEVED THAT TO DEFEAT THE LARGER TAIPING FORCES, THE QING TROOPS WOULD NEED EUROPEAN TRAINING AND MORE MODERN WEAPONS.

Toll of War: The Naked and the Dead

At first, most of the western world knew nothing of the carnage of the Taiping Rebellion, but by the early 1860s, reports began to drift out. These were carried mainly by letters written by foreign army officers or missionaries, or by journalists visiting the country.

These reports describe death on a scale that dwarfed even the killing going on in the battlefields of the American Civil War, which was considered mayhem of a new and modern type. Missionaries wrote of trying to pole their skiffs down the Yangtze River but finding the going slow because of the thousands of corpses that bumped monotonously against their hulls. One army officer wrote of stacks of dead on a recent battlefield, literally "walls 10 feet (3 m) high" around which the officer had to walk. Older battlefields saw "human bones bleaching among cannonballs."

In villages hit by endemic disease and starvation, "the houses are in ruins; streets filled with filth; human bodies are left to decay in open places or thrown into pools and cisterns, there to rot," an English missionary wrote. One American journalist saw a New Year's celebration occurring, firecrackers and streamers among piled dead, as if the dead were now simply part of the landscape.

Travelers near Shanghai and Nanjing, principal areas of fighting, found most houses destroyed; people slept on mats in the open, or in ruins. Children starved to death.

Young men were forced by Taiping or Qing forces into military service, and young women were abducted and sold into concubinage. Only the elderly remained, "with countenances showing their suffering and despair," according to the American journalist. Massive groups of refugees wandered the countryside, caught between the warring armies, and forced their way into Shanghai, which had not fallen to the Taipings. Shanghai was home to a sizeable contingent of foreigners, who soon saw their dogs disappearing, one by one, food for starving Chinese.

PICTURED: DEAD BODIES LYING IN THE TAKU FORTS DURING THE TAIPING UPRISING. AN ESTIMATED 20–40 MILLION SOLDIERS AND CIVILIANS DIED IN COMBAT, OF STARVATION, AND FROM DISEASE.

Getty Images

Century-Long Scars

The devastation of the Taiping Rebellion was not visited just on people, but on the Chinese ecology, as well. Some experts count the conflict as one of the greatest environmental disasters of the nineteenth century. With entire rural populations killed or driven away, the crop and property devastation was enormous. Experts estimate that central China did not recover from it until well into the twentieth century.

The scorched earth policy of both armies contributed to the disaster. Witnesses spoke of destroyed fields lying fallow for decades after the war's end, while erosion and increased flooding turned formerly fertile ground into wasteland. When the land finally became tillable again, whole families, villages, and towns did not exist to farm it. Either they had been killed or starved to death, driven to the larger cities, or forced into emigration.

Chinese emigration to Hawaii and California rose sharply during this period, similar to how the Irish departed Ireland during the Irish Potato Famine of the 1840s.

As late as the 1940s, there were still large areas of land forested by scrub brush and containing faded circles that were once villages along the Yangtze River and in central China— a legacy of the Taiping Rebellion.

"Good Words for Exhorting the Age"

The role of missionaries in the Taiping Rebellion—in particular, what responsibility they had in the incredible slaughter in mid–nineteenth century China—has long been debated among historians.

By the time Hong Xiuquan reached the city of Guangzhou in 1836 to take his test, Protestant missionaries, mainly from Great Britain and America, were hard at work trying to change the Chinese object of veneration from Confucius or Buddha to the Christian God. As Hong walked the streets of Guangzhou in despair after failing his exam, he was given the tract Good Words for Exhorting

the Age by a Christian street minister named Edwin Stevens, who adopted Chinese dress and spoke Chinese fluently. The pamphlet that so influenced Hong was written by a Chinese author schooled by missionaries. However, it colored Biblical stories and injunctions with a feverish and apocalyptic Chinese flavor, thus encouraging Hong and others in their delusions.

Hong and his followers focused in particular on the drama of the Book of Revelations, which they claimed foretold the need for bloody revolution in the country. When an aghast Christian missionary exhorted

Hong about the savage killings going on, he and his ministers pointed to other parts of the Bible where God, in his righteous wrath, smote thousands. Killing the unbelieving was a way of getting to heaven.

Some Christian ministers warned of the danger of blindly introducing such powerful texts to a country and a people who had no context whatsoever for understanding them. One Welsh Congregational minister wrote: "Protestant missionaries of China: This Insurrection is your offspring." But for the most part, missionaries, while horrified by the bloodshed, did little to change their way of preaching.

Mao and Hong

About thirty years after the death of Hong Xiuquan, a chubby young baby named Mao Zedong was born to Chinese peasants in a rural province. Mao, too, was a Hakka, a member of an outcast ethnic group. When Mao grew up and became China's most famous revolutionary, he took more than a few lessons from the rebellion of his predecessor, Hong Xiuquan.

The Qing Dynasty finally fell in 1911, but it had been weakened and almost entirely beholden to foreign governments since the Taiping Rebellion. Mao and his early Communists drew from that rebellion the important lesson that an independence movement based on egalitarian ideals could work. Mao even used some of the same terminology as Hong, referring to his enemies (chief among them the Japanese and his rival, Chiang Kai-shek) as "snakes" and "evil demons." Although Mao's impulse was for equality among the sexes, he, like Hong was rigidly puritanical and became, while ruling China, a paragon of lechery. Although Mao's rebellion was vastly more successful than Hong's, Mao, too, murdered millions and created a worshipful aura around his very person, thus belying the supposed "equality" of his movement.

After Mao took over China, he didn't forget his predecessor, building a museum near Hong's birthplace in Guangdong and planting a tree in his memory. The museum, still visited by tourists, ignores the seamier aspects of Hong's reign and focuses on him as a proto-socialist revolutionary.

MAO ZEDONG MODELED HIMSELF AFTER HONG XIUQUAN, EVEN DOWN TO USING SOME OF THE SAME TERMINOLOGY. AFTER MAO TOOK OVER CHINA, HE BUILT A MUSEUM TO HONOR HIS PREDECESSOR, A MAN HE CONSIDERED UNJUSTLY IGNORED.

We wish Chairman Mao a Long, Long Life, 1969 (colour litho), Chinese School, (20th century) / Private Collection, © The Chambers Gallery, London / The Bridgeman Art Library

Frederick Townsend Ward: Destined for Obscurity

Frederick Townsend Ward, the man who created and trained the Ever-Victorious Army, wasn't destined to be as famous as Charles Gordon, who led it to its greatest victories, but without Ward the Qing Imperial Court would have had a hard time in winning its war against the Taipings.

Ward, an American born in Salem, Massachusetts, in 1831, was a freebooter or filibuster—a U.S. military adventurer who sought to overthrow foreign countries, or at least, profit from fighting in their wars as a mercenary. Darkly handsome, reckless, and adventurous, Ward sailed to China numerous times aboard clipper ships, fought with the filibuster William Walker's forces during the latter's invasion of Mexico in 1853, managed to find his way to the Crimean War battlefields a few years later, and finally ended up in China by about 1860, working as a trader for a family business.

But soon the Chinese "Pirate Suppression Bureau" gave Ward command of an armed steamboat called "Confucius," with which Ward did an admirable job of protecting conveys on the Yangtze River from Taiping pirates. Thereafter, Chinese functionaries in Shanghai allowed him to control a small group of foreign mercenaries armed with modern Colt pistols and rifles, arms that far outclassed the outmoded muskets of the Taipings. Ward led this "Shanghai Foreign Arms Corps" in a successful assault on a Taiping fortified town in 1860. Although Ward was badly wounded in a subsequent action, he returned to action and began recruiting Chinese as soldiers—with the difference that he trained them in western tactics (See "The Qing Empire Soldier," p. 95).

In 1862, the Ever-Victorious Army, numbering perhaps 1,500 men, was ready to take the field. Under a banner inscribed with Ward's name rendered in Chinese, Ward led them in a series of actions against Taiping forces far larger than his. Due to Ward's unit's superior tactics and weaponry, they were victorious. Ward's forces growing to 5,000 men, he attacked the fortified town of Cixi in September of 1862, but he was mortally wounded near its walls. After Ward's death, command of his army would pass to Charles Gordon, who would become far more famous. But it was Ward who had finally discovered the key to beating the Taipings.

AMERICAN FREDERICK TOWNSEND WARD BEGAN TO TRAIN CHINESE FORCES IN WESTERN TACTICS AND WON A SERIES OF VICTORIES. THE DASHING WARD WOULD GO DOWN IN OBSCURITY, HOWEVER, AFTER BEING MORTALLY WOUNDED IN 1862.

Prints & Photographs Division, Library of Congress, LC-USZ62-91561

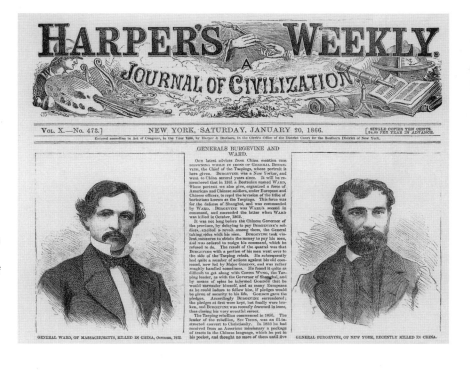

6

THE CRIMEAN WAR

1854–1856

Europe's most costly nineteenth-century conflict, the Crimean War had far-reaching results, inhibiting the southward expansion of Russia, extending the life of the Ottoman Empire, and introducing a type of warfare that would foreshadow that of World War I.

Combatants
- Great Britain, France, the Ottoman Empire
- Russia

Theater of War
Crimean Peninsula, Balkans, Black Sea, Baltic Sea, Pacific Ocean

Casualties
Great Britain: 6,000 combat deaths, 16,000 dead from disease

France: 30,000 combat deaths, 70,000 dead from disease

Ottoman Empire: 95,000 dead in combat and from disease

Russia: 400,000 dead in combat and from disease

Major Figures
GREAT BRITAIN
Lord Raglan, who led British land forces in Crimea
Earl of Cardigan and **Earl of Lucan,** whose rivalry caused the Charge of the Light Brigade
Admiral Sir Charles Napier, commander of the British fleet in the Baltic
William Howard Russell, British journalist who reported on the war
Florence Nightingale, whose nursing improved conditions for British wounded in Crimea

FRANCE
Louis-Napoleon Bonaparte III, who provoked war with Russia to increase his prestige

Marshal Jean-Jacques Pelissier, commander in chief of French forces around Sevastopol

OTTOMAN EMPIRE
Sultan Abdülmecid I, who rejected the Russian ultimatum
Omar Pasha, major Ottoman commander of the war

RUSSIA
Tsar Nicholas I, who sought war with the Ottoman Empire to expand his southern empire
Prince Alexander Menshikov, diplomat whose blunt maneuvering in Constantinople helped cause the outbreak of war
Tsar Alexander II, who took control after the death of his father

The Crimean War was fought ostensibly to protect the rights of pilgrims visiting the Holy Land, but the real story was that the major European powers were threatened by Russia's commercial and strategic designs on the tottering Ottoman Empire. When Russia, Great Britain, and France clashed on the battlefields of the Crimean Peninsula and the Baltic, using steam-driven warships, trains, the telegraph, powerful new rifles, and exploding artillery shells, the tone was set for the type of war that would be fought for generations to come. By the end of the war, a defeated Russia's ambitions were checked in southeastern Europe and the Ottoman Empire was preserved for the next half century.

1853:

May: Russia issues ultimatum to Ottoman Empire to allow Russian protectorate of Eastern Orthodox Churches. Ottoman Sultan refuses Russian ultimatum.

June: British fleet sails for the Dardanelles Straits, which connect the Black Sea to the Mediterranean.

July: Russia seizes Danubian principalities of Moldavia and Walachia, on the Danube River.

October: Ottomans declare war and cross the Danube River to defend their territory; British fleet enters the Bosporus Strait.

November: Russian fleet destroys Ottoman squadron at Sinop in northern Turkey.

1854:

March: Great Britain and France formally declare war against Russia.

April: Russians besiege Silistra, in Bulgaria.

June: Russians evacuate Moldavia and Walachia in the face of Austrian threats to enter the war.

August: Allies force the surrender of Bomarsund, in the Baltic.

September: Combined British and French army lands in Crimea, near Sevastopol. Allies defeat Russians in the Battle of Alma; Russians on Kamchatka Peninsula beat off landing force from French and British Pacific fleets.

October: Allies surround Sevastopol and begin bombardment. The Battle of Balaklava, which included the charges of the Heavy and Light Brigades, takes place.

November: Florence Nightingale arrives in Scutari, Turkey, with forty nurses, begins treating wounded from Balaklava; British and French defeat Russia at Battle of Inkerman; siege of Sevastopol continues.

1855:

March: Tsar Nicholas I dies and is succeeded by Tsar Alexander II.

May: Allied naval forces enter Sea of Azov, threatening Russian supply lines to Sevastopol.

August: British destroy Russian dockyard at Sveaborg, outside modern Helsinki, thus controlling the sea approaches to the northern cities of Kronstadt and Saint Petersburg.

September: Sevastopol falls to the French and British.

1856: Treaty of Paris is signed, ending the hostilities.

THE ALLIES INITIALLY THOUGHT THE BATTLE OF SEVASTOPOL IN 1854 WOULD BE QUICK AND THEY'D BE HOME WITHIN SIX WEEKS. THE BATTLE LASTED NEARLY A YEAR, HOWEVER, AND ALLIED TROOPS FOUGHT UNEXPECTED STIFF RESISTANCE FROM THE RUSSIANS.

The Bombardment of Sebastopol, 1858 (oil on canvas), Carmichael, John Wilson (1800-68) / © Royal Hospital Chelsea, London, UK, / The Bridgeman Art Library

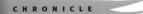

A BAD JOKE OVER A SICK MAN

Two famous phrases have come out of the Crimean War, a short war that would become notorious for a good many things. One of the phrases is historian Philip Guedella's statement that the conflict is "one of the bad jokes of history." The other is Tsar Nicholas I's repeated depiction of the Ottoman Empire as "the sick man of Europe." Both statements are accurate, but the joke turned out to be on Nicholas.

The Crimean War was in large part sparked by French Emperor Louis-Napoleon Bonaparte III's ambitions. In early 1852, having dispensed with representative government in France after his coup of December 2, 1851, Napoleon cast about for an issue that would unite the French people, predominantly Catholic, behind him. He found it in a seemingly insignificant spat in the Holy Land over which branch of the Catholic Church—Greek Orthodox or Roman Catholic—controlled the key to the Church of the Nativity in Bethlehem, birthplace of Jesus Christ (see "The Key," p. 112). Napoleon pressured the Ottoman government of Sultan Abdülmecid I to give the Roman Catholic Church (widespread in the west and France) control of all holy places in Palestine, which the Sultan finally did.

Tsar Nicholas I found this offensive because his country had nearly 50 million worshipping Greek Orthodox Catholics. He demanded that the Orthodox Church be given authority. But the Sultan, heavily influenced by frantic French and British diplomacy, refused, and in revenge the Russians occupied the Turkish principalities of Moldavia and Walachia, along the Danube River. Turkey then declared war.

Naturally, the Crimean War was about far greater issues. The Ottoman Empire was, indeed, "the sick man of Europe," corrupt and unwieldy in government and unable to defend its borders. Russia wanted to use that weakness to expand south and west into the Black Sea, while France, Great Britain, and to some extent, Austria (which did not appreciate the Russian presence just across the Danube) desperately needed to check these ambitions.

Russia delivered the first blow of the war by destroying a Turkish fleet at Sinop on the Black Sea in November 1853, but the Anglo-French fleet and invasion forces were already coursing toward the Black Sea. The allies' strategy was twofold. After protecting Constantinople, the Turkish capital, they wanted to bottle the Russians up in their main Crimean port of Sevastopol, while at the same time threatening the Baltic and the capital of Saint Petersburg in the north.

In September 1854, the combined Anglo-French invasion forces landed in the Crimea and planned to destroy Russian forces and take Sevastopol within six weeks. They defeated the Russians at the Alma River in the same month, but they hesitated in attacking Sevastopol. This miscalculation forced them to entrench around the city and besiege it.

The Russians fought valiantly to break through to their beleaguered town, attacking the Allied flanks in the battles of Balaklava and Inkerman in October and November, but they were unsuccessful. The Allies settled into a long siege of Sevastopol, both sides suffering dreadfully from disease and winter weather, before finally forcing the Russians out of the city on September 9, 1855. However, the Crimean campaign cost the French and British hundreds of thousands of casualties and would change the course of public opinion about "heroic" warfare, as the English public in particular was influenced by telegraph dispatches sent back by *London Times* reporter William Howard Russell. Russell, often known as the first war correspondent, described futile actions, such as the Charge of the Light Brigade (see "The Charge of the Light Brigade," p. 114) as well as the decimation of British soldiers through unchecked disease.

In the Baltic, the combined Anglo-French fleet initially commanded by Admiral Charles Napier saw the capture of the Russian fortress of Bomarsund in 1854 as well as the bombarding of valuable Russian shipping ports. This tied down 200,000 Russian troops in the area, even if the allies were unable to destroy the pivotal Russian cities of Kronstadt or Saint Petersburg.

With the near involvement of the Austrians—who threatened war unless Russia withdrew from Moldavia and Walachia, which it did—the actions of the King of Sardinia in sending forces to fight alongside the French, and the potential interest of the United States; the Crimean War, had it gone on much longer, could have conflagrated into the first World War.

As it was, the Treaty of Paris, signed in March 1856, would preserve Ottoman rule until the First World War, cripple Russia in the west, and unite

NAPOLEON III, PICTURED HERE, SOUGHT A CAUSE TO UNITE THE FRENCH PEOPLE, BUT HIS PROVOCATION OF THE RUSSIANS CAUSED A BLOODY AND UNNECESSARY WAR.

French and Britain, at least temporarily. Tsar Alexander II, seeing the weaknesses the war revealed in his country, which included a poorly trained peasant army that lacked any real sense of initiative, a byzantine bureaucracy, and an almost nonexistent supply system, set about making reforms that included freeing Russian serfs, streamlining the Russian civil service, and attempting to build railroads and industrial infrastructure.

Moreover, the war changed nineteenth-century warfare from its Napoleonic tradition to the type of conflict that would see its full, destructive fruition in the trenches of the First World War.

THE SIEGE OF SEVASTOPOL: 1879

The French and British troops who huddled in trenches and tents beyond the looming walls, towers, and earthworks of the Russian-held town of Sevastopol had been through a good deal. They had arrived in the Crimea in September, expecting to destroy the port city and return home within six weeks, no more. This little war would be a lark, a chance to gain some experience, and have stories to tell their children.

But the lark had never materialized. Dogged from the very beginning by typhus, cholera, and dysentery, the allies met unexpectedly stiff resistance from the poorly armed but tough and numerous Russian army. The Russians had been driven back at the Battle of Alma, whereupon the allies had surrounded Sevastopol instead of immediately attacking the city, which was a major error. The entire Russian army remained at liberty on the Crimean Peninsula and was able to supply Sevastopol through coastal roads that the allies had been unable to effectively cut off.

In October, the Russian army made a major effort to destroy the allies at the Battle of Balaklava, which had failed. On November 5, Russian forces from within the city under Prince Alexander Menshikov desperately attempted to break out, driving straight at the heart of the thin British and French lines around the city. In savage hand-to-hand fighting over uneven ground and through scrub brush—with much of the killing being done by bayonet—the Russians had been driven back, losing 12,000 men.

But the allies had little time to rest after their victory. On November 14, as the weary and bloody troops sat freezing inside their tents, a huge storm arose on the Black Sea, destroying the British supply ships in harbor at Balaklava. One ship, the *Prince,* went down with the loss of everyone on board— some 150 sailors—except for six who managed to crawl to shore. Almost worse from the point of view of the shivering British troops, the *Prince* had carried a cargo of 40,000 winter uniforms and boots, a cargo that was now completely lost.

Boots for Bread

Shivering in their thin summer uniforms, the British soldiers cursed their luck. "All life is a blunder," wrote one Scottish officer. "All matters, weather included, look sad and murky." The British especially had reason to complain. The British government bureaucracy, as one historian has put it, was "unfit to prosecute war so far from its home base." Either the proper supplies did not get through to British soldiers outside Sevastopol or, more frustrating, they did and sat on the docks at Balaklava, the tiny harbor through which British war materials were funneled. Commissary officers were too overwhelmed with red tape to move them. As December weather set in, the 3-mile (5-km) long road from the harbor to the British camp was almost knee deep in mud, making it difficult to bring in the food and clothing that the commander in chief, Lord Raglan (see "Commanders," p. 108) had begged Constantinople and London for.

The French, under the command of General François-Certain Canrobert, had fared better, with a stronger supply and commissary system, and became used to the pitiful sight of British soldiers coming to their portion of the lines, offering to trade boots for bread. The situation was so outrageous that the British public—alerted by letters back home and the *London Times* dispatches of journalist William Howard Russell—clamored for a change. The government began considering relieving Lord Raglan of command. In the meantime, the British army was so weakened that the French became the stronger force to reckon with outside Sevastopol.

The Malakov Tower

In the meantime, of course, the allies had the Russians to contend with. Had they attacked Sevastopol in September, they might have had a much easier go at it, but now it was formidably fortified, mainly through the attentions of the Russians' chief engineering officer, Count Frans Todleben, who had worked frantically to shore up its defenses. The centerpiece of the city's defense was the Malakov Tower. This huge stone tower, bristling with gun embrasures, and protected by fortifications on each side, enfiladed the ground for 180 degrees in front of it.

As the allies pushed closer to Sevastopol by means of interlocking trenches, Todleben made their lives hell by digging countertrenches of his own outside the city's walls and filling them with sharpshooters. These Russian snipers would so bedevil the attackers that, on a regular basis, several hundred British troops—drawn from different regiments, so as to evenly spread out casualties—would

crawl over the top of their trenches and launch a surprise attack with bayonets on the sharpshooters, hacking them to death, foreshadowing actions that would occur in World War I.

In fact, the whole stalemated scene outside Sevastopol foreshadowed the 1914–1918 war—the bursting of artillery shells, the crack of sniper rifles, the misery of freezing soldiers in muddy trenches, and the indecision of high command. As winter finally turned into the spring of 1855, with severe pressure being placed on them by their respective governments, Raglan and Canrobert decided they needed to crack the siege of the city.

"An Iron Shower"

On April 9, the Allies opened up with the most intense artillery barrage of the war, with 400 French and British guns battering Todleben's fortifications at Sevastopol. It went on for a week, with both defenders and besiegers nearly deafened by the continuous noise, and with Russian walls seeming to crumble in places. Lord Raglan was strongly in favor of an immediate infantry attack, despite the fact that the Russian guns, by no means silenced, continued to pound Allied trenches with return fire. But the French, who with 75,000 men seriously outnumbered the British forces, which counted only 35,000 troops able to do combat (there was also a Turkish army of some 60,000 in the trenches outside Sevastopol) were reluctant to attack without further reinforcements.

The waiting continued until June 7. Russian writer Leo Tolstoy, a young artillery officer, was inside Sevastopol and later published his *Sevastopol Sketches*, which capture what it was like inside the beleaguered, blacked-out town:

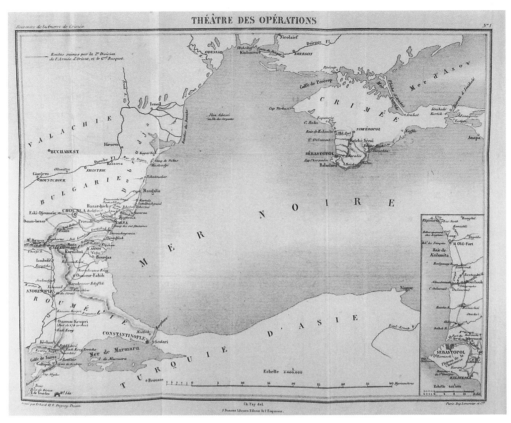

"The stars were high in the sky but shone feebly. The night was pitch dark, only the flashes of the guns and the bursting bombs made things around suddenly visible. The soldiers walked quickly and silently…only their measured footfall on the dry road was heard besides the incessant roll of the guns, the ringing of the bayonets when they touched one another, a sigh, or the prayer of some poor soldier lad, "Lord, O Lord, what does it mean?"

Finally, on the morning of June 7, the French and British troops attacked after another fierce artillery barrage. The French had snaked their trenches to a point only 60 yards (55 m) from the city's fortifications and leapt out of them with great élan, shouting as they surged forward, clearing the Russian sharpshooters from their rifle pits immediately in front of the walls. The French took the Russians' most forward position, a low, fortified hill known as the Mamelon, while the British stormed a Russian entrenchment called the Quarries, seizing artillery guns in a frenzied fit of bayoneting and close-quarters shooting that cost almost 700 lives.

The French casualties were far more shocking—more than 5,000 killed or wounded in a few hours—but the allies persisted. Seven days later, they launched an attack that unfortunately was so poorly coordinated that they had no hope of success. Here, the comparisons to the First World War are stunning. The French and British attacked through a hail of bullets, over open ground studded with primitive land mines, under heavy artillery fire from an enemy in prepared positions. It was, as one participant put, it "an iron shower," and a slaughter.

Final Attack

As September 1855 arrived, nearly 322 days after the initial British invasion, Sevastopol still held. It had cost much in human life on both sides, as well as careers. Prince Menshikov, the inept Russian commander, had been relieved in favor of Prince Michael Gorchakov. The French commander Canrobert had been replaced by General Jean-Jacques Pelissier. And Lord Raglan had died, some say of a broken heart (see "Commanders," p. 108) after the attacks of June, to be replaced by Major General James Simpson.

But from an Allied point of view, things were starting to look up. They had beaten off a major Russian attack on their lines on August 16 and then intensified their barrage fire. Their forces had been increased, and their supply situation bettered considerably, so that both the French and the British were able to pour artillery shells into the city, counting on counterbarrage fire, which destroyed Russian guns as soon as they fired. One Russian commander called it "the infernal fire" and bemoaned that the loss of guns and gun crews "can hardly be replaced."

On September 8, the last attack on Sevastopol began. Instead of having it take place at dawn, as usual, Pelissier sent his French forces in at mid-day, interrupting the Russian gunners as they ate lunch and so surprising them that only six artillery pieces even returned fire. Vicious hand-to-hand fighting ensued, but inside of ten minutes, the Malakov Tower was taken, and Russian forces subdued. In the meantime, the English charged their objective, a fortified area known as the Great Redan, but they were driven back at bayonet point, with great loss of life, most of their officers having been killed.

However, it turned out that the French had saved the day. Their capture of the Malakov Tower made the entire Russian position in Sevastopol essentially indefensible, and Gorchakov began to withdraw his forces from the city in orderly fashion, systematically blowing up their ammunition dumps and food stores. By the evening of September 8, they had left the embattled city. The British and French entered to find only ruined buildings and the moan of the wounded left behind.

The battle had cost the Russians 13,000 dead and the allies 10,000. Because the Russians had not had to surrender, they styled their withdrawal a strategic retreat, but both sides knew better. Despite the fact that the British had to swallow the bitter pill of having the French responsible for the fall of Sevastopol, the war was now all but ended. The Russians could not achieve their goal of broadening their influence in southeastern Europe, and Tsar Alexander II would capitulate the following March.

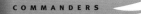

LORD RAGLAN:
"THEY WOULD STONE ME TO DEATH"

FitzRoy James Henry Somerset, Lord Raglan, was born in England in 1788, educated at Westminster, and commissioned an officer in the 4th Light Dragoons in 1804. He took part in the Duke of Wellington's peninsular campaign during the Napoleonic Wars, acquitted himself bravely in several battles, and was commissioned a lieutenant colonel by Wellington himself. Raglan lost his right arm in the Battle of Waterloo in 1814, retaining enough presence of mind after the amputation (which was done without anesthesia) to ask an orderly to pull a ring given to him by his wife off the cold fingers of the amputated limb.

So Raglan was distinguished and had behaved under duress in the fine tradition of a nineteenth-century British officer. But by the time of the outbreak of the Crimean War, Raglan was sixty-five years old and had not heard a gun fired in anger for forty years. Wellington had described him as a man "who wouldn't tell a lie to save his life," but honesty and Raglan's unfailing courtesy did not help him much in what he was about to face.

Both Lord Cardigan and Lord Lucan were officers under Raglan, yet he did little to stop their raging feud, born of mutual jealousy and family conflicts. While Raglan's English troops had performed with extraordinary bravery at the Battle of Inkerman, that Anglo-French victory was less due to his generalship than to luck and the Russians' failure to launch a coordinated attack.

Raglan's worst moments came during the siege of Sevastopol, which found the British army starving to death, without proper clothing, and ridden with disease. Press reports reaching home blamed Raglan. Although Raglan could have done more to stop the disaster, the ultimate blame lay with the British War Office and Commissary system, which was revamped after the war. Nevertheless, Raglan, weary and discouraged, wrote in the spring of 1855 that "I could never return to England now. They would stone me to death."

After the failure of the attack on Sevastopol on the fortieth anniversary of the Battle of Waterloo, Ragland fell ill, probably with dysentery, and was dead within ten days. Some members on his staff felt he had died of a broken heart.

LORD RAGLAN, LEFT, MEETS WITH OMAR PASHA, CENTER, AND MARSHALL PELISSIER, RIGHT, DURING THE CRIMEAN WAR.

TSAR NICHOLAS I

In 1852, Tsar Nicholas I of Russia was a man looking for war, and Emperor Louis-Napoléon Bonaparte III gave him an excuse for one.

Nicholas, born in 1826, son of Alexander I, who had ruled Russia since 1825, was and remains one of the most reactionary of Russian tsars. A well-built man with curling moustache and cold blue eyes, Nicholas ruled Russia by dint of a dreaded secret police force, known as the Third Section, which enforced all of the tsar's myriad rules with draconian efficiency. Opponents of the tsar were executed or declared insane and sent to asylums. Nicholas's own courtiers were forced to grow moustaches (like the tsar's own) and, if they were blonde, to dye them black to match his.

In the meantime, Russia was the most backward major power in the world. It had few roads, only one railroad line, a great mass of uneducated serfs, and a government bureaucracy that was so ponderous and inefficient that the only way to accomplish anything was through bribery.

Like Russian tsars before him, Nicholas had long dreamed of a southern outlet for his empire, and the port of Constantinople would do quite nicely. When Louis-Napoleon moved to force the Turks to put Palestine's holy places under French control, it was the perfect excuse for Nicholas to try to bully the Ottoman Sultan into capitulating to him.

Unfortunately for the Russians, Nicholas had miscalculated the extent to which the French

TSAR NICHOLAS I'S QUEST FOR DOMINATION OVER THE OTTOMANS SEEMED A FARFETCHED IDEA FOR A COUNTRY WITH FEW ROADS, A LARGELY UNEDUCATED POPULATION, A CORRUPT GOVERNMENT BUREAUCRACY, AND AN UNTRAINED ARMY.

and British were willing to support the Muslim Ottomans, and the Crimean War began. Nicholas had an army of nearly 750,000 men at his disposal, but because he hadn't bothered to properly arm or train them, they lost most major battles.

Ironically enough, replacing Prince Menshikov—the incompetent commander of Russian forces at Sevastopol—was Nicholas's last official act. In March 1855, before he came down with pneumonia and died, he encouraged his son Alexander to "serve Russia." Alexander would do so by reforming the country's economy and industrial might, as well as granting freedom to serfs. Had his father taken these steps, the Crimean War might have turned out very differently.

The British Soldier

Allied soldiers in the Crimean War had it slightly better than their Russian counterparts, but not by much. Although the Crimean War would change public perception of the common soldier's role and ultimately do a great deal to improve his lot, British, French, and Ottoman soldiers in the Crimea suffered a good deal.

The British expeditionary forces sent to the Crimea were members of a volunteer army that was paid meagerly and subjected to harsh discipline. Perhaps worse, British general officers in the Crimean War were some of the most incompetent men who ever put on a uniform. The officers' incompetence was partly because of the "purchase" system, which allowed aristocratic but otherwise unqualified men to buy commissions in army or infantry regiments. (This system would be abolished as a direct result of the debacle at the Charge of the Light Brigade.) The officers' incompetence was also partly because most high-ranking officers were in their fifties and sixties, yet had little experience in war.

Of the 22,000 British dead, only one-third died in combat or because of wounds. The vast majority died of cholera, which raged through the British camps in Turkey and the Crimea, camps where even basic sanitation was lacking. British soldiers wrote home about walking past their own dead lying in the streets between tents in Varna, the British staging area on the Black Sea. Other corpses were weighted and dumped into the ocean, but because the weights were too light, their gas-filled bodies popped to the surface to accompany transport vessels heading off to the Crimean Peninsula, heads and shoulders bobbing above the water like dreadful dolls.

Despite these hardships, British soldiers—like their French counterparts—were tough and hardy, armed with the new Enfield rifle and ably led on the noncommissioned officer level. That was why the allies were able to finally triumph over far more numerous Russians.

The Russian Soldier

The Russian soldier in the Crimean War was a conscripted serf, poorly armed, and ordered to attack by officers who cared little about his life.

The Russian army at the time of the Crimean War numbered about 750,000 men, far more than any of the armies that could be put up by the Allied countries. But the Russian army was spread out over a much vaster territory because the Russians had to defend the Baltic and also its western flanks near Austria, which had threatened to join the war. Because Russia did not have control of the sea lanes, reinforcements for the army in the Crimean Peninsula had to march over land, which was a time-consuming process.

The period of service in the Russian army was fifteen to twenty-five years, the pay was poor, and the Russians were mainly armed with flintlocks and smoothbore cannon, the weapons of another era. Russian officers paid a good detail of attention to parade-ground show. This was something that had trickled all the way down from Tsar Nicholas I, who enjoyed a good parade. But the officers had neglected firearms training, with the result that the fire of Russian soldiers was often erratic. Yet with their backs against the wall, they could be magnificent soldiers. They tenaciously defended Sevastopol throughout the long winter of 1854 to 1855 and only broke under heavy artillery bombardments and a determined Allied assault.

The Russian army, too, changed after the Crimean War. Tsar Alexander II, seeing what the armies of the western nations could do, freed the serfs in 1861 and sought to make other innovations to bring his army up the standards of the other combatants in the Crimea.

A War of Firsts

Although it began in the old Napoleonic tradition, with its officers seeking set-piece battles and massive frontal charges, the Crimean War ended as something very different indeed.

First there were the rifles. Although the armies of all sides in the field began the war with Napoleonic-era black powder muskets, the British and French shortly began to use the Enfield rifled musket, accurate at greater ranges, which fired a minié ball. This powerful slug greatly increased casualties and eventually contributed to the opposing forces facing each other over long lines of trenches, a foreshadowing of World War I. The telegraph was used extensively for the first time. Trains brought supplies and troops to the front and took back the wounded, something noted carefully by the young U.S. officer George McClellan, who was observing the war and would later become commander in chief of Union forces in the U.S. Civil War.

The Crimean War also heralded out the era of the man-of-war under sail. In the British naval bombardment of the Russian port of Odessa, the last full-sail frigate saw action—and heralded in the armored steamship. The Russians were the first to use exploding shells rather than round shot, whose effect, on the Turkish fleet at Sinop, was devastating. The British navy employed rocket ships

that fired 24-pound (11 kg) projectiles from metal tubes. The Russians made good use of mines and torpedoes developed by Immanuel Nobel, father of Alfred Nobel.

Of course, because of all these innovations, the slaughter of the Crimean War was enormous. Matched only by the U.S. Civil War when it came to total casualties, the Crimean War saw a new way of fighting break bloodily on the shores of old custom. The result would be the slow transformation of the armies involved to adjust to the new way of doing combat.

THE CRIMEAN WAR WAS A WAR OF FIRSTS, SUCH AS THE USE OF MORE MODERN WEAPONS. IN ADDITION, THE TELEGRAPH WAS USED EXTENSIVELY FOR THE FIRST TIME. WORKERS IN THIS NINETEENTH CENTURY IMAGE ARE SHOWN LAYING SUBMARINE TELEGRAPH CABLE BETWEEN ENGLAND AND FRANCE.

Getty Images

The Key to the Church of the Nativity

Strangely (and ironically) enough, a key to one of the holiest Christian places on Earth was the catalyst for one of the bloodiest European wars of the nineteenth century.

The key in question opened the main doors of the Church of the Nativity in Bethlehem, the place where, by Christian tradition, Jesus Christ was born in a straw manger. The church and other holy places in Palestine had long been sacred places of worship for pilgrims coming from all over Europe and Russia. One reason why the Crusades were fought was to maintain open access to these shrines while Muslims controlled the area. However, the Latin and Eastern Orthodox Churches had split apart completely by the mid–fifteenth century. By the mid–nineteenth century, Greek Orthodox monks controlled the key to the Church of the Nativity by dint of the fact that Palestine, now controlled by the Ottoman Empire, was much closer to Russia and its 50 million devout Eastern Christians.

This did not keep the Latin monks in Bethlehem from squabbling over the key. There are records of fistfights between clergy over its possession. Then, in 1852, Louis-Napoleon Bonaparte III, to shore up his standing with French Catholics after his dissolution of the French parliament, used cajolery and threats of force to convince the Ottoman government to have the key to the Church of the Nativity surrendered to the Latin monks, as well as give control of all holy places in Palestine to the French church.

This enraged Nicholas I, who thought of Louis-Napoleon as a pretender to imperial power. (Nicholas refused to add "the Third," to Napoleon's name, simply calling him "the Ruler of France.") Nicholas saw the French encroachment as a prelude to gaining a foothold in the tottering Ottoman Empire. Nicholas was also quite devout and felt the Ottoman action as an insult to millions of Orthodox Christians. He demanded that Russia be given control of all Palestinian holy places. When Nicholas's demands were not met, the Crimean War began.

IRONICALLY, THE CRIMEAN WAR BEGAN OVER THE CONTROL OF A KEY THAT UNLOCKED ONE OF THE HOLIEST CHRISTIAN PLACES. THE CHURCH OF THE NATIVITY, PICTURED HERE, IS SAID TO BE WHERE JESUS CHRIST WAS BORN AND THOSE WITH THE KEY HAD ACCESS TO IT.

Prints & Photographs Division, Library of Congress, LC-DIG-ppmsca-04331

Florence Nightingale and the Angel Band

The suffering of the wounded and cholera-stricken British soldiers was reported by William Howard Russell (see "Turning Point," p. 104), but also by a little-known *London Times* Constantinople correspondent named Thomas Chenery, who telegraphed stories of dismal conditions in British field hospitals immediately after the Battle of Alma. This brought an outcry for what one British observer called an "Angel Band," nurses who could ease the pain of the men who had so bravely thrown their bodies in harm's way.

The woman who would answer the call to lead these angels was Florence Nightingale. Born in 1820 to a well-off English family, she had a religious awakening while still a teenager, decided to devote her life to the plight of England's poor. Nightingale became prominent for improving the treatment of people in poorhouses and hospitals. When an outcry arose for better treatment of sick and suffering British troops in the Crimea, the government sought to assuage the public concern by appointing Nightingale superintendent of a band of forty nurses who would minister to the troops in the Crimea.

Not all was as selfless and altruistic as it might seem. Many observed that the conditions at home for the poor were far worse and that the British government had only been forced to act by the newfound power of the press. Nightingale herself later admitted that the chief inducement for her "angels," many of whom were illiterate and had to be warned not to get drunk and have sex with the soldiers, was money.

Nonetheless, Nightingale at least attempted to do something about the intolerable conditions in military hospitals in Turkey. Sanitation was almost nonexistent; sewers overflowed and vermin were everywhere. British authorities had failed to provide basic medicines or even food for the wounded. It was an almost insurmountable task, and Nightingale was only able to make incremental changes in the way the sick were treated. Nonetheless, she brought the idea of proper sanitation and health care very much before the public eye. This helped immensely to improve conditions in hospitals, both military and civilian, in the future.

THE OBSTACLES THAT FLORENCE NIGHTINGALE FACED WERE NEARLY INSURMOUNTABLE—NONEXISTENT SANITATION, A VIRTUAL LACK OF FOOD AND MEDICINE, AND AN UNRULY GROUP OF FEMALE AIDS. DESPITE THESE CIRCUMSTANCES, SHE ACHIEVED INCREMENTAL IMPROVEMENTS, THOUGH HER BIGGEST VICTORY MAY HAVE BEEN BRINGING THE IDEA OF PROPER HEALTH CARE AND SANITATION TO THE PUBLIC EYE.

Getty Images

The Charge of the Light Brigade

Among the many reasons why the Crimean War foreshadowed the world wars of the twentieth century (see "World War I," p. 233 and "World War II," p. 316) was the sense, after the Crimean War was done, that men had been sacrificed at the whim of a bumbling high command. In fact, this was often true, due in part to so many of the British general officers being aging men whose last memories of war—if they had such memories at all—were of Napoleonic battlefields (see "The British Soldier," p. 110).

The most famous slaughter of the war was, of course, the Charge of the Light Brigade, as immortalized by Lord Alfred Tennyson's poem of the same name, which he scribbled down almost immediately after reading of the attack in his morning paper. The charge took place at the Battle of Balaklava, on the Crimean Peninsula,

on October 25, 1854, as the Russians attacked to dislodge Allied troops from around Sevastopol. In charge of the British brigade of light cavalry was James Brudenell, the seventh Earl of Cardigan, a handsome but notoriously empty and arrogant man who usually dressed in a resplendent uniform. He was known sarcastically as "the Noble Yachtsman," because he spent evenings on the yacht he had parked in the nearby port of Balaklava. Cardigan's commanding officer was George Charles Bingham, the third Earl of Lucan, his former brother-in-law.

Lords Cardigan and Lucan hated each other. To make matters worse, both of them disliked the commander of the British army at Crimea, Lord Raglan, who sat high on a cliff watching the progress of the battle below. When Raglan decided he wanted his cavalry to charge a battery of Russian guns on the side of valley that sprawled out below him, he sent an aide, Captain Louis Edward Nolan, to tell Lucan to order Cardigan to make the attack. Unfortunately, Nolan did not translate the orders properly, and he gave Lucan the impression that Cardigan must attack the Russian battery at the very end of the valley,

which was more than 2 miles (3 km) away. Because the two men were estranged, Cardigan and Lucan were unable to use enough common sense together to question this order.

Instead, Cardigan led his 673 troopers straight down the valley, muttering "Here goes the last of the Brudenells." As Tennyson was to write, there were "cannon to the left of them, cannon to the right of them," in Russian emplacements, as well as the guns straight ahead. For a long ten minutes, the light brigade was exposed to merciless fire as it galloped forward. The survivors noted being spattered with the flesh of men who had been blown up riding next to them. The brigade actually made it to the Russian battery at the end of the valley. In an act of extraordinary bravery, they held the guns momentarily before being driven back by an overwhelming force of Cossacks.

Lucan had not accompanied the charge, but Cardigan had, sitting straight up on his horse in his brilliantly colored uniform. Cardigan made it through without a scratch, and then he turned and rode back down the valley. Behind him straggled 195 men—all that remained of the light brigade. The charge would forever go down in history as brave but futile slaughter. As one French officer watching said, "It's glorious, but it's not war."

THE CHARGE OF THE LIGHT BRIGADE WAS IMMORTALIZED IN TENNYSON'S POEM OF THE SAME NAME. AN ONLOOKER SAID ABOUT THE ATTACK AND THE 195 MEN— OUT OF 673—WHO MANAGED TO SURVIVE, "IT'S GLORIOUS, BUT IT'S NOT WAR."

Lord Cardigan (1797-1868) leading the Charge of the Light Brigade at the Battle of Balaklava, 25th October 1854, 1884 (chromolitho), Payne, Henry A. (Harry) (1868-1940) (after) / National Army Museum, London, / The Bridgeman Art Library

Napier's Forgotten War

Vice Admiral Sir Charles Napier, commander of British naval forces in the Baltic, was, to say the least, a colorful character. He was a Scotsman known as "Black Charlie" for his tempers and dark complexion; he was also a practicing alcoholic. One Swedish naval officer left behind a fascinating description of Napier, possibly under the influence of a hangover: "He was wearing a blue tunic with short trousers and big shoes, a civilian hat with gold stripes, an enormously big handkerchief in all the colors of the rainbow hanging out of his shirt tunic pocket. His face was very badly washed, some yellow spots—probably from the egg at breakfast—round the lips and lower part of his face."

Yet Napier, for all his eccentricities, was a brilliant and aggressive naval officer charged with leading his British fleet into the Baltic to join forces with a French fleet, and there do battle with Russia's navy and series of heavily gunned coastal fortresses. The idea was to harry the tsar's northern flanks as the allies assaulted Sevastopol in the Crimean, threaten the important ports of Kronstadt in the Gulf of Finland and perhaps even Saint Petersburg itself.

The war in the Baltic was a frustrating one for Napier. Although Napier's fleet outnumbered the Russians, the shallow waters of the sea made it difficult for the heavier British warships to maneuver. Plus, the most important Russian coastal fortresses —such as the one at Kronstadt— were too heavily defended to defeat, although the Allies were victorious in destroying smaller fortifications, such as the ones at Bomarsund and Fort Slava. And the blockade they instituted and kept despite the terrible weather of the Baltic area badly hurt Russia, which was hugely dependent on imports for its economy.

Despite this and the fact that more than 200,000 Russian troops were tied down guarding the region, Napier was criticized heavily in the British press and admiralty. This criticism was due to his seeming lack of success, as well as his bombarding of targets that were nonmilitary and thus out of bounds. Napier responded acerbically to such attacks on him.

He was relieved of command at the end of 1854, although historians now credit him with playing a major role in Russia's defeat.

VICE-ADMIRAL SIR CHARLES JAMES NAPIER, COMMANDER OF THE BRITISH FORCES IN THE BALTIC WAS A STUDY IN CONTRASTS: A PRACTICING ALCOHOLIC PRONE TO MOODINESS AND A BAD TEMPER BUT A BRILLIANT AND AGGRESSIVE NAVAL OFFICER.

Portrait of Sir Charles James Napier (1782-1853) (oil on canvas), Pickersgill, Henry William (1782-1875) / Private Collection, © Philip Mould Ltd, London / The Bridgeman Art Library

7

THE U.S. CIVIL WAR

1861–1865

An event that indelibly altered U.S. history,
the Civil War cost 600,000 lives and turned the country from
a collection of states into a nation, yet left lingering scars

Combatants

- Northern States
- Southern States

Theater of War

United States from the Mississippi
River to the Atlantic Ocean

Casualties

Union: 360,000 soldiers dead and
275,000 wounded

Confederacy: 260,000 soldiers dead
and 130,000 wounded
Perhaps 50,000 civilians dead, mainly
in the South

Major Figures

NORTH
Abraham Lincoln, U.S. president
during the conflict

General Henry Halleck, chief of staff
of the Army of the Potomac
General Ulysses S. Grant, commander
in chief of all Union armies
General George McClellan, slow-
moving Army of the Potomac commander dismissed by Lincoln, but
who later became the Democratic
presidential candidate in 1864
General Ambrose Burnside, who
engineered the Union's disastrous
loss at Fredericksburg, Virginia
General George Gordon Meade,
victor at Gettysburg, Pennsylvania
Admiral David G. Farragut who
captured New Orleans, Louisiana
General William Tecumseh Sherman,
who captured Atlanta, Georgia, and
drove the war home to the South

SOUTH
Jefferson Davis, president of the
Confederate States of America
General Robert E. Lee, commander
of the Army of Virginia
**General Thomas "Stonewall"
Jackson,** the most brilliant Southern
commander
General James Longstreet, legendary
commander who failed at Gettysburg
General Braxton Bragg, commander
of the Army of Tennessee
General Jubal Early, tough Confeder-
ate infantry commander who took his
army to within sight of Washington,
D.C.
General Jeb Stuart, brilliant cavalry
commander whom Lee called "my
eyes"
General Joseph E. Johnston, who
surrendered the last Confederate
army in April 1865

With a combined military death total of more than 600,000—a total higher than the death count in all U.S. wars put together until the end of the Vietnam conflict—the U.S. Civil War was the bloodiest war in the nation's history. Was it a war fought to keep the Union together? To free the nearly 4,000,000 slaves held by the southern states? To decide whether the future of the county would be controlled by the industrial North or the agrarian South? It was because of a combination of all these factors that the United States went to war against itself in 1861, with military campaigns raging in the east and the west—2,400 battles and skirmishes fought over thousands of miles of countryside. The result of the Union victory was the preservation of the United States, but lingering racism and bitterness still remain, 150 years after the last shot was fired.

1860:

November: Abraham Lincoln elected president.

December: South Carolina secedes from the Union.

1861:

January–February: Mississippi, Florida, Alabama, Georgia, Louisiana, and Texas secede. The Confederate States of America is formed, with West Point–graduate Jefferson Davis as president.

April: Confederates open fire on Fort Sumter in Charleston, South Carolina—the first shots of the Civil War; Sumter surrenders. Virginia secedes. Lincoln calls up 75,000 men and orders a blockade of southern ports. Robert E. Lee resigns his commission in the U.S. Army and becomes head of Confederate forces in Virginia.

May–June: Arkansas, North Carolina, and Tennessee secede from the Union.

July: Congress authorizes Lincoln's call for 500,000 soldiers. First Battle of Bull Run takes place, with Union Army defeated 25 miles (40 km) from Washington, D.C.

November: Lincoln appoints George McClellan commander in chief of all Union forces.

1862:

February: In the western theater of the war, General Ulysses S. Grant captures Fort Henry and Fort Donelson on the Tennessee River, earning the nickname "Unconditional Surrender" Grant.

March: The Confederate ironclad ship *Merrimac* fights the Union ironclad *Monitor*. Neither ship is the victor, but naval warfare is changed forever. McClellan's Army of the Potomac begins Peninsula campaign, marching to attack the Confederate capital at Richmond, Virginia.

March–June: Thomas "Stonewall" Jackson campaigns through the Shenandoah Valley in Virginia, drawing valuable union forces away from McClellan's efforts to attack Richmond.

April: The Battle of Shiloh occurs when Grant is surprised by Confederate forces along the Tennessee River. Grant finally forces Confederates from the field at a cost of 13,000 Union and 10,000 Confederate casualties. Admiral David Farragut takes New Orleans with the Union fleet, putting the mouth of the Mississippi in Yankee hands.

June–July: In the Seven Days' Battles, Lee attacks McClellan, driving him away from Richmond.

August: James Longstreet beats the far stronger Union Army at the Second Battle of Bull Run; Union Army retreats to Washington, D.C.

September: Lee invades the North with 50,000 Confederates, but he is checked at the Battle of Antietam in Maryland.

November: Lincoln replaces the slow-moving McClellan with General Ambrose E. Burnside.

December: Burnside leads the Army of the Potomac into disastrous slaughter at Fredericksburg, Virginia, losing 12,000 men.

1863:

January: The Emancipation Proclamation takes effect. Lincoln appoints Joseph Hooker commander of the Army of the Potomac, replacing Burnside. Grant is made commander of the Army of the West.

May: Hooker's Union Army is defeated by Lee's Army of Virginia at Chancellorsville, Virginia. Stonewall Jackson is killed, mistakenly, by his own men.

June: Lee again invades the North with 75,000 Confederates, heading through Pennsylvania. Lincoln replaces Hooker with General George Gordon Meade.

July: Meade decisively defeats Lee at the Battle of Gettysburg. Grant captures the important Mississippi River fortress of Vicksburg after a long siege. Draft riots in New York kill well over 100 people before being quelled by Union troops.

November: Lincoln delivers the Gettysburg Address. The Union Army defeats the rebels besieging Chattanooga, Tennessee.

1864:

March: Lincoln appoints General Grant commander of all armies in the United States.

May: Grant launches a major invasion of the South, attacking Lee's Army of Northern Virginia with bloody battles at Wilderness, Spotsylvania Courthouse, and Cold Harbor. William Tecumseh Sherman marches on Atlanta from the west.

June: The Union forces begin a siege of Petersburg, Virginia.

September: Sherman's forces capture Atlanta.

November: Sherman begins to march through Georgia to the sea.

December: Sherman reaches Savannah, Georgia, having destroyed a 300-mile (485-m) swath of the old South.

1865:

March: Lee begins his last offensive against the North, with an attack on Union forces surrounding Petersburg. It fails.

April: Grant's forces break through Lee's lines at Petersburg. Lee evacuates Petersburg and the Confederate capital of Richmond. Union forces enter Richmond. On April 9, Lee surrenders his army to Grant at the Appomattox Court House in Virginia. On April 14, Lincoln is assassinated in Washington, D.C. On April 18, General Joseph E. Johnston surrenders the last major Confederate force to Sherman in North Carolina.

A WAR TO SAVE THE UNION

The inciting event of the U.S. Civil War was the election, in November 1860, of Abraham Lincoln as president. Lincoln was an avowed anti-slavery Republican, which spelled trouble to the United States' Southern states. For years, the Southern states had been locked in what they saw as a life-and-death struggle with their counterparts in the North over the morality and legality of slavery. There were some 4,000,000 slaves in the South at the beginning of the Civil War, and they were needed to grow the cotton and tobacco crops that were the engines driving the Southern economy.

Every time a new western state was added to the Union, the South wanted it to be a slave-holding state, while the North wanted it to be free. The more populous, industrialized Northern states were better represented in the House of Representatives, where representation depended on population. The South, afraid that the North would gain enough power to abolish slavery, sought to have new states become slave states to at least keep the balance of power in the U.S. Senate.

But the election of Lincoln made this a hopeless cause, because he had made it known during his campaign that he would vigorously oppose any additional slave states. Within several months, eleven states, beginning with South Carolina, had seceded and formed the Confederate States of America, whose president was Jefferson Davis and whose leading general would become Robert E. Lee (see "Commanders," p. 130).

The first shot of the Civil War was fired on April 12, 1861, when a Confederate mortar lobbed a shell at Fort Sumter, the Union fort in the harbor of Charleston, South Carolina. Within a few days, Sumter was forced to surrender, and the North and South were at war.

At the very beginning, it appeared the North held the advantage. There were twenty-two Union states versus eleven Confederate ones. The North was far more populous, having 22 million people to the 9 million belonging to the South (of which 4 million were slaves). Also, the North possessed far more heavy industry than the South.

Yet the advantage was not all on the Union side. Most of the regular army officers of the United States, West Point graduates who had seen action in the Mexican War, opted for the

ABRAHAM LINCOLN FAMOUSLY DECLARED IN HIS GETTYSBURG ADDRESS THAT HE WANTED TO CREATE A NATION "OF THE PEOPLE, BY THE PEOPLE, FOR THE PEOPLE." HE WOULD NOT LIVE TO SEE HIS DREAM REALIZED.

Prints & Photographs Division, Library of Congress, LC-USZ62-95719

Southern side. Northern generals tended to be political appointees. The South early on had a conscription system, while the North, for the first two years of the war, depended on a volunteer army. More important, the South did not need to invade and conquer Northern territory to win the war. It needed simply to hold its own and win enough major victories to convince the North to sue for peace and allow the Confederacy to secede and become a separate nation.

At the start of the war, Lincoln immediately blockaded Southern ports, the first step in the "Anaconda Plan" to squeeze the Confederacy into submission, which entailed opening up the Mississippi River to Union forces and capturing the South's capital city of Richmond, Virginia. At first, the Confederate army under Robert E. Lee was successful in the eastern theater of operations, beating the Union at the Battle of Bull Run (also known as the First Battle of Manassas for the town near where it was fought) in Virginia in July 1861.

In the beginning of 1862, however, a relatively unknown Union major general named Ulysses S. Grant captured Fort Henry and Fort Donelson on the Tennessee River, severely crippling the Confederates in the western theater of operations. In the spring of that year, Lincoln's new commander of the Army of the Potomac, General George McClellan, launched his campaign on the

Virginia peninsula to capture Richmond, but, moving far too slowly and hampered by Stonewall Jackson's campaign in the Shenandoah Valley (see "The Shenandoah Campaign," p. 135), he was badly beaten by Confederate forces in the Seven Days' Battles and forced back toward Washington.

In the meantime, Grant fought the Confederates to a draw in the bloody Battle of Shiloh, Tennessee. That battle convinced both sides that this war would be unlike any other to date. The only bright lights for the Union were Admiral David Farragut's capture of New Orleans in the spring

and the fact that George McClellan was able to stem Lee's advance north at the battle known as Antietam by the North (for a stream in the middle of the battlefield) and Sharpsburg by the South (for a nearby village) in September 1862.

However, McClellan did not follow up on his victory, and Lincoln relieved him of command. In the next twelve months, Lincoln would appoint five different generals head of the Army of the Potomac, seeking to find a man aggressive enough to beat Lee. At the end of December 1862, the Union Army under General Ambrose Burnside suffered a disastrous defeat at Fredericksburg,

THE BATTLE OF ANTIETAM, FOUGHT TO A BLOODY DRAW, STEMMED LEE'S ADVANCE NORTHWARD, BUT COST 22,000 KILLED ON BOTH SIDES.

The Battle of Antietam, 1862 (colour litho), Thulstrup, Thure de (1848-1930) / Private Collection, Peter Newark Military Pictures / The Bridgeman Art Library

Virginia. His successor, General Joseph Hooker, was decisively defeated by Lee at Chancellorsville, Virginia, in May 1863, although Stonewall Jackson was killed, which was a severe blow to the South.

Lincoln appointed General George Gordon Meade as his new commander in chief. Meade at last was able to decisively defeat Lee at the pivotal Battle of Gettysburg, Pennsylvania, (see "Turning Point," p. 122) in July. At the same time, General Ulysses S. Grant, now commander of Union forces in the west, was able to capture the pivotal Confederate fortress of Vicksburg, on the Mississippi. Grant's further destruction of Confederate forces at Chattanooga, Tennessee, meant that the Confederates were now being driven into a corner.

The year 1864 saw Lincoln appoint Grant as commander of all Union forces. The Union's manpower was increased due to conscription, and its massive industrial might provided endless munitions and supplies. Grant now waged a vicious war of attrition against a South weakened by irreplaceable manpower shortages and the Union's effective blockade. As Grant advanced on Virginia, major battles were fought in May and June in Wilderness, Spotsylvania Courthouse, and Cold Harbor, and by June 1864, Union soldiers were besieging Petersburg, near Richmond.

In the meantime, General William Tecumseh Sherman, now commander of Union forces in the west, had been sent to attack the major rail terminus and supply city of Atlanta, Georgia. He achieved this goal in September, and then he marched famously through the South to the coast at Savannah, Georgia, leaving a trail of death and destruction 300 miles (485 km) long and 60 miles (95 km) wide.

In March 1865, Lee's army was defeated at Petersburg, and Richmond fell soon after. Lee surrendered his army to Grant at Appomattox Court House in Virginia on April 9. The last major Confederate force, that of General Joseph E. Johnston, surrendered to Sherman near Durham, North Carolina, on April 18.

But Lincoln had been assassinated by Southern firebrand John Wilkes Booth in Washington, D.C., on April 14, leaving the war-torn country with an uncertain future. After a Reconstruction period that was more corrupt and vindictive than healing, the South would take at least a century to fully rejoin the Union. Scars of the war, especially in terms of racism and a Southern sense of "apartness," still remain today.

THE BATTLE OF GETTYSBURG: JULY 1863

In June 1863, the finest soldiers on the North American continent—or so they considered themselves—began pouring into the lush and peaceful fields of south-central Pennsylvania. They were the Army of Northern Virginia, 75,000-Confederates strong, and they had marched west and north from Virginia, through Maryland, to find themselves in the rich heartland of their enemies.

Their general, Robert E. Lee, had forbidden plundering, but these soldiers were hungry, and they needed supplies. So they took what they could—food, clothing, horses, and even money that they "requisitioned" from banks and stores—leaving Confederate IOUs in their wake. When one farm woman complained after her livestock was stolen, General James Longstreet politely told her: "Yes, madam, it's very sad, very sad, and this sort of thing has been going on in Virginia more than two years, very sad."

Looking back, many Confederate soldiers saw this pleasant month of June—seemingly endless days of fine, balmy weather and rich Yankee buttermilk—as a dreamlike idyll. In fact, the rebel soldiers under one of Lee's division commanders, A.P. Hill, felt supremely confident as they approached a small crossroads town called Gettysburg. They had destroyed the Federals at Fredericksburg, Virginia, the previous December and outfought them at Chancellorsville, Virginia, just a month before. Now they were heading north to bring the war to the hated enemy and win independence for the Southern states.

But first they would stop at Gettysburg. There was a shoe factory there, and one thing A.P. Hill's men needed was good shoe leather.

"Those People"

War is inextricable from politics, and as Lee accompanied his men north that late spring, he had powerful political goals in mind. Lee so wanted to impress the Northern peace party, the Copperheads, with his good intentions that he ordered his soldiers not to hurt civilians or plunder their belongings.

More important, Lee wanted to destroy the Army of the Potomac under Joseph Hooker, whom he had beaten handily at Chancellorsville. Hooker was now belatedly following the Army of Northern Virginia as it headed into Union territory. Once Lee had beaten the Army of the Potomac, he was sure that foreign countries such as Great Britain and France would recognize the Confederacy and that Washington would sue for peace.

These were fine political goals, but a great general like Lee allowed himself to forget that the shedding of blood to gain political ends is an unpredictable matter. Lee may have been convinced of his army's invincibility and that "those people"—as Lee called the Yankee soldiers—would turn tail and run, as they had before. But Lee's force was not without its weaknesses. His boldest and most aggressive commander, Stonewall Jackson, had been killed by friendly fire in May at Chancellorsville after essentially winning that battle for Lee. And Lee's eyes and ears, the cavalry of Jeb Stuart, were not with him. Stuart had exploited Lee's order to go on a wild end run around Hooker's entire Union Army.

Thus, as Lee marched north, he did not know where the Army of the Potomac was, quite, nor did he know that, on June 28, Lincoln had replaced Hooker with General George Gordon Meade, a Union officer who had worked his way up through the ranks by excelling at combat. Meade was determined to stop Lee and—with his own cavalry—found out quickly that the Confederates had entered Pennsylvania. Meade aggressively moved his 90,000-man army north from Maryland, where it was stationed, to confront the Confederates.

Lee had split his forces to achieve his objectives in Pennsylvania, which included capturing the state capital of Harrisburg and blowing up key railroad bridges. But when Lee finally got word of Meade's men approaching, he sent orders for all of his commanders to bring their forces to Gettysburg. This was not because Lee wanted to fight a battle there, but simply because the town was the nexus of numerous highways.

The Battle Begins

But when A.P Hill's men arrived in Gettysburg on the morning of July 1, they did not care about this grander strategy. They wanted shoes, and they figured they would get them before the rest of the Confederate army showed up. But instead of the few Union militiamen they had been expecting, they found two brigades of Union cavalry under John Buford, who had ridden into town the previous day ahead of Federal forces. Buford

is recognized as one of the Union heroes of the battle, men who, acting independently, saw opportunities and seized them. He realized that the hills and ridges proximate to Gettysburg were important defensive points, and he was determined to hold them.

And so Buford dismounted his men and stationed them on the high ground northwest of Gettysburg. When A.P. Hill's men showed up, Buford's men made a fight of it, holding them off for two hours until a Union infantry corps showed up to reinforce them. What had been a hot skirmish began to turn into a real battle, as couriers were sent by both sides for more and more troops.

By the afternoon of July 1, 24,000 Confederates fought 19,000 Yankees along the ridges northwest of town. Lee realized that he had the enemy outnumbered and might be able to break their lines. He launched a Confederate attack that turned the Yankee right flank and finally forced their line to crumble. Union forces fled back through the town of Gettysburg to Cemetery Hill, to the south.

However, the battle was far from over. Lee knew that the Army of the Potomac was almost certainly moving quickly to Gettysburg. He needed to gain the high ground of Cemetery Ridge before the enemy could dig in there in strength. Late on the afternoon of July 1, Lee ordered General Richard Ewell, commander of Second Corps and the man who had replaced Stonewall Jackson, to attack Cemetery Hill "if practicable." It was therefore a discretionary order, and Ewell decided the enemy was already too well dug-in and thus declined. Although Ewell was a capable commander, he lacked Jackson's acumen and

bulldog aggressiveness. But had Ewell attacked that afternoon, he would almost certainly have broken the Union lines.

"The Enemy Is There"

That night, Meade and the rest of the Union forces had shown up and built a line of defensive breastworks several miles long. The Union line extended across Cemetery Hill and Cemetery Ridge, all the way to a hill called Little Round Top.

On the morning of July 2, Longstreet and Lee surveyed these defenses and had their first,

but not last, dispute of the battle. Longstreet felt that the Union line was now too strong to attack. He wanted Lee to flank the Yankees to the south and take up defensive positions. This would put the whole Army of Northern Virginia between Washington, D.C., and Gettysburg, something that would certainly make the Yankees leave their own defensive positions and attack. Once they did, the Confederates would cut them to pieces.

Lee would have none of this. He thought going on the defensive would make his troops lose their supreme confidence, their almost palpable desire to attack the enemy. Lee pointed at Cemetery Ridge and said to Longstreet, "The enemy is there, and I am going to attack him there."

Longstreet replied, "If he is there, it will be because he is anxious that we should attack him; a good reason, in my judgment, for not doing so."

But Lee dismissed this and ordered Longstreet

named General Gouverneur K. Warren saw the problem, too. Galloping pell-mell to the nearest Union brigade, he convinced its officers to send men storming up the other side of Little Round Top. They got to the summit just before the Confederates, and a pitched battle ensued. For more than two hours, on the slopes of a hill covered with rocks and trees and cut with ravines, an Alabaman regiment and a Maine regiment fought and struggled bitterly.

> *Little Round Top was saved because Union soldiers had acted most unlike the Union soldiers the Confederates had come to know: They had refused to yield.*

to attack. Smarting under the rebuff, Longstreet took almost the entire day to prepare his forces, so the attack did not kick off until 4 p.m. Longstreet sent his 15,000 hardened soldiers screaming their rebel yell straight at the Union lines. The fighting was fierce, in places that have become famous in U.S. history—the Peach Orchard, the Wheat Field, and a tumble of huge rocks known to the local townspeople as the Devil's Den.

Despite the lateness of the attack, the Confederates found extraordinary opportunity. Inexplicably, the Union had neglected to occupy Little Round Top, the hill that anchored the south flank of their line. If Longstreet's men could reach it, they would be able to fire down on the Yankees and send a flanking force into the Union rear.

The rebels realized this and raced for the hill. At the same time, a Union engineering officer

Leading the Maine regiment was another one of Gettysburg's Union heroes, Colonel Joshua L. Chamberlain, who was a former professor of rhetoric at Bowdoin College. As twilight lengthened, Chamberlain found that a third of his men were casualties and that the rest were rapidly running out of ammunition. Down the hill, through the drifting smoke and hoarse cries of the wounded littering the slope, Chamberlain could see the Alabamians preparing for another charge.

And so Chamberlain made one of the most important decisions of the war: He shouted for his men to fix bayonets and charge. Racing in a frenzy down the hill, the Mainers took the Confederates by surprise, shattered their charge, and forced most of them to surrender. Little Round Top was saved because Union soldiers had acted most unlike the Union soldiers the Confederates had come to know: They had refused to yield.

"The Hopeless Slaughter"

The Confederate assaults on the Union line on July 2 were poorly coordinated, and they had failed to make a significant dent in the enemy. Late that evening, as both sides were licking their wounds (18,000 Confederates and Yankees had died or been wounded that day), Lee called a conference of his officers. Much to their surprise, Lee told them that it was his intention, to attack the center of Meade's lines the next day. Lee was convinced that the Union commander had weakened his center to make his flanks strong enough to face the Confederate attacks.

The other Confederate officers, particularly Longstreet, did not see the logic in this, and they

p.m., Longstreet ordered the massed guns of the Confederates to open up in a huge bombardment of Union lines—the largest rebel bombardment of the war.

After two hours, what became known as Pickett's Charge, after General George Pickett, who commanded a Virginia division in the attack, began. Nine Confederate brigades participated—belonging to Pickett, General Isaac Trimble, and General James Johnston Pettigrew. The brigades arrayed themselves, flags flying, over a front 1 mile (1.5 km) long with three-quarters of a mile (1 km) of gently sloping fields before them. In the distance, the Yankees waited behind stone fences and barricades.

At Pickett's command, the rebels marched off. People present on both sides were awed by the beauty of the beginning of the charge, which

The aura of invincibility of the Army of Northern Virginia was shattered. The Union was given renewed hope.

protested, to little avail. Lee—perhaps weakened by a bout of diarrhea he was suffering or lacking intelligence that might have been provided by Jeb Stuart (whose troopers had only just joined the Confederate camp, wretchedly tired from their long ride)—was determined to push this battle to achieve his goals.

Once again, it was up to Longstreet to prepare this attack, and, once again, he dallied. "My heart was heavy," he later wrote, "I could see the desperate and hopeless nature of the charge and the hopeless slaughter it would cause." But at 1

seemed, as historian James M. McPherson put it, "a picture-book view of war." But the picture book view didn't last very long. The Confederate barrage hadn't significantly harmed the Yankee artillery. And as the Yankee artillery got within range, it opened up, shattering the perfect ranks of gray. Then, as the rebels ran screaming at the Yankee lines, the Union soldiers opened up from 200 yards (185 m) away. As Longstreet predicted, it was a slaughter, with men being blown apart where they stood. Union regiments raced out from their positions on the sides of the battlefield to flank the Confederates with fire. The rebels were caught in a killing zone in which it was difficult to even move without being hit.

Half an hour after the attack began, 200 Confederates, led by General Lewis Armistead, forced their way through Union lines. They were all killed within a few minutes. Armistead died with his hand on a Yankee cannon—the supposed "high water mark" of the Confederate effort in the Civil War. The soldiers who survived the attack streamed back toward Confederate lines. Of the 14,000 Confederates who charged, only 7,000 returned. Lee himself met with the soldiers who survived, telling them: "It is all my fault. It is I who have lost this fight."

"My Inability for the Duties of My Position"

Lee expected Meade to attack the next day, July 4, but the new general and his Union forces were worn out and chose to follow Lee's retreating men only desultorily. It was pouring rain as the Confederates retreated, carrying their wounded. Civil War soldiers noted that it often rained after a large battle, and they theorized it might be because the clouds were disturbed by the artillery fire.

They had lost 28,000 men killed, missing, or injured (Union losses were 23,000), but they had, in fact, lost a great deal more. The aura of invincibility of the Army of Northern Virginia was shattered. The Union (heartened also by Grant's great victory at Vicksburg on July 4) was given renewed hope.

Lee returned to Richmond, where he tendered his resignation to Jefferson Davis. "No one," he wrote, "is more aware than myself of my inability for the duties of my position." Davis refused to accept this, and Lee soldiered on. Lee performed brilliantly in the last two years of the war, but he would never again find himself with an undefeated army at his back, entering the territory of the enemy with victory within his grasp.

GENERAL ULYSSES S. GRANT: "I PROPOSE TO STAND BY HIM"

Ulysses S. Grant went through desperate journeys during the course of his life that would have daunted his namesake—the wandering hero of the *Odyssey*. Grant's Cyclops were whole Confederate armies, and his Siren was the seductive call of alcohol.

Grant was born in 1822 in a two-room cabin in Point Pleasant, Ohio, where his father ran a tannery. Grant's boyhood was mainly undistinguished except for his love of horses, and he was an excellent rider all his life. Nonetheless, he managed to secure an appointment to the U.S. Military Academy at West Point, from which he graduated, in the middle of his class, in 1843. He went on to serve bravely in the Mexican–American War of 1846–1848, which was a proving ground for many future Union and Confederate officers. During that war, Grant was promoted to captain.

But after the war, Grant became a journeyman officer, serving in desolate and depressing western outposts, at which point he began to drink heavily. Grant left the army in 1854 and—after working as a farmer and bill collector—brought his wife, Julia, and his growing family to Galena, Illinois, where he went to work in his family's leather goods shop as an assistant to his younger brother.

Grant—a short, gruff, and rather taciturn figure—served a kind of exile in Galena. He continued to drink (although how much is disputed) and probably suffered from some kind of clinical depression, finding himself, at the age of thirty-eight

in 1860, working in the family store. But as the Civil War broke out, at a time when experienced Union officers were needed, Grant used a connection he had made with Illinois Congressman Elihu Washburne to become a brigadier general of the Twenty-First Illinois Regiment.

In February 1862, supported by gunboats, Grant set off on a campaign to capture the key Confederate Forts Henry and Donelson, which protected the Tennessee and Cumberland Rivers, major Confederate waterways. At a time when the Union was receiving little good news, Grant took the forts, and he became famous for telling Donelson's Confederate commander: "No terms except an unconditional and immediate surrender can be accepted."

Suddenly the U.S. in Grant's initials stood for "Unconditional Surrender." Grant, after besieging and taking Vicksburg, was on his way to becoming the premier Union general of the war. He was a fighting man at a time when the Union desperately needed these. He did not make a lot of friends with his gruffness, and tales of his drinking abounded, many of them apocryphal. It appears that Grant could go long periods of time without drinking, but when he did touch alcohol, he binged. Fortunately, his wife, Julia, and Chief of Staff John A. Rawlins were able to keep him away from alcohol most of the time.

Grant's other staunch supporter was President Abraham Lincoln. Lincoln may not have said (to those who complained about Grant's drinking):

"Find out what whiskey he consumes; I want to send some to all my generals!" but he did proclaim: "What I want are generals who will fight battles and win victories … Grant has done this, and I propose to stand by him."

This was a wise move on Lincoln's part. After Grant was made commander in chief of all Union armies in early 1864, he attacked Robert E. Lee's dwindling army with vigor, sending William Tecumseh Sherman to take Atlanta while attacking with the Army of the Potomac into Virginia, cornering Lee, and forcing him to surrender in 1865. A grateful nation made Grant an enduring hero and twice elected him president, in 1868 and 1872. His administrations were not notably successful. Although Grant himself was an honest man, he was surrounded by scandals. But it is not an exaggeration to say that Grant was one of the most important military commanders in U.S. history.

GENERAL ROBERT E. LEE: "IT IS WELL THAT WAR IS SO TERRIBLE"

Despite the fact that Robert E. Lee was the losing general in a massive and destructive war effort fought, at least in part, to preserve the institution of slavery, Lee was (and still is) revered as a military genius and hero.

Unlike Grant, Lee's life before the war was one of unchecked successes. Born in Virginia in 1807, the son of Revolutionary War hero "Light-Horse Harry" Lee, Robert E. Lee graduated from West Point second in his class, received a commission to the Army Corps of Engineers, and fought heroically in the Mexican–American War, emerging with the rank of colonel and the admiration of his commander, General Winfield Scott, who called him "the very best soldier I have ever seen in the field."

After that war, Lee was appointed Superintendent of West Point, and then he served as a cavalry colonel in West Texas. Lee stayed in the regular army right up to Virginia's secession from the Union. (It was in this capacity that Lee and his chief lieutenant, Jeb Stuart, captured abolitionist John Brown at Harpers Ferry). When Virginia seceded, Lee resigned his commission, saying that he could not fight against the land of his birth.

Lee was soon named a full general of the Confederate army, and he served as a military advisor to Confederate President Jefferson Davis. Lee planned Stonewall Jackson's Shenandoah Valley campaign (see "The Shenandoah Campaign," p. 135). Lee took over command of the Army of Northern Virginia in the spring of 1862 and repeatedly rebuffed the efforts of General George McClellan to capture Richmond that summer.

In the fall, Lee's own invasion of Maryland was stopped at the fierce battle of Antietam—the single bloodiest day in U.S. history—where he suffered 10,000 casualties to McClellan's 12,000. But with an army of only 38,000 men, Lee managed to intimidate McClellan's Union force of some 75,000. The next year, Lee won his signal victory at Chancellorsville, where he divided his forces in front of Joseph Hooker's larger Union army and sent Jackson crashing into the northern right flank.

Some historians believe that Lee's momentous string of victories in 1862 and early 1863 had less to do with his tactical acumen than with the timidity of the Federal commanders he faced. But Lee certainly knew how to aggressively exploit the weaknesses of his opponents. Despite the fact that Lee had the demeanor of a southern gentleman, he was an iron-fisted commander who waged war hard.

After repulsing Ambrose Burnside at Fredericksburg, Virginia, Lee viewed the slaughtered Union dead who had charged the entrenched Confederate lines and remarked to General James Longstreet: "It is well that war is so terrible. We would grow too fond of it." But Lee himself would make the same mistake of attacking an entrenched enemy armed with modern rifles in July 1863 at Gettysburg, Pennsylvania, where he sent a massive infantry assault against the Union Army in what is called Pickett's Charge. The result was his defeat and the beginning of the end for the Confederacy (see "Turning Point," p. 122).

Increasingly cornered by Grant, Lee fought a series of brilliant but costly rear-guard actions in 1864, before finally surrendering to Grant at Appomattox Court House in April 1865. Lee became president of Washington College (now Washington and Lee University) in Virginia, a state where he was held in reverence. By his demeanor and military successes, he had made the cause of the Confederacy seem a holy one, even though, in the end, he had failed to win the single victory needed to bring the North to its knees. Lee died in 1870 of heart failure. He had actually applied to have his citizenship restored by the Federal government, but the application was lost. It was found again in 1970 and granted posthumously.

ROBERT E. LEE IS STILL CONSIDERED ONE OF THE MOST REVERED MILITARY LEADERS OF THE SOUTH. HIS HUNGER FOR VICTORY OVER THE NORTH LED TO POOR JUDGMENT IN THE BATTLE OF GETTYSBURG. THE DEFEAT SERIOUSLY WOUNDED LEE'S SPIRIT. HE LATER SAID, "IT IS ALL MY FAULT. IT IS I WHO HAVE LOST THIS FIGHT."

Prints & Photographs Division, Library of Congress, LC-DIG-pga-03298

The Confederate Soldier: Johnny Reb

It can probably be said that for at least the first two years of the war, the average Confederate soldier outfought the average Yankee soldier. Both of them were about eighteen years of age, but the Confederate soldier initially had two advantages. One, he was better led. Almost all the officers in the United States regular army prior to the war went to the Southern side once secession occurred. Second, Johnny Reb was fighting in his homeland much of the time. The strongest soldier is the one with a good officer who is fighting to protect his own backyard. Most Confederate infantrymen had never owned slaves in their lives (although many of their officers had), but they were fighting for what they considered to be their state, their freedom, and their way of life.

From the very beginning, Confederates had a much poorer supply system than the Union Army, and rebel soldiers almost always were scruffier looking and far more hungry. One Virginia woman—a rebel

sympathizer—describes Confederate soldiers in the late summer of 1862 (barely a year and a half after the war started) coming to her door with a look of "gaunt starvation" and "cavernous eyes." They begged for food: "I been a-marchin' and a-fightin' for six weeks...and I ain't had n-a-rthin' to eat 'cept green apples and green corn." That these men could fight at all, the woman concluded, was incredible. The Confederates lost

one important battle to the forces of General Philip Sheridan late in the war because they were so hungry they had stopped to plunder Union stores.

Still, carrying the Confederate infantryman's primary weapon, the Enfield rifle, and supported by superb cavalry, the likes of which the Union could never equal, the rebel soldier fought bravely under far more trying conditions than his Union counterpart. In the end, the Confederate soldier lost not because he was outfought, but because he was out-supplied and outmanned.

THE CONFEDERATE SOLDIER WAS NOT SO NEARLY WELL-SUPPLIED WITH ARMS AND FOOD AS HIS COUNTERPART IN THE UNION ARMY, BUT, FOR MUCH OF THE WAR, HE WAS FIGHTING TO DEFEND THE HOMELAND HE HELD DEAR.

Edwin Tennison, Confederate Army soldier (b/w photo), American Photographer, (19th century) / Private Collection, Peter Newark Military Pictures / The Bridgeman Art Library

The Union Soldier: Billy Yank

Similar to the Confederate soldier, the average age of a Yankee private was eighteen years old. Despite the stereotype that Union soldiers came from industrial cities, the great majority of them hailed from farms. Many of these had never even seen a large town before they enlisted or were drafted.

Of the two soldiers, the Union soldier was better provisioned and

better fed. But, at least in the first part of the war, they were not better led. Union generals at the beginning of the war tended to be political appointees who knew little about fighting. This doesn't mean they lacked courage, necessarily. At the start of the war, it was considered de rigueur for a higher officer to expose himself calmly to fire. (This is what led to the astonishing

statistic, for both sides, of generals having a 50 percent higher mortality rate than privates.) But Union generals were unimaginative in their tactics, and they often overestimated the size of Confederate forces—as at the battles of Antietam and Chancellorsville. This allowed Robert E. Lee to divide his army and outmaneuver them (see "Commanders," p. 130).

UNION ARMY TROOPS WERE BETTER PROVISIONED AND BETTER FED THAN SOUTHERN TROOPS, BUT AT THE BEGINNING OF THE WAR THEY WERE LED BY ILL-EQUIPPED AND INEXPERIENCED MILITARY LEADERS, WHICH LED TO THEIR EARLY DEFEATS.

Civil War Photograph Collection, Prints & Photographs Division, Library of Congress, LC-USZC6-48

Prussian General Helmuth von Moltke once likened the soldiers of the Civil War on both sides to "two armed mobs chasing each other around the countryside." But by mid-war, the Union soldier who had survived had become a wily veteran. Armed with his 1861 U.S. Model Springfield Rifle musket, which fired a .58 caliber minié ball (see "Weaponry," p. 134), he had learned how to fire from cover as much as possible, as well as to avoid exposing himself to the enemy.

One telling fact: Early in the war, the position of flag-bearer was coveted because of the chance of dying a glorious death as Confederates poured fire upon the man carrying a unit's battle banners. Toward the end of the war, with slaughter endemic and all hopes of glory disappearing, most Union soldiers shunned the position at all costs. They wanted to fight, but they wanted to survive, as well.

The *Monitor* vs. the *Merrimac:* Epic Clash of the Ironclads

On March 9, 1862, two opposing ships exchanged fire off Hampton Roads, Virginia. They were the USS *Monitor* and the CSS *Merrimack,* and they were both sheathed in iron. The battle between them became the first in history that was not conducted between wooden ships.

The *Merrimac* actually began its life as a Union frigate, which was sunk when Confederate forces approached the Norfolk Navy Yard. The Confederates raised her, cut the hull down to the waterline, put slanting sheets of iron over it, bolted iron plates over the entire ship, and added a huge battering ram at the bow. The *Merrimac* looked, as one wag said, like a "floating barn roof," and it was extremely slow, but much to everyone's astonishment, it floated.

The *Monitor* was not improvised like the Merrimac, but it was purpose-built by Union engineer John Ericsson. Covered with iron, it looked a little like today's submarines, with a hull so low to the water that ocean waves splashed over it and a revolving turret with two huge guns.

The ships made their debuts during the Peninsula campaign. The *Merrimac,* not realizing the *Monitor* was there, steamed out among the wooden-hulled Union ships in the Hampton Roads Harbor off the coast of southeastern Virginia and proceeded to sink one Union ship and run the other aground. When the *Merrimac* attacked another Union vessel, the *Monitor,* which had been lying in wait, fired on her.

For four hours, the two ironclad monsters exchanged shellfire, but neither was able to appreciably damage the other. They finally broke off the engagement. So impressed were the navies of both sides, however, that they stopped building new wooden warships and immediately began turning out iron battleships. The future of naval warfare had changed irrevocably.

Abraham Lincoln and the Gettysburg Address

One of the greatest speeches ever given in U.S. history was also one of the most unnoticed at the time it was spoken.

The date was November 19, 1863. The place was the new Soldier's National Cemetery being dedicated outside the town of Gettysburg, Pennsylvania, where, four months earlier, thousands of young men of both the North and South had given their lives in a battle that had finally stopped the northward advance of Robert E. Lee's Army of Virginia. The Confederate dead had been roughly tumbled into mass graves. The Union corpses had been dug up from the hasty graves prepared for them that summer, arduously identified by which states their units were from (if that was possible), and then reburied in wide semi-circles around a monument to their valor.

Abraham Lincoln arrived the night before to address the crowds at the dedication, but he was not the principal speaker. That honor had gone to the famous orator Edward Everett, who spoke for more than two hours. This was not a snub to Lincoln, as legend has it, but merely a reflection of the fact that, at the time, U.S. presidents had little involvement in state affairs. Lincoln rose to speak after Everett was through, however, and in just three minutes and 272 words focused his listeners on the purpose behind the horrible casualties such as the dead young men who surrounded them—that of creating a nation "of the people, by the people, for the people."

Although most of the attention at the time was focused on Everett, it was Lincoln who summed up the meaning of the solemn day in words that have run through history. In fact, Everett wrote the president the next day, saying: "I should be glad, if I could flatter myself, that I came as near to the central idea of the occasion in two hours, as you did in two minutes."

Weaponry: Mighty Minié

The relatively rapid-firing rifled muskets and repeating rifles of the Civil War (see "The Confederate Soldier" and "The Union Soldier," p. 132) caused unheard of slaughter on U.S. battlefields between 1861 and 1865, but the carnage would not nearly have been as great without a half-inch lead slug incongruously called the minié ball.

The minié ball, named after its inventor, French army Captain Claude F. Minié, was not really a ball, but a cylindrical slug with a cone-shaped tip. The minié was smaller than most of the slugs that were then currently being jammed down into muskets with ramrods—with the result that it could be more easily and rapidly fired. It also had a small lead "skirt" or edging around the base of the bullet, which expanded with the powder gases released after firing to hug the rifling grooves in the inside of the musket barrel, thus ensuring better accuracy. Finally, the minié had a hollow tip and large caliber (.58), which combined to cause horrendous wounds as the slug tumbled inside the human body.

The result was a bullet that was accurate at 300–400 yards (275–365 m), but still deadly at half a mile, which could be fired rapidly, and which killed and maimed easily. Almost immediately the minié became the favored bullet on both sides of the conflict. However, for the first several years of the war, generals did not fully understand the carnage it would wreak, thus continuing to order old-style frontal charges against defensive positions that cost thousands upon thousands of lives. The minié ultimately made the favored tactic of the Civil War defensive in nature: dig in, lay your rifle on your breastworks, and wait for the enemy to charge. The mighty minié would do the rest.

The Shenandoah Campaign: The Valley of Death

General Thomas "Stonewall" Jackson has been called the most remarkable soldier of the Civil War, on either side, but you certainly couldn't tell that by looking at him. A backwoodsman from western Virginia who graduated seventeenth in his class of fifty-nine from the U.S. Military Academy at West Point, served in the Mexican–American War, then settled down to the humdrum life of a mathematics instructor at the Virginia Military Academy, Jackson was not impressive. Jackson was extremely religious, adhering rigidly to the tenets of the Bible. He wore dilapidated old Virginia Military Academy hat into battle, sucked lemons for his indigestion, refused to eat pepper because he claimed it made his legs ache, and stood in a certain posture at all times to keep his alimentary canal straight. He spoke little and confided his plans in almost no one.

Jackson had fought so stubbornly at the First Battle of Bull Run that many had nicknamed him "Stonewall." But before the spring of 1862, most of his men knew him as "Old Tom Fool" because of his eccentricities. But that was before Lee unleashed Jackson in the Shenandoah Valley. Located in Virginia and West Virginia, the Valley is a beautiful southwest to northeast corridor, 140 miles (225 km) long, between the Blue Ridge Mountains on the east and the Appalachians and Alleghenies on the west.

At the beginning of the Civil War, Confederate planners knew that the Shenandoah was a natural roadway through which Confederate troops could stream to threaten the northern cities of Baltimore and Washington. In the spring of 1862, with General George McClellan threatening the Confederate capitol of Richmond, Virginia, Jackson's 22,000-man army, using cavalry to screen the east–west gaps in the Blue Ridge Mountains, headed down the valley to harry the North. This forced the Union to detail thousands of troops to protect the nation's capital, troops that otherwise might have helped McClellan take Richmond.

In three months, Jackson's army marched up and down the Shenandoah Valley no less than five times, playing hide and seek with Federal troops searching for them. The infantry moved so fast, and marched so long, that they became known as Jackson's "foot-cavalry." At one point, Jackson—fooling even his disappointed men—loaded them on a train heading back down the Valley, as if in retreat, but then unloaded them at another station, put them on another train heading back into the Valley, and led them in a successful surprise attack against Union forces.

Using extraordinary maps drawn by his topographical engineer Jedediah Hotchkiss, Jackson directed his men through the smallest and most obscure mountain passes, emerging again and again in the enemy's rear. He drove his men at a relentless pace. "If a man's face was as white as cotton and his pulse so low you could scarcely feel it, [Jackson] looked upon him as an inefficient soldier and rode off impatiently," said one man. But Jackson's actions had saved Richmond, and none of his men again called him "Old Tom Fool." When Jackson was killed the next spring at Chancellorsville, after another brilliant flanking move that had defeated a Federal army, Lee mourned that he had lost his "right arm."

GENERAL THOMAS J. "STONEWALL" JACKSON WAS ORIGINALLY CALLED "OLD TOM FOOL" BECAUSE OF PERSONAL ECCENTRICITIES. THE NAME LATER BECAME "STONEWALL" BECAUSE OF HIS IMPRESSIVE FIGHTING AT THE FIRST BATTLE OF BULL RUN.

Thomas J. 'Stonewall' Jackson mortally wounded in the left arm at the Battle of Chancellorville, Virginia, 2nd May 1863 (litho), Redwood, Allen Carter (1844-1922) (after) / Private Collection, Peter Newark Military Pictures / The Bridgeman Art Library

Marching to the Sea: "Making Georgia Howl"

William Tecumseh Sherman, whose middle name was that of the famously warlike Indian chief of the Ohio Valley, was one of Ulysses S. Grant's new breed of generals. These men were not political appointees. They were fighters, and it was their business to bring the bloody and seemingly interminable Civil War to an end.

To achieve this result, in 1864, Grant sent Sherman, with an army of 110,000 men, to march on the city of Atlanta, Georgia, the South's second most important city, a vast railway terminus and manufacturing center. After defeating Confederates under John Hood, Sherman took Atlanta on September 2 and, the next month, burned about a third of the city to the ground to deny it to the Confederates. Then Sherman set off on his famous march through Georgia to the sea. His goal was to punish the Confederacy and bring it to its knees through total war.

Sherman, who had a knack for being quotable, said at the time: "The utter destruction of Georgia's roads, houses, and people will cripple their military resources...I will make Georgia howl." (It was only after the war, in a speech in the 1870s, that Sherman uttered his famous phrase, "War is hell."). Leaving behind his supply lines and living off the land, Sherman marched 62,000 men, with 35,000 horses, and 2,500 wagons, overland 300 miles (485 km) to Savannah, Georgia.

The effect of this Union horde on this land previously unspoiled by war was catastrophic. There were almost no Confederate troops to oppose them. Sherman's "bummers" as they were called, "foraged liberally on the country," to use the euphemism employed by one Union officer. Not so euphemistically, a bummer wrote: "We destroyed all we could not eat, stole their niggers, burned their cotton & gins, spilled their sorghum, burned and twisted their R. Roads and raised hell generally."

The march ended in Savannah in December, having destroyed little of actual military value, but having had an incalculable effect on Southern morale. Sherman sent Lincoln a triumphant telegram that stated: "I beg to present you the city of Savannah as a Christmas gift."

WILLIAM TECUMSEH SHERMAN WAS CONSIDERED ONE OF THE NEW BREED OF NORTHERN GENERALS.

General William T. Sherman (1820-91) in Atlanta, GA (b/w photo), Brady, Mathew (1823-96) / Private Collection, Peter Newark American Pictures / The Bridgeman Art Library

Black Soldiers: "Staking Their Lives"

Abraham Lincoln issued the Emancipation Proclamation on New Year's Day, 1863, which freed all slaves and called for them to be enlisted in the Union Army and Navy.

This was easier said than done because a good deal of prejudice existed on the Union side toward blacks. Ironically, the Northern War Department called the conflict "a white man's war," and initially refused to accept blacks into the armed forces as soldiers. This was not solely due to racism. It was recognized that armed black men were the Confederates' worst nightmare and that they would fight all the harder against the Union should black soldiers be sent against them. However, abolitionists and more radical Republicans soon put enough pressure on the War Department, and the recruitment of black soldiers began.

The most famous black regiment was the 54th Massachusetts, led by a white man, son of a famous abolitionist family, Colonel Robert Gould Shaw. In July of 1864, the 54th attacked Fort Wagner, a Confederate fort that defended the entrance to

Charleston Harbor. During this frontal assault, Shaw was killed, and the 54th lost nearly half its men. But the unit managed to hold the fort for an hour before retreating before a counterattack.

Northern newspapers compared this battle to Bunker Hill in its importance to the abolitionist movement,

but Confederates were not moved. They refused to return Shaw's body to his family, saying "we have buried him with his niggers." There were numerous incidents during the war of Confederates bayoneting black soldiers who tried to surrender. But by war's end, 130,000 black soldiers and sailors were fighting for the Union—men whom, as Lincoln put it, had "staked their lives" for their country.

THE 54TH MASSACHUSETTS INFANTRY WAS THE MOST FAMOUS REGIMENT OF BLACK FIGHTERS. INITIALLY THERE WAS RESISTANCE ON THE PART OF THE WAR DEPARTMENT, WHICH BELIEVED THAT HAVING BLACK SOLDIERS FIGHT AGAINST THE CONFEDERATES WOULD ONLY ENRAGE THEM MORE AND CAUSE EVEN GREATER DESTRUCTION TO UNION FORCES. AFTER ENOUGH PRESSURE, HOWEVER, THEY FINALLY GAVE IN.

William J. Netson, 54th Massachusetts Infantry, c.1863 (tintype), American School, (19th century) / © Massachusetts Historical Society, Boston, MA, USA, / The Bridgeman Art Library

8

THE FRANCO-PRUSSIAN WAR

1870–1871

This ten-month-long war between France and Prussia had
an outcome far more outsized than its time span, creating the
European order that would last until World War I and radically
changing the way the world's armies would train and fight

Combatants

- France
- Prussia, German states

Theater of War

France and Germany

Casualties

Prussia: 117,000 dead and wounded
France: 140,000 dead and wounded
and 400,000 captured

Major Figures

GERMANY
Wilhelm I, king of Prussia
Premier Otto von Bismarck, Prussian
leader who provoked France into war
General Helmuth von Moltke, brilliant
Prussian commander in chief

FRANCE
Emperor Napoleon III, formerly known
as Louis-Napoleon Bonaparte and
nephew of Napoleon Bonaparte
General Patrice de MacMahon,
severely wounded at the Battle
of Sedan
Field Marshal Achille Bazaine,
commander in chief of French forces,
later convicted of treason

Bubbling into existence from the poisonous alchemy of a Prussian statesman seeking war and a French emperor wanting to save face, the Franco-Prussian War of 1870–1871 was a short, vicious "modern" conflict that cost hundreds of thousands of lives on both sides. It was the first war fought by a united Germany, the last by an imperial France, and it featured weaponry (see "Chassepot versus Krupp," p. 154) and tactics that determined the way armies would do battle for the next half a century. It also featured a loss of territory (especially Alsace and Lorraine), which became a major source of resentment to the French for many years to come and escalated a French–German enmity that would burst bloodily onto the killing fields of the First World War.

But on the plus side for the victorious Prussians, a unified Germany was finally created, which became a European powerhouse and set the stage for the German nation of the nineteenth and early twentieth centuries.

1870:

June: Spain offers crown to German prince Leopold von Hohenzollern. France threatens war if Leopold accepts. French ambassador arrives at Ems in western Germany to demand apology from Prussian King Wilhelm I. Wilhelm refuses, but Premier Otto von Bismarck alters a telegram sent to him by Wilhelm to make it deliberately incendiary.

July 19: France declares war on Prussia.

August: French forces capture Saarbrücken in their only victory of the war.

Prussians defeat French at the battles of Weissenburg, Wörth, and Spichern; French retreat to fortress at Metz. Prussians pin down French forces under Marshal Achille Bazaine at the Battle of Borny and begin encirclement of Metz, defeating the French in a series of battles.

September 1: French forces are surrounded and defeated at the Battle of Sedan; Napoleon III captured.

October 26: After a fifty-four-day siege at Metz, Bazaine surrenders an army of 170,000 men to the Prussians.

September 1870–January 1871: The Prussians besiege Paris, which surrenders on January 28, 1871.

1871:

March: The French Civil War sees the creation of the Paris Commune, made up of independent French republican leaders who battle the new French government.

May: The Treaty of Frankfurt ends the Franco-Prussian War, forcing the French to pay Germany $1 billion in reparations and cede territory. Germany is united.

WILHELM I, KING OF PRUSSIA, PRESIDED OVER A WAR WITH FRANCE THAT HAD BEEN EAGERLY SOUGHT, AND WAS MAINLY RUN, BY HIS CHANCELLOR OTTO VON BISMARCK.

Portrait of William I (1797-1888) King of Prussia and Emperor of Germany, engraved by William Holl (1807-71) pub. by William Mackenzie (engraving), / Private Collection, / The Bridgeman Art Library

GERMANY'S RISE, FRANCE'S FALL

Ostensibly, the Franco-Prussian War began because the Spanish offered their vacant crown to Leopold, a prince of the Prussian house of Hohenzollern.

The French (feeling rightly that they would be hemmed in between two Prussian-controlled states) demanded that the offer be withdrawn. It was, but a telegram between King Wilhelm I of Prussia and his premier Otto von Bismarck (see "Commanders," p. 146) was released (see "The Ems Telegram," p. 153) whose language was so inflammatory that both the Prussian nation and Emperor Napoleon III of France (see "Commanders," p. 148) clamored for war to avenge the insult.

In reality, things were far more devious and complex. France and Prussia had been enemies since they fought on opposites sides of the Napoleonic Wars. In the 1860s, Prussia had 19 million inhabitants (compared to 35 million French). But Prussia had become an industrial powerhouse, with 5,000 miles of railroad track and booming, smoke-belching cities such as Berlin, Breslau, Düsseldorf, and Cologne.

In 1866, in what became known as the Seven Weeks' War, the Prussians, with their brilliant fifty-one-year old premier, Otto von Bismarck, and his legendary military genius, General Helmuth Karl von Moltke, (see "General Helmuth Karl von Moltke," p. 151) destroyed Austria's army and replaced the old German confederation of states (controlled by Austria) with the Prussian-led North German Confederation.

Bismarck sought to unite the North German Confederation with the still-independent south German states. The best way to do that was to provoke a war with France to stir up nationalist feelings. This he did by encouraging Spain to offer its crown to Prince Leopold and then altering the Ems telegram (see "The Ems Telegram," p. 153) so that not only France, but also Prussia, felt insulted after what should have been a bloodless diplomatic dispute.

Seeing his fortunes falling at home, Emperor Napoleon III, aging, corrupt, often sick, and ill-advised, took the bait and declared war on Prussia on July 19, 1870. He had been assured that the French army was invincible, which turned out to be far from the case. France had a few initial advantages, which included the ability to call on a larger standing army (at first) and the rapid-firing and highly accurate Chassepot rifle, which far outclassed the Prussian "needle-gun."

French troops marched east to their border with Prussia and won a minor early victory at

Emperor Napoleon III had been assured that the French army was invincible, which turned out to be far from the case.

Saarbrücken, but then a fully mobilized Prussian army led by the redoubtable Helmuth von Moltke, swollen to nearly twice the size of the French, attacked.

The French, under General Patrice de MacMahon, were defeated at the battles of Weissenburg, Wörth, and Spichern, in early August. Napoleon III put Marshal Achille Bazaine in charge of all French armies, but Bazaine was encircled and trapped in September in the fortress city of Metz in northeastern France and was ultimately forced to surrender in October 1870 after a fifty-four-day siege.

In late August, Napoleon III had joined a French army under MacMahon at the city of Sedan, in the Ardennes region of France. On September 1, his forces were destroyed by the attacking Prussians. The next day, Napoleon surrendered along with 83,000 French troops.

With the Prussians now marching on Paris, a French provisional government of national defense deposed the captured Napoleon, thus ending the Second French Empire, and established the Third Republic. While guerilla fighting broke out in the provinces, the Prussians besieged France from September to January 1871.

The starving Parisians were forced to capitulate on January 28. The French Civil War began in March; this bloody action saw independent republican elements in Paris battling with the leaders of the Third Republic, which had signed the armistice with the Prussians. Almost 20,000 members of this Paris Commune were executed before the revolt was suppressed by the Third Republic.

The Treaty of Frankfurt, on May 10, 1871, ended the Franco-Prussian War, with France forced to pay an indemnity of 5 billion silver francs and cede territories that included Alsace and part of Lorraine. This sowed the seeds for resentment that would ultimately end in the fighting of World War I.

But for the time being, a new, unified Germany reigned supreme in Europe. Although the French often fought valiantly, German mobilization through its railroad system; its rapid-firing, breech-loading Krupp artillery guns; and its swarming, intelligent, squad-level military tactics (see "The Prussian Soldier," p. 150) ultimately won the day.

THE BATTLE OF SEDAN:
SEPTEMBER 1, 1870

At the end of August 1870, 85,000 French soldiers of the Army of Châlons were caught in a landscape that formed an enormous shallow bowl with a radius of about 1,000 yards (1 km). At the center of the bowl, on the Meuse River, was the picturesque old city of Sedan, but no one was paying much attention to the scenery. Far more immediate were the more than 700 Prussian guns that ringed the French positions. They were fast-firing Krupp six- and twenty-four pound cannon that the French troops knew from experience were horrifyingly deadly.

The French were caught in what the Prussians liked to call (and loved to fight) the *Zirkel-Schlacht,* or "circle-battle," but French General Auguste Ducrot had a far simpler term for it. "Here we are in a chamber pot, about to be shitted upon," he told his commanding general, Patrice de MacMahon, urging him to seek new positions. But MacMahon—and Emperor

BY THE END OF THE BATTLE OF SEDAN, THE FRENCH EMPIRE CEASED TO EXIST AND THE GERMAN NATION BEGAN.

The defeated French troops at the battle of Sedan, 1st September 1870 (coloured engraving), German School, (19th century) / Musee de la Ville de Paris, Musee Carnavalet, Paris, France, Archives Charmet / The Bridgeman Art Library

Napoleon III, who had picked this inopportune time to join the French army in the field—were strangely passive, confused, and paralyzed, like most of the French field generals during the war. And the result would be a battle that would end the French Empire forever.

Surrounded

Throughout August, the Prussians had repeatedly outmaneuvered the French in a series of victories that had sent French armies reeling back in disarray. Finally, Napoleon III had made the grand old French soldier, Field Marshall Achille Bazaine, commander in chief of French forces, but Bazaine was slow and indecisive. The result was that he became trapped by the Prussians with an entire army in the fortress city of Metz. This was a huge blow to the French. Bazaine had nearly 170,000 men with him, and Napoleon and Patrice de MacMahon had formed the 90,000-strong Army of Châlons to relieve him. They had embarked on a left-flanking move, north along the Belgian border, with more patriotism than forethought.

When General Helmuth von Moltke saw how the French maneuver was developing, he took two Prussian armies northward, leaving two behind to hold Metz. They caught up with the French at Beaumont on August 30. After a short but fierce action that cost the French 5,000 casualties, they drove them back toward Sedan.

Here Napoleon III and MacMahon were going to rest and regroup their forces, resupply with ammunition, and move out. But they hadn't counted on the fact that their troops were exhausted by the long series of forced marches they

had been subjected to. They also hadn't counted on swift-moving Germans, who quickly encircled the French at Sedan in a series of swift thrusts. On the morning of September 1, the French looked up to see themselves ringed by Prussians.

"Now We Have Them in a Mousetrap"

Because of the natural amphitheater quality to the battlefield, the Prussian general staff and their visitors were afforded a birds-eye view of the impending battle. These visitors included King Wilhelm I, Otto von Bismarck, famous U.S. Civil War officer General Philip Sheridan, and numerous foreign dignitaries, as well as the press of many countries. In luxurious enclosures on a grassy slope above the village of Frénois, these men waited for the guns to open up.

Sheridan, who was there as a neutral observer but found himself quite partial to the Prussians, was impressed by the energy with which the Prussian troops positioned themselves: "The German troops moved with … a peculiar swinging gate, with which the men seemed to urge themselves over the ground with ease and rapidity. There was little or no straggling, and being strong, lusty young fellows and lightly-equipped … they strode by with an elastic step."

At around the same time on the evening of August 31, a French officer described a group of French soldiers lying down in a field. The men insisted on sleeping, even as an advancing Prussian skirmish line poured fire into them—until finally, with the Prussians only 500 yards (450 m) away, they were able to bestir themselves to drive them back with their Chassepots.

GENERAL PATRICE DE MACMAHON LED TROOPS INTO THE
FATEFUL BATTLE OF SEDAN. HE FOUND HIMSELF TRAPPED
BY THE SWIFT-MOVING PRUSSIANS.

Comte Maurice de MacMahon (1808-93), 1860 (oil on canvas), Vernet, Emile Jean
Horace (1789-1863) / Chateau de Versailles, France, / The Bridgeman Art Library

It was easy to foresee the outcome of such a battle. Von Moltke, watching the envelopment take place from high on a ridge, told King Wilhelm: "Now we have them in a mousetrap." Hostilities would commence early in the morning of September 1.

"The Hiss of Chassepot Rounds"

At four o'clock in the morning, a Prussian division attacked French forces in the town of Bazeilles, outside Sedan, a point considered the most likely one from which the French might launch a breakout attack. But the French were waiting for them. In savage house-by-house fighting, with French civilians grabbing shotguns and taking part, the Prussian troops were stalemated.

The fighting spread outward from this point, with German forces attacking north of Bazeille and French forces holding them off with a series of counterattacks. As Patrice de MacMahon was inspecting the scene of these actions, his horse was blown out from under him, and he was severely wounded. Unable to continue, he turned command of the Army of Châlons over to Auguste Ducrot, who had previously tried to get MacMahon to position the army anywhere but in Sedan. Ducrot now ordered a "retreat to the west," but it was too late for a breakout. Two Prussian corps blocked his way. There was nothing for the French to do but fight.

In the heights above Frénois, the observers watched as smoke erupted around the entire encirclement, and the rolling rattle of rifle fire echoed across the hills. Even from above, they could hear screams of men cut down in combat. The French were not about to give up without a fight.

A Bavarian infantry officer described the withering fire the French laid down as they attacked on the northern side of the encirclement: "Left and right of me, my men fell…I saw my best soldier killed by three bullets…Our colonel died in the storm, shot twice at 200 yards. I remember trying to flatten myself in the furrows of the potato fields and then crawling among the dead and wounded to scavenge cartridges. I found a piece of sugar in a Frenchman's backpack and sucked on it while hearing the hiss of the Chassepot rounds, *pfft, pfft*."

Blown to Bits

As outlying French units were driven into the killing grounds around Sedan, more and more of the Krupp guns opened up. "The ground trembled," wrote one witness, and "shells passed like storm winds." It was a massacre. There was nowhere for the French to shelter, and the Prussian guns pounded them on all sides. French troops raced panic-stricken through the streets of Sedan, leaving "mutilated, dying men," as one observer wrote, "without arms, feet, legs, many with open skulls, their brains oozing out."

A Bavarian officer, coming into the town after the battle, found a general and his entire staff literally blown to bits. The only way to identify the general was through a piece of his underwear, upon which was written: "General T."

As the afternoon wore on, Sheridan, high on the heights, wondered to Bismarck and von Moltke whether Napoleon III would survive it. They laughed at him. "Oh, no," Bismarck said. "The old fox is too cunning to be caught in such a trap; he had doubtless slipped off to Paris."

"My Sword in the Hands of Your Majesty"

But the old fox had not, in fact, slipped off. Late on the afternoon of September 1, realizing that there was no escape and that his situation was hopeless, Napoleon III sent an adjutant with a white flag through the front lines, with a note addressed to King Wilhelm I. It read: "Having failed to die amongst my troops, there is nothing left for me to do but place my sword in the hands of Your Majesty."

Above Frénois, the king had the letter read aloud to the assembled. After a moment of silence, a cheer went up. Bismarck hoisted a bottle of brandy and shouted (in English, for the edification of Sheridan and members of the press) "Here's to the unification of Germany!"

The Prussians set harsh terms for the French—the surrender of the entire army, with all nonofficers being sent to prison camps, rather than being paroled. On September 2, Napoleon III set out from the city to find Kaiser Wilhelm, hoping for some mercy. He was intercepted by Bismarck, who explained to him that no gentler terms would be forthcoming—that the French were now well and truly beaten.

The war would drag on until May, but the Battle of Sedan was, as one Austrian observer put it, "one of the most stunning events in [European] history." In the course of one long and bloody day, the French empire ceased to exist, and the German nation began.

PREMIER OTTO VON BISMARCK: THE IRON CHANCELLOR

Without Otto von Bismarck, it is most likely there would have been no Franco-Prussian War. But without Bismarck there would have been no German nation either.

Bismarck, like Helmuth von Moltke (see "General Helmuth Karl von Moltke," p. 151) is something of a surprise. Although his nickname became "the Iron Chancellor" and he often wore a uniform he had no official right to wear (he had only spent a year in the Prussian army, before retiring to the reserves) he was a man with a wide education and sophisticated tastes. Born in 1815 to a rigid Prussian military officer and landowner, he had a mother with more sophisticated and cosmopolitan leanings, which Bismarck would also cultivate. He loved art, dance, and literature, and he even tried his hand at writing a novel.

When Bismarck became a member of the newly created Prussian legislature at the age of thirty-two and rose to deputy parliamentarian the following year (1847), it was as an ultraconservative champion of Prussia's Junker class (the ancient, landowning nobility). When revolutions burned their way across Europe in 1848, Bismarck attempted (in a classic feat of Bismarckian manipulation) to rally peasants in defense of the Prussian king.

Yet—and this is also classic Bismarck—he quickly recognized the changing political climate and within a few weeks made a speech to the legislature claiming "the past is dead...no human power can bring it back to life." This was the first example of the concept of Realpolitik that Bismarck would pioneer and that would have such a profound effect on European politics for the next seventy-five years.

As Bismarck rose in Prussia to become premier, fighting wars against Denmark, Austria, and finally France, he had one goal in mind—the unification of Germany into a great power. Bismarck had numerous means of achieving that goal, which meant making alliances with enemies (where necessary) and resorting to such trickery as the Ems telegram.

146

In the meantime though, Bismarck believed, along with military thinker Carl von Clausewitz, that "war is merely an extension of politics by other means." Bismarck's famous "iron and blood" speech in the Prussian parliament in 1862 called for the unification of Germany through military means, and he was to write: "After all, war is, properly speaking, the natural condition of humanity."

Bismarck's wars were smashingly successful. After 1871, Germany was the premier power of Europe, and Bismarck had been named its first chancellor. Yet the man who had so hungered for violence was chastened by the death toll of the Franco-Prussian War—117,000 Prussian casualties in less than a year. Bismarck argued with von Moltke and his other generals and soon came to realize that entrusting the fate of a nation to generals was never a good idea.

Bismarck's post-Franco-Prussian War career, therefore, was devoted to keeping down the many-headed hydra of military expansionism while spinning alliances with other nations, with the goal of avoiding conflicts and keeping Germany supreme. For a while he was successful, but when the militaristic Kaiser Wilhelm II began his rule in 1890, he dismissed Bismarck from his post. A new and dangerous period in German politics—which Bismarck had helped to engender, but which he now wished to avoid—was about to be embarked upon, and there was no room for the Iron Chancellor. Bismarck was deeply concerned about the future in his country, but he died in 1898, covered with honors.

PREMIER OTTO VON BISMARCK, "THE IRON CHANCELLOR," WAS THE CAUSE OF BOTH THE FRANCO-PRUSSIAN WAR AND THE FORMATION OF THE GERMAN NATION.

Chancellor Otto Von Bismarck (1815-98) c.1871 (colour litho), German School, (19th century) / Musee de la Ville de Paris, Musee Carnavalet, Paris, France, Archives Charmet / The Bridgeman Art Library

EMPEROR NAPOLEON III:
"ALL IS FINALLY LOST."

Like his uncle, Napoleon I, Emperor Napoleon III was in many ways a man who defies description. He staged a coup to become emperor of France, yet he was responsible for many liberal reforms that included a freer press and the implementation of numerous programs to help the poor. He was ruthless in crushing opposition, yet he nowhere near as ruthless when it came to prosecuting the one war that he needed to win—the Franco-Prussian War.

Napoleon III—known as Louis-Napoleon Bonaparte before he took the title of emperor—was born in Paris in 1808, the third son of Napoleon's brother Louis who along with his wife, Hortense, had been made King and Queen of Holland by Napoleon. Along with all Bonapartes, Louis-Napoleon had been forbidden by the Bourbon monarchy, restored after Waterloo, to live in France. Thus, he spent much of his early life in exile in Switzerland, Austria, and Italy. In the latter country, he took part in various revolutionary schemes to unify the country, which, while unsuccessful, showed a talent for intrigue and a desire to gain the same prominence as his uncle.

On two different occasions, Louis-Napoleon stole back into France and attempted quixotic revolutions designed to oust what he called the "illegitimate" Bourbon dynasty governments. The first time Louis-Napoleon was caught, he was sentenced to exile in the United States; after the second attempt, in 1840, he was jailed in a French fortress "in perpetuity."

Louis-Napoleon, while seen by some as a foppish and romantic young man, was resourceful. Six years into his jail sentence, he disguised himself as a construction worker and simply walked out of prison. Then, after the French revolution of 1848, which freed the Bonapartes to return to France, Louis-Napoleon ran for president. In the main, because of nostalgic yearning for the greatness of Napoleon I, he actually won in a landslide. During Louis-Napoleon's term in office, he displayed an adroitness most people would not have expected, uniting conservative and liberal factions, making reforms, creating public works projects to help the unemployed, and beginning a glorious, $15 billion (in today's currency) redesign and rebuilding of Paris.

But term limits set after the 1848 revolution would put Louis-Napoleon out of office in 1852. This Louis-Napoleon could not abide; hence, on December 2, 1851—on the date of his uncle's great victory at Austerlitz—he seized power in a coup, named himself "prince-president," and, a year later, Emperor Napoleon III.

Napoleon III ruled successfully for many years, but by 1870 he was simply outclassed by Prussian leaders such as Bismarck and King Wilhelm I. With a large and corrupt family kept on the French payroll (his own personal reserves in foreign banks amounted to about $75 million), his foreign mistresses, and, increasingly, his illnesses (hemorrhoids, gout, and bladder stones), Napoleon III was out of touch.

He believed his generals when they told him the French army was invincible, with its quick-shooting Chassepots (see "Chassepot versus Krupp," p. 154) and heavy fortresses, and he also made the mistake of thinking he could outbluff Bismarck. When he was finally disabused of this notion—as a captive of the Prussians after Sedan (see "Turning Point," p. 142), he said to Bismarck, as if the revelation had just struck him: "All is finally lost."

It was. In a few short months, France would fall, and Napoleon would be overthrown. He was to spend his final days in luxurious but ignominious exile in London, dying in 1873 haunted by regrets.

NAPOLEON III, THE NEPHEW OF NAPOLEON I, ROSE TO THE THRONE ON A WAVE OF NOSTALGIA FOR THE FRANCE OF OLD UNDER RULE OF HIS UNCLE. WHILE HE MADE SOME POSITIVE CHANGES DURING HIS REIGN, THEY WOULD BE EXTINGUISHED AFTER THE LOSS OF THE FRANCO-PRUSSIAN WAR.

Portrait of Napoleon III (1808-73) 1862 (oil on canvas), Flandrin, Hippolyte (1809-64) / Chateau de Versailles, France, Lauros / Giraudon / The Bridgeman Art Library

The Prussian Soldier

On the eve of the Franco-Prussian War, the Prussians possessed the finest army hosted on the fields of Europe, and perhaps anywhere in the world. This is one reason why military observers from many countries, including U.S. Civil War General Philip Sheridan, accompanied its army as it crushed the French in less than a year.

For one thing, the Prussians depended on universal conscription to amass an army, which gave them a great advantage in numbers over the smaller, professional army of the French. Every Prussian male served in the military for three years, beginning at age twenty, then in the reserves for four years, and then in the *Landwehr* (or national guard) for five more.

Although there might be an initial delay while calling up reserves, the Prussians could field a huge, relatively experienced army quite quickly.

Unlike the French, the Prussians depended on an educated soldiery. Good maps (something the French lacked at all levels of command) were passed out to noncommissioned officers in the field. Plus, the huge ability of the Prussians to organize helped in moving hundreds of thousands of troops over five different railroad lines to attack the French all along its eastern borders in the summer of 1870. And, once on the attack, the Prussians were a marvel. They seemed to excel when they were separated from each other on the battlefield, with squads and companies probing the opposing line and seeking the French flanks. Yet when threatened, their excellent communication allowed these seemingly chaotic and disparate elements to come together to defend themselves.

All of these qualities were held together by the marvelous Krupp big guns (see "Chassepot versus Krupp," p. 154), which destroyed French lines with uncanny and horrifying precision. For the day, the Krupp big guns were extraordinarily mobile. When the Franco-Prussian War was over, foreign military advisors returned home, and the armies of the world began to change. The Prussian model was followed, beginning with conscription and moving on to training, maneuvering, and fighting.

The French Soldier

The French army in 1870 could muster only 400,000 men, while the Prussians could call on fully 1 million, as a result of its conscription system. But the French depended on professional soldiers—men who went into the army and stayed there for life. Although initially, observers thought that this gave France the advantage, because it had a fully prepared army theoretically ready to strike Prussia the minute war was declared, this was in reality a paper advantage.

The quality of many of the French troops was sometimes lacking. Unlike their highly disciplined Prussian counterparts, the professional French soldiers, long accustomed to barracks life and a certain laxness, contained large numbers of thieves and scavengers who would rather steal then fight. The consumption of alcohol among French troopers was astonishing even for soldiers of the day. They drank all day and then switched to a brandy they called *le tord-boyaux* ("the gut-wringer") at night.

Then, too, the tactical thinking of French generals was poor. Before the Franco-Prussian War, after observing the Prussian tactics of sending troops in smaller units scrambling over the battlefield, French military thinkers decided that this could be defeated by massing French troops, with the superior firepower of their Chassepots, on the defensive and simply waiting for the Prussians to come within range. This was the French tactic in rushing troops in July 1870 to the German frontier and then simply entrenching them. But keeping the troops in a close front (rather than a long offensive line) actually weakened the firepower of the Chassepots (as did the French regulation of allowing its soldiers to fire only five shots before having an officer verify whether the trooper was shooting at a proper target).

While the outnumbered and outled French troops fought with marvelous bravery, they were simply unable to overcome Prussian tactics and Prussian artillery.

General Helmuth Karl von Moltke: War As an Art Form

Born in 1800 and dead in 1891, Helmuth Karl von Moltke's life spanned the century in which he is now considered to be second only to Napoleon as the premier military innovator. Yet he was not the stiff, stern Prussian taskmaster of popular imagination, but rather a man with a supple, imaginative turn of mind. "In war as in art," he once wrote, "there exist no general rules; in neither can talent be replaced by precept."

There was never any question that von Moltke's raw talent could be replaced by anything. Born into a family of ancient but impoverished nobility, he went early into military service. By 1832, von Moltke had risen quickly enough to be named to the Prussian General Staff. Yet he was a far more well-rounded man than most of his military peers. Von Moltke spoke seven languages, published fiction under a pseudonym, and was a talented travel writer and sketch artist.

By 1855, von Moltke had become adjutant to Prussian Crown Prince Wilhelm; by 1857, he was named chief of the Prussian General Staff. In three ensuing wars—with Denmark (1864), Austria (1866), and France (1870–71), he perfected his theory of battle, which can be summed up in his famous statement: "No battle plan survives contact with the enemy."

This did not mean that von Moltke was not prepared for war, just that he wanted his entire army, from general staff officers right down to new recruits, to be able to think independently on the battlefield. Von Moltke decentralized command structure and gave authority to his young officers to take advantage of new situations—one way he was able to do this was by making sure the Prussian army made full use of the new technology of railroad and telegraph, so that troops and information darted quickly around the front lines. Von Moltke's trademarks were the scrambling independent companies and squads of Prussian infantry that confounded conventional military wisdom by not massing in large groups and by always seeking the enemy's flanks, rather than its front lines.

Despite von Moltke's great victories, he was far from a warmonger. Later in life, he became alarmed by the belligerent militaristic posturing of Kaiser Wilhelm II and his inner circle, even going so far as to rise in the German Reichstag, at the age of ninety, to speak out against them. If these men got the war they wanted, he told the German legislature, "its length will be incalculable, and its end nowhere in sight." Von Moltke died the next year, but this farseeing soldier had correctly predicted the unimaginable conflagration of World War I.

HELMUTH KARL VON MOLTKE IS CONSIDERED SECOND ONLY TO NAPOLEON IN NINETEENTH CENTURY MILITARY INNOVATION. HE SPOKE SEVEN LANGUAGES, PUBLISHED FICTION, AND WAS A TRAVEL WRITER AND SKETCH ARTIST.

General Fieldmarshal Helmuth Graf von Moltke (1800-91), 1890 (oil on canvas), Lenbach, Franz Seraph von (1836-1904) / Hamburger Kunsthalle, Hamburg, Germany, / The Bridgeman Art Library

The Siege of Paris: Night Flying

The siege of Paris is one of the grimmest episodes in that proud city's history. Beginning in mid-September of 1870, the encircling Prussian forces slowly strangled the city while a French army tried mightily to fight its way through to relief. French irregular forces known as *franc tireurs* harried von Moltke's troops in the Parisian suburbs with savage guerilla actions, which prompted equally savage reprisals.

In the meantime, inside, Paris, 1 million people starved. By early January, they were eating horsemeat, cats, dogs, rats, insects, and anything else they could get their hands on. Still they hung on, which finally prompted the Germans to start shelling the city with their heavy guns, something they had avoided for fear of raising the ire of the rest of Europe. Four-thousand Parisian civilians died every week in January under the shelling, until the French finally surrendered on January 28.

One of the biggest reasons Parisians were able to survive a five-month long siege was their use of the balloon, whose early employment in war they had pioneered during the French Revolutionary Wars. This time, the Parisians used balloons—sixty-six in all—to carry messages to the rest of the country and to smuggle important people and spies out of the city. It was a dangerous game. Most of the balloons were sent up at night,

but the Germans captured at least six balloonists, while one was blown by strong winds all the way to Norway, 875 miles (1,410 km) away.

It was impossible to send balloonists back into Paris. Although many tried, all failed because it was difficult to control the balloons of the day with that kind of accuracy. But the fact that the rest of the country—and the world—knew of the plight of the Parisians was success enough, although in the end of the crushing weight of Prussian military might carried the day.

PICTURED: THE SIEGE OF PARIS REMAINS ONE OF THE MOST HORRIFIC EPISODES IN THE CITY'S HISTORY. THE PRUSSIAN ARMY ENCIRCLED THE CITY, CHOKING IT OF ITS SUPPLIES. ONE MILLION PEOPLE STARVED, AND YET THOSE WHO REMAINED CONTINUED THE FIGHT, INCITING EVEN HARSHER RESPONSES FROM THE PRUSSIANS.

The Battle of Villejuif, Siege of Paris, 1870 (oil on canvas), Detaille, Jean-Baptiste Edouard (1848-1912) / Musee d'Orsay, Paris, France, Lauros / Giraudon / The Bridgeman Art Library

The Ems Telegram: "A Red Rag to Taunt the Gallic Bull"

In July of 1870, while taking a morning stroll at Bad Ems, Germany—a favored spa—King Wilhelm I of Prussia was, as he put it later, "waylaid" by Count Vincent Benedetti, French Ambassador to Prussia. Benedetti had been instructed by his superiors to demand that the king never approve the candidacy of a Hohenzollern (see "Chronicle," p. 140) to the throne of Spain.

The ambassador was somewhat too forthright in his importuning (for the diplomatic standards of the day), and Wilhelm responded firmly (but politely) that he would not guarantee any such thing. Instead, Wilhelm said that, as his private secretary later wrote in a telegram to Premier Otto von Bismarck, "surely [Benedetti] must see that my government was not concerned in the matter."

The issue would have ended there, except that Bismarck, who received the telegram in Berlin, decided to alter the communication to inflame passions for the war he so devoutly sought with France. Striking out the king's diplomatic words, he doctored the language to make it seem like both the king and Benedetti had been far more brusque and angry than they really were. That night at dinner, Bismarck read the new version to General Helmuth von Moltke, saying that he was seeking "a red rag to taunt the Gallic bull." Von Moltke heartily approved. "Now the telegram has a different ring ... [not] a parley but a response to a challenge," he said. He was sure war would ensue: "If I may but live to lead our armies in such a war, the devil may come afterward and fetch away my old carcass."

Von Moltke was to have his wish. When the new version of the telegram was released to the public, both sides felt their honor had been insulted, and a French declaration of war came by July 19.

COUNT VINCENT BENEDETTI, FRENCH AMBASSADOR TO PRUSSIA, PICTURED HERE, SPOKE WITH KING WILHELM I ABOUT PRUSSIA'S APPROVAL OF A HOHENZOLLERN CANDIDATE TO THE THRONE OF SPAIN. HIS DIPLOMACY WAS TWISTED BY OTTO VON BISMARCK TO PROVOKE WAR BETWEEN FRANCE AND PRUSSIA.

© Mary Evans Picture Library / Alamy

Chassepot versus...

One day in the fall of 1868, a French army surgeon staged a macabre demonstration for a group of French infantry officers and medics. He took the corpse of a middle-aged man who had died of natural causes, set it up against the wall of a firing range, and then had a soldier fire five rounds into the body with the newly issued French infantry rifle known as the Chassepot.

The damage, even to these onlookers versed in the horrors of war, was incredible. "Bones smashed all out of proportion," one medic reported observing exit wounds up to thirteen times greater than the entry wounds, which indicated severe damage to internal organs. Amazingly enough, no bullet could be found inside the man's body. All had passed through two mattresses placed behind the corpse, as well as the firing range wall itself.

Such was the power of this short, carbine-like infantry rifle designed by French inventor and gunsmith Antoine

Chassepot and a team of army engineers. Its superior stopping power lay in the fact that although its bullet was a smaller caliber than the rifle carried by the Prussian infantryman (the Dreyse "needle rifle," named for its needle-like firing pin), each cartridge had more powder and thus packed an extra punch.

The Chassepot had many more advantages, as well. It was a light breech-loader that could fire eight to fifteen rounds per minute (as compared to four or five for the needle rifle) and was accurate at 1,000 yards (915 m), compared to 400 to 600 (365 to 550 m) for the Dreyse. And its cartridges were so light that French riflemen could carry more than 100 rounds in their pouches (as compared to only 70 for the Prussians).

The Chassepot was indeed, as one German officer would later say, "a gorgeously worked murder weapon." But instead of improving tactics and morale, the French high command

depended too much on the Chassepot to win the war for them. It certainly accounted for most Prussian casualties, but was not the decisive weapon of the conflict. That accolade would go to the breech-loading, rapid-firing Prussian artillery.

PICTURED: THE SUPERIOR CHASSEPOT RIFLE USED BY THE FRENCH DURING THE FRANCO-PRUSSIAN WAR.

Getty Images

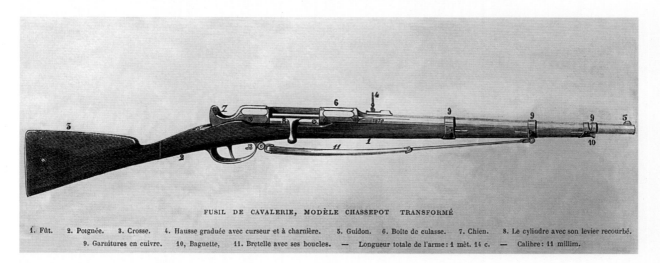

FUSIL DE CAVALERIE, MODÈLE CHASSEPOT TRANSFORMÉ

1. Fût.   2. Poignée.   3. Crosse.   4. Hausse graduée avec curseur et à charnière.   5. Guidon.   6. Boîte de culasse.   7. Chien.   8. Le cylindre avec son levier recourbé.
9. Garnitures en cuivre.   10, Baguette,   11. Bretelle avec ses boucles.   —   Longueur totale de l'arme: 1 mèt. 14 c.   —   Calibre: 11 millim.

…Krupp

The artillery gun that trumped even the brilliantly powerful and accurate rifle of the French was indeed revolutionary. Manufactured by Krupp Industries, designed by Albert Krupp himself, it was a cannon of cast steel whose extraordinary accuracy was due to a superior rifled barrel, whose shells could be fired more quickly because it was breech-loading, and which had devastating explosive power. While the French clung to their old, brass muzzle-loading cannon, the Krupp guns, using six-pound or twenty-four pound shells, could fire twice as fast with three times the accuracy.

It wasn't just the guns themselves, but the way the Prussians used them. Instead of placing them in huge, immobile batteries where they could lay down immense barrages but were hard to maneuver, the Prussians pioneered a concept they called *artillerie-massen* ("artillery masses"), in which smaller units of guns, pulled by horses, would mass together to deliver a deadly fire on any given target, then disband to head for the next objective.

Because the guns stayed close to the ever-maneuvering Prussian infantry (unlike the French artillery, which was kept well back by its commanders

and fired at maximum range) Prussian artillery could be directed by infantry observers. This method of close fighting with artillery remains with modern armies to this day.

As historian Geoffrey Wawro wrote in his history of the Franco-Prussian War: "Cumbered with a rifle that was already obsolete in 1870, the Prussians relied almost entirely in the war on their breech-loading, steel-tubed Krupp guns. The major battles of 1870–71 were decided by the Prussian artillery."

KRUPP ARTILLERY WAS THE CROWNING GLORY OF THE PRUSSIAN WAR EFFORT, DECIDING MAJOR BATTLES FOR THEM.
Getty Images

9

THE ANGLO-ZULU WAR

1879

The British destruction of the sixty-year-old Zulu
nation in just six months signaled a bleak future for all such
independent African countries for almost a century to come.

Combatants
- Great Britain
- Zulu nation

Theater of War
Zululand, Africa

Casualties
Great Britain: 1,083 dead, 243
wounded
Zulu: 8,000 dead, 16,000 wounded.

Major Figures
GREAT BRITAIN
Sir Henry Bartle Frere, high commissioner of Southern Africa, who pushed
for the Zulu army to be eliminated and
gave Cetshwayo an ultimatum

**Lieutenant General Frederick
Augustus Thesiger, Lord Chelmsford,**
leader of British invasion forces
General Sir Garnet Wolseley,
Chelmsford's replacement

ZULU
Cetshwayo, king of the Zulus

It took the British, with their repeating rifles, howitzers, and Gatling guns just six months to destroy the mighty nation founded by Shaka Zulu sixty years before. However, during the course of the short conflict, the Zulus, with a population of about 300,000, were able to bring about the worst defeat the British ever suffered at the hands of an indigenous people in Africa and even managed to drive the first invasion force from Zululand. But when the dust settled in August 1879, the British had divided the once-proud nation among thirteen different pro-British chieftains, thus setting the stage for a civil war that would tear the country apart and cause Great Britain to finally annex Zululand into South Africa.

After the Anglo-Zulu War, no independent African nation of any power would exist until the end of the colonial era, post World War II.

1878: Sir Henry Bartle Frere issues ultimatum to Cetshwayo, telling him to disband Zulu army. Cetshwayo refuses.

. . . .

1879:

January: First invasion of Zululand: Lord Chelmsford's forces enter Zululand in three columns on January 15. One column is attacked and destroyed by Zulus at Isandhlwana on the 22nd. Later that day, British forces from the same column remaining at Rorke's Drift outpost hold off another Zulu attack. The second column engages the Zulus at Hlobane Mountain on January 24, but retreats upon hearing of the disaster at Isandhlwana. A third column is besieged by the Zulus and forced to fight its way out.

March: British under Colonel H.E. Wood are defeated by the Zulus at Hlobane; the next day, Wood defeats Zulu forces at Kambula.

April: Chelmsford relieves British forces trapped at Ekowe and retreats with them back to Natal.

May: Second invasion of Zululand. Chelmsford invades again with stronger British force.

July: British destroy Zulu army at their capital of Ulundi.

August: British capture King Cetshwayo.

. . . .

A ZULU WARRIOR IN FULL WAR DRESS IN 1875. THE ZULUS INFLICTED THE WORST DEFEAT THE BRITISH HAD EVER SUFFERED AT THE HANDS OF AN INDIGENOUS FORCE IN AFRICA AT THE BATTLE OF ISANDHLWANA IN 1879.

2007 Getty Images

THE END OF THE ZULU NATION

The Zulu nation, in territory that is now a part of South Africa, was started by Shaka Zulu (see "The Great and Murderous Shaka," p. 172) in the early 1820s. It became the most powerful and most populous independent African nation of the nineteenth century, known for its military prowess and willingness to annex neighboring states by force.

In the 1830s, the Zulu kings who followed Shaka to power battled with the Boers, Dutch farmers who had trekked to southern Africa to escape British rule farther north in Africa. The Boers came face to face with the Zulu people, with both groups wanting the same land. The British took over the Boer territory of Natal in 1843 and, at first more amenable to peaceful dealings than the Boers, co-existed with the Zulus. But in the 1870s, the high commissioner appointed for southern Africa, Sir Henry Bartle Frere, wanted to unite the odd grouping of British, Boer, and black states into one Confederation of South Africa, under British rule. However, Frere knew that this was impossible while the fiercely independent Zulu nation and its 40,000-man-strong army were intact.

Although the British government in England did not want war, Frere exaggerated the Zulu threat. Late in 1878, Frere issued an ultimatum to Zulu King Cetshwayo (see "Commanders," p. 168), calling for, among other things, the dismantling of the Zulu army. Cetshwayo rejected this demand, as Frere knew he would. A month later, on January 11, 1879, the English invaded Zululand with 5,000 white soldiers and 8,000 Africans under the command of Lieutenant General Frederick Augustus Thesiger, Lord Chelmsford.

The English plan to send three separate columns to converge on Cetshwayo's capital of Ulundi almost immediately ran into trouble. On January 21, Chelmsford took two-thirds of his army to chase what he believed to be a large army of Zulu warriors to the southeast. Eighteen hundred British soldiers, including 400 African auxiliaries, were left behind near the small mountain of Isandhlwana. They were attacked by 20,000

Zulu warriors. After a pitched battle, only fifty-five British troops managed to escape.

The next day, a small group of British soldiers at Rorke's Drift, a nearby river crossing, managed to hold off further Zulu attacks. The Zulus had inflicted the worst defeat the British had ever suffered at the hands of an indigenous force in Africa. They followed it up the next month by scattering and defeating a British attacking force under Colonel H.E. Wood at Hlobane. However, the Zulu warriors, with the lack of discipline and tactical direction that was to be their downfall during the war (see "The Zulu Soldier," p. 170) the next day attacked Wood's main camp and were driven back by the massed firepower of the British, losing 2,000 men to the twenty-nine English soldiers.

After relieving a besieged British column at Ekowe in April, Chelmsford took his battered British forces back to Natal, and then reinvaded Zululand at the end of May with an increased force of 16,000 British soldiers and 7,000 Africans. This time, badly needing a victory over the Zulu to keep his personal reputation intact, Chelmsford ignored peace overtures from Cetshwayo and drove 5,000 British troops to the king's capital city of Ulundi. The British formed into a fighting square and were attacked by 20,000 Zulu warriors on July 4, 1879. The massed fire of British repeating rifles and Gatling guns killed 1,000 Zulus at the cost of only ten British dead.

The British seized and burned Ulundi, and Cetshwayo became a fugitive who was captured during mopping up operations in August and exiled from his people, whose independence, after sixty years, had now been lost forever. The British divided the nation up into areas governed by thirteen different pro-British chieftains. This was recipe for civil war that would lead to the complete destruction of the Zulu Kingdom.

SIR HENRY BARTLE EDWARD FRERE WANTED TO UNITE THE AFRICAN STATES UNDER BRITISH RULE BUT KNEW HE WOULD HAVE TO NEUTRALIZE A 40,000 MAN ZULU ARMY.

Sir Henry Bartle Edward Frere (1815-84) (engraving), English School, (19th century) / Private Collection, Ken Welsh / The Bridgeman Art Library

BATTLE OF ULUNDI: 1879

The kraal, or village, of the great King Cetshwayo at Ulundi, which means "the high place," was vast. Some 1,500 mud huts were connected by a maze of fenced-in passageways. At the end of June 1879, it buzzed with activity. Thousands of women and children worked and played in the streets, while some 20,000 Zulu warriors streamed through on their way to tend cattle in the pastures nearby or keep watch over the approaches to the town.

Despite British rumors of a grand palace filled with treasures, Cetshwayo's own hut was modest, only one-story high. In it were treasures, but of a different sort than the British imagined: a silver snuffbox, an English newspaper with photographs of Cetshwayo's inauguration ceremony in 1873, and numerous empty champagne bottles that Cetshwayo, although a modest drinker, kept around because he liked the way the light struck the glass.

Right now, however, Cetshwayo had little time to ponder his treasurers. Reports had come from his lookouts that the massive British column that had invaded the country the previous month could now be seen from the heights surrounding Ulundi, meaning that it was, perhaps, 30 miles (48 km) away. Cetshwayo rose and spoke hurriedly to an envoy. Attempts had been made in the past month to reach the leader of the British, Chelmsford, but each time messengers had been unable to contact him. Cetshwayo urged his latest messenger to head straight for the British, to show himself with a white flag, and to tell the English commander that the king of the Zulus desired peace.

The False Peace of Chelmsford

Cetshwayo did indeed want peace, but Lieutenant General Frederick Augustus Thesiger, Lord Chelmsford, did not. Even as Cetshwayo spoke to his envoy in the dimness of his hut, Chelmsford was at the head of his Flying Column, urging his troops on. Smoke from burned and blackened kraals spiraled in his wake, as thousands of British soldiers spread out over the countryside dealing out death and destruction.

This was Chelmsford's second invasion of Zululand. During the first (see "Bloody Isandhlwana," p. 174) he had been dealt a severe and severely embarrassing loss at Isandhlwana, mainly because he had underestimated his enemy. Although Chelmsford's respect for the Zulu had not much increased, he had learned his lesson. Arriving back in Zululand at the end of May, he had brought with him a force three times as large, which he did not separate into three columns. And he was currently driving straight at the heart of Zululand and at Cetshwayo's heart as well.

When the Zulu envoy reached Chelmsford, the latter listened cursorily to him and then made a list of demands: Cetshwayo was to return everything taken from the British since the war started (this would include horses, cattle, and the two pieces of field artillery the Zulus had seized at Isandhlwana). Moreover, several Zulu regiments must surrender in a very public and humiliating

fashion by approaching the British camp and laying down their arms. The envoy protested that captured British material was spread all over Zululand and that it would take weeks to return it all and that it would be almost impossible to get three of the war-like Zulu regiments to surrender in such a manner.

Finally and impatiently, Chelmsford agreed to accept all the British goods and livestock that were currently at Ulundi, and only one regiment need symbolically surrender in this way. The envoy headed back to Ulundi, and Chelmsford continued on with his army, spreading his cavalry out in front of him to avoid ambush, intent on saving his reputation by destroying the Zulu nation.

"I Am Astonished at Not Hearing from You"

In reality, Chelmsford's biggest problem, as he saw it, was the fact that he had received word that London, finally impatient with his blundering in

the first invasion, had replaced him with General Sir Garnet Wolseley, who had now arrived in Africa. Wolseley had begun to send a series of importuning telegrams from the rear. His latest, postmarked June 30, had been quite peremptory:

"Concentrate your force immediately and keep it concentrated. Undertake no serious operations with detached bodies of troops. Acknowledge receipt of this message at once and flash back your latest moves. I am astonished at not hearing from you."

Wolseley's astonishment was no greater than that of Chelmsford. How dare Wolseley send him a telegram written in such a tone? Wolseley was Chelmsford's superior officer, but between men of such high rank, such discourtesy was unforgivable. But, even more, it was apparent that Wolseley wanted Chelmsford to stay in one place and await his arrival—an arrival that might take weeks, because Wolseley was at least 250 miles (400 km) behind Chelmsford. Chelmsford could see that

Wolseley wanted the honor of leading the attack against the Zulus. But that was an honor that Chelmsford had worked hard for, the only honor that would restore his reputation after the disaster at Isandhlwana.

This Chelmsford would not stand for. The telegram had been sent on June 30 and reached Chelmsford on July 2, when he was but 5 miles (8 km) away from Ulundi. He sent a deliberately vague reply and ordered his men forward.

Napoleon's Sword

As the European column moved closer to Ulundi, Cetshwayo began to despair. It was obvious from Chelmsford's reply that he knew little about the way the Zulu nation truly worked. Cetshwayo had had the same experience with Sir Henry Bartle Frere, whose ultimatum demanding that Cetshwayo disband his army had started the war. Cetshwayo could not comply with a demand for

Zulu surrender then, and he could not now, either, because many of the Zulu *impi* ("regiments") were not directly under his control. It was not like a European army, where the generals obeyed the king and politicians. Each regiment was commanded by a different Zulu warrior-leader who might, or might not, obey the order of the king.

Here, the Zulu warriors could see the English threatening their capital and homeland, and they were already preparing to attack them. Women and children were now streaming out of Ulundi, the Zulus' precious capital city, leaving the town to the warriors.

Cetshwayo could not force the public surrender of even one regiment. What he hoped for was a negotiation that would lead, say, to reparations being paid on the part of the Zulus and then the withdrawal of British forces from his land.

Cetshwayo decided to send Chelmsford, as a sign of his good faith, a gift of one hundred valuable white oxen. And he would add one thing more: a European sword, with handle and pommel trimmed in gold, obviously made by a fine craftsman. The sword had been taken from the body of the young officer killed recently in a nearby Zulu kraal and brought to Cetshwayo. The King had very soon realized from his sources in Capetown that the officer was Prince Louis-Napoleon IV and that the sword had belonged to none other than Napoleon Bonaparte (see "The End of Louis-Napoleon IV," p. 173).

Sitting on the floor of his hut, Cetshwayo hefted the weight of the sword in his hands. He knew the British placed great store in such relics and decided that perhaps it, plus the rare white cattle, might be enough to stop the Chelmsford forces from attacking. On July 3, he sent the cattle to Chelmsford, who was camped on the other side of the White Mfonzi River. The cattle were driven to the river by a group of Cetshwayo's Zulus, who also had in their possession Napoleon's sword. But when the Zulu regiment guarding the crossing saw this peace offering, they stopped it and refused to let the cattle or the emissaries cross. The English would not get away with invading their homeland. They would pay with their lives.

Usuthu!

The next day, July 3, the British sent a mounted reconnaissance across the river, only to have it attacked in force by 3,000 Zulu warriors. It only escaped through the alert actions of its commander, who sensed an ambush. That night in camp, the British could hear the sounds of Zulus singing all night, preparing for combat. Even worse, they could also hear the screams of a lone British soldier, who had been captured in that afternoon's skirmish and was being tortured to death by Zulu women.

Chelmsford gathered his officers and informed them that they would cross the White Mfonzi River and attack the Zulus the next day on the plains below Ulundi. They would move in a "laager" formation—essentially, in a large square or rectangle, with cavalry in front and on either wing. In all, there were about 4,100 British soldiers and 1,100 native troops in the attacking force. As the sun came up full, these men could see Zulu warriors flowing down from Ulundi, joining their regiments, and spreading into a large semicircle as they moved toward the British troops.

There were about 20,000 Zulus, all of them moving inexorably toward the British, who had now stopped and formed themselves into a square, with two riflemen kneeling in front, two standing behind, and the rest of the ranks in the rear, ready to take the place of any man who had fallen. Inside the square, boxes of ammunition were opened up, while wagons were prepared to receive the wounded. The British soldiers also had several seven-pound artillery pieces as well as two Gatling guns, which could pour concentrated fire into the Zulu ranks.

The Zulus were doing exactly what Chelmsford hoped they would do by attacking, but he didn't want them to have any second thoughts. He ordered the British cavalry to ride in close to the advancing horde, shoot at them, and then dart away, almost taunting the Zulus. Back in the British square, the men could hear a distant throbbing sound that was an amalgam of noises—the Zulus clapping their spears against their rawhide shields and the sound of their fleet hitting the ground as they ran faster and faster. When the Zulus got close enough, they began screaming their war cry, "Usuthu!" which meant, "Kill!"

The Bloody Half Hour

The cavalry raced into the British square, which closed behind them just as the British artillery began to open up, sending shells into the packed Zulu ranks. Zulus did not understand how artillery worked and believed that each shell, upon exploding, sent British soldiers leaping out, so they stabbed their spears at the dark smoke drifting up from the explosions. At about 1,000 yards (915 m), the British infantry opened up with the Martini-Henrys and the rattle of the Gatling guns could be heard.

A MILITARY SKETCH-
MAP OF ZULULAND IN
THE EARLY PART OF
THE 19TH CENTURY

Wyld's Military Sketch
of Zululand, 1879 (colour
engraving), Wyld, James the
Elder (1790–1836)/British
Museum, London, UK/ The
Bridgeman Art Library

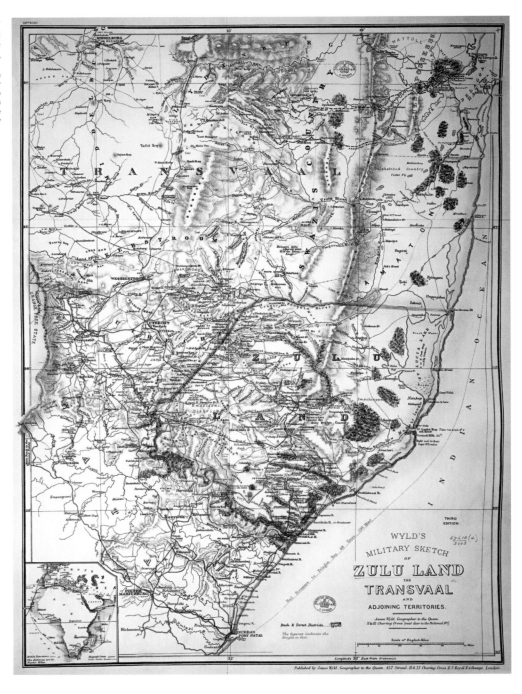

Gaps began to open in the Zulu ranks, but still they came on, screaming and waving their shields and spears. Many of the Zulus had rifles captured at Isandhlwana, and they knelt and fired at the British. Typically, unused to the kick of the gun, they fired high, but casualties began to pour back through the ranks into the center of the square, where bullet wounds were treated by pouring water on them and bandaging them up.

The Zulu attacked on every side, and the British poured fire into them. Chelmsford strode around the center of the square, giving orders to shift men from one hard-pressed side of the square to another. At one point, Zulus threatened to get close enough to break through, and he ordered a Gatling gun to be moved, whose automatic fire sent the Zulus tumbling to the ground. The noise of the battle was astounding, especially to Zulu ears, who had never heard the sound of so much firepower expended all at once. Prisoners later told the British that the din had terrified them.

The attack lasted half an hour. That was all the time it took for modern firepower to break the back of the Zulu nation. Finally unable to take it any more, the Zulus turned and ran. At that point, Chelmsford ordered his cavalry out of the square. For once, the horsemen found the Zulus out in the open and running, and they raced joyfully after them. People watching from the square could see British horsemen spearing Zulus with their lances, tossing their bodies in the air to clear the spearhead, and then racing after more, as if they were on a hunt. When the retreating Zulus were far enough away to clear the threat of a new attack, the British moved from within their square and began to walk among the fallen enemy on the field, shooting any who moved.

The attack had killed ten British and wounded sixty-nine, all by bullets. Because the Zulus had not been able to get within 30 yards (27 m) of the square, they hadn't been able to use their feared assegais, their short stabbing spears. At least 1,000 Zulus were dead, and probably many more.

The End of the Zulu

Cetshwayo had not taken part in the attack, and when it turned against the Zulus he fled into the countryside, only to be captured by British troops in August. British troops sauntered into the now deserted Ulundi and hopped its fences, seeking long-hoped-for treasures. Finding nothing but trinkets and glass, the soldiers set fire to the place and joined the long column of troops heading back across the White Mfonzi River.

The black smoke rising into the blue winter sky spelled the end of the Zulu nation, begun by Shaka so many years before. Chelmsford rode at the head of his men, satisfied. He had outwitted both Cetshwayo and Wolseley. The former was scrabbling through the bush, on the run, and the latter was now forced to send him congratulatory telegrams to not come across as a poor loser.

It was time for Lord Chelmsford to retire and rest on his laurels, and he would do exactly that.

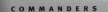

LIEUTENANT GENERAL FREDERICK AUGUSTUS THESIGER, LORD CHELMSFORD: "HOW HOPELESSLY INFERIOR THEY ARE"

Lord Chelmsford is a paradox, a typical British upper-class officer of his day, right down to his bushy moustache, chest full of medals, and gentleman's club, who consistently underestimated the Zulu enemy he would face. "If I am called upon to conduct operations against [the Zulus]," he wrote in July 1878, "I shall strive to be in a position to show them how hopelessly inferior they are to us in fighting power, altho' numerically stronger."

This type of thinking caused the great British defeat at Isandhlwanda, where a small British force was slaughtered by the "hopelessly inferior" Zulus. At the same time, Chelmsford was ultimately responsible for the British victory in the war when he doggedly marched a British square to the Zulu capital of Ulundi and dared 20,000 warriors to attack him. They did, and he destroyed them.

Chelmsford was born in 1827 in London, the son of a lawyer who became Lord Chancellor of Great Britain. He was determined to pursue a military career and saw action in the Crimean War and later in the Indian Mutiny in 1858. Despite his bluntness and outspoken ways (or because of them) he became a favorite of Queen Victoria's and rose rapidly through the ranks to become major general. On the eve of the Zulu War, he was promoted to lieutenant general and put in charge of the British invasion force of 5,000 troops.

Chelmsford's first invasion of Zululand proved notably unsuccessful, in the main because he overestimated his troop's ability to beat off mass attacks of Zulu warriors simply by dint of superior firepower. Responsibility for the terrible British defeat at Isandhlwana lies with Chelmsford, who divided his force to search for the main Zulu impi without fully scouting the area and then, when messages reached him of the battle taking place, refused to switch course and return to the aid of the beleaguered defenders, once again because he felt that only a few British soldiers were needed to fight off native warriors like the Zulus.

After Isandhlwana, when Prime Minister Benjamin Disraeli was writing Queen Victoria that his "whole Cabinet had wanted to yield to the clamours of the Press, & Clubs, for the recall of Ld. Chelmsford," Chelmsford tried to foist the blame on a more junior officer at the scene.

Chelmsford knew he had to redeem himself and his reputation, and he was right. He returned to Zululand in late May with a much larger force determined to destroy Cetshwayo at his capital city. He was moving one step ahead of the British effort to recall him, for Disraeli, no longer able

166

to protect Chelmsford from mounting public outcry, had replaced him with General Sir Garnet Wolseley, who had landed in Capetown and was sending Chelmsford telegrams ordering him to cease operations. But Chelmsford ignored these and provoked his fight with the Zulus at Ulundi on July 4 (see "Turning Point," p. 160). Then Chelmsford was able to resign his commission, his honor assuaged.

Chelmsford was never quite able to escape the stigma of Isandhlwana, but at the same time he never felt that he had done anything wrong, and he could point to his victory at Ulundi as the battle that finished the Zulus. Heavy with honors in his old age (mainly bestowed upon him by an admiring Queen Victoria) he collapsed and died of a heart attack at the age of seventy-eight while playing billiards at his club.

CETSHWAYO,
LAST KING OF THE ZULUS:
"I AM A VERY OLD MAN"

In many ways, Cetshwayo can be considered one of the most tragic figures of the Anglo-Zulu War. Fighting a conflict he could not possibly win—one he did not even fully understand—he mourned what he saw as the inevitable loss of his entire nation. It is no wonder that when captured by the British, dressed in European clothes, and taken as a prisoner to Capetown, he muttered to one of his captors: "I am a very old man."

He was then fifty-two.

Cetshwayo was born in 1826 in Zululand, the son of King Mpande, and the grand-nephew of Shaka Zulu. In 1856, with the aging Mpande still on the throne, Cetshwayo fought a bitter civil war for control of Zululand with his brother. Cetshwayo won in a bloodbath that killed thousands of members of his brother's clan. Thereafter, although Mpande remained a figurehead on the throne, Cetshwayo ruled the country from behind the scenes, finally emerging as king when Mpande died in 1872.

Cetshwayo understood that he needed to get along with the British for his nation to survive, even making a point of asking Queen Victoria to recognize his position as king of the Zulus (she did). But he had not bargained on the ambitions of British High Commissioner Sir Henry Bartle Frere, who decided—often contrary to the wishes of the British Colonial Office, which would have preferred to avoid a war with the Zulus—that he needed to provoke a conflict with Cetshwayo to destroy his army and unite southern Africa.

This Frere did in December 1878 by sending Cetshwayo an ultimatum demanding that he disband his 40,000-man force immediately. Had Cetshwayo even tried to do this, he would have been killed by his own people. Cetshwayo barely had a chance to reply, in any event, when Chelmsford launched his invasion. After this, in a very real sense, events were out of Cetshwayo's control. "The warlike spirit of the [Zulu] regiments," as historian Donald R. Morris wrote, then took over, leading both to the major victory at Isandhlwana and the defeat at Rorke's Drift and finally Ulandi.

Even the victory at Isandhlwana cost thousands of Zulu lives, which is why Cetshwayo attempted to make peace with Chelmsford as the latter led a new column into Zululand, aimed straight at Cetshwayo's capital city of Ulundi, in June 1879. But Chelmsford was, for personal and political reasons (see "Turning Point," p. 160), intent on finishing the Zulus. While bargaining with Cetshwayo through emissaries, he never really made a serious effort to make peace before the final battle at Ulundi. Thereafter, Cetshwayo went on the run, finally surrendering to British cavalry after being cornered in a tiny kraal in the bush in August.

Deposed and exiled to London by the British, Cetshwayo was brought back to reign in Zululand in 1883 when the English division of the country brought about bloody civil war. However, by that time he had lost all credibility with his people, and the attempt to set him up as a puppet ruler failed. Cetshwayo died on February 8, 1884, supposedly of a heart attack, but, according to the suspicions of the British medical examiner, possibly poisoned by rivals.

The Zulu Soldier

The Zulu warriors of King Cetshwayo were the most feared indigenous soldiers in Africa in 1879. They formed an army whose discipline, unit cohesion, and tactics were directly descended from those fashioned by Shaka Zulu some sixty years before.

The Zulu army was essentially a citizen-army, with warriors spending their time between conflicts as farmers and herders who were liable to be called into military service until they were forty or so. Zulu warriors were divided into units of some 300 soldiers, each identified by the color pattern of its shield. The Zulu shield was another innovation of Shaka's. Smaller and easier to carry than previous shields, the Zulu shield could be hooked under an opponent's shield in hand-to-hand combat to knock him off balance.

Regiments also had their own songs, chants, traditions, and customs. They were so competitive with each other that they often had to be separated, lest they get into brawls. Each unit of the Zulu army was commanded by officers, with a strong chain of command leading right up to the grizzled veterans who acted as generals and gave orders for the army to attack.

The Zulu were renowned for traveling fast, covering more than 20 miles (32 km) a day on foot. However, the Zulu's lack of horses impeded their efforts against the British, who could easily outpace them when mounted. The Zulu's efforts were mainly aimed at surprising and attacking the enemy with overwhelming force. These tactics were effective against other African tribes, but they worked only sporadically against the British because of their superior firepower. King Cetshwayo's men carried firearms—and the Zulus captured more from the British—but when using them they tended to fire high. They relied mainly on their spears and clubs, and they lost the war because they were ultimately unable to get close enough to the British to use them and they never learned to adapt their "human wave" tactics to confront modern firepower.

THE ZULU WARRIOR WAS ONE OF THE MOST FEARED FIGHTERS IN AFRICA, BUT THE BRITISH HAD HEAVY ADVANTAGES WITH THE USE OF HORSES AND FIREARMS.

Zulu Warrior (gouache on paper), McConnell, James Edwin (1903-95) / Private Collection, © Look and Learn / The Bridgeman Art Library

The British Soldier

At the time of the Anglo-Zulu War, the British soldier was armed with the rifle that would serve the empire well for the next thirty years: the breech-loading, lever-activated Martini-Henry. It fired a heavy cartridge that did enormous damage to the human body, and it fired quickly by the standards of the day—five or six rounds per minute.

British commanders had much faith in the Martini-Henry. Lord Chelmsford said, "I am inclined to think that the first experience of the Martini-Henrys will be such a surprise to the Zulus that they will not be formidable after the first effort." British commanders thought that a British soldier armed with one could hold off ten Zulus. In a sense they were right: In their epic defense of Rorke's Drift, 137 British forced away 4,000 Zulus. But the Martini had its problem in the heat of Africa, jamming frequently because the thin case of its copper cartridge expanded in the heat. In the meantime, when fired rapidly under combat conditions, the barrel and even the wooden stock became so hot that most soldiers had scorched hands after a fierce engagement.

Although the British soldier was every bit as brave as the Zulu warrior—eleven Victoria Crosses were handed out after Rorke's Drift, a record for one engagement—he was less motivated and probably had less information and understanding of why he was fighting.

The lower ranks of the British army were filled with young volunteers from poorer classes who were subjected to rigid discipline. During the short Anglo-Zulu War, according to British army records, more than 500 British soldiers were flogged for offenses that included falling asleep on guard duty. This caused such an outcry back in Great Britain that flogging was completely banned. However, in its place came the almost equally barbaric "Punishment Number One": tying a man to a wagon wheel and letting him broil in the hot sun for several hours.

The British soldier was separated from his officers, whose existence, even in camp in Zululand, was far more luxurious than that of the common soldier. Hundreds of common soldiers died of disease in Zululand and were subjected to privations that included poor rations and lack of basic shelter, due to incompetent supply systems. When the veterans returned home, many of them were lionized by the British press. But these same soldiers—knowing the incompetence of even their most senior officers—found the opportunity to leave the army as soon as possible.

THE ZULU WERE NO MATCH FOR THE FAR BETTER EQUIPPED BRITISH SOLDIER.
Getty Images

The Great and Murderous Shaka

Before the birth of Shaka in 1787, the Zulus were a part of a small tribe in southeastern Africa, a breakaway group of ethnic Bantus who raised their cattle near the White Mfozi River in what is now KwaZulu/Natal. Most of their intertribal wars involved a good deal of fist-shaking and the shouting of insults, but little in the way of casualties. That changed when Shaka came of age.

Shaka was illegitimate, the son of the first Zulu chieftan (the word Zulu means "the heavens") and grew up as an outcast, subject to taunts from other children. He left his village to work for a nearby chief, Dingiswayo, to whom the Zulus paid tribute. By the time he was twenty-four, Shaka had become a fearsome warrior.

Dingiswayo's goal was to capture slaves, and his way of doing battle was far fiercer than Zulu practice. Shaka carried it a few steps further. He felt sandals slowed his men down, and so made them run for miles over thorns to toughen their feet. If a man so much as winced, he was killed by club-wielding guards. Shaka improved the long Zulu spear into what became the tribe's primary weapon, the assegai (see "Weaponry," p. 173).

Shaka's other military innovation was training a large body of Zulus, an impi, to maneuver. Previously, Zulus and other African tribes had simply crept up and attacked their enemy. But Shaka developed a simple strategy, the *impondo zankomo,* or "horns of the bull," based on the figure of the Zulu's beloved cattle. The main body of the impi, trotting toward the enemy, was the "chest" of the bull. The "loins" of the animal were the soldiers kept in reserve. And the all-important "horns" were the Zulu warriors who streamed out from the chest on either side, to envelop their enemy.

Shaka's tactics, ruthlessness, and training were so innovative that, once Dingiswayo had been murdered by a rival, he took control of the Zulus and led them to victory after victory. By 1824, Zulu territory stretched from the Indian Ocean west to the Kalahari Desert. While creating a great empire, Shaka was a brutal and capriciously cruel leader. He ordered vengeful reprisals on those who had taunted him and his mother in his youth. Shaka was followed everywhere by his personal executioners, and he had people clubbed to death for the most insignificant infractions.

It's no wonder that Shaka was assassinated by two of his half-brothers in 1828. But, despite his failings as a ruler, he had created the greatest independent nation that Africa would know until the twentieth century.

SHAKA WAS ABLE TO CREATE THE GREATEST INDEPENDENT AFRICAN NATION UNTIL THE TWENTIETH CENTURY.

Shaka, the Zulu warrior, English School, (20th century) / Private Collection, © Look and Learn / The Bridgeman Art Library

Weaponry: The Soul-Sucking Assegai

Although King Cetshwayo armed some of his Zulu warriors with rifles, their main weapon was their traditional spear, the assegai, which had been developed by Shaka Zulu some sixty years before the Anglo-Zulu War (see "The Great and Murderous Shaka," p. 172). Previous to Shaka, the Zulus had used a javelin-like throwing spear with a slimmer blade. Shaka had considered it absurd that one hurled a weapon and then lost it for good.

Shaka cut down the handle of the Zulu spear, made it heavier, and added a wide, flat blade to create the assegai, a stabbing spear that forced warriors to closely engage with the enemy. Once a few feet away, the Zulus either threw the spear or, preferably, rammed it into his opponent's gut.

Actually, assegai is the European term for the Zulu spear. Zulus called it by the much more descriptive term *ikwa,* which was an onomatopoetic word for the sound the spear made being wrenched from a fallen foe's abdomen. The assegai was such an important weapon for the Zulus that rituals sprang up around it. The Zulus would cry, as Shaka first did so many years before, "I have eaten!" after killing an enemy. Then he would use his assegai to eviscerate the man—a process known as "the washing of the spears"—believing that otherwise evil spirits would be trapped within the corpse's body and come back to haunt the Zulu warrior. Although the assegai would prove no match, ultimately, for the repeating rifle (see "The British Soldier," p. 171), the assegai dealt murderous destruction to anyone unfortunate enough to get in its way.

The End of Louis-Napoleon IV

The sere plains and rocky hills that provided the setting for the Anglo-Zulu War also served as the unlikely backdrop for the death of Prince Louis-Napoleon IV, the only child of Emperor Napoleon III of France (see "The Franco-Prussian War," p. 138).

Louis-Napoleon was born in 1856, the subject of great rejoicing by his father and mother, Empress Eugenie. He was trained early to the French military tradition and became a crack rider. At the age of sixteen, he saw limited action in the Franco-Prussian War, but he was forced to flee with the rest of his family to England, once the war turned against the French and his father was captured. After his father died in exile in 1873, Louis-Napoleon was proclaimed Napoleon IV by the Bonapartists, who agitated to get him back on the throne of France.

Louis-Napoleon attended various British military academies during this period, and he was a well-liked young man who impressed those around him with his horsemanship. One of his favorite tricks was using an old sword of his grand-uncle's, Napoleon I, to cut in half potatoes hurled at him while he raced at full gallop. His friendships extended throughout the young elite of the English upper classes, with whom he loved to socialize.

THE FRENCH BONAPARTE DYNASTY ENDED WITH THE DEATH OF PRINCE LOUIS NAPOLEON.

Eugene-Louis-Napoleon Bonaparte (1856-79) 1874 (oil on canvas), Lefebvre, Jules Joseph (1836-1912) / Chateau de Versailles, France, Lauros / Giraudon / The Bridgeman Art Library

(continued on p. 174)

When the Anglo-Zulu War broke out, the twenty-two-year-old Louis-Napoleon begged Queen Victoria for a chance to fight for his adopted country, as way of saying thank you. However, he had other reasons, chief among them the fact that seeing combat might enhance his youthful reputation and force people in France to take him seriously when the inevitable attempt came for this last Bonaparte to try to regain power in his home country.

With some reluctance, the queen allowed young Louis-Napoleon to join Chelmsford's forces with the rank of lieutenant. Officially, he was one of Chelmsford's *aides-de-camp*; unofficially, he made it known that he wanted to see as much action as possible. Louis-Napoleon went on several reconnaissance missions, once endangering himself by chasing off on his own to try to kill solitary Zulus.

On the morning of July 1, 1879, Louis-Napoleon foolishly overruled the orders of the officer accompanying him and made camp in what he thought was a deserted Zulu kraal. He posted no lookouts, and thus he and his squad were taken by surprise when forty Zulus sprang from cover and attacked. Louis-Napoleon attempted to escape on his horse, but he fell and was set upon by his assailants while the rest of the English fled. When Louis-Napoleon's body was recovered, it had eighteen assegai wounds in it.

Louis-Napoleon's death caused a great stir in Europe. Some Bonapartists even accused Queen Victoria of having him killed, but in fact he had caused his own demise through his incaution. His death ended the last hope of restoring the Bonaparte dynasty to the throne of France.

Bloody Isandhlwana

The Battle of Isandhlwana stands as the worst defeat ever inflicted upon British forces in Africa in the nineteenth century. It came about because of the miscalculations and overconfidence of Lord Chelmsford (see "Commanders," p. 166) who, only ten days after his invasion of Zululand, abandoned a large portion of his force to go hunting Zulus where there weren't any.

On January 21, about 1,700 members of the British central attacking column, including 750 native soldiers, set up camp near the mountain of Isandhlwana, near the Buffalo River. They did not bother to entrench because they thought there were no Zulus around. In any event, their modern weapons were more than a match for the primitive spears of any enemy who might lurk nearby. Behind the British force was the sheer rock face of Isandhlwana; in front of them, a vast and seemingly empty plain. While Chelmsford led a column out to seek the Zulus (see "Chronicle," p. 158),

THE BRITISH DEFEAT AT THE BATTLE OF ISANDHLWANA CAME ABOUT BECAUSE OF THE MISCALCULATIONS AND OVER-CONFIDENCE OF LORD CHELMSFORD.

The Battle of Isandlwana: The Last Stand of the 24th Regiment of Foot (South Welsh Borderers) during the Zulu War, 22nd January 1879, c.1885 (oil on canvas), Fripp, Charles Edwin (1854-1906) / National Army Museum, London, / The Bridgeman Art Library

the rest of the British waited in camp under the command of Lieutenant Colonel Henry Pulleine.

On the afternoon of January 22, Pulleine sent mounted scouts out to reconnoiter the area a few miles in front of the British camp. Much to their astonishment, as they rode up to a previously hidden ravine, they peered down and saw 20,000 Zulu warriors, sitting in complete silence, perfectly hidden. When the Zulus spotted them, they arose as one body, and the British scouts raced furiously back to camp to spread the news. As Pulleine screamed orders at his men, the Zulus charged,

screaming their battle-cry *"Usuthu!"* ("Kill!"). They were spread out in their traditional "horns of the bull" formation, but on a massive scale, with the Zulu main line 5 miles (8 km) across, and one of the horns reaching well behind Isandhlwana. The British, at first, did not even see it.

As soon as the Zulus came close, the British began firing, beating off wave after wave of Zulus, but soon the Zulu's superior numbers began to tell. Bursting into the British camp, they hacked and speared anyone in their path, and the fighting degenerated into a hand-to-hand brawl. British soldiers clubbed with their empty

guns and stabbed with bayonets while the Zulus threw their own dead at them and charged behind cover of the bodies.

When the smoke cleared, thousands of corpses littered the ground around Isandhlwana and the Buffalo River, where many of the British soldiers had tried to flee. Out of 950 Europeans who started the day alive, only fifty-five survived. Native troops supporting the British lost 500 of their number. At least 2,000 Zulu died, probably many more. It was a great Zulu victory, but it would be their last major blow against the British.

Aftermath: The Zulu Today

Although the Zulus failed to survive as an independent nation after the Anglo-Zulu War, they have managed to thrive as a people.

When the war ended in 1879, the British divided the country into thirteen different kingships, each run by a pro-British king who was generally supported by Boer mercenaries. Factionalism and infighting were naturally the order of the day after this—as the British, who did not have the manpower to occupy

Zululand after defeating the Zulus, may have hoped. They did reinstate Cetshwayo as king in 1883 (see "Commanders," p. 168), but this did little to stop the violence of civil war. Within a few years, the British decided to absorb Zululand into their Cape colony.

The British then taxed the Zulus heavily and used them as common laborers. This mistreatment caused the final uprising of the Zulus, the Bambatha Rebellion of 1906 (named

for the Zulu chief who led the rebels). But Bambatha was killed, along with about 3,000 of his followers, while thousands more were sent to prison.

Despite these hardships, the Zulu population has increased. Today perhaps 10 million people of Zulu descent live in the South African province of KwaZulu/Natal. They're the most numerous ethnic group in South Africa—where they are famous for their music and culture.

10

THE SPANISH–AMERICAN WAR

1898

The four-month-long war that ended the Spanish Empire
and placed the United States as a major player on the world stage

Combatants
- United States
- Spain
- Cuban rebels
- Filipino rebels

Theater of War
Cuba, Puerto Rico, Philippines

Casualties
United States: 380 combat deaths
and 5,000 dead of disease
Spain: 2,100 combat deaths and esti-
mated 50,000 dead of disease
Cuban rebels: 5,000 combat deaths
Filipino rebels: 5,000 combat deaths

Major Figures
UNITED STATES
President William McKinley, who
declared war on Spain
**Lieutenant Colonel Theodore "Teddy"
Roosevelt,** who led the Rough Riders
in victory at San Juan Heights
Commodore George Dewey, who
destroyed the Spanish fleet at
Manila Bay

SPAIN
General Valeriano Weyler y Nicolau,
governor-general who implemented
the *reconcentrados* policy in Cuba
Admiral Pascual Cervera, commander
of the Spanish fleet in Santiago Bay
General Arsenio Linares y Pombo,
commander of the Spanish army in
Santiago

CUBAN REBELS
Máximo Gómez, military leader of
the Cuban revolution
Calixto García Íñiguez, who provided
crucial intelligence about Spanish
forces in Cuba to the U.S. Army
José Marti, Cuban activist killed by
the Spanish in 1895, who became a
martyr to the Cuban people

FILIPINO REBELS
Andrés Bonifacio, who founded the
Katipunan, a group of Filipino nationalists committed to independence
Emilio Aguinaldo, leader of Filipino
guerillas who fought both Spain and
the United States

The Spanish–American War only lasted 113 days, but when it was over, it had changed the course of history for two world powers. Spain, beaten badly, would end its days as an imperial force; while the United States, acquiring new territory in the Caribbean and Pacific, would start its days as a major power on the world stage of the new twentieth century.

Referencing American victories at Manila Bay and San Juan Heights, a gleeful officer said, "An hour or two at Manila, an hour or two at Santiago, and the maps of the world were changed." However, just as the war ended, a bloody insurgency against the United States arose in the Philippines. The United States put it down with cold-blooded brutality, to the shock of the Filipino citizens who had so relentlessly promoted the war against what they saw as the ruthless country of Spain.

1895:

February: Second Cuban revolution against Spanish rule begins.

June: U.S. President Grover Cleveland issues proclamation of neutrality in Cuban affairs.

....

1896:

February: Cuban Governor-General Valeriano Nicolau y Weyler places the first of what will be hundreds of thousands of Cubans in concentration camps. U.S. Senate passes resolution calling for censure of Spain and recognition of Cuban independence.

August: Filipino rebels rise against Spanish rule.

December: Cleveland reverses himself and says that the United States may take action against Spain if the atrocities in Cuba continue.

....

1897: Hundreds of thousands of Cubans die in concentration camps. U.S. President William McKinley threatens Spain with American intervention.

....

1898:

January: McKinley sends the battleship USS *Maine* on a "friendly" visit to Havana.

February: The *Maine* is blown up in Havana Harbor, with loss of 268 men.

March: U.S. Naval Court of Inquiry find that the *Maine* was destroyed by a submerged mine. U.S. prowar sentiment grows, fanned by the newspapers of William Randolph Hearst.

April: United States declares war against Spain. U.S. North Atlantic Squadron blockades Cuba.

May: U.S. Asiatic Squadron, under Commodore George Dewey, attacks and destroys the Spanish fleet in Manila Bay in less than six hours.

June: U.S. Marines capture Guantánamo Bay. Sixteen thousand American troops land east of Santiago de Cuba, the second largest city in Cuba. Teddy Roosevelt and the Rough Riders fight the Battle of Las Guasimas against Spanish troops and successfully storm Kettle and San Juan hills.

July: Roosevelt and the Rough Riders assault San Juan Hill. A Spanish squadron bottled up in Havana Bay attempts to run the U.S. blockade, but all of the Spanish ships are destroyed. Spain surrenders Santiago de Cuba. The United States begins an invasion of Puerto Rico.

August: Spanish and U.S. officials sign a peace protocol to the end fighting. Unaware of peace, Dewey attacks Manila; Spain surrenders in the Philippines.

December: The Treaty of Paris ends the Spanish–American War. Spain cedes Puerto Rico and Guam to the United States, agrees to sell the Philippines for $20 million, and grants Cuba independence.

....

1899:

February: The Filipino insurrection against the United States begins, and it does not end until July 1902.

....

PRESIDENT WILLIAM MCKINLEY PRESIDED OVER THE WAR THAT BROUGHT AMERICA TO THE FOREFRONT AS A WORLD POWER.

Prints & Photographs Division, Library of Congress, LC-USZ62-97097

"A SPLENDID LITTLE WAR"

The Spanish–American War was a war tailor-made for the might of a youthful United States at the end of the nineteenth century. In that conflict, the United States would gain major power and prestige, satisfy its mercantile interests, and liberate a suffering people.

The war only took four months in 1898, although it had its beginnings years earlier. In 1895, Cuban rebels led by José Marti and others (see "El Apóstol and the Cuban Revolution," p. 189) began the latest in a series of revolts against Spanish rule on the island. Marti was killed, and the insurrection was brutally repressed by the Spanish governor-general of Cuba, Valeriano Weyler y Nicolau, who placed hundreds of thousands of Cubans in *reconcentrados,* concentration camps, guarded by Spanish guards. He also placed the entire country under martial law.

United States businesses had more than $50 million dollars invested in Cuba, having bought up large tracts of land there in the late 1800s. These business interests were being threatened by actions of the Spanish government, while the popular press in the United States (see "The Yellow Press," p. 193) pushed for war because of the injustice being done to the Cuban people. When the USS *Maine,* visiting Havana Harbor, blew up in February 1898 for reasons still unknown (see "Remembering the *Maine,*" p. 193), killing 268 American sailors; the American people and Congress seized upon this as a *casus belli.* War was declared against Spain in April. The first major blow was struck by Commodore George Dewey, whose fleet entered Manila Bay on May 1 and destroyed an entire Spanish squadron.

In the meantime, preparations for war rose to fever pitch in the United States. The U.S. Army made contact with Cuban rebel General Calixto García Íñiguez, who supplied it with maps, intelligence, and rebel officers to guide U.S. forces in an invasion, which occurred in June, when Marines captured Guantánamo Bay.

Seventeen thousand U.S. troops then landed east of Santiago de Cuba, the second largest city on the island, in July. American troops, including the Rough Riders commanded Lieutenant Colonel Teddy Roosevelt, former assistant secretary of the navy, inflicted a serious loss on the Spanish army during the ensuing battle. When the Spanish fleet attempted to escape from Havana Bay and was destroyed, the battle for Cuba was essentially over. The two countries signed a peace protocol in August. Unaware of this, Commodore Dewey had invaded the Philippines.

The Treaty of Paris, signed in December 1898, ceded Puerto Rico and Guam to the United States, allowed the United States to purchase the Philippines for $20 million, and established the independence of Cuba. The war cost the United States more than 5,000 soldiers, most of whom died of yellow fever. It seemed like a cheap price to pay for a new empire stretching from the Philippines to the Caribbean, but the United States would soon be involved in a bloody war against Filipino guerillas (see "The

Philippene–American War," p.192) that, ironically, saw the country of liberators implement a concentration camp policy to destroy its enemy.

In all, though, the United States was quite satisfied with the Spanish–American War. "It has been a splendid little war," wrote John Hay, the U.S. ambassador to London, "begun with the highest motives, carried on with magnificent intelligence and spirit, favored by that fortune which loves the brave."

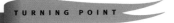

BATTLE OF THE SAN JUAN HEIGHTS: JULY 1, 1898

The little village of Daiquiri on the southeast coast of Cuba, about 14 miles (23 km) from the city of Santiago, would later become famous for the drink of the same name. But on June 22, 1898, it was the place where General William R. Shafter landed his First Army Corps, 15,000 troops who swarmed ashore ready to teach the Spanish a thing or two about American might and power.

Among those swarming troops was Teddy Roosevelt, now a lieutenant colonel in charge of the First Volunteer Cavalry—also known as the Rough Riders, although there were few horses in evidence (see "The U.S. Soldier," p. 188). Roosevelt had with him a special sidearm: a Colt .45 revolver that he had salvaged from the wreck of the USS *Maine* and refurbished. Roosevelt intended to use it in the combat that he wanted to be in the thick of, to "kill his man," as he put it, and revenge himself for the 268 men who had died in that explosion.

"A Long Z-z-z-z-z-e-u!"

General Shafter and U.S. planners had targeted Santiago, the second largest city in Cuba, to destroy the defending army of General Arsenio Linares y Pombo (some 10,000 strong) as well as attack the Spanish squadron at harbor in Santiago Bay, led by Admiral Pascual Cervera. To do this, Shafter divided his forces on July 1, sending 6,500 men to attack the Spanish stronghold town of El Caney, north and east of the city, and sending out

another group of some 8,000 troops to assault San Juan Heights, just one mile east of Santiago. The heights consisted of San Juan Hill and the smaller hill the Americans would call Kettle Hill, for the large kettle, probably used in sugar refining, that was found at the base of it.

Teddy Roosevelt's Rough Riders were among the troops that would assault the San Juan Heights. Setting off early in the morning, he found himself on his horse negotiating thick jungle, occasionally broken by "glades or rounded hill shoulders," as Roosevelt later remembered. He found it pleasant to imagine going on a hunting excursion here.

But as the men got closer to the Heights, they began to hear overhead what Roosevelt called "a long z-z-z-z-z-e-u," and what journalist Richard Harding Davis called "a rustling sound." It was the sound of bullets—Mauser bullets to be exact—fired by Spanish snipers high on a ridge in front of the advancing U.S. columns. For most of the Americans, this was their first experience with smokeless powder. They were unable to see the tell-tale tufts of smoke rising up from the barrels of the enemy rifles. It seemed the bullets were coming out of nowhere, which was a particularly terrifying phenomenon. Another journalist watched as the bullets began to strike home randomly, and Rough Riders began to fall.

"Every one went down in a lump, without cries …They just went down like clods in the grass," Davis wrote. Soon the journalist heard what he called a "chug," and he fell to the ground

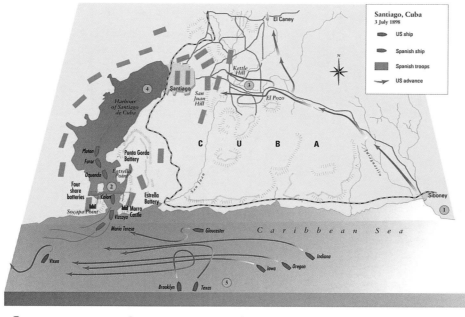

THIS MAP DEPICTS
THE FIGHTING AT THE
VERY CLOSE OF THE
AMERICAN INVASION
OF CUBA, AS THE
SPANISH ATTEMPTED
TO RETREAT.

1. 22 June 1898: General William Shafter's V corps lands at Daiguiri and moves inland through Siboney.

2. On the night of 2-3 July USS *Merrimac* is sunk to block the harbor entrance.

3. 1 July: U.S. forces seize San Juan Hill, forcing the Spanish back toward Santiago. The city is now within artillery range of the Americans.

4. 3 July: Admiral Pascual Cervera is ordered by Madrid to attempt to run the American blockade. The *Maria Teresa* leads the Spanish squadron out past the wreck of the *Merrimac*.

5. Commodore Winfield Scott Schley, deputized for Admiral William T. Sampson, immediately gives chase; in under two hours all except one Spanish ship are destroyed. The sole survivor, the *Colón*, is caught some 50 miles west of Santiago when she runs out of fuel

himself, quite surprised to be hit, his spine nearly shattered by a Mauser bullet fired by an unseen enemy.

Buffalo Soldiers

By 8 a.m., Roosevelt and his Rough Riders had been pinned down in a valley by Spanish soldiers' firing volleys at them, soldiers whom they still couldn't see. Finally, Roosevelt saw a group of them running up a clearing on the side of nearby hill and ordered his men to shoot at them, forcing them to retreat. Soon all was quiet except for the occasional snapping shot of a Krag or a Mauser. The Rough Riders joined the regular army, coming up on their flanks, and advanced to the base of the San Juan Heights.

These men included about 2,000 black soldiers of the 9th and 10th cavalry, the fabled buffalo soldiers who formed the very first post–Civil War all-black troops. They had mainly fought against Comanche and Kiowa Indians in the far west (and had been named by them, for their thick, shaggy hair). The buffalo soldiers were now prominent among the troops who reached the base of the hills.

The buffalo soldiers, the Rough Riders, and the rest of the regular U.S. Army had reached their objective, but they were now drawing heavy fire from Spanish troops entrenched in fortifications atop San Juan Hill and Kettle Hill. The Americans were awaiting the arrival of the 6,500 men who had attacked El Caney, but these troops had become

THIS PICTURE SHOWS A TROOPER FROM THE 9TH CAVALRY,
THE HISTORIC GROUP OF ALL-BLACK POST-CIVIL WAR TROOPS
NICKNAMED THE "BUFFALO SOLDIERS."

Gladstone Collection, Prints & Photographs Division, Library of Congress,
LC-USZ62-132221

bullet hit him in the carotid artery, and he fell across Roosevelt's knees, dead.

Then two things happened. Roosevelt saw the regular army begin swarming up San Juan Hill, having finally been ordered to charge. And, nearly simultaneously, orders reached Roosevelt that he should "move forward and support the regulars in their attack." The instant Roosevelt received the order, he sprang on his horse and ordered his men to attack.

The Charge Up Kettle Hill

Directly in front of the Rough Riders was the smaller of the two hills, Kettle Hill. Roosevelt, the only man on horseback, led his men directly up it, bullets whizzing around him. Regular army troops and buffalo soldiers intermingled around them, but journalist Davis, watching, thought that "someone had made a terrible mistake." The Rough Riders seemed so few, a thin black line of figures, and the charge seemed "merely terribly pathetic."

The men moved up the hill, with their rifles held across their chests, "slipping and scrambling in the smooth grass, moving forward with difficulty, as if they were wading in water, moving slowly, carefully, with strenuous effort."

Bullets knocked men down, and still they kept coming. There were ranch buildings at the top of Kettle Hill, occupied by Spanish soldiers, and Roosevelt galloped toward them. He was forced to dismount when he reached a wire fence and was there grazed by a bullet.

Soon, however, Roosevelt was joined by Rough Riders and black troops, all of whom were cheering and shouting. They cut through the wire and

bogged down and did not show up. To make matters worse, Shafter and other U.S. commanders were unable to pass on any useful orders. Shafter had become ill, while other commanders were not sure of the exact location of American forces.

Growing frustrated at being shot at, Roosevelt later wrote that, "I was just about making up my mind that in the absence of orders I had better 'march to the sound of guns.'" He attempted to send an orderly back to find a general officer who would provide him with the order to charge, but as soon as the orderly arose and saluted him, a

drove the Spanish out of the ranch buildings, but found they were still under fire. A blockhouse filled with Spanish troopers on higher San Juan Hill was relentless in raining bullets down at the crest of Kettle Hill, as well as at the regular army troops who were storming it.

Roosevelt, greatly excited, saw U.S. troops attacking the block house and ordered a charge from Kettle Hill up San Juan Hill. Roosevelt took off running, but, at 100 yards (91 m), realized that he was only being followed by half a dozen Rough Riders. The rest of Roosevelt's soldiers claimed they hadn't heard him call for the charge. Somewhat disgruntled, Roosevelt tried it again, and now all of his Rough Riders, combined with a large group of black troopers, charged up to the crest of San Juan Hill. Two Spanish soldiers sprang out of a trench in front of Roosevelt. He described what happened next:

"As they turned to run, I closed in and fired twice, missing the first and killing the second. My revolver was from the sunken battleship *Maine.*"

The Legend of Teddy Roosevelt

The charge up Kettle, and then San Juan, hills, would make Roosevelt's reputation and catapult him directly to the presidency of the United States.

He was nominated for a Congressional Medal of Honor, which his political enemies quashed. (Although Roosevelt received the award posthumously in 2001.)

Wags at the time of the Spanish–American War suggested that Roosevelt's memoirs should have been called "Alone in Cuba," because his postwar writing so relentlessly credited himself and his Rough Riders for the victory on the San Juan Heights. It's true that numerous other brave men made the charge, and also that Roosevelt, in his memoirs, slurred the buffalo soldiers who accompanied the Rough Riders by claiming many of them were trying to retreat under enemy fire, which was simply false.

But Roosevelt's example that day displayed relentless courage under fire. He was the only man on horseback, a prominent target, leading his men onward. And the result of Roosevelt's charge—and the charge of all the other Americans who participated—was victory in Cuba. Two days later, on July 3, the Spanish fleet attempted to leave Santiago Bay and was destroyed by U.S. forces. Cut off, the Spanish army in Santiago surrendered within two weeks. Three weeks later, a peace protocol was agreed upon by Spanish and U.S. diplomats.

TEDDY ROOSEVELT: "PURE ACT"

U.S. historian Henry Adams once described Teddy Roosevelt as "pure act"—meaning the human embodiment of spirit and energy, a person whose instincts dictated his actions. Whether you admired this about Roosevelt depended entirely on your point of view. (Writer Henry James, not a fan, called Roosevelt "a monstrous embodiment of unprecedented and resounding noise.") But whatever you thought, you couldn't ignore the man.

Theodore Roosevelt, Jr., was born into a prominent New York family in 1858 and overcame an asthmatic condition with constant exercise. He graduated from Harvard College in 1880, became a lawyer, a New York State assemblyman, a historian, and (briefly) a western cattle rancher, before returning to politics. He became police chief of New York City before serving as assistant secretary of the navy in William McKinley's first administration. When the Spanish–American War broke out, Roosevelt resigned his office to help form the First U.S. Volunteer Cavalry Regiment, known as the "Rough Riders" (see "The U.S. Soldier," p. 188). This colorful group of horsemen would see heavy action in Cuba.

Roosevelt was determined that he would take part in combat. At the Battle of the San Juan Heights, he led his dismounted regiment on a charge straight into the teeth of enemy fire on Kettle Hill, having become tired of waiting for orders while his men were shot up. With journalist Richard Harding Davis present (and William Randolph Hearst as well—see "The Yellow Press," p. 193), Roosevelt's exploits made him famous.

Roosevelt and Commodore George Dewey (see "You May Fire When You Are Ready, Gridley," p. 191) became the prominent U.S. heroes of the war. The acclaim catapulted Roosevelt to the position of New York governor, then to McKinley's vice president in 1900. When McKinley was assassinated in 1901, Roosevelt became president of the United States.

WITH THE HELP OF THE AMERICAN YELLOW PRESS, THEODORE ROOSEVELT GARNERED AN UNPRECEDENTED REPUTATION THAT WOULD CATAPULT HIM TO NEW YORK GOVERNOR, VICE PRESIDENT TO MCKINLEY, AND FINALLY PRESIDENT WHEN MCKINLEY WAS ASSASSINATED IN 1901. HE WAS EXTREMELY PATRIOTIC AND PROUD OF HIS ECCENTRIC MIX OF ROUGH RIDERS. HE CARRIED WITH HIM INTO THE SPANISH–AMERICAN WAR A COLT.45 REVOLVER HE REFURBISHED HIMSELF, SALVAGED FROM THE WRECK OF THE USS MAINE.

GENERAL VALERIANO WEYLER Y NICOLAU: "A FIENDISH DESPOT—A BRUTE!"

In 1895, Arsenio Martínez Campos, the Spanish governor-general of Cuba, faced yet another rebellion of Cuban guerilla fighters seeking to be free of Spanish rule. Writing back home to the Prime Minister of Spain, Campos saw clearly what steps he needed to take. He proposed a *reconcentrado* plan in which the peasant farmers, or *pacíficos,* whom the guerillas needed to feed and support them, be herded into concentration areas—essentially government-controlled towns—and kept from their homes, their food supplies, and the guerillas.

Campos concluded that these steps would be quite effective. Yet, he said, "the misery and hunger would be horrible." He could not bring himself to institute such a step ("I have scruples that come before everything else") but recommended that he be replaced by the one man in Spain who could carry out such a policy: General Valeriano Weyler y Nicolau. Weyler, born in Spain in 1838 of mixed Prussian and Spanish heritage, did indeed have a fearsome reputation. In the army since the age of sixteen, he had fought fiercely against the Cuban rebels during the Ten Years' War and had then gone on to uproot and destroy uprisings in the Philippines and in the Basque region of Spain.

Weyler took control as governor-general in Cuba in February 1896. His reputation from previous engagements in Cuba and elsewhere

GENERAL VALERIANO WEYLER Y NICOLAU WAGED A CRUEL WAR AGAINST CUBAN GUERILLA FIGHTERS, FORCING HUNDREDS OF THOUSANDS OF CUBAN PEASANTS INTO CONCENTRATION CAMPS.
© CORBIS

186

preceded him. He was a special target of the U.S. yellow press, with the *New York Journal* calling him "a fiendish depot…a brute…an exterminator of men." By contrast, the short, abstemious, and energetic Weyler considered himself a professional soldier just trying to get a job done.

"How do they want me to wage war?" he asked, referring to U.S. newspapers criticism of him. "With bishops' pastorals and presents of sweets and money?" Shortly after Weyler's arrival, he issued a series of orders that set up the reconcentration areas and forced hundreds of thousands of peasants to move into them. If the peasants refused, they were shot.

The *reconcentrado* camps were, essentially, fortified towns. On paper, there was provision made to house and feed the peasants who crowded into them, but this was on paper only. The *pacificos* were not allowed to bring their livestock with them, there was little food available, and housing was usually in abandoned warehouses or ruined houses. There was little in the way of fresh water, and there were no sanitation facilities for the overcrowded areas.

Almost immediately, people began to die from starvation and disease. According to a Spanish government report, "at least a third of the rural population, that is to say, 400,000 human beings, died" in the reconcentrado camps in about a year's time. (Some modern historians, however, put the death toll at half this number.)

The camps had a significant effect on the ability of the rebels to wage war, but they had a far greater effect on public opinion in the United

THE RECONCENTRADO CAMPS, ON PAPER, WERE FORTIFIED TOWNS THAT WOULD HOUSE PEASANT FARMERS TO KEEP THEM AWAY FROM THEIR HOMES AND FOOD SUPPLIES SO THAT THEY WOULD NOT BE ABLE TO SUPPORT THE EVER-RESISTANT GUERILLA FORCES.

Prints & Photographs Division, Library of Congress, LC-USZ6-1815

States. As more and more reports came back to the United States from journalists and Cuban émigrés, such an outcry arose that the Spanish government ultimately recalled Weyler. But the damage was done. Most Americans believed that Spain was a country of repressive and cruel brutes who deserved a good beating. When the USS *Maine* blew up, Americans were only too glad of an excuse to go to war.

As for Weyler? Still protesting that his was only the work of a soldier interested in getting a job done, he lived until the ripe old age of ninety-two and died peacefully in his bed.

The U.S. Soldier: Rough Riders

In 1897, in response to the threat of war with Spain, U.S. Secretary of War Russell Alger wanted to create a highly mobile unit of mounted riflemen—"young, sound, good shots and good riders." He offered command of this unit, to be called the First Volunteer Cavalry, to Teddy Roosevelt, but Roosevelt felt he didn't have enough experience and suggested his friend, army chief surgeon and Medal of Honor winner Leonard Wood, for the job.

Roosevelt would serve as his second in command and help create the First Volunteers, which were, he wrote, "as typical an American regiment as ever marched or fought...including a score of Indians, and about as many of Mexican origin; then there are some fifty Easterners—almost all graduates of Harvard, Yale, Princeton, etc....the rest are men of the Plains and Rocky Mountains."

In other words, the unit was comprised of an extraordinary mix of adventurers, cowboys, and Indians, New York City policeman who had served with Roosevelt when he was that city's police commissioner, plus a national tennis champion, polo players, and one or two Protestant ministers. The men trained near San Antonio, Texas. Roosevelt insisted that they be armed with the new Model 1896 Krag-Jorgenson rifle, which had a five-shot magazine and used smokeless powder. The Rough Riders were therefore one of the few units in the U.S. Army to receive the weapon. (Most regular army troopers of the time carried the breech-loading,

single shot, 45.70 "Trapdoor" rifle, which shot black powder bullets.) The Rough Riders made good use of the Krags against the Spanish on the San Juan Heights.

The Rough Riders—named after a Buffalo Bill Wild West show by an admiring press—were a unit of extraordinary esprit. Roosevelt, who had taken command of the unit when Leonard Wood was promoted to brigade level, was a constant and energetic presence among them. At one point, Roosevelt hijacked a railroad train to make sure the Rough Riders got to their point of disembarkation in Tampa, Florida, on time. They did no riding in Cuba because space limitations on shipboard forced them to leave all but their officers' horses

behind. But their charge up Kettle Hill (see "Turning Point," p. 180) was an extraordinary display of bravery and made the unit famous in U.S. history.

THE ROUGH RIDERS WERE AN INCREDIBLE MIX OF ALL THAT WAS AMERICA AT THE TIME—INDIANS, COLLEGE GRADUATES FROM HARVARD AND YALE, MEXICANS, POLICEMEN, POLO PLAYERS, AND PROTESTANT MINISTERS.

Roosevelt's 'Rough Riders' storm San Juan Hill/ Kettle Hill, Cuba, 1898 (colour litho), McBarron, H. Charles, Jr. (1902-92) (after) / Private Collection, Peter Newark Pictures / The Bridgeman Art Library

The Spanish Soldier: Fighting "to the Knife"

While most of the attention historians give to soldiers of the Spanish–American War rests on the Rough Rider, the Spanish soldier of the war in Cuba was an extremely tough opponent, although not one who was extremely well led.

When the U.S. troops approached the Spanish-held positions near the San Juan Heights, they discovered, to their dismay, that the Spanish were well hidden. During the long years of civil unrest in Cuba, they had learned to fight like guerillas, taking advantage of cover, and using stealth in their approaches. The average Spanish soldier also possessed a weapon that completely outgunned most U.S. rifles—the 1893, bolt-action Spanish Mauser, which had a five-round magazine firing new bullets that used smokeless powder. This made the Spanish troops very difficult to spot (see "Turning Point," p. 180).

Despite the attitude of many Americans that the Spanish would be easy opponents, they were, in fact, men who would fight to the death, or "to the knife," in the phrase of the time. The Spanish soldiers would defend themselves with knives or bayonets when all ammunition ran out. Even when Spanish soldiers were captured alive, they could not believe that the Americans were not going to kill them (as they would have done to their opponents). "The [captured] Spaniards persisted in preparing for instant death," one officer remembered, "and would not be comforted either by encouraging smiles or the offer of water or hardtack."

Spanish forces on the island of Cuba actually outnumbered those of the U.S. invaders, but Spanish officers did not do their men a service, employing them poorly. At San Juan Heights, only 750 Spanish soldiers stood off against thousands of Americans. Despite the fact that 10,000 Spanish troops stood idle in nearby Santiago de Cuba, their over-cautious commander decided not to commit them.

THE SPANIARDS WERE ARMED WITH THE 1893 MAUSER, WHICH OUTGUNNED MOST AMERICAN RIFLES.

Springfield Armory National Historic Site

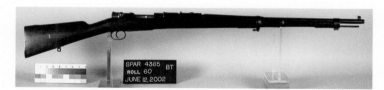

El Apóstol and the Cuban Revolution

Cuba became one of the earliest islands of the Caribbean to be colonized by Spain. For a long time Cuba was known as "the Pearl" of the far-flung Spanish empire. It was an island of unsurpassed beauty, with rugged mountains and jungles and pure white beaches stretching away into the distance. Cuba was also an island of great plenty. Its sugar cane plantations produced vast amounts of revenue for a Spanish empire, which, by the late nineteenth century, was becoming increasing moribund.

From 1868 to 1878, Cuban insurrectionists led by Maximo Gómez y Báez and others fought the Ten Year War against the Spanish. The insurrectionists ultimately did not prevail, but they trained others in revolution. One of these was José Marti who, at the age of sixteen in 1869, fought with the guerillas, was arrested and sentenced to six years imprisonment, and then exiled to Spain. There, Marti found himself, not just as a political activist, but as a poet and writer. He is still considered one of Cuba's leading poets of the period.

In 1895, after spending time lobbying for support in the United States, Marti joined forces with Maximo Gómez, the aging Cuban revolutionary

(continued on p. 190)

leader, to publish a manifesto demanding full independence for Cuba. He then landed with a small group of armed men on the Cuban coast in April 1895, an act that began the Cuban Revolution of 1895. Marti was killed by the Spanish barely a month later, during a reckless charge against entrenched Spanish forces.

While there were numerous heroes of the Cuban revolution, including Gómez and Calixto García Íñiguez, who secretly gave important Spanish military information to invading U.S. forces, Marti, pale, darkly handsome, and poetic, became the martyr of the movement. He was a man who gave everything for his country, and he is still known as *El Apóstol*, "the Apostle" of Cuban independence.

Remembering the *Maine*

When the United States battleship USS *Maine* arrived in Havana Harbor on January 25, 1898, it was there on what the U.S. government officially described as a "friendly visit." The *Maine* fired an official salute to Spanish authorities, was saluted in return by a Spanish battleship, and its officers presented their papers to Spanish officials.

But, in reality, the *Maine's* visit was anything but friendly. It was a not-so-subtle reminder to Spain that the Americans did not approve of their conduct of the war against Cuban guerillas. It was also a sign of encouragement to the suffering Cuban people, hundreds of thousands of whom had died at the hands of Governor-General Valeriano Nicolau y Weyler.

Seething, the Spanish accepted the *Maine's* presence. There were no outward signs of hostility. But, on the evening of February 15, Havana Harbor was lit up with what one observer called "an intense light." This was followed by a deafening roar that shattered windows all over the city. All eyes turned to the harbor, where it was discovered that the *Maine* had exploded, turned in a few moments from proud U.S navy ship to a piece of hissing, twisted wreckage. Two-thirds of the crew—more than 268 men—died in the explosion.

Given the nature of the *Maine's* mission, there were immediate suspicions that it had blown up from hostile action. In March, a U.S. naval court of inquiry returned with a finding that the ship had exploded

because of a mine, although it could provide no evidence as to where the mine originated. This was enough. With William Randolph Hearst's newspapers demanding a war, the cry "Remember the *Maine,* to Hell with Spain," rang through the United States, and the country took up arms.

However, more than a century later there is still no consensus as to what really happened to the *Maine.* Four separate inquiries agree that the explosion originated in the ship's forward ammunition magazine. The second naval court of inquiry, in 1911, also agreed that an external explosion had done the *Maine* in, but in 1976, Admiral Hyman Rickover launched an investigation using more modern scientific techniques. His scientists found that it was likely the ship had exploded due to spontaneous combustion in a coal bunker near the forward ammunition magazine.

Finally, on the 100th anniversary of the sinking, *National Geographic* magazine undertook an investigation, using computer modeling, which suggested that it was "probable" that a mine had caused the sinking. If so—a big "if"—no one will ever know whether it was a mine that had somehow come adrift from a minefield in the harbor, one deliberately set by the Spanish, or even one placed there by Cuban guerillas looking to provoke the United States into war.

"You May Fire When You Are Ready, Gridley"

These words were spoken by Commodore George Dewey in Manila Bay on May 1, 1898. They became among the most famous sentences uttered in nineteenth-century U.S. history.

Right up there with Teddy Roosevelt's charge up San Juan (actually Kettle) Hill and the blowing up of the USS *Maine,* came the total defeat of the Spanish navy by Dewey's Asiatic Squadron. This defeat would cost the Spanish its Filipino colony.

Dewey, born in 1837, graduated from the U.S. Naval Academy in 1857, and had long sought his heroic moment. He had served ably as a lieutenant with the forces of Admiral David Farragut in the U.S. Civil War, taking part in the capture of New Orleans. Dewey continued his long rise in the peacetime U.S. Navy, finally being appointed a commodore in 1896 and then given charge of the Asiatic Fleet by Assistant Secretary of the Navy Theodore Roosevelt in 1897.

The Asiatic Fleet, stationed in China, was ready as soon as war

broke out on April 25, 1898. Consisting of Dewey's flagship, the cruiser-class USS *Olympia,* commanded by Captain Charles Vernon Gridley, two other cruisers, and several support vessels, the fleet sailed quickly to the Philippines, arriving outside of Manila Bay on the evening of April 30. At this point, Dewey decided to enter the bay with his ships in single file, with the *Olympia* leading the way. After Dewey gave this order, he was approached by his nephew, an officer on another

THE ASIATIC SQUADRON, LED BY COMMODORE GEORGE DEWEY ON MAY 1, 1898, WOULD SOUNDLY DEFEAT THE SPANISH FLEET AT MANILLA BAY AND COST SPAIN ITS CONTROL OF THE PHILIPPINES.

Prints & Photographs Division, Library of Congress, LC-DIG-pga-01865

(continued on p. 192)

vessel, who begged for the honor of taking his own ship through first.

But Dewey told him: "I have waited sixty years for this opportunity. I am leading the squadron in myself."

And he did. At about 5:30 a.m. on May 1, the Spanish Pacific fleet under Admiral Patricio Montojo y Pasarón was sighted. At 5:40, Dewey calmly told his captain, "You may fire when you are ready, Gridley," and all guns opened up. After six hours of bombardment, the eleven Spanish vessels, outgunned by Dewey's more powerful cruisers, were either destroyed or forced to surrender. The Spanish suffered 300 dead and wounded. Dewey lost only one man, to heatstroke.

Because of Dewey's great victory, the Philippines were lost to Spain. Dewey returned home to great honors, being appointed admiral of the navy, a rank no officer before or since has held. He had at last found his opportunity.

The Philippines–American War: A Nasty Little War

There had been numerous revolts against the inequities of Spanish colonial government during its 300-year-long rule of the Philippines, including one as recently as 1872. That revolt, in the province of Cavite was unsuccessful, but it inspired a young Filipino nationalist named Andres Bonifacio to found a revolutionary society called Katipunan, in 1892.

Soon, Bonifacio drew to him a charismatic young Filipino named Emilio Aguinaldo, who became leader of the independence movement in Cavite province, taking the code name Magdalo, for Mary Magdalene. In 1896, the revolution began with attacks by Katipunan guerillas in Manila. Aguinaldo defeated the Spanish in a number of battles, then rose to become leader of the movement, after which he ruthlessly had Bonifacio, who had become his rival, executed.

In 1898, when the United States and Spain went to war, Aguinaldo and his rebels joined the U.S. side and declared the independence of the Philippines from Spain. However, once the United States had defeated Spain (and paid $20 million for the Philippines), McKinley's administration refused to recognize Aguinaldo's new government, which the Filipino commander saw as a deep betrayal.

The Filipino rebels then went to war against the United States in one of the bloodiest small wars in U.S. history. A series of vicious battles forced the Americans to escalate their military presence there to some 130,000 troops, which was a massive commitment for the time. U.S. atrocities abounded in the war, with the murder of numerous unarmed civilians (any suspected insurgent over the age of ten could be shot on sight) and the use of torture, including what is now known as "waterboarding," on captured Filipino guerillas.

Many prominent Americans, including Andrew Carnegie and Mark

A Sacrifice to Aguinaldo's Ambition—Behind the Filipino Trenches after the Battle of Malabon, P. I. Copyright 1899 by Underwood & Underwood.

THE PHILIPPINES-AMERICAN WAR PROVED TO BE ONE OF THE BLOODIEST, MOST BRUTAL SMALL WARS IN AMERICAN HISTORY.

Twain, spoke out vigorously against the war. But, despite the capture of Emilio Aguinaldo in 1901, the fight continued on until 1902, with further guerilla actions against U.S. forces occurring sporadically until 1913. In the end, 40,000 Filipino soldiers and 4,000 Americans would die. Some 200,000 Filipinos died of starvation or disease. Ironically, given what had happened in Cuba (see "General Valeriano Weyler y Nicolau," p. 186), the United States ultimately won by partitioning off Filipino villages into concentration camps guarded by U.S. soldiers, wherein thousands of Filipino citizens died.

The Yellow Press

Journalists had first become important figures in warfare during the Crimean War when *London Times* reporter William Howard Russell sent back dispatches that had a heavy influence on public opinion as to the conduct of the war.

But Russell looked like Shakespeare in comparison to the journalists who labored for the yellow press, which was the sensational rival daily papers of Joseph Pulitzer and William Randolph Hearst, the *New York World* and the *New York Journal.* Both papers engaged in circulation wars as fierce as those of any modern-day tabloid (their direct descendants). They were called the "yellow press" because both ran a comic strip about a ghetto urchin known as *The Yellow Kid*. Gradually, this was shortened to the *yellow kid papers* and, finally, the yellow press.

Both papers, but especially the *Journal,* were highly influential in stirring up U.S. public opinion during the run-up to the Spanish–American

War. Stories of the brutality of Cuban Governor-General Weyler and of indignities supposedly perpetrated on U.S. citizens by the Spanish, such as the supposed strip-searching of U.S. women touring Cuba, were daily fare.

Once the war began, the fighting attracted scores of U.S. journalists, in part because of the proximity of Cuba, only 90 miles (145 km) from Florida. Richard Harding Davis, Hearst's premier reporter, was there, as was the U.S. novelist Stephen Crane. Hearst himself accompanied the Rough Riders during the attack on San Juan Heights. Wounded *Journal* reporter James Creelman, lying in the grass in the aftermath of the action, felt a hand on his forehead. He opened his eyes to see Hearst bent over him, with "a straw hat with a bright ribbon on his head, a revolver at his belt, and a pencil and notebook in his hand."

"I'm sorry you're hurt," Hearst told Creelman, grinning broadly. "But wasn't it a splendid fight? We must beat every paper in the world."

WILLIAM RANDOLPH HEARST WAS THE FOUNDER OF THE *NEW YORK JOURNAL,* ONE OF THE SENSATIONALIST PAPERS COVERING THE WAR.

Getty Images

11

THE RUSSO-JAPANESE WAR

1904–1905

In a war fought for control of northeast Asia, Japan's swift and decisive victory over Russia marked its debut as a major world power.

Combatants

- Russia
- Japan

Theater of War

Manchuria, Korea, Yellow Sea

Casualties

Russia: Estimated 40,000–70,000 combat dead
Japan: Estimated 50,000 combat dead

Major Figures

JAPAN
Emperor Meiji, who approved the request of his war ministers to attack Russia
Admiral Heihachiro Togo, seminal Japanese naval figure and victor of the Battle of Tsushima
Marshal Iwao Oyama, commander of Japanese forces at Mukden

RUSSIA
Tsar Nicholas II, who favored an expanded Russian Empire at the cost of war with Japan

Vice Admiral Stepan Makarov, trusted Russian naval commander killed early in the fighting at Port Arthur, Manchuria
General Aleksey Nikolayevich Kuropatkin, minister of war and commander in chief of the Russian land forces in Manchuria
Rear Admiral Zinovy Petrovich Rozhestvensky, commander of the Russian fleet defeated at Tsushima
Sergey Witte, who led the Russian peace delegation at Portsmouth, New Hampshire

It was the war that was supposed to make Russia's fortune in northeast Asia. In 1904, after half a century of being denied entrée to Western Europe by Germany, and Austria and to the Mediterranean by France, Great Britain, and Turkey (see "The Crimean War," p. 100), the Russians sought in northeast China (Manchuria) and Korea the unfettered sea access and trade influence they lacked. But here they ran straight into the Japanese, who were expanding westward and whose ambitions in the region were historic and bolstered by a Japanese victory over a faltering China in the Sino-Japanese War of 1894–95. The Russo-Japanese War, fought in bloody Manchurian land battles and naval clashes between armored, steam-powered battleships using torpedoes and explosive shells fired from miles away, was to set the scene for revolution in Russia while bringing Japan to supernation status for the first time.

1904:

February: Japan breaks off diplomatic relations with Russia and then launches a surprise attack on Port Arthur, Manchuria, damaging three Russian ships, and lands troops at Chemulpo (modern-day Inchon), Korea. Japan declares war. Japanese try, but fail, to sink ships to block Russian ships at Port Arthur Harbor.

March: The second Japanese attempt to block Port Arthur Harbor fails.

April: Russian Admiral Stepan Makarov is killed at Port Arthur when his flagship is destroyed by a Japanese mine. Japanese troops landed at Chemulpo (modern-day Inchon) and reach the Yalu River. The Battle of Yalu River begins.

May: Russia retreats after losing the Battle of Yalu River. Japanese troops land in the Liaodong Peninsula in Manchuria. Russia loses the Battle of Nanshan. Port Arthur is isolated.

July: Japanese began a siege of Port Arthur.

August: Russian Port Arthur fleet attempts break out to Vladivostok but fails and is forced to return. Japanese attempt unsuccessfully to storm Port Arthur.

September: Russians defeated at the Battle of Lioyang, Manchuria.

October: Russians launch counteroffensive. Russian 2nd Pacific Squadron leaves the Baltic on a journey to the Pacific. Russian counteroffensive stalls, and it retreats.

December: Japan breaches Port Arthur defenses, taking three different forts. Russia requests surrender terms.
....

1905:

January: Port Arthur surrenders.

February: The Battle of Mukden begins.

March: The Battle of Mukden ends with Russian defeat, but both armies are exhausted. U.S. President Teddy Roosevelt offers to mediate a peace treaty.

May: Russian navy decisively defeated by forces of Admiral Heihachiro Togo at the Battle of Tsushima.

June: Japanese invade Sakhalin Island.

September: The United States–mediated Treaty of Portsmouth (New Hampshire) is signed.
....

THE BATTLE OF MUKDEN WOULD SEE 500,000 RUSSIAN AND JAPANESE KILLED BY THE SOPHISTICATED RAPID FIRE WEAPONRY OF THE TIME. PICTURED HERE ARE THE DEFEATED RUSSIAN SOLDIERS PREPARING TO EVACUATE MUKDEN AFTER BEING ABANDONED BY THEIR GENERAL.

Getty Images

"LORD OF THE EAST"

In 1860, the Chinese—in a treaty forced upon them after the Qing Dynasty was weakened by the Taiping Rebellion and the Second Opium War—ceded Russia the entire eastern coast of Manchuria. It is instructive that the Russians had named their new port on the Sea of Japan Vladivostok, which means "Lord of the East." That is exactly what the Russians wanted to be. But Vladivostok was locked in by ice part of the year and could also be bottled up by any nation with a navy large enough to stopper the southern end of the Sea of Japan.

Russia therefore sought a port open year-round and found Port Arthur, in southern Manchuria's Lioyang Peninsula, facing the Yellow Sea. The Japanese had won this area after beating China in the Sino-Japanese War of 1894–95, but Russia, backed by France and Germany, forced Japan to renounce these gains. So the Lioyang Peninsula and Port Arthur were leased to Russia, although they remained under nominal Chinese rule. This move and spreading Russian influence in Korea, which was traditionally a country Japan considered within its own sphere of influence, convinced Japanese war planners that they must fight Russia if their country were to survive.

When it came to war, Japan had the advantage. After living isolated from the rest of the world for two centuries, Japan saw in the mid–nineteenth century how powerful western military forces were. They moved quickly to adopt western tactics and armament. The British Royal Navy was a special model. Japan's officers were educated in British schools, and by 1904, Japan had purchased six new battleships from Great Britain. The ships had massive cannon that could fire from miles away, radio communications, and torpedoes. The latter became a highly effective weapon of the Russo-Japanese War.

Japan understood that while the Russian land army approached an incredible 4.5 million men (as opposed to their own effective troop strength of perhaps 300,000), much of the Russian strength was based in European Russia, some 6,000 miles (9,600 km) away. Supply and reinforcement from the west, on the just-completed single-track Trans-Siberian Railroad, could take anywhere from two weeks to a month and a half. In February 1904, with much of the Russian Pacific fleet bottled up by ice in Vladivostok, Japan gambled. It decided on a surprise attack on Port Arthur on Manchuria (see "Attacking by Surprise," p. 209) to beat the Russians before they could be substantially reinforced.

Japan's attack severely damaged Russian ships; it also landed troops at Chemulpo (modern-day Inchon) in Korea. Moving swiftly up the Korean Peninsula, the Japanese arrived at the Yalu River by April, defeated the Russians at the Battle of the Yalu River, and forced them to retreat northward. Another Japanese sally through the Lioyang Peninsula drove the Russian back into Manchuria, at which point the Japanese had effectively surrounded Port Arthur, which would surrender in January 1905. In February and March, the Russian and Japanese armies fought a costly battle near Mukden, over a 50-mile (80 km) front, which ultimately forced the Russians to retreat still further, but bloodied and exhausted both armies.

In the meantime, the Russian Baltic fleet had begun the long journey through the Atlantic, around the Cape of Good Hope, and up the Pacific to the Sea of Japan, where it intended to attack the Japanese fleet and relieve the siege of Port Arthur. But in May 1905, at the Battle of Tsushima, the Japanese under Admiral Heihachiro Togo almost completely destroyed the Russian fleet, while losing only three torpedo boats (see "Turning Point," p. 198). At this point, U.S. President Theodore "Teddy" Roosevelt offered to mediate an offer that resulted in the Treaty of Portsmouth, signed on September 5, 1905, in which Russia recognized Japan's "political, military and economic interests" in Korea and returned to Japan parts of the Lioyang Peninsula.

More than the relatively minor territorial and economic gains—which angered many in Japan—Japan's swift victory and highly professional military force gained it recognition as a major world power and *the* major player in Asia. Five years after the war, Japan would annex Korea, and twenty years later it would invade Manchuria.

Russia, which had underestimated the Japanese, proved itself to have a woefully unprepared army, lost two of its three fleets (Baltic and Pacific, with only the Black Sea fleet remaining), and had shown that its government, under Tsar Nicholas II, was out of touch with its populace. Discontent over the war helped foment the failed Russian Revolution of early 1905, which in turn set the stage for the Russian Revolution of 1917.

TSAR NICHOLAS I DID NOT UNDERSTAND FULLY THE POWER OF MODERN WEAPONRY AND, LIKE MANY RUSSIANS, UNDERESTIMATED THE COURAGE AND EFFICIENCY OF THE JAPANESE SOLDIER.

THE BATTLE OF TSUSHIMA: 1905

The Battle of Tsushima has been called "the greatest naval engagement since Trafalgar," and it ushered in a whole new era where steel-clad dreadnoughts pounded away at each other, sending shells shrieking across the sky from miles away to inflict horrendous damage, blowing men and ships to bits. It also spelled the end of one nation's dreams of expansion before it slid into civil war and the beginning of another nation's bright hopes for the future.

On May 22, 1905, Japan and Russia were about to change history in a little known strait off the tip of the Korean Peninsula, between Korea and Tsushima Island, whose southernmost point is about 45 miles (72 km) from Japan. As the commander of the Japanese fleet, Admiral Heihachiro Togo, was to write in his after-action report, "By the help of Heaven, our combined squadron fought with the [enemy] and succeeded in almost annihilating him."

"This Hopeless Business"

In the fall of 1904, the war was looking grimmer and grimmer for the Russians. The Japanese had besieged Port Arthur. While that city was holding out, it was only a matter of time before the weight of Japanese guns and infantry would cause it to surrender. In the meantime, the Russian army was being driven farther north into Manchuria, where it would soon fight to a stalemate with the Japanese in the costly Battle of Mukden.

It seemed that the only answer to the Russian predicament was their navy, but much of the Russian Pacific Squadron had either been disabled or was holed up in Vladivostok, trapped by the Japanese navy. That left only the Baltic fleet and the Black Sea fleet, which was comprised of mainly older and slower vessels that were needed, it was thought, to keep the sultans of the Ottoman Empire honest.

Tsar Nicholas II and his advisors therefore decided that the fate of the Russian empire hinged on the vessels in the Baltic. The fleet—which it renamed the 2nd Pacific Squadron—contained fourteen large warships (eleven battleships and three cruisers) as well as destroyers, torpedo boats, repair and supply vessels, and hospital ships. But the ships were not staffed properly, and their sailors were poorly trained.

It was the job of Admiral Zinovy Petrovich Rozhestvensky to whip the fleet into shape. Fifty-five years old, mercurial in temper, stubborn as a mule, but with the ability to work eighteen-hour days, Rozhestvensky labored since the spring to bring on 12,000 new officers and men, train them in gunnery, and practice fleet maneuvers in the Gulf of Finland. Once the fleet attained a state of readiness, Rozhestvensky, aboard his flagship, the *Suvorov,* was to lead it on a 20,000-mile (32,000 km) journey through the North Sea, down the Atlantic, around the Cape of Good Horn, into the Pacific and up the coast of Asia, to confront the Japanese fleet near Port Arthur.

It is any wonder that Rozhestvensky confided to one of his officers in an unusual moment of candor, "We should not have started this hopeless business, and yet how can I refuse to carry out orders when everyone is so sure of success?"

Togo Awaits

Admiral Heihachiro Togo, commander of the Japanese fleet that had surprised and trapped the Russians in Port Arthur, was aware of the Russian fleet's intentions; Japan had numerous spies in the Baltic. Togo had fewer ships than the Russians—twelve warships, including four battleships and eight cruisers—but this did not disturb him. Above all else, Togo preferred speed and maneuverability, and the top speed of his vessels was 17–20 knots (8.7–10.2 meters per second), compared with only 14–18 knots (7.2–9.3 meters per second) for the Russians.

Togo's ships were more modern than those belonging to Rozhestvensky, with hydraulically operated gun turrets. Togo also had faith in his superbly honed crews. His sailors had trained so thoroughly that they could target from miles away with precise accuracy, as opposed to the Russian crews, who were forced to spend six months ashore in the winter because the Gulf of Finland froze and who were not allowed much gunner practice because of a shortage of ammunition.

Finally, Togo's confidence lay in a new type of shell the Japanese had developed from a material called *shimose* (essentially, the highly explosive substance known as melnite). These shells had four times the explosive force of Russian shells. Although they were not armor-piercing, they released picric acid, a poisonous gas, on contact.

BECAUSE OF ADMIRAL TOGO'S BRILLIANT MANEUVERING, THE BATTLE OF TSUSHIMA BECAME A JAPANESE VICTORY AND THE TURNING POINT OF THE RUSSO-JAPANESE WAR.
© DeA Picture Library / Art Resource, NY

"Odyssey and Ordeal"

The 2nd Pacific Squadron, after passing in display for the Tsar, left Saint Petersburg for its long journey. There were fifty ships in all, and they would need about half a million tons (450,000 kg) of coal to operate. Normally, the deep sea fleets of the world set up coaling stations in advance of their squadrons. The Russians had difficulty doing this, partly because Great Britain, which supported Japan in the war, refused to allow Russia to stop in any of its ports for coal and twisted the arms of other nations, such as France and Spain, in an attempt to get them to go along.

Finally, Kaiser Wilhelm II of Germany—who encouraged Russia's involvement in the Far East because it kept Russia out of trouble along his borders—agreed to sell the fleet sixty colliers worth of coal, which would meet the ships at various points along the journey to the Pacific. But even this wasn't enough, and every corner and nook and cranny of each ship in the fleet was filled with coal, overloading the ships, slowing them down, and making life hell for the sailors, who got what they called "black fever" from the amount of coal dust they inhaled daily. It was as if they were working in coal mines. "We are tormented by thirst," wrote one sailor.

They were tormented by other things, too. After shooting up British fishing boats in the North Sea (see "The Incident at Dogger Banks," p. 208), the wallowing, overloaded Russian fleet was followed as far as the Rock of Gibraltar by Britain's navy. One sailor wrote in his diary: "It's disgusting to treat us this way, following us about like we're criminals." But, watching the superb maneuvering of the British fleet, Rozhestvensky said to a fellow officer: "Those are real seamen. Oh, if only we…." He broke off and left the *Suvorov's* bridge, apparently to regain his composure.

On the fleet went, surviving a hurricane off the Cape of Good Hope and heading up the east coast of Africa. Sailors fell ill to fever. Some committed suicide, unable to take any more of a journey that one historian has called both "odyssey and ordeal." Arriving in Madagascar in February, the fleet received two bits of unwelcome news: First, Port Arthur had fallen. Second, civil unrest in Russia had caused the massacre of unarmed civilians at the Winter Palace in Saint Petersburg.

Upon hearing this news, the sailors aboard the cruiser *Nakhimov* mutinied, fed up with the 120-degree temperatures, the constant inhalation of coal dust, the execrable food and water, and the huge, 3-inch (7.6-cm) long cockroaches the sailors called "cannibals" for the way they set upon human flesh.

Rozhestvensky randomly picked fourteen *Nakhimov* sailors and had them shot to quell the rebellion. Then, on March 16, the fleet left Madagascar and sailed for Singapore and Indochina, where it was joined by another group of older, slower Russian vessels, known as the 3rd Pacific Squadron and recruited from the Black Sea fleet, which was forced upon Rozhestvensky by political machinations in Saint Petersburg. The combined Russian forces did not arrive in the vicinity of Japan until late May, after a journey of seven and a half months. And Admiral Togo, informed by spies and newspaper accounts, knew they were coming.

"The Fate of the Empire"

Because of the fall of Port Arthur, Togo knew that the only possible destination for the Russians could be Vladivostok. The only question was which route they would take— the long one that would take the fleet east of Japan or the much shorter and direct one that traveled west of Japan, through the Tsushima Strait, which lay between the southeast corner of the Korean Peninsula and the island of Tsushima.

Togo knew the Russians were short on fuel. He gambled that they would take the shorter route, stationing most of his warships on the Korean south coast, in Masan Bay and sending out his cruisers to scout to the south. On May 25, he learned that Russian colliers had arrived at Shanghai, which meant that the Russians intended to take the westerly route.

The only piece of information Togo was missing now was whether the Russian fleet would pass east or west of Tsushima Island. That was resolved when, at about 3 a.m. on May 27, a patrolling Japanese cruiser spotted a Russian hospital ship, brightly lit in accordance with international law, passing west of the island. The ship brought up the rear of the Russian column. Immediately, Togo took four battleships and eleven cruisers to sea, leaving his torpedo boats behind. The seas were too rough for them that day, and they operated best at night, by stealth. Togo headed to the north of Tsushima Island to meet the Russians, who were approaching from the south.

By this time, it was about 1:45 on the afternoon of May 27, a cloudy day with high seas that pitched over the bows of the Japanese warships as they raced to battle. Togo, aboard his battleship *Mikasa,* spotted the Russian fleet heading for him, about 10 miles (16 km) distant. He sent out a radio signal to his fleet: "The fate of the empire depends upon this event. Let every man do his utmost." The men cheered and drank a toast.

"They Are All There!"

Aboard the Russian ships, a very different mood prevailed. No one had slept as they neared Tsushima, and clusters of sailors and officers huddled tensely on the decks. To the horror of the superstitious sailors, rats began appearing above deck, as if preparing to abandon ship. The Russians had not yet spotted Togo's main fleet. Still, they passed several of the Japanese scouting cruisers, none of whom fired on them. (They were under orders to let the Russians proceed to come under fire by Togo's battleships.) Many of the officers and men had hopes that the Japanese were letting them pass.

"Head for No. 23," Rozhestvensky ordered. Number 23 was code for Vladivostok, and he drove his ships, himself at the head on *Suvorov*—in a single line 4 miles (6 km) long, bouncing through the seas at eleven knots. But as Rozhestvensky got farther into the strait, more Japanese ships appeared out of the distant haze. Rozhestvensky realized that they were blocking his way.

Rozhestvensky decided to change formation and signaled his ships to form a line abreast so that they would charge at the Japanese fleet with the additional firepower such a move provided. But the maneuver failed badly. The Russians had not trained properly to perform such a complex tactic in the face of oncoming enemy ships. Rozhestvensky canceled the maneuver, which left his twelve ships cruising in two columns, side by side. Now they could clearly see Togo's fleet.

The Great U-Turn

Admiral Togo's ships were now headed right at the Russians, but he had a major problem. If he kept on course, his column would split right between the double lines of the Russians, exposing it to fire on both sides. There was no room for him to pass on the west, and if he maneuvered his warships to the east, the Russians would easily pass him and head for Vladivostok.

Togo's only option, or so it seemed to British naval observers aboard his ship, was to turn his ships in place, so that the Japanese could sail north in a battle line parallel with the Russians. But that would place Togo's weakest ships (which were currently in the rear of his column) against Rozhestvensky's strongest battleships, and it would deprive Togo of his fierce desire to lead his fleet into combat.

So Togo, just 3 miles (5 km) ahead of the advancing Russians, decided on an extraordinary maneuver. He turned his ships in a giant semi-circle in front of the Russian fleet so that, when the tactic was completed, his ships would run parallel to the Russians, with his heaviest battleships able to square off with the heavy Russian ships. The only problem was that this maneuver entailed something called "crossing the T." This was a risky exercise in which Togo's ships, the horizontal cross-bar of the T, had to cross in the path of Rozhestvensky's vessels, the vertical stem of the T.

When the Russians saw this, they were ecstatic. "In another minute, we shall be hammering their flagship," cried one Russian officer on the *Suvorov*. Aboard the *Mikasa*, a British observer said: "The Japanese approach could hardly have been worse."

Essentially, Togo was making a U-turn in the face of ships with enough firepower to blow him and his entire fleet out of the water. At exactly 1:49 p.m., the *Suvorov* opened fire at the *Mikasa*. The battle was on.

"Hell Has Started"

As each ship turned in front of the Russian fleet, Rozhestvensky's battleships had about five minutes to hammer it to pieces. None of the Japanese were firing because Togo had ordered them to complete their maneuver before attacking. This was Russia's chance to destroy the enemy, to change the entire course of the war. But the Russian gunners simply were not up to the task. They had been poorly trained, due to their high command's unwillingness to expend ammunition in practice, and most of their shots missed as the enemy fleet made its turn.

An astonished Russian officer later wrote of the Japanese maneuver, "The Japanese ships were in perfect order at close intervals, steaming parallel to us." Togo ordered them to open fire at a range of almost 4 miles (6 km). This was an extremely long distance for the time, but here the superbly trained Japanese gunners came into play. Within minutes, the *Suvorov* was burning badly, and another new battleship, the *Oslyabya*, was holed and would sink within an hour.

In the meantime, the *shimose* shells hit the Russian ships with fierce effect, causing the sides of the vessels to explode in fire from the paint burning on contact. Russian binoculars were useless because the air became so hot that heat vapors obscured everything. Six- and twelve-inch shells blasted into Russian gun emplacements, blowing men literally to bits. Survivors were assigned to gather hands and feet off the decks to keep people from tripping on them.

A shell smashed into Rozhestvensky's conning tower on the bridge of the *Suvorov*. The shell did not pierce the armor, but it sent splinters of the wall flying through the cabin, turning it into an abattoir of the dead and dying. One splinter entered Rozhestvensky's brain, "opening it like an envelope," as one observer stated. Another hit Rozhestvensky in the left leg, rendering that limb immobile. Rozhestvensky was taken below, out of the fight, and the slaughter went on. A Russian officer who remained on the bridge looked around and repeated numbly to himself, over and over: "Hell has started."

By seven o'clock that evening, four Russian battleships, including the *Suvorov*, had been sunk. (Rozhestvensky had evacuated to a destroyer.) Unrelenting, Togo ordered night torpedo boat attacks that continued to harass the remains of the Russian fleet. The next morning, the remaining Russian admiral, Nikolay Nebogatav, decided to surrender the remains of the fleet. First he raised a white bed sheet high on his flagpole, but the Japanese continued to fire. Next he ran up Japanese flags, but Togo refused to see this as a clear sign of surrender, because he was so intent on utterly destroying his enemy. It was only when Admiral Negogatav ordered the Russian ships to turn off their engines and stop dead in the water that Togo relented.

The Battle of Tsushima was over, and the Japanese victory was complete. Out of forty-two Russian ships, thirty-one had been captured or sunk. The Russians lost 10,000 who were killed or wounded, but the Japanese lost only three torpedo boats and 116 men.

The Russians, now utterly defeated, would turn to President Theodore Roosevelt to help them end the war with Japan. Togo's victory had forced Nicholas II to the peace table.

In a final, ironic note, Admiral Rozhestvensky, captured by the Japanese, was placed in a hospital, where he gradually recovered from his wounds. Two weeks after the battle, Rozhestvensky was visited by Admiral Togo, who brought with him an aide, Captain Isoruku Yamamoto, who had been wounded at Tsushima, losing two fingers to a shell fragment. Yamamoto listened quietly as Togo pointed to his missing fingers and remarked to Rozhestvensky: "We fighting men suffer whether we win or lose. The only question is whether or not we perform our duty. You performed your great task heroically."

The two Japanese officers then left the room. Thirty-six years later, Admiral Yamamoto would plan the Japanese surprise attack on Pearl Harbor, hoping to fell another giant.

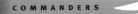

ADMIRAL HEIHACHIRO TOGO: LORD NELSON OF THE EAST

In the extraordinary career of Heihachiro Togo—one of the most brilliant naval tacticians ever to sail the oceans—we can also trace the rise of Japan's fortunes as a military power. Togo was born in 1848 in southern Japan during the period when the country had cut itself off completely from the west. His father was a *daimyo,* a samurai warrior who was a feudal lord, but this way of life would soon start to die off, after the first visits by U.S. Commodore Matthew Perry in 1853.

Ten years later, when Togo was fifteen, British warships paid a visit to the port of Kagoshima, near his hometown. The warships relentlessly destroyed the town with six hours of gunnery, in retaliation for the killing of a British citizen.

Togo—and Japan—now saw for the first time the power of steam warships equipped with modern guns. Togo joined the tiny Japanese navy. In 1871, Togo was sent along with other young naval officers for training to Great Britain, where he graduated second in his class from the Thames Nautical Training College, training and living aboard a British Royal Navy ship that circumnavigated the globe. Togo learned a great deal, but he nearly lost his eyesight to a strange malady that was finally cured by British ophthalmologists. During this period, Togo also learned about the great English Admiral Horatio Nelson (see

"French Revolutionary Wars," p. 10), whose daring at Trafalgar depended on shedding naval orthodoxy and doing something completely new.

Back at home, Togo rose in the ranks of the Japanese navy as it grew ever more powerful while purchasing ships from the British. During the Russo-Japanese War, Togo saw combat with a Japanese fleet that destroyed a much larger Chinese armada, adding both to Togo's confidence and that of Japan. When Togo took command just before the Russo-Japanese War, the Japanese navy was one of the most powerful in the world, but Togo had also insisted on speed, and his ships could outmaneuver any on the oceans.

As head of the Japanese fleet, Togo was deeply respected by his men. They knew that short, barrel-chested Togo was completely committed to his duty to his country. Even when the Russians had given up at Tsushima and raised the white flag, Togo stopped firing only with the utmost reluctance. After this victory, journalists began calling him "the Nelson of the East," a colorful name that he rejected, but which was apt. Togo had faced down a massive fleet and won through daring, speed, and bravery—something Nelson himself would have been proud of. Togo went to his death at the age of eighty-six in 1934, revered by the Japanese, and a man whose success cast its long shadow into World War II.

REAR ADMIRAL ZINOVY PETROVICH ROZHESTVENSKY

Admiral Zinovy Petrovich Rozhestvensky was a hard man to miss, even in a room filled with Russian naval officers in full uniform. Fifty-five years old in 1904, he was six feet, three inches (190 cm) tall, thickly built, and powerful-seeming. His chest and arm muscles filled his uniform, and his large, bald head towered above everyone in the room.

Born in 1848, the same year as his opponent Admiral Togo, Rozhestvensky graduated from the Russian naval college and went on to distinguish himself in action against the Ottomans in the Russo-Turkish War of 1874–75. After serving as a naval attaché in London, he was promoted to gunnery officer for the Russian Baltic fleet and then, in 1902, made admiral.

With the death of the aggressive and well-liked Admiral Stepan Makarov, Rozhestvensky became one of the preeminent admirals in the Russian fleet. Tsar Nicholas II appointed Rozhestvensky to command the Baltic fleet, now renamed the 2nd Pacific Squadron, on its 20,000-mile (32,000 km) journey to Port Arthur.

Rozhestvensky was not well-liked by his men. He had a habit of physically striking sailors who did not perform to his liking—hitting them with his large fists, which he hardened by sparring for exercise. Men aboard ship would literally hide from him while they waited for one of his towering rages, usually set off by something as insignificant as a fleck of dirt on his binoculars, to subside.

At the same time, however, Rozhestvensky was a brave, capable, and scrupulously honest officer, which was rare in the Russian navy at the time. Perhaps only someone of his iron will could have held together the 2nd Pacific Squadron on its incredible journey, dealing with issues of poor morale, refueling problems, and the Dogger Banks incident.

By the time Rozhestvensky reached the Tsushima Straits, it was almost as if he was beaten already. He had prepared his own ships poorly for the fight, not meeting with his admirals or captains to confer on strategy, although in the end, the major factors in his defeat were Admiral Togo's superior tactics and the fighting preparedness of the Japanese.

Badly wounded, Rozhestvensky was well-treated by the Japanese. After he was released to the Russians, he did not fare so well. He was court-martialed for dereliction of duty. While he was finally exonerated, his career was at an end, and he died in 1909 at the age of sixty-one.

The Japanese Soldier

As there would be later in World War II (see "World War II," p. 316) there were numerous racist stereotypes among western countries and Russia about the supposed lack of fighting ability of the Japanese soldier. In fact, the Japanese army that fought in the Russo-Japanese War was on a par with all western countries and decidedly better equipped and more professional than the Russian forces it faced.

Both Japanese soldiers and sailors had been imbued with a love of country and emperor, and a deep sense of duty and dogged fatalism. (One soldier in the trenches before Port Arthur described his role as that of a "human bullet.") The average Japanese fighting man, although usually a conscript from a rural area, was far better educated than his Russian counterpart, having been the beneficiary of universal primary education.

Most of the Japanese soldiers who fought in the war had been trained rigorously for at least twelve months. They were at the peak of their physical strength, and they knew and understand their mission. In this, they were helped by the fact that their officers usually came from the same towns and villages and were of the same social class. In the Russian army, officers tended to be aristocrats, or at least autocratic in outlook.

Japanese infantrymen carried a state-of-the-art .256 caliber rifle with a five-shot magazine whose maximum range was 3,000 yards (2.75 km) but that was truly effective at about 100–300 yards (91–275 m). In the second year of the war, many regiments were supported by rapid-firing Hotchkiss guns. The main support of the Japanese infantry was the artillery, both field howitzer and heavier guns, the latter of which were set on reverse slopes or mounted in earthworks to protect them from counterbattery fire.

Japanese tactics emphasized surprise and flanking movements whenever possible. Because their supply lines were closer and better organized than those of the Russians, they were generally able to maneuver more adeptly and were more mobile. However, in the 90-mile (145 km) front along Mukden, facing a massed force opposite them, the Japanese bogged down, just as the Russians did. While the infantry war stalemated, the war on the seas (see "Turning Point," p. 198) would ultimately decide the war in favor of the Japanese.

ADMIRAL HEIHACHIRO TOGO WAS THE SON OF A SAMURAI, BUT RECEIVED HIS CRUCIAL MILITARY TRAINING IN ENGLAND. LIKE HIS HERO, ADMIRAL NELSON, HE BELIEVED IN UNORTHODOX AND DARING NAVAL MANEUVERS.
Getty Images

The Russian Soldier

One example of the difference between the Russian army and that of the Japanese is the fact that the Russians thought nothing of placing their men on a train and transporting them for days without feeding them or giving them water. The Japanese set up special feeding halls at specified points along their routes, which could serve up to 800 men at a time.

Like the Japanese soldier, the Russian infantryman was usually a rural conscript. While hardy and brave, the Russian soldier was illiterate and generally did not enjoy good relations with his officer, who was, if not an actual aristocrat, then from landed gentry. Class divisions added significantly to the problems of the Russian army, as did racial and ethnic divisions between the soldiers themselves. The European Russians considered those from the Far East and in particular Siberia as unintelligent and unreliable, whereas Siberians thought their counterparts from the West poor soldiers who had underestimated the Japanese threat.

Likewise, soldiers and sailors did not get along well. One Russian officer wrote home that some gunners in the forts protecting Port Arthur had seriously considered opening up their heavy guns on the Russian ships trapped in the harbor by the Japanese "to force the squadron to put to sea and fight."

Like the Japanese, the Russian infantryman was armed with a modern .256 caliber magazine rifle. Unlike the Japanese, the Russian generally attached a 2-foot (61 cm) bayonet to it at all times, due to the Russian belief in the efficacy of the bayonet attack. Unfortunately, such an attack made little sense as a major tactic in the face of massed firepower. Plus, the bayonet overweighted the rifle, which made the Russian soldier, according to one historian, "the worst shot among the European quality armies." (Contributing to this was the fact that the Russian army still fired in volleys at an officer's command, which was not the optimum way of shooting fast-moving small squads of Japanese soldiers approaching at wide intervals on the battlefield.)

Still, Russian common soldiers could put up with a great deal of hardship. Many European observers accompanying both armies to battle thought that the Russian officer was the most problematic part of the tsar's forces. Russia had a large officer corps (42,000 men ranked lieutenant and above, which is more officers than the U.S. Army had men at the time), but many of the most senior officers owed their jobs solely to social position. They did not buy their commissions, as the British army had at one time, but they were, as one historian as written, "effete, idle, preoccupied with social pursuit [and] promoted prematurely and beyond their level of competence." They simply did not know, or care, much about the welfare of their men, or about the tactics involved in modern warfare. Therefore they sent their troops in hopeless massed attacks against Japanese forces. Thousands fell on the Manchurian killing fields, and still the generals did not learn.

RUSSIAN REAR ADMIRAL ZINOVY PETROVICH ROZHESTVENSKY WAS BRAVE, CAPABLE, AND HONEST, ALTHOUGH NO MATCH FOR ADMIRAL TOGO.

© The Print Collector / Alamy

The Incident at Dogger Banks

On October 11, 1904, when the Russian Baltic Fleet, now renamed the 2nd Pacific Fleet, set sail to rescue the trapped ships at Port Arthur, Tsar Nicholas II prayed in his diary: "Bless its voyage, Lord."

But a more star-crossed beginning to the venture (see "Turning Point," p. 198) could not be imagined than what happened ten days later, on October 21. The commanders of the Russian fleet were horribly paranoid about attacks by Japanese torpedo boats—the same ones that had wreaked such havoc at Port Arthur—although how a Japanese torpedo boat could have survived in the North Sea (some 20,000 miles [32,000 km] from its base) was something the Russians apparently did not ask themselves.

In any event, the gunners aboard the Russian fleet were jumpy, and searchlights pierced the cold foggy seas, searching for danger. One ship set its sirens shrieking, reporting that it was being chased by no less than eight Japanese torpedo boats. The report proved to be unfounded, but it forced the entire fleet to change course.

But on the late evening of October 21, passing Dogger Banks, a popular fishing place for British trawlers, Admiral Zinovy Petrovich Rozhestvensky thought he saw a torpedo boat boring in to attack and ordered his flagship to open fire. Several other Russian vessels erupted in gunfire, as well. In the aftermath of the fire, one observer onboard a Russian destroyer looked across the dark seas to see that "a small steamer was rolling helplessly. A funnel, a bridge, and the red and black paint on her side were clearly visible." These ships—no bigger than 100 tons—were fishing boats—the Gamecock fleet out of Hull, in northern England. Rozhestvensky would claim to the end of his days that there were torpedo boats among the ships, and Russian gunners kept on firing for some twenty minutes, one ship loosing off 500 rounds. At one point, the Russian fleet even opened fire on itself, mortally wounding a ship's chaplain.

Aboard the fishing vessels, numerous men were wounded, and two English fishermen were beheaded by Russian shells as crew members

frantically waved fish at the Russian fleet, to show they were harmless. Finally, the Russians stopped firing. They understood that there were innocent fishermen present, but they still believed that Japanese torpedo boats had mixed themselves in among the Gamecock fleet. Therefore, they did not stop and pick up any of the helpless men in the water, but instead continued on their journey.

Such was the rage in England when the Gamecock fleet limped back into Hull that Great Britain very nearly declared war on Russia and sent its cruisers to follow the 2nd Pacific Fleet southward. The Russians avoided war with Great Britain only by apologizing and paying reparations, but their attack on these innocent ships—and the impunity with which the British squadrons sailed circles around them as they headed into the South Atlantic—had a serious effect on morale as the Russian fleet sailed toward its fateful meeting with the Japanese.

ON OCTOBER 21, 1904, ENGLISH FISHING BOATS WERE MISTAKEN FOR JAPANESE TORPEDO BOATS AND THE RUSSIAN FLEET OPENED FIRE ON THEM. THE INCIDENT AT DOGGER BANKS NOT ONLY ENRAGED ENGLAND, BUT DEVASTATED RUSSIA'S MORALE JUST PRIOR TO ITS FATEFUL MEETING WITH JAPAN.

© The Print Collector / Alamy

Attacking by Surprise: Port Arthur to Pearl Harbor

On the evening of February 8, 1904, Russian officers attended a grand party in Port Arthur, thrown by the commander of the Russian fleet at anchor there, Vice Admiral Oscar Stark. Port Arthur had a reputation as a town where people loved to have fun. Common soldiers and sailors naturally not invited to Admiral Stark's soiree roamed up and down Pushkin Street, the main thoroughfare, partaking of the pleasures to be found in the numerous gin mills and brothels.

Out in the dark waters of the Yellow Sea, Admiral Heihachiro Togo, aboard his flagship *Mikasa,* sent ten destroyers aiming like a knife right at the heart of the Russian fleet anchored at harbor. It was snowing lightly, but the Japanese destroyers—guided by the searchlight of the lighthouse at Port Arthur—had no trouble finding the Russian ships. The attacking vessels increased their speed to twenty knots, closed to within 1,000 yards (915 m), and released their torpedoes.

Many aboard the Russian ships knew nothing of the Japanese presence until torpedoes slammed into their steel hulls, shattering them and causing concussive blasts that tossed men overboard. At Admiral Stark's party, the blasts caused the band to stop playing, and the Russian officers raced outside into the frigid air to see fires leaping up from the harbor. Two Russian battleships and a heavy cruiser would be badly damaged in the attack.

While the Japanese had severed diplomatic relations before their surprise attack on Port Arthur, they had not declared war and would not until February 10. Surprise attacks without declaration of war were not illegal by international law (although they become so after the Russo-Japanese War), but they were normally frowned upon. The Russian tsar and his ministers were stunned by this attack, but much of the rest of the world was not. Great Britain and the United States, sympathetic to the Japanese in what was publicly seen as a kind of David and Goliath battle, shrugged off the lack of a declaration of war as something necessary for the Japanese to do to beat their overwhelming foe.

It is much harder to learn lessons from victory than from defeat, and lessons learned were in short supply after the Russo-Japanese War (see "The Lessons Not Learned," p. 210). But the Japanese surprise attack worked so well, and exposed them to so little criticism, that they felt they could pull it off again. More than thirty-five years later, another Japanese fleet approached another unsuspecting naval base, this time with mighty aircraft carriers. In fact, one of those aircraft carriers proudly flew the same battle flag carried by Togo's *Mikasa* as it launched planes to attack Pearl Harbor. However, this roll of the dice would ultimately doom Japan, because it would meet more than its match in the awakened wrath of an industrial giant like the United States.

JAPANESE ADMIRAL TOGO IS SEEN VISITING RUSSIAN ADMIRAL ROZHEST-VENSKY, RECOVERING IN THE HOSPITAL FOLLOWING THE BATTLE OF TSUSHIMA. THERE TOGO COMPLIMENTED THE RUSSIAN ON HIS BRAVERY DURING THE BATTLE. TOGO WAS ACCOMPANIED BY CAPTAIN ISORUKU YAMAMOTO, WHO, THIRTY-SIX YEARS LATER, WOULD PLAN THE JAPANESE SURPRISE ATTACK ON PEARL HARBOR.

© The Print Collector / Alamy

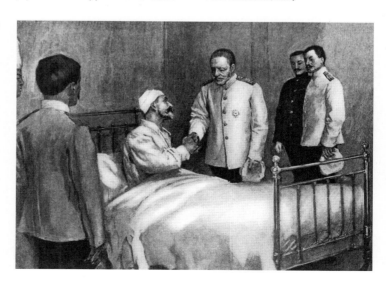

The Horror of Mukden

The ancient city in Manchuria is now called Shenyang, but at the time of the Russo-Japanese War it was known as Mukden, from a Manchu word meaning "to rise." To western ears, however, the name, with its echoes of "muck," is descriptive of the horrors that took place south of the city during a slogging month-long battle that saw 500,000 men pitted against each other.

By the early winter of 1905, Japanese infantry under Marshal Iwao Oyama had driven Russian forces under General Aleksey Nikolayevich Kuropatkin back through Manchuria from the coast. The Japanese had captured Port Arthur, and all of their forces were committed now to destroying the Russian army.

Russian forces were arrayed over an incredible 90-mile (145 km) long front, with their extreme left in high mountains, which made it difficult for them to mass troops and attack from that sector. In any event, the line was extremely thin, and there were no central reserves the Russians could call upon. The Japanese had decided to try to flank the Russians, catching them in a pincer movement on both sides. Before the major battle kicked off, numerous skirmishes between the two forces cost thousands of casualties in winter weather that was so cold the wounded simply froze to death where they lay.

On February 21, the Japanese attack kicked off along a 40-mile (65 km) front. The Japanese feinted toward the Russian lines in the mountains, but then sent a column around the Russian forces to wreak havoc in their rear. As the Japanese advanced, however, the Russians slowly retreated, avoiding being encircled. The Russians fielded 275,000 men, the Japanese 200,000, and neither side could summon more for the moment.

The battle became a grinding war of attrition, with the frozen bodies of the unburied dead lying between both sides. Men went out at night to scavenge ammunition from the pockets of the corpses. British war correspondent Douglas Story, who wrote the classic book, *The Campaign with Kuropatkin,* describes how many of the Russians had prepared themselves to die: "The dead hands clutch tender love messages...the laboured scrawl of infants sending their love to Daddy at the war."

Finally, after a two-and-a-half week battle that cost Japan 50,000 dead and wounded, and Russia about 78,000 casualties, Kuropatkin withdrew still farther north into Manchuria, and the city of Mukden fell into Japanese hands. (Kuropatkin offered his resignation to the tsar and it was accepted.) Both sides were almost literally unable to take a step further, and it fell to Admiral Togo at Tsushima to wrest complete victory from the Russians.

The Lessons Not Learned

Hindsight, as we all know, provides twenty–twenty vision in a way that the muddled events of present time cannot. But even so, it is remarkable that so many wrong lessons were drawn from the Russo-Japanese War.

Because the land war in Manchuria was the first war to be fought between large bodies of men armed with rapid-firing, breech-loading rifles and artillery, as well as machine guns, one would think that the Russians in particular would have learned not to make massed frontal attacks against entrenched troops. But immediately after the war, the Russian military engaged in some quick revisionist thinking. The Russians had not been conquered; in fact, they had inflicted heavy casualties on the Japanese. The problem was they had suffered from a kind of spiritual malaise. As one Russian officer put it, "Our moral strength was less than that of the Japanese, and it was this inferiority rather than mistakes in generalship that caused our defeat."

Well, partly right. The Russians did lack moral fiber, but it was also a torrent of automatic weapons fire that caused their defeat, coupled with Japanese genius at defense. But other European countries, with no small touch of racial stereotyping, accepted this. The failure of the massive Russian offensives had to be mainly due to the Russians themselves, not to any superiority on the part of the Japanese. This, in fact, was another lesson to be learned. The Russian and European sense of racial superiority to the Japanese should have been dispelled by the way the Japanese had fought. But it was not, and it would not be until World War II.

Ultimately, the many foreign observers of the Russo-Japanese War decided, as historian R.M. Connaughton put it, "that the Japanese had been such fanatics and the Russians had been such a poor opposition as to negate the value of military observation." But the failure of these same observers to fully appreciate the strength of automatic weapons fire coupled with strong defense would, as Connaughton writes, "cost the British and French thousands of lives in the First World War."

Sergey Witte: Finding Victory in Defeat

Ironically enough, the many prominent Russians in Tsar Nicholas's court didn't like Sergey Witte (pronounced "Vitte") very much, despite the fact that the tsar had appointed him to lead Russia's delegation at the peace negotiations to be presided over by U.S. President Theodore "Teddy" Roosevelt in Portsmouth, New Hampshire. Witte, who used to be finance minister of Russia, was a large, sloppy, brusque, arrogant, and brilliant man. He made no secret of the fact that he opposed the policies that had started the war with Japan in the first place.

However, Witte was the most able of Russian diplomats, and the tsar overcame his personal distaste for Witte and appointed him. Whatever Witte's personal feelings, he launched an insidious propaganda campaign against the victorious Japanese, one that began as he spoke to reporters while crossing the Atlantic. Well aware the public opinion in the United States favored Japan (which most Americans considered a little country that had fought back against a bully), Witte enthusiastically praised the Japanese, but then he began to emphasize their differences with Americans. In New Hampshire, Witte insisted that talks be suspended on Sunday mornings while he went to church with his entire delegation, forcing the Japanese ambassador to do the same. Witte went out of his way to seem as if he loved "the common man," tipping porters and shaking hands with people on the street, even though he was in reality the picture of an autocratic upper-class Russian.

Witte disliked Roosevelt (Witte described him in his memoirs as "selfish and totally without ideals"), but he hinted none-too-subtly in private meetings that the Americans might not like an expansion-minded Japan threatening their newly won Philippines (see "The Spanish American War," p. 176). And when the Japanese asked for indemnities to pay for a war that Russian land aggression had in reality started, Witte successfully portrayed them publicly as rapaciously greedy. In the end, the Japanese gave up their claims for money and did wring concessions from the Russians. The long-term gains from Japan's victory would continue to resonate, but they seemed to the Japanese public so little for so much blood shed that weeks of rioting ensued in Tokyo.

SERGEY WITTE WAS APPOINTED TO RUSSIA'S DELEGATION AT PEACE NEGOTIATIONS IN THE UNITED STATES. WHILE ARROGANT, WITTE KNEW HOW TO SWAY PUBLIC OPINION.

12

THE MEXICAN REVOLUTION

1910–1920

The first major revolution in what was to be a century of revolutions, the Mexican Revolution ushered radical changes in Mexican government, economy, and society

Combatants
• Factions within Mexico

Theater of War
Mexico

Casualties
Estimated 200,000 battle deaths on all sides, with another 1,000,000 Mexican noncombatant civilians dead of warfare, starvation, or disease

Major Figures
MEXICO
Pancho Villa, revolutionary leader from northern Mexico, head of *villistas*
Emiliano Zapata, revolutionary leader from southern Mexico, head of *zapatistas*
Porfirio Díaz, longtime autocratic president of Mexico
Francisco Madero, revolutionary who issued call to arms against Diaz and replaced him as president
Pascual Orozco, revolutionary leader in northern Mexico who staged a counterrevolution against Madero but was overthrown by Villa

General Victoriano Huerta, who overthrew Madero and murdered him
Venustiano Carranza, who ousted Huerta, became the new head of Mexican government, and had Zapata assassinated
General Álvaro Obregón, who assassinated Carranza, replaced him as president, and assassinated Villa

UNITED STATES
General John J. Pershing, who sought to capture Villa in Mexico

As Mexico entered the twentieth century, the fine promises of its revolts of the previous century—in which the country threw off first Spanish and then French rule—had turned into bitter lies. Long-term president Porfirio Díaz had gone from a liberal war hero to an autocratic dictator who refused to consent to fair elections or allow land redistribution from the wealthy oligarchs to the suffering peasants. But in 1910, Díaz's reign came to an end when he was overthrown and forced into exile by Francisco Madero, a United States–educated lawyer who called upon the Mexicans to revolt. What followed was ten years of bloody revolution that featured severe and treacherous factional infighting between Mexican radical groups. But when the dust settled—and the blood of more than 1,000,000 people had soaked into the ground—the outlines of the modern nation that Mexico would become were drawn.

1910:

July: President Porfirio Díaz jails his presidential election opponent, Francisco Madero, and wins a rigged election by a landslide.

September: Madero escapes from jail and flees to San Antonio, Texas.

October: Madero issues the Plan of San Luis Potosí, calling for a general uprising in Mexico on November 20.

November: Madero invades Mexico, but he is joined by only a few poorly armed rebels and returns to San Antonio.

1911:

May: Pancho Villa's forces capture Ciudad Juárez. Emiliano Zapata leads a peasant army against Díaz in the south of Mexico; Díaz resigns and heads into exile in Europe.

October: Francisco Madero is elected the new president of Mexico.

November: Zapata issues his Plan de Ayala, calling for rich landowners to immediately turn their land over to the peasants.

1913: In a counter-revolt that
begins on February 9, 1913, General Victoriano Huerta overthrows Madero and has him assassinated.

1914:

April: American troops occupy Veracruz.

July: Huerta is forced to resign and go into exile. Venustiano Carranza becomes "First Chief" of Mexico, with Álvaro Obregón fighting Pancho Villa as commander in chief.

December: Pancho Villa and Emiliano Zapata meet to try to organize a government. They march on Mexico City with 55,000 men, causing Carranza and Obregón to flee.

1915: Obregón defeats Villa at
the Battle of Celaya in April. The United States recognizes Carranza's government as the official one of Mexico and Carranza as president.

1916: Villa crosses the border
and attacks Columbus, New Mexico. U.S. President Woodrow Wilson sends General John J. Pershing into Mexico to catch and punish Villa.

1917:

January: Pershing is forced to return with his troops to the United States without capturing Villa.

February: The Mexican constitution is signed in the town of Querétaro. Zapata refuses to accept it or to recognize Carranza as president.

1919: Carranza traps Zapata and
has him murdered.

1920:

September: Obregón assassinates Carranza and assumes the presidency.

1923:

July: Obegrón has Villa assassinated.

WHILE FRANCISCO MADERO USHERED IN THE POSSIBILITY OF CHANGE AND OF NEW GOVERNMENT, IT WOULD BE HIS PRESIDENCY THAT WOULD SPARK A SECOND PUSH FOR REVOLT WHEN IT WAS FELT THAT MADERO WAS NOT IMPLEMENTING THE PROMISED CHANGES FAST ENOUGH.

Francisco Indelecio Madero (b/w photograph), Mexican Photographer, (20th century)/ Private Collection/Peter Newark American Pictures/ The Bridgeman Art Library

"LAND AND LIBERTY"

In 1876, Porfirio Díaz was a national hero in Mexico. He was the general who helped oust the French (who had invaded Mexico in service of Emperor Napoleon III's dreams of empire there), and he was elected president, promising to serve only one four-year term.

Yet, in 1910, the now-eighty-year-old Díaz was still president, having coerced and bribed his way into thirty-five years of unbroken power. In some ways, Díaz's leadership had been good for the country. He brought stability to the political process. Between Mexican independence from Spain in 1821 and Díaz's rise to power, the country's presidency had changed hands seventy-five times. And Díaz built factories, dams, and better roads, while bringing in an influx of foreign capital, especially from the United States.

But Díaz's rule was a disaster for the average Mexican because most of this foreign money went to the wealthy ruling families for whom the huge masses of *peons* ("peasant laborers") worked. Not only that, but Díaz had made it illegal for peasants to own the formal title to the land they worked, even if such land had been in their families for a century. This made it easier for Díaz to pass out huge gifts of rich farmland to the oligarchy or to large foreign companies. (By 1900, one out of every five acres [20,000 m²] of Mexican land was owned by a foreign interest.) But this policy left ordinary farmers with no security and a sense of displacement from their heritage.

In 1908, Díaz had hinted that he might allow a free election in 1910, and so Francisco Madero, a lawyer from a wealthy family in northern Mexico, ran for president on a platform of land reform. At first, Díaz thought Madero was a harmless candidate who might give the election an appearance of true democracy. But when anti-Díaz forces flocked to Madero, Díaz had Madero jailed until after the election, which Díaz won.

Madero escaped from jail and fled to the United States, where he issued the Plan of San Luis Potosí (named for the Mexican city in which he had been jailed). The plan called for the nullification of the 1910 election and a general uprising to begin in Mexico on November 20, 1910.

On that day, Madero invaded Mexico from San Antonio with a small force, but he found only a small group of rebels ready to join him, and so he returned temporarily to the United States. But even as Madero did so, major rebel leaders began rallying people to his cause. In northern Mexico, Pancho Villa, a charismatic one-time bandit who, having met a representative of Madero's, became convinced of the rightness of his ideals and joined forces with other rebel commanders under the overall command of Pascual Orozco. Villa's forces, which came to be called *villistas*, were mainly armed cowboys and ranch foremen who began to make lightening raids on isolated Mexican government outposts and armories.

The major leader in the south of Mexico was Emiliano Zapata a man heavily influenced by the political writings of Russian anarchists, who formed an army of peasants seeking dramatic

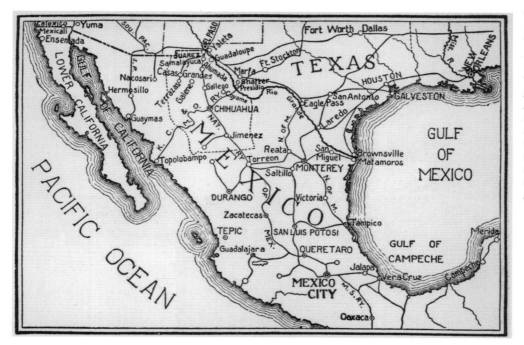

agrarian reform—the redistribution of land, violently if necessary, from the *hacendados,* or big landowners, to the peons. Zapata's poorly armed but passionate followers, many of whom, like Zapata himself, were half-Indian or Indians, formed the Liberation Army of the South, whose slogan was "Land and Liberty!" They were more generally known as known as *zapatistas.*

In the spring of 1911, rebel forces commanded by Villa captured the northern city of Ciudad Juárez. Seeing the handwriting on the wall, Díaz agreed to resign and go into exile in Europe. In elections held in the fall of 1911, Francisco Madero became president, but he soon faced major challenges from numerous other rebel leaders. Madero was a political moderate and moved slowly in implementing the radical land reform demanded by Zapata, who soon repudiated

Madero and instituted his own plan, the Plan of Ayala, which called for immediate land transfers from the hacendados to the peons. Zapata fled to the mountains to build up his forces and plan military action against Madero. Madero also offended Pascual Orozco, now commander in chief of Madero's army, who had played a major role in ousting Díaz and who felt he had not been adequately rewarded.

In a counter-revolt that began February 9, 1913, bitter factional combat broke out in the nation's capital, as Madero's General Victoriano Huerta, with Pancho Villa fighting on his side, defeated Orozco's army. (Orozco escaped to Texas, where he was killed in a shoot-out with Texas Rangers.) After ten days of struggle, with civilian casualties mounting, Huerta had Madero assassinated and seized control of the government

PORFIRIO DIAZ BEGAN HIS PRESIDENCY AS A NATIONAL HERO, HAVING DRIVEN THE FRENCH OUT OF MEXICO. HE PROVIDED POLITICAL STABILITY WHEN IT WAS SO DESPERATELY NEEDED, BUT THAT STABILITY CAME AT THE COST OF DICTATORSHIP. HIS PROMISED FOUR-YEAR TERM BECAME THIRTY-FIVE YEARS OF SUFFERING FOR PEASANT FARMERS, WHO LOST CENTURIES-OWNED FAMILY LAND UNDER UPPER CLASS AND FOREIGN INTERESTS.

Prints & Photographs Division, Library of Congress, LC-USZ62-100275

himself. Huerta also tried to execute Pancho Villa, whom he saw as a threat, but Villa escaped.

Huerta's rise to power only began another cycle of violence. Revolutionary forces known as "the Men of the North"—Villa, Álvaro Obregón, and Venustiano Carranza—joined forces to overthrow Huerta. In this they were aided by the U.S. government and its president, Woodrow Wilson, who objected to the way Huerta had come into power and refused to recognize his government, which made it difficult for him to purchase arms from U.S. suppliers. Wilson also sent U.S. forces to occupy the port city of Veracruz, further cutting Huerta off from arms supplies.

Finally, Huerta was forced to relinquish the reins of government and went into exile in Spain, with Carranza replacing him as so-called "First Chief" of Mexico in July 1914. Once again, regime change did not stop the cycle of violence. Villa was now at the height of his powers. Having plundered numerous Mexican banks, he had a growing army, railroad cars to transport them, and even mobile hospital units to care for his wounded, something that made both Carranza and Obregón afraid of him.

Zapata, for his part, refused to recognize Carranza's government (because it had not been duly elected by the Mexican people). He and Villa sought to form an alliance, entering Mexico City with 55,000 men of both their armies, causing Carranza and Obregón to temporarily flee. But two such disparate personalities were not able to fully cooperate, and the opportunity was lost. Zapata returned to the south, and Villa went to the north, where the latter was beaten in a series of battles beginning with the Battle of Celaya in the spring and summer of 1915 by the forces of Obregón.

At this point, Villa, angered that the United States had recognized Carranza's rule as legitimate, began killing U.S. citizens in Mexico. In 1916, he crossed the border to Columbus, New Mexico, and burned the town, killing eighteen people. In return, Wilson sent General John J. Pershing, later to become famous in World War I on a punitive raid to catch and imprison Villa, but Pershing was unable to capture him.

When Pershing finally withdrew in 1917, Villa recovered to become a power in northern Mexico, undefeated by Carranza, but unable to expand his base. In the meantime, Zapata was fighting a bloody war of attrition in the south, using a new strategy of attacking infrastructures—bridges, factories, and railroads—in the hopes that the government of the foreign countries that owned most of these structures would intervene to oust Carranza.

Despite this, Carranza stayed in office, created a constitution for Mexico in 1917, which struck a few hopeful notes—restricting the power of foreign companies to own Mexican land and establishing at least the principles of a minimum wage and unionization for laborers—but at the same time investing more power in the hands of the presidency. Carranza was also able to trap Zapata and have him assassinated in 1919. But shortly thereafter, while traveling from Mexico City to Veracruz in May of 1920, Carranza was killed by supporters of Obregón, who became president in September 1920.

Villa was still too strong for Obregón to attack directly, so the latter bribed Villa to retire from politics and remain in northern Mexico. Villa at first agreed to this, but Obregón was afraid he might try to return to power, and so had him ambushed and killed in July 1923. (Obregón himself would die by an assassin's hand five years later—see "Die Killing," p. 228.)

The bloody Mexican Revolution had lasted roughly ten years and profoundly changed the country. It cost more than a million lives, and it is remembered by many mainly because of its assassinations and counter-assassinations. All of the major personages of the revolution died violently.

While the revolution did not create the perfect democracy in Mexico, it forced the Mexican government to take an interest in the lives of its people, laying the basis for a social welfare system and a massive land redistribution effort, as well putting in place the notion of minimum wage and eight-hour working days. (Although it would be two decades before these finally came into effect.) The role of the military in politics was also reduced, as was that of the Catholic Church. Especially in the south, the revolution promoted nationalism as well as pride in the indigenous peoples in Mexico who had once marched under Zapata.

BATTLE OF CELAYA: APRIL 6, 1915

The army was spread out across a 4-mile (6 km) front, a wide flat area of fields and drainage ditches, and dug deeply into the earth, with barbed wire strung in glittering coils in front of its trenches. Banked earth and logs indicated machine gun emplacements, while behind the lines, artillery guns pointed darkly at the sky.

It could have been a scene from the Western Front in France, thousands of miles away, except for the fact that, facing this army across the plains, were thousands of men on horseback, wearing wide sombreros and serapes. The men belonged to the famous *División del Norte*, the Division of the North, and they were the finest irregular cavalry force in the world.

It was about four o'clock in the afternoon on April 6, 1915, and the leader of the Division rode out in front of them. He was Pancho Villa, a compact, muscular man with extraordinary self-confidence, and he swept an arm across the plains at the men waiting silently in what he disparagingly called their "holes" in the earth. "Muchachos!" he shouted at his men. "Before it gets dark, we'll burst into Celaya in blood and fire!" He gave the command, and the ground shook as thousands of horse hooves thundered at the troops of General Álvaro Obregón, who thumbed off the safeties on their Mausers and carefully took aim.

Two Generals

The battle that was about to take place near the little north-central Mexican town of Celaya would be the decisive one of the Mexican Revolution, which had now raged violently for five years. Mexico's autocratic President Porfirio Díaz was long gone, and those who had sought to replace him were fighting desperately for control of the country (see "Chronicle," p. 214). Francisco Madero had ruled, only to be overthrown and assassinated by General Victoriano Huerta, who had in turn been replaced by Victoriano Carranza and his fighting general Obregón.

In the meantime, the two rebel leaders perhaps closest to the people of Mexico, Villa and Emiliano Zapata (see "Commanders," p. 222), had been unable to ally with each other and thus were fighting virtually separate wars against Obregón and Carranza in the north and south of the country, respectively.

In early 1915, Obregón considered the strategic situation in his country. On the face of it, he and Carranza faced a desperate situation fighting a two-front war against two sizeable armies. (Villa's alone was larger than those belonging to Carranza and Obregón.) Obregón, a student of the military philosopher Clausewitz, understood that the only way to defeat these enemies was to isolate one army and destroy it before turning on the other.

He chose Villa's army, in the north, for two main reasons. One, Villa had spread his forces over too vast an area and was at least 1,000 miles (1,610 km) from his base in Chihuahua. But more important was Villa's personality. Villa had become famous—literally a movie star, because he had appeared in Hollywood director Raoul Walsh's 1914 movie *The Life of General Villa*—for his daring cavalry charges, mass attacks in which his horsemen swept aside any opposition, crashing to victory with guns blazing. Villa's weakness was that he did not seem to know any other tactic. Obregón, who had taken a close look at the fighting on the western front in France, understood that modern weapons and entrenchment would decimate any frontal attack.

It was only a question of getting the volatile Villa to take the bait.

"I Came into This World to Attack"

Obregón headed north from Mexico City at the end of March for the town of Querétaro, in the Bajío, a 250-mile (400 km) long valley in Mexico's high central plateau. He captured the ancient Toltec capital of Tula, which was connected to Veracruz on the coast by railroad. Veracruz was where Obregón would be supplied from, and where Carranza and his government had gone once Obregón's 11,000 men had abandoned Mexico City, and zapatistas had started swarming into the city in the vacuum of power.

Obregón then advanced to the town of Celaya, digging in with 6,000 cavalry, 5,000 infantry, 86 machine guns, and 13 artillery pieces. When Villa heard of Obregón's presence, he took it as a personal affront and began to advance toward Celaya, even as his close advisor, General Felipe Angeles, suggested that he attack Mexican forces at Veracruz rather than risking a frontal battle with Obregón—or, at the very least, retreat north in true guerilla fashion and force Obregón to come after him.

But Villa would have none of it. "I came into the world to attack," he told Angeles, and he said that even if his attacks failed to work today, they would work tomorrow. Besides which, his men's morale would never stand for a retreat, even a strategic one. On the afternoon of April 4, Villa's men clashed with an advance force belonging to Obregón, which then retreated in disarray toward Obregón's fixed lines outside of Celaya. The retreat was real, but Obregón also understood that such a tempting target of panicked troops would be irresistible to Villa. Telling his men that they would be in Celaya by dark, Villa sent them thundering on their way.

"If Death Should Surprise Me"

Thousands of Villa's horsemen now raged toward Celaya, shouting, shooting their guns in the air, and waving their hats. The men in Obregón's trenches let them get close and then, at a word from their commanders, opened fire, followed by their artillery and scores of machine guns.

The carnage was incredible. One U.S. journalist who watched from the rear with Villa said it was as if the men and horses had been knocked over like ninepins by invisible bowling balls rolled into their midst. Obregón, with the help of his German mercenary Colonel Maximilian Kloss, had set up interlocking fields of fire, in the best European tradition, so that there were no blind spots that the machine guns could not reach.

The attack failed. As the survivors streamed back, what historian Frank McLynn has called "the bankruptcy of Villa's generalship" became evident. Instead of pulling back and regrouping, Villa sent another attack, and then another, wave after wave of villistas riding straight to their deaths. He did not bother to reconnoiter for weak spots, nor did he try to mass his forces at a certain place and punch a hole through. He simply sent his squadrons of cavalry against the barbed wire, entrenchments, and machine guns of Celaya. Although the attacks were not skillful, the sheer weight of them—there were ten charges in all—nearly broke through. Obregón sent a telegram to Carranza that read: "I will consider it my good fortune if death should surprise me as I strike a blow in the face of its fatal onslaught."

But darkness intervened, and Villa was forced to withdraw, at least temporarily.

"My Men Could Hardly Advance"

The next morning, the fields in front of Celaya were littered with thousands of dead men and huge mounds of dead horses. Yet at dawn, Villa kicked off another round of attacks by blasting away at Obregón's lines with his own field pieces. Yet the range of Villa's guns was so poor that he was forced to move them close to Obregón's lines so that, as Villa himself later recalled, "The enemy machine gun bullets rang off our gun shields."

Villa then sent his forces in thirty charges against the enemy lines. Once again, he had made no attempt to probe for the spots weakened by his previous attacks. Even worse, he kept no troops in reserve. Thirty times between sunup and noon, the villistas attacked. Thirty times, they were sent reeling back by, as Villa later recalled bitterly, "those hundred machine guns of Álvaro Obregón and the [soldiers] firing from the cover of their holes."

Despite Villa's losses, his attacks were sending some of Obregón's regiments (mainly those who had run out of ammunition) retreating from the forward lines. Slowly, the villistas pushed a salient, or bulge, into Obregón's lines. Thinking quickly, Obregón sent for a bugler, an eleven-year-old boy whom he ordered to sound the villistas' call for retreat. The ploy worked. Villa's men stopped, confused, "halting their advance and assuming defensive positions," Obregón later recalled. Obregón found ammunition to bring to his men, and his forces carried the day.

Villa now was forced to fall back, leaving 2,000 dead on the field. Surrounded by his 400 *Dorados* ("Golden Ones"), his personal cavalry escort, he retired with what was left of his forces and in the next few days tried to win a propaganda battle. First, Villa sent a letter to the French, British, German, and U.S. consuls of Celaya, saying that he had only retreated to spare the town's inhabitants and its colonial-era cathedrals. In the same letter, he challenged Obregón to come out and fight him in the open, a challenge Obregón scornfully ignored.

None of this had any effect on Obregón's troops, who remained right where they were, and Villa decided he had to attack again.

"Villa Directed the Battle"

A week later, on April 13, the defenders of Celaya noticed huge pillars of dust hovering off in the distance. The dust was raised by Villa's new army of 20,000 horsemen, who had come to deal a death blow to them, once and for all. But Obregón now had 15,000 men and had improved his defenses with more barbed wire and machine guns.

Without having learned anything at all from his experience a week before, Villa sent in his men in bloody charge after bloody charge.

The attacks went on for three days. The second day, a heavy rain fell, bogging Villa's men and horses down in mud, where they were slaughtered by the hundreds. On April 15, just as Villa's men were at their weakest point, a cavalry reserve of 4,000, which Obregón had cleverly hid in some nearby woods, attacked the villistas' flanks. Obregón's men roared out of their trenches, and Villa's troops were routed, fleeing for their lives.

They surrendered by the thousands, 6,000 prisoners taken in one day, standing with their hands up on the battlefield surrounded by 3,000 corpses, men who had once been their comrades. Terrified, hundreds of Villa's officers put on private's uniforms, pretending to be ordinary citizens. Obregón magnanimously declared that there would be a general amnesty for all captured officers. When more than one hundred villista officers accepted this and declared themselves of senior rank, Obregón put them all in front of the firing squad.

It was a great and decisive victory for the man who would, within five years, become Mexico's president. Although there was more hard fighting to come (fighting in which Obregón would shortly lose his right arm), Villa was no longer a threat to the country at large, but rather a force who could be confined to northern Mexico. Almost more important, the myth of Villa's invincibility, his impenetrable aura, was finally shattered. When Obregón was asked why he had won at Celaya, he replied sarcastically, "Fortunately, Villa directed the battle personally."

It was a cutting reply, yet one that held a great deal of truth. While charismatic and personally brave, Villa was no tactician; his personal stubbornness cost dearly the men who fought for him at Celaya.

PANCHO VILLA:
THE CENTAUR OF THE NORTH

Although many other major figures from the Mexican Revolution have been lost in history, no matter what their accomplishments, rebel leader Pancho Villa remains famous, nearly mythological, as his nickname—the Centaur of the North, given to him for his supposedly unparalleled riding skills—can attest.

The trick with Villa's life is to separate the fact from the fiction. Villa was born Doroteo Arango in 1878 in the central Mexican state of Durango, to a family of poor sharecroppers. Doroteo's father died when he was still young, and he and his siblings were forced into what was virtually slave labor for a rich landowning family, the Negretes.

When Doroteo was sixteen, he came home one day and found a member of the Negrete clan attempting to rape his sister. Doroteo shot the man and killed him or so he later said. In other versions of the story, Villa claimed he only wounded him, but he was then forced to flee into the rugged Sierra Madre mountains, where he became a bandit.

He took on the pseudonym Pancho Villa, which had been his maternal grandmother's name. Villa lived a hand-to-mouth existence, constantly chased by the police, until he joined a much larger gang of bandits led by Ignacio Parra. With these men, Villa began robbing wealthy miners and landowners, a story that in his own personal mythology Villa turned into a version of Robin Hood, although in fact he did not redistribute this wealth to the poor, but spent most of it in cantinas in remote mountain towns.

As the Mexican Revolution was kicking off, Villa met Abraham Gonzales, an aide to future Mexican President Francisco Madero, who saw something in this rough-hewn, handsome, and seemingly happy-go-lucky young man. Villa thereafter joined the forces of Madero and waged war against Porfirio Díaz in northern Mexico, gathering a following around him.

He attacked and defeated Díaz's forces at the battle of Ciudad Juárez, near enough to the U.S. border town of El Paso, Texas, that U.S. reporters and newsreel cameras could record the action, and thus a legend was born. Villa made incredible copy for reporters. He was thirty-two years old, well-built, with curly black hair and apparently mesmerizing brown eyes and a way of moving that reminded a lot of people of a wild animal—a wolf or cougar.

One moment Villa could be extraordinary merry, yet he could turn violent and cruel the next. (Some modern analysts have speculated that he was manic-depressive.) He could be extremely gallant, but he was also known to rape women— literally kidnapping them and arranging a fake "marriage" in front of a "justice of the peace" as if to justify the act.

It can be said that Villa fought well, but not, ultimately, wisely. His failure to cement an alliance with Emiliano Zapata spelled the end of any hope that he might have had of defeating

THE LIFE OF PANCHO VILLA, SEEN HERE ON HORSEBACK, IS ONE OF BOTH BANDIT AND REVOLUTIONARY. FROM A VERY HUMBLE BIRTH, HE BECAME ALMOST MYTHOLOGICAL DURING HIS LIFETIME. HIS LEGEND WAS FURTHERED IN THE NEWSREEL CAMERAS OF THE AMERICAN REPORTERS.

Getty Images

Álvaro Obregón and Venustiano Carranza, and his provocation of the United States (see "Chasing Villa," p. 229) by invading U.S. territory was ultimately foolish. Villa was a man in service of his own appetites, a bandit as much as a revolutionary, although he loved the common men who served him.

In the end, seeing the handwriting on the wall, Villa took a deal from Obregón to stay out of his hair: $100,000 U.S. dollars and a vast estate in northern Mexico, where Villa was free to do whatever he wished. But his continual bragging to the press that he could summon an army of 40,000 at any time made Obregón (already nearly clinically paranoid) deeply suspicious. Although Villa's words were empty ones, Obregón sent gunmen for him as Villa visited his mistress in a nearby village in July 1923. Villa was riddled with bullets while driving his car and died far more like a bandit than a revolutionary.

EMILIANO ZAPATA: VIVA ZAPATA!

Emiliano Zapata, as powerful leader in the south of Mexico as Villa was in the north, was born in 1879 in the tiny Mexican state of Morelos, some 60 miles (97 km) south of Mexico City. While Villa was born poor, Zapata was both poor and a *mestizo*—half Indian and half white—which made his lot even more difficult. While mestizos made up half the population of Mexico at the time, they were looked down upon with scorn and the objects of racial prejudice.

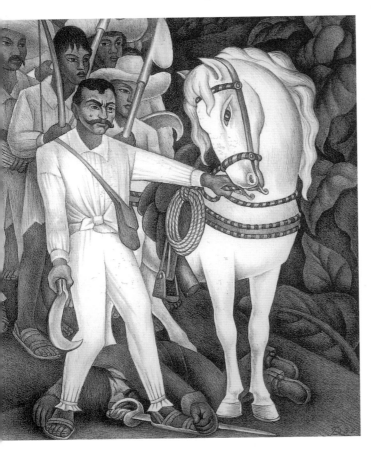

It can be accurately said that Zapata grew up smoldering with rage, rage that can easily be seen in his dark, suspicious eyes in almost any photograph taken of him. Aside from being a mestizo, he was a member of a family of minor landowners that saw their ancestral acres of sugar cane taken away from them when the railroad reached Morelos and wealthy landowners, enabled by Díaz, were simply able to steal whatever land they wanted.

By the time Zapata was sixteen, he had vowed to take revenge on Díaz and the ruling oligarchy. His revenge took shape in 1906, when an itinerant bookseller visited Zapata's village. Through him, Zapata learned about the theories behind Russian anarchism and socialism. Zapata began to see himself as a revolutionary, an image that was, at least on the surface, at odds with a young man who wore the fanciest clothes he could find (he had a suit with sparking silver pesos sewn onto it) and was a fine horsemen.

At the age of twenty-eight, Zapata became a village chief and attempted, though legal means, to win back the land stolen from local peasants. But when that didn't work, he formed a group of armed peons who engaged in guerilla warfare against Mexican government interests. It was 1910, and war was in the air.

THIS FAMOUS PAINTING BY DIEGO RIVERA DEPICTS EMILIANO ZAPATA, WHO STANDS WITH A SICKLE IN HAND OVER A FALLEN LANDOWNER. IT IS SYMBOLIC OF EVERYTHING ZAPATA STOOD AND FOUGHT FOR WITH HIS PEASANT ARMY.

Prints & Photographs Division, Library of Congress, LC-USZC4-3908

Zapata called his peasants the Liberation Army of the South, and they were much different group than Villa's tough bandits (see "The Zapatistas," p. 227). Zapata saw himself and his army as true revolutionaries who needed to destroy the ruling class. He believed firmly that there was no compromise. As his peasant fighters swept north shouting "Viva Zapata!" they killed the rich wherever they could find them. In fact, Zapata's army was the first to enter Mexico City, ahead of that of Villa and Madero.

But Zapata was never comfortable with government and seats of power and did not attempt to become president himself. Instead, he waited for Madero to make promised land reforms, and when the latter proved too slow in moving forward, Zapata simply began fighting him. Zapata lost an opportunity to join forces with his natural ally from the north, Villa, mainly because Zapata was too unwilling to compromise and suspicious of Villa's materialistic side. When they both rode into Mexico together, causing Carranza and Obregón to flee, Villa took Zapata to the grand presidential palace and suggested that Zapata sit in the presidential chair.

Zapata scowled: "I didn't fight for this, I fought to get the lands back. We should burn that chair," a statement that was utterly foreign to Villa. Had the two of them come together—Zapata with his powerful revolutionary vision and Villa with his stronger military force—they might have stopped the revolution then and there. Instead, they went their separate ways, with Zapata heading south to continue to do battle, his army of peons ultimately dwindling from attrition.

In 1919, Carranza lured Zapata into a trap, having one of his most prominent officers offer to defect to Zapata with his entire force. Zapata let down his guard for just a moment. Visiting the officer's camp, he was gunned down by a guard of honor that lifted their rifles, supposedly to fire a salute to the great rebel leader. Instead, they shot Zapata at point blank range, killing him instantly.

The Villistas

The men who fought in Pancho Villa's army naturally were, like those who fought for Emiliano Zapata, loyal to the charismatic personality of a single man—Villa. They came from hard peasant stock in northern Mexico, and many of them had spent most of their time on the wrong side of the law. Perhaps more so than most zapatistas, the villistas were prone to looting, drinking, and causing general mayhem, but they were ferocious fighters.

Because of Villa's greater wealth and access to arms from the United States, the villistas were generally better equipped for combat than the zapatistas, most of whom were armed with smokeless Mauser rifles and repeating pistols. As the war went on, Villa brought artillery, machine guns, trains, mobile medical units, and fine horses for his fighters. Like their leader, they were often seen armed to the teeth, with bandoliers of ammunition criss-crossing their chests.

And they were loyal to Villa even in his most difficult days, such as the period in the first half of 1916 when he was wounded and on the run from the U.S. Army. When one of his officers was wounded during the raid on Columbia (see "Chasing Villa," p. 229), he was turned over to Mexican authorities and placed in front of a firing squad. Before he died, he told a foreign reporter: "When the call came, I was one of the first to join [Pancho Villa] and have been his faithful follower ever since....I would much prefer to die for my country in battle, but since it is decided to kill me, I will die as Pancho Villa would wish me to...with my head erect and my eyes unbandaged."

When placed in front of the firing squad, this man refused a blindfold and even gave the firing squad the command to shoot. It was the type of loyalty no amount of money could buy, and Villa commanded it.

SHOWN BELOW, THE VILLISTAS WERE FEROCIOUS FIGHTERS AND INTENSELY LOYAL TO PANCHO VILLA.

Followers of Pancho Villa in Action at the Battle for Matamoros, 1913 (b/w photo), Mexican Photographer, (20th century) / Private Collection / Peter Newark American Pictures / The Bridgeman Art Library

The Zapatistas

The zapatistas were an army possessed of a true revolutionary fervor, if not the modern arms needed to carry it out. In 1911, following Zapata in a five-month journey that culminated in their entering Mexico City in triumph (see "Commanders," p. 224) they became for a time the most feared force in Mexico. Zapata's 4,000 or so peon followers dressed all in white and carried banners with pictures of the Virgin of Guadeloupe as they attacked army installations, police stations, and the homes of wealthy landowners. Armed in some cases only with machetes, they charged into the teeth of rifle and machine gun fire shouting "Viva Zapata!"

The zapatistas were feared everywhere because they were possessed of extraordinary revolutionary fervor, much more so than the men of Villa, who fought hard but were less revolutionaries than opportunists, like their leader.

An example of the kind of bloody warfare that occurred when the zapatistas entered the fight took place in the heavily armed government town of Cuautla in May 1911, when Zapata sent his 4,000 men against the elite Fifth Cavalry of the federal government. The fighting took six days, and Zapata's soldiers matched their machetes against bayonets

in hand-to-hand combat all over town. No quarter was given. When the zapatistas discovered that some federales had hidden in a boxcar, they poured gasoline on it and set it alight, cremating the screaming men.

There are pictures of the zapatistas entering Mexico City and sitting down at a local coffee shop—scarred men who look ill at ease in civilization and still wear thousand-yard-stares from the shock of their combat experiences. Never again would they reach such a peak, but at war's beginning, they were the best fighting force in the country.

SEEN HERE ARE THE ZAPATISTAS, THE FIGHTING FORCE LED BY EMILIANO ZAPATA. WHAT THEY LACKED IN ARMS (OFTEN TIMES CARRYING ONLY MACHETES), THEY MADE UP FOR IN FERVOR.

Followers of Emiliano Zapata in 1914 (b/w photograph), Mexican Photographer, (20th century) / Private Collection, Peter Newark American Pictures / The Bridgeman Art Library

"Die Killing": The Life and Death of Álvaro Obregón

ALVARO OBREGON AND VENUSTIANO
CARRANZA, PICTURED HERE, WERE ONCE
ALLIES—OBREGON SERVING AS COM-
MANDER-IN-CHIEF UNDER CARRANZA AS
PRESIDENT. BUT GIVEN THE OPPORTU-
NITY, OBREGON WOULD ASSASSINATE
CARRANZA AND TAKE THE PRESIDENCY.

Alvaro Obregon with Venustiano Carranza, 1916 (b/w
photograph), Mexican Photographer, (20th century) /
Private Collection, Peter Newark American Pictures /
The Bridgeman Art Library

Here is a classic story from the life of General Álvaro Obregón, the last man left standing after the dust of the Mexican Revolution settled. During a battle with Villa's forces in 1915, he climbed a bell tower to get a better look at the action and was hit by a shell that tore off his right arm. Assuming the wound was fatal, Obregón decided to commit suicide. He put his gun to his head, pulled the trigger—and heard only an empty click. It turned out his orderly had been cleaning the pistol the night before and forgotten to reload it.

Obregón survived, one-armed, to become president of Mexico. While he is nowhere near as famous as Zapata or Villa, he was the most brilliant and certainly most death-obsessed general of the war. Once, when asked by a foreign journalist what his goal in the revolution was, he replied simply and starkly: "Die killing." He continually exposed himself to fire and was known to break out into laughter when shellfire burst around him.

His courage was extraordinary and so was his skill in tactics and battle. When Mexican government patrol boats refused to join his side of the conflict, Obregón hired airplanes to bomb them miles out at sea, one of the world's first air-to-sea attacks (see "The Wild Blue Yonder," p. 231).

At the Battle of Celaya (see "Turning Point," p. 218), he defeated Villa by studying the rebel leader's impetuous tactics and then, taking a page from the battlefields of Europe, digging in his troops behind barbed wire and supporting them with artillery and machine guns, leaving Villa to make hopeless frontal assaults.

After Venustiano Carranza was assassinated by Obregón's supporters in May 1920, Obregón became president and (after killing Villa) the sole remaining major figure of the revolution left on the Mexican political scene.

There were numerous plots on his life, but Obregón scoffed at them, saying that anyone who wanted to kill him would have to be willing to trade his life for Obregón's. On July 17, 1928, someone was. A young Catholic named Jose de Leon Toral, upset with the fact that Obregón was trying to diminish the power of the Church in Mexico, pretended to be a sketch artist to gain admittance to a banquet Obregón was attending. He drew a more than passable likeness of the president and was allowed to show it to him. Obregón was impressed and told Toral to fill out the details, to which Toral replied by pulling out a gun and shooting Obregón five times. Obregón died, at the age forty-eight, and Toral was executed two days later.

Chasing Villa: John J. Pershing's Punitive Expedition

At 4:45 a.m. on March 9, 1916, the tiny town of Columbus, New Mexico, awakened to the sound of shouts and gunfire as 500 armed men raced on horseback through its streets. The men were villistas, and they had crossed the border from Mexico to make their attack, the first invasion by a foreign country since the War of 1812.

Pancho Villa—who waited across the border in Mexico—had directed his soldiers to attack the U.S. Army garrison first, but the peasants assumed that the stables were the barracks, because they were by far the largest building, and hence opened fire only on horses. The army battled back fiercely, as another contingent of villistas entered the town to rob the bank and exact vengeance on a U.S. arms dealer who had reneged on a deal with Villa (and who was fortunately out of town that morning, visiting his dentist). By the time the Mexicans rode out of town, they had lost one hundred men to U.S. machine guns and rifles, but they had killed eighteen U.S. citizens.

Villa's raid was mainly in revenge for Woodrow Wilson's recognition of Venustiano Carranza as chief of the new Mexican state. It is possible that he wanted to provoke exactly what he got—an invasion of Mexico by the U.S. Army. Public outcry in the United States was so great that Wilson (who did not want to be drawn into war with Mexico as the possibility of the United States' joining the European conflict of World War I loomed) was forced to commit 10,000 troops, led by General John "Black Jack" Pershing to track Villa down.

Pershing's punitive expedition began on March 15 when he crossed the Rio Grande with three brigades and penetrated deep into Villa's home state of Chihuahua, seeking the outlaw leader. At first Villa stayed one step ahead of Pershing, even though Pershing was using eight scout planes to try to find him, partly because conditions in the near-desert of Chihuahua were so difficult for infantry to march through. The sun blazed during the day, yet at night the air was so cold that water froze in canteens.

But with the help of Carranza's men, Pershing began to close in on Villa. Villa was wounded in a skirmish and taken to a mountain hideout to recover, while his men dispersed throughout the rough country in small groups that were hunted down by U.S. commanders, including young officers such as George Patton and Douglas MacArthur, both to become famous in World War II.

Even though Pershing had not yet caught Villa, Wilson was urged by his advisors to withdraw U.S. troops, because Villa's army was so obviously neutralized. But he refused to, which was a political error. The longer the American stayed in Mexico, the more Carranza was seen as a puppet of the hated government of Uncle Sam and the more people began to return to Villa's side, who was to recover from his wound and became a resurgent force in Mexico after the Americans had finally left, in early 1917.

AFTER PANCHO VILLA RAIDED THE TOWN OF COLUMBUS IN NEW MEXICO, U.S. PRESIDENT WOODROW WILSON COMMITTED 10,000 MEN UNDER GENERAL JOHN PERSHING, PICTURED HERE, TO CAPTURE VILLA.

General Pershing (U.S. Army) crossing the Rio Grande into Mexico in Pursuit of Pancho Villa, 1916 (b/w photograph), Mexican Photographer, (20th century) / Private Collection, Peter Newark American Pictures / The Bridgeman Art Library

In the meantime, Germany observed that the Americans could not even catch an outlaw like Villa. Germany felt it had little to fear from the United States and entered into unrestricted submarine warfare, and also, in the Zimmerman Telegram urged Carranza's government to attack the United States. This was an error of great magnitude, because the United States' intervention helped sink Germany's last hope of winning World War I.

"An Explosive and Authentic Revelation"

As with many epochal conflicts, one effect of the Mexican Revolution was to inspire generations of artists and writers. One such artist was Diego Rivera, who was born in 1886 in Guanajuato, Mexico, studied painting at a young age, and moved to Europe to advance his technique in 1907. He stayed there for fourteen years, thus missing out on the entirety of the Mexican Revolution, although he was not indifferent to the sweeping effects it had upon the society of his native country, where a loosening of the repressive ties of church and government had come about.

He returned to Mexico in 1921 and, inspired by Renaissance frescos he had seen in Italy, began working in mural form—murals being the only canvas big enough to capture the events of the previous decade. Rivera's public images of men and women fighters, done on fresh plaster in universities and other public buildings, fit in with his Marxist-inspired idealistic views. In works like "The Night of the Rich," "In the Arsenal," and others, Rivera translated the revolution for the people. In his stirring scenes, all the gray areas of the revolution—the greed and violence of the men who clashed for power in Mexico, including President Alvaro Obregon, who sponsored Rivera's murals—disappeared, leaving only the narrative of the heroic, simple peasant fighting against repressive capitalism.

An important Mexican writer whose work was profoundly influenced by the Mexican Revolution was Octavio Paz. Paz was born in 1914 and so was too young to take part in the conflict, but had deep ties to it nonetheless. His father, Octavio Paz Solórzano, was a lawyer who supported Emilio Zapata during the revolution and made notable contributions in the area of agrarian reform, while Paz's grandfather was a brilliant writer who was one of the first to write a novel about the plight of the Mexican Indians. After Zapata's assassination, the family was forced to flee Mexico for a time.

As Paz grew into his position as Mexico's preeminent poet and essayist, he returned again and again to themes of the revolution. "The Mexican Revolution," he wrote, "was an explosive and authentic revelation of our real nature." Despite its violence, the revolution was necessary for Mexico to come to grips with its past and move on into the future. Paz was awarded the Nobel Prize in 1990, the first Mexican to be so honored. He died in 1998.

THE MEXICAN REVOLUTION INSPIRED MANY ARTISTS AND WRITERS, INCLUDING MEXICAN-BORN POET AND ESSAYIST OCTAVIO PAZ, WHO RETURNED TO THE THEMES OF THE REVOLUTION MANY TIMES IN HIS WORK. PAZ WON THE NOBEL PRIZE IN 1990, THE FIRST MEXICAN TO BE SO HONORED.

Time & Life Pictures/Getty Images

The Big Bang

One of the major weapons of the Mexican Revolution was dynamite, which, along with the machine gun, was one of the reasons why the casualty count in relatively small-scale battles was so high.

Dynamite was invented in the late 1860s and was made up of nitroglycerine mixed with a powder that stabilized it. But it didn't really reach its full potential until Alfred Nobel came up with a substance that could absorb far more nitroglycerine than the powder previously used, yet remain stable until lit by a fuse. The explosive was cheap, powerful, and readily available, especially in northern Mexico, because of its use in mining. Therefore, Mexican rebels made ready use of dynamite as a hand explosive, lit and thrown after creeping close enough to a machine gun position, or as a bomb, which was set off from ambush and exploded via a long fuse when the enemy passed by a certain position.

Dynamite played a large part in numerous battles between various factions in the fighting in northern Mexico, as well as in smaller ambushes where it was used as a weapon to shock opponents before cavalry charges. It was even dropped as bombs from airplanes (see "The Wild Blue Yonder," below).

Dynamite also loomed large in the way the U.S. public imagined the Mexican Revolution. It was a staple of movies about the revolution right up to 1971 and movie director Sergio Leone's *A Fistful of Dynamite,* which featured a rebel plot to fill a locomotive with the explosive and send it crashing into government forces. Sounds far-fetched, but in March 1912, one of Pascual Orozco's commanders did exactly that, sending a locomotive filled with dynamite straight into Francisco Madero's forces in northern Mexico, killing sixty men and causing wild panic.

The Wild Blue Yonder

The Mexican Revolution turned out to be one of the very first proving grounds for the use of airplanes as combat weapons. This development was almost simultaneous to what was happening in the battlefields of Europe as World War I developed (see "World War I," p. 232).

Numerous foreign mercenary pilots fought for both sides in the Mexican Revolution. In early 1911, the government of Porfirio Díaz hired Rene Simon, an American of French descent, to scout rebel positions near Juarez. A much more aggressive use of the airplane came from U.S. Captain John Hector Worden, who dropped dynamite bombs on rebel positions. In May 1913, Didier Masson, a French-born U.S. aviator, was sent by Obregón (see "Die Killing," p. 228) to bomb the government gunboat Guerrero in Guaymas Bay. Most of Obregón's air force in his war against Villa consisted of Americans, one of whom, Charles Niles, actually blew up a rebel locomotive with a dynamite bomb.

Villa's air force, which suffered from flying older model planes, was also almost entirely made up of U.S. adventurers. Two of these warring Americans, Dean Ivan Lamb and Phil Raider, engaged one afternoon in flying duel, using revolvers, which many think to be the first ever aerial dogfight, although there is some dispute over the date (either 1913 or 1914) and whether Lamb was even involved. Even if he wasn't, Lamb was an incredible character. After leaving Mexico, he ended up (like many of the U.S. mercenaries who had fought in the revolution) in France, where he fought for Great Britain and shot down eight German planes. He was awarded the British Distinguished Conduct Medal for "conspicuous gallantry," the French *Croix de Guerre,* and numerous other decorations.

13

WORLD WAR I

1914–1918

A series of interlocking alliances placed Europe at the epicenter of a conflict that cost 20 million lives, destroyed centuries-old empires, and set the stage for World War II

Combatants

MAJOR ALLIED POWERS
- France
- Great Britain
- Russia
- United States
- Italy

MAJOR CENTRAL POWERS
- Germany
- Austria-Hungary
- Ottoman Empire

Theater of War

Europe, Middle East, Africa, Russia

Casualties

Allies: 5,250,000 dead, 12,800,000 wounded
Central Powers: 4,386,000 dead, 8,388,000 wounded
Civilian deaths: Estimated 10 million

Major Figures

ALLIES

GREAT BRITAIN
King George V, inspirational leader of British people during the war
Sir Winston Churchill, First Lord of the Admiralty
Field Marshall Sir John French, commander in chief British Expeditionary Force (BEF)
Sir Douglas Haig, second commander of BEF
Admiral Sir John Jellicoe, commander of the British Grand Fleet
T.E. Lawrence, "Lawrence of Arabia," British officer who helped lead the Arab revolt against the Turks

FRANCE
General Joseph Joffre, aging French chief of staff who refused to be panicked by the German attack at the war's beginning
General Joseph Gallieni, whose flank attack on German forces saved Paris
Marshal Henri-Philippe Pétain, defender of Verdun who became the commander in chief of the French army by 1917
Georges Clemenceau, prime minister who revived French morale
General Ferdinand Foch, supreme allied commander, March 1918

RUSSIA
Tsar Nicholas II, Russia's last tsar
General Paul von Rennenkampf, Russian general of German ancestry who helped lose the Battle of Tannenberg
General Aleksey Brusilov, whose successful offensive in 1916 drove back Austrian forces
Alexander Kerensky, leader of Russian provisional government

UNITED STATES
President Woodrow Wilson, who failed to keep the United States out of war
General John J. Pershing, head of the American Expeditionary Force
General Peyton Conway March, U.S. Army chief of staff who modernized the United States' war efforts

ITALY
King Vittorio Emanuele III, who brought Italy into the war on the side of the allies

General Luigi Cadorna, chief of staff of Italian army

CENTRAL POWERS

GERMANY
Kaiser Wilhelm II, emperor of Germany, militaristic ruler
Field Marshall Alfred Graf von Schlieffen, who developed the famous Schlieffen Plan
General Helmuth von Moltke, the German chief of staff in 1914
General Erich von Falkenhayn, who succeeded von Moltke as chief of staff
General Pavel von Hindenburg, chief of staff after Falkenhayn
General Erich Ludendorff, von Hindenburg's deputy, who planned the Ludendorff Offensive
Admiral Alfred von Tirptiz, creator of the modern German navy

AUSTRIA-HUNGARY
Emperor Franz Joseph I, who issued an ultimatum to Serbia after the assassination of his nephew and heir, Archduke Franz Ferdinand
General Franz Graf Conrad von Hötzendorf, chief of staff of the Austro-Hungarian army

OTTOMAN EMPIRE
Sultan Mehmed V, who joined the war on the side of Germany and Austria-Hungary in 1914
Mustapha Kemal, victor at Gallipoli
Enver Pasha, minister who convinced the sultan to fight on the side of the Central Powers

1914:

June 28: Austro-Hungarian heir to the throne Archduke Franz Ferdinand is assassinated in Sarajevo by Serbian nationalist.

July 28: Austria-Hungary declares war on Serbia. Russia mobilizes forces against Austria-Hungary.

August: Germany declares war on Russia, France, and Belgium. Germany invades Belgium on its way to attacking France. Great Britain declares war on Germany. Germans defeat Russians at the Battle of Tannenberg on the eastern front.

September: The First Battle of the Marne, France, halts the German advance; trench warfare begins.

October: The First Battle of Ypres, in Belgium, begins, ending in an Allied victory that keeps the Germans from flanking them at the North Sea. Turkey enters the war on the side of the Central Powers.

December: Troops on the front line declare an unofficial Christmas truce.

1915:

January: The first German zeppelin bombing attack on England.

February: The first German U-boat attacks on neutral shipping as Germany declares a blockade of England.

March: The British announce a blockade of German ports.

April: The allies begin the nine-month-long Battle of Gallipoli, which they will ultimately lose. Germany attacks Russia in Poland, eventually driving it out of the country. The first use of poison gas occurs by Germans at the Second Battle of Ypres.

May: A German submarine sinks the passenger liner *Lusitania*.

September: Tsar Nicholas II takes personal command of the faltering Russian forces. The British use poison gas near Loos, Belgium.

December: Sir Douglas Haig takes command of the British Expeditionary Force. The allies begin to withdraw troops from Gallipoli.

1916:

February: The British began conscription as losses on the western front cause severe manpower shortages. The Battle of Verdun begins with a German attack on French positions. It will be fought for nine months, cause more than 1 million casualties, and end in a draw.

March: Beginning in March and lasting through November, Italy and Austria-Hungary fight a series of battles in northern Italy. Italy loses them all, but refuses to surrender.

April: British forces in Mesopotamia begin an advance on Baghdad.

May: The Battle of Jutland, the war's biggest naval battle, ends in a draw but with the British still in control of the North Sea.

June: In the Middle East, T.E. Lawrence leads an Arab revolt against the Turks.

July: The Battle of the Somme begins with a British attack. It will end six months later with more than 1 million casualties and no Allied breakthrough.

September: Tanks are introduced for the first time at the Battle of the Somme.

1917:

January: Germany declares unrestricted submarine warfare. The United States severs diplomatic ties with Germany.

February: Arthur Zimmerman, undersecretary for foreign affairs, sends a telegram urging Mexico to go to war against the United States. It is intercepted by the British and turned over to the United States.

March: The British capture Baghdad. Tsar Nicholas II abdicates. A provisional government is formed in Russia.

April: The United States declares war on Germany. The French Nivelle Offensive fails as it advances only 500 yards (457 m) while 250,000 are killed or wounded. French soldiers mutiny.

June: The American Expeditionary Force arrives in France.

July: A major British offensive is launched at Ypres, but it bogs down without breakthrough and with 700,000 casualties on both sides. Russian forces begin a last offensive against the Germans, which fails badly.

October: Austrian and German forces defeat Italy at the Battle of Caporetto on the Italian front.

November: The Russian Revolution installs a Communist government in Russia.

December: British forces capture Jerusalem.

1918:

March: Russia makes a separate peace with Germany. Germany launches a major spring offensive on the western front, designed to break the allies' will to fight before the Americans arrive. German forces are finally stopped in June.

May: U.S. forces stop the Germans in their first major test under fire, at the Battle of Cantigny. They also defeat the German offensive at Chateau-Thierry.

August: The Allied counteroffensive along the Somme pushes the Germans back to the Hindenburg line.

September: A mainly United States' counter-offensive against German forces in the Meuse-Argonne region deals the death blow to German hopes on the western front.

November: Kaiser Wilhelm II abdicates. An armistice is signed.

1919:

June: The Treaty of Versailles is signed.

"A TRAGIC AND UNNECESSARY CONFLICT"

World War I was a historic clash that caused unprecedented bloodshed, mainly because of the joining of old world diplomacy and expectations with modern firepower and mass armies.

As the twentieth century began, Germany's military and economic ascendancy since the Franco-Prussian War continued unabated. This rise was watched nervously by Russia, Great Britain, and France, which had formed an arrangement to go to each other's aid if attacked, known as the Triple Entente. In the meantime, Germany's ally, Austria-Hungary, grew increasingly concerned about nationalistic forces in the Balkans, to its south, especially in Serbia, which was Russia's ally.

Germany, Austria-Hungary, and Italy had formed the Triple Alliance, to defend each other in the event of war. All of these interlocking alliances were, in some ways, meant to encourage war. The countries involved each felt that they had something to gain by a limited conflict. France and Great Britain felt Germany could be contained, Austria-Hungary wanted to quash Baltic nationalism once and for all, and Germany wanted to increase its status in the world.

Thus, when Serbian nationalist Gavrilo Princip killed the heir to the Austro-Hungarian throne, Archduke Franz Ferdinand, on June 28, 1914, most of those concerned thought that a short war might not be the worst thing that would happen. This was because they were going by nineteenth-century standards of warfare. But the result was a twentieth-century war that historian John Keegan has called "a tragic and unnecessary conflict."

On July 28, 1914, Austria-Hungary declared war on Serbia. Shortly thereafter, Russia mobilized its forces for war against Germany, Germany declared war on Russia and France, and France declared war on Germany and Austria-Hungary. On August 4, Germany declared war on neutral Belgium and invaded as part of the right-flanking move, a giant wheeling movement to attack France from the northeast, which lay at the heart of the famous Schlieffen Plan to neutralize France in six weeks. As a result of this invasion, Great Britain declared war on Germany, and the sides coalesced.

The Central Powers—so-named because they were located between Russia and France—were Germany and Austria-Hungary, shortly to be joined by the Ottoman Empire (Turkey and the Middle East). The allies were France, Russia, and the United Kingdom, later to be joined Italy—which had balked at entering the war on the Central Power side—the United States, and numerous other smaller countries.

Almost every country involved in the conflict had a war plan at the ready. Germany, well aware of the problem of fighting a two-front war against Russia and France, sought to knock out France with the Schlieffen Plan, named after its originator, former German Chief of Staff Alfred von Schlieffen. The plan called for a blocking army to face the French in the west, while seven other German army groups swung northeast through Luxembourg and Belgium to smash down into France and capture Paris. But von Schlieffen's successor, General Helmuth von Moltke, fatally weakened the thrust by depleting the armies sweeping through Belgium to strengthen Germany's western defensive positions.

The French and British were able to blunt the German attack in the First Battle of the Marne in September, beginning a stalemate in France that would last for four years. However, in August, German forces had inflicted 150,000 casualties on the Russians at the Battle of Tannenberg, in East Prussia (near the modern-day Polish town of Olsztyn—see "The Battle of Tannenberg," p. 260). This resulted in the almost complete destruction of the Russians in that area and kept them at bay for almost a year.

On the western front, a rapidly growing line of trenches, ultimately 470 miles (756 km) long, snaked from Switzerland to the North Sea, containing the armies of either side. A series of attritional battles were then fought. At the First Battle of Ypres (October–November 1914), the Germans lost 130,000 casualties, the British and French 108,000. The Second Battle of Ypres (April–May 1915) saw poisonous chlorine gas used by the Germans against French troops. From February to December 1916, the Battle of Verdun, in the Lorraine region of eastern France was fought, costing 1 million French, British, and German casualties. The Battle of the Somme, in northern France (July–November 1916) counted 57,000 British casualties on its first day alone—making it the bloodiest day in

THE BRITISH LOST 60,000 CASUALTIES ON THE FIRST DAY OF THE BATTLE OF THE SOMME, MAKING IT THE BLOODIEST SINGLE DAY IN THE HISTORY OF THE BRITISH ARMY. HERE, GERMAN SOLDIERS FIGHT BACK FROM THEIR STRONG DEFENSIVE POSITIONS.

Getty Images

the history of warfare—while ultimately costing a combined total of 1,265,000 French, British, and German dead and wounded.

Old ways of making war, especially the frontal assault, had come head to head with modern weapons, such as the rapid-firing machine gun (see "Weapons of the Land War," p. 254), the might of heavy artillery, poison gas, tanks, and air power. The commanders on both sides were discovering that the massive size of modern armies and the relatively small battlefield areas left almost no room to maneuver by attacking the enemy flanks.

Frontal assaults caused almost apocalyptically large casualty counts. Historian Dennis Showalter wrote that the killing came eventually to seem

(1,448 km) of trenches. However, with a larger territory within which to maneuver, the Germans outflanked the Russians in June 1915 and drove them out of Poland. Russia rebounded a year later with an offensive against Austria-Hungary, which successfully pushed the enemy back 50 miles (80 km) along a 250-mile (402 km) front. But the Russian army, plagued by poor morale, desertions, and a lack of supplies from the tottering tsarist government back home, was force to stop short of its goals.

Far from Europe, the Germans, French, and British fought over German possession in sub-Saharan Africa, while the British prevailed over Turkey's possessions in the Middle East, ultimately bringing down the old Ottoman Empire. On

The German announcement that it would begin unrestricted submarine warfare, combined with the British interception and decoding of the Zimmerman Telegram, prompted the United States to declare war in April 1917.

"mechanical," as if bodies were simply being fed to the engines of warfare. Digging deeper and deeper into the earth resulted in stalemate. When the allies attempted to break the stalemate by attacking the Turks in the Gallipoli Peninsula—hoping to gain a foothold in southeastern Europe and ultimately draw German troops away from the western front—it failed miserably.

The same stalemate happened on the eastern front as the Germans, Russians, and Austro-Hungarians fought each other along 900 miles

the high seas, Great Britain had imposed a successful blockade in the North Sea to keep all shipping away from Germany. From May 1–June 31, 1916, the naval clash many had predicted between the great dreadnought class battleships of Great Britain and Germany took place at the Battle of Jutland (see "The Sea War," p. 257). Both fleets fought to a draw, although the British were able to keep their supremacy in the North Sea.

By January 1917, the Germans had decided to resort to a policy of unrestricted U-boat warfare, sinking any ship of any country, merchantman or warship, that approached Great Britain's ports. It was thought that this policy would force Great Britain to sue for peace within five months. Instead, it helped bring the previously neutral United States into the war.

In 1915, the Germans had torpedoed the British ocean liner *Lusitania,* which carried on it 128 Americans. The United States had merely protested the incident. But the German announcement that it would began unrestricted submarine warfare, combined with the British interception and decoding of the Zimmerman Telegram (in which the German undersecretary of foreign affairs encouraged Mexico to declare war on the United States) caused the United States to declare war in April 1917. From the Allied point of view, it was just in time. British and French forces were exhausted by years of bloodshed, and the German blockade was taking its toll. The American Expeditionary Force of 500,000 men that arrived in France in June infused fresh strength into the British and French forces. The French in particular were exhausted, having lost hundreds of thousands of men in a failed spring offensive that had caused the troops to mutiny.

The Russian Revolution had caused the collapse of the Russian provisional government that October, and Austrian-German forces had defeated the Italians at the Battle of Caporetto, thus freeing Germans troops and resources for the western front. In the spring 1918, the Germans launched their massive, last-ditch Ludendorff Offensive, designed by Erich Ludendorff to force the British and French to the peace table before the Americans arrived in full force. However, the combined forces of the French, British, and, finally, the Americans were able to drive the Germans back.

In September, the allies launched the last major offensive of the war, fought mainly by U.S. forces in the Meuse-Argonne region of France. As they pushed the Germans farther and farther back, the Ottoman Empire sued for peace, as did Austria-Hungary. Fighting alone, the Germans finally agreed to an armistice as war-weary citizens revolted. Kaiser Wilhelm II abdicated on November 9, and an armistice was signed on November 11, 1918.

After World War I, the world felt enormous political changes. The Russian monarchy fell, the Ottoman Empire finally crumbled, and the Austro-Hungarian Empire was torn apart into numerous small states. The Treaty of Versailles, which ended the war, forced Germany to admit guilt for the war, give up 25,000 square miles (64,750 square kilometers) of territory, pay heavy reparations, and limit its army to 100,000 troops without heavy weapons, submarines, or airplanes. German anger over what it perceived as harsh conditions was a significant contributing factor to the beginning of World War II.

THE FIRST BATTLE OF MARNE: 1914

On the last day of August 1914, the citizens of Paris heard a low buzzing noise that sounded irritatingly like a bee trapped behind glass in summer's waning heat. The noise grew louder and louder. When they looked up in the sky, they saw a German bi-plane overflying the city. The plane circled ever lower and lower, insolently ignoring the few rifle shots loosed at it by soldiers racing to the roofs of buildings. When the plane arrived over the huge square called the Invalides Esplanade, it dropped a message tied to an iron rod, waggled its wings, and flew off at a leisurely pace.

The message read: "The German army will arrive in three days."

Almost no one in Paris doubted this. Already, all over the French countryside, the forces of the French and the British Expeditionary Force (BEF) were reeling back from a German onslaught that had swung five armies down through Belgium like "a great hour hand in counterclockwise motion," as one historian put it. At the very tip of the hour hand was the German First Army, north and west of Paris, racing to capture the city with the Second Army on its left, northeast of the city.

As the Germans advanced, the roads around the capital filled with retreating soldiers, still in their bright red and blue uniforms. But now, as no less an eminence than French Commander in Chief General Joseph Joffre noticed while inspecting his troops, the "red trousers had faded to the color of pale brick, coats were ragged and torn, shoes caked with mud, eyes cavernous in faces dulled by exhaustion …Twenty days of campaigning seemed to have aged the soldiers as many years."

"It Is the Thirty-Fifth Day!"

To be closer to the progress of the new war, Kaiser Wilhelm II had shifted his headquarters from Berlin to Luxembourg, some 170 miles (274 km) to the north of Paris. On September 4, he was exultant. "It is the thirty-fifth day," he told a delegation of German politicians. By this he meant that the German armies were in the middle of the period when the Schlieffen Plan called for a decisive battle for Paris. Thirty-one days would see the armies nearing the French capital, and this in fact was happening. By forty days, according to Schlieffen, there would be a battle to control the city.

The kaiser and most officers in the German high command followed the invasion schedule of Count Albert Graf von Schlieffen almost as if it were the Bible. The former chief of staff of the German army, von Schlieffen had essentially finished his plan by 1905 but kept tinkering with it until his death in 1913. It called for a blocking force of two German armies to be arrayed on Germany's western border with France, to ward off any attack, while five other armies would swing down through Belgium and into France, destroying the French army and capturing Paris within six weeks.

This timetable was important because Schlieffen had figured it would take forty days before the Russian army would be able to mount an offensive from the east, at which point Germany would be fighting the two-front war it dreaded. So taking Paris within this forty-day period was essential. But despite the headlong rush of the German troops to Paris, there were certain problems. To begin with, the Allied troops, while retreating, were retreating toward their supply lines, while the German troops were moving away from theirs. Second, the German soldiers were exhausted. A French prisoner later wrote that he had seen the German troops of General Alexander von Kluck, head of the First Army, which was supposed to capture Paris, reach the end of their ropes after a long march on September 3. "They fell down exhausted, muttering in a dazed way,

'Forty kilometers! Forty kilometers!' That was all they could say."

But finally, and most important, at the penultimate moment, the Germans decided to change the plan.

Changing the Plan

German Chief of Staff Helmuth von Moltke—who was with the kaiser in Belgium, directing the operation, but who might have been better served being far closer to the action—had already changed the Schlieffen Plan once, by weakening

A CHARGE OF FRENCH SOLDIERS AT THE BATTLE OF THE MARNE IN SEPTEMBER 1914. THE FRENCH FOUGHT AN EPIC BATTLE THAT WOULD FORCE A STALEMATE ON BOTH THE FRENCH AND THE GERMANS FOR THE REST OF THE WAR.

The Charge of French Soldiers at the Battle of the Marne, 8th or 9th September 1914, 1915 (oil on canvas), Chaperon, Eugene (b.1857) / Musee de l'Armee, Paris, France / Archives Charmet / The Bridgeman Art Library

his attacking forces to shore up Germany's border, which made progress through Belgium more slowly than von Schlieffen had intended. But now, almost miles away as the tactical situation was rapidly unfolding, von Moltke acquiesced to changing the plan again.

Kluck's First Army—exhausted but still moving with a will west of Paris—had seen the French Sixth Army under General Michel-Joseph Maunoury fall back to within 30 miles (48 km) of the capital. To the right of the French Sixth were the British Expeditionary Forces of General Sir John French, which had been defeated in several large battles and were falling back hastily. French, giving in to discouragement, thought the war lost. Three other French armies, badly beaten up but refusing to give in, were racing in from the east to help protect the capital city.

According to the Schlieffen Plan, the German army on the far west—Kluck's First Army— was to swing west of Paris before turning to take the city from the south. But on August 31, seeing the disarray of the forces facing him, Kluck thought he had a better idea. He radioed von Moltke that instead of attacking Paris, he wanted to wheel north of the capital to roll up what remained of Maunoury and French's forces and cut them off from Paris, as well as stop those French forces now arriving from the east. After this was accomplished, he could join with the German Second Army, under General Karl von Bülow, and attack the French capital and end the war in the west.

Von Moltke, who believed in giving his field commanders wide latitude, agreed to this plan, even though he and Kluck realized that it would leave the First Army's right flank exposed to the city. But, they decided, it didn't matter because the French were beaten anyway. What forces could possibly challenge the Germans?

"They Offer Us Their Flank!"

Von Moltke and Kluck hadn't counted on General Joseph Gallieni, military governor of Paris in its present emergency. Gallieni, born in 1849, had a background in France's colonial wars, much like General Joseph Joffre. In fact the two men were rivals, with Joffre more than a little envious of Gallieni's influence and the respect with which he was held by most officers in the French army. Gallieni was offered the commander in chief job, but he turned it down, citing ill health, and retired from the army in April 1914. Joffre brought him back and made him military governor of Paris as German forces threatened, which meant that Gallieni was in charge of any French forces defending the city.

Gallieni immediately set about building barricades and rifle pits and repairing old fortifications. He reorganized Maunoury's Sixth Army, reinforcing it with whatever troops he could lay his hands on. Gallieni—one of the few in the French army who then understood how important airplanes were for reconnaissance—sent his small fleet of biplanes out from the city, probing for the German forces. And by September 3, Gallieni had realized that Kluck's army was no longer heading west of the city, but was now north of Paris, moving east.

When this news set in, Gallieni and his officers stared at the huge map on the wall of his headquarters, the German advance marked with colored pins. "They offer us their flank!" Gallieni's chief of staff, General Clergerie, exclaimed. The Germans had placed no blocking force between them and the capital. They could be hit, and hit hard, on their vulnerable rear and sides while their attention was elsewhere.

Gallieni leaped at once into action. On his own responsibility, he ordered General Maunoury to prepare to attack. He then called Joffre and tried to convince him over the telephone of the importance of Kluck's exposed flanks and how the French must take advantage of it. Slow to move—and distrustful of his rival—Joffre said he would have to think about it.

Seeking support for such an attack, Gallieni got into his car and headed for BEF headquarters to confer with Sir John French, but French wasn't there and Gallieni found the British officers he talked to dispirited and defeatist in manner. They were suspicious of this voluble little man with spectacles, a shaggy moustache, and a rather messy uniform. "No British soldier would be seen speaking to such a comedian," one present said.

But the comedian would not give up, even as the forces of French and Joffre were retreating. Gallieni relentlessly pushed forth his arguments until Joffre abandoned his initial reluctance. Joffre even went to BEF headquarters to try to convince Sir John French, at one point grasping the English commander's hands and begging him to have his troops join in the attack. French was so moved that tears rolled down his cheeks. He tried to speak in French, but failed. "Damn it, I can't explain," he told an interpreter. "Tell him that all man can do our fellows will do." Joffre—who would henceforth take credit for Gallieni's ideas—then sent a telegram to the ministry of war in Paris: "The struggle which is about to take place may have decisive results. It may also, in the case of a reverse, have the gravest consequences for the country."

The Taxis of Paris

The British had fallen too far back to immediately take part in the attack, so it was up to the French. Joffre sent Maunoury and his Sixth Army forward, and advance elements of it made contact with the German First late on September 5. But an alert German corps commander put up a fierce resistance when he sensed the French counterattack, and the French stalled.

Kluck and von Moltke now began concerned about that flank exposed to Paris and decided to withdraw the First Army farther north, but it was too late. On the morning of September 6, the French Sixth Army hit them hard while the Fifth Army attacked the German Second Army under von Bülow. The French threw everything they had into the attack. Gallieni had scoured Paris for every last French soldier home on leave, every last reservist, every last malingerer. He found that a train carrying the North African 45th Algerian Division, still in their far-too-colorful Zouave uniforms, was headed east, and he commandeered it and brought it to Paris.

But Gallieni had no way to get these and other extra troops to the front, some 40 miles (64 km) distant, because trucks were in short supply and railroads hard pressed. It was then that Gallieni hit upon using Paris' taxicabs and their famously irascible drivers to transport the troops to the fighting that was raging as the Germans began to slowly withdraw to the River Marne north

and east of Paris. Gallieni sent troops out all over Paris to stop taxis, expel their protesting passengers, and tell them to gather at the Invalides Esplanade, the same place where the insolent biplane had dropped its insulting message.

Once there, Gallieni piled troops into them, five per cab, and sent them in a long procession to the front. When the drivers wanted to know who would pay them, Gallieni told them, "France will pay you!" and then jibed: "Are you afraid of gunfire?"

As the taxis left the square, hundreds of French civilians cheered. Only 6,000 French troops actually reached the battle in this way, not enough to materially affect its outcome, but the legend of the heroic taxis of Paris became a huge morale booster for France in the long war to come.

The Battle of the Marne

And the reason it *was* a long war to come—the reason why the war didn't end that hot early September—was because of the battle French and British troops fought for the next four days, one that Winston Churchill was to reference as one of the most important battles in the history of the world. The front line stretched 100 miles (161 km) from Verdun on the east to Paris on the west; most of the fighting raged around the River Marne and its tributaries. The area was a beautiful scene of streams, pastures, deep valleys, and wooded hills, although it was cut through east and north of Paris by the marshes of St. Gond, a wide swath of then nearly impassable swampland.

The Battle of the Marne was a series of fast, furious fights between forces that knew just how pivotal its outcome would be. The French knew that to lose the battle meant losing the war, while the Germans understood that any failure to take Paris would mean the failure of the Schlieffen Plan. As the Allied forces hit the German First and Second armies, a gap slowly widened between the German armies. The allies exploited that gap with attacks by French's BEF and General Ferdinand Foch's Ninth Army. Foch's army then withstood ferocious German counterattacks in the St. Gond marshes. The weather had turned from hot and sunny to cold and rainy, and the swamp became a horrible morass where wounded men drowned in shell holes while others fought hand to hand, knee deep in muck.

This was not the classic war of the trenches—that would soon start—but a more mobile war of attack and counterattack, of deadly skirmishes in woods and valleys, of bayonet attacks on farmhouse positions. Men on both sides were exhausted, using their last ounces of energy. A French officer described "men emaciated, in rags and tatters, most without haversacks, many without rifles, marching painfully, leaning on sticks…."

Yet the French held. Gradually realizing their position as untenable, the Germans withdrew to positions behind the River Aisne. They had sustained 250,000 casualties, the French about the same, while the BEF suffered about 12,000. But Paris was saved. Yet both Germans and Allies realized their northern flanks were not anchored. Now the race to the North Sea began, with the Germans seeking to turn the Allied flank and seize the channel ports and the allies fighting to keep them from doing so. Ten separate battles were fought throughout the fall of 1914, with neither side gaining the advantage, until a stalemate was reached, trenches were dug, and the war on the western front, as we know it, began.

Directly after the Battle of the Marne, General Helmuth von Moltke wrote his wife: "The appalling difficulties of our present situation hang before my eyes like a dark curtain through which I can see nothing." Within a few days, he had suffered a nervous breakdown, and he was relieved of command. On the face of it, the battle ended as a draw, but, in reality the failure of the German army to break through would set the stage for the long war of attrition that would eventually be won by the allies. In that sense, the Battle of the Marne was the battle that saved France, and the allies, from defeat.

MARSHALL HENRI-PHILIPPE PÉTAIN:
"ILS NE PASSERONT PAS!"

Following the career of Marshall Henri-Philippe Pétain is like watching the ups and downs of a roller coaster, because this most popular of French World War I generals would also become one of the most reviled politicians in France twenty years later.

When World War I began, Pétain was fifty-eight, only a colonel in charge of an infantry brigade. He was on his way to retirement, in part because he advocated a defensive war in the face of modern weapons, a stance at odds with prevailing wisdom. But Pétain's meticulous defensive arrangements and intuitive knowledge of how to use artillery against attacking forces was very much in demand after his performance at the First Battle of the Marne, which helped keep the German forces from taking Paris.

IN THIS PHOTO, FRENCH MARSHALL PÉTAIN, LEFT, STANDS NEXT TO AMERICAN GENERAL PERSHING. BOTH MEN WOULD PROVE THEMSELVES VALIANT MILITARY LEADERS.

George Grantham Bain Collection, Prints & Photographs Division, Library of Congress, LC-DIG-ggbain-28128

As 1916 began, Pétain was named commander of French forces holding the front south of Verdun as the Germans launched their massive attack. Unlike previous French commanders, Pétain knew how to hold the line during nine months of apocalyptic battle. He developed a system for rotating divisions in and out of the front lines without allowing those at rest to become combat-ineffective. He became extremely popular with the common soldiers and French people, as well, who thrilled to his refusal to retreat. *"Ils ne passeront pas!"* he said. "They will not pass."

And he meant it, finally succeeding in halting the German advance. However, when Marshall Joseph Joffre was relieved as commander of French forces, he was replaced not by Pétain, but by General Robert Nivelle, whose insistence on offensive attack, beginning with his ruinous offensive in April 1917, helped bring the French army to mutiny. Pétain replaced him, and in the ensuing months executed forty-nine mutinous French soldiers, but he also attempted to redress some of the wrongs inflicted on them. Pétain remained commander of French forces for the rest of the war and emerged as one of its premier heroes.

Unfortunately, his reputation was besmirched when he became head of the collaborationist Vichy government in France after the German takeover in 1940. He was condemned to death after the war, but his sentence was commuted to life imprisonment by Charles de Gaulle, who had served as a junior officer in Pétain's regiment in 1914.

GENERAL JOHN J. PERSHING:
"AS COOL AS A BOWL
OF CRACKED ICE"

Just as George Patton would become the United States' warrior general in World War II (see "World War II," p. 316), John J. Pershing was the country's fiercest soldier of World War I. Commander in chief of the U.S. forces that reached France in the summer of 1917, the fifty-seven-year-old general brought with him an impressive resume.

He had fought Apache and Sioux Indians in the American West with the black buffalo soldiers of the 10th Regiment (see "The Spanish–American War," p. 177), which is where he got his nickname "Black Jack." In 1898, when he went up the San Juan Heights with the same black troopers, a fellow officer said he looked "as cool as a bowl of cracked ice" leading his men against the withering fire of Spanish sharpshooters.

Following this came a tour fighting Moro rebels in the Philippines, then a fortunate marriage to Helen Frances Warren, daughter of the head of the Senate Military Affairs Committee. Along with Pershing's varied combat experience and friendship with then-president Theodore Roosevelt, this connection vaulted him from captain to brigadier general in the space of seven years. When World War I began—after a brief sortie invading Mexico in search of Pancho Villa (see "The Mexican Revolution," p. 212)—Pershing was the natural choice to lead the Americans "over there."

In France, Pershing refused to allow his soldiers to be combined with the French and British troops, insisting on a separate U.S. fighting force, despite heavy political pressure to do so.

In September 1918, he showed the mettle of U.S. troops by defeating the Germans in a massive attack against the St. Mihiel salient (a huge bulge in the French lines). However, the next month, during the Meuse-Argonne attack, Pershing's aggressive tactics cost American lives until he rallied his troops—relieving division commanders until he found the officers who would fight, no matter what the cost—and they prevailed.

Pershing became army chief of staff after the war and retired from active duty in 1924, having been named "General of the Armies," which was a title given to no one in United States' history except for George Washington.

QUARTERMASTER GENERAL ERICH LUDENDORFF: "AN INTERVAL BETWEEN WARS"

Born in 1865, Erich Ludendorff was Field Marshal Pavel von Hindenburg's chief of staff at the Battle of Tannenberg, but this title—as well as that of quartermaster general—obscures his true worth to the German army.

Ludendorff was bourgeoisie-born, not one of the noble "vons" who held most command positions in the German army prior to World War I. This had held him back in his career. As the war began, he was in his own particular version of Ulysses S. Grant's exile in Illinois (see "The U.S. Civil War," p. 116). Ludendorff had been assigned to command a regiment in the bleak industrial city of Düsseldorf. But through connections, he was able to acquire a deputy chief of staff job with the German Second Army, then attacking Brussels. Ludendorff was so energetic in pursuit of his duties that he was soon sent to join the German Eighth Army in East Prussia, where it would shortly face the invading Russians.

Here Ludendorff became chief of staff for Marshal Pavel von Hindenburg, and they proved the perfect pair. Hindenburg was a man of noble birth and sterling character, if not intellect. Ludendorff possessed a brilliant military mind, although he was perhaps too bluntly aggressive for his own good. He had once said that peace was merely "an interval between wars."

It was probably Ludendorff who came up with the plan for destroying the Russian Second Army

at Tannenberg (see "The Battle of Tannenberg," p. 260), but, in any event, both men became celebrated for Tannenberg and other eastern victories. Hindenburg became chief of the army, taking over from General Erich von Falkenhayn in 1916. In conjunction with Ludendorff, other generals, and prominent German civilian leaders, Hindenburg formed what was known as the "Third Supreme Council," which essentially took over the running of the country from the kaiser and the Reichstag until the end of the war.

With this kind of power behind him, Ludendorff was given free reign to try to bring about a breakthrough on the western front, but here his aggressiveness did him in. In the fall of 1917, after the Russians had sued for peace and the Italians were defeated at the Battle of Caporetto (see "Chronicle," p. 234), Ludendorff might have been able to find amicable grounds to convince the allies to make a treaty.

Instead, he launched his massive Ludendorff Offensive in the early spring of 1918, which achieved a 40-mile-deep (64 km) German breakthrough on the western front. The breakthrough ultimately stalled because of the lack of German supplies and reinforcements and because so many German soldiers were suffering from influenza (see "The Influenza Pandemic," p. 262).

In November, when the German government fell apart, Ludendorff fled to Sweden, where he

wrote numerous books and articles claiming that the German army had been betrayed by left-wing politicians. He returned to Germany in 1928 and became a front man for the Nazis, serving in the Reichstag and taking part in the Munich Putsch. Ludendorff died in 1937, still insisting that he had been betrayed, not by his own blind aggressiveness, but by faithless politicians.

FIELD MARSHAL SIR DOUGLAS HAIG: "A MUCH OVER-RATED WEAPON"

Douglas Haig, commander in chief of the British Expeditionary Force (BEF), is perhaps the most controversial of all World War I Allied generals. Was he a thoughtless and unimaginative leader who sent a generation of men marching off to slaughter at the Somme? Or was he a man who understood that only attrition would wear down his enemy?

Haig, born in 1861, studied at the Royal Military Academy at Sandhurst and then became a cavalry officer in India, rising through the ranks to take part in Lord Kitchener's campaign in the Sudan in 1897–1898 as well as the Second Boer War in 1899. When World War I started, he was a lieutenant general heading the First Army Corps in the BEF, which was then commanded by Sir John French. Haig performed admirably and was then chosen to replace French when the latter proved too dispirited by the slaughter taking place in the trenches.

Haig took over at the end of 1915, and the British government thought it had found its man. Haig, the ex-cavalryman, believed in going on the offensive—using "hurricane" artillery bombardments followed by massive attacks to break through enemy lines. Haig did not really understand modern firepower and, in fact, went on record saying: "The machine gun is a much overrated weapon," even as thousands of British troops were being mowed down by that deadly gun.

In the Battle of the Somme, which kicked off on July 1, 1916, Haig had a chance to put his theories into action. He blew up ten giant mines under German positions, followed it up with a massive artillery barrage, and then sent hundreds of thousands of British troops straight at German lines. The plan was to have them punch a hole in enemy lines, a breakthrough that would then be exploited by cavalry.

More than 57,000 British troops were killed or wounded on that day, the greatest number of single-day casualties in history. No breakthrough was achieved. By the battle's end (some six months later), more than 1 million men would die or be wounded. Haig, throughout the war, kept looking for the giant breakthrough battle, but he failed to find it. (To be fair, so did Erich Ludendorff.) While Haig never fully understood that a cavalryman's mobility was not what was called for in this new war, he was stubborn enough to keep wearing away at the Germans. He knew that ultimately, if it came down to a war of attrition, his enemies must lose.

A PORTRAIT OF FIELD MARSHAL SIR DOUGLAS HAIG, ONE OF THE MOST CONTROVERSIAL ALLIED FIGURES OF WORLD WAR I.

Field Marshal Earl Haig of Bemersyde, copy after Sir James Guthrie (1859-1930), Anderson, J.B.A. (19th century) / The Crown Estate, / The Bridgeman Art Library

The Allied Soldier

THE BRITISH SOLDIER

At the beginning of the war, Britain depended on an all-volunteer army raised by such famous recruiting techniques as the poster showing the stern visage of Secretary of War Lord Herbert Kitchener pointing a finger and declaring: "Britons: Lord Kitchener Wants You! Join Your Country's Army!"

But because of the extraordinary British losses, England was forced to turn to a conscription system by early 1916, in which all men between eighteen and forty-one were required to join the army. The British soldier was nicknamed "Tommy." The name's origins are nebulous, but it's believed to have been used as early as the eighteenth century, deriving from "Thomas Atkins," a sort of "John Doe" name signed for illiterate British soldiers and later popularized the world over by the poems of Rudyard Kipling. The Tommy carried his SMLE—Short

Magazine Enfield Rifle, or "Smiley"— the beloved gun of the British infantry, shooting a .303 caliber bullet with a ten-shot magazine and a smooth bolt-action. Experienced British infantry shooting Enfields could put out such a rapid rate of fire that opposing Germans thought they were facing machine guns.

The morale of the Tommy was generally good during the early stages of the war. But devastating and poorly handled battles such as the Somme caused thousands of soldiers to lose faith in their senior officers. By the time the Americans arrived in 1917, British armies were tottering on their last legs. The British in the First World War suffered the second highest rate of shell shock, or combat fatigue, among soldiers. (Germany had the highest incidence.) After the war, 15 percent of British soldiers on disability pay from the government (about 120,000 men) received such checks because of psychiatric problems caused by combat. In 1924, four years after the war had ended, about 6,000 British veterans of the western front were in insane asylums.

THE FRENCH SOLDIER

The French started 1914 with 3.7 million men in uniform, who were poorly prepared for the war that was to come. Their officers tended to be overage men who had fought in colonial wars of the nineteenth century and who taught infantry tactics that focused on bayonet attacks involving dense columns of men who wore brightly colored red and blue uniforms. By the end of the fall campaigns in 1914, 600,000 French troops would be dead. It was such an appalling number that the French were forced to begin conscription of men up to the age of forty-five. The French also got rid of their colorful uniforms, changing to gray-blue (supposedly the "blue of the horizon"). They were the last army to do so. (The British wore brown, the Germans gray-green, the Americans khaki, and the Russians olive-green.)

The French soldier, or *poilu* (a French term of endearment dating back to the Napoleonic Wars, which meant "hairy one," because so many French soldiers had moustaches or beards) carried the Lebel 8mm rifle, which fired smokeless cartridges with an effective range of up to 1,000 yards (914 m). But the Lebel had one major design flaw. The cartridge magazine was a long tube into which bullets had to be loaded nose to nose, after which the tube was placed under the barrel of the rifle. This highly cumbersome process could be dangerous if one bullet hit the primer of the bullet in front of it, causing an explosion.

THE BRITISH SOLDIER, OR "TOMMY," ENJOYED HIGH MORALE DURING THE FIRST YEARS OF THE WAR, BUT DEVASTATING LOSSES CAUSED THE MEN TO SUFFER THE SECOND HIGHEST RATE OF "SHELL-SHOCK" AMONG ALL SOLDIERS DURING WORLD WAR I.

British Infantry Charge near Ypres in 1915 (litho), English School, (20th century) / Private Collection, The Stapleton Collection / The Bridgeman Art Library

FRENCH *POILU,* SEEN HERE WITH A
HEAVY MACHINE GUN.
Getty Images

The French fought bravely throughout the war, but massive losses at Verdun and other battles caused a major mutiny in May 1917. (Out of a total population of 20 million, 1,300,000 Frenchman would become casualties.) As many as 30,000 soldiers refused to obey orders to go to the front. Henri-Philippe Pétain was brought in to restore order and after almost 4,000 court-martials and some fifty-five executions—as well as assurances that he would no longer spend blood as freely as French generals had in the past—the mutiny was over.

The U.S. Soldier

Americans were reluctant to get involved in World War I, but once they did, they did so with a will. Two million Americans would ultimately serve in France. They were known as "doughboys," a term whose derivation is obscure. It dates back to the nineteenth century and may have been a pejorative reference to the number of young baker's apprentices who went to war and who were thought to be quite dull. By the time

of the First World War, however, it was a friendly term applied both to and by the U.S. soldiers.

Well supplied, well fed, energetic, and young (the average U.S. soldier was nineteen years old, younger than most of the British and French fighting on the front), the doughboy was a welcome addition to the Allied war effort. His weapon of choice was the Springfield Model 1903, a bolt-action, smokeless powder rifle with a five-round magazine modeled after the Mauser rifles that had so bedeviled the U.S. soldiers in Cuba during the Spanish–American War. Some Americans carried the Enfield Model 1917, based on the British rifle, which was a heavier rifle than the Springfield,

A WORLD WAR I POSTER PROMOTING
AMERICAN MEN TO JOIN THE CAUSE.
THE UNITED STATES WAS AT FIRST
RELUCTANT TO GET INVOLVED, BUT
ONCE COMMITTED, PROVED TO BE AN
INVALUABLE ASSET TO THE ALLIED WAR
EFFORT.

'Be A US Marine', 1st World War poster (colour litho),
American School, (20th century) / Private Collection,
Peter Newark Pictures / The Bridgeman Art Library

but it was extremely rugged under combat conditions.

U.S. casualties in the war were a good deal less than those of the other Allied countries (116,000 dead, compared to more than 800,000 for the British, 1,300,000 for the French, and 1,800,000 for the Russians), but they fought for only a little over a year, so these casualties do represent a fairly high proportion of soldiers committed to combat. The casualty rate reflects the U.S. inexperience in the war, as well as General John J. Pershing's determination to attack. But gradually the doughboys learned how to proceed in trench warfare, and they can be seen as the deciding force that forced the Germans to sign the armistice.

SUFFERING FROM A LACK OF EDUCATION, INSUFFICIENT SUPPLIES, AND POOR LEADERSHIP, THE 4.5 MILLION RUSSIAN SOLDIERS QUICKLY LOST MORALE.

Russians cheering King George: Infantry of our gallant Allies honouring this country and its Ruler, from 'The Illustrated War News' (b/w photo), Russian Photographer, (20th century) / Private Collection, The Stapleton Collection / The Bridgeman Art Library

THE RUSSIAN SOLDIER

Within a week after the war started, the Russians had 4.5 million men in the field ready to fight the Germans and Austro-Hungarians. However, the problems of the Russian soldier varied little from those he had experienced in the Russo-Japanese War and even the Crimean War. The average Russian infantryman was a poorly educated peasant led by a poorly trained aristocratic officer.

Supply problems bedeviled the Russian infantry to a far greater extent than they had in previous wars. In some divisions in the battle on the eastern front in 1916, only 30 percent of soldiers had rifles. They were simply expected to trail along into battle and pick up weapons from those who died around them. As political unrest continued at home, Russian soldiers mutinied, deserting by the thousands.

By 1917, the Russian officer corps was severely demoralized by their losses and by the desertions among the troops. Russian industry, crippled by a lack of men and material, was no longer able to manufacture small arms and ammunition in large enough quantities. Russia was ultimately forced to sign a separate peace with Germany and Austria at Brest-Litovsk in the fall of 1918.

Central Powers

THE GERMAN SOLDIER

The Germany army in World War I was the most battle-ready in Europe. Within a week of war having been declared, the German government was able to put 3.8 million men into the field. Although this was not as many as the Russians, the German soldiers reserve training was a part of their civilian life, and they were far better supplied, led, and motivated.

The German soldier marched off to war wearing his distinctive spiked helmet, known as the *Pickelhaube,* which had been worn since the nineteenth century. (The little spike on top was removed in combat, because it made a distinctive target for snipers.) But it turned out that the leather Pickelhaube did not protect against concussive shock from the heavy artillery fire German soldiers in the

trenches experienced, and so it was saved for ceremonial occasions and replaced by the steel helmet that German soldiers would wear into World War II. The Germans had a superior rifle, the 7.92mm Mauser Gewehr, which fired accurately and rapidly. Its only drawback was a five-shot magazine, which meant it had to be reloaded often.

THE GERMAN SOLDIER, SEEN HERE IN THE TRENCHES, WAS THE MOST READY AND ABLE SOLDIER TO INITIALLY ENTER WORLD WAR I.

Prints & Photographs Division, Library of Congress, LC-USZ62-98186

Even so, the German army was by far the best equipped for the new type of warfare, with many more machine guns than either the French or British, and with far superior defensive strategies. As the war went on, the Germans pioneered "defense in depth," which were nearly impregnable trench systems with bunkers 30 feet (9 m) deep, interlocking fields of fire, and second and third defensive lines set back well away from the front. It was this type of system that the British and French ran into at the Battle of the Somme, and which caused so many Allied casualties.

Finally, the weight of fighting a massive war nearly on its own caused the Germans to surrender, but many German soldiers felt that they had not been defeated on the field—that they had been betrayed by politicians back home. Even though the German war dead accounted for 52 percent of all deaths among the Central Power countries and German casualties surpassed those of any country in World War I, with an incredible 6,300,000, they were ready to fight on.

THE AUSTRO-HUNGARIAN SOLDIER

Like the Russian soldiers it so often faced, the Austro-Hungarian army of World War I was not well supplied and well fed. Like the Russians, the Austro-Hungarians had internal problems. Many of its soldiers were conscripts from Austria's various Slavic countries and would often refuse to follow orders from the Austrian officers, especially after suffering huge losses in the first year of the war. These losses were in part because the Austrians had underestimated the toughness and durability of the Serbian forces they were fighting after a Serbian nationalist assassinated Austrian Archduke Franz Ferdinand.

The main weapon of the Austro-Hungarian soldier was the Steyr-Mannlicher, a durable rifle, although not one that fired rapidly. However, it was produced in large quantities and hardly ever broke down. After the war, it became the main weapon for many years of the Italian army, because so many were taken as war reparations from the Austro-Hungarians.

In an offensive launched in 1916 by Russian forces, Austrians were pushed back all along the borders of Galicia and Transylvania. It was soon apparent that the empire, suffering from explosive political difficulties and supply problems, was moribund. As one German officer said at the time: "We are shackled to a corpse."

LIKE THE RUSSIANS WHOM THEY WERE FIGHTING AGAINST, THE AUSTRO-HUNGARIANS SUFFERED FROM MANY INTERNAL PROBLEMS—POOR FOOD AND SUPPLY SYSTEMS AND A CONSCRIPTED ARMY THAT OFTEN TIMES REFUSED TO FIGHT AFTER A STRING OF LOSSES.

Getty Images

Weapons of the Land War

THE MACHINE GUN

The machine gun, after trial runs in the Civil War, the Franco-Prussian War, and the Russo-Japanese War, had at last come of age in World War I. What a murderous coming of age it was.

Different countries used different versions of this rapid-firing automatic weapon. The French employed the Hotchkiss, the Americans used the Lewis or the Browning, and the Germans fired the Maxim. Typically, the German were the first to appreciate the full uses of the machine gun, beginning the war with 12,000 of the guns (rising by war's end to 100,000) while the French and British had only a few hundred at first. (Inventor Hiram Maxim first offered his water-cooled Maxim machine gun to the British government. But it was rejected by some British officers as being an "immoral" weapon of war.)

Unlike the light machine guns that would follow in World War II, most machine guns of the First World War were cumbersome and needed to be manned by crews of four or five. The machine guns were water-cooled, meaning water was recycled through the barrels to keep them from overheating. They needed large quantities of water, which was often impracticable under combat conditions. Later in the war, they were mainly replaced by the air-cooled variety. Machine guns were considered roughly the equivalent of eighty rapid-firing rifles. Under optimal conditions, the machine guns of the First World War could fire perhaps 300 rounds per minute.

Both sides learned to use this weapon as the chief defensive tool to break up massed infantry attacks. Machine gun companies were formed that set up positions containing several guns with interlocking fields of fire, which proved murderous to attackers. Entire lines of assaulting infantry would be scythed down in seconds by heavy automatic fire whose sound was invariably described as that of "hammering." It was a sound dreaded by all those who heard it.

ARTILLERY

"The war of 1914–1918 was an artillery war," historian John Terrain wrote "Artillery was the battle-winner, artillery was what caused the greatest loss of life, the most dreadful wounds, and the deepest fear."

The long-range artillery gun was not a new innovation. Large guns and howitzers had been pounding enemy emplacements at great distance since the Franco-Prussian War. But the stalemate caused by the trench system caused commanders to seek out heavier and heavier weapons with which to attack soldiers dug into trench systems and hiding in bunkers. Howitzers were developed that could hurl heavy shells 15 miles (24 km) or more, screaming across the front with the sound of rushing freight trains. Mortars lobbed shells on high trajectories to land in trenches, and the 75mm guns barked away at infantry attacks, recoiling sharply on their gun carriages.

GERMAN SOLDIERS GATHER WATER FOR THEIR MACHINE GUN. THE MACHINE GUNS EARLY ON IN THE WAR REQUIRED LARGE QUANTITIES OF WATER TO BE RECYCLED THROUGH THE BARREL IN ORDER TO KEEP THEM FROM OVERHEATING.

Getty Images

Germany had the heaviest guns—150mm to 255mm—while the French and British used 75mm to 105mm, which were more transportable. Artillery constantly ranged through enemy lines and behind, even when no attack was being made. Bombardments could be the most horrifying experiences a soldier would ever have. The feeling of lying helpless under heavy fire by high explosive shells drove many of those men who managed to survive mad, hence the term "shell shock."

However, sometimes even artillery failed. To "soften" up the enemy prior to the attack on the first day of the Battle of the Somme, the British used 1,000 pieces of artillery to fire some 3 million shells. However, the weakness of artillery bombardment was evident here, because the Germans had dug themselves into 30-foot (9 m) dugouts that sheltered them from the massive British bombardment. When it was over, they climbed from their holes, manned their machine guns, and cut down the oncoming British forces. In this case, the British high command placed to too much value on its big guns and lifted their fire too soon. To make matters worse, they failed to prepare the battlefield properly by cutting the barbed wire that the British troops became hung up on.

Still, artillery was to prove the greatest killer in the war. It was the reason such a high percentage of the dead could not be located and buried. (Seventy thousand British soldiers are "missing" from the Battle of the Somme alone.) They were simply blown to pieces.

THE TANK

Interestingly enough, the classic land vehicle first belonged to the British navy, which had developed an armored car (at the behest of the imaginative Winston Churchill, first lord of the admiralty) that saw action in Belgium in August 1914. The first tank—called a landship—was developed into a working model in December 1915 and introduced into action with the British Fourth Army on September 15, 1916. The British attacked with fifty of these strange-looking creations, which were oblong, had giant treads, and could only travel at about 4 miles (6 km) an hour. The so-called "male" tanks had a cannon that could fire a six-pound shell; the "female" ones only machine guns.

At the Somme, the tank attack initially terrified the Germans and achieved some success, but the Germans soon learned that these behemoths were vulnerable to artillery fire and mechanical breakdown. However, new and improved tanks were introduced later in the war, most dramatically in a massed British attack at Cambrai in November 1917, which punched a hole 7 miles (11 km) wide in German defenses. Although tanks were ultimately not a decisive factor in World War I, they would become the most important land weapon in World War II.

THE TANK, FIRST CALLED A LANDSHIP, WAS INITIALLY DEVELOPED BY THE BRITISH NAVY UNDER THE DIRECTION OF WINSTON CHURCHILL. TRAVELLING JUST FOUR MILES PER HOUR, IT OFTEN SUFFERED MECHANICAL BREAKDOWNS AND FELL PREY TO HEAVY ARTILLERY FIRE.

Tanks, Somme (w/c), Handley-Read, Captain Edward Henry (1869-1935) / Topham Picture Source, Edenbridge, Kent, UK, / The Bridgeman Art Library

Poison Gas

The Germans first used poison gas in October 1914 in an attack against the French, but the quantities were so small that the French did not even notice it. The Germans then tried tear gas on the Russian front in January 1915, but the low temperatures there froze it. It was not until April 1915, at the Second Battle of Ypres, that the Germans unleashed chlorine gas in massive quantities. They had experimented with putting the gas into shells fired from artillery, but this did not work well, and so they chose pressured cylinders from which to spread the gas.

The trick was to wait for a favorable wind, and at Ypres, on April 22, the Germans had one. Six-thousand cylinders released 160 tons (145,149 kg) of gas in the direction of the French and Algerian troops opposite the German lines. At first, the French were simply puzzled by the gray-green cloud they saw floating toward them, but then the gas—which kills by causing fluid to be produced in the lungs, essentially drowning its victims—hit them. Thousands of men died, choking, while thousands of others raced for the rear. Unfortunately, from the German point of view, they did not have large enough stockpiles of gas on hand to cause a breakthrough.

After this, both sides began using gas, but both Germans and allies switched to mustard gas. Although it was generally disabling (it blinded and could cause permanent respiratory damage), it was not as deadly as chlorine gas, it could be fired by shell, and it lingered in low-lying areas, which could pollute an enemy's trenches and supply dumps for some time. Gas masks were developed to ward off the agent, which were generally effective, but gas was to cause hundreds of thousands of casualties during the war, as well as lingering health problems for veterans afterward.

Despite its use by both sides, all combatants dreaded poison gas, and it was banned internationally in 1925.

THE GERMANS WERE THE FIRST TO EXPERIMENT WITH GASES, TRYING TEAR AND CHLORINE GAS BEFORE SETTLING ON MUSTARD GAS THAT BOTH BLINDED AND CAUSED RESPIRATORY DAMAGE. GAS MASKS WERE DEVELOPED, ABOVE, AND WERE GENERALLY EFFECTIVE, HOW-EVER, HUNDREDS OF THOUSANDS OF LIVES WOULD BE LOST TO THE POISON-OUS GASES DURING THE WAR.

Getty Images

The Sea War

The Germans and British had been at pains to develop bigger and better battleships for some time. These were known as dreadnoughts, after the HMS *Dreadnought,* built in 1906, which outclassed every ship on the high seas at the time. This naval arms race contributed greatly to tensions between Great Britain and Germany, particularly because it was known that developing the finest naval fleet in the world was an obsession with Kaiser Wilhelm II. At the beginning of the war, both nations had fleets that contained heavily armored battleships—now in what was called the "super-dread-nought" class—which were studded with 12- or 15-inch (30 or 38 cm) guns that could fire heavy shells at a distance of 17,000 yards (16 km).

The question was what to do with them? The naval arms race had been predicated on the theory that the very heart of a modern nation's defense was a strong navy. But World War I, with its massive land battles, wasn't turning out quite that way. The German High Seas Fleet was from the first bottled up in the North Sea by Great Britain's Grand Fleet. The British had the greater number of dreadnoughts, which meant they would almost certainly win any large scale battle between the two fleets, so the Germans hoped to lure the English into minefields or actions in which the ships could be destroyed piecemeal.

The first two years of the war were a stalemate (helped in part because the British were reading the German naval code and hence knew their plans). But in 1916, the two mighty fleets finally clashed in the Battle of Jutland, which was the only battle ever fought between dreadnoughts in the First World War. On May 31, a British naval group made contact at about 3:30 in the afternoon with part of the German fleet and engaged in a running gun battle with it. The clash brought in the main German fleet, which chased the British ships, inflicting serious damage and sinking two ships. But now the main British fleet was brought into the battle. By 6 p.m., the first and only struggle between dreadnoughts occurred, with the British losing three battle cruisers, but with the Germans eventually withdrawing. It turned out to be a tactical draw, although the fact that the British fleet continued to control the North Sea gave it the ultimate victory.

To the surprise of both sides, the most influential naval weapon of the First World War turned out to be the submarine. Submarines had been around, in theory, for centuries, with crude ones in use as far back as the American Revolution, but the first fully functioning submarine, one that could dive, cruise on the surface with diesel engines, and fire torpedoes, was invented by an Irish-American named J.P. Holland in 1901. It was quickly seized upon by the navies of the world. At the beginning of World War I, the British and French had the largest fleets of submarines, totaling some 300 boats, while the Germans had only twenty-nine U-boats (*Unterseeboots)*. But the Germans

BOTH BRITAIN AND GERMANY HAD FLEETS OF ARMORED BATTLE SHIPS OF THE SUPER-DREADNOUGHT CLASS, ONE SUCH IS SEEN HERE.

would build 390 U-boats during the course of the war, and they were by far the most effective practitioners of undersea warfare.

At the beginning of the war, German U-boat commanders would warn merchant ships before they sank them, allowing their crews to abandon ship, but as the war turned more deadly, this was abandoned. Not only that, but Germans, as they blockaded England, began to practice "unrestricted" submarine warfare, which meant they torpedoed any ship, civilian or military, approaching British ports. This was highly effective for blockading purposes, but it had a highly negative impact on the German war effort, because it helped bring the United States.

The Air War

The first military use of aviation came during the French Revolutionary Wars when the French used observation balloons to spy on the Austrians. The balloon had been used for observation in numerous wars since that time. But in 1900, Count Ferdinand von Zeppelin developed the "guided rigid airship"—in other words, a dirigible powered mechanically, which one could use for purposeful reconnaissance. After the Wright brothers developed the fixed-wing aircraft in 1903, the sky could bristle with weapons.

At the beginning of the war, the French, British, and Germans all had military air commands whose fixed bi-wing aircraft were used mainly for reconnaissance. Soon, however, the crews of these airplanes began to shoot at each other (in one case, throw bricks), and they were soon equipped with machine guns.

German aircraft designer Anthony Fokker developed "interrupter" gear, so that machine guns could fire through the plane's propeller. This gave the Germans, at first, a great advantage over British and French aircraft, whose guns were perched atop their bi-wings or fired by gunners in rear seats. Soon however, planes such as the Sopwith Camel and Spad 13 evened the playing field, and the era of the great aces began. Flyers such as Manfred von Richthofen (the Red Baron), Ernst Udet, René Fonck, William Bishop, and Eddie Rickenbacker, captured the public imagination as they led squadrons into aerial battle over the western front.

Because fixed-wing aircraft at the time were relatively small, long-range German bombing raids at the beginning of the war were carried out by zeppelins, which had top speeds of more than 100 miles (161 km) an hour and could drop 4,000 pounds (1,814 kg) worth of bombs. The first zeppelin raid on London in May 1915 killed twenty-eight people. Subsequent attacks killed as many as 600 British, but the zeppelin proved too vulnerable to British fighters and anti-aircraft attack, and so the German High Command stopped such attacks in 1917, after losing seventy-seven zeppelins. King George V refused to evacuate during these raids, despite being urged to do so by advisors, setting an example that inspired the British people, who would in just over twenty years endure far worse bombings.

IN THE PAST, WARFARE HAD SEEN ITS BATTLES ON LAND AND ON SEA, BUT NOW, WITH THE WRIGHT BROTHERS' INVENTION OF THE FIXED-WING AIRCRAFT IN 1903, THE BATTLES WOULD TAKE TO THE SKY.

Royal Aircraft Factory SE5, single seater with Vickers and Lewis gun, powered by Hispano-Suiza, 1914-18, Withams, B. (20th century) / Private Collection, / The Bridgeman Art Library

Life in the Suicide Ditch

The trench—the "suicide ditch" as frontline British soldiers called it—is the symbol of World War I on the western front, the place where soldiers on both sides lived in the mud, the holes in the ground from which they went "over the top," often to die.

Facing each other over a no-man's-land that averaged about 200 yards (183 m) across, but sometimes could be as small as 50 feet (15 m)—the trenches snaked across Europe from Switzerland to the North Sea. Perhaps 12,000 miles (19,312 km) of trenches were dug in total on the western front. Some were elaborate affairs. The German trenches later in the war were deep, interlocking tunnels dotted with reinforced concrete pillboxes, but many were merely shallow depressions in the earth. However, most trenches were part of a system. The front line trench, with its wooden firing step built in, from which the troops could shoot their enemy, was backed up by supply trenches further in the rear, and they were all connected by communications trenches.

The purpose of all the trenches, of course, was to hide from the overwhelming artillery fire that rained down upon both sides. In between shellings and attacks, soldiers followed highly unpleasant daily routines, which included delousing each other with candles, treating their "trench" or immersion foot, which was a serious disease caused by prolonged exposure to the puddles that inevitably formed in the bottom of the trenches, and peering at the other side through periscopes—sticking one's head up inevitably invited a sniper's bullet. At night, no-man's-land was alive with scouting parties, each out to seek information and capture prisoners.

Everywhere, the constant companion of the living was the dead. Left in no-man's-land, because to remove them was generally too dangerous, the dead became part of the landscape. British officer Edwin Vaughan wrote in his diaries about sitting in his trench staring at a corpse: "He had a diamond-shaped hole in his forehead through which a little pouch of brains was hanging, and his eyes were hanging down. He was very horrible, but I soon got used to him."

PICTURED HERE ARE BRITISH SOLDIERS IN THEIR TRENCHES. THE TRENCH WAS OFTEN CALLED THE "SUICIDE DITCH" AND IT BECAME A SYMBOL OF WORLD WAR I ON THE WESTERN FRONT.

Prints & Photographs Division, Library of Congress, LC-USZ62-75152

The Battle of Tannenberg: Horror on the Eastern Front

Tsar Nicholas II called it "a great calamity," and so it was—although for the Germans it was their most complete and decisive victory of the war, the victory that would elude them on the western front after the First Battle of the Marne (see "Turning Point," p. 238). Yet, it almost certainly should have turned out the other way.

When the Germans committed most of their forces to attacking Belgium and France, they had only one army group, the Eighth Army, left behind to guard East Prussia. The Eighth Army was outnumbered by the two Russian army groups that faced it. Thus, as the Russians invaded Prussia in August 1914, it should have been easy for their First and Second armies to simply grab the German Eighth Army in a pincer movement and squeeze it to death. But the Russian commanders, General Rennenkampf of the First Army and General Samsonov of the Second, disliked each other powerfully, ever since Samsonov complained that Rennenkampf had not supported his division at the Battle of Mukden in 1905. In fact, the two men had come to blows over the incident.

This old grudge was to cost the Russians dearly, but at first didn't matter because the two armies advanced on separate wings, probing for the German flanks as the Germans retreated. But then the German Eighth Army commander was replaced by Field Marshall Pavel von Hindenburg, called out of retirement for the occasion, who brought along with him his chief of staff, General Erich Ludendorff.

These two men, particularly Ludendorff, changed the tide of history (see "Commanders," p. 246). Through superior intelligence the German generals realized that the two Russian armies, whose commanders were not communicating with each other, had drifted further apart than each apparently knew. Therefore Hindenburg and Ludendorff turned their forces on Samsonov's army alone, enveloped it, and destroyed it during two days at the end of August, while Rennenkampf, still nursing his old grudge, made no move to come to the Second Army's aid.

Ninety-five thousand Russians were captured, 50,000 were killed or wounded, and perhaps 10,000 escaped. Samsonov, unable to face the tsar, shot himself. Hindenburg and Ludendorff would then go on to push Rennenkampf's army back into Russia. The ultimate effect of the battle—what has been called the most complete German victory of the war—was to allow the Germans to concentrate on the western front, knowing that they faced no serious threat from the east. For the Russians, defeat at Tannenberg helped spell the demise of the tsarist government, which had pinned its hopes for survival on victory against Germany.

THE BATTLE OF TANNENBERG WOULD BE GERMANY'S RESOUNDING VICTORY ON THE EASTERN FRONT, PROVING ITS MILITARY EXPERTISE. IT WOULD BE QUITE THE OPPOSITE FOR THE RUSSIANS, WITH 50,000 WOUNDED OR KILLED AND 95,000 CAPTURED (PICTURED HERE).

Getty Images

Lawrence of Arabia: "The Nature and Power"

"Some Englishmen...believed that a rebellion of Arabs against Turks, would enable England, while fighting Germany, simultaneously to defeat Turkey. Their knowledge of the nature and power and country of the Arabic-speaking peoples made them think that the issue of such a rebellion would be happy, and indicated its character and method.

So they allowed it to begin...."

These laconic lines—brilliantly understated and ironic—are from the introduction of T.E. Lawrence's classic autobiography *The Seven Pillars of Wisdom*. They set the scene for his depiction of one of the most glorious and romantic, although ultimately tragic, episodes of World War I. Lawrence— soon to be known to the world as Lawrence of Arabia—was born illegitimate in 1888 to an Anglo-Irish baronet who had an affair with a nursemaid for whom he left his wife. Lawrence was educated at Oxford and traveled during his undergraduate years in the Middle East. (His thesis was on crusader castles.) When the war came, Lawrence was enlisted into the British Army's Arab Intelligence bureau in Cairo, and he was eventually sent to forge a military alliance with Hussein, the sharif of Mecca and Medina, the Muslims' most holy places.

As Lawrence wrote in Seven Pillars, the British encouraged Arab revolt to weaken the Ottoman Empire, one of the Central Powers. Lawrence joined with Hussein's son Faisal in a series of attacks with desert Bedouins against Turkish trains and supply routes, with Lawrence arming the Arabs with British munitions. Lawrence and Faisal's most notable achievements were the conquest of Aqaba, in modern day Jordan, in 1917, and the capture of Damascus in 1918.

The Middle East was still an obscure theater of a very big war, and Lawrence might have remained unnoticed, but his exploits were captured on film and publicized by American journalist Lowell Thomas. Lawrence, who had become a passionate believer in Arab self-government, was made famous throughout the world as Lawrence of Arabia.

Lawrence, a complicated man who struggled with homoerotic desires and who may have been raped by a Turkish commander when captured during the war, was extremely disappointed by the betrayal by the British of the Arab cause for independence. After unsuccessfully representing Arab interests at the Versailles peace conference, he tried to disappear from view, disguising himself under two different names as he enlisted first in the Royal Air Force, and then in the Royal Tank Corps. He died in a motorcycle accident in Dorset, aged forty-six, in 1934.

IT WAS DURING HIS UNDERGRADUATE CAREER AT OXFORD, DURING WHICH TIME HE TRAVELLED EXTENSIVELY THROUGOUT THE MIDDLE EAST, THAT T.E. LAWRENCE DEVELOPED A LOYALTY AND UNDERSTANDING FOR THE PEOPLE THERE. AFTER BEING ENLISTED IN THE BRITISH ARMY'S ARAB INTELLIGENCE BUREAU IN CAIRO, HE HAD THE OPPORTUNITY TO AID THEM AND LEAD THE ARAB REVOLT AGAINST THE TURKS.

"The Yanks Are Coming!" The United States in World War I

When President Woodrow Wilson was elected to a second term of office in 1916, his successful slogan was: "He kept us out of war." That, in any event, was Wilson's hope. Wilson was a decidedly unsentimental man who rejected the calls of many Americans to aid the British and French in their war and who tried to bring the Great Powers to the mediation table prior to 1917.

Wilson hoped that the vast Atlantic Ocean would keep the United States distant from the conflict, but in fact, the Atlantic brought the war to U.S. shores when a German U-boat torpedoed the passenger liner *Lusitania* in 1915, with the loss of more than one hundred American lives. The Germans apologized for this, but later declared that they would resume "unrestricted" submarine warfare in their attempts to blockade Great Britain, which meant that U.S. merchant ships and passenger liners were in serious danger. When the British turned over to the U.S. government an intercepted telegram in which the Germans urged that Mexico go to war against the United States to recover territory lost in the Mexican–American War, even Wilson had had enough. At his urging, the United States declared war in April 1917.

As the Japanese would learn in World War II, the might of the industrial United States was overwhelming. By war's end, 2 million Yankee "doughboys" (see "The Allied Soldier," p. 250) were serving in France, tons of badly needed supplies had poured in, and the powerful U.S. Navy, with five dreadnoughts, spelled the end of any German hopes of survival on the high seas. Although Americans had initially favored staying out of the conflict, they went to war with will and enthusiasm, with massive recruiting campaigns, Broadway musicals, and popular songs.

Could the allies have won World War I without the Americans? While the brash Yankees didn't like to think so, the British and French probably could have, but it would have taken a good deal longer without the infusion of fresh energy, men, and material the Americans provided.

The Influenza Pandemic: God's Judgment

In June 1918, when the Germans tried to advance across France in the latest in a series of spring offensives, the French and Americans counterattacked and quickly brought them to a halt—far too quickly to the minds of most veteran observers, who were used to the usual German tenaciousness in combat.

It turned out that what was bothering the German troops was not shot and shell, but a bug—the influenza bug, part of the first outbreak of the "Spanish flu." By July 1918, the horrifying influenza pandemic would affect nearly half a million German soldiers.

It hit them much harder than their Allied counterparts because their immune systems had already been weakened by their poor diet, unlike the French, British, and Americans, who were supplied plentifully now that the United States had entered the war.

The 1918 flu pandemic was caused by a particularly virulent A virus strain that mainly targeted people in their twenties and thirties, rather than the elderly and the very young, as influenza usually did. Modern tests on the strain—which has survived in corpses frozen in permafrost—has shown that it stimulated people's immune systems to ravage their own bodies. Although the flu pandemic probably would have occurred had there not been a war, it seemed a direct outgrowth of the horrors of the First World War. To some people, it was as if nature itself was punishing humankind for engaging in such a dreadful conflict. By 1920, the flu had disappeared as mysteriously as it had come. It if was a "judgment from God," as one afflicted soldier wrote his family, it had done its work. An estimated 20 to 40 million people worldwide died of the disease.

Hitler's War: "The Greatest Villainy of the Century"

On August 1, 1914, a massive crowd gathered in the Odeonplatz, a huge pedestrian square in Munich, celebrating the German declaration of war against France, Great Britain, and Russia. A photograph exists from the day, which captures people milling about, smiling, talking excitedly—obviously a festive day, a moment when Germany, it must have seemed, was about to capture its place in the sun.

In the middle of this crowd, one can see with the aid of photo enhancement, is a young man immediately recognizable as Adolf Hitler. Hitler was then an Austro-Hungarian citizen living in Munich and eking out a bare existence as an artist. Despite his impoverished circumstances, the photograph shows him transfigured with happiness, smiling radiantly. Hitler, born in Austria in 1889 to a brutal father and a deeply loving but helpless mother, had drifted through Germany and Bavaria, sometimes living in homeless shelters, railing against the middle-class Jews he saw living prosperous lives, as he sought to find his calling. Now, it appeared, the war would find it for him.

Hitler immediately enlisted in the 16th Bavarian Reserve Infantry Regiment, trained for a few weeks, and was sent to the western front in time to see the final German autumn offensive at Ypres. It was the beginning of a long and arduous war for Hitler. A corporal, he served as a runner delivering messages, a job that was later denigrated by Allied propagandists, but which in fact was one that exposed Hitler to fire a good deal of the time. He won two Iron Crosses and was twice wounded—once by a shellburst at the Battle of the Somme in 1916 and then, when he had returned to the front, by mustard gas in October 1918.

Even so, Hitler was prepared to fight on, and the armistice in November of that year caught him, as it caught thousands of Germans, by surprise. When the Treaty of Versailles (see "Chronicle," p. 234) forced Germany to admit guilt for the war and exacted punishing reparations, Hitler called it "the greatest villainy of the century." While hunger and economic ruin swept Germany, this former infantrymen began to gather other veterans about him, men who, like him, were in search of a terrible revenge.

IN THIS PHOTO FROM 1914, AMID A CROWD OF ENTHUSIASTIC AND EXCITED GERMANS EMBRACING THE DECLARATION OF WAR, STANDS THE YOUNG ADOLF HITLER. WORLD WAR I COULD NOT HAVE COME AT A BETTER TIME FOR HITLER, WHO WAS UNSATISFIED AND UNSURE OF WHAT TO DO WITH HIS LIFE. WITH THE WAR THERE CAME A NEW EXCITEMENT—HE HAD FOUND HIS CALLING.

Hitler singing with the crowd in the Odeonplatz, Munich, 1914 (b/w photo), German Photographer (20th Century) / Private Collection, Peter Newark Pictures / The Bridgeman Art Library

14

THE RUSSIAN CIVIL WAR

1918–1921

One of the most bitter and costly civil wars of the
twentieth century directly shaped the future of communism
and the Soviet Union for the next seventy years

Combatants

- Red army
- White army
- Nationalist factions of Ukraine, Poland, and other countries
- Intervening forces of France, Great Britain, United States, Japan, and other countries

Theater of War

Former Russia Empire

Casualties

Estimated 1 to 2 million battle deaths on all sides. Another 7 to 8 million dead of executions, starvation, or disease

Major Figures

REDS

Vladimir Lenin, founder of the Bolsheviks and head of the Soviets

Leon Trotsky, commissar of war who helped shape the Red Army

Joseph Stalin, obscure party functionary from Georgia who rose to rule the Union of Soviet Socialist Republics (USSR) after destroying all rivals

Mikhayl Tukhachevsky, Russian nobleman who joined the Bolshevik cause and helped win key victories on the Volga River

Alexander Kerensky, prime minister of the provisional government ousted by the Bolsheviks

Fanya Kaplan, whose attempted assassination of Lenin helped touch off the Red Terror

WHITES

Tsar Nicholas II, Russia's last emperor

General Mikhail Alekseev, key figure in forming the first White army in south Russia

General Lavr Kornilov, commander of the Volunteer army in south Russia until killed in combat

General Anton Denikin, commander of the White forces after Kornilov, whose attack on Moscow nearly succeeded

General Alexander Kolchak, commander of all White forces in Siberia

Alexey Kaledin, commander in chief of the Don Cossacks

Baron Peter Nikolaevich Wrangel, leader of the last major White army evacuated in the Crimean

In one of the ugliest civil wars of the twentieth century, the new Bolshevik government of Russia consolidated its power, fighting off numerous White armies consisting of monarchists and those who favored a less drastic form of socialism, as well as nationalist armies from border states such as the Ukraine, and the intervening forces of fourteen different foreign countries. In a conflict that raged across the length and breadth of the former Russian Empire, millions of lives were lost and the Soviet Union was eventually born, with its leaders scarred by terror, deeply paranoid, and xenophobic. The result was the autocratic USSR of Stalin's terror purges, the gulag, and the Cold War.

1917:

October: The Bolsheviks seize Petrograd and oust Alexander Kerensky and the provisional government.

November: Former tsarist officers arrive in south Russia to begin forming the White army of resistance to the Bolsheviks.

1918:

February: Lenin orders the formation of the Red army.

March: Leon Trotsky named war commissar; Bolsheviks negotiate separate peace with Germany.

May–June: Czech Legion begins fighting the Bolshevik forces in Siberia.

July: The Reds murder the Romanov family in Yekaterinburg; Whites capture the city five days later.

August: Lenin shot. U.S., British, and Japanese forces land at the Pacific port of Vladivostok, and British and U.S. troops arrive at Archangel to support the Whites.

September: The Red Terror begins. Trotsky helps hold the Red forces at Sviyazhsk, on the Volga River, stemming the White assault.

1919:

January–March: White armies advance against the Reds on three fronts—from the south, northwest, and east. The Reds recapture Yekaterinburg.

October: Denikin's White army stopped at Orël, 200 miles (322 km) south of Moscow.

November: Admiral Kolchak's White army defeated at Omsk as the Reds retake Siberia.

December: Kolchak's White army ceases to exist in Siberia. Czech Legion negotiates safe passage home.

Red armies defeat the Whites around Petrograd and in the Ukraine, retaking the city of Kiev.

1920:

The White army under Baron Peter Nikolaevich Wrangel evacuates Crimea.

Kolchak is executed.

1921:

March: The Kronstadt Uprising is put down.

February: The Green Rebellion of peasants is put down.

LEON TROTSKY WAS THE MOST ABLE ORGANIZATIONAL AND MILITARY MIND AMONG THE RUSSIAN REVOLUTIONARIES, BUT WAS LESS POLITICALLY ADEPT THAN HIS RIVAL, STALIN.

Portrait of Leon Trotsky (1879-1940), from 'The Illustrated London News', 16th October 1920 (b/w photo), / The Illustrated London News Picture Library, London, UK, / The Bridgeman Art Library International

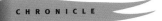
"UNBOUNDED HATRED EVERYWHERE"

By the fall of 1917, the Russian Empire had lost millions of people in the horrible conflagration of World War I, not only soldiers—many of whom were sent into battle unarmed, to be turned into "gruel" by German cannon fire, as one commander wrote—but also civilians who had died of starvation and disease. The Romanov dynasty, as represented by Tsar Nicholas II, had been overthrown. The tsar and his family were now prisoners, and a provisional government under the relatively moderate Alexander Kerensky was put into place.

But in the famous October uprising of 1917, the far more radical Bolsheviks, led by Vladimir Lenin and Leon Trotsky, seized Petrograd (the former Saint Petersburg), ousted Kerensky from power, and, in March 1918, made a separate peace with Germany. The Bolsheviks, known as the Reds, were only in control of European Russia, and so began to fulfill their goal of consolidating their rule over all of what had formerly been the Russian Empire. Arrayed against them were the counterrevolutionary forces of the White army, consisting of former monarchists (many of them officers from the tsar's army), moderate socialists who wished to see a more democratic form of government; and a broad coalition of men and women dismayed by the iron hand the Bolsheviks had already begun to display.

Other forces fighting against the Reds were the Don Cossacks (Cossack horsemen from the Don River region in west Russia, who had long supported the tsar); armies from the Ukraine, Poland, Lithuania, Georgia, and other border states, who sought their independence; and the expeditionary forces of fourteen foreign countries, most notably Great Britain, France, the United States, and Japan, who were dismayed that the ideas of Bolshevism might spread to their own countries.

The war can be divided roughly into three phases. The first phase began in November 1917 when generals of the former Imperial Army, especially Mikhail Alekseev, Lavr Kornilov, Anton Denikin, and Alexey Kaledin, disguised themselves and found their way to south Russia, where, under Alekseev's direction, they formed the first White army, called the Volunteers. Kaledin was also the *hetman*, or leader, of the Don Cossacks in the area, and he organized them to fight against the Reds.

In response to this military threat, Vladimir Lenin, head of the Bolshevik government, proclaimed the establishment of the Red army in February 1918 and made Leon Trotsky the country's first commissar of war. The Treaty of Brest-Litovsk was negotiated with Germany in March, ending the war. Around the same time the Bolsheviks dissolved the Constituent Assembly (the country's first parliament-style stab at democracy), convincing even more moderate Russians to join the White army.

They also put into place a series of measures known as War Communism, which allowed the seizure of grain from Russian peasants—"those who have grain and fail to deliver it to properly designated rail stations … are to be declared enemies of the people," Lenin declared in May. The initiatives may have been necessary to feed the Red army, but they caused famine, disease, and further unrest among the peasants of Russia.

In mid-1918, a group of 10,000 Czech soldiers, known as the Czechoslovakian Legion, who had fought on the side of the tsarist army during the war, embarked on a journey east along 5,400 miles (8,690 km) of the Trans-Siberian Railroad, where they planned to disembark at Vladivostok, ship to the western front, and join the Allied Powers fighting against the Germans (see "The Incredible Journey of the Czech Legion," p. 277).

(see "The Incredible Journey of the Czech Legion," p. 277).

TSAR NICHOLAS II, SEEN HERE, WAS IMPRISONED WITH HIS FAMILY AFTER ABDICATING. BUT EVEN IN ISOLATION THEY WERE SEEN AS A THREAT FOR BOLSTERING THE RESISTANCE OF THE WHITE ARMY AND LENIN HAD THEM EXECUTED.
Getty Images

When the Bolsheviks ordered them to give up their arms after the Treaty of Brest-Litovsk ended the Russian part in the war, the Czechs joined the White forces and in June set up anti-Bolshevik governments in Siberian towns. With their joint forces swelling to some 50,000, the Czech Legion and the White army, united under the command of former tsarist admiral Alexander Kolchak, eventually captured almost all of Siberia. In July 1918, as White forces and the Czech Legion neared the royal family's place of captivity in Yekaterinburg (modern-day Sverdlovsk), Tsar Nicholas II and his entire family were murdered on the orders of Lenin (see "The Fate of the Romanovs," p. 278).

advance of the White army at Sviyazhsk, changing the course of the war.

In September 1918, after Lenin was nearly assassinated, the Bolsheviks launched the Red Terror (see "The Red Terror," p. 279), which was aimed at eliminating political opponents inside the civilian population. The second stage of the Russian Civil War began after the Allied defeat of the Central Powers in November 1918. Kolchak, who had been named head of the White army in Siberia, planned a spring 1919 offensive to capture Moscow. He attacked east from Siberia, while General Denikin's armies headed north from southern Russia.

The Russian Civil War resulted in the creation of the USSR. However, it also caused widespread destruction of infrastructure, famine, disease, economic devastation, the emigration of millions of Russians, and the deaths of many millions more.

In August 1918, U.S., British, and Japanese forces landed at the Pacific Russian port of Vladivostok to support the Whites. U.S. and British troops also arrived at Archangel on the White Sea and helped establish a new White provisional government there. They also funneled supplies of munitions into the White effort, but without the full backing of their war-weary nations, the intervention of foreign countries had relatively little effect on the war. While this was happening, the Bolsheviks, inspired by Leon Trotsky (see "Turning Point," p. 270) stopped the

In the meantime, the army of General Nikolay Yudenivich attacked Petrograd from the Baltic region. Fighting raged all throughout Russia, with Denikin's forces coming within 200 miles (322 km) of Moscow while Yudenivich reached within 10 miles (16 km) of Petrograd, but by the end of the year, the better-supplied and more cohesive Red army had defeated the Whites in the Siberia, the south of Russia, and the Baltic.

In the third and final stage of the war, the White forces made a fighting retreat to the Crimean Peninsula under their capable commander Baron Peter Nikolaevich Wrangel. But decimated by casualties and disease, the White forces eventually had to be evacuated by the British and French navies in November 1920. Within the next year, the Kronstadt Uprising (see "Kronstadt Uprising," p. 281) and the Green Rebellion, in which various peasant groups joined together to protest near-starvation conditions, would be bloodily put down.

Although the Bolsheviks had not been successful in reclaiming all of the Russian Empire (the Ukraine, Poland, and Finland became separate republics), they had fought a successful war that they had won mainly because of a unified purpose and command, and because they held the factories and manpower of the geographic center of the country. The disparate groups of Whites were never able to effectively find common cause, and they often lacked supplies and munitions.

The Russian Civil War resulted in the creation of the USSR. However, it also caused widespread destruction of infrastructure, famine, disease, economic devastation, the emigration of millions of Russians, and the deaths of many millions more. The emotional effects of such a savage war—what White Commander Anton Denikin later described as the "unbounded hatred everywhere"—lasted for a long time. The Bolsheviks had been arrayed against forces not only within their own country, but invading armies from without, and this militarized the Russian communist party.

After the death of Lenin and the ouster of Trotsky, Russia would be led by Joseph Stalin, whose dark paranoia resulted in the Great Terror of the 1930s, in which many of the methods put in service by the Bolsheviks in the Russian Civil War—including mass executions and a form of War Communism in which agriculture and industry were collectivized for the common good—were employed in the murder, by bullet or starvation, of millions of people.

TROTSKY AT SVIYAZHSK: SEPTEMBER 1918

S viyazhsk, some 250 miles (402 km) south-west of Moscow near the Volga River, is not a village advancing in the world. Its population is only about 300 or so, down from more than 1,000 a half century ago. This may be because Sviyazhsk is now located on a small island, in the middle of the deep, light-blue waters of the far-flung Kuybyshev Reservoir, created when a part of the Volga was dammed in the 1950s in a vast Soviet hydroelectric project.

Sviyazhsk's change of circumstance and dwindling size makes it one of the most obscure but important places in Russian and world history. It's not a place you read about in guide books. But in late August 1918, well before it became an island, the Russian Revolution was saved at Sviyazhsk because of the efforts of Leon Trotsky, an armored train, and a few thousand dedicated Bolsheviks. As W. Bruce Lincoln, one of the premiere historians of the Russian Civil War, wrote:

"During August of 1918, Sviyazhsk became the Valmy (see "French Revolutionary Wars," p. 10) of the Russian Revolution, the point where the Bolsheviks, like the armies of revolutionary France in 1792, first halted the advance of armies that marched to restore the old order."

The Hungry Spring

By the summer of 1918, the Russian Revolution had fallen on hard times. The initial euphoria of the great events at Petrograd in the fall of 1917, when the Bolsheviks had seized the Winter Palace and ousted Alexander Kerensky from power, had now broken against some very hard realities. The Russian people were starving. The masses in Russia at the time lived mainly on bread, but the harvest the previous fall had been poor, and the infrastructure of Russia's railways—falling apart as the old regime fell apart—proved inadequate to transport what grain supplies there were to the big population centers. Men and women in cities such as Petrograd, Moscow, and Novgorod ate what was called "famine bread," because the dough from which it was made was filled with water and vegetable shavings. And even then, they were on quarter rations.

The spring of 1918 later became known as "the Hunger Spring." Under orders of Vladimir Lenin, the Reds confiscated grain from peasants for the Red army. Starving crowds pleaded for bread; demonstrations turned hostile and had to be put down violently. Unemployment spread across the country, and soldiers newly released from the Russian army after the March peace treaty with Germany returned home to find no jobs and no food. Their response was to commit violent crimes against the citizenry. The Bolsheviks estimated that, during the early winter of 1918, 800 robberies were committed every single day in Petrograd.

Even worse, the military situation was becoming untenable. The successful spring and early summer offensive of the White army (see "The Whites," p. 276) and Czech Legion (see

"The Incredible Journey of the Czech Legion," p. 277) robbed Russia of the vast grain stores of Siberia and pushed Red armies back toward the Volga River. The United Kingdom and France had already sent troops to Russia, supposedly to protect the massive piles of munitions they had sent to the tsar for use against Germany. But in reality, as everyone knew, they were hostile to the Bolshevik government. The Japanese, with designs on Siberia, had 70,000 troops there, and the Americans were soon to land 10,000.

"Everything Was Crumbling"

Everywhere, it seemed to a harried Leon Trotsky, Bolshevik war commissar, the revolution was coming apart at the seams. "A rumor began to spread," he later wrote, "that the Soviets were doomed … Everything was crumbling, there was nothing to hold to. The situation seemed hopeless."

As the White army, coupled with the units of the Czech Brigade, swept west, heading for the Volga, news came that an army under Alexey Kaledin, hetman of the Cossacks, and General Mikhail Alekseev, former supreme commander of Russian Imperial forces, had been formed south of the Don River, and was pushing back Red forces there.

It was what Trotsky called "the first wave of the counterrevolution," and it was graphically marked by the little blue flags he stuck in the map on the wall of his Moscow office, each flag marking another counterrevolutionary force taking another bit of Russia from the Bolsheviks. Educated socialist theorists like Trotsky and Lenin had expected the counterrevolution, but not such a rapid destruction of revolutionary forces. That summer of 1918, Trotsky received word that entire units and garrisons were deserting.

1917 RUSSIA WAS RIPE FOR REBELLION, AND THE PEOPLE WERE READY FOR RADICAL CHANGE, COMING IN THE FORM OF THE BOLSHEVIKS, LED BY VLADIMIR LENIN AND LEON TROTSKY.

Mass Demonstration in Moscow in 1917, 1917 (oil on canvas), Meshkov, Wassily (1867-1946) / Art Museum of Ryasan, Russia, / The Bridgeman Art Library International

Despite the large amount of work Trotsky had put into constructing his Red army, it seemed like even he would be hard put to hold back the flood. He told a subordinate that "it is essential to start producing tanks in the Urals… using tractor parts, if necessary," despite the fact Whites, even as he spoke, threatened Red factories there. He desperately cabled Lenin: "We need to find a possible way of using asphyxiating gases." (This cable was ignored.)

By August 1918, White forces, along with units of the Czech Legion, had closed on the Volga and captured the town of Kazan, the easternmost terminus of the Moscow–Kazan railway line, which put them within striking distance of Moscow.

Trotsky in Sviyazhsk

Fifteen miles (24 km) west of Kazan was the small town of Sviyazhsk, which had been founded by Ivan the Terrible in the 1550s, but had no other claim to fame than this. Monitoring events at the front from Moscow, Trotsky learned that Sviyazhsk was where the Red soldiers fleeing the Whites around Kazan were gathering, pausing for breath before they continued their journey westward. With Trotsky's extraordinary energy, organizational skill, and ability to improvise, he decided at once to head to Sviyazhsk aboard a special train that contained a printing press, a telegraph, a radio station capable of receiving signals from Moscow, and a shipment of boots, medicine, food, watches, and arms.

Arriving at Sviyazhsk, Trotsky could hear the sound of heavy guns in the distance and found Red army soldiers wandering the streets, some in a state of panic. Just as Trotsky arrived, while he was still on his train, a White army brigade broke through to raid the rear of the Bolshevik lines and made an attack on Sviyazhsk. "This move caught us quite off our guard," Trotsky later wrote. As gunfire cracked against the armored sides of the train, he armed everyone he could, "even the cook." They moved about a mile from the train, and Trotsky himself set up a battle line. "We had a good stock of rifles, machine guns, and hand grenades," he said. "The train crew was made up of good fighters. The battle went on for eight hours …Finally, after they had spent themselves, the enemy withdrew."

After the fight, Trotsky learned that one cause of the breakthrough had been the desertion of an entire Red regiment from the front lines, including the regimental commander and political commissar who accompanied each regiment. Steeling himself, Trotsky had the commander and the commissar executed immediately. He then told his guards to pick out every tenth man in the ranks of the regiment—an old Roman method of discipline called decimation—and shoot them.

"A red-hot iron has been applied to a festering wound," Trotsky wrote Lenin. "[The Red soldier] must choose between the possibility that death lies ahead and the certainty that it lies behind."

"The Holy Demagoguery of Battle"

Trotsky's repressive discipline had its effect, but so did his supplies. Staying at Sviyazhsk for an entire month, he shuttled his and other trains from the front to the rear and back again "tens, even hundreds of times." He wrote that the resources brought by the train "served as that one shovelful of coal needed at a particular moment to keep the fire from dying out."

Apprised of the needs of the front line soldiers, Trotsky sent for 126 machine guns, three armored cars, sixteen aircraft (some carrying 1,000-pound bombs), and even gunboats, which arrived on the Volga to bombard Kazan. He sent an urgent plea to Moscow for any fighters willing to come and risk their lives on this front, and boys as young as fifteen responded, impressing even the hardened fighters at Sviyazhsk.

At last, Trotsky was ready to attempt to re-take Kazan. He named as his commander General Ioakim Vatsetis, the squat, good-humored son of a Latvian peasant who had served in the tsarist army before joining the Bolsheviks the previous October. Vatsetis had been driven out of Kazan— in fact, he and his orderly had been the last to leave, under fire from the Whites—and now he was ready to battle his way back in. Before the attack Trotsky told Vatsetis and his fighters that "the taking of Kazan means merciless revenge against the enemies of the revolution." Then he shouted: "Do not allow the enemy to move a step further. Tear Kazan from his hands. Drown him in the Volga!"

Vatsetis and his men launched their attack at 3:30 in the morning on September 10, 1918, as gunboats boomed from the river. Kazan was an ancient fortress town with high walls, but they were no match for modern artillery, nor could they withstand the Red infantry pouring through the rubble-strewn breaches from three sides. Thousands of Whites fled to the east, hundreds died, and the city fell by the early afternoon.

At Sviyazhsk with Trotsky during those days was a twenty-two-year-old female soldier named Larissa Reisner, the wife of the commander of the Volga fleet of gunboats; Reisner headed the flotilla's intelligence-gathering section. Like so many Russians of her generation, she would not live long. (She died of typhus before she was thirty.) But watching Trotsky in action that month, she confided to her journal that she and her comrades "could die in battle with the last cartridge gone, oblivious to our wounds, for Trotsky incarnated the holy demagoguery of battle. This we used to whisper among ourselves on those nights of a quick-freezing autumn, lying jumbled in our heaps across the floor of [Sviyazhsk] station."

Although the next year, 1919, would bring extraordinary challenges to the Bolsheviks, Trotsky's intervention at Sviyazhsk had been decisive. To Bolshevik soldiers like Larissa Reisner and her comrades, he became a living symbol of what the Red cause had been missing—backbone and inspiration.

LEON TROTSKY:
COMMISSAR WITH A PURPOSE

Despite the fact that Leon Trotsky did not command a Red army in the field, his contributions to the building of the Red army did as much as any field commander to gain victory for the Bolsheviks.

Trotsky was born Lev Bronstein in southern Russia in 1879 to a small landowner who worked hard to provide for his wife and children. The handsome, blue-eyed Trotsky was a brilliant student whose intellect helped him overcome the stigma of being Jewish as he went through a state high school in Odessa. Radicalized early by harsh tsarist treatment of workers and peasants, he demonstrated against the imperial government, and he was arrested and placed in jail. When he got out, he went into exile, took on the pseudonym Leon Trotsky (an ironic tribute to one of his jailers of the same name), and began writing in support of the Marxist cause.

At the outbreak of the Russian Revolution, Trotsky was second only to Vladimir Lenin in power among the Bolsheviks, so it was no surprise when Lenin named him commissar of the new Red army in March of 1918. Trotsky set to his job with a will, proclaiming that "the Soviet Republic must have an army that can fight battles and win." A brilliant organizer, Trotsky knew that the raw recruits of the Red army must have experienced officers leading them, and so, against the advice of many of the Bolsheviks in power, insisted on allowing tsarist officers (eventually as many as 75,000) to serve.

"It is essential for us to have a real military force, one that is properly organized according to scientific military principles," he stated. He then convinced many of these tsarist officers (who, with good reason, feared for their lives) to serve with the Bolsheviks. Without this masterly task of persuasion, the Red army would have been stillborn. (Trotsky also made sure he used persuasion of a different sort. If a former tsarist officer seemed likely to desert, Trotsky would have him closely watched by loyal Bolsheviks with pistols drawn.)

Trotsky's actions at Sviyazhsk are a showcase for the ways in which a tough-minded, but compassionate and resourceful, commander could act to change the fortunes of his army. Yet Trotsky's service in the Civil War was to be the highpoint of his career, mainly because of the machinations of his rival, Joseph Stalin. Stalin was a member of the Revolutionary Military Committee and a political commissar on several Civil War fronts who criticized Trotsky openly for his use of tsarist officers and set traps for him (demanding absurdly large amounts of supplies for a certain area, for instance, and then complaining to Lenin when Trotsky could not produce them). After Lenin's death, Stalin won the power struggle to become the new leader of Russia and forced Trotsky—far more talented, but less skilled in political infighting—out of the country. When Trotsky continued to write from exile in Mexico criticizing Stalin's regime, the latter had him murdered in 1940.

GENERAL ANTON DENIKIN:
THE MAN IN THE TATTERED UNIFORM

It is a sign of how diverse were the ranks of the White army that one of its principal leaders came from as humble an origin as the most committed Bolshevik.

General Anton Ivanovich Denikin was born in 1872, the son of a Russian serf and a Polish Catholic seamstress. He spent most of his childhood in a squalid two-room shack in Poland, but he grew up speaking two languages and possessed an incredible desire to overcome his circumstances. Denikin entered a Russian military academy and then joined the tsarist army in 1889, at the age of seventeen. He showed such promise that he was allowed to join the General Staff Academy, graduated an officer, and saw action in the Russo-Japanese War, where he distinguished himself in hand-to-hand fighting during cavalry raids behind Japanese lines. By the beginning of World War I he was the major general in command of the Kiev Military District and became an innovative and successful corps commander, fighting in Romania against the Austrians in what would be the last major successful Russian offensive of the war.

When the revolution broke out, Denikin was on the staff of Russian Supreme Commander Mikhail Alekseev and joined him in forming the White army of the Don River region. When General Lavr Kornilov, commander of the Volunteers, was killed in action against the Bolsheviks, Denikin took over command. He was an interesting man—literate and a fine writer (as his later memoirs would attest), and he was also honest. He refused to take graft, and he even cut his own salary in half, wearing a tattered uniform for most of his campaign against Moscow.

Unfortunately, the bulk of Denikin's men stole food and clothing from the civilians of the lands they passed through, and they were in general so drunken and corrupt that Denikin complained that "I cannot foretell when [my men] will rise from the mire." Yet, tellingly, he did not take the harsh line taken by other White commanders, which involved shooting drunks and looters.

At first Denikin found resounding military success as the premiere commander of the Whites. In the spring of 1919, he launched a spectacular offensive from the south, aimed at Moscow. His forces captured hundreds of miles of Russian territory and reached the town or Orël, only 200 miles (322 km) from Moscow, by October. Unfortunately, Denikin was struck hard by Lenin's forces in a series of counterattacks that drove a wedge between the Cossacks and the Volunteers and turned the White advance into a retreat that became a rout as winter weather set in.

Driven all the way back into the Crimea, this most talented of White officers was harshly criticized by his fellow Whites and replaced by Baron Peter Nikolaevich Wrangel in 1920. Disillusioned, he left Russia and lived in Europe and eventually the United States, at near poverty levels, supporting himself by writing and lecturing against the Reds. He died in Ann Arbor, Michigan, in 1947, a long way from home.

The Reds: "A Model Army"

The Red army was formed by decree of Vladimir Lenin in January 1918 and was known officially as the Workers and Peasants Red Army. It originally consisted of a core of Red Guards—the early military force of the Bolsheviks—as many as 75,000 former tsarist officers, and (although the force was officially supposed to be a volunteer one) hundreds of thousands of peasant conscripts.

Although the Reds outnumbered their White opponents—the army would grow to more than 5 million men (and women) by the end of the Civil War—it had numerous problems.

Chief among them was desertion, which reached such endemic proportions that in 1919 alone, Bolshevik authorities re-captured some 1.7 million AWOL soldiers. Conditions were harsh, rations were short, and many members were "barefoot, naked, hungry, and lice-ridden," as Leon Trotsky, the army's commissar put it.

Although it may have been an exaggeration to say that Trotsky turned them into a "model army," as Lenin said, he was able to bring order and cohesiveness to large, untrained group. As the fighting intensified in all areas of the country, the Red army was divided up into numbered units (the 1st Red Army, the 12th Red Army,

VLADIMIR LENIN IS SEEN HERE ADDRESSING THE RED ARMY IN 1920. TO FEED THE ARMY, LENIN PUT INTO PLACE A SERIES OF MEASURES CALLED WAR COMMUNISM, WHICH ALLOWED FOR THE SEIZURE OF GRAIN FROM PEASANTS.

Vladimir Ilyich Lenin (1870-1924) Addressing the Red Army of Workers on 5th May 1920, 1933 (oil on canvas), Brodsky, Isaak Israilevich (1883-1939) / Private Collection, RIA Novosti / The Bridgeman Art Library International

etc.) and sent wherever they were needed in the country. Each "army" consisted of perhaps 30,000 infantrymen supported by light artillery and cavalrymen. Although most of the country's Cossack horsemen had joined the Whites, the Reds had excellent cavalry units in the *Konarmiia,* or "horse army," an irregular but elite unit comprised of peasants who had learned to ride and who sometimes went into combat in civilian clothes.

Because the Reds operated from the center of the country, they were able to get resupplied from Russia's factories and also have use of its transportation system and were thus shuttle from one area to another much faster than the Whites. And, desertions notwithstanding, those millions who remained in the army to fight had become indoctrinated with the Bolshevik spirit and became extremely difficult to beat.

The Whites: The Volunteer Army

One day in the late fall of 1917, a short, thin, bespectacled man of about sixty arrived in Novocherkassk, the capital of the Don Region of southern Russia, where Cossack forces, tsarist officers, and other refugees from the Bolshevik takeover of Russia had begun to gather.

The man's name was General Mikhail Alekseev, and he had an

impressive resume. He had been the imperial chief of staff of the Russian army in 1915 and helped reorganize it to fight the Germans, despite the interference of the inept Tsar Nicholas II. After the provisional government of Alexander Kerensky took over, Alekseev became head of all Russian armies, but Kerensky's ouster had sent Alekseev, too, into flight. A fierce

patriot and anti-Bolshevik, he was dying of cancer (he would live only nine months longer) but he wanted to organize an army to fight Lenin and his compatriots.

Using a base of fugitive tsarist officers, military cadets, and noncommissioned officers who had left the front, Alekseev joined forces with anti-Communist Cossack cavalrymen, to create what he called the Volunteer army. At first it numbered only about 600 men. Anton Denikin (see "Commanders," p. 275), who would later take over the Volunteers, wrote that "it was touching…to see the former supreme commander of Russian armies…fretting about getting a dozen cots, a few sacks of sugar, and a tiny amount of money."

But gradually the Volunteers grew to encompass about 23,000 men and was then joined by other groups, including nationalists and moderate social democrats, as well as partisan fighters who often changed sides, and became known as the Whites. (They were named possibly because white was the color traditionally associated with Russian aristocracy, although some White officers also initially wore the white uniforms of the former tsarist officer corps.)

The Whites were never as cohesive a group as the Reds, and they were given to far more internecine squabbling. There were three major White armies operating in Russia during the war (see "Chronicle," p. 266) with, for a time, one overall commander in chief in Admiral Alexander Kolchak, but the armies never truly coordinated with one another. Nor did they have a social or political agenda beyond their common hatred of the Reds, and thus allowed chaos and disorder to follow in their wake in the territory they did conquer. Too, many of the Whites committed serious civilian atrocities, which further alienated them from the peasants of the countryside.

The last fully functioning White army, under the command of Baron Peter Nikolaevich Wrangel, beat a fighting retreat through the Crimean Peninsula and was evacuated (146,000 soldiers and civilians who had supported them aboard 125 ships) in November 1920. Despite a

THE WHITE ARMY WAS SO NAMED BECAUSE WHITE WAS THE COLOR ASSOCIATED WITH THE RUSSIAN ARISTOCRACY.
Getty Images

few sporadic pockets of resistance, and a White expatriate organization in Europe for two decades to come, the White movement was essentially over.

The Incredible Journey of the Czech Legion

The story of the Czechoslovakian Legion that, in effect, started the hostilities in the Russian Civil War is one of history's most incredible ones.

The Czech Legion began in 1914 as a brigade of fewer than 1,000 Czechs and Slovaks, who had traditionally been a nationality repressed by the Austro-Hungarian Hapsburg Empire, which controlled Bohemia, the Czech homeland. The tsarist government enlisted and trained the men and encouraged them to fight alongside Russian forces against the Austrians and the Germans. The legion fought bravely as political changes swept out the tsarist forces and put the provisional government of Alexander Kerensky in place (see "Chronicle," p. 266). At that point, the ranks of the legion were swelled by thousands of Czech prisoners of war taken in the fighting with the Austrians.

With the war on the eastern front seemingly coming to an end, the Czech nationalist leader Tomàs Masaryk negotiated a deal with the new government of Vladimir Lenin to allow the legion to travel east on an extraordinary journey that would take them on the Trans-Siberian Railroad (more than 5,000 miles [8,047 km]) all the way to Vladivostok, where they would disembark in U.S. ships, travel across the Pacific to North America, and across the United States and the Atlantic Ocean. Arriving in France, they would fight on the side of the allies against the Germans.

In reality, Masarayk wanted to have a force ready-made to invade and take over Czechoslovakia just as soon as the Germans capitulated in the west. No sooner had the legion begun its journey east, however,

(continued on p. 278)

THE CZECH LEGION BEGAN AS A BRIGADE OF FEWER THAN 1,000 CZECHS AND SLOVAKS, ENLISTED BY TSARIST RUSSIA TO FIGHT AGAINST THE AUSTRIANS AND GERMANS IN WORLD WAR I. THEIR RANKS WOULD SWELL TO 50,000.

Prints & Photographs Division, Library of Congress, LC-USZ62-62917

when the Bolshevik government signed a peace treaty with Germany, which demanded that the Czechs surrender to them as prisoners of war. The Bolsheviks in turn demanded that the Czechs disarm, which they refused to do. On May 25, as the Czechs moved east, they discovered that Leon Trotsky had sent a telegram to all the towns along the Trans-Siberian Railroad saying that "every Czech who is found carrying a weapon anywhere along the route of the railway is to be shot on the spot."

Seeing that the Bolsheviks planned to return them to the Germans, the Czechs went on the attack, immediately capturing small Siberian railroad towns, dispersing the sparse Red forces on the ground there, and then moving on to larger Siberian cities such as Chelyabinsk and finally the Siberian Provincial capital of Tomsk, which contained an armory the Czech fighters gratefully looted. Joining forces with anti-Bolshevik White fighters, they simply destroyed all Bolshevik resistance in Siberia by the end of June 1918. By this time the Czech Legion numbered some 50,000 strong.

The shifting fortunes of war, however, make strange bedfellows. The Czechs, after all, were not there to settle Russia's Civil War, but to get back home. After World War I ended in November 1918, a new Czech Republic was born, and it ordered the Czech Legion back home. The Czechs, tired of fighting in someone else's war, stopped supporting the White army and only defended themselves against attack. Worse was to follow. The Czech Legion had been entrusted by Admiral Alexander Kolchak with guarding a trainload of gold that belonged to the White army. Not only did the Czechs use the gold to barter their safe passage from the Bolsheviks (they gave up nine of ten cars of bullion), but they also revealed the location of Kolchak and his staff, who were captured and executed. Fifty-six thousand Czech soldiers would return to their new country aboard forty-two ships provided by the Soviets, which sailed from Vladivostok in 1920.

In another odd twist, it was the seeming fate of the Czech Legion, trapped in Russia while trying to help the Allied cause, which helped convince Woodrow Wilson that U.S. troops should be sent to Siberia (see "America's Polar Bears," p. 280).

The Killing of the Romanovs

After Tsar Nicholas II had abdicated in March 1917, he, his wife, and five children became prisoners of Russia's first provisional government, headed by Alexander Kerensky. At first, with the British government offering asylum, it was assumed that the tsar and his family would soon be on their way to foreign land to live out their days as expatriates.

But the British withdrew their offer when it was thought that giving shelter to the tsar might stir social unrest in their own country at a time when Britons were already being bled dry by the war. As the Russian Revolution turned more to the left and the radical Bolsheviks gained power, Kerensky was afraid he might not be able to keep the Romanovs safe near Petrograd and thus had them transferred in August 1917 to the isolated town of Tobolsk, in western Siberia, some 1,500 miles (2,414 km) away. After Kerensky lost power in the fall of 1917, the Bolsheviks in turn sent the Romanovs to another isolated town, Yekaterinburg, in the Urals.

There the Romanovs lived in a large stone house with whitewashed windows (so they could not look out and no one else could look in), eating peasant rations of black bread and tea, playing card games, singing hymns, and praying for deliverance. They were surrounded by guards with machine guns. In the meantime, Russia's Bolshevik leaders debated what to do with them. Lenin wanted a show trial in which the tsar would be tried for his crimes, but it was now the summer of 1919 and White army forces were advancing on Yekaterinburg with the express purpose of rescuing Nicholas and his family. Deciding that the Bolsheviks would be foolish to "leave the Whites with a live banner to rally around," Lenin ordered the execution of the tsar and his entire family.

Early in the morning of July 17, 1919, with the sound of White artillery thundering in the distance, the Romanovs were awakened and told they were going to be moved to a different city because the Whites were about to attack. They were then taken to the cellar of their house — Nicholas and his wife, Alexandra; their hemophiliac son and heir to the throne, Alexei; and their daughters, Olga, Anastasia, Maria, and Tatiana. Several servants and the family doctor accompanied them.

Once there, their chief jailer, Yakov Yurovsky, read a statement

condemning them to death. The tsar only had time to stand up and exclaim: "What!" when Yurovksy shot him twice in the head and then pumped two more bullets into Alexei. The rest of the guards opened fire on the other Romanovs as the room filled with screams, the echoing sound of gunfire, and the smell of cordite. When some semblance of silence returned, they heard groans from Anastasia, who had apparently only been wounded slightly. A guard pierced her abdomen with a bayonet several times, killing her. "Their blood flowed in streams," one witness later recalled.

No member of the royal family escaped, despite later persistent rumors that Anastasia had survived. The Whites arrived in Yekaterinburg less than a week later, to find no trace of the Romanovs' bodies. It wasn't until the late 1980s that it was finally discovered that Yurovksy had taken them to a nearby forest, had the corpses chopped apart and burned in gasoline fires, and then had pushed the bones into the bottom of the shaft of an abandoned mine and covered them with dirt. No trace of the Romanovs was to remain — not even a bone — for the Whites to use as an icon of a bygone age.

The Red Terror: "Floods of Blood"

On August 30, 1918, Vladimir Lenin went to a Moscow hand grenade factory, where he spoke to the workers about socialist theory — "the dictatorship of the proletariat and the dictatorship of the bourgeoisie." Watching him that night was a plain young woman, who took notes on almost everything he said and nervously chain-smoked cigarettes. After the speech, as Lenin was walking to his car, she walked up behind him and fired three times. One bullet hit him in

the chest, another in the arm, and he fell heavily to the ground, before his chauffeur dragged him into this car and they raced away down Moscow's darkened streets.

Lenin would survive these wounds, and his would-be assassin, a disillusioned socialist named Fanya Kaplan, would be executed by the Russian Cheka, or secret police. But the attempted assassination of Lenin (as well as the successful killing of the head of the Petrograd Cheka on the

morning of Lenin's shooting) opened the doors for what even Bolshevik officials tagged the Red Terror — an extraordinarily brutal campaign to kill anyone even remotely suspected of being disloyal to the Bolsheviks. The next day, the Bolshevik party newspaper *Krasnaia gazeta* shouted in a lead article: "We will kill our enemies in scores of hundreds. Let there be thousands, let them drown themselves in their own blood...Let there be floods of blood of the bourgeois."

(continued on p. 280)

And there was. Within a week, the Petrograd Cheka had shot more than 500 people. Thousands more were executed in provinces all over Russia. The first to go were former policemen, tsarist bureaucrats, opposition leaders, and property owners. It was not necessary to be proven guilty of anything. One Cheka chief proclaimed: "Do not look in the files for incriminating evidence as to whether the accused rose up against the Soviets with arms or words. Ask him instead to which class he belongs...These are the questions that will determine the fate of the accused."

In other words, it wasn't what you did but who you were. Historians differ on how many lives the Red Terror, which lasted into mid-1919, took. In the fall of 1918 alone, 10,000 to 15,000 people were executed, many of them having been tortured first. (A common practice was to take a husband hostage and then allow his wife to come and ransom him—with her own life.) Perhaps 50,000 in all were killed. And those who weren't executed were sent to prison camps, perhaps 70,000 in all, in what scholars peg as the beginning of the Russian gulag system, which would eventually grow to 14 million prisoners in 476 camps.

U.S. Polar Bears

When word of the plight of the Czech Legion became public, a great amount of sympathy arose for them in western countries, particularly the United States. Here were fighters making a journey halfway around the world to fight for the Allied cause, and the hated Bolsheviks were attempting to send them to the equally hated Germans as prisoners.

As the civil war in Siberia raged, U.S. President Woodrow Wilson ultimately decided to send troops, but it is unlikely that merely taking the pressure off the Czech Legion was his only goal. The United States had transported tons of munitions and other supplies to Vladivostok to help the tsarist government in its fight against the Central Powers and wanted to keep them from falling into the hands of the Bolsheviks—or into the hands of the Japanese, who had already sent troops to Siberia, where they had held territory ambitions since the Russo-Japanese War. Wilson's main goal for his American Expeditionary Force was defensive, but as subsequent history has shown, it is very difficult for an armed military force to intervene in a highly volatile civil war and function purely in a guard or police capacity.

Led by Major General William Graves, a force consisting of some 8,000 men landed in Vladivostok in September 1918, while another contingent of 5,000, which would become known as the Polar Bear Division, was sent to Archangel. Graves's force, while skirmishing with the Bolsheviks, managed to stay out of major trouble, mainly because of Graves's ability to stand up to British, French, and Japanese commanders in the region, who wanted the Americans to take a more active role in fighting the Bolsheviks. Still, 189 Americans died before the force was pulled out in 1920.

The experience of the Polar Bears in Archangel was far different. These Americans had been placed under the command of the British, whose troops predominated in the region, and so their first task was to go on offensive operations against Bolsheviks who had stolen U.S. supplies. By October 1918, this thin U.S. force was engaged in fighting on fronts hundreds of miles long.

On the day that the armistice was signed on the western front, the U.S., British, and Canadian forces were involved in a pitched battle with Bolshevik forces in temperatures that reached -30°F (-34°C). As a bitter Russian winter set in—which froze the harbor at Archangel and trapped the Americans there—casualties mounted and the U.S. forces began to question their officers as to why they were here fighting when the rest of the world had stood down. These questions turned into open mutiny when four members of the Polar Bear Division wrote a note to their commanding officer that began: "After this March 15, 1919, we positively refuse to advance on the Bolo [Bolshevik] lines." This was smoothed over, and no actual mutiny occurred, but morale was so low among the Americans in Archangel that they were evacuated within nine months, well before the forces in Vladivostok, having suffered more than 250 deaths to combat and disease.

The Kronstadt Uprising: The Sailors' Rebellion

The naval base of Kronstadt lay on Kotlin Island in the Gulf of Finland some 20 miles (32 km) west of Petrograd and had served as a protector of Russia's grand city every since Peter the Great had built his capital in the eighteenth century. Kronstadt's fortifications were thought to be "impregnable," in the words of one non-Russian military expert, bristling not only with massive guns, but with a population of 25,000 sailors, artillerymen, and dockyard workers.

Kronstadt had something of the air of a small, isolated country. The men who worked there were self-sufficient and highly independent. Thus it was no surprise that, as the Russian Revolution broke out, it was the black-jacked sailors of Kronstadt who were among the first to protest against tsarist rule, who took part of the storming of the Winter Palace as the Bolsheviks captured Petrograd, and who fought with the Red army.

Therefore, however, it should also be no surprise that these fiery partisans should rebel when Bolshevik rule became oppressive. In the winter of 1921, conditions around Petrograd had become almost intolerable. Citizens lived on half-rations while being forced to work endless hours in factories, and any protest

was put down savagely by the Red government. Inflation had increased to such an extent that the price of a pound of sugar cost 22,000 rubles. In the meantime, War Communism took grain from starving peasants in the countryside and funneled it to the army.

In the ice-bound harbor of Kronstadt, the sailors formed committees to discuss the emergency facing them. They had heard that civilian bread protests had been ruthlessly suppressed by Cheka firing squads. While this was not true, armed squads of soldiers had forced hungry strikers back to their work benches, convincing one visiting sailor from Kronstadt that "these were not factories but the forced labor prisons of tsarist times." Sixteen-thousand sailors and soldiers formed the Kronstadt Provisional Revolutionary Committee and challenged any attempt by the Bolsheviks to regain control over them.

In early March, the Reds decided that the only alternative was to attack the heavily armed fortress. If they waited any longer, the thick ice around Kronstadt would break up and the island would be virtually impregnable to attack. Not only that, but the Reds might be able to sail the two Russian battleships at

anchor to freedom. On the night of March 7 and the morning of the 8th, a force of Red soldiers attacked across the ice in a swirling snowstorm, moving in thin lines widely spread out, in case the ice might break, and clad in white shrouds to diminish their visibility. But the defenders of Kronstadt picked out the attackers by searchlights and opened fire with machine guns and artillery. Huge shells blasted from the fortress and the battleships exploded among the Reds, breaking the ice and sending the men screaming to their deaths in the freezing water.

Two more attacks five days later were also destroyed in like fashion, and those defending Kronstadt began to believe that they might be able to hold out until the ice broke up. But on March 17, the Red army attacked in great force with handpicked veterans who were also fanatical Bolsheviks. Despite heavy losses, they managed to break into Kronstadt, where vicious house-to-house fighting took place before the Reds secured the city a day later. Those rebels who weren't killed were either sent to the gulag camps or dispersed in small numbers to remote outposts. The last major rebellion against Bolshevik rule had ended.

15

THE CHINESE CIVIL WAR

1927–1949

Fought in two lengthy phases over twenty years, this struggle between the forces of Chiang Kai-shek and Mao Zedong resulted in the creation of the People's Republic of China.

Combatants

- Chinese Nationalist Party (KMT)
- Chinese Communist Party (CPC)

Theater of War

China

Casualties

More than 3 million military dead and wounded on both sides; 5 million civilian casualties from war, famine, and disease

Major Figures

NATIONALISTS

Sun Yat-sen, initial revolutionary who overthrew the Qing Dynasty and created the Republic of China
Chiang Kai-shek, head of the Nationalist Party and of the Republic of China
Madame Chiang Kai-shek, his advisor and often co-strategist
Du Yuming, Chiang's liaison with the Nationalist army
Liu Zhi, Chiang's commander in the field in Manchuria

COMMUNISTS

Mao Zedong, head of the Communist Party and Red army
Zhou Enlai, his close advisor
General Su Yu, mastermind of the final campaign of victory in 1948
Deng Xiaoping, one of Mao's top field commanders and future premiere of the People's Republic

From 1927 to 1949, breaking only to ostensibly join forces to defeat the Japanese in the Second Sino-Japanese War, the forces of Mao Zedong and Chiang Kai-shek fought to determine who would rule over China after the fall of the tottering Qing Dynasty. While the personalities of both Chinese leaders figured large in the war (see "Commanders," p. 290), the conflict was an iconic twentieth-century struggle in which the new order of Communism wrestled with a more traditional nationalism. When Communist forces emerged victorious in 1949, China was set to step forward for the first time in its history as a major player in world politics, but internal problems would keep it from fulfilling that role for another fifty years.

1911: Sun Yat-sen's uprising begins.

1912:

February: Qing Dynasty dissolves; China becomes a republic.

September: Sun Yat-sen forms the Nationalist Party.

1925: Sun Yat-sen dies of cancer; Chiang Kai-shek assumes the main position of power in the Nationalist Party.

1926:

As commander in chief of the Nationalist army (KMT), Chiang launches the Northern Expedition, a joint "Unified Front" with the Communists, to defeat northern bandit warlords.

1927:

April: After success of the Northern Campaign, Chiang launches a surprise attack on the Communists in Shanghai, killing and capturing thousands. Mao flees the city.

September: Mao leads the first uprising against KMT forces with newly formed guerilla forces, is defeated, and retreats to the mountains of the Jiangxi Province.

1930–1932: The Nationalist Party under Chiang launch five separate offensives, attempting to encircle and destroy the Communist army. Each time they are unsuccessful.

1933: The KMT army surround Mao in his Jiangxi base, building fortified pillboxes and entrenchments and slowly strangling his sources of supply.

1934: Mao and the Communist army break out from Jiangxi and begin the Long March to Shaanxi, some 6,000 miles (9,656 km) to the north.

1936: Mao kidnaps Chiang and forces him to agree to the "Second United Front" against the Japanese.

1937–1945:

The Second Sino-Japanese War/World War II, in which both Mao and the Chinese fight Japanese invaders. Mao conserves forces in the guerilla war in north, while Chiang suffers great losses fighting the Japanese in the south.

1945: In August, Chiang orders Japanese troops in Manchuria to remain at their posts and surrender only to KMT, not Communists. United States–sponsored peace talks in Chongqing began, with both Mao and Chiang attending. They end inconclusively in October.

1946: The truce between the two side falls apart, and full-scale fighting begins.

1947:

March: KMT seize the Communist capital of Yanan and go on to take over major northern cities.

June: More United States–brokered peace talks; Chiang agrees to a temporary truce.

1948:

August: Communist forces launch a major offensive against KMT, whose soldiers begin to surrender in droves.

November: The decisive battle of Huai-Hai begins and lasts for sixty-five days, ending with victory by the People's Liberation Army.

1949:

October: Mao Zedong proclaims the People's Republic of China.

December: Americans withdraw aid from Chiang Kai-shek, who flees to Taiwan.

SUN YAT-SEN'S WRITING HELPED TO BRING ABOUT THE DOWNFALL OF THE 250 YEAR OLD QING DYNASTY AND CREATE A CHINESE REPUBLIC.

Prints & Photographs Division, Library of Congress, LC-USZ62-5972

THE VIOLENT TRANSFORMATION
OF CHINA

In the late nineteenth and early twentieth centuries, when both Chiang Kai-shek and Mao Zedong were born and came of age, China was seeing the last days of the corrupt and enfeebled Qing Dynasty, which had ruled the country for 250 years. The Qings had been severely weakened by the Taiping Rebellion (see "The Taiping Rebellion," p. 84) and were being eaten away by foreign powers. The Japanese held onto large portions of Manchuria after the First Sino-Japanese War of 1894 and annexed the island of Taiwan, while the British, French, and Germans expanded their influence over the rest of the country.

In 1911, the Qing Dynasty was finally toppled by reformer Sun Yat-sen, and China became a republic. The following year Sun Yat-sen formed the Nationalist Party, or Kuomintang (KMT), but he was pushed out of power by a former Qing general named Yuan Shikai, who proclaimed himself emperor. Sun Yat-sen, with his young follower and close advisor Chiang Kai-shek (see "Commanders," p. 292) fought a series of battles against the forces of Yuan and were eventually able to defeat him, but the KMT was now too weak to consolidate its gains, and the country fell into warring factions as different warlords vied with each other for control.

In 1925, Sun Yat-sen died of cancer, and Chiang became the leader of KMT forces. At this time, Mao Zedong (see "Commanders," p. 290) was a rising young member of the Communist Party who had organized labor strikes in major cities. Before his death, Sun Yat-sen had insisted on merging the KMT with the Communists, hoping the two groups would make a common cause in China. At first they did, forming the "United Front" in 1926 against the warlords who controlled the country, but then the alliance began to fall apart. The two had basically different goals. The KMT wanted to turn China into a republic and become a military and industrial power along western lines, while the Communists hoped for a mass peasant revolution along socialist lines.

Watching the growing power of the Communist Party—nearly 60,000 members strong—Chiang Kai-shek decided to strike first and attacked the Communists in Shanghai in the spring of 1927, rounding up and killing thousands. Mao Zedong barely escaped with his life. Fleeing to a provincial city, Mao famously proclaimed: "Political power is obtained from the barrel of a gun." He raised a guerilla army that battled Chiang Kai-shek's more numerous and better-equipped Nationalist army from 1929 to 1934.

Each time it seemed that the KMT had Mao and his forces encircled in the mountains of Jianxi Province in southern China, Mao would escape. But in 1933, a 700,000 strong Nationalist force, advised by German generals and with the aid of modern planes and artillery, cornered Mao. The latter responded by beginning, in March 1934, what would become known as the Long March (see "The Desperate Journey," p. 296) a brutal, year-long trek to a remote base in northern China that cost the Communists nearly 150,000 casualties but saved Mao's army.

In December 1936, as Nationalist forces were closing on him once again, Mao audaciously kidnapped Chiang Kai-shek (see "Kidnapping the Generalissimo," p. 296) and held him hostage. In a stunning propaganda move, Mao announced he would release Chiang if the latter joined forces with him in fighting the Japanese, who were advancing through Manchuria. Chiang, under duress, agreed and the first portion of the Civil War ended as the Second Sino-Japanese War began, coinciding roughly with the outbreak of World

led and motivated. Even so, the Nationalists slowly pushed the Communists and their newly renamed People's Liberation Army (PLA) back, until, at United States–brokered peace talks held in 1947, Chiang fatefully agreed to temporarily halt his advance. This gave the Communists breathing space, and in the summer of 1948, they began their final advance, destroying KMT forces at the pivotal Battle of Huai-Hai in November (see "Turning Point," p. 286), taking, killing, or capturing 550,000 Nationalist prisoners.

In October 1949, Mao and his victorious army proclaimed the People's Republic of China,

Fleeing to a provincial city, Mao famously proclaimed: "Political power is obtained from the barrel of a gun."

War II. Here KMT forces in the south, armed and equipped by the Americans, fought pitched battles with the Japanese and suffered massive losses, while Mao's northern army took few casualties in its guerilla-style conflict in the north.

As World War II ended, the Chinese Civil War began again in earnest. With the Soviet Union's takeover of Manchuria, the Chinese Communists under Mao had a ready base (as well as significant amounts of captured Japanese arms) with which to attack Chiang's KMT army in the south. The Nationalists, while well-supplied with American equipment, were poorly

with their capital city of Beijing. In December, Chiang and his Nationalist government fled to the island of Taiwan. Perhaps 8 million people had died as a result of the Civil War since 1927; millions more faced starvation and runaway inflation, but Mao had won his war against overwhelming odds. Western observers expected China to takes it place with the Soviet Union on the world stage, but, torn apart by internal difficulties (see "The Great Leap Backward," p. 299) largely due to Mao's miscalculations, it would be decades before China would begin to come into its own.

THE BATTLE OF HUAI-HAI: OCTOBER–DECEMBER, 1948

In the late summer of 1948, Communist forces under the overall command of Mao Zedong went on the attack in an offensive that would change the course of Chinese history. No longer were they guerilla warriors, hitting and then ducking for cover, the way they had been against the Japanese for the eight long years of the Second Sino-Japanese War. Nor were they the grim fighters on the run from overwhelming Nationalist forces, as they had been at the outset of the first phase of the Chinese Civil War, back in 1927–1934.

Instead, they were the People's Liberation Army (PLA), a modern army bearing modern arms, accompanied by tanks, airplanes, and heavy artillery, and they were intent on nothing less than the total destruction of the KMT forces that had plagued them for so long. The war had stretched for twenty years, involved millions of men and women, and was, in the way of civil wars, a highly personal conflict. The Communists knew that Nationalist leader Chiang Kai-shek hated them and had done—and was continuing to do—everything in his power to stamp them out as if they were cockroaches scuttling across his kitchen floor.

At the same time, the KMT troops knew that there was no place for them and their way of life in a China run by Mao. Across the wide plains and sere mountains of northern China and Manchuria, as the fall of 1948 began, there was finally a sense that endgame had been reached for both sides.

No Parlay

Peace treaty talks instituted by U.S. President Harry Truman immediately after World War II had failed to produce any results, despite the fact that both Mao and Chiang personally attended the conference in the then–capital city of Chongqing in August–September 1946. But as one English observer noted: "Neither Mao nor Chiang trusts one another. Each wants territorial, military, civil, political control. Yet each claps hands for democracy, union, freedom [and] nationalization."

When the Russians withdrew from the parts of Manchuria they had occupied after the Japanese defeat, they bequeathed to Mao's PLA a cornucopia of captured Japanese arms—700,000 rifles, 14,000 machine guns, and 700 military vehicles, including trucks, tanks, and armored cars. The PLA, husbanded as a guerilla force by Mao during the fighting against Japan, and never taking huge losses, had grown to nearly half-a-million-men strong, while the Nationalists had spent the war being bled dry by the Japanese in the south (see "Chronicle," p. 284). It was apparent that final battle for the fate of China would take place in the north, and here the PLA had another advantage. Their political commissars had been careful to treat the local peasantry with respect, and now had a ready-made labor force to prepare for the immense battles ahead.

Intensive fighting broke out in the summer of 1946, fighting in which Chiang's forces, with the aid of hundreds of millions of U.S. dollars, made headway. With U.S. air power supporting them, they were able to airlift masses of troops to bases in Manchuria—Mao's territory—and bring the battle to him. The Nationalists were even able to take the Communist capital city of Yanan in March 1947. Chiang was now possibly close to winning the war. But, pressured by the Americans, he agreed to a truce with Mao while peace talks resumed.

That was all Mao needed. By the following year, he and the PLA were ready to launch their historic offensive.

Dividing by Three

During the summer of 1948, the PLA had engaged in a series of hard-fought battles with KMT forces that resulted in pushing the main Nationalist army into an area of central China bounded by Nanjing on the south, Tsinan on the north, Kaifeng to the west, and Soochow (known as Suzhou today) on the east. Following the tenets of *The Art of War,* by Sun-tzu, Mao decided these troops should be surrounded, separated, and destroyed one by one.

On October 11, Mao secretly issued the orders to attack the 500,000 KMT troops between the Huai River and the Lung Hai railway (the combination of locales giving the battle its name). The plan was carefully worked out ahead of time between Mao and his chief strategist Su Yu, who was the originator of the idea for the offensive. The PLA divided the KMT territory into three primary targets. Beginning in November, each segment would be attacked in turn. The PLA's half a million men matched those of the Nationalists; it was to be a set piece battle such

as these two armies had never fought before. The Huai-Hai area where the battle would take place was enormous, about 7,600 square miles, and relatively flat. As November approached, the PLA commissars used hundreds of thousands of peasants to set up supply dumps and dig communications trenches as the PLA troops moved forward.

Then, at the end of October, the PLA attacked the Jinpu railway line, the crucial link to Nanjing and Nationalist headquarters there. This was to bait the trap; they knew that the attack would draw Nationalist forces to the railroad. On November 3, Huang Baitao, the nervous commander of KMT 7th Army in nearby Xuzhou begged Chiang Kai-shek for permission to move his men toward the Jinpu railroad to fight off an entire PLA army (the so-called East Chinese Field Army, or ECFA) which was said to be moving in that direction. On November 5, Chiang approved this plan.

The Plan: Part One

On November 7, as the KMT 7th Army crossed a large canal on its way toward Jinpu, the ECFA opened fire on it with heavy artillery and then struck hard, with combined forces of tanks and infantry. Part of the 7th Army fled back to Xuzhou; the rest was trapped by the canal. The ECFA easily broke through and thus cut the 7th Army in half. It then turned in two massive flanking movements to destroy each half. Half of the fighting took place in Xuzhou; the other half on open ground around the city. The Nationalist defenders did not give in easily, and fierce fighting took place in the freezing cold. There was house-to-house combat in Xuzhou, with Communist

SOLDIERS OF A CHINESE NATIONALIST MORTAR DETACHMENT WATCH HEAVY ARTILLERY SHELLS EXPLODE SHORT OF THE COMMUNIST LINES FROM THEIR POSITION, SOUTH OF SUCHOW, CHINA, NOV. 25, 1948.

Associated Press

forces having to burst through the doors of each building and home, throwing grenades and spraying rooms with their burp guns, whose barrels often became so hot that they melted.

Huang Baitao threw more and more reinforcements into the battle, only to see each unit chewed up by a PLA unit that had been waiting for just such an eventuality. Finally, by November 22, the 7th Army had ceased to exist, with more than 100,000 men killed, wounded, or captured. Huang Baitao committed suicide, and the PLA turned to Phase Two of its plan.

Part Two

The second phase called for the destruction of the Nationalist 12th Army, which Su and Mao had correctly assumed would come to the aid of the 7th Army. Led by one of Chiang's top commanders, General Huang Wei, the 12th attacked another PLA army, the Central Plains Field Army (CPFA), which retreated enough to lead the 12th Army into a trap sprung by ECFA, which surrounded and attacked Wei's forces. Encircled, the only way Wei could be supplied was by airdrop. Finally, at the end of November, the Nationalist general decided to try a breakout. But when the attempt was launched, the division leading the way—Chiang Kai-shek's elite 110th Division, which had fought bravely for the generalissimo during the war—unexpectedly defected to the Communists.

The destruction of the 12th Army now seemed inevitable. Chiang monitored the fighting from Nanjing with increasing concern. Part

THE CHINESE CIVIL WAR

of his problem was his officer corps. Most of his senior officers were rivals with each other, men who were almost warlords in the old Chinese tradition, and in some cases they did not want to go to the aid of the trapped troops of another general. Some of these officers considered that the war was lost already, and defected or deserted. And all of them, even the brave ones, offered only passive resistance, not striking out at the enemy but waiting to be attacked.

On December 12, a combined attack of the ECFA and CPFA spelled the end for Wei's entire army. Wei himself was captured.

Part Three

The end of the 12th Army left the PLA leaders with only one more goal to be obtained, the destruction of the KMT 13th Army (as well as parts of the 2nd Army—the rest of this unit was the only KMT unit to escape the trap in northern China.) Unexpectedly, Mao called a halt to the fighting for ten days. This was to allow the PLA, some of whose units were badly shot up, to regroup. But it was also a propaganda ploy. As December continued, heavy winter weather set in, including a severe snowstorm that made it impossible to supply the Nationalist 13th by airdrop. Su Yu then presented relatively lenient surrender terms to General Du Yuming, Chiang Kai-shek's personal protégé and representative in the field. Du rejected them, but the PLA made sure that

common Nationalist soldiers freezing and starving on the field knew about them. Units of the 13th Army began to desert en masse, to the point where Du had lost half his army by the end of December.

The only thing left for Du to do was order a breakout, which he planned for January 6th. Unfortunately from the Nationalist point of view, that day was the same day Su had decided that his combined PLA forces would attack. The collision of both armies created intense fighting, but two days later, the 13th Army had completely collapsed. Attempting to escape to the west, Du was himself captured on January 10, 1949, and the great Huai-Hai battle was at an end.

"The Campaign That Won China"

In total, the PLA killed, wounded, or captured 500,000 men in the two-month-long battle. Within weeks, major Chinese cities like Beijing fell to the Chinese as they swept south. On January 20, Chiang resigned his leadership of the Nationalists. By the following December, he had fled to Taiwan, leaving Mao in possession of China.

Today, the flat battlefields of Huai-Hai are visited often by tourists and students, who reverentially walk from monument to monument. The PLA Military Academy, and with good reason, calls the Battle of Huai-Hai "the campaign that won China."

MAO ZEDONG:
"THE BARREL OF A GUN"

When most westerners think of Mao Zedong, they summon up an image from propaganda posters of the 1960s, which show a corpulent Mao, face beaming, pointing the way to victory for the Chinese masses. The Mao of the Chinese Civil War was tall and lanky, an awkward young man from the country, who loved spicy hot food and plump peasant girls.

But both Maos shared the same burning desire: to unite China, whatever the cost, under the banner of Communism. Or perhaps it would be more accurate to say the banner of Communism as held by Mao himself—because Mao's main goal, like his antagonist, Chiang Kai-shek, was to be in total and complete control of China.

Mao Zedong was born in 1893 in the rural province of Hunan. Although Mao had a later tendency to exaggerate the poverty of his upbringing, his parents, who owned a small farm, were considered prosperous by the standards of Chinese peasantry. At the age of thirteen, Mao—able to read and use an abacus—left school and went to work for his father to whom he was not close. (His father was "the first capitalist I struggled against," Mao told a journalist in 1936.) His mother arranged a marriage for him with a peasant girl who was, at age nineteen, five years older than Mao. The girl died of unknown causes two years later, and Mao later denied having been married at all, but it is possible that the trauma of her death forced him to look outward, to discover the world around him.

One thing Mao discovered was new books that urged readers to change China—saying that the old order of the Qing Dynasty was dead. Mao was not then a Communist—he was most impressed by a book about George Washington's role in winning the American Revolution—but was encouraged in the spring of 1911 when Sun Yat-sen's successful uprising was launched against the Qings.

By 1918, Mao had left Hunan Province to study at Beijing University, where he read Marxist theory and joined a group of students inspired by the Bolshevik uprising in Russia. By 1921, Mao had joined the Communist Party and had begun to work organizing unions in China. When Sun Yat-sen decreed (see "Chronicle," p. 284) that the Communist Party and the KMT would work together, Mao became head of the KMT Propaganda Department, where he met, for the first time, his future rival Chiang Kai-shek. After the United Front fell apart and Chiang attacked Communists power centers and party centers in Shanghai and other areas, Mao fled to the country (his second wife would be executed by KMT troops) and began the brilliant guerilla resistance for which he is known.

"We must know that political power is obtained from the barrel of a gun," Mao wrote at the time. If he was the gun, the masses of Chinese that he rallied to him were the bullets. Despite enormous hardships, despite being outnumbered and outgunned by KMT forces, Mao and his men

THE VICTORIOUS MAO
ZEDONG PROCLAIMS
CHINA THE NEWLY
APPOINTED PEOPLE'S
REPUBLIC OF CHINA.

Chairman Mao announces the
birth of the People's Republic
of China on top of Tiananmen
in 1949, August 1959 (colour
litho), Chinese School, (20th
century) / Private Collection,
© The Chambers Gallery,
London / The Bridgeman Art
Library International

survived time and time again to fight again. The first phase of the civil war, culminating in the Long March and Mao's audacious kidnapping of Chiang, was a hard-won victory for Mao. The second phase, beginning at the end of World War II, had actually been won during the war, when Mao kept his forces in remote areas of China and harried the Japanese with guerilla actions, rather than fighting pitched battles, as did Chiang.

Mao's historic victory in 1949 came because he had outwitted and outfought Chiang Kai-shek almost every step of the way. When the two men met at the failed U.S. attempt to broker a peace treaty in 1945, Chiang pointed to Mao at a cocktail party and said sarcastically: "Look—isn't he a prize exhibit?" But the "prize exhibit" had won the greatest prize of all: the entire country of China.

CHIANG KAI-SHEK: RUTHLESS OPPORTUNIST

The figure that Chiang Kai-shek presented to the word was quite different than that presented by Mao Zedong. Chiang stood ramrod straight, wore a western-style military uniform, and appeared quite cultured and in control. During the first phase of the Chinese Civil War, before the shine wore off his reputation, he was a darling of the U.S. press and government, who saw him as best representing U.S. interests against the unruly Communism of Mao.

The press didn't report upon Chiang's volcanic temper or his bouts of debauchery with alcohol and Shanghai "sing-song girls," or the fact that he was so opportunistic that he proposed marriage to Sun Yat-sen's widow almost immediately after Sun Yat-sen died. When she turned him down, he married her younger sister, so he could be called Sun Yat-sen's brother-in-law.

This streak of ruthless opportunism would take Chiang Kai-shek far, although ultimately he overplayed his hand. He was born in 1887 in the eastern seaboard province of Zhejiang, to parents who owned a salt shop, but who claimed to be descended from nobility. Imperious, controlling, and reckless—on a dare, he once stuck his head in a large water jar and nearly drowned—Chiang always needed to be the center of attention.

At the age of sixteen, he left his village to attend school in the district capital, and there became inflamed with revolutionary ideas on liberating China from the Qing Dynasty. In 1905, Chiang cut off his queue, or long pigtail, which was worn as a sign of submission to the imperial dynasty, and sailed to Japan to attend military school.

Chiang returned in 1911 as commander of an artillery company that helped Sun Yat-sen destroy the Qings, and he became a key player in later fighting against those who sought to wrest the new republic from Sun. When Sun Yat-sen died, Chiang assumed the mantle of leadership, even thought it meant murdering several rivals (one of whom he personally shot while the man was in his hospital bed). After briefly forming a "United Front" with Communist forces, he became alarmed by their growing power and decided to make what he hoped would be a preemptive strike against them. Allying himself with Chinese underworld powers, Chiang rounded up and killed thousands of Chinese labor union members in Shanghai in 1927, thus setting off the Chinese Civil War.

In the years to follow, Chiang, who did not command his army in the field, saw his Nationalist forces come close numerous times to wiping out the Communists, only to have the Communists escape time and time again. Gradually, the sympathy of the people of China began to side with Mao. This was less because of Mao's Communist teachers and more because of the fact that Chiang's forces were notably corrupt and that Chiang himself was seen to be in the pocket of the Americans because of his reliance on them and their money. Ultimately, after World War II, even the Americans turned against Chiang, tired

SUN YAT-SEN, SITTING, WITH CLOSE ADVISOR CHIANG KAI-SHEK, WAS THE IMPETUS OF THE CIVIL WAR, LAUNCHING THE FIRST SUCCESSFUL UPRISING AGAINST THE QING DYNASTY. IT WAS THROUGH SUN YAT-SEN THAT CHIANG RECEIVED HIS MILITARY AND POLITICAL EXPERIENCE AND IT WAS THROUGH HIS DEATH THAT CHIANG ROSE TO POWER, GOING SO FAR AS TO MARRY THE YOUNGER SISTER OF SUN YAT-SEN'S WIDOW TO CLAIM TIES TO THE FORMER GREAT LEADER.

Sun Yat-Sen (1866-1925) and Chiang Kai-Shek (1887-1975) (b/w photo), Chinese Photographer / Private Collection, Archives Charmet / The Bridgeman Art Library International

of the corruption of his government, his scheming (his wife even tried to influence the outcome of an U.S. presidential campaign—see "Madame Chiang Kai-shek," p. 298), and the fact that his "democratic" National Party was merely a mechanism to give power to Chiang.

When Chiang was defeated, he and about 2 million of his followers proclaimed the Republic of China on the island of Taiwan. Chiang lived a long and inconvenient exile there, recognized as the real Chinese government by western powers only because of the exigencies of the Cold War. Dying in 1975 at the age of eighty-four, Chiang lived long enough to see Richard Nixon visit China and shake hands with Chiang's old nemesis, Chairman Mao, beginning the first step in formalizing relationships between the two countries.

The Nationalist Soldier: Brave but Unsupported

The Chinese Nationalist soldier has been much maligned through history because the KMT army came apart with such rapidity at the end of the Civil War, but recently his role has been reappraised by historians.

It's true that from the very beginning, KMT soldiers were better supplied than their Chinese counterparts, especially with United States–made weapons, but a closer look reveals that many KMT units went into battle poorly armed and uniformed because of the corruption of their commanders, who sold military equipment and supplies on the black market (sometimes to middlemen working for the Communists). KMT soldiers, aware of the fraud endemic around them, were also less motivated than their Communist counterparts. A final problem for any Nationalist soldier was leadership. While many individual KMT company-level officers and noncommissioned officers were brave soldiers and good leaders, staff level officers tended toward panicky retreats and contradictory orders. In the second phase of the Civil War, they—and Chiang Kai-shek—were consistently outthought strategically by military leaders like Mao and Zhou Enlai.

However, it needs to be taken into account that KMT forces had been bled dry fighting against the Japanese during World War II, suffering the loss of hundreds of thousands of casualties, while Mao had carefully husbanded his men. And when the

last offensive of the Civil War began in 1948, the Americans, who had consistently shored up the KMT, abandoned them (see "Americans in China," p. 298), essentially leaving Chiang's army to its unhappy fate.

MANY NATIONALISTS, OR KMT, SOLDIERS WENT INTO BATTLE POORLY ARMED AND UNIFORMED BECAUSE OF THE CORRUPTION OF THEIR COMMANDERS.

The Communist Soldier: "A Revolutionary Army"

The Chinese Communist soldier was for the most part a peasant recruit or conscript, because generally speaking Mao drew his forces from rural areas whereas Chiang's men came from the larger cities. Aside from being tough and resilient, Mao's men were highly motivated. Mao wrote that "a revolutionary army must have discipline that is established on a limited democratic basis," by which he meant that soldiers could not be coerced to fight, to face the dire situations Mao's men faced. They must fully understand why they were fighting and believe in it.

To foster this, Mao developed a system, first used in his guerilla forces and then put into effect in his regular army. He encouraged men to form small, ostensibly informal relationship units within squads and companies, as, in fact, soldiers the world over do. These social groups met regularly, without officers, to talk about the meaning of what they were fighting for. Thus, at the time they were fighting Chiang—that is to say, at the height of their motivation—the Chinese Communist soldiers had passionate beliefs that made them akin to what one historian has called "the closely-knit military religious orders of the past"—the Knights Templar of the Crusades, for instance.

Arms were a problem for Mao's Chinese guerilla fighters in the first stage of the war. They used rifles and machine guns made in the Soviet Union as well as whatever arms they could capture from KMT forces or buy on the black market. They had no air force, little artillery, and few armored

vehicles. In the second phase of the Civil War, after the end of World War II, Mao's newly renamed People's Liberation Army now functioned as a regular army mass, rather than a guerilla force, and was fully provided with captured Japanese or Soviet-made tanks, planes, artillery, etc.

MAO'S COMMUNIST SOLDIERS WERE HIGHLY MOTIVATED THOUGH INITIALLY POORLY ARMED.

Kidnapping the Generalissimo

On a freezing cold morning in December 1936, a middle-aged man wearing a pair of fine silk pajamas huddled shivering in a Chinese mountain cave while the sound of shouts and gunfire rang in his ears. The man's was Chiang Kai-shek—the generalissimo, as he liked to be called. While we have no idea exactly what he was thinking, we can have a pretty good idea that he was cursing the name of his chief rival, Mao.

When Chiang had awoken that morning—December 12—and begun his daily tai chi in the lovely Ming-era palace he had appropriated in the northern city of Xiang, all had looked good for the generalissimo. Despite the fact that Mao and his legions had made their stunning Long March, escaping the clutches of the Nationalist army in the south, Chiang had followed them north to their new base and was that very morning about to give the orders for a major KMT offensive. Normally, Chiang did not get

so close to the action, but this time he wanted to be there when his armies crushed those of Mao, his longtime nemesis. But just as he began the calming ancient motions of tai chi, he and his bodyguards heard shouts and the sound of loud motors. Chiang raced to the palace window to see two trucks come careening to a halt outside the palace compound gates. Drab-uniformed Communist soldiers leaped out, firing.

Chiang knew immediately what had happened and tried to escape, racing to the rear of the compound, climbing the mountain behind it, and hiding in a cave. But soon, freezing and surrounded, he was forced to give up. He was taken to the headquarters of a local warlord who had allied himself with Mao, there to await his fate. It was too dangerous for Mao to go near Chiang. In fact, KMT generals wanted to mount a massive air attack against the city where the warlord was holding the generalissimo, only

to be dissuaded by Madame Chiang herself, who told them it would endanger her husband's life.

At first Mao wanted to have the generalissimo—whose forces had after all beheaded his second wife and killed thousands of his followers—shot. But then a much better idea came to him. Why not use Chiang as an unwilling propaganda tool? So he announced that Chiang would be released as long as he joined with Mao in a "Second United Front" (the first had been way back in 1927) to defeat the Japanese who were attacking throughout Manchuria.

Chiang reluctantly agreed, and he was released. No one would have blamed him if he renewed his attack against Mao, but the kidnapping had affected his health. He fell ill, and it took him awhile to recover, which was all the breathing space the Communists needed. Without that kidnapping, there might not be a People's Republic of China today.

The Desperate Journey

It began with the sound of artillery roaring on a cloudy October day in 1934. After holding off KMT troops for almost a year, the sound of their guns were getting closer and closer, and the Chinese Communist troops in their mountain base in the southern province of Jianxi knew that it was time to break out to bases an incredible 6,000 miles (9,656 km) to the north.

The men and women of the army left carrying typewriters, desks, printing presses, bedrolls, everything they could get their hands on. Surrounding them was an army of 500,000 Nationalist soldiers who, for once, were being skillfully led by a German advisor, and so they were entrenched, with barbed wire and pillbox strongpoints that the Chinese would have to battle through.

Mao was leading the Chinese 8th Army—his advisor Zhou at his side—but the man who unofficially had the most power in the army was a Russian advisor named Otto Braun. It was Braun who advised the Chinese to bring with them all they could carry, and it was Braun who directed them in a frontal attack on Nationalist positions at Xiang, which resulted in 45,000 Chinese casualties.

After Braun was suspended from command, Mao became the March's effective leader. He immediately changed their Communist way of marching, taking a circuitous route and breaking up the army into smaller units. In a year's time, Mao and his armies crossed eighteen mountain ranges—including the Snowy Mountains, which contain some of the highest mountains in the world—twenty-four rivers, and a vast swamp known as the Chinese Grasslands, which claimed hundreds of lives with men simply sinking in quicksand.

They fought off not only the KMT, but the armies of provincial warlords as well. When Mao arrived in Shaanxi Province in October 1935, only 50,000 of the original 200,000 men remained, but the Communist army had survived and the march itself became the stuff of legend, a huge propaganda coup: "The Long March is a manifesto," Mao wrote in December 1935. "It has proclaimed to the world that the Red army is an army of heroes...."

IN OCTOBER OF 1934, MAO AND A FORCE OF 200,000 COMMUNIST SOLDIERS LEFT FOR THE LONG MARCH, A DESPERATE 6,000 MILE TREK ACROSS MOUNTAINS, RIVERS, AND SWAMPLANDS.

Mao Zedong (1893-1976) with Zhou Enlai (1898-1976) during the Long March in the north of Shensi, c.1935 (colour litho), Chinese School, (20th century) / Private Collection, Archives Charmet / The Bridgeman Art Library International

Americans in China: The Deep Betrayal

Like many foreign governments, the United States had had a foothold in China for some time. In the 1840s, during the First Opium War, it dispatched troops to protect U.S. business interests and missionaries, and by 1892 had established the Yangtze River patrol to keep bandits away from U.S. civilians.

After Sun Yat-sen's revolution of 1911 the Americans sent two regiments to protect U.S. lives and property, but otherwise did not interfere in the Civil War between Mao and Chiang. However, it was natural for U.S. political and business leaders to prefer Chiang as an alternative to the Communist Mao, and during World War II, U.S. supplies and material poured into KMT coffers, while U.S. strategic leaders such as General Joseph Stilwell and General Claire Chennault helped train the Chinese army. In the meantime, Chiang was feted as the man who would bring democracy to his sprawling country.

Unfortunately for Chiang, as World War II ended, U.S. leaders became tired of the corruption they saw among Chiang's advisors and of his inability to bring order to the chaos that was China. As Mao and Chiang squared off to fight round two of their Civil War, the Americans, at the behest of President Harry Truman and retired General George Marshall, called two different truce talks, but all these did was give the Communists breathing space. As KMT forces were being overwhelmed by Mao's troops in 1948 and 1949, the Truman administration gave up on Chiang as a lost cause and pulled support away from him, something Chiang, who always thought Americans would actually bring combat troops into the war on his side if necessary, felt as a deep betrayal.

Madame Chiang Kai-shek: "A Totally Mad Proposal"

Madame Chiang Kai-shek, Chiang's third wife, was a fixture in the U.S. media in the 1940s. Reporters loved her for her sleek beauty and elegant mandarin-collared dresses, her wit, and the access she provided to Chiang himself. (Chiang did not speak English and in any event disliked speaking to foreigners, so Madame Chiang translated for him.)

Most journalists knew that she and Chiang had a stormy marriage, plagued in no small part by Chiang's numerous infidelities. Madame Chiang—who had been born Meiling Soong and educated in U.S. schools—did not easily play the part of the devoted and submissive wife. She was brilliant and ambitious and, in her own way, as opportunistic as Chiang himself, particularly when it came to the enticement she knew that she had for men, especially foreign ones. One U.S. reporter who met

MADAME CHIANG KAI-SHEK, SEEN HERE WITH PRESIDENT TRUMAN, REMAINED A PROMINENT PART OF AMERICAN MEDIA. SHE KNEW HOW TO USE HER CHARM AND DEVISED A PLAN OF HER OWN FOR OBTAINING POWER.

New York World-Telegram and the Sun Newspaper Photograph Collection, Prints & Photographs Division, Library of Congress, LC-USZ62-114737

her described her as "quite dishy—it isn't fright that sends shivers down your spine when you shake hands with her."

At a crucial moment in 1943, Madame Chiang decided to use her charms to try to change the course of U.S. political history. Wendell Willkie, the Republican who had unsuccessfully run against Franklin Delano Roosevelt in 1940 and was considering another run in 1944, went on a good will mission to China and there met Madame Chiang at a tea party. The two of them began disappearing together for hours at a time—so

much so that Chiang's bodyguards, toting submachine guns, once tore up a house looking for them—and it became apparent to all that they were having an affair.

The rumpled, alcoholic, affable, and very married Willkie might have thought it was his good looks that drew the woman nicknamed "the Dragon Lady" to him, but it was all part of Madame Chiang's plan. The Roosevelt Administration seemed to be losing faith in her husband, she told Willkie political backer Gardner Cowles. She thought that if she had an affair with Willkie and secretly

backed him financially in a run against Roosevelt, he might win, at which point she would become highly influential in U.S. politics.

It was, as Cowles later put it, "a totally mad proposal," but the woman proposing it was so beautiful he was mesmerized. Fortunately— or unfortunately—Willkie failed to get the Republican nomination in 1944 and died that year of a heart attack. Madame Chiang, the ultimate survivor, would outlive her husband and all of her contemporaries, dying in New York City in 2003 at the age of 105.

The Great Leap Backward

After Mao won his war against overwhelming odds, he seems to have thought that there was nothing he could not do. When the People's Republic of China was born in 1949, he decided to move drastically forward to turn the country into a Communist state, despite the advice of more conservative aides who felt that the country—torn apart by years of war and undergoing rampant economic inflation—needed to move more slowly.

In 1958, Mao instituted what he called "the Great Leap Forward," an

attempt to modernize Chinese industry and communize its agriculture. First steel factories were built on fertile rice fields, and then 24,000 communes were created nationwide, each controlling its own means of production. But many peasants were now forced from farming to becoming steelworkers (many of them creating their own backyard forges) while a great deal of fertile land was lost to the factories, and also to incorrect agricultural techniques foisted on Chinese peasants by Maoist officials who wanted a higher rice yield.

The result was the disastrous Great Famine, in which anywhere from 20 to 40 million people died by the end of 1962. Mao's reputation, both within China and without, never really recovered from this. The disaster—coupled with the ensuing Cultural Revolution, in which Mao, trying to divert attention from his policy failures, used militant Red Guards to purge his political enemies—ensured that China's entry into the modern world would still be decades away.

16

THE SPANISH CIVIL WAR

1936–1939

This harsh conflict between Nationalist rebels seeking to wrest control of Spain from the elected Republican government became the stage for a larger struggle between Fascism and Communism.

Combatants

- Republicans
- Nationalists

Theater of War

Spain

Casualties

Republicans: 110,000 killed in combat; between 100,000–200,000 estimated executed after the war
Nationalists: 90,000 killed in combat

Major Figures

REPUBLICANS
President Manuel Azana, who headed the Republican administration during the war
Juan Negrín López, Republican prime minister
Indalacio Prieto, Republican minister of war who urged the Republicans to seize Teruel
Juan Hernández Saravia, chief commander of the Republican forces at Teruel

NATIONALISTS
General Francisco Franco, head of the Nationalist military forces and government
General Manuel Goded and **General Emilio Mola,** fellow plotters and chief lieutenants

If there were a dress rehearsal for World War II, it took place in Spain between 1936 and 1939, when the Nationalist forces of General Francisco Franco rebelled against the duly elected Republican government and sought to take over control of the country by military force. Supporting Franco and the Nationalists were the Fascist regimes of Germany and Italy. Opposing them on the Nationalist, or Loyalist, side were the Soviet Union and various volunteer "International Brigades" made up of a mix of Communists, socialists, and those who believed in a democratic form of government. Essentially, two completely different ideologies, one socialist, one fascist, were now fighting for control of Spain. With western powers such as Great Britain, France, and the United States staying out of the war, the forces of fascism finally won out.

1936:

February: The leftist Popular Front, representing the Republican side, wins national elections.

April: The new parliament replaces President Niceto Alcalá Zamora with President Manuel Azana, a liberal politician.

July: Military uprising begins in Spain and Spanish Morocco. Republican warships blockade General Francisco Franco and the Army of Africa in Morocco. Adolf Hitler and Benito Mussolini agree to airlift the Army of Africa across the Strait of Gibraltar.

August: The First International Brigades arrive in Spain. Nationalist forces relieve the siege of Toledo.

October: Franco is named "Chief of Spanish State" by Nationalist rebels. Joseph Stalin sends the first aid to the Republican government.

November: Germany and Italy recognize Franco as the head of Spain's government. Franco launches a major offensive against Madrid.

December: The Republicans win the Battle of Boadilla del Monte.

1937:

February: The Republicans win the Battle of Jarama.

March: The Republicans win the Battle of Guadalajara, ending Franco's bid to take Madrid.

April: The town of Guernica destroyed by bombing of Condor Legion.

June: The Republicans lose the strategic city of Bilbao to the Nationalists.

December: The beginning of the Battle of Teruel.

1938:

February: The Nationalists defeat the Republicans at Teruel. They launch a major offensive designed to cut Spain in half.

April: The Nationalists reach the Mediterranean.

March: The Republican forces begin to collapse after losing the Battle of the Ebro River.

October: The International Brigades leave Spain.

1939:

January: Barcelona falls to Nationalist forces.

March: Fall of Madrid.

April: The Republicans surrender unconditionally.

RALLYING INTERNATIONAL SENTIMENT TO THEIR CAUSE, SUPPORTERS OF THE REPUBLICAN ARMIES WAGED PROPAGANDA WAR WITH POSTERS LIKE THIS.

Rue des Archives/The Granger Collection, New York

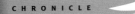

"OVER ALL OF SPAIN,
THE SKY IS CLEAR"

After undergoing its long fall from power during the seventeenth to nineteenth centuries, Spain veered from monarchy to republic (for a short period of time beginning in 1873) and then back again to monarchy. King Alfonso XIII would reign from 1887 to 1931, at which point he agreed under pressure to democratic elections. When the people of Spain overwhelmingly voted for a republic, he resigned and went into exile in Rome.

The new Republican government was centrist in nature, but constant strife between political radicals on both the right and left during the Great Depression made it hard for moderates to stay in power. In 1936, the leftist "Popular Front"

Manuel Azana, a liberal politician abhorred by conservative groups such as the Falange (Fascist) Party, run by General Francisco Franco. There ensued a period of violence and political assassinations on both sides as Franco and other military officers such as General Manuel Goded and General Emilio Mola plotted a military coup.

On July 17, 1936, the phrase, "Over all of Spain, the sky is clear," was broadcast on numerous radio stations. It was the signal for a right-wing uprising. The rebellion was almost immediately successful in the south and west, in rural and highly Catholic provinces, but it was pushed back by Republicans in Madrid, Barcelona, and other major northern industrial cities. In the very begin-

The Spanish Civil War was widely seen as the opening battle of World War II, one in which the world powers had failed to defend against the evils of fascism, encouraging Hitler to continue his plans for world domination.

won the elections and began agrarian reforms, which many in Spain saw as inspired by the Soviet Union, and also continued railing against the power of the Catholic Church, a stance that was partly based in the reality that the Church had a strong influence on Spanish politics, but which was also partly anti-clerical in nature.

In April 1936, the new parliament replaced President Niceto Alcalà Zamora with President

ning, the war featured untrained workers militias fighting on the Republican side against the newer conscripts who made up the rebellious Spanish army in Spain, which had almost completely sided with the Nationalists.

Republican warships had barricaded the Spanish Army of Africa, a formidable fighting force led by Franco, in Morocco. However, Adolf Hitler and Benito Mussolini agreed to airlift

Franco's army across the Strait of Gibraltar to Spain, the first but not the last aid they would give to Franco, thus turning what would have been a stalled coup d'état into a serious civil war.

After the Army of Africa arrived, it moved swiftly to relieve the besieged Nationalist garrison at Toledo. It named Franco its "Chief of the Spanish State" on October 1, 1936, and he attacked Madrid, but the city held out against his forces, with the Republicans defeating him at the battles of Boadilla del Monte (December 1936), Jarama (February 1937), and Guadalajara (March 1937).

Despite this, the Nationalists had certain advantages. The Republican government was rife with dissension between Communists, moderate socialists, a hodge-podge of anarchists, Trotskyites, and social revolutionaries, as well as Basque separatists. And while the Soviet Union had started to send aid to the Republicans, the closer and far wealthier powers of France and Great Britain, mired in economic difficulties and fearful of war with Fascist powers, stayed out of the conflict.

The Nationalists, on the other hand, were well supported by Germany and Italy. With the assistance of the ace German Condor Legion, they captured much of northern Spain using terror bombing as a particularly new and frightful tool of war. The Republicans, aided by volunteer "International Brigades" that had rushed to Spain as world opinion fell on the side of the beleaguered government, fought back hard and

in a strong counteroffensive in the fall of 1937 recovered some of the ground lost, although at an almost Pyrrhic cost of men and material.

However, these victories were offset by the victory of the Nationalists at the Battle of Teruel (see "Turning Point," p. 304) and a sweeping offensive launched by Franco in early 1938, involving 100,000 men and more than 600 German and Italian planes. Using mass panzer attacks and carpet bombing techniques, they swept through the province of Aragon and reached the Mediterranean on April 15, cutting the Republic in half.

Republican forces held on, hoping the world would come to their aid. But in January 1939, Nationalist forces captured Barcelona, the new seat of the Nationalist government, which caused the collapse of Nationalist resistance throughout the country. The Republicans surrendered on March 28, 1939, and Francisco Franco became the head of Spain, a country he would rule until his death in 1972. Despite the pleas of western countries, more than 100,000 Republican sympathizers in Spain were executed after the war, while others died in concentration camps. Nearly 400,000 Spanish citizens went into exile to avoid such treatment.

Spain was to remain neutral during the Second World War, but the Spanish Civil War was widely seen as the opening battle of World War II, one in which the world powers had failed to defend against the evils of fascism, encouraging Hitler to continue his plans for world domination.

BATTLE OF TERUEL:
DECEMBER–FEBRUARY, 1937–1938

Battles are, by their very nature, grim affairs. They can be nothing else, because they are essentially abattoirs where human beings are slaughtered.

But the Battle of Teruel—what Spanish Civil War historian Hugh Thomas calls "the atrocious battle of Teruel"—was the darkest conflict in the history of the war, both because of the amount of men who lost their lives there and because of the landscape itself.

Teruel is an ancient walled town located in the extremely poor province of Lower Aragon in northeastern Spain. It is surrounded by bizarre geological formations—singular sawtooth peaks; deep, narrow gorges; and ridges that twist up and away from the town like arthritic fingers.

Teruel is the most remote provincial capital in Spain and also, because of its elevation, it has the lowest average temperature in the country. To add to the glum aura of Teruel, it has its own legend, the maudlin story of two separated lovers who died of longing in the thirteenth century. As if that isn't enough, the town has been a battleground for centuries, beginning in the twelfth century when it was a spark point of conflict between the Moors and Christians, a place where opposing forces collided.

And now, in the late fall of 1937, this oppressive place was about to see new conflicts—and about to create a new legend.

"Teruel's Tooth"

By December 1937, the war in Spain had raged for a year and a half. Generalissimo Francisco Franco, after early losses to the rebels, had conquered much of northern and western Spain and planned to renew his attacks on Madrid by first launching a preliminary attack on Guadalajara just before Christmas. But the Republicans got wind of these plans. One story has it that a Republican spy disguised himself as a shepherd and infiltrated Franco's headquarters—although this may be as apocryphal as Teruel's lovers—and decided to derail them with an attack that would draw off Franco's forces from his planned attack.

Teruel was the target of the Republican offensive for two reasons. One, it was a Nationalist-held town that stuck like a thumb jabbed into the belly of Republican-held Spain—a bulge, or salient, in the military term—and was thus surrounded on three sides by Republican forces. Second, the town's garrison numbered only about 4,000 men commanded by Colonel Rey d'Harcourt, and seemed easy pickings, especially because the Republicans could summon up an army of 100,000 of their finest fighters to make the attack. And there would be no International Brigades here, just the fighters of Spain, commanded by General Juan Hernández Saravia, to show the world that Republican Spain could still hold its own against Franco.

For days, moving in at night, Saravia's army crept into trenches around Teruel as the weather began to turn colder. Then, on the night of December 15, they attacked, without artillery preparation to preserve the element of surprise. It had started to snow as the attackers climbed out of their trenches and advanced on the town, dark figures darting through the wind-blown flakes. First one shot, then several, then a ragged fusillade rang out from the town as its defenders caught sight of the attackers. Moving swiftly to the west, a large force of Republicans climbed the solitary peak known as "Teruel's Tooth," which commanded the town. There was bitter fighting there throughout the night, much of it hand-to-hand, with both Nationalists and Republicans hurtling to their deaths over the peak's sheer and slippery sides, but by dawn the town was in Republican hands.

"Confidence in Spain"

D'Harcourt withdrew his forces from Teruel's Tooth that day and pulled back his lines from the edge of town. Seeing that he was facing a much larger force, he wanted to consolidate his men into a tight defensive line. In the meantime, word of the attack reached Franco's headquarters. The normally level-headed generalissimo was infuriated that the Republicans launched their attack, because it now made it very difficult for him to begin his scheduled offensive against Guadalajara.

Despite German and Italian advisors who were telling Franco to ignore Teruel, he knew better, knew that it would not do to allow the Republicans the propaganda victory of re-capturing even one provincial capital, lest it seemed (especially to foreign observers) that the tide of the war was turning. However, because of logistical reasons, he could not send a relief force to Teruel until December 29. He wired d'Harcourt, telling him to "have confidence in Spain as Spain has confidence in you" and to fight to the last man.

By December 21, Republican forces had entered the town and were engaged in street-by-street fighting with the vastly outnumbered Nationalists. In this strange battle, the Republicans were for once the more numerous and better-armed, the Nationalists reduced to holding bank and government buildings and retreating as they left bloody trails in the snow behind them. The fighting was savage. Within a week, d'Harcourt's numbers were reduced by half, to about 2,000 men. The Republicans would approach the buildings they held with tanks and armored cars and blast them with shell fire. Then Republican machine gunners would open up from neighboring roofs, hosing windows with bullets while the infantry snuck up close and threw dynamite bombs through; then, a final charge, with bayonets fixed. Prisoners were not taken.

The Blizzard

While this house-to-house fighting was taking place in the city, however, Franco's forces had launched their counteroffensive. Attacking on December 29, they recaptured Teruel's Tooth, which meant that they could now shell Republican forces within the city from the heights. But just as this happened, a huge blizzard set in—the worst anyone had seen for twenty years. The temperature dropped to -18°F (-28°C). Both machines and men froze up and stalled. The snow was 4 feet (1.2 m) deep in the street of Teruel, yet the fighting continued deep in the cellars, with hand grenades, knives, and fists. Soldiers from the different armies inhabited different floors of the same building, firing at each other through holes they smashed in the floors and ceilings. In the meantime, frozen and twisted bodies—solders and civilians alike—littered the streets like grotesque statuary.

With the Nationalist artillery and the Condor Legion (see "Birds of Prey," p. 311) held at bay by the weather, the Republicans were able to drive d'Harcourt's forces to ground. Finally, on January 8, without food, water, or ammunition, and encumbered by hundreds of civilian refugees, d'Harcourt emerged from the cellar of the Civil Governor's Building, waving a white flag. Next to him were the bishop of Teruel and the chairman of the local chapter of the Red Cross. Honoring his extraordinary stand, the Republicans treated the Nationalist wounded and the civilian refugees well. D'Harcourt and the bishop of Teruel were taken to Republican-held Valencia as prisoners, and the Republican government trumpeted a great victory.

The fighting, however, was far from over.

Besiegers Besieged

On January 17, with the weather clearing, Franco's forces unleashed a huge artillery barrage on Teruel, and then the Nationalist army advanced while planes from both sides held dog-fight duels in the gray skies above. For days the battle wavered; the Republicans, losing men, brought in International Brigades and flung them into battle, 10,000-men strong. But gradually the Republican lines gave way. By the end of January, the besiegers, themselves now besieged, had been driven into the core of the city. Many could no longer take the strain of fighting for a month and a half under such horrible conditions and refused to go to their positions anymore. (Fifty men, including three noncommissioned officers, were shot for dereliction of duty.)

On February 7, the Nationalists, now 90,000 in number, made their last attack on Teruel's offenses, an attack that included a massive cavalry charge, one of the last in the history of warfare. It was too much for the demoralized Republican forces. Soon after, the survivors fought their way out of the ruined city, the last leaving in the dead of night in late February. Seventeen thousand Republicans were captured in the attack and forced to bury 10,000 corpses that their comrades had left behind in the city. There were another 4,000 Republican dead on the battlefields around Teruel and probably 20,000 wounded in all. This meant that the Republicans had essentially lost nearly half their original attacking forces after a two-month-long battle.

The Battle of Teruel depleted the resources of the Republican army, which was simply unable, at this point in the war, to replace men and munitions. Because of the Republican losses there, the army was incapable of offering any real resistance to Franco's spring 1938 offensive, in which he pushed east to the sea, cutting Spain in half. Teruel was a bitter blow to Republican hopes internationally as well, because Joseph Stalin soon began to withdraw aid, seeing that he was supporting a losing cause.

The strange and desperate battle of Teruel engendered one more cruel stroke of fate. D'Harcourt, the heroic Nationalist commander who had held out so long (and who had been called a "traitor" by Franco when he surrendered his ragged forces) was held captive for a year by the Republicans. In the winter of 1939, as the last of the Republican forces retreated toward the safety of France, his guards put him up against a wall and shot him. His heroism meant nothing in a war where there was little room for honor, on either side.

GENERALISSIMO FRANCISCO FRANCO: RUTHLESS AND OBSTINATE

Franco was born in Spain in 1892, the son of a naval postmaster. He grew up to become a young man who was on the surface not prepossessing. He was physically small, almost delicate, with soft features and an almost child-like look to his large, olive-shaped eyes. But hidden within was a person of sterner stuff. Franco went to the Toledo Military Academy and was posted to Morocco in 1913, where he proved his bravery battling against rebel Moorish factions. By 1920 and now a major, he became second in command of the Spanish Foreign Legion, a unit that was known for its cruelty when putting down rebellions. One man, who served under Franco in Morocco, wrote: "When it attacked, the Legion knew no limits to its vengeance. When it left a village, nothing remained but fires and the corpses of men, women, and children."

Franco was a staunch Catholic, political conservative, and supporter of the monarchy. A member of King Alfonso XIII's court attended his 1923 wedding to Carmen Polo, a wealthy aristocrat. When Alfonso abdicated in 1931 after widespread unrest, a Republican government took over, one that distrusted Franco and assigned him to minor posts, including one that amounted to quasi-exile in the Balearic Islands. However, Franco and numerous other officers began plotting to overthrow the Republicans and in July 1936 staged their history-changing military coup.

Franco had numerous rivals for military leadership of the Nationalist armies, but he forced most of them into exile while possibly arranging for the deaths of at least two more in plane crashes. Just as he was in his Foreign Legion days, he was ruthless in prosecuting the war against the Republicans, whose way of life he violently hated. Franco did not stop his forces from executing Republican prisoners, either during or after the war, and he was especially disturbed by the way many Republicans held the Catholic Church in disdain. In the end, he demanded unconditional surrender and got it, and then ruthlessly purged anyone who had supported the Republican cause.

A STAUNCH CATHOLIC, CONSERVATIVE, AND SUPPORTER OF THE MONARCHY, FRANCO WAS RUTHLESS IN WAGING WAR AGAINST THE REPUBLICANS.

Official Portrait of General Francisco Franco (1892–1975) (coloured photo), Spanish School, (20th century) / Private Collection, Archives Charmet / The Bridgeman Art Library International

MANUEL AZANA:
AT HISTORY'S CROSSROADS

anuel Azana, the last president of the Second Spanish Republic, was one of those unfortunate politicians whose spirit lay on the side of truth and justice, but whose body lay directly in the hurly-burly of history's crossroads.

Azana was born to a wealthy Madrid family in 1880, but orphaned at a young age when both his parents were killed. Despite this, Azana, a brilliant student, became a lawyer at the age of seventeen and received a doctorate in history and political science when he was twenty. By 1920, he had become a writer, a member of a reformist Spanish political party, and a minor politician. He was a strong critic of the power of the Catholic Church in Spain, as well as of King Alfonso XIII. He became prime minister of a Republican coalition government when Alfonso was ousted. Azana's radical ideas about redistributing land and wealth belonging to the Church put him on a collision course with some of the most powerful forces in Spain, and he resigned.

In 1934, Azana founded the Republican Left Party, which staged bloody uprisings in several major Spanish cities, including Barcelona. Accused of fomenting these, Azana was incarcerated aboard a Spanish naval vessel, but was eventually acquitted of all charges. He was elected president of the Spanish Republic only two months before the military coup that threw the

FROM LEFT TO RIGHT, JUAN NEGRIN (IN DARK COAT), REPUBLICAN PRIME MINISTER, MANUEL AZANA Y DIAZ, PRESIDENT OF THE REPUBLIC, AND TWO REPUBLICAN GENERALS, JOSE MIAJA AND VALENTIN GONZALEZ, INSPECTING TROOPS GOING TO THE FRONT.

Getty Images

country into civil war. In fact, it was his assuming that post that pushed military plotters such as Franco over the edge, because it was assumed that the military reforms Azana had declared (which included cutting the defense budget) would severely impact Spain's army.

When the war started, Azana attempted to bring together the various squabbling factions of left-wing groups that made up the Republican political party, urging them to unite to beat off the fascists. He was not successful and then tried to resign his office, protesting that he was ineffective and did not, in any event, want to preside over a country at war with itself. He was persuaded to stay on, however, and with his cabinet fled across the French border in February 1939 as Nationalist forces spread across Spain. He died in France in 1940.

The Republican Soldier

When the war began, the Republican army immediately dwindled to half its former size because many of its soldiers—and most of its officers—went over to the Nationalist side. When Nationalist units in Spain rose up and began to seize territory in July of 1936, the Republican government gave out arms to trade unions and left-wing organizations, hoping to swell their numbers.

Although at the very beginning of the war, the Republicans outnumbered the Nationalist forces, that would soon change. The Republican forces during the war in all totaled perhaps 450,000, including 60,000 members of the various International Brigades—and so in general was at a disadvantage, because Nationalist forces would ultimately number 600,000. While the Republicans were armed by Joseph Stalin—and by the fall of 1936 had a large number of Soviet tanks and airplanes, as well as military advisors, pilots, and mechanics—the quality of the armament was not as good as that of the Condor Legion of the Germans. Still, Republican forces held out much longer in the war than many people thought they would, refusing to give in at Madrid and fighting to the bitter end elsewhere. Not all of the Republicans had the fervor of the International Brigades. Many of them were conscripts, some even men who had passed out in their local taverns and when they awoke found themselves impressed into the army. They suffered from a lack of noncommissioned officers, most of whom had defected to Franco's army. But as the war progressed, they fought harder and better, until overwhelmed by the advantage in numbers and arms that the enemy possessed. Unfortunately, most Republican soldiers who surrendered in Spain in 1939 were treated harshly—either executed or sent to concentration camps (see "The Bloody Aftermath," p. 315).

The Nationalist Soldier

Generalissimo Francisco Franco started out his civil war with an advantage, because at least half of the soldiers in the Spanish army—and, significantly, most of the officers—defected to his side. But his problem at the outset was that he commanded the Army of Africa which, while a tough and superior fighting force, consisting of the regular Spanish Army, the Spanish foreign legion, and Moroccan fighters, numbered only about 34,000 men. The bulk of the army—the so-called Peninsular Army—was in Spain, but was considered the more poorly trained and undependable of the two forces.

But Adolf Hitler's airlift of the Army of Africa into Spain in late July 1936 changed the equation of the war. Franco was able to use his experienced officers to bolster the experience and morale of the Peninsula Army in the initial fighting. Very soon, with the aid of arms from Germany and Italy, the Nationalists had taken over one-third of Spain, and at that point Franco began forced conscription, raising an army of some 270,000 thousand men by 1937. As well as the German aviators of the Condor Legion, the Nationalist forces were joined by some 30,000 so-called "Blue Shirts" sent from Italy by Benito Mussolini.

With better arms and training, the Nationalist Army, pushed back during the fall of 1936, eventually destroyed the enemy in a series of key battles, which culminated in its victory in the stubborn and hard-fought Battle of Teruel (see "Turning Point," p. 304) in the winter of 1937–1938. But victory was by no means certain until that point.

The Condor Legion: Birds of Prey

Within a month of the beginning of the Spanish Civil War, the Germans were supplying Franco's legions with men and material. Starting in August 1937, streams of freighters (waving the flags of various South American countries) left Hamburg carrying bombers and fighter planes, trucks, land mines, flame-throwers, machine guns, and even entire radio field stations. They also carried pilots, gun crews, and radio and other equipment operators, although at first Germany did not publicly acknowledge their presence.

Beginning in September 1937, Colonel Walter Warlimont, a member of the German general staff, arrived to become General Franco's military advisor, and it was he who suggested forming a "condor" legion of German flyers—a bomber group, a fighter group, a reconnaissance group, and a seaplane group. The Condor Legion originally had about 100 aircraft and 5,000 men, although the number of planes and men would nearly double during the course of the war. Although commanded by a German officer, the unit was responsible directly to Franco. The Condor Legion took part in numerous engagements in the war, and many people suspected that Hitler wanted them there not so much because of his ideological kinship to Franco's fascists, but because he wanted to use Spain as practice for the war he was planning.

There is some truth in this. While in Spain, the Condor Legion perfected the technique of carpet bombing (all planes dropping all their bombs at once on a target, rather than dropping

them in turn). It was also apparent during different attacks on civilians (see "The Sorrow of Guernica," p. 314) that Condor Legion planes were rehearsing different methods of strafing. Hermann Göring, head of the Luftwaffe, said as much during the Nuremberg Trials after the war, when he testified that "I urged [Hitler] to give support [to Franco], under all circumstances, firstly in order to prevent the further spread of communism in that theater and, secondly, to test my young Luftwaffe at this opportunity in this or that technical respect."

ON APRIL 26, 1937, GERMAN PILOTS FLYING UNDER THE SPANISH NATIONAL-IST BANNER DEMOLISHED THE CITY OF GUERNICA.
Getty Images

The International Brigades: Fascist Bombs, Innocent Blood

The idea for brigades of men and women from around the world committed to ousting the fascists from Spain belonged to French Communist Party leader Maurice Thorez, who came up with it shortly after German planes had airlifted Franco's Army to Spain (see "Chronicle," p. 302). Joseph Stalin himself approved the plan, and the Comintern—the international arm of the Communist Party—helped raise the groups.

In all during the war, there were 59,000 foreigners serving on Spanish soil. They came from all over the world—France, Great Britain, the United States, Czechoslovakia, Canada, Mexico, Yugoslavia, etc. Both men and women fought, and the brigades represented a fairly large spectrum of political thinking on the left—from radical Communists to moderate democrats. However, Communists always led the battalions from the different countries, which caused friction among those in the brigades who were not so radical in their political thought.

Most members of the brigades were young and idealistic. Those who volunteered faced harsh fighting against a generally better-trained and equipped enemy, and the horrible scenes of war sometimes tested their resolve, as in the young recruit who, entering a Madrid under Nationalist siege, saw "the gaping bodies of a dozen innocent women lying among scattered milk cans and bits of Fascist bombs, turning the pavement red with their gushing blood." The International Brigades saw women fighting side by side with men, and blacks leading racially mixed units into combat, for the first time.

Americans featured strongly in the fighting, entering the war with both the Abraham Lincoln and George Washington Battalions, which suffered casualties so severe that the two units were eventually merged into one. Two thousand eight hundred Americans enlisted in International Battalions, and one-third of them were killed or wounded, a casualty rate about on a par with what most volunteers from other countries suffered.

THE INTERNATIONAL BRIGADES, SEEN HERE, CONSISTED OF MEN AND WOMEN FROM ALL OVER THE WORLD COMMITTED TO FIGHTING FASCISM. BEGUN BY MAURICE THOREZ, THE COMMUNIST PARTY LEADER OF FRANCE, THE BRIGADES TOTALED 59,000 FIGHTING FOR THE REPUBLICAN CAUSE.

Getty Images

The Writer's War: "A Cause To Fight For"

"The ivory tower is no place for writers who have in democracy a cause to fight for. If you live, your writing will be better for the experience gained in battle," wrote French Communist André Malraux in a speech he gave in the United States in November 1938. "If you die, you will make more living documents than anything you could write in ivory towers."

Like the war in Vietnam a quarter century later (see "The Vietnam War," p. 362), the Civil War in Spain drew writers with fierce partisan views. Some of them actually fought in battle, as Malraux urged. Writer George Orwell, a devout socialist, went to Spain and was seriously wounded

there. But when he found that Communists had outlawed the socialist party he belonged to, which put him in danger of being executed, he returned to England and wrote *Homage to Catalonia*, a classic that decried the tyranny of both left and right. American writer Ernest Hemingway reported on the war and was strongly on the Republican side, visiting Popular Front lines near Madrid and making fund-raising speeches back in the United States and elsewhere.

Another writer in Spain—but one who provided an entirely different perspective—was Kim Philby, who was a correspondent for the London *Times,* covering the war from the

Nationalist side and writing fawning reports about Francisco Franco. After a Republican shell hit a car in which Philby and three other journalists were driving, killing all but Philby, Franco decorated Philby. Philby found this quite ironic, because the future British spy and traitor was already in the employ of the Communists and secretly reporting to Joseph Stalin.

ANOTHER WEAPON OF WAR CAME IN
A WAVE OF INTERNATIONAL WRITERS,
INCLUDING ERNEST HEMINGWAY,
PICTURED HERE.
Getty Images

The Sorrow of Guernica

In 1937, April 26 was a Monday afternoon, and Monday afternoon in the Basque town of Guernica always meant market day. Despite the fighting that had been going on nearby between Nationalist forces and Republicans and Basque separatists, it was important to the thousands of people who gathered in Guernica that they could come and trade their goods as they had done for centuries. Guernica has often been described as the spiritual and cultural center of the Basque world, the place where the independent Basque assembly had historically met under an oak tree in the town square. In these troubled times, it was good to keep up tradition.

Late on Monday afternoon, those in the square turned their heads upward at the approach of airplane engines, squinting open-mouthed at the sky. But before they had time to react, the planes were upon them. Although they had Nationalist markings, the planes were German—Junker JU-2 bombers, and Heinkel He-111 fighters—and flown by German pilots of the Condor Legion. Without fanfare, they began dropping bombs directly on Guernica, first satchels of hand-grenades tied together with fuses, then explosive bombs and incendiaries. Explosions tore through the panicked crowds racing from the market. For three hours, twenty-five planes dropped 100,000 pounds of explosive and incendiary bombs on Guernica, gutting the entire town. People raced for the shelters. One man—a boy at the time—recalled huddling in a basement: "I didn't think about my parents, mother, house, nothing. Just escape."

But those who tried to escape were gunned down by the HE-III's, who machine-gunned anything moving on the streets. "[The planes] just kept going back and forth, sometimes in a long line, sometime in close formation," said one witness. "It was as if they were practicing new moves." In the end, the Basque government reported 1,600 people were killed and 900 wounded, although these figures have since been disputed as too high—it is possible 300–400 died that day. Seventy percent of Guernica was destroyed. The attack immediately caused an international incident, with even Nationalist supporters in other countries denouncing it. The Nationalists denied involvement, and said that the town was burned by retreating Republican troops. It was a myth, but it remained a crime in Spain for the next thirty years to say that Guernica was bombed.

It is probable that the Nationalists and their German advisors decided to bomb Guernica precisely because it was the center of the Basque world, to teach their enemies a lesson. The bombing ultimately backfired, because world outcry (stoked by writers and artists such as Pablo Picasso, who began his famous painting *Guernica* within fifteen days of the attack) forever branded the Nationalists and Germans as barbarians.

SPANISH NATIONALIST SOLDIERS SURVEY THE DAMAGE AND RUBBLE OF GUERNICA, WROUGHT BY GERMAN PILOTS OF THE CONDOR LEGION IN THIS MAY 1, 1937 PHOTOGRAPH.

ullstein bild / The Granger Collection, New York

The Bloody Aftermath

At the end of the Spanish Civil War, in the fine and balmy spring of 1939, there was a feeling of great relief among those of the middle and upper classes who supported Franco's military rebellion. Men and women began to flock to cafés again in major cities, while priests once again walked the streets in clerical garb. (They had become target for the more radical Communist fighters during the war.)

For the failed Republicans, however, there was no rejoicing. All who could fled across the Pyrenees to France or booked passage to England or the United States. Those who remained behind found themselves in grave jeopardy. Franco's military rounded up known Republican supporters—teachers, politicians, journalists—and placed them in concentration camps. Many were shot there. Others were forced to work at hard labor under thirty-year sentences and to give the fascist salute every morning. There are estimates that by the early 1940s, Franco's concentration camps held up to 2 million men and women.

Outside the concentration camps, Republican sympathizers were hunted down by death squads and accused of "revolutionary excesses," which could mean anything from burning down a church to simply voting the wrong way. In July 1939, once visitor to Madrid wrote, "there are trials going on every day at a speed which I would call almost summary...There are still a great number of shootings. In Madrid alone, between 200 and 250 a day, in Barcelona, 150, in Seville, 80."

The exact number of Republican deaths after the fighting concluded is unknown. Estimates range from 100,000 to 200,000. It needs to be remembered that this was a civil war, despite the help of outside parties, like the Soviet Union and Germany, and therefore there was blood on the hands of both sides. Republicans are estimated to have executed 75,000 Nationalists during the war, including 6,000 clerics (among them thirteen bishops). Even so, most liberal governments were shocked at the carnage unleashed by Franco. However, their protests went in vain, and soon the greater carnage of World War II would obscure what was going on in Spain.

BY THE EARLY 1940S, IT IS ESTIMATED THAT THERE WERE AROUND 2 MILLION PEOPLE IN FRANCO'S CONCENTRATION CAMPS. WHEN THE WAR ENDED, REPUBLICAN SYMPATHIZERS WERE ROUNDED UP AND EXECUTED OR PLACED IN THE CAMPS UNDER THIRTY-YEAR SENTENCES OF HARD LABOR. SEEN HERE, REPUBLICAN SOLDIERS IN A CAMP RAISE THEIR FISTS IN DEFIANCE.

Getty Images

17

WORLD WAR II

1939–1945

The deadliest conflict in human history was fought by soldiers from every part of the world in the service of the Allied or Axis powers and ended with the rise of two great postwar superpowers, the United States and the Soviet Union.

Combatants

MAJOR ALLIED POWERS

- China
- France
- Russia
- Great Britain
- United States

MAJOR AXIS POWERS

- Germany
- Italy
- Japan

Theater of War

Europe, Middle East, Africa, Russia, Southeast Asia, China, Korea, Japan, Pacific islands, Pacific and Atlantic Oceans

Casualties

50 to 70 million dead on all sides, both military and civilian

ALLIES

Great Britain: 344,000 military dead
Soviet Union: 7,000,000 military dead
United States: 292,000 military dead
France: 200,000 military dead

AXIS POWERS

Germany: 4,000,000 military dead
Japan: 1,200,000 military dead
Italy: 165,000 military dead

Major Figures

ALLIES

UNITED KINGDOM
Winston Churchill, prime minister who held Britain together in the dark days of the Blitz
Neville Chamberlain, prime minister who appeased Nazi Germany
Hugh Dowding, air marshall of the Royal Air Force
Field Marshal Bernard Law Montgomery, preeminent British field commander
Alan Brooke, chief of staff of the British army

FRANCE
General Charles de Gaulle, head of the Free French Forces
Marshal Henri-Philippe Pétain, who headed Vichy government

SOVIET UNION
Joseph Stalin, leader of the Soviet Union
Field Marshal Georgy Zhukov, who fought off the German invasion
General Vasily Chuikov, who deflected the Germans at Stalingrad

THE UNITED STATES
President Franklin D. Roosevelt, who led his country until his death in 1945
President Harry S. Truman, who replaced Roosevelt
Dwight D. Eisenhower, supreme commander of the Allied forces in Europe
General George Patton, the most famous field commander of the war

General Douglas MacArthur, head of the U.S. forces fighting in the Pacific

CHINA
Generalissimo Chiang Kai-shek, whose Nationalist forces fought the Japanese in southern China
Mao Zedong, head of the Communist guerilla forces

AXIS POWERS

GERMANY
Chancellor Adolf Hitler, who planned to conquer Europe and devised the Final Solution to exterminate Jews
Hermann Göring, the second in command and the leader of the Luftwaffe
Heinrich Himmler, who established the system of concentration camps
Joseph Goebbels, minister of propaganda
Field Marshal Erwin Rommel, the best German general of the war

JAPAN
Emperor Hirohito, ruler of Japan
Prime Minister Hideki Tojo, the main proponent of war against the west
Admiral Isoroku Yamamoto, who planned the Pearl Harbor attack
Hajime Sugiyama, chief of staff of the Japanese Imperial Army

ITALY
Benito Mussolini, leader of the Italian Fascist Party and de facto leader of Italy until 1943
Rodolfo Graziani, head of the Italian Tenth Army in Libya

1939:

September: German forces attack Poland. Great Britain and France declare war on Germany. Warsaw surrenders to the Germans.

October: The last Polish armed forces surrender to the Germans.

1940:

February: The first parts of the German "Enigma" machine are captured from a sunken U-boat.

April: Germany invades Norway, Denmark, and the Netherlands.

May: Neville Chamberlain resigns as British prime minister and is replaced by Winston Churchill. German forces attack Belgium and France. The Netherlands surrender. Great Britain begins a strategic air campaign against Germany. The British evacuate at Dunkirk. Belgium surrenders.

June: The Battle of France begins. The French government evacuates Paris for Tours; German forces enter Paris.

August: The Battle of Britain begins as Germany starts bombing Royal Air Force military targets.

September: Switching to civilian bombing, Germany begins the bombing of London and other cities. Germany, Italy, and Japan sign the Tripartite Pact. Italy invades Egypt.

October: Italy invades Greece.

December: British troops defeat the Italians at the Battle of Sidi Barrani in Egypt as the first British offensive in North Africa begins.

1941:

January: British troops surround the Italians at Tobruk, Libya.

February: The first German troops land in North Africa at Tripoli.

March: The U.S. Congress passes Lend-Lease Act, allowing for the sale of war materials to Allied powers.

April: British-held Tobruk is surrounded by Afrika Korps. The Greek army surrenders to the Germans.

June: Germany invades Russia.

July: General Douglas MacArthur is appointed the head of U.S. troops in the Philippines.

September: The Siege of Leningrad begins.

December: The Japanese launch a surprise attack against the U.S. base at Pearl Harbor. Japanese forces attack the Philippines. The United States declares war against Japan, Germany, and Italy.

1942:

January: The Japanese attack British-held Singapore.

April: British forces in Mesopotamia begin to advance on Baghdad.

May: U.S. forces surrender at Corregidor in the Philippines.

Americans defeat the Japanese at the Battle of Coral Sea.

June: Americans sink four Japanese carriers at the Battle of Midway. The Germans take Tobruk from the British.

July: The Battle of El Alamein in North Africa begins.

August: U.S. marines land on Guadalcanal in the Solomon Islands. The Battle of Stalingrad begins. The British defeat the Germans at El Alamein.

November: Allied forces land in North Africa.

1943:

February: The German Sixth Army surrenders at Stalingrad.

May: The allies take Tunisia. German forces in North Africa surrender.

June: The Allied Combined Bomber Offensive begins a strategic bombing campaign against Germany.

July: The allies launch an invasion of Sicily.

September: The allies invade Italy, and Italy surrenders. German troops seize control of Italian areas and rescue Mussolini from captivity.

November: U.S. Marines land on Tarawa, in central Pacific, experiencing heavy losses.

1944:

January: The Battle of Anzio begins as the allies attempt to outflank the Germans. The German Siege of Leningrad is lifted.

February: The battles of Monte Cassino and Monte Carlo are fought by the allies; Italy surrenders.

June: The allies invade Normandy, France. The Germans launch first V-I rockets at England. U.S. troops attack Saipan in the Pacific.

July: After the Battle of St. Lô, Allied troops break out of Normandy and begin to drive German forces back.

August: The allies capture Paris.

September: The allies capture Antwerp, Belgium. U.S. Marines land on the island of Peleliu in the Pacific.

October: U.S. forces land in the Philippines. The U.S. Navy wins the Battle of Leyte Gulf.

December: The Battle of the Bulge begins, with a massive German counterattack in Ardennes.

1945:

January: The Battle of the Bulge ends with German forces beaten back.

February: The Yalta Conference begins. U.S. Marines land on Iwo Jima.

March: The U.S. Third Army crosses the Rhine River.

April: Americans invade Okinawa. President Franklin Delano Roosevelt dies and is replaced by Harry S. Truman. The Battle for Berlin begins. Mussolini is assassinated. Hitler commits suicide.

May: The Soviet Union takes Berlin. Germany surrenders.

August: The United States drops two atomic bombs on Japan.

September: A formal surrender ceremony is held aboard the USS *Missouri* in Tokyo Bay that officially ends World War II.

NO "PEACE IN OUR TIME"

After the end of World War I, many millions of Germans were left in a state of smoldering resentment by the harsh terms of the Treaty of Versailles. The Great Depression of the 1930s was exacerbated in Germany by the billions of dollars of war reparations owed, as well as by the fact that large portions of its territory had been taken away. Germany, with a population of 65 million, was also forbidden to have a large standing army, but during the Weimar Republic that governed Germany immediately after the war, secret armed paramilitary groups had arisen. When Adolf Hitler took power in 1933, these powerful groups (the *Sturmabetilung,* or SA, and the *Schutzstaffel,* or SS) became the nucleus of the new German army.

Hitler led the German National Socialist, or Nazi, Party, which is to say he was a fascist. Essentially, he preached the message that Germany needed to push its boundaries outward to accommodate its expanding population, and thus wars for territory needed to be fought. Further, a demographic restructuring of Germany along racial lines was essential—all those races, in particular the Jews, which were deemed "impure" or "undesirable" would be (it was soon clear) liquidated, particularly if they lived in territory that Germans desired to possess.

To this end, Hitler stepped up German re armament throughout the 1930s, ignoring the ineffectual protests of the governments of countries such as France and Great Britain, which were themselves mired in economic difficulties because of the Great Depression. These countries (and the equally ineffectual League of Nations, which was the precursor to the United Nations) did nothing when Hitler sent an army into the Rhineland (a zone along the French-German border demilitarized after World War I) in 1936, and in 1938 annexed Austria, and took control of the Sudetenland, a Czechoslovakian region of German-speaking people.

In the latter case, British Prime Minister Neville Chamberlain acquiesced to Hitler's demands, in return for an agreement that he would not move into the rest of Czechoslovakia. Chamberlain came back home to Great Britain announcing "peace in our time," but within six months Hitler had annexed the rest of Czechoslovakia. Within a year, on September 1, 1939, the date traditionally given as the beginning of World War II, Hitler had begun his invasion of Poland. (Hitler intended to invade the Soviet Union, but he had for the time being signed a nonaggression pact with Soviet leader Joseph Stalin, agreeing to divide up Poland.)

Hitler's rapid assault on Poland—with Stuka dive bombers, tanks, and infantry—was the very first blitzkrieg, or "lightning war." France and Germany were bound by treaty to help Poland and thus declared war against Germany on September 3, 1939. The following April, Hitler's mechanized legions invaded Norway, and in May they attacked Holland, Belgium, and France. The French army was utterly defeated, and a British expeditionary force sent to help was driven back to the English Channel coast, where it was evacuated at Dunkirk.

In the meantime, in the Far East, the Japanese were pursuing a policy of expansion as well. They had invaded and seized Manchuria from the Chinese in 1937, and they were engaged in a continuing war with China. Border skirmishes with the Red Army in western Manchuria proved the Russians a tougher nut to crack than they were during the Russo-Japanese War.

The Japanese turned their attentions south, planning an invasion of oil-rich Southeast Asia. The United States–owned Philippines stood in their way, and Japanese war planners knew that they would sooner or later have to attack the United States. Seeing the string of German victories, the Japanese reached a mutual defense agreement with Germany and Italy, which was ruled by Benito Mussolini. This Tripartite Pact established the Berlin–Rome–Tokyo Axis, and Germany, Italy, and Japan became known as the Axis Powers.

Beginning in August 1940, Hermann Göring, the head of Germany's powerful Luftwaffe, launched a massive bombing campaign against England, beginning with Royal Air Force bases (RAF), to soften up England prior to a German invasion. The RAF suffered horrendous losses, but it held out. (During one two-week period, one in four English pilots was killed.) The Germans then switched tactics, bombing British cities in terror bombings. but the British, led by their resolute prime minister, Winston Churchill (see "The Men of Yalta," p. 334), refused to give up. German victories in Greece and the Balkans made 1940 a victorious year for the Axis.

By the spring of 1941, however, as Great Britain suffered devastating bombing as well as a German submarine naval blockade, the country's situation was dire. But in March of that year, the United States, officially neutral, passed Lend-Lease legislation that allowed it to send war material to countries whose security affected its own. Massive supplies were sent in convoys to Great Britain through the perilous North Atlantic seas, which were infested with German U-Boats.

Great Britain's situation became somewhat better when Hitler made the huge blunder of attacking the Soviet Union in June 1941 with a force of a 1.5 million soldiers. Caught at first by surprise, the Soviets reeled back, losing some 3 million soldiers—dead, wounded, and captured—before the Soviet line stabilized and the Russian winter set the Germans back.

On December 7, 1941, Japan launched a surprise aerial attack on the U.S. naval base of Pearl Harbor, Hawaii. Devastating though it was, the attack—devised by Admiral Isoruku Yamamoto—missed the United States' aircraft carriers, which were out at sea, and thus was only a limited tactical success. The United States quickly declared war against the Axis Powers.

In the Far East, the Japanese attacked and captured the Philippines, Burma, Malaya, the Dutch East Indies, and Singapore by April 1942 and occupied numerous South Pacific islands. But an attempt to capture Port Moresby, New Guinea, and thus cut off communications between the United States and Australia failed when the Americans turned back and destroyed the Japanese invasion force at the Battle of the

Coral Sea in May 1942. A month later, an attempt to destroy the U.S. fleet was thwarted at the Battle of Midway when the carrier-based airplanes of the U.S. Navy sank four Japanese aircraft carriers, and the Americans began to turn the tide against the Japanese in the Pacific.

In May 1942, an offensive by the famed German Afrika Korps, under General Erwin Rommel had driven the defending British forces in Libya nearly back to Cairo, but then British resistance stiffened and they stopped the Germans in two battles at El Alamein, in July and October 1942. A month later, British and U.S. troops entire German army would surrender within four months' time, forever blunting Hitler's invasion.

In the meantime, in the Pacific, U.S. war planners had decided upon a two-prong offensive against the Japanese. One arm of the offensive, based in Australia, would attack up the New Guinea coast, through the Solomon Islands, and on to the Philippines and Tokyo, bypassing and cutting off numerous Japanese-held islands along the way. The other offensive arm would thrust along some of the smaller islands of the Central Pacific, to the Marianas, the Philippines, and the Chinese coast, and from there to the Japanese

The German offensive attacked Stalingrad in August 1942. But unexpectedly tough resistance from the Russians turned the battle for the city into an epic bloodbath in which 400,000 Germans would lose their lives.

(commanded by General Dwight D. Eisenhower) landed in Morocco at the rear of the Germans and caught them in a pincer. German troops in Africa were forced to surrender in May 1943. With their southern flanks secure, the allies invaded Sicily in July and Italy in September.

Another blow to the Germans came with their stalled attack on the Russian city of Stalingrad. The German offensive had picked up steam since the winter of 1941–42, and they attacked Stalingrad in August 1942. But unexpectedly tough resistance from the Russians turned the battle for the city into an epic bloodbath in which 400,000 Germans would lose their lives and an home islands. This latter strategy made it crucial to keep the Nationalist Chinese government in the war, to protect the United States' left flank. Masses of arms and material were sent to Chiang Kai-shek's armies, which even so barely held their own against the Japanese.

The U.S. "island-hopping" began with an attack on the Japanese-held Solomon Island of Guadalcanal in August 1942, where a hard-fought six-month battle ended in U.S. victory in February 1943. In the meantime, U.S. Marines fought battles at coral atolls such as Tarawa, Peleliu, and Bougainville, building bomber bases as they went. By November 1944, B-29 bombers operating out of airfields in the northern Marianas and China were able to reach targets in Japan.

After much debate, the allies finally decided to invade France along the Normandy coast on June 6, 1944. With an armada of 6,000 ships containing an attacking force of 175,000 British, Canadian, and U.S. troops, the allies won a hard-fought toe-hold in France (see "Turning Point," p. 322). After bloody fighting during the summer months, the allies were able to drive the Germans into full-blown retreat that August.

However, the Germans were far from down yet. In December 1944, secretly assembling some 250,000 troops and 1,000 tanks, they launched the Battle of the Bulge in the Ardennes Forest in Belgium, very nearly breaking through U.S. and British lines. Despite a fierce struggle, they were thrown back, and the allies continued their march toward Berlin, using powerful bombers to destroy German cities, factories, and troops. All the while, the victorious Soviet Army pushed the Germans back from the east. After Hitler committed suicide in his Berlin bunker, Germany surrendered on May 7, 1945.

This left the allies free to concentrate all their might on the Japanese. U.S. air raids over Japan increased in intensity, targeting civilian populations. U.S. Marines island-hopped right to Japan's Bonin (Iwo Jima) and Ryukyus (Okinawa) islands by April 1945, but Japanese resistance had become even more ferocious as their homeland was invaded, especially with the introduction of the kamikaze, or suicide, pilot.

Fearful of the casualties that would ensue if the Americans and British invaded Japan as planned that November, the new U.S. President Harry S. Truman opted to drop the newly developed atomic bomb on Japan. The first bomb was dropped on Hiroshima on August 6, 1945. Three days later, another bomb was dropped on Nagasaki. With 200,000 dead from these two bombs alone, the Japanese capitulated. On September 2, 1945, aboard the U.S. battleship USS *Missouri*, the Japanese signed the surrender agreement that ended World War II.

After the war, the United Nations was formed in the hopes of keeping peace, but no one was able to say with equanimity that the war to end all wars had been fought. World War II, with its millions of dead, had simply been too awful. The immediate result of the war was the elevation of the United States and the Soviet Union to superpower status, where they almost immediately squared off in the Cold War, each threatening the other with potential nuclear annihilation.

The colonial world order was now gone forever, with countries vying for self-determination. The discovery that Hitler had perpetuated the Holocaust (see "The Holocaust," p. 343) in which more than 6 million Jews were killed in concentration camps changed how people everywhere viewed the notion of evil. It also helped hurry the state of Israel into existence.

D-DAY: JUNE 6, 1944

As the huge flotilla crossed the dark, choppy waters of the English Channel, the roar of protecting planes overhead, reporters in the holds of ships with the troops of the different Allied countries—the Americans, British, and Canadians—noticed an interesting phenomenon take shape. Most of the U.S. soldiers were green recruits who had never seen combat before. Normally one might expect these to be the most nervous, but in fact these young GIs appeared to be the coolest, almost glad to be taking part in history. They were, after all, about to make the first assault on Fortress Europa, Hitler's territory since 1940, and strike right at the heart of the German empire.

The GIs laughed, cleaned their rifles, and sharpened their bayonets. They knew there was a tough task ahead and that some of them would die, but they all thought that someone would be someone else.

It was a different picture with the British and Canadian battalions that had seen three years or more of warfare. In their case, as one observer wrote, "Everybody who was any good had been promoted or become a casualty." These men had faced Hitler's *Wehrmacht*, his proud and combative infantry, and they knew how fiercely they could fight, especially now, defending their own territory. As the sky lightened—but did not clear—on this overcast early morning of June 6, 1944, these men knew just what was in store for them. They did not kid themselves that they, personally, would be the targets of a hailstorm of death and destruction.

The Beginning of Overlord

Green recruit or veteran, the hopes of the allies rested on these 150,000 men who were approaching 60 miles (97 km) of French coastline in some 6,500 ships. Despite the fact that the might of the world was stacked against Hitler, he was proving remarkably difficult to finally beat. In Italy, Allied forces were pushing up through the peninsula, but at a glacial pace over rugged terrain. Meanwhile, in Russia, the Soviets were also winning victories, but the German troops were giving way slowly. Nightly, Allied forces pounded German cities and industry, and yet the Germans kept on fighting.

Everyone, Germans or allies, knew that there would be a major invasion somewhere along the channel coast. The Germans defenses stretched all the way from Scandinavia to Spain, but they could not possibly fortify all areas equally. Their war planners had come to the conclusion that the Allies would attack across the Straits of Dover, heading for the Pas de Calais, the area of France closest to England. Calais had a natural harbor that the Allies could use. It made so much sense to the Germans that they stationed their main reserve—the Fifteenth Army, containing about 100,000 men—there.

It was not that the rest of the Atlantic Wall, as the Germans called it, was poorly fortified. Field Marshal Erwin Rommel—the famed Desert Fox—had been given charge of building up the defenses and was determined not to let the Allies get a foothold in France. He was certain that they would exploit any foothold with their massive advantage in armor and bombers.

Allied war planners—knowing from their top secret Ultra intercepts (see "The Secret War," p. 342) that the Germans were massing around Pas de Calais—had no intention of attacking there. The allies did stage a massive and elaborate deception to make the Germans think that an attack on Calais was imminent. However, the real target of Allied leaders, such as General Dwight D. Eisenhower, commander of Supreme Headquarters Allied Expeditionary Force, and General Bernard Law Montgomery, head of Allied ground forces, was Normandy, France. Here, specifically at the Cotentin Peninsula, on five beaches designed Juno, Gold, Sword, Utah, and Omaha, the beginning of the end of World War II would begin in an attack aptly named Operation Overlord.

The Largest Flotilla

As the Allied troops fought off seasickness and climbed down into their landing boats, bobbing up and down in the heavy chop of the English Channel, they watched a preparatory bombardment of the enemy positions. It was an awesome sight. Thousands of planes flew overhead, dropping bombs that turned the coastline into a curtain of smoke. Heavy booming thuds echoed back across the water, the footsteps of a thousand giants. The Allied air force had full ownership of the sky, with barely 200 Luftwaffe planes to oppose them.

Unbeknownst to those soldiers on the boats, the land battle for Normandy had begun the night before, when 20,000 men of the U.S. 82nd and 101st Airborne Divisions and the British Sixth Airborne had been dropped by parachute behind enemy lines. Their goal was to block off approaches to the Normandy beaches to keep the Germans from reinforcing them. But most of

SOLDIERS SCRAMBLE UP THE BEACHES ON D-DAY, JUNE 6, 1944. OUT OF AROUND 155,000 MEN COMPOSED OF AMERICANS, BRITISH, AND CANADIANS, 11,000 DIED THAT DAY, BUT THE HARD FIGHTING WAS THE TURNING POINT OF THE WAR AND THE BEGINNING OF THE END FOR HITLER.

Soldiers disembarking from landing craft at Ouistreham and Bernieres in the St Aubin Sector on 6th June 1944, from a collection of 102 photographs collected by A.D.C. Smith of the Army Commandos (b/w photo), English Photographer, (20th century) / National Army Museum, London, / The Bridgeman Art Library

the jumpers went astray in the inevitable confusion of a combat parachute drop in darkness, and only one in twenty-five paratroopers landed in his assigned drop zone. Nevertheless, the chaos served its purpose, keeping the Germans guessing about what was coming. Many German commanders dismissed the disorganized paratrooper attacks as just another commando raid, even after one German general was ambushed and killed by 101st Airborne troopers who happened upon his staff car.

But there was a moment, as the sky brightened but just before the Allied bombers swept in, that the German gunners in their pillboxes on the shore could see exactly what was happening. Spread out on the waters before them was the largest flotilla the world had ever known. Then the bombers came, and the gunners put their heads down.

When the gunners manned their machine guns again, troops in landing craft were nearing the shore.

The Attack

The beaches being invaded were, from east to west, Sword, Juno, Gold, Omaha, and Utah. The first three were attacked by Canadian and British forces, and the last two were attacked by Americans. On Sword Beach, the British, although confronted with minefields and beach obstacles, managed to land 28,000 troops with only 600 casualties and push to within a few miles of their objective, the town of Caen.

What happened on Juno Beach depended on what part of the beach you landed on and when you landed on it. In the first wave on Juno, Canadian

casualties were nearly 50 percent, but in other areas of the beach where resistance was not so stiff, the allies made it ashore almost unopposed.

On Gold Beach, however, the British took extremely heavy casualties. Their landing craft lowered their ramps in 6 feet (1.8 m) of water, and numerous soldiers, weighed down by heavy equipment, drowned. Other soldiers got to the beach, only to face withering fire and an unreal scene of chaos. As one soldier remembered: "The beach was strewn with wreckage, a blazing tank, bundles of blanket and kit, bodies and bits of bodies. One bloke near me was blown in half by a shell, and his lower half collapsed in a bloody heap on the sand."

On Utah Beach, mass confusion reigned. Stiff currents had carried the U.S. Fourth Division almost 2 miles (3 km) from where it was supposed to be, and the troops had no idea where they were. However, this turned out to be a stroke of luck, because they had landed in an area that was not quite so heavily defended. They managed to quickly break through the seawall and link up with paratroopers from the 101st Airborne.

Bloody Omaha

It was on Omaha Beach that the slaughter truly reached epic proportions. Because the beach there was the only stretch of open sand in either direction for some miles, the German planners knew that the Allies would have to make use of it.

Omaha Beach is only 6 miles (9 km) long and about 400 yards (365 m) deep at low tide, which it was when the invasion was taking place. Much of the beach was shingle or shale, and there were high bluffs facing it in the front and on either side, making it a kind of natural amphitheater. German defenses here were formidable. Every inch of the beach was pre-sighted by machine guns, mortars, artillery, and underground ammunition chambers and pillboxes at the top of the cliffs, which were connected by a series of well-dug trenches. Five small ravines led up the cliffs, but at the top of each was an 88, the ubiquitous, and deadly, German light artillery gun of choice.

The minute U.S. soldiers landed here at about 6:40 a.m., the German defenders opened fire. The Germans were amazed at the Americans' audacity. "They must be crazy," one of them said to one of his comrades. "Are they going to swim ashore right under our muzzles?" The first landing craft on the beach simply disappeared in a hail of fire. Other GIs crawled up the beach, hiding in long snaking lines behind beach obstacles, while the machine guns raked up and down, like deadly garden hoses. (One German gunner would fire 12,000 rounds that day.) Finally, the Americans, urged on by brave noncoms and officers, realized that if they stayed where they were, they would die. And so they began to move forward, singly, in ones and twos, until they reached the comparative shelter of a seawall near the base of the cliff. By afternoon, a few men had made it up the draws, and more followed.

Ultimately, 40,000 men would land at Omaha Beach during the course of the day and spread out for about a mile from the top of the cliffs, where they dug in—as forces were digging in all up and down the 60-mile (97-km) stretch of Normandy beaches—waiting for the inevitable German counterattack.

The Beginning of the End

The counterattack might have been inevitable, but it never came. German commanders thought that the real objective of the Allied attack was still the Pas de Calais, and that Normandy was just a diversion. It would take German commanders weeks to figure out otherwise, and by that time the allies had secured a firm beachhead 120 miles (193 km) long and 10 miles (16 km) deep, while more men and material poured into the man-made harbors that the Allies created in Normandy.

All told, about 10,000 men were killed or wounded out of a total of about 155,000 on D-Day, but this high price meant the final destruction of Hitler's Germany. A lot of hard fighting still lay ahead, but the first major step had been taken.

DWIGHT D. EISENHOWER: THE MODERN WARRIOR

Even if Bernard Law Montgomery sneered at Dwight D. Eisenhower as a desk jockey with no combat experience, Eisenhower has to be ranked the most successful general in World War II. Other generals might have a better grasp of battlefield strategy and tactics, but no one was better at getting a coalition army to function—and win—than "Ike."

Eisenhower was born to a poor family in Abilene, Texas, but he won a commission to the U.S. Military Academy at West Point and graduated in 1915. However, he was not sent overseas when the United States entered World War I, as he hoped. Instead he was billeted to an army camp near Gettysburg, Pennsylvania. After the war, he was stationed in the Panama Canal Zone, and in the early 1930s he became an aide to General Douglas MacArthur in the Philippines.

Eisenhower clashed with MacArthur and his huge ego, as many people did. But after Eisenhower returned to the States, he continued his rise through the ranks.

After Pearl Harbor, Eisenhower was promoted to major general, and he was assigned a prominent place in the United States' War Plans department. In June 1942, he was made commander of all U.S. troops in Europe. Many people, like Montgomery, decried Eisenhower's lack of combat experience when he headed the U.S. Army invading North Africa. Still, after some rocky early moments, Eisenhower learned quickly, although he remained a somewhat conservative and cautious general.

Eisenhower's joint invasions of Sicily and Italy with the British were successful and taught him how to work with difficult allies. This experience stood him in good stead when he was named head of the Allied Expeditionary Force planning the invasion of Europe. Smoking four packs of cigarettes and drinking fifteen cups of coffee a day, he helped plan the massive invasion of Normandy in June 1944. Then he kept the coalition army fighting together all the way to Berlin.

Historians have called Eisenhower "the modern warrior"—a general who fought by overseeing large armies over vast areas and making sure alliances remained stable. He went on to become a two-term U.S. president, where his experience and vision kept the country in a cold war and out of a hot one.

DWIGHT D. EISENHOWER UNDERSTOOD THE NEW PRIORITIES NEEDED IN MODERN WARFARE—THE ABILITY TO CONTROL LARGE ARMIES OVER AN IMMENSE AREA AND THE IMPORTANCE OF MAINTAINING STABLE ALLIANCES.

General Dwight D. Eisenhower (photo), American Photographer, (20th century) / Private Collection, Peter Newark American Pictures / The Bridgeman Art Library

FIELD MARSHAL
BERNARD LAW MONTGOMERY:
"I TRY HARD NOT TO BE TIRESOME"

Bernard Law Montgomery, who would have to be considered the preeminent British commander of the Second World War, was also one of the most irritating men that many of his fellow general officers, both English and American, had ever met. Montgomery was a stickler for details, hated to be wrong, and had a nasty habit of attempting to take credit for others' triumphs.

Montgomery knew that he rubbed people the wrong way, but, as he put it, "I have seen so many mistakes during this war, and so many disasters happen, that I am desperately anxious to see that we have no more, and this often means being very tiresome."

Born in London in 1887, Montgomery was the son of an Anglo-Irish priest who was made bishop of Tasmania, where Montgomery spent much of his early years. When Montgomery arrived in England, he attended the military academy at Sandhurst, where he was seen as a "gauche figure," a bit of a drone or grind who did nothing but study. But as a lieutenant in World War I, he was badly wounded (and nearly buried by gravediggers who thought he had passed on) and came out as a lieutenant colonel wearing the Distinguished Service Cross. Between the wars, Montgomery—"Monty," as he was now known to one and all—focused on improving military intelligence and being able to pinpoint the exact area of an enemy's weakness for an attack, to avoid the massive and bloody frontal assaults of World War I.

When Montgomery arrived in North Africa in August 1942 to take command of Britain's Eighth Army, reeling under assault from Rommel's Afrika Korps, his confidence was infectious. "We are going to finish this chap Rommel once and for

BERNARD MONTGOMERY, PICTURED AT RIGHT WITH GENERAL GEORGE PATTON AND GENERAL OMAR BRADLEY, WAS A TOUCHY MAN WHOM MANY FOUND HARD TO GET ALONG WITH. HOWEVER, HE WAS GREAT BRITAIN'S MOST DECORATED WAR HERO.
Prints & Photographs Division, Library of Congress, LC-USZ62-58989

all," he told his troops, the famous "Desert Rats." They responded, beating the Germans at the Battle of El Alamein, the first large-scale Allied victory of the war.

After forcing the Germans from North Africa, Montgomery—now knighted and lionized—led the British part of the Allied invasions of Sicily and Italy. Here his prickly personality caused him to run afoul of General Eisenhower, who told a subordinate, "Dammit, Montgomery is the only man in either army I can't get along with." (Monty, for his part, said of the bureaucratic Eisenhower: "Nice chap, but no general.")

Tensions came to a head after the D-Day Invasion when Montgomery, whom Eisenhower, as supreme Allied commander, had made temporary head of Allied ground forces, was promoted to field marshal by the British. Because this rank did not exist in the U.S. Army, Monty thought it made him permanently in charge. It did not, and Eisenhower let him know it, causing Monty to claim he had been "demoted." However, tensions aside, Montgomery's tenacious personality was trouble for the Germans more than for the allies, and he ended the war a viscount and England's most decorated general.

ERWIN ROMMEL: THE DESERT FOX

Very few German officers were able to come out of World War II with their reputations intact, but Erwin Rommel was one of them. He was a master military tactician admired by friend and foe alike, and he is the only German general who has his own museum (in Ulm, Germany).

Rommel was born in 1891, the son of a German school headmaster. During World War I, he fought in France, Romania, and Italy. He gained a reputation as a daring, aggressive, and brilliant young officer, being wounded three times and winning the Iron Cross, First and Second Class. Between the wars, Rommel taught in German military academies, but he was soon singled out by Adolf Hitler to become head of his personal protection battalion. After the war began, Rommel asked Hitler for a command, and he was made head of the Seventh Panzer Division as it attacked France in 1940. Rommel very quickly became one of Germany's foremost adherents of fast-moving armored warfare, blazing through France all the way to the English Channel.

Rommel's reward for his brilliant performance was to be made commander of the two panzer divisions that made up the newly formed Afrika Korps, which, in early 1941, was sent to Libya to shore up the Italian army, which had been driven back by the British. Rommel made his mark in history there as a master of mobile operations who acted with boldness and initiative, striking at the enemy when he least expected it.

When the worn-out and outnumbered Afrika Korps was finally driven out of North Africa, Rommel was given the new assignment of preparing the Atlantic Wall defenses in western France against the expected Allied invasion. By this time, Rommel had lost faith in Hitler (whom he had once admired for reviving the morale of the German people post–World War I), but he hoped to build a strong defense to push the allies back into the sea and win a negotiated peace.

This was not to be. As the allies began to push through France in the summer of 1944, Rommel tried personally to convince Hitler to sue for peace. Hitler refused to do so. Shortly thereafter, an assassination plot nearly succeeded in killing Hitler, and it was assumed that Rommel had been one of the plotters. Although this was not the case, Rommel was approached at his home—where he was recovering from injuries sustained in an Allied air attack in France—and given the choice of a public trial for high treason, with his family disgraced, or a private suicide, with his death officially announced as a heart attack. Rommel chose the latter, and took poison.

ERWIN ROMMEL IS THE ONE GERMAN OFFICER WHOSE REPUTATION SURVIVED WORLD WAR II UNSCATHED. HE WAS A MASTER MILITARY STRATEGIST ESTEEMED BY BOTH SIDES.

Marshal Erwin Rommel (1894-1944) from 'Signal' Magazine, No. 17, first edition of September 1942 (photo), German School, (20th century) / Private Collection, / The Bridgeman Art Library

ADMIRAL ISOROKU YAMAMOTO: OVERPLAYING HIS HAND

There are few more controversial figures in the Pacific War than the brilliant Japanese Admiral Isoroku Yamamoto. Yamamoto was at the helm of the Japanese navy when it overran much of Southeast Asia, the East Indies, the Philippines, and the islands of the Central Pacific at the beginning of World War II. But he was also at the helm for Japan's worst naval defeat—the Battle of Midway—arguably because he overreached himself and his country's strategic resources.

Yamamoto brought an illustrious personal history into World War II. Born in 1884, he had attended the naval academy and been wounded at the Battle of Tsushima in the Russo-Japanese War (see "Russo-Japanese War," page 194). After World War I, he spent a year at Harvard University and another at the Japanese Embassy in Washington, getting to know Americans quite well. They were a people he liked, but whose stamina for a long fight he found suspect. Yamamoto was promoted to the rank of rear admiral in the 1930s. He fought against traditionalists in the Japanese navy who saw battleships as the combat vessels of the future. Like many farseeing U.S. strategists (see "The Sea War," p. 339), he believed that naval air power would be the key to winning the upcoming war.

As part of Yamamoto's strategy, he pushed for the surprise attack on Pearl Harbor on December 7, 1941. He thought that the attack would cripple the Americans and allow the Japanese to carry on their operations in Southeast Asia without interference. But the U.S. carriers were not at port that day, so while the blow was crippling, it was not fatal. And Americans responded with a ferocity that Yamamoto underestimated.

Still, with Japanese in control of much of the Pacific, Yamamoto could have fought a defensive battle; allowing the Americans, their supply lines stretched thin over thousands of miles of ocean; to come to him. But Yamamoto had been taught to play poker during his days in the United States, and he loved to play a strong hand—even if he didn't have one. He planned a trap for the U.S. Navy at Midway. But that trap failed when Americans discovered his carrier task force first and destroyed it in June 1942.

In April 1943, alerted by radio intercepts that Yamamoto's personal plane would be visiting the Japanese-held island of Bougainville, U.S. fighters—under personal orders to "Get Yamamoto" from President Franklin Delano Roosevelt—stalked the Japanese admiral and shot down his plane, sending him to his death.

ADOLF HITLER: THE LUCKY MAN

Adolph Hitler shouldn't have survived. He should have been killed in the trenches of World War I where he was wounded twice, or he should have been shot dead or blown up in one of the seventeen planned attempts on his life between 1939 and 1945. It's hard to know what this simple fact says about God, the fates, or the mysterious powers of the universe, but Hitler was a lucky man.

People who came into contact with him, however, were not quite so blessed.

Hitler was born in Austria in 1889 to a coarse custom's inspector named Alois Shicklgruber who changed his last name to the less rural-sounding Hitler. (The rumor that Hitler had a Jewish grandparent, however, was false, planted by Allied propagandists.) Alois, who physically abused young Adolf, died when Hitler was thirteen.

At the age of sixteen, Hitler dropped out of school and moved to Vienna, where he sought to find himself, attending art school, often living on the streets, and envying the rich Jewish families he saw walk by. At last, with the outbreak of World War I, Hitler found some purpose in his life. Swept up in patriotic fervor, he volunteered for duty on the western front, reaching the rank of corporal and being twice wounded and decorated with the Iron Cross.

When the war ended and the Treaty of Versailles forced Germany to pay expensive and humiliating reparations, Hitler, like so many Germans, was depressed and enraged. He joined those who were forming the *Freikorps*. These urban paramilitary organizations battled Bolsheviks and the German politicians and generals they called "the November criminals," men who had urged the November 1918 armistice on Germany.

Hitler was a politician, though, not a street fighter, and he rose to lead the new National Socialist German Workers Party, known as the Nazis, from the German pronunciation of the beginning of the word "National." With Hitler's paramilitary force of Stermabetilung members behind him, led by Ernst Röhm (whom Hitler would purge when he became too powerful), Hitler became a force to reckon with in German politics, and he ultimately seized power in 1933.

Hitler's doctrine of racial purity called for the elimination of people who were not of pure Aryan blood. Those Aryans remaining would have large families; eventually, the German people would need to expand into surrounding areas. Thus, as Hitler rearmed Germany in the mid-1930s, he planned several wars—a small one against Czechoslovakia, followed by a larger one against Poland, Great Britain, and France, then one against the Soviet Union, followed by a final massive war against the United States.

When war came, everything went Hitler's way at first. But his decision to invade Russia was a Napoleonic example of overreaching, and after losing at Stalingrad, Germany's expansion was thwarted and then began to shrink back on itself. In the meantime, Hitler had been systematically purging the Jewish population of Germany and the Nazi-occupied countries, in a deliberate and

ADOLF HITLER WAS A MAN WITH MANY SECOND CHANCES. IN THE TRENCHES OF WORLD WAR I, HE WAS WOUNDED TWICE AND BETWEEN 1939 AND 1945 THERE WERE SEVENTEEN ATTEMPTS ON HIS LIFE. EVENTUALLY TRAPPED IN HIS BERLIN BUNKER, HE COMMITTED SUICIDE, SUCCEEDING WHERE ALL OTHERS HAD FAILED.

Prints & Photographs Division, Library of Congress, LC-USZ62-72155

scientific genocide that humankind had never before seen (see "The Holocaust," p. 343).

In the end, despite grand schemes like his plan to destroy London with V-1 and V-2 rockets, Hitler found himself in the rubble of his capital city of Berlin, with the Russian army only two blocks away from his headquarters. It was April 30, 1945. Hitler's luck having finally run out, he put a bullet to his head at the same moment that he bit down on a cyanide capsule.

BENITO MUSSOLINI: *IL DUCE*

Benito Mussolini has been much caricatured as the jackbooted, fist-waving, guttural-sounding epitome of mid-century fascism (and always second to Hitler in this regard, at that). But in fact Mussolini—*Il Duce*, or "the Leader," as he liked to call himself—started out far more promisingly.

Mussolini was born in rural Italy in 1883. His father was a blacksmith who was also a fervent socialist, and his mother was a schoolteacher. Like his father, young Benito became a socialist, a political belief that was heightened by the treatment he received when he emigrated to Switzerland to look for work. Unable to feed himself, he wandered the streets as a vagrant (an early sojourn not unlike that of Hitler a few years later in Vienna), and he was eventually deported. Back in Italy, Mussolini became the editor of a socialist newspaper and a labor leader in Milan. He firmly believed, as he wrote, that workers should unite "in one formidable *fascio* (bundle)," before seizing power. Some historians believe this to be the beginning of the first fascist party.

Italy had in the meantime joined World War I and was fighting against the Austrians and Germans. At first Mussolini held pacifist views, but as the war progressed he supported it, apparently hoping that the conflagration would end in the collapse of the Italian government and lead to his own rise to power. In 1919, he founded the first fascist party, *Fasci di Combattimento*, and entered the Italian parliament in 1921 fully a right-winger, a man whose goon squads now crushed communist opposition.

Mussolini became prime minister of Italy in 1923 and assumed dictatorial powers in 1925, censoring all political opposition as well as the press. Within the next fifteen years, he had made Italy a completely fascist state, with all laws rewritten to reflect his will, while at the same time completing numerous public works projects that met with the approval of the people. Moving aggressively militarily, he also conquered Somalia, Ethiopia, Libya, and Albania, as well as helping the forces of Francisco Franco in the Spanish Civil War.

As World War II began, Mussolini was a full partner of Hitler's, but Il Duce's forces, poorly led and trained, suffered serious setbacks in Greece and North Africa. In both places, Hitler's armies had to bail out the Italians. When the allies invaded Sicily, King Victor Emmanuel III and the Italian high command overthrew Mussolini and placed him in prison as they prepared to surrender to the allies. A daring German commando raid freed Il Duce, who was then installed as the puppet leader of northern Italian states not yet conquered by the advancing allies. On April 28—just two days before Hitler's death—Mussolini was caught by communist partisan fighters and executed. His body was hung upside down from the roof of a gas station and stoned.

THE MEN OF YALTA

The three men were in all their power and glory—Winston Churchill, cigar in hand, Franklin Delano Roosevelt, cape thrown over his shoulders, and Joseph Stalin, in military uniform—when they met in February 1945, at Yalta, in the Crimea to decide the fate of the postwar world.

Each had been instrumental in helping bring the defeat of the Axis Powers closer and closer to reality. Churchill was prime minister of Great Britain, replacing Neville Chamberlain, who had appeased Hitler and his Nazis and thus lost all credibility with the people of Great Britain. Churchill knew that he needed to provide inspiration for Great Britain to continue against the odds. His speeches during the dark days of the summer and fall of 1940 resounded with powerful inspiring language, as in his "finest hour" speech to the British parliament, where he declared that the Battle for Britain had begun. He said: "If the British Empire and its Commonwealth last for a thousand years, men will say, 'This was their finest hour.'"

President Franklin Delano Roosevelt, who had ably led his country through the Great Depression, also began to subtly steer the United States toward war, despite numerous isolationists who thought that the United States should not interfere in what was going on in Europe. But Roosevelt, through Lend-Lease legislation (see "Chronicle," p. 318), was able to provide aid to Great Britain. Then, when the Japanese attacked Pearl Harbor, Roosevelt declared war with the ringing words: "December 7, 1941…was a day which will live in infamy." He, like Churchill, presided over a country that saw defeats in the early days of the war but that found its war footing very quickly and accepted rationing and other forms of privation on the civilian front so that the military might make greater strides against Germany, Italy, and Japan.

Premier Joseph Stalin was a different case. He was the totalitarian dictator of a country whose citizens he had ruthlessly purged (or starved because of his agricultural collectivization) by the millions. And he had been fooled into thinking that Hitler was his ally early in the war. Nevertheless, as Russians reeled back under the initial onslaught of Operation Barbarossa, Hitler's massive attack on Russia, Stalin, too, provided the backbone that kept his country from capitulating.

At Yalta, these three leaders came together to decide what would happen after Germany and Japan had been defeated. It had already been decided that Germany would be divided into zones overseen by Russia, Great Britain, and the United States. But at Yalta, Stalin agreed to allow France to rule a zone—as along as it came from English or U.S. territory.

Foremost on Stalin's agenda was Poland. He wanted the country in the Soviet Union, claiming that it had traditionally been "the corridor through which the enemy passed into Russia." Roosevelt agreed to this, although it constituted selling out Poland to Russia. This was much to Churchill's dismay, because Great Britain had

already recognized that Poland should become a free state after the war. But Roosevelt wanted something in return—Stalin's promise to attack Japan, with which it had a nonaggression pact, within ninety days after Germany's defeat.

Roosevelt has been heavily criticized for this decision, but at the time he did not know whether the atomic bomb would be developed in time to use against Japan, and he knew that any invasion of the Japanese home islands would be a bloodbath. He hoped that the creation of the United Nations—which Stalin agreed to join at Yalta—would help ameliorate Poland's plight. Roosevelt would die of a cerebral hemorrhage in just over two months after Yalta. At the war's end, Stalin did attack Japan, but mainly as a power grab in Manchuria. And Poland was unfortunately sucked back behind what Churchill would later name the "Iron Curtain."

Allied and Axis Soldiers

THE BRITISH SOLDIER

Just after the evacuation at Dunkirk, where the Germans forced the British out of continental Europe in 1940, the British army totaled about 1,650,000 men. The individual British soldier was still known as the Tommy, as he had been in World War I. He carried a Lee-Enfield .303 caliber rifle—an improved version of his World War I weapon—and in some cases a Sten submachine gun, which provided rapid fire in close quarters, although it was known to jam.

The most famous group of British soldiers in the war were the Desert Rats, who served under Montgomery. They were members of the Seventh Armored Brigade that first drove the Italians out of North Africa, then ferociously battled the Afrika Korps before forcing them to defeat as well.

By the end of the war, the British army had grown to nearly 3 million men and fought on every continent involved in the war, both on the western front and in the Pacific.

THE AMERICAN SOLDIER

Just before the outbreak of World War II, the U.S. Army was only a small professional force of some 175,000 men. But the largest draft in the history of the United States brought the number to 1,400,000 by the time of Pearl Harbor. The conscripts were truly a wide-ranging group—farmboys, factory workers, office clerks. They were the sons of rich and poor alike, men from all over the United States. (However, the significant exception were African-Americans who, though they were drafted and volunteered in great numbers, were relegated to service units and generally restricted from combat, although by war's end there were black units fighting, in particular the Tuskegee Airmen.)

The U.S. Army infantryman was known as the GI, for "Government Issue." He carried an M1 Garand rifle, which had replaced the Springfield as the country's primary infantry weapon. Although the GI had less experience at the war than his European counterparts who had started fighting in Europe and Africa earlier, he quickly caught up.

Wearing his 1-pound (455 g) steel helmet, with fragmentation grenades hanging in the webbing of his pack, he was a formidable force in combat. But by the time the war in Europe neared its end, U.S. resources were becoming depleted. Soldiers were rushed into combat with little training, simply to fill the gaps in the lines. Consequently, they suffered a higher percentage of casualties.

Most of the fighting in the Pacific was done by U.S. Marines, who faced different challenges than the GIs in Europe—less heavy armor, artillery, and bombardment from airplanes, but a more tenacious, dug-in Japanese enemy who in the main refused to surrender.

THESE BRAVE FLIERS WERE PART OF THE MASSIVE BRITISH WAR EFFORT THAT EVENTUALLY PUT MILLIONS OF MEN IN UNIFORM.

MEMBERS OF THE FRENCH RESISTANCE PLAYED A KEY PART IN WORLD WAR II, HELPING TO SABOTAGE GERMAN RAIL LINES AND COMMUNICATIONS. THEY OFTEN FACED HARSHER CONSEQUENCES THAN OTHER SOLDIERS CAPTURED BY THE GERMANS, BEING TORTURED AND KILLED OR SENT TO CONCENTRATIONS CAMPS.

THE RUSSIAN SOLDIER

When World War II broke out, the Russian army numbered an estimated 1,800,000 men, but more than half of them were stationed in the east, to meet the threat posed by the Japanese. The Red army in the west scored its first victory of the war when, still on the Axis side, it invaded Finland in November 1939, but the victory also showed that the Reds were poorly prepared and poorly armed, as the much smaller Finnish army was able to keep the Russians off-balance until the spring of 1940.

When Hitler turned the tables on the Russians and invaded a year later, the Red army, although its numbers were now about 3 million, lacked armor and mechanized transport, and were supported instead by cavalry. The Nazis outmaneuvered and encircled them (see "Chronicle," p. 318), capturing 1 million men. But the Russian victory at Stalingrad, against all the odds, stiffened the backbone of the Red army, as did the influx of arms and material from the United States. Advances in Russian technology made its T-34 tank a formidable force on the battlefield, and the Russians began to slowly push the Germans back. By 1944, with a force of 3,000 tanks and formidable air cover from fighters and bombers, the Soviet Union was winning its war against Germany.

THE FRENCH GUERILLA FIGHTER

When the French were driven out of France, a nucleus of about 7,000 former soldiers, under Charles de Gaulle, formed the Free French Fighters. The force grew and took part in actions against the Germans in North Africa, Italy, and, after the Normandy invasion, France itself.

Another group of fighters remained within France and were exposed to great danger—the men and women of the French Resistance. Many of them were French soldiers who had been unable to escape the country, others were communist fighters who wanted to strike a blow at fascism, and still others were patriotic citizens who wanted to oust the Germans. These groups formed in rural and forested areas and were known as the *Maquis,* after a small bush that grew plentifully in France.

Eventually supplied with arms by the Americans and British, they performed acts of sabotage against German targets, helped rescue downed airmen and escaped Jews and prisoners, and fought small-scale actions against the Germans. It was a precarious existence—if they were caught they were tortured and then generally killed or sent to concentration camps. People caught harboring them were killed as well. But when the D-Day invasion came, the Maquis played an important role in helping the Allied invasion by sabotaging German rail lines and communications.

THE GERMAN SOLDIER

As the triumphant German army prepared to invade Russia in 1941, one German male in four was in uniform—2,500,000 men in all. The Germans also possessed 2,500 of the then-finest tanks in the world—the Tiger, with its heavy armor and extraordinarily accurate 88 artillery rifle.

Germans soldiers at the beginning of World War II were highly trained and extremely well armed. Infantry carried Mauser rifles, "potato masher" hand grenades (so named because of their shape), submachine guns, and sidearms. Mechanized Panzer divisions (see "The Land War," p. 339) were the central focus of the army, slashing ahead of the regular infantry divisions to initiate breakthroughs in German lines. The Germans were also the first to use parachutists. Their successful attack on Crete was the first ever all-parachute assault.

At the beginning of the war at least, German troops were supremely motivated. Most of them believed totally in Adolf Hitler, or at least had powerful patriotic feelings for their country. As the war went on, many German troopers stopped believing in their *führer,* but they continued to fight out of patriotism—and became tougher and tougher. Their defense of the hedgerow country in Normandy right after the D-Day landing was an example of a superior soldier led by experienced noncommissioned officers who knew small unit tactics extremely well and refused to give up any territory without a fight. The German soldier—known generally as "Jerry"—to the allies, won the grudging respect of those who fought against him.

THE JAPANESE SOLDIER

The Japanese infantryman probably endured more hardship than any common soldier fighting in World War II. Although at the beginning of the war, the army—some 1,700,000 men strong—was well motivated and well supplied, the gradual stranglehold the allies applied to the Japanese supply lines in the Pacific forced many Japanese soldiers to live off bare subsistence rations. In some cases, they turned to cannibalism of Allied dead for sustenance.

The Japanese infantryman was generally a conscript, with a powerful and unquestioning love of home, family, and the emperor. As the Pacific war continued, the fighting became more and more savage because the warrior code of Bushido made it difficult for a Japanese soldier to surrender with honor. Therefore, many thousands of Japanese lives were lost in useless actions against their enemy, like the brave but wasted banzai attacks, where they made frontal charges into Allied machine guns. The stigma against surrender was so great that Japanese soldiers turned up alive in jungle settings on remote Pacific islands more than twenty-five years after the war. Sometimes even then they were unwilling to believe that the war had ended, and that Japan had lost.

THE ITALIAN SOLDIER

Of any soldier fighting on the Axis side during World War II, the Italian soldier was probably the weakest. When Mussolini joined the war on the side of the Axis Powers in 1940, he did not consult with any of his generals, many of whom were opposed to such an action. Numerous officers rebelled and were replaced by others of lower quality, who had far less military experience.

In quick succession, the poorly armed and led Italian forces (who were also paid barely a subsistence wage) were driven from Albania, Greece, and North Africa. Each time the Italian forces had to be bailed out by the Germans, who restored order to the situation and took over Albania and Greece and very nearly North Africa. When the allies invaded Italy on September 3, 1943, the Italians had just over 1 million men, most of whom had little or no will to fight. The Italian government surrendered only five days later.

Weapons of War

THE LAND WAR: PANZER ATTACK

While tanks and armored vehicles were just being introduced in the First World War (see "World War I," p. 232), they were to become a decisive factor in the Second World War. In between the wars, military planners at first thought that tanks should merely be used as support tools for infantry.

However, numerous forward-thinking war planners—including Englishmen J.F.C. Fuller and Basil H. Liddell Hart and German general Heinz Guderian—believed in the use of all-mechanized armored divisions. The Germans in particular pioneered the idea of panzer (armored) divisions, creating the first ones in the mid-1930s. Infantry accompanied these divisions, in armored half-tracks, and there was mobile artillery as well, but the real killing force was two regiments of tanks that could be used to punch holes through enemy lines in advance of regular infantry. The Germans put this to good effect in Poland and France and during the initial stages of their rapid advance into Russia.

The primary German tank of the war was the Tiger I, which was put into battle in early 1941. It was heavily armored, so much so that it had a problem crossing most bridges. It carried (along with two machine guns) the powerful German 88 gun, along with an extremely effective Zeiss optical aiming sight, so that the Tiger could knock out enemy tanks at a range of 1,600 yards (1.5 km).

This spelled trouble for U.S. Shermans and Russian T-34s, which had to close to 500 yards (457 m) or so before they could hope to penetrate the Tiger's armor. But a major drawback of the Tiger was how long it took to produce. In the same amount of time that German factories could turn out 1,300 Tigers, 40,000 Shermans and 60,000 T-34s could be built. Ultimately, even with its overwhelming firepower, this doomed the Tiger.

THE SEA WAR: THE AIRCRAFT CARRIER

Just as the tank was the symbol of land warfare in World War II, the aircraft carrier represented the sea. After World War I, many naval commanders continued to pin their strategic dreams on the huge dreadnought-class battleships, and these certainly played a crucial part in the naval war.

But aircraft carriers were pivotal. At the end of World War I, certain ships in the U.S. and British navies had been converted so that biplanes might take off from their decks, but the first purpose-built aircraft carrier was the HMS *Hermes,* built in 1918. This and other carriers built by the British, Japanese, and Americans in the interwar years carried ever larger planes whose function changed from mere scouting ahead of a task force of ships to bombing and torpedoing enemy vessels.

The first real blow from aircraft carriers came when British carrier ships destroyed half the Italian fleet at anchor at Taranto, Italy. The

(continued on p. 340)

THE TIGER I, DEVELOPED BY THE GERMANS, SEEMED THE ULTIMATE OFFENSIVE MACHINE, BUT IT TOOK SO LONG TO PRODUCE THAT AMERICAN SHERMANS AND RUSSIAN T-34S QUICKLY OUTNUMBERED IT.

Prints & Photographs Division, Library of Congress, LC-USZC4-4415

Japanese planes that devastated Pearl Harbor came from aircraft carriers. In return, aviator Billy Mitchell shocked the Japanese by bombing Tokyo only a few months after Pearl Harbor with sixteen B-25s secretly launched from a U.S. aircraft carrier.

In the most famous naval battle of the war, the Battle of Midway, fought mainly with naval aircraft, the Americans destroyed four carriers belonging to the Japanese and changed the course of the war in the Pacific

THE AIR WAR: THE HEAVY BOMBER

World War II's most destructive power, bar none, came from the sky, with the advent of the heavy bomber and its ability to drop tons of high explosive and incendiary bombs on both military and civilian targets. While the iconic image of World War I is long trenches snaking off through a barren wasteland, the one that

most fully symbolizes World War II are the haunting ruins of a city, piles of rubble with a few scattered walls standing upright.

The British used the Wellington or the Lancaster; the Americans flew the B-25, B-17 Fortress, or B-29 Super Fortress; and the Germans employed the Junkel 88 or the Heinkel III, or even a jet bomber developed in late 1944, which was almost impossible to intercept because of its speed but came too late to affect the course of the war. The Japanese bomber was the fast but thinly armored Betty.

All of these airplanes were used against military targets, and all were used against civilian ones, as well. Deliberate terror bombing of civilian targets in an attempt to break enemy morale was a chief weapon of World War II, used most extensively after 1943 by the allies. In total, the United States and Great Britain dropped 2 million tons (1.8 billion kg) of bombs

on Europe, killing 600,000 German civilians, 60 percent of them women and children. (About 60,000 British civilians died from German bombing.)

In the war in the Pacific, Americans wreaked havoc on the Japanese civilian population. In the low-level night bombing perfected by U.S. General Curtis LeMay, U.S. Superfortresses dropped incendiary bombs of jellied gasoline on the enemy, burning the wooden cities to the ground and creating huge firestorms. (Japan no longer had the air defenses to fight off the bombers, thus it could fly closer to its targets.) Two hundred thousand Japanese were killed, and another 13 million were made homeless. However, until the atomic bomb was dropped on Hiroshima, killing 80,000 people within a few hours, Japan refused to surrender.

In general, since the war's end, it has been recognized that strategic bombing of military targets is highly effective in helping defeat an enemy. However, bombing population centers, far from bringing about a loss of morale, actually stiffens one's opponents' resistance.

WHAT THE TRENCHES SYMBOLIZED FOR WORLD WAR I, THE AIRPLANE DID FOR WORLD WAR II, WITH THE HEAVY BOMBER TAKING OUT WHOLE CITIES AND HUNDREDS OF THOUSANDS OF CIVILIANS. THE GERMAN HEINKEL III, PICTURED HERE, WAS ONE OF THE MAIN PLAYERS UNTIL THE GERMANS DEVELOPED A NEW JET BOMBER IN 1944, SURPASSING THE CAPABILITY OF ALL OTHER HEAVY BOMBERS OF THE TIME BUT COMING TOO LATE TO CHANGE THE MOMENTUM OF THE WAR.

The Atomic Bomb: "An Extremely Powerful Bomb of a New Type"

In August 1939, Albert Einstein wrote several letters to President Franklin Delano Roosevelt, informing him that nuclear fission—fragmenting a uranium atom's nucleus by bombarding it with neutrons—might result in "an extremely powerful bomb of a new type." Einstein also told Roosevelt something even more alarming: The Germans had forbidden the export of uranium and were already working on this experimental weapon. He urged Roosevelt to help set up a program to develop an atomic bomb ahead of the Germans.

At Roosevelt's request, scientists who had already been working on nuclear fission—including Enrico Fermi, Edward Teller, and J. Robert Oppenheimer—came together with numerous others in the early 1940s. Fermi, at the University of Chicago, built the first successful nuclear reactor, which showed that controlled nuclear fission could work. This was a huge step in the development of the atomic bomb, whose complex mystery was solved step by step by the top secret Manhattan Project, headed by Oppenheimer, with locations in New York and all over the country, including the Los Alamos Laboratories in New Mexico.

On July 16, 1945, the first atomic bomb, its core the more stable and powerful plutonium rather than uranium, was exploded atop a tower near Alamogordo, New Mexico. Fermi wrote that the explosion resulted in "a huge pillar of smoke with an

expanded head like a gigantic mushroom." The blast, more powerful than even the scientists thought, brought on temperatures so hot (7,000°F [3,871°C]) that the nearby sand was fused together.

President Roosevelt had died earlier that year, but President Harry S. Truman made the decision to drop the atom bomb on Japan only a month after this first test. It was a decision that ended World War II, and helped begin the Cold War.

IN A STILL-CONTROVERSIAL DECISION, PRESIDENT HARRY TRUMAN DROPPED THE ATOMIC BOMB ON JAPAN; THE MUSHROOM CLOUD OVER NAGASAKI IS SEEN HERE. IT TOOK THE TWO ATOMIC BOMBS AND THEIR COMBINED KILLING OF 200,000 BEFORE THE JAPANESE SURRENDERED.

Prints & Photographs Division, Library of Congress, LC-USZ62-39852

The Secret War: Station X

The story of how the British deciphered encrypted German radio messages during World War II, leading to a bonanza of intelligence information and possibly shortening the war (this from no less an authority than Dwight Eisenhower) by two years, was kept secret until the 1970s. When it came out—in a series of books written by participants—it read like the stuff of spy novels.

The British eavesdropping on German radio traffic took place at Bletchley Park, an estate located in the town of Bletchley, in Buckinghamshire. It was also known—with appropriate intelligence flair—as Station X. There expert British decoders worked on deciphering transmissions from secret German coding machines, most notably the Enigma machine, used to code radio transmissions, and the Lorenz coder, used for teletype communications.

The Germans felt these codes—essentially strings of letters and numbers—were unbreakable because the machines translated them into thousands of possible combinations. But with an early Enigma model provided by Polish intelligence, with brilliant scientists and mathematicians such as Alan Turing, and with one of the earliest digital computers, developed in 1943, the British were able to crack German codes with an astonishingly high degree of accuracy. They knew beforehand of the German attack on Crete in 1941, of the sailing of reinforcement convoys to German troops in North Africa,

and especially to the tracking of German U-boat wolf packs during the Battle of the Atlantic, as the German submarines destroyed any resupply shipping headed for England.

Pooling their resources with the Americans, who had made great strides in breaking the Japanese "Purple Code," the Allies together used the best code-breaking effort of any war to date.

WHAT HELPED TO SHORTEN THE WAR BY AN ESTIMATED TWO YEARS WAS THE GENIUS OF THE BRITISH. USING THE COMBINED EFFORTS OF MATHEMATICIANS, SCIENTISTS, AND THE EARLIEST OF DIGITAL COMPUTERS, THEY WERE ABLE TO ACCURATELY DECIPHER THE GERMAN CODES, SKILLFULLY PREDICTING GERMAN ATTACKS AND CONVOYS.

Getty Images

The Holocaust: The Massacre

As historian John Keegan has pointed out, one of the things that makes Hitler's killing of more than 6 million Jews (as well as other "undesirables," such as Gypsies, the mentally challenged, Polish and French resistance fighters, and clergy) even more shocking is that, while hundreds of thousands, even millions, were killed in campaigns by the likes of the Romans, Mongols, and Spanish, "massacre had effectively been outlawed from warfare in Europe since the seventeenth century." With Hitler, massacre on an unimaginable scale was back.

After the Nazis took power in the 1930s, Jews in Germany suffered under a series of restrictive legal measures that culminated in the Nuremberg Laws of 1935, in which Jews were deprived of German citizenship. There were about a half a million Jews in Germany at the time and while a fifth of this population attempted to migrate, many of them went to nearby countries that were soon subsumed in the Nazi onslaught. Heinrich Himmler, head of the German SS, devised four task groups divided into *Sonderkommandos,* or Special Commandos, which killed roughly 1,000,000 Jews in the newly conquered areas of Poland and Russia. But these deaths were

mainly by shooting, which Himmler considered unproductive and slow.

In 1942, he proposed what he called the *Endlosung,* or Final Solution, at the behest of Hitler. The Endlosung took Jews from the ghettos in major cities to where they had been confined and brought them to concentration camps. Some of these were work camps, where inmates were literally worked to death. Others, like Treblinka and Sobidor, were simply extermination camps where Jews were herded into gas chambers as soon as they arrived.

By the spring of 1944, there were twenty concentration camps and some 160 smaller labor camps, and some 6 million Jews—40 percent of the world's Jewish population—had been killed. The fact that a supposedly civilized people in the middle of the twentieth century could massacre so many is one the world has struggled with ever since. However, the wave of sympathy for the plight of the Jews immediately after World War II was in part what helped them gain their own homeland and statehood (see "Arab-Israeli War," p. 344).

SEEN HERE ARE TWO INMATES OF THE AMPHING CONCENTRATION CAMP IN GERMANY JUST AFTER BEING LIBERATED BY U.S. TROOPS.

Prints & Photographs Division, Library of Congress, LC-USZ62-128310

18

THE ARAB-ISRAELI WAR

1948–1949

This war saved the existence of the fledgling state of Israel,
but it created circumstances that would cause almost unceasing
conflict between Jews and Arabs for the next half a century.

Combatants

- Arab Palestinians
- Israel
- Egypt
- Transjordan
- Syria
- Lebanon
- Iraq

Theater of War

Palestine

Casualties

Israel: 4,000 military dead, 2,300 civilians dead.
Palestinian Arabs and Arab countries: Estimated 8,000 to 15,000 military dead. Estimated 2,000 civilians dead.

Major Figures

PALESTINIAN ARABS AND ARAB COUNTRIES
King Abdullah of Transjordan, who led the Pan-Arab invasion against Israel
Commander Abd al-Qadir al-Husseini, head of the army of the Holy War
Fawzi al-Qawuqji, leader of the Arab Liberation Army
Hassan Salame, important Palestinian militia commander neutralized by Operation Nachshon

ISRAEL
David Ben-Gurion, head of the Yishuv and political leader of the Haganah, the Jewish army, destined to be first Israeli prime minister

Golda Meir, head of the political office and future Israeli prime minister who tried to negotiate with King Abdullah to stop the war
Yigael Yadin, military leader of Haganah
Yigal Allon, Yitzhak Rabin (future Israeli prime minister), and **Shimon Avidan,** major Haganah officers
Menachem Begin, head of the Irgun Zvai Leumi (IZL), a militant offshoot of the main Jewish paramilitary forces of the Haganah, and future Israeli prime minister

The Arab-Israeli War of 1948 began when the new United Nations attempted to partition the ancient land of Palestine into a Jewish and a Palestinian Arab state, but the roots of the conflict reach back millennia, to when the Jews were expelled from Israel by the Romans in the second century AD and the Muslims took over the country in the seventh century. But in the late nineteenth century, new waves of Zionist settlers sought to re-establish the ancient land of Israel on territory Arabs considered their own. After the end of World War II and the horrors of the Holocaust were revealed, the world decided to give the Jews back their ancestral homeland. But a war broke out between the new state of Israel, the Palestinian Arabs, and neighboring Arab states. Against the odds, the Israelis won the war, but in the process 700,000 Palestinian refugees were created, and the essential conflict between Arabs and Jews remains unresolved.

1946:

May: An Anglo-American commission delegated by the newly formed United Nations (UN) recommends that 100,000 Jewish refugees from Europe be allowed to create a Jewish state in Palestine.

June: Arab countries reject the idea of a Jewish state.

. . . .

1947:

February: Great Britain, protectorate of Palestine, refers the issue to the UN.

August: A UN committee suggests dividing Palestine into a Jewish state and a Palestinian state, with Jerusalem shared by both factions under UN protection.

November: The UN General Assembly endorses the partition of Palestine.

December: Civil war begins in Palestine, still under British mandate, with Arab attacks on the Jewish community in Palestine (the Yishuv). Israeli forces of the IZL place car bombs near Damascus Gate, killing twenty Arabs. The Arab Liberation Army (ALA) attacks a Jewish supply convoy outside Jerusalem.

. . . .

1948:

January: Civil war continues, with ALA fighting forces of the Haganah, IZL, and Lohami Herut Yisrael (LHI), another radical Jewish armed group, for control of roads leading into Jerusalem.

March: An Arab car bomb destroys the Jewish National institute compound in Jerusalem. Three Jewish convoys to Jerusalem are ambushed and more than eighty Jewish fighters are killed.

April: Jewish forces launch Operation Nachshon, an offensive to open the road to Jerusalem. Palestinian leader Abd al-Qadir al-Husseini killed in action during this operation. Massacre of Arabs at village of Deir Yasin by IZL and LHI forces. Haganah captures Haifa.

May: Arab attacks on Jewish settlements in Galilee. Haganah attacks Arab villages. Arabs finally capture Etzion Bloc, and a massacre ensues. The British mandate over Palestine ends, and Great Britain withdraws its forces. Israel proclaims itself a sovereign state on May 14. On May 15, armies of Egypt, Syria, Transjordan, Lebanon, and Iraq invade Israel. Egyptian forces besiege Jerusalem. Haganah commandos raid Syria and Lebanon. Haganah captures Acre and occupies western Galilee. A major attack by Syrians, Egyptians, and Transjordanians fails. Israeli Defense Force (IDF) is formed. The Jewish quarter of the Old City of Jerusalem falls to Arab infiltrators. The Egyptians besiege isolated Israeli settlements in the Negev Desert, in southern Israel.

June: A combined Syrian-Lebanese-ALA army captures the strategic settlement of Malkiya, in northern Israel near the Lebanese border. Egyptian forces occupy towns within twenty-five miles (40 km) of Tel Aviv. IDF tries and fails three times to capture the Arab town of Latrun, key to the Arab siege of Jerusalem. After international intervention, a truce is declared June 11.

July: The Israelis capture central Galilee. The Iraqis force IDF out of Jenin, just south of Galilee. Egyptian attacks on Israeli settlements south of Jerusalem fail. IDF opens a road corridor to supply Israeli settlements in the Negev Desert besieged by Egyptian army. A second truce is declared.

August: The Egyptians prevent Israeli convoys to Negev in violation of the truce, and Israeli and Arab forces in Jerusalem skirmish with each other.

October: The IDF launches the largest offensive of war to date, to reestablish communications with Negev settlements, defeating large Egyptian army in the south. In the north, IDF forces push the ALA and Syrians from Upper Galilee.

December: The last major Israeli attack against the Egyptians in the south.

. . . .

1949:

January: The Israelis expel the last of the Egyptian army from Israeli territory and enter the Sinai Peninsula, but withdraw under international pressure.

February–June: Israel and the Arab states of Egypt, Syria, Jordan, and Lebanon agree to armistice in separate peaces. Israel gains far more territory than it was originally given under the UN Partition.

. . . .

"THE LAND OF MILK AND HONEY"

It was all about a narrow strip of land between the Mediterranean Sea and the Jordan River that has been inhabited almost continuously since Paleolithic times. The land goes by many names—Canaan, Israel, the Holy Land, and Palestine (derived from the Latin name for some of the land's early inhabitants, the *Philistinus*, or Philistines). The Old Testament called it "the land of milk and honey." The Jewish people had their origins in Palestine, in the land they called Israel, and which they ruled from the twelfth century BC to the second century AD. But the conquering Romans drove them from Palestine after successive Jewish revolts, and the country was eventually ruled by numerous occupiers—Byzantines, Arabs, Seljuk Turks, Crusaders, and Mamluk and Ottoman Turks.

All of these, with the exception of the Byzantines and Crusaders, were Muslims, and the law of Mohammed was the law of the Palestine—which for centuries had become a quiet backwater, considered of little use to anyone. By the 1880s, some 25,000 Jews lived there, well outnumbered by the Arabs who surrounded them. But then Jewish emigrants from Eastern Europe began arriving, swept along by the Zionist movement, which called for a return to the Jewish homeland. (Zion was the name for one of the hills of Jerusalem and became the name for Israel itself.) By 1914, there were almost 100,000 Jews in Palestine, in a community known as Yishuv, 15 percent of the total population. The Jews, like their Arab-speaking neighbors, were subjects of the Ottoman Empire.

Palestine was not viewed as a separate state, merely an area between Jerusalem and Beirut.

After World War I these former Ottoman territories became a British protectorate. The British, in return for their help in defeating the Ottomans, had promised self-determination to both the Zionists and Arabs of Palestine. In 1922, the British divided Palestine into two different territories. The land east of the Jordan River became Transjordan (today's Jordan) while the land to the west, from Egypt in the south to Lebanon and Syria in the north, remained Palestine. Jews and Arabs then began terrorist attacks against each other, and the British tried to keep the lid on the growing violence. However, the Zionists slowly acquired more and more territory because they were more organized, because of steady immigration to Israel, and because they had more money to make land purchases.

After World War II ended and the world became aware of the Holocaust, sympathy turned to the Zionist cause. A clamor grew to allow a Jewish homeland in Palestine. The British government, which would soon leave Palestine to self-determination, and whose enthusiasm about a Jewish state had waned, decided to turn the matter over to the United Nations (UN).

In November 1947, against British wishes, the UN passed Resolution 181, which called for the partition of Palestine into both a Jewish and an Arab Palestinian homeland. The Jews accepted this proposal, but the Arabs rejected it, and the first of two distinct stages of the Arab-Israeli War

began. While the differing sides obviously worshipped different religions, the Arab-Israeli War was not a religious war, per se, because for centuries, with some exceptions, Muslims had allowed Jews freedom of religion in Muslim-controlled lands. Instead, it was a war over precious territory, with each side considering that its survival as a people was at stake.

The first stage, from November 1947 to May 1948, saw a ragtag Jewish army known as the Haganah (meaning "defense")—aided by its more radical terrorist arms, the LHI and the IZL—fighting against Arab guerilla fighters who coalesced into a group called the Arab Liberation Army (ALA). There were 650,000 Jews in Palestine, compared to twice that many Palestinian

347

THIS MAP OF THE
SOUTHEASTERN
MEDITERRANEAN
SHOWS HOW ISRAEL,
OCCUPYING A NARROW
STRIP OF LAND ALONG
THE OCEAN, WAS
SURROUNDED BY ITS
ARAB ENEMIES.

United States Military
Academy

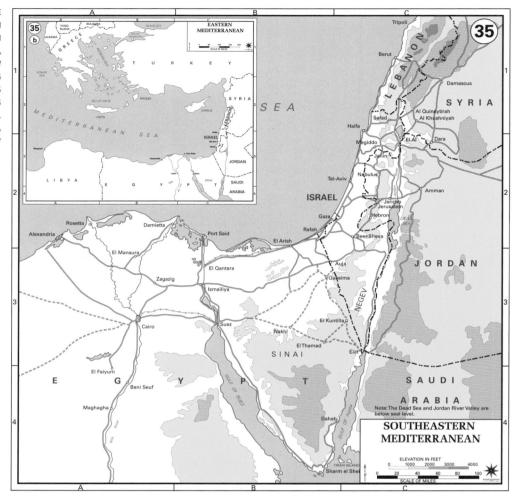

Arabs and 40 million Arabs in surrounding states. But the Jews, led by David Ben-Gurion had organized themselves for war, while the Arabs, among whom there was a great deal of factional infighting, had not. Still, the civil war from November to May was a vicious one, with terror groups on both sides setting off car bombs among civilian populations.

Jerusalem, sacred to both Arabs and Jews, was to be at the center of the fighting. The Jews held most of the so-called New City of Jerusalem, while the Arabs surrounded much of the Old City. Haganah and the ALA clashed over supply roads going into the city, while Arab snipers infiltrated Jewish areas and shot civilians. Arabs also attacked outlying Jewish settlements, or kibbutzim, like those at Kfar-Szold and Etzion Bloc, where outnumbered settlers held out against the odds, buying precious time for Israel.

By April, although the Jews had not yet lost a single settlement to the Arabs, they were reeling under heavy losses and suffering a shortage of men and materials. But then David Ben-Gurion mounted Operation Nachshon, the largest Jewish operation of the war to date (see "Turning Point," p. 350), which opened up a corridor out of besieged Jerusalem and also killed the Arab militia commander Abd al-Qadir al-Husseini, which was a grievous blow to Arab morale.

Despite being outnumbered, the Jews held their own in this first part of the war and even expanded their territory. But when the British mandate ended and Israel proclaimed itself a sovereign state, there was a Pan-Arab attack on the new state, consisting of an invasion by the armies of Egypt, Syria, Transjordan, Iraq, and (on a smaller scale) Lebanon. Jordanian troops took control of the Old City of Jerusalem, while Egyptians attacked and overran Jewish settlements in the Negev Desert in the south. But by July, the consolidated army of the Israelis—now called the Israeli Defense Force (IDF)—had taken central Galilee and pushed the Arabs back.

In July, the UN brokered a four-week truce, but when the Egyptians began fighting again, the Israelis pushed back the Arab countries on all fronts, gaining possession of all of the Negev Desert in the south (with the exception of the Gaza Strip). After another truce, broken by the Egyptians who refused to allow the IDF to supply Jewish settlements in the Negev, Israel pushed the Egyptians back into the Sinai Peninsula and forced the other Arab countries to withdraw as well.

Between February and May 1949, Israel signed separate peace agreements with all the combatants except Iraq, which withdrew its forces but would not agree to a treaty. In a stunning victory, Israel had taken more than 400 Arab villages and towns, had increased its original land allotment under Partition by one-half, and had swelled its armed forces to more than 200,000 strong.

But in the process, 700,000 Palestinian refugees had been created, expelled to other Arab states, and a smoldering resentment would grow against Israel. In a sense, the Arab-Israeli War of 1948 never really ended. There were further wars—in 1956, 1967, and 1973—as well as Palestinian uprisings as the descendants of those original refugees sought their homeland, as the Zionists once so fervently sought theirs.

OPERATION NACHSHON: APRIL 1948

On March 28, 1948, Jewish leader David Ben-Gurion cabled a political ally in New York from his headquarters in Tel Aviv: "This is the most terrible day since the beginning of the war."

It was an uncharacteristic note of despair from the resilient leader, but, indeed everything seemed to be going wrong for the Jews. Although the civil war was barely four months old, they had already lost 1,000 men. Jerusalem was surrounded by ALA forces and, as one Haganah captain reported, "there is starvation in the city." On March 27, a Haganah convoy filled with food and ammunition had tried to force its way into the city to re-

men in the Galilee convoy committed suicide rather than risk capture.

There was even worse news on the political front. The Americans, who had supported the partition of Palestine and the creation of a Jewish state, now seemed to be wavering in their support as the bloody civil war continued. The United States' ambassador to the United Nations, Warren Austin, told the UN Security Council in mid-March that "there seems to be general agreement that the [partition] plan cannot now be implemented by peaceful means …. we believe that a temporary trusteeship for Palestine should be established."

The attack would begin on April 5, and it would be called Operation Nachshon after the Biblical figure of Nachshon Ben Aminadav, who was the first to stride into the parted Red Sea.

lieve the population, only to be ambushed by the ALA and nearly destroyed. (During this last week of March, 136 supply trucks were sent through to Jerusalem, but only 41 made it.)

On March 28, the day Ben-Gurion sent his cable, another Jewish convoy had been attacked while trying to reach isolated Jewish settlements in western Galilee. In bitter fighting that lasted into the night, forty-seven Haganah soldiers were killed, and their bodies were mutilated by the Arabs. That fate awaited any convoy soldier caught by the ALA, which is why many of the

President Harry Truman tried to reassure Zionist leaders in the United States that Austin had spoken without his permission. (In his diary, Truman complained the State Department "pulled the rug out from under me today.") But Ben-Gurion knew that any delay in the creation of Israel might cause the shaky political coalitions within the Yishuv to collapse. With the British ready to pull out of Palestine in May, and with the armies of neighboring Arab countries massing to invade, something needed to be done, and quickly.

"If Jerusalem Falls…"

On March 31, Ben-Gurion called a meeting of the political and military wings of the Haganah. He told them that it was necessary to loosen the Arab death grip on Jerusalem by any means possible. "If Jerusalem falls, the whole country might fall," he told Yigael Yadin, chief of staff of the Haganah. He wanted a huge Haganah force to clear the road from Tel Aviv to Jerusalem.

Yadin pointed out the difficulty of this. The Haganah forces were hard-pressed everywhere in the country, he said. Not enough could be spared for such an effort. There weren't even enough weapons to arm them all.

Ben-Gurion retorted: "We'll take men, arms, and mortars from the settlements."

Yadin replied that this would leave these communities unprotected, but Ben-Gurion was insistent. "The fall of Jewish Jerusalem could be a deathblow to the Yishuv," he said. "The risk is worth everything." Finally, he won the day. It was decided to create a Haganah brigade of 1,500 men, organized into three battalions, by thinning ranks of Jewish troops all over the country. This was to be the first time that the Haganah had operated on such a large scale. Its goal would be to secure the Tel Aviv–Jerusalem road by creating a corridor 2 to 6 miles (3 to 9.5 km) wide. They would do this by clearing all Arab forces away from the road and by considering all Arab-held villages along the route as possible bases of ALA operations.

The attack would begin on April 5, and it would be called Operation Nachshon after the Biblical figure of Nachshon Ben Aminadav, who was the first to stride into the parted Red Sea when the Jews escaped ancient Egypt. The operation was part of a larger strategic calculation by Ben-Gurion and his military planners, one that they called Plan D. They knew the British would be withdrawing from Palestine in six weeks' time and that Arab countries would almost certainly invade shortly thereafter. Plan D called for destroying or severely weakening the capabilities of the Palestinian Arabs and the ALA before such an invasion began. The Jews must regain control internally before facing a foe from the outside, or they were doomed.

Arms from the Sky

On the very night that Ben-Gurion was meeting with his advisors, a chartered U.S. Skymaster cargo plane landed secretly in a remote airfield near the Arab village of Beit Daras, north of the Gaza Strip. It held 200 rifles, 40 machine guns, and 160,000 bullets—a shipment of Czech arms that the Haganah had long been trying to arrange. Two days later, another plane landed, carrying 200 machine guns, 450 rifles, and 5 million bullets, its crates of arms covered with potatoes and onions. The arms were taken by sea to Tel Aviv, where they were handed out to the gathering Haganah fighters. The soldiers were so joyful that they kissed the guns, "which were still coated in grease," as one soldier later noted.

With this relatively huge stockpile of weapons, Operation Nachshon was ready to begin. The official kick-off date for clearing the Jerusalem road was April 6, but two important small operations began earlier. On the night of April 2–3, a Haganah company attacked and captured the small but strategic village of al-Qastal, some 5 miles (8 km) west of Jerusalem, which overlooked the road into the city.

And on the night of April 4–5, a group of Israeli commandos snuck through an orange grove west of Jerusalem, near the village of Ramla, and attacked the four-story building that was the headquarters of Hassan Salame. Salame was a dreaded, Nazi-trained Palestinian militia leader, whose men had been responsible for numerous attacks on Jewish convoys into Jerusalem. The Haganah commandos blew up the headquarters and killed two dozen Arabs. Although Salame himself escaped (he was to be killed in action against the Israelis the following June), his prestige was dealt a serious blow by this incident. Many of his militia deserted him, which kept his forces from any real role in the fighting to come.

The Road to Jerusalem

Operation Nachshon launched in the early morning of April 6, and for the most part it took ALA forces and Arab militia completely by surprise. In the past, the Jews had played a mainly defensive role and operated on a company-strength level, but now they came down the Jerusalem road 1,500 strong, well armed, and on the offensive. Two Arab villages along the road, Khulda and Deir Muheizin, fell almost immediately. With al-Qastal in the hands of the Jews, the Haganah quickly launched a sixty-truck convoy, which made it to Jerusalem and was met by cheering crowds.

But the battle was far from over. Abd al-Qadir al-Husseini, commander of the army of the Holy War, understood the strategic significance of the village of al-Qastal, which the Jews now held and

AN ICONIC PICTURE OF DAVID BEN-GURION, THE FOUNDER AND GUIDING LIGHT OF THE EARLY ISRAELI NATION.
Getty Images

which commanded the main road that ran into Jerusalem from the west. If the Arabs could recapture it, they might stop the Jewish convoys once again. After being denied arms and reinforcements by Arab High Command, al-Husseini decided to attack the village anyway. Because of a shortage of men, Haganah leaders had garrisoned it with raw recruits. They then compounded this mistake by arguing over who was responsible for its command.

In the meantime, al-Husseini's men gathered by the hundreds and began laying down mortar and sniper fire on al-Qastal. On the night of April

352

7–8, al-Husseini launched his attack, sending hundreds of men at the perimeter of the village. The Haganah held on, but barely, as streams of machine gun tracers lit up the air and grenade and mortar explosions rocked the town.

Early on the foggy morning of April 8, a Jewish sentry heard a noise and fired at it. There were cries and the sound of a body thudding to the ground. It turned out that he had killed al-Husseini, who had gotten lost on a reconnaissance mission with two aides. The Jews at al-Qastal knew they had killed someone big when they examined his body, but they could not figure out who it was. But then they heard the radio waves filled with Arabs frantically wondering where their commander was. As the day wore on, more and more Arabs showed up at the foot of the hill below al-Qastal. "I saw thousands of Arabs," one Jewish survivor wrote. "Buses, trucks, and donkeys brought them from Suba." Determined to find al-Husseini, or at least his body, they attacked that afternoon "like madmen," said the same Jewish survivor.

With their ammunition depleted, the Jews defending al-Qastal could no longer hold on and tried to retreat eastward down the slope, with the Arabs now filling the village. While their officers heroically covered their retreat from an orchard, dozens of Haganah were able to escape, but anyone left behind was killed and mutilated by the Arabs. By nightfall, al-Qastal belonged to the Arabs, and they had also found the body of Abd al-Qader al-Husseini.

Parting the Red Sea....

Early on the morning of April 9, the Haganah counterattacked al-Qastal, only to find it empty except for dozens of Jewish bodies. The Arabs had simply left the strategic village, abandoning it to go to the funeral of al-Husseini, which was held in the Arab-controlled Old City of Jerusalem. The Haganah immediately razed the village and then built a defensive perimeter around it. From up on the hill, they could watch another convoy snaking its way safely into Jerusalem.

The battle for Jerusalem would continue for the rest of the war. In just a month's time, the British would leave, David Ben-Gurion would proclaim Israel's statehood, and the Pan-Arab invasion would begin. But for now, Operation Nachshon had parted the Red Sea just enough to allow the Jews to survive another few weeks.

DAVID BEN-GURION:
FOUNDER OF A NATION

Any number of brilliant leaders helped Israel rise to nationhood, but the one indispensable person was David Ben-Gurion, who would go on to become the nation's first prime minister. Ben-Gurion was born in small-town Poland in 1886, the son of a lawyer who believed deeply in the Zionist movement. Ben-Gurion acquired this belief, further strengthened by the pogroms that occurred in Poland while he was there, the almost casual attacks that seemed to come in historic waves.

In 1906, Ben-Gurion, like so many Zionists, immigrated to Palestine, which was then a part of the Ottoman Empire. He became a farmhand and was also a socialist, but his main ambition in life was the creation of a Jewish state in Palestine. Although small of stature, Ben-Gurion was fiery and charismatic, yet somewhat authoritative and didactic.

He was expelled from Palestine in 1915 for his political activism and went to the United States, where he became involved with Zionist groups in New York. His experiences in the United States left him less enchanted with the byzantine, ever-changing socialist groups, as well as more democratic in inclination. After World War I, he returned to Palestine, which was then governed by the British, and rose to become a prominent leader in the Yishuv, or Jewish community,

there. In the 1930s, as reports reached the Jews in Palestine of the atrocities being perpetuated on Jews in Nazi Germany, Ben-Gurion became even more dedicated to creating a homeland for persecuted Jews.

With World War II in the offing, Ben-Gurion crafted a brilliant strategy. The British (and other countries in the world) refused admission of Jewish refugees, so Ben-Gurion set up an underground rescue system that brought them from Europe to Palestine, where the British authorities promptly locked them up in camps, thus creating world sympathy for the Zionist plight.

At the same time, Ben-Gurion encouraged thousands of young Jews to enlist in the British army to fight the Nazis and gain valuable combat experience. Although Ben-Gurion did not hate the Arabs, he knew that any Jewish state would have to be forged in the crucible of war, and so during the years leading up to 1948 created a shadow army, the Haganah (see "The Israeli Soldier," p. 356), which was ready to fight when the time came.

In the end, Ben-Gurion's planning was the key to the Israeli triumph in the war. He became prime minister in 1948 and would hold that position until 1963 (with the exception of a two-year period in the middle 1950s), guiding the state of Israel through its crucial formative period.

ABD AL-QADIR AL-HUSSEINI:
"SOMETHING BURNS IN MY HEART."

Abd al-Qadir al-Husseini was born in 1907 to a prominent Jerusalem family, and he grew up to become a fervent believer in Arab Palestinian nationalism. While still in his teens, he became a member of the Arab Nationalist Party, which fought to expel the British from the country. In 1938, he was exiled for his involvement with an underground militia group. He secretly returned to Palestine before the 1948 war to organize the army of the Holy War, the best-organized among the Arab militia groups.

Al-Husseini was a charismatic leader, darkly handsome, often pictured with bandoliers crossed over his chest, who was fearless in battle. He had little patience for Arabs who would not join his cause. He was responsible for expelling Palestinians from numerous villages, yet those who flocked to him found him a man who would never retreat from fighting the Jews.

When Operation Nachshon began he immediately recognized the importance of the Jewish offensive and journeyed to ALA headquarters in Damascus to plead for more arms and artillery with which to retake the critical village of al-Qastal, which overlooked one of the main supply roads into Jerusalem. None of the ALA leaders were willing to give him what he wanted. Finally, he threw a map of Palestine in the face of an ALA staff officer and said: "You traitor. History will condemn you. I am returning to al-Qastal … and will die fighting." That night, he wrote a poem to his young son, Faisal:

The land of the brave is the land of our forefathers

The Jews have no right to this land.

How can I sleep while the enemy rules it?

Something burns in my heart.

My homeland beckons.

Returning to the fighting, al-Husseini ordered an assault against al-Qastal that failed. He and several staff officers then attempted to get closer to the village to see what was going on, but he became lost in the fog and stumbled on an Israeli sentry, who fired a burst of submachine gun fire, killing al-Husseini almost instantly.

The Arabs recovered his body when they successfully attacked the village the next day and drove out the Jews. They held a massive funeral for al-Husseini in Jerusalem. The Arabs who held al-Qastal simply abandoned their posts to attend the funeral, leaving the strategic village wide open to the Israelis, who retook it the next day to find many dead Jewish soldiers mutilated beyond recognition by Holy Army members angered over al-Husseini's death. Without al-Husseini, this most important Arab militia group fell apart and was never again an effective fighting force.

The Israeli Soldier

As civil war between the Jews and Arabs began in late 1947, many observers did not give the Jewish army—the Haganah—much of a chance. The total Jewish population in Palestine was less than half that of the Arabs of Palestine let alone the millions of Arabs in surrounding nations.

The Haganah, which would be renamed the Israeli Defense Force in June 1948, was not to be underestimated. It had been established in the 1920s to fight the underground war against the Palestinian Arabs and had evolved in that time into a tightly knit, highly organized fighting force

of about 25,000 men and women. In general, 5,000 of the Haganah were on active duty, and the rest were ready as reservists who trained on weekends. Political control of the Haganah at the start of the war rested with David Ben-Gurion (see "Commanders," p. 354) although the military leader was Yigael Yadin. Other commanders, many of whom would become prominent figures in Israel, included Yigal Allon, Yitzhak Rabin, and Shimon Avidan.

A British blockade kept arms and reinforcements from reaching Palestine. Although the blockade

was meant to keep a lid on the war, it hurt the Jews more than the Arabs. But the Haganah had underground arms factories, which, at the end of 1947, provided it with 10,000 rifles, 3,500 pistols, 900 machine guns, and almost 1,000 mortars. Most of the weapons were sent to Jewish settlements, which became fortified camps, but even so, at the beginning of the war, only one Jewish soldier out of three could be armed, and they had no tanks or heavy artillery.

Nonetheless, the Haganah's success in holding off the Arab attacks at the very beginning of the war lay with its training, unit cohesion, leadership, and preparation. Jewish leaders had long planned for this war. They knew what their strategic initiatives were—essentially, keeping Jerusalem open at all costs, while making the Arabs pay a heavy price for attacking outlying settlements. Plus the Jewish leaders were able to communicate this to the men and women who gave their lives on the front lines.

HAGANAH SOLDIERS CELEBRATE A SEDER MEAL, STEN SUBMACHINE GUN AT THE READY.
AFP/Getty Images

The Arab Soldier

Although the Arab Palestinians who faced the Haganah in the early part of the war were better armed—a Jewish intelligence estimate put the number of rifles and machine guns at 50,000—they were a far less organized and disciplined group.

The Arabs who had fought the Jews in Palestine since the 1920s consisted of large armed bands that formed and re-formed somewhat spontaneously after attacks by Jews. Each band had a core of 200 to 300, with more armed men added in times of crisis. But many of these groups fought with each other as well as the Jews. One Arab commander described the bands as "unreliable, excitable, and difficult to control and in organized warfare virtually unemployable."

However, the best organized and largest of these armies was the Arab Liberation Army (ALA), which was led by Fawzi al-Qawuqji, although the most charismatic commander was the leader of the Arab militia group army of the Holy War, Abd al-Qadir al-Husseini (see "Commanders," p. 355). Al-Qawuqji told his men that they were "fighting Jihad in order to help the persecuted Arabs of Palestine." However, despite the fervor displayed by many members of the ALA, and despite the fact that they were more heavily armed (with armored cars and some artillery) and numerous, the ALA was unable to overcome Jewish resistance.

Lack of cohesiveness was still a problem. Although the ALA consisted of four battalions with Palestine divided into territories the responsibility for which was given to one commander, the Arab High Command (AHC) was ineffective as a central authority. Each battalion operated more or less on its own, supported by local militias that might or might not be relied upon in battle. When al-Husseini, the commander of the Jerusalem district, was killed in battle in early April, no overall commander could replace him quickly and effectively because he was a militia group leader whose men had close ties to him. Thus the Arabs lost this crucial early battle for the most important city in Palestine.

AT CENTER, NOTABLE FOR HIS CROSSED BANDOLIERS, IS ABD AL-QADIER AL-HUSEINI, THE FORMIDABLE ARAB WARRIOR WHOSE DEATH CAUSED IRREPARABLE DAMAGE TO THE ARAB MILITIA.
AFP/Getty Images

357

The Palestinian Refugees: "There are Enough Arabs Around"

One of the most enduring problems created by the 1948 Arab-Israeli War was the Palestinian Arab refugee. By April 1948, a month before Israel declared itself a state, 100,000 Arabs, mainly from the more heavily populated centers of Jaffe, Haifa, and Jerusalem, had already left the country. By June, 400,000 had left and by war's end, in early 1949, about 700,000 refugees had left their homes.

Why did the Arab Palestinians flee, but not the Jews? In one sense, this was because the Jews had nowhere to flee to, surrounded by hostile Arab countries. But much more important, the Jews had faith in their leadership and a strong central political organization. The Palestinians had none of this. In fact, ordinary Palestinians became disillusioned with their leaders, many of whom were fleeing the country as fast as they could. The flight of the Arab elite—intellectuals, politicians, community leaders— was one part of the exodus that was disheartening.

Even more problematic was the fact that the ALA and other Arab military organizations had decided to force Palestinian women and children out of their homes and into exile. The professed reason was so that they would not become targets for Jewish attacks. Another underlying reason was that the Arab military did not want these people to become citizens of a new Jewish state. But the ALA failed to bargain on the fact that many Palestinian men did not want to leave their families and thus went with them into exile.

While some historians, both Arab and Israeli, have written that the Israelis had a plan to evict Arabs from Palestine, this was probably not the case. In fact, the chief of staff of the Haganah, in preparing for the Pan-Arab invasion that did in fact take place, called on his officers to ensure "the full rights, needs, and freedom of Arabs in the Hebrew state."

The Palestinian refugees were in fact treated far more cruelly by Arabs in countries such as Egypt, Syria, and Jordan, which refused to take responsibility for them, or even allow them self-determination in the parts of Palestine (the Gaza and the West Bank) that the Arabs retained after the war. As one Egyptian diplomat said to a British journalist, "We don't care if all the refugees will die. There are enough Arabs around."

THE SPRAWLING DHEISHEH REFUGEE CAMP, FOUNDED IN 1949, HOUSED REFUGEES FROM 45 ARAB VILLAGES WEST OF JERUSALEM. TODAY, IT HAS 12,000 INHABITANTS.
Associated Press

The Secret Meeting of Golda Meir and King Abdullah: "I Will Treat You Very Well"

As the end of the British mandate in Palestine drew near, David Ben-Gurion became increasingly concerned. He knew—as in fact did every other Jew and Arab in the region—that the minute the British pulled out and Israel declared itself a state, the neighboring countries were going to attack. And, although Ben-Gurion's Haganah had fought so well and bravely that they had actually expanded their territory, only 60 percent of them were armed, and there were severe shortages of ammunition and other supplies. It was one thing to hold out against the disorganized Arab Palestinian forces, but how could Israel take on the massed might of the Egyptians, Lebanese, Transjordanians, and Syrians?

Ben-Gurion decided to send a secret emissary to King Abdullah of Transjordan, who had been named commander in chief of the Pan-Arab invasion forces. That person was Golda Meir. Born in the Ukraine in 1898, Meir had emigrated with her family to the United States, become a Zionist, and eventually went to Israel, where by 1947, after a career as a fundraiser and political activist for Jewish émigrés, she had risen to the position of acting head of the political department of the Jewish Agency, which was the Jewish government before the state of Israel was declared.

In this job she had spent much time negotiating various issues with British Palestine authorities, and Ben-Gurion had admired her forcefulness and intelligence.

On May 11, just three days before Israel was to declare its statehood, Meir arrived in Transjordan to speak with King Abdullah. She was willing to give him certain territory in Palestine in return for stopping the invasion, but he insisted that he wanted all the Arab parts of Palestine. And he didn't like the idea of Jewish statehood, either. "Why are you in such a hurry?" he asked Meir. "Why not wait a few years?"

Meir replied: "We've been waiting for 2,000 years. Is that hurrying?"

King Abdullah told her that Israel should wait just a few more years. In the meantime, he would allow it to be represented in his parliament, as a kind of subject state. Meir refused this, but, as she was leaving, Abdullah told her politely she should reconsider his reply, and if the Jews wanted to acquiesce they would need to tell him by May 15, no later. "I will treat you very well," he told her. Meaning that he would rule benevolently over the Jews.

There would be no Jewish reply. On May 14, Israel declared its statehood. On May 15, led by Transjordan, the Arab countries attacked.

GOLDA MEIR, SECRET EMISSARY TO KING ABDULLAH OF TRANSJORDAN, AND FUTURE PRIME MINISTER OF THE ISRAELI STATE, IS PICTURED HERE.

Time & Life Pictures/Getty Images

Two Massacres …

Both sides in the Arab-Israeli War of 1948 accused each other of indiscriminately killing civilians, charges that would be debated for years to come. In fact, as in any civil war, both sides were guilty of atrocities.

DEATH AT DEIR YASIN

During the same Operation Nachshon that saw the death of Abd al-Qadir al-Husseini and the fighting around al-Qastal, Israeli forces attacked and captured the small Arab village of Deir Yasin, which lay on the road between Jerusalem and al-Qastal. Deir Yasin had little military significance, but the aftermath of the battle, as historian Benny Morris has written, "proved to be one of the key events of the war."

There had long been a history of hostility between the Arabs of Deir Yasin and the Jewish inhabitants of

MANY OF THE VICTIMS OF THE MASSACRE ARE BURIED IN DEIR YASIN CEMETERY, WHICH IS PICTURED HERE.

Popperfoto/Getty Images

the nearby Jerusalem suburb of Giv'at Shaul, which had been attacked more than once by gunmen from Deir Yasin in the years preceding the war. Since the 1948 war started, the two villages had signed a nonaggression pact, but Arab snipers in Deir Yasin still fired occasionally on Jews in Giv'at Shaul, although it is not known whether the Arab villagers supported them.

In any event, on April 9, as the battle for al-Qastal raged, Jewish forces advanced on Deir Yasin. These were mainly irregular troops of the LHI and the IZL. The LHI (the initials come from the Yiddish initials that stand for Freedom Fighters of Israel) was a radical Jewish militia also known as "the Stern gang" after one of its initial leaders. The IZL (its initials stood for National Military Organization) was also known as the Irgun; one of its leaders, Menachem Begin, would become a future prime minister of Israel. Regular Haganah forces also assisted, but they were in the minority.

The attack on the village began with IZL and LHI forces using bullhorns to urge the villagers to surrender. But when fire from the village was unexpectedly heavy, Jewish forces moved in and indiscriminately began tossing grenades in homes, blowing up some entirely, and shooting women and children as they tried to flee. Some male villagers were taken to an LHI base in western Jerusalem

and executed. Altogether about 120 villagers were killed that day, both combatants and noncombatants.

The Palestinian Arabs made effective propaganda use of this massacre in radio broadcasts that fired up the sentiments of Arabs in neighboring states. King Abdullah of Jordan, who had earlier promised the Jews and Golda Meir he would not invade, pointed to the massacre as the reason why he had changed his mind.

DEATH AT ETZION BLOC

In the weeks before the Pan-Arab invasion of the newly declared state of Israel in May 1948, both sides within Palestine fought with renewed vigor, the Israelis to prepare defenses against the oncoming invasion, the Arabs to clear a path for the invading armies of Syria, Jordan, Egypt, and Lebanon.

The so-called Etzion Bloc lay on an important road between Bethlehem and Hebron and consisted of four kibbutzim that had been established there in the early 1940s. Relations between the kibbutzim and their Arab neighbors were never good, and as the war began, the Arab mayor of Hebron warned the Jews to leave their land or "you will be removed by force." This the Jews refused to do, and the Etzion Bloc kibbutzim became a major staging ground for Jewish forces attacking Arab or British convoys along the road.

The British wanted these attacks to stop and allowed the Jordan Legion, which at this time was still officially a part of the British army, to capture the kibbutzim, which contained about 500 Haganah fighters and armed kibbutz members. On May 12, the legion attacked in the early dawn hours, accompanied by artillery, armored cars, and a large force of Arab militia. During fighting that lasted all day, the legionnaires overran Jewish positions at the Kfar Etzion, and the next day the one hundred Jewish defenders who were left surrendered. A Jewish eyewitness reported that a photographer came up and took pictures of the prisoners. After the photographer left, the Arabs, yelling "Deir Yassin!" opened fire with machine guns and threw hand grenades into the mass of prisoners.

Almost all of these one hundred prisoners were murdered; some of the women fighters were raped and afterward killed, despite the efforts of a few Jordanian officers to stem the bloodshed. The other three Jewish settlements, subjected to continuous attack, were too terrified to surrender until the Red Cross arranged for their safe transport. Even then many were killed by legionnaires and militia. In the end, 350 prisoners were taken to Transjordan and held there safely until the war was over. Still, the Etzion Bloc massacre enraged Jewish forces and apparently figured in a number of smaller killings of Arab prisoners as the war progressed.

The British in Palestine: "Partners in Adversity"

In late 1947, Sir John Troutbeck, head of the British Middle East Office, wrote: "We [and the Arabs] are partners in adversity on this question. A Jewish state is no more in our interest than it is in the Arabs'...."

Although the British had in the years after the First World War promised statehood to both Jews and Arabs, it was really the Arabs they favored because of the Arab countries' vast oil reserves and strategic location near the Suez Canal. The idea of a Jewish state was one the British tried to put off as long as possible — "No solution of the Palestinian problem should be proposed which would alienate Arab states," one British diplomat wrote. This attitude enraged the Zionist population of Palestine, particularly after the British refused to allow refugees from the Nazi death camps to land there during the war.

After the war, as the British mandate over Palestine was ending, they handed off the "Palestinian problem" to the United Nations, while trying to convince other countries (especially the United States, whose president, Harry Truman, had gone on record supporting a Jewish state) that a Jewish homeland would probably be a "Red" or communist state. Certain Americans believed this, but Truman's support for Israel was firm, in large part because he did not want to offend the large and influential Jewish population in the United States, which had traditionally supported Truman's Democratic Party.

When the United Nations voted for the Partition, Great Britain tried to obstruct the plan, claiming it would not accept any change in status in Palestine that was not accepted by both parties. And when the Partition became a reality, Britain instituted a blockade that hurt the Jewish army, but not the armies of Transjordan, Syria, and Egypt, which had, since World War II, been armed by the British themselves.

Great Britain also supported the Transjordanians in their invasion of Israel immediately after Great Britain's mandate had ended. One diplomat went so far as to write: "It is tempting to think that Transjordan might transgress the boundaries of the United Nations' Jewish state...this would have immense strategic value for us."

However, after continued Israeli victories in the war, and after world opinion began to turn against the British, Great Britain begrudgingly reversed course, although it still threatened to send an armed force into the Sinai Peninsula when Israel entered that territory early in 1949 while pushing back the Egyptians.

19

THE VIETNAM WAR

1955–1975

North Vietnam inflicted a devastating and historic defeat
on a United States seeking to stop communism in Southeast Asia,
but unable to come up with a coherent strategy to fight
what became the longest war in U.S. history.

Combatants

- United States, South Vietnam
- North Vietnam and National Liberation Front (NLF or Viet Cong)

Theater of War

Vietnam, Cambodia, Laos

Casualties

United States: 58,000 dead, 303,000 wounded, 2,000 missing
South Vietnam: 220,000 dead, 1,170,000 wounded. Civilian dead estimated at 1,500,000
North Vietnam and Viet Cong: 1,176,000 dead or missing. Civilian dead estimated at 3,000,000

Major Figures

UNITED STATES

President John F. Kennedy, who committed small amounts of troops and material to Vietnam
President Lyndon Johnson, who escalated the war until troop levels reached 500,000
Secretary of Defense Robert McNamara, senior U.S. policymaker who fervently promoted the bombing of North Vietnam, but later turned against the war
General William Westmoreland, senior U.S. officer in Vietnam, in charge of all combat troops
President Richard Nixon, who authorized the secret war in Cambodia, but also reduced troop levels and eventually pulled U.S. forces out of Vietnam
Henry Kissinger, senior U.S. diplomat and Nixon's national security advisor, who negotiated peace with North Vietnam in Paris

SOUTH VIETNAM

Ngo Dinh Diem, first president of the Republic of South Vietnam, who was ousted and murdered in a coup
General Duong Van Minh, who led the coup that assassinated Diem
General Nguyen Khanh, who subsequently ousted Minh
Air Force Vice Marshal Nguyen Cao Ky, who became president by toppling Khanh
Nguyen Van Thieu, who, backed by the United States, became president while Ky stayed on as prime minister

NORTH VIETNAM

Ho Chi Minh, president of North Vietnam, early communist and guerilla fighter, who declared independence from the French in 1945, thus beginning the long battle for Vietnamese independence
Vo Nguyen Giap, brilliant military leader and architect of the U.S. defeat in Vietnam
Le Duc Tho, Hanoi's chief negotiator at the Paris peace talks
Colonel Dong Si Nguyen, who constructed the Ho Chi Minh trail
General Van Tien Dung, who led the final, successful invasion of South Vietnam in 1975

1954:

May: The French base in northwestern Vietnam falls to Viet Minh forces.

July: Vietnam is divided at the 17th parallel into the Democratic Republic of North Vietnam and the Republic of South Vietnam.

1955:

January: Direct U.S. assistance to South Vietnam begins as U.S. advisors arrive.

October: South Vietnam national referendum replaces Emperor Bao Dai with President Ngo Dinh Diem.

1959:

January: The Hanoi Politburo passes Resolution 15, turning the struggle against South Vietnam into a military, not just a political, one.

1960:

November: John F. Kennedy is elected president of the United States. A military coup against Diem fails.

December: Hanoi announces the formation of the National Liberation Front of South Vietnam (the Viet Cong).

1961:

October: U.S. General Maxwell Taylor visits Vietnam on a fact-finding mission and one month later recommends that Kennedy send U.S. combat troops to South Vietnam. Kennedy refuses but does increase U.S. aid.

1962:

February: The United States creates the U.S. Military Assistance Command, Vietnam (MACV). There are now 4,000 U.S. military advisors in South Vietnam.

1963:

January: In the Mekong Delta village of Ap Bac, 200 Viet Cong hold off 2,000 ARVN troops and their U.S. advisors.

November: U.S. officials give at least tacit approval to a coup attempt against Diem by South Vietnamese generals led by Duong Van Minh on November 1. Diem and his brother Nhu are murdered the next day.

1964:

January: South Vietnam General Nguyen Khanh ousts Minh.

August: North Vietnamese torpedo boats exchange fire with a U.S. destroyer in the Gulf of Tonkin. The U.S. Congress gives Johnson broad powers to wage war against Vietnam.

1965:

February: Air Force Vice Marshal Nguyen Cao Ky takes control of South Vietnam, ousting Khanh.

Johnson sends two Marine battalions to guard the U.S. base at Da Nang, the first U.S. combat troops stationed in South Vietnam.

March: The United States begins large-scale bombing of North Vietnam.

July: Johnson approves the request of General William Westmoreland for forty-four more U.S. battalions in South Vietnam.

November: U.S. troops meet regular North Vietnamese Army (NVA) troops in the first conventional battles of the war, in the Ia Drang Valley.

1967:

April: Westmoreland asks Johnson for another 200,000 troops to be sent to Vietnam; Johnson has already committed 470,000 but sends 45,000 more.

September: The United States maneuvers Nguyen Van Thieu into becoming president of South Vietnam, with Ky now prime minister.

1968:

January: Communist forces in the south launch the Tet Offensive, which turns out to be a military defeat for both the NVA and the Viet Cong, but the U.S. public is shaken.

March: Lyndon Johnson says he will halt bombing of North Vietnam and negotiate with Hanoi. He also says he will not run for re-election.

May: The Paris peace talks, between the United States and Hanoi—Saigon does not join until January 1969—begin but make little headway.

November: Richard Nixon becomes U.S. president.

1969:

March: Nixon, aided by National Security Advisor Henry Kissinger, begins secret bombing of Cambodia. Vietnamization begins.

September: Ho Chi Minh dies.

December: 25,000 U.S. troops are withdrawn from Vietnam.

1970:

May: The Ohio National Guard opens fire on protesting students at Kent State University, killing four.

December: U.S. troop strength in Vietnam is reduced to 334,000.

1971:

January: ARVN troops, without U.S. ground forces, attack NVA bases in Laos, but they are easily driven back.

December: U.S. troop strength is further reduced to 156,000.

1972:

October: Henry Kissinger and Le Duc Tho, Hanoi's chief diplomat, reach agreement in Paris on peace terms.

December: Nixon bombs Hanoi and Haiphong for eleven days, claiming that Hanoi has stopped negotiating.

1973:

March: Last U.S. combat troops leave South Vietnam. North Vietnam releases 591 U.S. POWs three days later.

1974:

August: Nixon resigns from the presidency rather than be impeached.

1975:

March: Under General Van Tien Dung, North Vietnamese troops take major cities in South Vietnam's Central Highlands and capture Hue. Dung's forces take Da Nang and march on Saigon.

April: Thieu and other government officials evacuate Saigon. The last Americans in Saigon evacuate.

THE LONGEST WAR

The country of Vietnam had been divided at the 17th parallel in 1954 after the forces of Ho Chi Minh defeated the French in 1954 at the battle of Dien Bien Phu. North of the demarcation line was the Democratic Republic of North Vietnam, and south lay the Republic of South Vietnam.

Elections were mandated to be held in 1956, but then civil war broke out between the communist government of the north and the corrupt, but nominally democratic government of the south, backed by the United States, which was afraid that a communist victory in Vietnam would lead to a communist takeover in all of Southeast Asia.

At first U.S. aid to South Vietnam and its series of presidents was confined to military advisors and financial assistance. But soon it became clear to U.S. President Lyndon Johnson that the Army of the Republic of Vietnam (ARVN) was losing the war against the Viet Cong guerillas operating in the south and supplied by North Vietnam. After North Vietnamese patrol boats clashed with a U.S. intelligence-gathering destroyer in the Gulf of Tonkin in August 1964, Johnson secured the approval of Congress to send U.S. combat troops to South Vietnam and begin bombing North Vietnam.

The war then escalated as North Vietnam sent regular army (NVA) troops to infiltrate the south. The first major clashes between these two forces took place in the Ia Drang Valley in South Vietnam in November 1965 and underscored the differences in their approaches to the war. The Americans favored the new tactic of air mobility—moving large bodies of men quickly from battlefield to battlefield via the helicopter—as well as using close support of artillery and fighter strikes. Without this technology, the North Vietnamese pursued a strategy of getting as close as possible to their enemy, rendering bombs and artillery useless.

The war raged through 1968, with Americans under General William Westmoreland seeking to deny Viet Cong guerillas the help of the populace by moving thousands of Vietnamese to so-called "strategic hamlets" built for them and guarded by ARVN troops, while at the same time attacking the NVA from firebases built around the country. The massive bombing of North Vietnam continued unabated until 1968. But the strategic hamlet program was a failure because it alienated the peasant population by taking them away from their homes. Plus the Americans were never able

PICTURED: VIET CONG TROOPS SHOOTING AT THE ENEMY AIRCRAFT

to trap the NVA into a large enough set-piece battle to inflict irreparable harm on them.

In January 1968, the Viet Cong and North Vietnamese launched the Tet Offensive, a major, concerted attack against thirty-six cities in South Vietnam. They caused widespread destruction there, but they were defeated on the battlefield with heavy losses. Despite this, the attack shook the U.S. public. Calls for ending United States' involvement in Vietnam, which had been growing, now reached fever pitch.

President Johnson stopped the bombing of North Vietnam and began negotiating with the North Vietnamese in Paris, while announcing that he would not run for a second term. In March 1969, U.S. strategy switched to that of "Vietnamization," which meant gradually allowing the South Vietnamese to do all the fighting themselves. The next year, under President Richard Nixon, the United States gradually withdrew its 500,000 troops, as civilian protestors in the United States grew steadily more vocal, especially after news of the My Lai Massacre was revealed.

After the killing of students at Kent State University by the Ohio National Guard in May 1970, most of the country wanted war to end. At last, Nixon's negotiator Henry Kissinger and North Vietnam diplomat Le Duc Tho reached a peace agreement in Paris in October 1972. The last U.S. combat troops were withdrawn from the country in March 1973, although the South

PRESIDENT LYNDON JOHNSON PREPARES TO ADDRESS AMERICANS AND ANNOUNCE HIS DECISION TO HALT BOMBING OF NORTH VIETNAM IN MARCH 1968.

Time & Life Pictures/ Getty Images

Vietnamese would continue to fight on, supplied with U.S. weapons, until they were overwhelmed by the North Vietnamese army in April 1975.

The war in Vietnam—the longest war in U.S. history—was also the first war ever lost by the United States and is probably the most traumatic event in its twentieth-century history. U.S. citizens were divided against each other during the war and developed a powerful distrust of their government, while the United States also lost face around the world. However, a triumphant North Vietnam had united the country at last, despite severe losses, and it would gradually became apparent after a period of postwar adjustment that it would not march in lockstep with Soviet Russia or communist China.

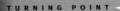

THE TET OFFENSIVE: 1968

It seemed to a lot of people, many of them in the U.S. intelligence community, that something was simmering that January of 1968. In the fall, North Vietnamese Army (NVA) regular troops had launched strong attacks against U.S bases at Khe Sanh and Con Thien along the 17th parallel, attacks that would retrospectively be seen as successful attempts to draw U.S. reinforcements north, away from Saigon.

Early in January, a document found on the body of a dead Viet Cong officer talked about a "concerted offensive" to be held very soon. And as Tet—the annual Vietnamese celebration of the lunar New Year—approached on January 31, it appeared to many Americans that there were more and more Vietnamese men in major cities such as Saigon and Hue who appeared strong and whippet-thin, yet pale, as if they had been spending a good deal of time trekking through shady jungles.

In fact, they had. In the month before January 31, 1968, thousands of Viet Cong and NVA troops had shed their uniforms and blended into the civilian population, prepared for the mightiest offensive the North had ever launched against the south and the Americans. It would involve attacks on thirty-six provincial capitals, more than one hundred towns and cities, with almost 200 Viet Cong and NVA battalions—70,000 would take part in the initial attack.

And it would all occur to the sound of fireworks, horns, and drums.

"An Allied Intelligence Failure"

On the night of January 30–31, most Americans in South Vietnam were listening to and taking part in Tet celebrations. In fact, in Saigon, more than 200 colonels assigned to the U.S. embassy went to a boisterous drinking bash at the home of a fellow officer, leaving only one extra guard on the embassy, despite the high level of alert.

Later, one U.S. officer would call the fact that so many warnings had been ignored "an allied intelligence failure ranking with Pearl Harbor." But most U.S. troops in Vietnam were on high levels of alert at least half the time, and no one had passed on any sense of urgency to those around Saigon. After all, wasn't there a truce in place for the Tet celebrations?

Certainly, the North Vietnamese had agreed to one, and in response the South Vietnamese gave half its troops home leave. And while everyone was celebrating, the North Vietnamese and Viet Cong infiltrators picked up their guns and hand grenades and left their hiding places. Through the haze of gunpowder from fireworks and the shrieks of laughter, they headed for their assigned targets as part of a plan that had been designed mainly by General Vo Nguyen Giap. He had decided that the south was ready for a general uprising, that people there would oust the Americans and corrupt South Vietnamese governments. In fact, this was not true, but it turned out to be the best miscalculation Giap ever made.

"What the Hell Is Going On?"

In the early morning darkness in Saigon—the most important target of the infiltrators—nearly 4,000 Viet Cong gathered in small teams and headed to their targets. Nineteen highly trained Viet Cong commandos piled into a truck and a taxi cab, arrived outside the U.S. embassy at about three o'clock in the morning, and blasted a hole in its wall with plastic explosives. Then they charged in, firing.

All across the country, other actions were taking place almost simultaneously. The Viet Cong attacked twenty-five military bases, putting frantic Americans under siege as the realization dawned that what they thought were Tet firecrackers were in fact actual bullets and explosives. Outside Saigon, the Viet Cong blew up the Long Binh ammunition dump, causing a spectacular explosion that could be seen for miles. The Saigon suburb of Cholon was turned into a staging ground for Viet Cong and NVA attacks that briefly were able to take over the national radio station, assault the presidential palace, and keep General William Westmoreland prisoner in his U.S. Military Assistance Command, Vietnam, headquarters.

But it was the assault on the U.S. embassy that gained the most notoriety in the first night and day of the attack. Despite the fact that one U.S. officer derisively referred to it as a "piddling platoon action," despite the fact that U.S. Ambassador Ellsworth Bunker was hustled off to safety, the Viet Cong sappers and guerillas had actually penetrated U.S. territory and killed GIs there. Because this was Saigon, U.S. reporters and camera crews were present, and they filmed

CIVILIAN DEAD IN HUE DURING THE 1968 TET OFFENSIVE. TENS OF THOUSANDS OF NON-COMBATANTS DIED BEFORE THE AMERICANS DROVE THE NORTH VIETNAMESE FROM THE CITY.

the chaos. Instead of the images the U.S. public had been seeing—images of smoke pluming from the jungle as jets launched air strikes at Viet Cong and NVA positions, or of GIs firing their M-16s from the relative safety of trees and bushes, the U.S. public suddenly saw rubble within Saigon and dead bodies. They heard the firing coming from infiltrators and the panicked voices of the television reporters.

It was pure chaos to a U.S. public that had been told, by none other than General Westmoreland, that they were winning the war. Trusted television announcer Walter Cronkite put it for most Americans when he asked, "What the hell is going on? I thought we were winning the war."

Hue City

Actually, within weeks, the Viet Cong and North Vietnamese were being pushed back with heavy losses, but this mattered little to a public with these images emblazoned on its mind. And there was worse to come. The iconic battle of the Tet

367

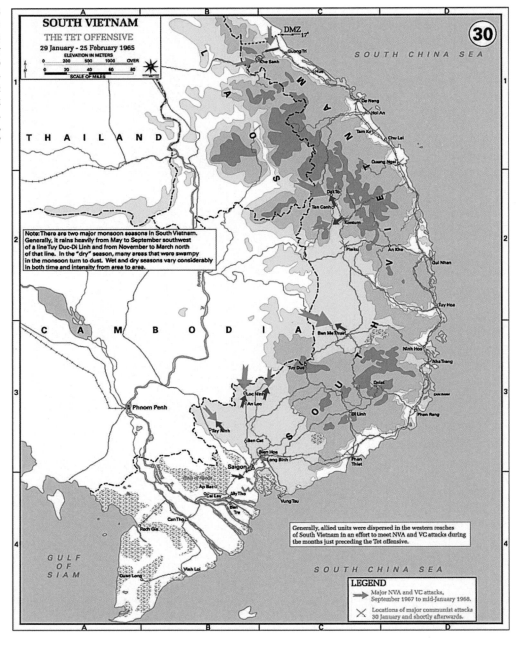

Offensive would take place at Hue City, in central Vietnam. A beautiful place situated on the Perfume River, Hue is the ancient "imperial city" of the Nguyen Dynasty, a place that was filled with museums, lovely parks, and about 140,000 people, including many foreigners (mainly French) and a large number of Catholics. As the Tet Offensive began, a division of NVA seized much of the city and then raised its flag over the Citadel, the fortified inner city of the ancient kings.

The soldiers then embarked on a preassigned massacre: to cleanse the city of all those who had spoken out against North Vietnam. NVA commanders had lists of people—including government officials, students, and priests—and rounded them up by the thousands. Many were shot. A favorite fate for the clergy was burying them alive.

But in early February, three battalions of U.S. Marines came to take the city back, attacking from the north in assault boats that crossed the Perfume River with NVA bullets pinging off their sides. In cold, foggy weather that often restricted the Marine's ability to call in air strikes, the Americans dug the NVA out of their spider holes and sniper's nests, fighting their way through streets littered with military and civilian dead. An estimated 5,000 NVA soldiers met their deaths in Hue, as well as tens of thousands of civilians, including 3,000 executed by the Communists. The stink of death was in the air; one officer commented that "the horrible smell was everywhere. You tasted it as you ate your rations, as if you were eating death." Marines blasted their way into the Citadel and at last removed the NVA flags.

But U.S. firepower destroyed the once beautiful city of Hue, leaving 116,000 citizens homeless. As one U.S. major commented, describing another fight for a nearby town: "We had to destroy the town in order to save it." Hue was saved, but devastated.

In the end, the Tet Offensive appeared to be a costly failure for Giap. After fighting that lasted into April, the NVA and Viet Cong had lost a staggering 50,000 men dead and had been pushed back from every position they had taken. In fact, the Viet Cong had ceased to exist as an effective fighting force.

But though they had lost in battle, it turned out that Giap and the North Vietnamese had won the propaganda war. Americans did not like what they were seeing on their television sets, in a war they were supposedly winning. When General Westmoreland, who could rightly proclaim an allied victory, asked for an additional 200,000 men, Lyndon Johnson turned him down, kicked him upstairs to chief of staff, and decided to ask for peace talks with Vietnam. The beginning of the end was at hand for the North Vietnamese—who had, after all been fighting since 1945. A poem written by the then-ailing Ho Chi Minh—he would die the following September—and broadcast on Hanoi Radio sums up the feelings of the North Vietnamese that pivotal early part of 1968:

This spring far outshines previous springs.

Of triumphs throughout the land come happy tidings.

Forward!

Total victory shall be ours!

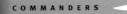

GENERAL WILLIAM WESTMORELAND: "A CORPORATE EXECUTIVE IN UNIFORM"

William Westmoreland, commander of the Military Assistance Command, Vietnam (MACV), was a solid U.S. soldier who had the misfortune to reach the apex of his career just as the United States was fighting its most unconventional war. Born in 1914, he served with distinction in both World War II and Korea, reaching the rank of brigadier general in 1953.

Westmoreland was known as a no-nonsense disciplinarian who, however, cared deeply about the welfare of his men. He was also, unusually, a graduate of Harvard Business School and believed in running his command almost as if it was a corporation. Historian of the Vietnam War Stanley Karnow called him "a corporate executive in uniform."

After serving in the Pentagon and as superintendent of the U.S. Military Academy at West Point, Westmoreland ("Westy," as he was known to intimates) arrived to take over command of U.S. forces in Vietnam in 1964. Westmoreland considered that he was fighting a conventional war. He wanted U.S. troops to engage in set-piece battles against regular North Vietnamese Army (NVA) troops, fighting a war of attrition to wear them down while the Army of the Republic of Vietnam (ARVN) battled Viet Cong guerillas and provided security for the "strategic hamlets" in provincial South Vietnam. Although Westmoreland succeeded in killing hundreds of thousands of NVA troops, he was never able to control the pace and tempo of the war, and the NVA, dodging most conventional battles, was never worn down. The irony is that when North Vietnam finally launched its massive Tet Offensive, Westmoreland's forces were able to defeat them, but by that time the U.S. public had grown sick of the war.

Still, despite 500,000 U.S. troops in Vietnam, Westmoreland kept returning to the United States to ask for more—requesting an additional 200,000 after Tet. He was always seeking that superior force that would finally corner an elusive enemy. Westmoreland's requests were denied, and he left Vietnam in the spring of 1968 to become army chief of staff. Like so many U.S. general staff officers of the time, Westmoreland had fought a war rooted in strategy twenty years old, and he had lost against a much more versatile and determined enemy.

GENERAL VO NGUYEN GIAP: "TOUGH AS NAILS"

General Vo Nguyen Giap—still alive as of this writing—is one of the fiercest patriots Vietnam has ever known, perhaps even fiercer than the legendary Ho Chi Minh. He was born into a moderately well-to-do family in Quang Binh province in what would later become North Vietnam, to parents who were also proud patriots who wanted to drive the French colonial forces out of Vietnam.

Giap went to an elite school in the ancient imperial capital city of Hue, and he turned more and more radical after reading Ho Chi Minh's Marxist-inspired writings. In the early 1940s,

When the war against the Americans reached a fever pitch in the 1960s, Giap was carving out strategy there, too. As commander of the People's Army of North Vietnam, which came to be called the NVA, he sought successfully to neutralize the superior firepower of the Americans by "grabbing the enemy by the belt" (see "The North Vietnamese Soldier and Viet Cong," p. 373) and fighting a war of small unit actions.

Giap was mainly responsible for the Tet Offensive of 1968—an offensive that failed militarily, with great loss of life. But in adversity, Giap was, as one U.S. historian later put it, "tough as

General Vo Nguyen Giap is one of the fiercest patriots Vietnam has ever known, perhaps even fiercer than the legendary Ho Chi Minh.

Giap left Vietnam for China, where Ho Chi Minh was in exile. French authorities threw his wife, a fellow Marxist, in prison, where she died.

In 1942, Giap returned to Vietnam to join a guerilla group that waged jungle warfare against both the Japanese and French. After 1945, when the Japanese were defeated and the French failed to recognize an independent Vietnam, Giap rose to become Ho Chi Minh's chief strategist in the Viet Minh war against the French, sculpting the tactics that defeated the French at the decisive battle of Dien Bien Phu, in 1954.

nails." He saw that Americans were unwilling to continue the war politically and thus continued to fight, even though severely weakened.

By war's end, Giap had been mainly replaced as active commander by General Van Tien Dung, after which he became defense minister. While there is currently some reevaluation of his reputation occurring among historians—Giap lost at least 500,000 NVA troops in battle, a startling number—there is little doubt that his contribution to the North Vietnamese victory was crucial.

The American Soldier

For a U.S. GI, brought to South Vietnam in a huge transport plane from his training base in the United States, the Vietnam War was an exercise in surreal terror. On one hand, South Vietnam had been turned into what one soldier called "a miniature America." By 1967, a million tons of supplies per month were being funneled to Vietnam to support the troops there. Saigon had previously been South Vietnam's main deep-water port; now, the U.S. Army engineers created six huge artificial harbors. South Vietnam became the scene of the busiest airports in the world as U.S. bombers and helicopters flew in and out. At their bases, GIs—or "grunts," as they were known in the slang of the war—could visit air-conditioned post exchanges (PXs) and bars and call home on long-distance lines.

But in the field, life was tough for U.S. soldiers. Sent out on search and destroy missions or stationed in remote fire bases, they faced a wily and elusive foe who knew the countryside far better than they did. The Americans sought to gain not territory, but body count. They were aided and equipped with the finest weapons in the world at the time, which included the M-16 rifle and grenade launcher, tanks, armored personnel carriers, and devastating claymore antipersonnel mines.

GIs were transported around the country in the ubiquitous Bell UH-I helicopter (called the Huey) to facilitate rapid strikes, and they were supported by fighter jets and B-52 bombers. But they often found themselves ambushed by NVA and Viet Cong forces who came to understand that the closer they got to their enemy, the less effect all the U.S. lethal firepower had.

At the height of the war, in 1968, the Americans had committed more than 500,000 troops to Vietnam. Fifty-three thousand of them were to die. The average U.S. soldier was a draftee who stayed in Vietnam for only a year's time before rotating out. While this system spared many a GI from excessive combat strain, it sent men home just as they were becoming experienced in the ways of jungle warfare and did not lend itself to unit cohesiveness or create high morale. In the end, influenced by the war protests back home and by the U.S. military's own conflicted goals in the war, most U.S. soldiers fought bravely, but came to the realization that the war was a futile effort.

AMERICAN TROOPS EMERGE FROM A HELICOPTER IN 1968, THE HEIGHT OF THE WAR. THE UNITED STATES HAD COMMITTED MORE THAN 500,000 TROOPS TO VIETNAM. FIFTY-THREE THOUSAND OF THEM WERE TO DIE BY THE WAR'S END.
Getty Images

The South Vietnamese Soldier

As the United States sought exit from the quagmire of Southeast Asia, its chief plan was one of "Vietnamization," (see "Chronicle," p. 364)—turning the fighting of the war over to the Vietnamese themselves.

But this was easier said then done. The Army of the Republic of Vietnam (ARVN) was plagued by poor leadership and training, and especially endemic corruption in its officer corps, many of whom became rich selling supplies and equipment to the Viet Cong, the very forces the ARVN was supposed to be fighting. The individual ARVN soldier could often be a brave fighter. Some 250,000 ARVN troops lost their lives in the war, and historians have credited them with doing a more than creditable job stopping the Viet Cong. But many ARVN units did flee the enemy during joint operations with the United States, causing U.S. troops to take over the brunt of the fighting in the war. Even so, the ARVN, when well-led, defeated the NVA numerous times on the battlefield.

When U.S. ground forces were withdrawn in 1973, many ARVN units, heavily supported by U.S. airpower, were able to score victories against the North Vietnamese. But in a series of final battles, the NVA finally defeated the ARVN, which disintegrated into chaos. Most captured ARVN soldiers were sent to re-education camps in North Vietnam.

The North Vietnamese and Viet Cong Soldiers

The first Communist fighter of the war between North and South Vietnam was the National Liberation Front soldier, or Viet Cong, short for *Viet Nam Cong San,* or "Vietnamese communist." U.S. soldiers called simply called him VC or Victor Charlie, shortened to Charlie. The VC soldier was in the main a guerilla fighter operating in small, semi-independent units, attacking ARVN and U.S. positions at night and carrying out terror operations in South Vietnam's larger cities.

Despite the VC's reputation as feared fighters, they were being steadily beaten back by ARVN and U.S. forces until the North Vietnamese Army (NVA) entered the war on a large scale by infiltrating down the Ho Chi Minh trail, beginning in 1964 (see "The Ho Chi Minh Trail," p. 376).

The NVA were extraordinarily resilient fighters. They had few of the high tech weapons the Americans had, relying mainly on the AK-47 rifle, hand grenades, light machine guns, and booby traps. They were subject to extraordinary hardship in the field, including B-52 bombings. Yet they could survive on rice from the canvas bags they carried over their shoulders, while they marched to engage an enemy who was almost always superior, at least in firepower.

After the battles of the Ia Drang Valley in 1965, where U.S. troops and the NVA first clashed, the NVA learned that to avoid the awesome U.S. fighters and bombers, they needed to get as close to the enemy as possible. They called the strategy "grabbing the enemy by the belt." That way, the Americans could not bring down their firepower without hitting their own men, which was a highly important factor in winning the war. NVA soldiers, however, fighting for their homeland, and encouraged by political officers who accompanied the troops into action, had unsurpassed morale that eventually translated into victory after a long, hard war that cost the Viet Cong and NVA combined 1,176,000 dead and missing.

NORTH VIETNAMESE SOLDIERS, PICTURED HERE, GOT AS CLOSE AS POSSIBLE TO THE ENEMY, RENDERING BOMBS AND ARTILLERY USELESS.

The My Lai Massacre: "Women and Children, too?"

A famous antiwar poster of the 1960s showed the bloodied bodies of Vietnam peasants, old women, and infants, lying in a ditch. The type on the poster posed this question: "Women and children, too?" And the answer was obvious: "Women and children, too."

Numerous atrocities were committed by both sides during the war in Vietnam—the North Vietnamese execution of civilians at Hue (see "Turning Point," p. 366) being just one of them. But the massacre of more than 300 unarmed civilians by U.S. troops, and the pictures the U.S. public saw on television, brought home the war home as never before.

On March 16, 1968, Charlie Company of the 111th Brigade, Americal Division, entered the village of My Lai in the South Vietnamese district of Son My. Viet Cong guerillas had a major presence in the district, and Charlie Company had fought a frustrating war against these shadowy figures in black pajamas who used hidden mines and booby traps as their main way of combating the far superior U.S. forces. Numerous members of Charlie Company had been killed or maimed by such devices in the weeks leading up to March 16. The men who entered the village on a typical search and destroy mission (searching for the enemy, destroying any of his munitions or supplies) were angry and frightened.

They were led by Captain Ernest Medina, who had previously told the troops that the only people left in the village would be Viet Cong. Some of his soldiers later claimed that he had ordered them to shoot women and children, but he denied this. In any event, one officer, Lieutenant William Calley, told his men to enter the village firing, even though there were no reports of enemy fire. A BBC reporter as well as a U.S. Army photographer were present and saw Americans round up men, women, and children, aged from one year to eighty-one years, and kill them with machine gun fire, bayonets, and hand grenades. Calley ordered a group of villagers into a ditch and mowed them down with his M-16.

Despite the efforts of a few heroic individuals who attempted to stop the killing, including a U.S. helicopter pilot who rescued a dozen villagers from certain death, Charlie Company killed more than 300 civilians that day. The massacre was covered up for more than a year. When news leaked out, the story angered the antiwar movement, and it caused the general public, which had not previously questioned the rightness of the war, to wonder about the morality of U.S involvement. Only one person present at the massacre, Lieutenant Calley, was ever convicted of murder. He was sentenced to life in prison after a court martial, but upon orders from President Richard Nixon, he served only a four-and-a-half-month sentence.

The Gulf of Tonkin Incident: "To Take All Necessary Measures"

If there was a *casus belli* for the stepped-up U.S. involvement in Vietnam, it came from what is now generally known as the Gulf of Tonkin incident. On August 2, 1964, the destroyer USS *Maddox* fought a brief battle with three North Vietnamese assault boats in the Gulf of Tonkin, off North Vietnam's east coast. Beyond that, much is in dispute. How close the *Maddox* was to the coast depends on who is telling the story. The *Maddox* reported that it was about 30 miles (48 km) away, in other words, well into international waters. The North Vietnam claimed it was within 5 miles (8 km) of the coastline, which they claimed as their territory.

It must be said that the *Maddox* was not on a pleasure cruise. It was crammed full of electronic eavesdropping equipment designed to listen in on North Vietnam communications. This was particularly sensitive for the North Vietnamese because on November 1, there had been numerous covert action incursions over its border by United States–sponsored South Vietnamese intelligence teams, which were trying to infiltrate the country. The North Vietnam boats that sortied out may have thought the *Maddox* was a part of these efforts.

In any event, the *Maddox* claimed that the assault boats fired torpedoes at the destroyer and returned fire, damaging one assault boat and destroying another. The North Vietnamese claimed that there were no torpedoes fired, but they admitted an exchange of surface fire initiated by the *Maddox* and that no North Vietnamese assault boat was damaged or destroyed.

On the night of August 4, the *Maddox,* joined by another destroyer, the *C. Turner Joy,* returned to the same area where they had been previously attacked and claimed that they were assaulted once again. Historians universally believe that this attack did not occur and was probably caused by a misreading of radar blips by edgy U.S. sailors.

These incidents were seemingly trivial, but they led to U.S. escalation of the war. Prodded by Lyndon Johnson, the U.S. Congress, on August 7, passed the Gulf of Tonkin Resolution, which allowed the president "to take all necessary measures to repel any armed attack against forces of the United States and to prevent further aggression." It was basically a blank check, signed and made out to Lyndon Johnson, to wage all-out war against North Vietnam without a formal declaration of war from Congress.

POW-MIA: An Undying Hope

For many years—and even to this day—many Americans wore bracelets with the names of servicemen who were, in the parlance, POW-MIA—either prisoners of war or missing in action.

During the Vietnam War, the North Vietnamese and Viet Cong forces captured hundreds of U.S. soldiers, sailors, and aviators.. Those captured by the Viet Cong were usually hidden in small jungle camps near the borders of Laos and Cambodia, traditional refuges for the Viet Cong. Ill-treated, poorly fed, and sometimes summarily executed, most of these Americans did not return home. The Americans captured by the North Vietnamese—many of these aviators, such as senator and former presidential candidate John McCain—were taken to more organized prisons, the most infamous of which U.S. POWs called "the Hanoi Hilton." The North Vietnamese generally notified the International Red Cross about the existence of these captives (something the Viet Cong did not usually do) but subjected many of them to harsh treatment that included torture.

At the end of the war, 591 American captives were released by the North Vietnamese and the Viet Cong, leaving about 2,000 Americans missing in action, or MIA. After U.S. personnel left Vietnam for good in 1975, the U.S. public sought answers as to what happened to these men. There were rumors of U.S. prisoners sighted postwar in Vietnam by "boat people"—Vietnamese fleeing the new regime—despite the fact that U.S. administrations subsequent to the war denied that any Americans were alive there. In 1980, a reliable CIA contact in Vietnam claimed to have seen about thirty Americans working there on a road crew, but this was never verified. By 1993, separate investigations by the U.S. Senate and House of Representatives concluded that no U.S. POWs were alive in Vietnam, although there might have been a small number alive after the war. Therefore, even though their bodies had never been recovered, most MIAs were in fact, dead.

Still, to this day, POW-MIA activists continue to try to find out what happened to the missing U.S. servicemen. The remains of sixty-seven of 2,000 have been identified since relations with Vietnam have normalized. Of the rest, there is no trace.

The Ho Chi Minh Trail: A Lifeline 12,000 Miles Long

Even before U.S. troops entered the war in the war in great numbers in 1965, the government of North Vietnam was infiltrating NVA troops into the south in order to augment the poorly armed and trained Viet Cong units there. The only way North Vietnam was able to move massive groups of men and huge amounts of material was over the Ho Chi Minh Trail, which the North Vietnamese called the Truong Son Strategic Supply Route, because it went across the long mountain chain of the same name that separates Vietnam from Laos. The trail was, even the United States' National Security Agency agreed, "one of the great achievements of military engineering in the twentieth century."

The Ho Chi Minh Trail went from North Vietnam, over the Truong Son Mountains and traveled for hundreds of miles down through Laos and Cambodia, just across Vietnam's western and southwestern borders. The trail, hidden beneath triple canopy jungle, culminated in South Vietnam, just north of Saigon. But in fact it had numerous entry points into the country across mountain passes. The first actual trail was just a footpath carved out over millennia by Vietnam's indigenous tribes, and it was then used by Chinese convoys carrying opium into Southeast Asia. The Viet Minh had used the trail on a smaller scale during their war against the French, mainly as a communications conduit,

and the Viet Cong also used this hidden trail system.

But after 1964, needing to widen this network of trails to bring in thousands of troops and hundreds of thousands of tons of food, ammunition, and other supplies, the North Vietnamese turned the trail into a modern logistical system. Under the command of Colonel Dong Si Nguyen, engineer battalions were sent in to widen roads and strengthen bridges for heavy trucks, while underground camps, hospitals, and fuel and ammunition dumps were set up.

The Ho Chi Minh Trail was a work in progress. By 1974, ten years after he began, Dong had turned it into a network of 12,000 miles (19,000 km) of major and secondary roads. A North Vietnamese solider could now reach South Vietnam in six weeks, rather than six months. It was not an easy journey. Untold thousands were lost to U.S. bombing attacks as well as to malaria, but without this lifeline, North Vietnam would never have won the war.

SOUTH VIETNAMESE TROOPS WALK ALONG A SECTION OF THE HO CHI MINH TRAIL INSIDE LAOTIAN BORDER, FEBRUARY 14, 1971. OVERHEAD, THE NORTH VIETNAMESE ERECTED A BAMBOO AND FOLIAGE CANOPY TO PREVENT TRAIL'S DETECTION FROM THE AIR.
Associated Press

Protests at Home: "Hey, Hey, LBJ!"

One of the major reasons the United States withdrew from the war in Vietnam without attaining victory was the antiwar movement in the United States. It was made up of numerous different (and often competing) groups whose interests coincided when it came to their desire to end the war in Vietnam.

While there had long been a small peace movement in the United States, made up mainly of conscientious objectors and those who protested against the use of the atomic bomb, the Vietnam War galvanized students all across the country. Two movements—Students for a Democratic Society (SDS) and the Free Speech Movement (FSM)—were created in the early 1960s to protest the Cold War and to participate in the civil rights struggle in the United States. After the United States began bombing North Vietnam in February 1965, these groups came together to organize protests against the war. In April 1965, SDS organized a protest march on Washington that brought 15,000 to 20,000 participants, many more than SDS members assumed would come. Obviously, they had tapped into something.

As the U.S. involvement in the war increased, the protests became larger and more boisterous. Students marched to Washington chanting: "Hey, hey, LBJ, how many kids did you kill today?" and staged mock funerals of Uncle Sam. More radical groups such as the Weather Underground began bombing federal institutions and university laboratories doing

government work. GIs returning from Vietnam were sometimes harassed in airports. By the late 1960s, the movement had grown large enough to bring 500,000 marchers to Washington in November 1969. Then, on May 4, 1970, at Kent State University, Ohio National Guardsmen fired on peaceful student protestors, killing four. At this point, for the first time, a majority of Americans from all walks of life demanded that the war be brought to an end. The 1960s antiwar movement was unprecedented in scale and power, one whose like had never been seen before or since in the United States.

CIVILIAN PROTESTS THROUGHOUT THE UNITED STATES GREW STEADILY MORE VOCAL, ESPECIALLY AFTER NEWS OF THE MY LAI MASSACRE WAS REVEALED.
Getty Images

20

THE SOVIET-AFGHAN WAR

1979–1989

The Soviet Union's entry into Afghanistan and subsequent defeat by Afghan mujahideen fighters helped bring about the dissolution of the USSR and the rise of Islamic fundamentalism.

Combatants

- Soviet Union
- Afghan mujahideen fighters

Theater of War

Afghanistan

Casualties

Soviet Union: 13,000 military dead, 400,000 wounded
Afghanistan mujahideen: Unknown number of military dead. Up to 1 million civilians dead from military action, starvation, disease, and exposure

Major Figures

SOVIET UNION AND AFGHAN ALLIES
President Nur Muhammad Taraki, assassinated by **Deputy Prime Minister Hafizullah Amin,** who was then assassinated by invading Soviet forces
Deputy Prime Minister Barbrak Kamal, who replaced Amin to become the Soviet puppet president
General Boris Gromov, commander of the Soviet 40th Army

AFGHANISTAN AND ALLIES
Ahmad Shah Massoud, who commanded mujahideen forces in the Panjshir Valley and was the most successful mujahideen leader
President Ronald Reagan, who signed NSDD-166, giving expanded aid to mujahideen **Jalaluddin Haqqani,** heroic leader of the Islamic fighters at the Zhawar cave complex
Osama bin Laden, the Saudi who brought foreign fighters to aid of the mujahideen

Soon after one Cold War superpower was humbled in Vietnam (see "The Vietnam War," p. 366), the other would fight a similarly disastrous and self-defeating war. The Soviet Union's invasion of Afghanistan on December 27, 1979, was an attempt to set up a pro-Soviet buffer state between itself and Pakistan, as well as to frustrate efforts of the United States to gain inroads in Afghanistan. More than 100,000 troops of the USSR's 40th Army attacked and took control of the country's major population centers. But they had not counted on the fierce resistance of the Afghan mujahideen (tribal Muslim fighters). Supported by billions of dollars in aid from the United States and other countries, the mujahideen fought a stubborn guerilla war that lasted a decade, ultimately forcing the Soviet Union to withdraw. The USSR's defeat hastened the dissolution of the Soviet Union and sowed the seeds for the rise of Islamic fundamentalism that would eventually result in Taliban rule in Afghanistan and Osama bin Laden's attacks on the United States.

1979:

September: Deputy Prime Minister Hafizullah Amin seizes power and kills President Nur Muhammad Taraki.

December: Russian forces capture Kabul and kill Amin; Barbrak Kamal declared the new president.

. . . .

1980:

January: The United Nations General Assembly condemns the Soviet invasion.

February: The Soviet offensives against the mujahideen begin with a sweep of the Kunar Valley in the northwest part of the country.

April: The Soviets sweep in the Panjshir Valley in north-central Afghanistan.

June: The Soviets launch an offensive in the Ghazni Valley in the east-central part of the country.

November: The Soviets launch an offensive in the Kunar Valley. The Soviets sweep in the Wardak Province in central Afghanistan.

. . . .

1981:

April: The Soviets launch an offensive in the Panjshir Valley.

July: The Soviets sweep through the Sarobi Valley east of Kabul.

August: The Soviets launch more attacks in the Panjshir Valley.

December: The Soviets launch an offensive in Nangahar in eastern Afghanistan.

. . . .

1982:

January: Heavy fighting in the Herat Province and the city of Herat in western Afghanistan wages into the summer with the mujahideen holding their own against Soviet forces.

February: Fierce fighting occurs in the city of Kandahar, which is the second largest urban center in Afghanistan.

May: The Soviets conduct another major sweep through the Panjshir Valley.

November: The Soviets launch an offensive in the Laghman Valley in eastern Afghanistan.

. . . .

1983:

January: The Soviets launch an offensive in the Lowgar Valley near Kabul.

August: The Soviets sweep in the Paktia Province in southeast Afghanistan.

November: The Soviets launch an offensive in the Shomali Plains near Kabul.

. . . .

1984:

April: The largest Soviet offensive of the war begins in the Panjshir Valley, as well as the Andarab and Alishang valleys. Heavy fighting rages through July.

July: There's a renewed Soviet offensive in the Lowgar and Shomali valleys.

December: The Soviets sweep the Kunar Valley.

. . . .

1985:

March: President Ronald Reagan signs the secret National Security Directive 166, expanding a covert war against the Soviets in Afghanistan.

June: The mujahideen, led by Ahmad Shah Massoud, capture the Soviet garrison at Pechgur. The Soviets launch a new offensive in the Panjshir Valley in retaliation.

August–September: One of the largest Soviet offensives of the war relieves the Soviet garrison besieged at Khost.

. . . .

1986:

April: A Soviet offensive captures the mujahideen base of Zhawar, near the Pakistan border, after a major battle, but it withdraws after a few days.

August: There's a renewed Soviet sweep of the Lowgar valley.

October: Six Soviet regiments are withdrawn from Afghanistan.

. . . .

1987:

May–June: The Soviet campaign is launched in Arghandab, a district in the Kandahar Province.

July: The Soviet garrison at Kalafghan in northeast Afghanistan is destroyed.

November–January: General Boris Gromov launches Operation Magistral to relieve the troops in Khost. The operation is a success, but when the Soviets leave, the mujahideen besiege Khost again.

. . . .

1988:

April: The Geneva Accords are signed, calling for the Soviets' withdrawal from Afghanistan.

October: Half of Soviet forces are withdrawn.

. . . .

1989:

February: The last Soviet troops leave Afghanistan.

. . . .

"THE BLEEDING WOUND"

The remote and mountainous country of Afghanistan has been a battleground for great powers ever since the nineteenth century, when Great Britain and Russia, which had clashed in the Crimean War (see "The Crimean War," p. 100), fought over which country would control western Asia. The British waged two wars in Afghanistan (1839–1842 and 1879–1880) that were in large part provoked by Russia's attempt to dominate the country, which would threaten the British presence in India.

In both cases, Britain was able to pacify Afghanistan, but only at great cost and with the realization that Afghan's legendary Muslim tribal fighters were never completely quelled. Eventually, through an Anglo-Russian agreement in 1905, Afghanistan became a buffer state between Russia and Great Britain's India, with Great Britain controlling its affairs. Finally, in 1919, Afghanistan won its full independence.

However, it is perhaps only natural, as Afghani historian M. Hassan Kakar wrote, that "seeing their country… sandwiched between two 'infidel' giants, the Afghans became xenophobic, inward-looking, and jealously guarded their independence."

A century after the last Anglo-Afghan War, Afghan suspicions of foreigners continued to be borne out. In the 1970s, the Soviet Union, which had aided Afghanistan financially and with military training during the 1950s, became concerned about the growing United States' influence in Pakistan, Afghanistan's neighbor to the southeast, with whom it shared many ethnic and tribal similarities. The Russian government was concerned that its access to the Persian Gulf—and the world's oil—might be impeded by an Afghanistan too overtly friendly to the United States, as Pakistan had become.

The Soviet Union therefore sought an opportunity to exert greater control over Afghanistan and found it in a civil war that had begun within the ranks of the People's Democratic Party of Afghanistan (PDPA). In September 1979, the hard-liners of the party led by Deputy Prime Minister Hafizullah Amin seized power and killed President Nur Muhammad Taraki. The Russians didn't trust Amin. Some of them even thought he was a Central Intelligence Agency (CIA) agent, although no proof exists of this.

By mid-December, the Soviet Union had decided to invade Afghanistan to protect its interests there. Soviet units had been infiltrating the country for some time, many in civilian clothes or wearing the uniform of the Afghan army. On the evening of Thursday, December 27, 1979, the USSR attacked Kabul. Seven-hundred KGB agents dressed in Afghan army uniforms seized the presidential palace and assassinated Amin. The Russians then installed former Deputy Prime Minister Barbrak Kamal as Afghan president.

Soviet troops of the 40th Army then spread out and took control of major population centers and supply routes in the country, intending to leave the fighting against the mujahideen guerillas to the Soviet-trained Afghan army. But the mujahideens didn't make it easy. Due in large part to decisions made by the administrations of U.S. presidents Jimmy Carter and Ronald Reagan to stem the Russian tide in Afghanistan, the CIA began to aid the mujahideen, eventually spending more than $10 billion to equip and train them to fight the Russians. The result was a powerful and

who, along with other militant Islamists, would form the terrorist group al-Qaeda in Afghanistan in 1988 (see "Osama in Afghanistan," p. 391).

In 1986, the Soviets realized that they had placed themselves in a quagmire. Soviet Premier Mikhail Gorbachev called Afghanistan "a bleeding wound" and needed to find a way to exit

Mujahideen fighters quickly became expert at firing the shoulder-held Stinger anti-aircraft missiles provided to them by the United States, knocking out hundreds of Soviet helicopters.

intractable insurgency that harried the Russians with hit-and-run attacks. Mujahideen fighters quickly became expert at firing the shoulder-held Stinger anti-aircraft missiles (see "Stung by Stingers," p. 390) provided to them by the United States, knocking out hundreds of Soviet helicopters.

By 1985, U.S. aid had reached its peak, and the war had turned even more brutal. Russian tactics changed, with their special forces (*spetsnaz*) attacking villages that had first been bombarded by plane or artillery. Most Afghan men of fighting age had fled to the mountains, and the Soviet goal was to destroy the homes of the Afghan people and create refugees. A third of the 15 million people who lived in Afghanistan at the time were forced to flee to Pakistan and Iran, creating a huge refugee population.

As the war continued, Islamic fighters from Arab countries began to join the mujahideen. These included Osama bin Laden, a Saudi millionaire

the country. Under the auspices of the United Nations, Russia signed the Geneva Accords in the spring of 1988, effectively ending Russian participation in the war. The last Soviet soldier left the country in February 1989.

However, a civil war continued within Afghanistan between competing moderate and fundamentalist Muslim groups. The war was ultimately won by the fundamentalist Taliban, which was supported by Osama bin Laden. Bin Laden's assassination of the United States–backed moderate Afghan military leader Ahmad Shah Massoud (see "Commanders," p. 386) came two days before his attacks on the United States on September 11, 2001, which precipitated the U.S. invasion of Afghanistan in November of that year.

THE CAVES OF ZHAWAR

Mikhail Gorbachev was elected general secretary of the Communist Party on March 11, 1985, shortly after the death of Konstantin Chernenko. One of his first orders of business that spring was the Afghanistan war—specifically, the fact that the Soviets had suffered thousands of casualties and were being outfought by the mujahideen fighters whom many Soviet officials called "bandits," albeit bandits well-armed by the U.S. Central Intelligence Agency (CIA).

After studying the matter, Gorbachev reached a conclusion. The Soviet army and its Afghan allies, the solders of the Democratic Republic of Afghanistan (DRA), had exactly one year to destroy the resistance of the Muslim tribespeople. If they were not successful, Gorbachev would try to bring about an end to the war through diplomatic channels, in which case the Soviet army would be handed the worst defeat of its history. In June, the Soviets launched a major new offensive against the forces of Ahmad Shah Massoud in the Panjshir Valley (see "Commanders," p. 386). That August, another massive offensive, the largest of the war to date and led by new 40th Army commander Boris Gromov (see "Commanders," p. 387), attacked and temporarily relieved the besieged Soviet and DRA garrison at Khost, near the border with Pakistan.

But neither of these offensives was successful enough to satisfy Mikhail Gorbachev. The Soviets decided that the next and last target for a major offensive, because Gorbachev's deadline was running out, would be the extraordinary mujahideen cave complex at Zhawar.

The New Face of the War

After initial losses to the guerillas when the war began, the Soviets had learned a much better, albeit cruel and inhumane, way of fighting them (see "Killing the Fish," p. 392). Attacking villages after the Islamic fighters had left, the Soviets targeted civilian populations and turned the rural towns and farms into wastelands, forcing the population to flee into refugee camps in Pakistan. That way, they would no longer be there to supply the mujahideen.

As a result of this, the mujahideen were forced to establish a series of supply depots and transfer bases within Afghanistan, much as a conventional army would. From these bases, supplies and rested fighters would make their way through the country to engage the Soviets. The new Soviet strategy then became one of attacking these bases, which were fortified and defended, in hopes of destroying the vital communications and supply links of the rebels.

One of the most important, and extraordinary, of these bases lay at Zhawar, in the rugged eastern Afghanistan province of Paktia, just 4,000 yards (3.6 km) from the Pakistan border. Zhawar lay in a remote canyon squeezed between two mountain peaks, the entrance to which faced southeast, toward Pakistan. It had originally been a mujahideen training base, but it had expanded into a supply and troop transfer base. The mujahideen had used bulldozers and explosives to carve eleven huge tunnels deep into the side of the canyon, some of them reaching back almost a quarter of a mile (400 m) into the rock. The tunnels actually contained a hotel (with overstuffed furniture), a mosque with brick facing, a hospital, a garage, an arms depot, a communications center, and a huge kitchen. It was all guarded by the 500-man-strong mujahideen "Zhawar Regiment," which had two tanks, several howitzers, and anti-aircraft defenses.

All in all, it was a formidable target, but an important one. If the Soviets and DRA could destroy Zhawar, their victory might be enough to forestall Gorbachev's peace overtures.

The First Attack

In September 1985, the DRA, backed by Soviet airpower, launched its first attack. Its intelligence units had told it that most of the mujahideen commanders, including Jalaluddin Haqqani, who was the highest ranking mujahideen commander, were away on a pilgrimage to the holy city of Mecca. It was a perfect time for an assault. The DRA, supported by air strikes and artillery bombardments, were able to take the mujahideen stronghold of Bori, a few miles from Zhawar, and then attack west toward the stronghold itself. But the mujahideen reacted swiftly after their initial disarray, sending in a blocking force of eighty fighters. In a furious night battle, the DRA lost two armored personnel carriers and four trucks and retreated.

However, the next day, prodded on by their Soviet advisors, the DRA returned, fighting their way across the mountains toward Zhawar until they were stalled by a twenty-man mujahideen blocking force in a pass called Manay Kandow.

The mujahideen, though few in number, were in a virtually unassailable position, firing machine guns and AK-47s from a cave beneath a huge slab of rock high on the side of a mountain. Every time the DRA would call in artillery, the mujahideen would simply retreat farther into the cave until the bombardment was over, then leap to their firing positions to beat back the advancing DRA infantry.

For ten days, the DRA tried to breech the pass, and for ten days the small force of mujahideen held them off. Finally, the Soviets called in heavy airstrikes that repeatedly battered the slab of rock that protected the mujahideen cave. Finally, the rock began to shift and shake over the heads of the Islamic fighters. Fearful that it had become unstable under the relentless pounding, the mujahideen retreated. The DRA took the high ground, advancing to within a mile (1.6 km) of the cave complexes at Zhawar. But now, in a last-ditch effort, mujahideen fighters brought up their two T-55 tanks and opened up on the DRA, who did not realize that the enemy had heavy weapons. Caught in the open, they were forced to retreat, hearing the victory shouts of the mujahideen ringing in their ears.

The Last Attack

What was to be the second and last attack on the fierce caves of Zhawar began in late February 1986. It involved a much larger force—12,000 DRA troops, with 2,000 Soviet advisors. By this time, Gorbachev had already announced that he was about to perform a phased withdrawal of half of the Soviet troops from Afghanistan, but the Russian commanders in the field still hoped that a

THIS MAP OF
AFGHANISTAN SHOWS
THE ELEVATION OF
THE COUNTRY, WHERE
RUGGED MOUNTAIN
HEIGHT MADE FIGHT-
ING AGAINST THE
MUJAHIDEEN SO MUCH
MORE DIFFICULT.

Dorling Kindersley

successful attack on Zhawar, performed mainly by the DRA, would change Gorbachev's attitude toward the army's plans in Afghanistan.

The chief element of this new attack on the mujahideen stronghold was an airborne assault by DRA commandos to be made on Dawri Gar mountain, which rose high above the eastern side of the Zhawar canyon. In the meantime, other DRA elements would attack through the passes. But the air assault was made at night and in the darkness confusion reigned. The commandos actually landed 5 miles (8 km) inside Pakistan, where they were surrounded by Pakistani troops and, after a firefight, taken prisoner.

Despite this, the rest of the DRA forces attacked in helicopter assault groups and were met at their landing zones by mujahideen fighters, who shot them as they piled out of their helicopters. At the same time, however, Soviet fighter-bombers made runs at the Zhawar caves, first flying southeast into Pakistan and then turning to make their attacks at the southern-facing entrances to the tunnels. Laser-guided precision bombs exploded into the caves, killing dozens of mujahideen or sealing them up inside the rubble. At one point, mujahideen commander Jalaluddin Haqqani was trapped in a cave with his fighters, but he managed to dig his way out.

A Hollow Victory

A major battle was now raging, with firestorms seen over the mountains and explosions echoing down the mountain passes. The mujahideen held steady, even as the Soviet artillery began to bombard their positions inside Zhawar twenty-four hours a day. Airplanes dropped illumination flares at night, and the eerie light they cast threw long shadows over the mountain walls as Soviet bombers arrived to drop their payloads on the cave complex.

The DRA commanders, having failed in their assault, left for Kabul on April 17 as the Russians in charge stepped in and ordered an all-out assault. The Islamic fighters, weakened by days of bombardment, their morale suffering because of a persistent, though untrue, rumor that Jalaluddin Haqqani was dead, finally evacuated Zhawar and fled to the nearby mountains.

When DRA and Soviet army units arrived in the cave complex, they were astounded. They discovered forty-one separate man-made caves, walls faced with brick, and entrances protected by iron doors. The hospital had ultrasound equipment manufactured in the United States. There was a library filled with books, in numerous languages. And none of it had been disturbed by the near continuous bombing. Ironically enough, after fighting so hard to get into Zhawar, the Soviets and DRA stayed for only five hours. They were cut off from their supply lines, and they knew that, even then, the mujahideen would be mounting a counterattack. Quickly booby-trapping and mining the cave complexes, the Soviet commander gave the order to retreat. The troops moved west with the sound of explosions ringing in their ears.

These explosions, however, had not come close to destroying Zhawar. The mujahideen arrived shortly after the Soviets left and immediately began restoring the place. It was up and running within four months. The battle to prove that the Soviets could be victorious in Afghanistan represented the final nail on their coffin. Gorbachev now had firsthand proof that the ineptitude of the DRA could simply not be overcome. After the war, Zhawar would continue to be used by Islamic fighters. Osama bin Laden's presence there in 1998 would cause U.S. President Bill Clinton to launch cruise missiles at the cave complex in an attempt to kill him and al-Qaeda members training there.

Clinton was unsuccessful, of course. Zhawar is far too tough a nut for a few cruise missiles to crack. And to this day, Osama bin Laden is thought to be hiding out in a similar complex, probably not far away from the caves of Zhawar.

AHMAD SHAH MASSOUD: "THE LION OF PANJSHIR"

Ahmad Shah Massoud was born in Afghanistan's Panjshir Valley in 1953—fittingly so, because it was in the Panjshir that he became famous fighting the Soviet invaders of his beloved country. Massoud was the son of a police commander and was relatively well-to-do and well-educated. He spoke several languages. He went to Kabul University in the early 1970s. There, like any number of young Muslims of the time, he became enamored of traditional Islamic tenets and joined a group of Islamic students that opposed the increasing Russian presence in Afghanistan.

In 1975, Massoud took part in a revolt against Mohammed Daoud Khan, a communist-backed politician who had taken over the country in a coup in 1972. The revolt failed, but Massoud gained valuable experience, especially in organizing guerilla cells in his home province of Panjshir. After this period, Massoud allied himself with the less radical Islamic groups that would battle the

communist PDPA party in a civil war in the late 1970s. When the Russians invaded, Massoud already commanded a small army.

As the war progressed, Massoud was the commander favored more and more by the Americans. While he was a devout Muslim, he was more tolerant of other beliefs than other, more radical jihadists. Massoud began to score important victories against the Russians fighting in the Panjshir against repeated offensives and bombing so heavy that, at one point, Massoud evacuated all 30,000 inhabitants of the valley.

Even though Massoud was nicknamed the "Lion of Panjshir" and became a national hero, he was controversial among other mujahideen leaders. In 1983, after fighting the Russians for three years, he arranged a cease-fire with them. While this was temporary, other Afghan rebel leaders saw it as Massoud caving in to Soviet pressure. But by the end of the war, Massoud led an army some 13,000 strong. After the Soviet withdrawal, he continued a civil war against other Islamic groups fighting for control of Afghanistan. But, without U.S. aid, which had been withdrawn at the end of the Soviet-Afghan War, Massoud lost to the Taliban fighters who by the early 1990s controlled 90 percent of the country.

Massoud then became leader of a group called the Northern Alliance, a loose confederation of fighters that continued to oppose the Taliban regime and radical Islamic terrorists like Osama bin Laden. On September 9, 2001, two days before

AHMAD SHAH MASSOUD WAS ONE OF THE PREMIER FIGHTERS OF THE SOVIET-AFGHAN WAR AND LED THE RESISTANCE AGAINST THE TALIBAN UNTIL HE WAS MURDERED BY AL-QAEDA ASSASSINS TWO DAYS BEFORE THE SEPTEMBER 11, 2001, ATTACKS ON THE UNITED STATES.

the 9/11 attacks on the United States, Massoud allowed himself to be interviewed by two journalists who were almost certainly al-Qaeda agents. One of them detonated a bomb in a video camera, killing the assassin and Massoud.

Most intelligence agencies believe that Osama bin Laden had Massoud killed to curry favor with the Taliban, who would soon need to protect bin Laden from the wrath of the Americans.

GENERAL BORIS GROMOV: HERO OF THE SOVIET UNION

Boris Gromov, commander of the Soviet 40th Army in Afghanistan from 1987 through 1989, personified everything that the USSR hoped to be—but had a hard time attaining—during its long and difficult war in that country. He was smart, brave, aggressive, resourceful, and even humane, but in the end it was not enough.

Gromov was born in Russia in 1943, attended cadet and general officer's school, and then was fast-tracked to the prestigious Frunze Military Academy in Moscow. Gromov rose rapidly in the Soviet army, earning the rank of general by the beginning of the Soviet-Afghan War.

In whatever sector of the county Gromov was fighting in, he managed to push back the mujahideen. The operation for which he was best known was Operation Magistral, in November 1987, in which he sought to lift the siege on the fortress of Khost, which had been cut off by the mujahideen for years. Coordinating attacks by artillery, air force bombers, and paratroopers, who jumped from planes ahead of the advancing Russian column, Gromov was able to take a strategic mountain pass away from the mujahideen and finally enter Khost on December 30.

Gromov was named a "hero of the Soviet Union" for his efforts at Khost. Gromov also became the last Soviet soldier out of Afghanistan on February 15, 1989, when he stopped his tank halfway across the Freedom Bridge, climbed out, and walked the rest of the way into Uzbekistan.

The Soviet Soldier

When the soldiers of the Soviet 40th Army invaded Afghanistan in 1980, they came behind the special KGB units that had first infiltrated the country and killed President Hafizullah Amin (see "Chronicle," p. 380). Most of them did not know really why they were there at all. One soldier recalled that he had been told that they needed to seize Afghanistan or the Americans would. Another soldier said that he thought he was bringing peace to Afghanistan and performing humanitarian acts such as bringing food and medical aid.

The reality for the average Soviet soldier, who was in his early twenties, was quite different. Soviet troops found themselves in an alien landscape, with high mountains and hot deserts, fighting an elusive enemy who hid easily among the civilian population. A quick mujahideen attack would kill several Russian infantrymen, but by the time the Russians could return fire, the mujahideen would melt away.

As happened with U.S. forces in Vietnam (see "The Vietnam War," p. 362), Soviet soldiers often took out their anger on innocents, killing and maiming women and children. But with some children working for the guerilla fighters, it was hard to know who was innocent and who was not. As the war continued, the morale of Soviet forces eroded, and drunkenness and drug use among units became endemic. Thirteen thousand Russians soldiers were killed in Afghanistan, but more than 400,000 were wounded. Soldiers returned home to bring the story of Soviet failures to a society that was largely shielded from them by a censored press.

However, the Soviet special forces units, known as spetsnaz, did not suffer from such a morale problem. These elite squads struck deeply into the heart of enemy country, carried in for quick raids on fast-moving helicopters. They used high technology, such as mobile communications intercept vehicles, to find convoys of arms coming over the border from Pakistan, then swooped down to attack them. Sometimes the spetsnaz wore the flowing robes of the mujahideen, which was a tactic that allowed them to get close enough to the real rebels to attack. Other times, they paid Afghans to dress as Islamic rebels, and then attack Islamic militants. Carrying sniper rifles, silenced 9mm. pistols, hand grenades, and knives, the spetsnaz were the most feared soldiers that the Russians employed in Afghanistan.

GENERAL BORIS GROMOV, AT LEFT, WAS THE LAST SOVIET SOLDIER OUT OF AFGHANISTAN WHEN THE SOVIETS LEFT IN 1989.

The Mujahideen

The word mujahideen means "holy warrior" or "one who fights in a jihad" and has been in use in Arabic for hundreds of years. It only entered the English language with the rise to prominence of the loosely knit associations of Afghan guerillas that fought against the Russian invasion. Although one term is used to refer to such fighters in general, there were a complex array of these groups, which were generally defined by how radically Islamic they were, as opposed to those who supported a more moderate form of Islam.

At the beginning of the war, stunned by the swiftness and brutality of the Russian invasion, Afghan opposition forces that had previously been fighting at cross-purposes in the civil war banded together to combat the Russians, calling themselves the Islamic Unity of Afghanistan Mujahideen. This group soon split apart into different fighting bands, such as the National Islamic Front of Afghanistan, the Islamic Revolutionary Movement, the Islamic Society (home to Ahmad Shah Massoud—see "Commanders," p. 386), and others that would sometimes unite to fight the Russians and other times fight local and separate wars against the invaders. All, however, were funded by the U.S. Central Intelligence Agency (CIA). The general rate for a local or district mujahideen commander was $25,000 a month, while a really prominent warlord could bring in $75,000–$100,000 a month, which

he used to pay his fighters and support their families, who might be in refugee camps.

Before CIA funds began flowing, many mujahideen groups were so short of weapons that they were forced to ambush Russian soldiers to acquire their arms. Other times, weapons were stolen or purchased through bribes from the armories of the Soviet-backed Afghan army. In the first twenty months of the war, 25,000 AK-47 automatic rifles disappeared from the Afghan army in this way. The mujahideen put these, and the more advanced weapons they later received from the United States, Saudi Arabia, and Egypt, to good use as they waged a tenacious war against the Soviet Union.

MUJAHIDEEN FIGHTERS WAGED A TENACIOUS WAR AGAINST THE SOVIET UNION, USING WEAPONS FROM THE UNITED STATES, SAUDI ARABIA, EGYPT, AND SOVIET SOLDIERS THEY AMBUSHED AND KILLED.

Stung by Stingers

If there is an iconic image from the Soviet-Afghan War, it is that of a mujahideen fighter standing on a rocky landscape with a Stinger missile launcher balanced on his shoulder, ready to take aim at a Soviet attack helicopter. The image is striking because of its combination of elements that personify the war itself—the traditional dress of the tribesman and the sleek modernity of the Stinger.

The Stinger, developed in the United States in the early 1980s, is a shoulder-held, battery-powered, surface-to-air missile that is light, relatively easy to use, and, most important, heat-seeking. It hones in on the heat signatures given off by helicopter and airplane exhaust. Therefore, one only has to aim it in the general direction of the target, and it will generally find it and kill it.

Because the Soviet Army in Afghanistan relied heavily on helicopters for troop transport, supporting fire, and evacuation of wounded, the Stinger was the perfect weapon for the mujahideen to employ.

William Casey, director of the CIA, gave the word in the mid-1980s that hundreds of Stingers should be sent to Afghanistan. CIA operatives trained Muslim fighters in the use of the weapon, which proved enormously effective. The Stinger could knock helicopters out of the air at 12,000 feet (3.6 km), which kept the Soviets from flying the low-level attack missions they had become accustomed to. The mujahideen were so successful in their attacks that Soviet field commanders became reluctant to call in medevac helicopters for the wounded, which further demoralized Soviet troops.

After the war, as documented in Steve Coll's book *Ghost Wars*, the CIA became concerned that Stingers in the hands of terrorists could be used to shoot down passenger liners. They then put in place what Coll calls "a kind of post-Cold War cash rebate system," buying back missiles from Afghan warlords to the tune of $80,000 to $150,000 apiece.

A MUJAHIDEEN FIGHTER WITH A SHOULDER-HELD STINGER MISSILE, ONE OF HUNDREDS PROVIDED BY THE CIA.
Getty Images

NSDD-166: A Powerful Escalation

The famous National Security Decision Directive 166 would change the way the war was fought in Afghanistan and ultimately defeat the Soviets.

By the spring of 1985, the CIA had been giving substantial aid to Afghan guerillas, but many in U.S. President Ronald Reagan's ideologically conservative administration wanted to do more, seeing Afghanistan as the perfect place to fight a proxy battle against the Soviets. In late February, the National Security Council—made up of representatives from the Pentagon, State Department, and CIA—met to consider giving the CIA legal authority to step up its aid to the mujahideen by giving them weapons such as Stinger missiles.

Working together, they produced document NSDD-166, entitled "Expanded U.S. Aid to Afghan Guerillas," that outlined a powerful escalation of the secret U.S. war against the Soviets. It was not just Stinger missiles, either. NSDD-166 called for providing the mujahideen with satellite information as to the disposition of Soviet troops and also for the assassination of Soviet generals stationed in Afghanistan with long-range rifles provided to the guerillas by the United States. It also endorsed using car bombs in population centers to kill Russian soldiers.

President Ronald Reagan signed the highly classified NSDD-166 on March 16, 1985, although it was without the specifics (the car bombs and assassinations) mentioned above. It merely said that it was now time to defeat the Soviets "by all means possible." To protect the president, the sixteen-page addendum containing these recommendations was instead signed by his national security advisor, Robert McFarlane.

Osama in Afghanistan: The Making of a Terrorist

It is an irony not lost on the U.S. government that the man who was the driving force behind the worst attack on United States soil since Pearl Harbor was trained and funded by the CIA.

However, Osama bin Laden, privately wealthy, would have targeted the United States anyway. Born in 1957 in Saudi Arabia to a wealthy and fecund construction business owner (bin Laden's father would ultimately sire fifty children), bin Laden grew up with close ties to the powerful Saudi royal family. Like many young men of his social milieu, bin Laden was well educated at a prestigious college, although in Jedda. He did not attend the private British boarding schools many of his brothers and sisters were enrolled at.

In 1979, when the Soviet-Afghan War began, bin Laden was a college sophomore with a $1 million annual

IN 1984, OSAMA BIN LADEN FOUNDED THE MAKTAB AL-KHADAMAT, A CONDUIT THROUGH WHICH HE FUNNELED RADICAL ISLAMIC FIGHTERS TO BATTLE THE SOVIETS IN AFGHANISTAN.

(continued on p. 392)

allowance and a teacher named Abdullah Azzam, a radical Palestinian who would later go on to found the terrorist organization Hamas. Through Azzam and other radicalized Islamic teachers, bin Laden learned about jihad—a holy war to restore Islam to its original purity and drive the West out of Islamic holy places.

Bin Laden probably first went to Pakistan in 1980, where he met with members of the mujahideen fighting the Soviets, a group that were at the time supported strongly by the Saudi government. Bin Laden's efforts to aid the mujahideen included providing money to build roads through the rugged countryside, roads that would be used to deliver weapons to the Islamic fighters.

By 1984, bin Laden—by all accounts a highly intelligent and personable young man—had founded an organization called Maktab al-Khadamat (MAK), which means "Office of Services." MAK was a conduit through which bin Laden funneled the increasing number of radical Islamic fighters who sought to battle the Soviets in Afghanistan. However, this was not enough for bin Laden. Soon he joined Arab forces fighting the Russians in eastern Afghanistan, just across the border from Pakistan. In April 1987, bin Laden and fifty Arab volunteer fighters held off 200 Soviet attackers for four or five days in a mountain stronghold. Osama bin Laden, despite the need for insulin shots to treat diabetes, fought bravely. His exploits

were reported to the public by two Arab journalists who were present.

Bin Laden was now seen in the eyes of the Arab world as a jihadist of the first order. He split with MAK, whose service and supply role he considered too tame, and he helped found al-Qaeda (see "The Birth of al-Qaeda," p. 392). After clashing with Saudi authorities over the increased presence of Americans in the country, bin Laden had his citizenship revoked by Saudis and was expelled from the country. He returned to Kabul, from where he and al-Qaeda launched numerous terrorist attacks against the United States, culminating in the attacks of September 11, 2001.

The Birth of al-Qaeda

Al-Qaeda—which means "the Base"—was founded by bin Laden from Maktab al-Khadamat (MAK), the "Office of Services" that he had created to fund and supply Arab militants arriving in Afghanistan to fight jihad against the Soviets. But with bin Laden moving more and more to direct military attacks against the Russians, al-Qaeda referred simply to the training camps he and his cohorts set up along the Pakistan border to train the Arab militants who would fight in Afghanistan.

But as Soviet withdrawal from the war neared, many militants, including bin Laden, wanted to expand their

war to include Islamic jihads in other countries, which would eventually include Egypt, Sudan, Saudi Arabia, Bosnia, and the United States. In August 1988, bin Laden met with representatives of these groups inside Afghanistan to plan such activities. Most intelligence agencies consider this the founding of al-Qaeda. After this meeting, bin Laden's former teacher, Abdullah Azzam, parted ways with him. (Azzam was assassinated by car bomb the next year; his killers have never been found.) Bin Laden, angered by the deployment of U.S. troops in Saudi Arabia during the first Gulf War, went on to plan operations

against the country he referred to as "the head of the snake."

After the attacks against the United States on September 11, 2001, and the United States' subsequent invasion of Afghanistan, where most al-Qaeda leaders had taken refuge along with bin Laden, al-Qaeda's operations were somewhat hampered. But the United States' National Intelligence Council considers the group "the most serious terrorist threat to the United States." It is still quite active, even though its main leaders have either been killed, captured, or are in hiding, along with bin Laden, probably in remote areas of Pakistan.

"Killing the Fish"

Much more so than in Vietnam, the war in Afghanistan was a war without major set-piece battles, a war that was carried by the Soviets all over the countryside through numerous operations or "sweeps," in which Soviet regular army and elite spetsnaz forces, supported by bombers, artillery, and attack helicopters, assaulted Afghan villages.

However, in most cases, the mujahideen fighters had already melted into the hills, unwilling to meet the Soviet juggernaut head-on. This was fine with the Soviets, who were following the time-honored anti-guerilla strategy of destroying the bases of irregular forces to rob them of support. The Soviets called this "killing the fish by draining off the water." After the Soviet army surrounded a village, it was bombarded indiscriminately, killing the elderly men, women, and children who remained. Villagers who did not die were forced to flee.

The Soviets then made sure that they would not return by poisoning their wells and placing booby traps that were designed to maim rather than kill. In particular, they used the "butterfly mine," a small, winged, anti-personnel weapon that was camouflaged the color of earth and dropped into fields by airplane. With these villages virtual wastelands, the villagers became refugees.

The Soviets also proclaimed that any large gathering of Afghan citizens—whether clan gatherings, weddings, or funerals—would be considered hostile demonstrations against the Soviet presence and treated as such. In September 1980, hundreds of men, women, and children were celebrating a wedding in the village of Ganjabad, near the Iranian border, when Soviet helicopters attacked without warning, killing 150 civilians with rocket and machine gun fire. This sort of attack was repeated numerous times during the war, until the previously convivial Afghans learned to keep their public gatherings private.

A final weapon of terror the Soviets used against the mujahideen was the abduction of Afghan women. Soldiers flying in helicopters would scan for women working in the fields in the absence of their men, land, and take the women captive. Russian soldiers in the city of Kabul would also steal young women. The object was rape, although sometimes the women were killed, as well. The women who returned home were often considered dishonored for life by their families.

21

THE IRAN-IRAQ WAR

1980–1988

In a costly and ultimately futile war, Iran and Iraq battled
each other for eight long years over territory and religion.

Combatants

- Iran
- Iraq

Theater of War

Iran, Iraq, and the Persian Gulf

Casualties

Iran: Estimated 500,000 military dead
Iraq: Estimated 500,000 military dead
Unknown number of civilian casualties on both sides

Major Figures

IRAN

Ayatollah Khomeini, Islamic cleric who led the Iranian people during the war
Mohammed Reza Shah Pahlavi, ousted in January 1979 by revolutionaries loyal to Khomeini
Abdol Hassan Bani-Sadr, first president of the Islamic republic of Iran
Ali Khamenei, who replaced Bani-Sadr as Iranian president
Ali Akbar Hashemi Rafsanjani, Khomeini's chief military leader

IRAQ

Saddam Hussein, president and dictator of Iraq who launched the first attack against Iran
Tariq Aziz, deputy premier of Iraq and close aide to Hussein, who survived an assassination attempt by an Iranian terror group
General Maher Abdul al-Rashid, who convinced Hussein to go on the offensive against the Iranians

T he Iran-Iraq War of 1980 to 1988 was the longest conventional war of the twentieth century and the largest war between two Third World countries. Although it began as a clash over a disputed waterway, it was more importantly a battle between the secular Arab nationalism of Saddam Hussein's Iraq and the feverish religious ideology of the Iranian regime of the Ayatollah Khomeini. More than a million Iraqi and Iranian soldiers died, plus an unknown number of civilians. Iraq used chemical weapons while Iran's *mullahs* ("holy men") sent children as young as nine in human wave attacks through Iraqi minefields. Because both countries were rich in oil, the superpowers of the Soviet Union and the United States played important roles. The war ended inconclusively, except for the fact that Hussein, having enhanced his position in the Arab world, would soon feel emboldened to attack another of his Arab neighbors: Kuwait, in 1990.

1979:

February: The Ayatollah Khomeini and his radical Islamic regime take power.

July: Saddam Hussein becomes president of Iraq.

November: Iranian students occupy the U.S. Embassy in Tehran and seize U.S. diplomats as hostages.

1980:

January: Abdol Hassan Bani-Sadr is elected president of Iran.

April: An unsuccessful attempt is made by an Iranian terror group to assassinate Tariq Aziz, deputy premier of Iraq and close aide to Hussein.

September: Hussein says the 1975 treaty with Iran is null and void and claims full sovereignty over the Shatt al-Arab waterway. Iraq invades Iran along a 400-mile (645 km) front. The fighting continues for three months.

1981:

January: An attempted Iranian counter-offensive is unsuccessful.

September–November: An Iranian counteroffensive pushes Iraqi forces back and retakes the important city of Abadan, near the Shatt al-Arab.

1982:

January: Kurdish guerillas sabotage an oil pipeline to Turkey. The Kurdish insurgency in Iran grows worse.

April: Hussein says he will withdraw from Iran if that will end the war. The Iranian government replies with major offensive against Iraqi positions in southern Iran.

May: The Iraqis are driven back to the international border.

June: Hussein evacuates forces in Iran, but still holds some Iranian territory.

July: An Iranian offensive inside Iraq to capture the city of Basra fails.

August: Iraq blockades Iran's Kharg Island oil refinery, stating that any vessel entering for oil is open to attack.

1983:

April: An Iranian offensive aimed at cutting the Basra–Baghdad highway fails. Iraq fires surface-to-surface missiles at the Iranian city of Dezful.

October: Iran mounts an offensive against Iraqi Kurdistan in the north, but makes only limited gains.

1984:

February: More Iraq missiles are fired at Dezful, as well as Iranian shelling of Basra and other Iraqi cities. Both parties then agree to a UN–sponsored mediation not to attack civilian targets. Tehran mounts a major offensive through the Haur al Hawizeh marshes, which straddle the Iran-Iraq border.

March: Iran gains control of Iraq's oil-rich Majoon Islands in the Haur al Hawizeh marshes.

April: Iraq planes begin attacking tankers in the Persian Gulf heading for Iranian oil facilities.

May: Iran uses planes and naval vessels to attack ships carrying Iraqi oil.

June: The UN Security Council condemns all Iranian and Iraqi attacks on international shipping. Both parties ignore the condemnation.

1985:

March: Iraq bombs several major Iranian cities, attacking civilian population centers. Iran replies by firing surface-to-surface missiles at Baghdad and launching a major offensive in the Haur al Hawizeh marshes, but Iraq pushes it back.

July: Iran says it will stop and search all ships in the Persian Gulf suspected of carrying supplies to Iraq and ends up inspecting some 300 ships.

September: Iran receives more than 500 surface-to-air missiles from the United States in a secret arms-for-hostages deal made by the Reagan Administration.

1986:

January: The United States secretly provides 4,000 more missiles to Iran.

February: Iran mounts three offensives against Iraq. One of them captures the strategic Fao Peninsula in southeastern Iraq, adjoining the Persian Gulf.

March: Iraqi attacks to regain the Fao Peninsula fail. The UN condemns Iraq for its use of chemical weapons in the counterattack.

May: Successful Iraqi airstrikes against oil refineries near Tehran force Iran to begin importing refined oil.

August: Iraq launches a long-range air raid on Iran's oil terminal on Sirri Island, in the Persian Gulf.

1987:

January: Iran launches a large offensive aimed at Basra, but the Iraqis drive it back with heavy casualties.

July: Because of attacks on Kuwaiti tankers by Iranian gunboats, the U.S. Navy begins escorting them in the Persian Gulf.

September: U.S. helicopters capture an Iranian mine-laying vessel.

October: The U.S. Navy sinks three Iranian patrol boats.

1988:

February: Iraq launches Scud missiles against Tehran and other major Iranian population centers in attacks that last through March, kill 2,000 people, and cause hundreds of thousands of Iranians to flee cities.

March: Attacking the rebellious Kurdish town of Halabja, Iraqi forces use gas, killing thousands of civilians.

April: Iraq recaptures the Fao Peninsula.

June: Iraq drives the Iranian army from the Manjoon Islands.

July: The USS *Vincennes* shoots down an Iranian passenger airliner, mistaking it for a fighter jet. Iraq pushes into Iranian territory for the first time in six years. Iran accepts a cease-fire by agreeing to UN Resolution 598.

August: The cease-fire begins.

"THE MAIN OBSTACLE TO THE ADVANCE OF ISLAM"

The main point of difference between Iran and Iraq before the bloody war that erupted between them in 1980 was control of the 120-mile-long (200 km) Shatt al-Arab ("the Arab River") waterway, the eastern portion of which separates the two countries. The Shatt al-Arab, into which the Tigris and Euphrates rivers flow, is nearly landlocked Iraq's sole outlet to the Persian Gulf.

Disputes over control of the Shatt al-Arab were settled in 1937 by dividing the waterway. However, in the early 1970s, Iranian Mohammed Reza Shah Pahlavi, attempting to make Iran the preeminent power in the region, claimed ownership over the entire Shatt al-Arab and began to charge tolls on Iraqi vessels using it. Iran exacerbated the situation through its military and monetary support of Kurdish rebels in northern Iraq. The two states nearly came to war before a new boundary line through the Shatt was drawn in a 1975 agreement. However, circumstances changed drastically in January 1979 after the Iranian Revolution ousted the shah and put into power the fundamentalist Muslim cleric Ayatollah Khomeini and his mullah, or holy men.

The revolution not only transformed Iran but sought to spread the radical Islam of Khomeini—what he called "the Government of Allah"—throughout the world and, especially to the neighboring state of Iraq, headed by the dictator Saddam Hussein. Although Sunni Muslims ruled Iraq, the majority religious group were Shi'ite, like the Iranians, and the new regime in Tehran began urging them to rebel against Hussein.

In April 1980, the Iranian terrorist group Al Dawa ("The Call") attempted and failed to assassinate Iraqi Deputy Prime Minister Tariq Aziz, but it was successful in killing numerous other high level Iraqi officials. Khomeini's government also began giving assistance to the Kurds, resuming the policy of the shah of Iran, which had been halted after the 1975 agreement.

Faced with all of these attempts to undermine his government, particularly the stirring up of the Kurds and Shi'ite majority, Hussein decided his only course was war. In September 1980, he launched a surprise aircraft attack across the Iranian border, striking Iranian air fields in an unsuccessful attempt to destroy the Iranian air force on the ground, while his mechanized infantry divisions pushed into Iran along a 400-mile-long (645 km) front extending from Iranian Kurdistan in the north to the Shatt al-Arab in the south. Hussein's goal was to cut off the Shatt from the rest of Iran and make it an Iraqi possession.

Khomeini's forces were caught off guard by this attack, with many of them stationed in the more central and eastern portions of the country. This may in fact have saved them from immediate defeat, because, purged of the shah's officers, the Iranian army was poorly led and trained. But Hussein's invasion galvanized the Iranian people, and hundreds of thousands, led by Pasdaran

(Revolutionary Guard) units, rallied to the calls of the mullahs to fight a holy war against Iraq.

The superior Iranian air force had not been destroyed and was able to fight back effectively, severely damaging Iraq's Abadan oil refinery, the largest in the world. In the meantime, its resistance on the ground stiffened, and the Iraqi advance was halted after nine days. Hussein called for a cease-fire, having reached his goal of controlling the Shatt al-Arab, but Khomeini refused to consider a cease-fire while Iraq occupied Iranian territory. The rainy season arrived, and the war settled into a stalemate, with each side entrenched and making sporadic attacks on the other, a pattern that would continue for the next eight years.

In 1982, Iran launched a fierce counterattack that drove the Iraqis back to the international border. Hussein, anxious to avoid more war, asked for a cease-fire, but still Iran refused. Iranian forces tried but failed to capture the important Iraqi port city of Basra.

Hussein began fighting a defensive war. Repeated Iranian attacks, often using preteen and teenage children, would push the Iraqis back temporarily, but the Iraqis would regroup as soon as the Iranian attacks wore themselves out and retake their positions. The longer the war went on, the more it began to favor the Iraqis.

The Iranians, having taken U.S. Embassy personnel hostage during the initial stages of the revolution, were now cut off from their traditional source of military aid, the United States. The United States supplied Iraq with military intelligence and significant credits for food and other supply purchases (by 1987, up to $1 billion worth of credit). Further, as the Iranian air force

mounted more attacks against Iraqi oilfields, the United States began patrolling the Persian Gulf to keep Iranian naval activity at a minimum and protect crucial oil supplies coming out of the region. (However, the administration of Ronald Reagan was also caught up in an embarrassing "arms for hostage" deal, in which it supplied Iran with surface-to-air missiles in return for the release of hostages held by terrorists in Lebanon.) And by 1982, the Soviet Union signed a $2 billion arms deal with Iraq, supplying Hussein's regime with tanks, sophisticated jet fighters and bombers, and surface-to-surface missiles.

Beginning in 1986, Iran launched a series of desperate last offensives, hoping to crack the Iraqi lines. But the Iraqis, who had now begun to use chemical weapons repulsed these. In the meantime, Iraq rained down Scud missiles on major Iranian cities, such as Tehran, causing panic and disillusionment among the Iranian citizenry.

In the spring of 1988, Hussein's generals convinced him it was time to go on the offensive once again. With an improved army and plenty of tanks and armored vehicles supplied by the Americans, the Iraqis attacked on a massive scale up and down their eastern front. Khomeini became convinced that peace was necessary. He agreed to United Nations Resolution 598, calling for an immediate cease-fire, which became effective in August 1988.

In the end, the outcome of this long and bloody struggle was relatively inconclusive. Iraq now controlled the Shatt al-Arab, but Hussein would voluntarily return part of the waterway to Iran in 1990, in return for a promise not to attack him when he invaded Kuwait.

THE IRAQI SPRING OFFENSIVE: 1988

In the winter of 1988, Iraqi forces dug in along their defensive lines just inside the eastern part of the country and looked expectantly to the west. Soon, as they had for the past five years, the Iranians would launch another all-out offensive, to break the Iraqi lines. It was a war of attrition, a series of "final" offensives meant to wear down the Iraqis.

But as winter turned into early spring, no major offensive occurred. For, while the long and vicious war had been costly to both sides, it had begun to cost the Iranians more than they could bear. While the Baathist ruling party of Saddam Hussein had been able to call up 1.6 million soldiers, the Ayatollah's army numbered only about 1.25 million men. Many men had become casualties or had gone into hiding to avoid the draft, and the Iranians were conscripting those as young as eleven and as old as fifty. In fact, the rigid and highly segregated Islamic society had recently begun to call up women to fight.

Then there was the edge Baghdad had in terms of war machines. Amply resupplied by the Soviets and foreign loans, Baghdad had 4,500 tanks to put into action, as compared to only 1,570 for Iran, and those were beginning to run out of spare parts. Armored vehicles gathered dust in supply dumps, unable to be repaired. In consequence of all this, Khomeini and his chief commander, Ali Akbar Hashemi Rafsanjani, decided to pursue a series of limited attacks against Iraqi lines. But doing this was like waving a red flag in front of a bull.

The General and the President

Hussein had fought a cautious, defensive war ever since the Iranians drove the Iraqis back out of their territory in 1982. But Hussein's generals, especially Maher Abdul al-Rashid, were convinced that Iraqi forces would be victorious if they went over to the offensive. Al-Rashid did something unheard of. He went to Baghdad and argued with the notoriously touchy Hussein, saying that the Iraqis must attack the Iranians as soon as possible if the war was to be won. Backing him up, a ring of group-level Iraqi commanders told Hussein that if anything happened to al-Rashid, they would refuse to continue fighting the war.

When al-Rashid arrived in Baghdad, a smiling Hussein stood publicly and decorated him for heroism, and then listened gruffly to what he had to say in private. Hussein listened because he was concerned that the international community, whose support Iraq held rather tentatively, would turn on him if he made massive attacks against the Iranians. Hussein gave his approval, and al-Rashid went back to the front lines to prepare. (However, Hussein did not forgive insubordination. Al-Rashid disappeared in 1990, two years after the war ended, and is presumed dead.)

The first stage in the spring offensive of 1988 was a renewal of the war of the cities, beginning on February 29. The Iraqis had developed a new Scud missile, the Al-Hussein, whose range was twice that of former ones and whose accuracy was greatly improved. On the night of February 29–March 1, sixteen of these struck Tehran, causing panic in the population. By April 20, 200 had hit targets in numerous Iranian cities, but mainly Tehran, killing more than 2,000 people. Iran, in turn, had been able to fire only eighty missiles at Baghdad, many of which went astray.

The Fao Peninsula

In response to the renewed missile attacks on Iranian cities, Iranian forces struck into Kurdistan in March and captured the Kurdish town of Halabja. Iraq struck back fiercely using chemical weapons to kill 5,000 people, many of them instantly. The Iranians possessed chemical weapons, although nowhere near as many as the Iraqis, but Ayatollah Khomeini, feeling that the use of them was contrary to Islamic law, forbade them. However, Iranian leaders kept that fact secret, wanting to let Hussein guess whether Iran might unleash them.

But if Hussein was deterred by this possibility, he did not show it. On April 16, Iraq attacked the Fao Peninsula, the strategic peninsula in southeastern Iraq that Iranian forces had captured in 1986. The attack began by the Iraqis sending planes with mustard gas bombs to drop well to the rear of Iranian lines, and then shelling Iranian frontline positions with both artillery shells and shells containing cyanide and nerve gases.

Because Iranian soldiers were not wearing their protective gas masks and clothing in the hot weather, they died by the thousands. Jubilant Iraqi soldiers easily took the Peninsula, setting off huge celebrations back in Baghdad.

The Final Push

On May 25, the Iraqis launched their final offensive, whose goal was to push the Iranians out of Iraqi territory for good. They attacked all along the front lines, beginning with a massive artillery bombardment that combined conventional explosives with nerve and mustard gas.

The Iraqis also used a surface-to-surface cluster missile that had a range of 40 miles (65 km) and exploded in the air 500 feet (152 m) above enemy positions, releasing tiny bomblets that tore into the masses of Iranian soldiers. The heat kept many of the Iranians from wearing protective clothing against chemical weapons. Combined with the cluster bombs, the bombardment caused thousands of deaths and sent the poorly armed and trained Iranian soldiers racing for the rear. Capitalizing on the disarray of the Iranians, the Iraqis attacked the oil-rich Manjoon Islands on June 25. The Iraqi attack was so swift and well coordinated that the Iraqis captured them (and their 7 billion barrels of oil) in a single day.

Iraq had now driven Iran from all its positions in Iraq, except for the land it held with the help of Kurdish rebels in Kurdistan. Hussein now warned Iran that unless it withdrew all its forces from Kurdistan, he would invade Iran. Iran complied, and the borders of the two countries were back to where they were when the war began. Finally, with Iranians fleeing major cities for fear of missile attacks and the Iranian army in retreat, the Ayatollah Khomeini agreed to UN Security Council Resolution 598, calling for a cease-fire.

SADDAM HUSSEIN:
"ONE WHO CONFRONTS"

At the time of the Iran-Iraq War, Saddam Hussein, president of Iraq, was forty-two years old and had made a meteoric rise through the thorny and highly dangerous stratosphere of Iraqi politics. He was born in 1937 to a Sunni clan in Auja, a village near Tikrit, about 100 miles (160 km) from Baghdad. His family was quite poor. Hussein's father died before he was born, and he was raised by his maternal uncle. His mother, seeing (or so she later claimed) great things in the boy, had named him Saddam, which means "one who confronts."

And, indeed, confrontation—not wisdom—was to be a hallmark of Hussein's life. He went to Baghdad at the age of ten to live with his uncle, and there joined the Baath Party, which espoused a pan-Arabism based on economic modernization (rather than Islamic beliefs) and sought to advance Iraq, with its rich oil fields, as a Middle Eastern power. In 1959, Hussein was part of a team of assassins that sought to kill Iraqi Premier Qasim, who had just taken power in a coup of generals. He failed and fled to Egypt, where he studied law at Cairo University, before returning to Iraq after the Baathists took power in 1963. By 1967, he had become secretary of the Baath Party and in 1968 took part in a coup that ousted the current Baathist premier and replaced him with a cousin of Hussein's maternal uncle, Ahmad Hassan Bakr.

Hussein then became vice president of the country, and he soon was considered the real power in Iraq, while the more senior and avuncular Bakr was relegated to the position of figurehead. Darkly handsome, charming, and ruthless, Hussein had a genius for seizing power. He did this by executing opponents (inside the Baath Party or out) while at the same time generously rewarding those close to him, particularly high commanders in the police and the military.

In July 1979, the year before the Iran-Iraq War began, Hussein finally seized ultimate power, by claiming that there was an "anti-state conspiracy" involving almost seventy Baathist military and civilian leaders. He then tried twenty-one of these men in front of a tribunal consisting of six of his closest friends. He had them summarily found guilty and executed, while the rest were imprisoned or exiled. When Bakr protested, he was forced to resign. Thereafter, Hussein purged dissident members of student and trade unions, the rank and file of the army, and the press, and had himself declared president of Iraq.

As president—in reality, a dictator in total control—Hussein created a cult of personality around himself, erecting monuments and emblazoning his face everywhere. But Hussein also pursued his goals of modernization, which included bringing women into more prominent roles in the Iraqi government and building roads, sewage systems, and better schools. At the same time, however, he dealt ruthlessly with anyone who rebelled against him, including the Kurds (see "Chemical Weapons," p. 409). And his instinct to

confront, rather than compromise, was ultimately his downfall. He allowed himself to be provoked into the Iran-Iraq War, from which he emerged with a stronger army, but an economy in ruins and a war debt of some $75 billion.

Hussein's attack on Kuwait, which precipitated the Gulf War of 1990 against a United States–led coalition, in part stemmed from a misguided sense of his own power. And it was this sense of arrogance that led to his confronting the Americans again in 2003 by self-destructively bluffing that he had huge stockpiles of chemical and even nuclear weapons. As his country lay in ruins around him, Hussein was discovered in a hole in the ground near his hometown of Tikrit. Tried and convicted of war crimes that included torturing men, women, and children, Hussein was hanged on December 30, 2006.

AYATOLLAH KHOMEINI:
"THE POISONED CHALICE"

Sayid Ruhollah Musavi Khomeini, who came to power in Iran in February 1979, was an unlikely revolutionary leader. Already seventy-seven years old at the time, he was pious, incorruptible, and strict, an Islamic cleric who had earned the high title of Ayatollah, which means "sign of Allah." He overthrew the pro-western dictatorship of Mohammed Reza Shah Pahlavi, but replaced it with a religious dictatorship, about which he declared, "We will export our revolution to the four corners of the world because our revolution is Islamic, and the struggle will continue until the cry of 'There is no god but Allah, and Mohammed is the messenger of Allah' prevails throughout the world."

Khomeini was born in 1902, the son of the chief cleric of Khomein, a town about 200 miles (321 km) from Tehran. At nineteen, the extremely religious young man joined a seminary and began training to become a cleric with a well-known ayatollah. When that man moved to the town of Qum, a center of Shi'ite worship in Iran, Khomeini followed him. Graduating from his studies in 1925 at the age of twenty-seven, Khomeini established himself as a traditionalist teacher with strict Islamic values who decried the secular, western-leaning government of Mohammed Reza Shah Pahlavi, which began in 1941. By the early 1960s, Khomeini had become an ayatollah and had stepped up his attacks against the Shah, who threw him in jail and eventually deported him to Turkey in 1964.

Ironically enough, Khomeini went the following year to Iraq, where he lived in the Shi'ite town of Najaf and continued his preaching against the shah. By this time he had many followers; when they would come to Iraq to visit Shia shrines, Khomeini would smuggle back taped speeches to be played to the faithful Shi'ites in Iran (who made up 90 percent of the Muslim population there). As the revolutionary movement inside Iran grew, Khomeini became its spiritual leader in exile, the incorruptible figure whom most devout Iranians wanted to replace the shah. And when the Shah was forced to leave the country in January 1979, Khomeini finally returned to take over Iran and received a tumultuous welcome.

Almost immediately, however, there was strife with Iraq. Khomeini fomented this strife because of his belief that the secular, pan-Arabic nationalism of Saddam Hussein was contrary to the goals of Islam. When a goaded Hussein finally attacked in the fall of 1980, Iran was sent reeling, but was able to recover and rally around the central figure of Khomeini, who remained a symbolic pillar of the Iranian state during the long and horrible eight years of the war. But finally, the huge losses and the war of the cities became too much for the Iranian people, as did Iraq's final offensive in the spring of 1988, and Khomeini was forced to agree to a United Nations ceasefire. The by-now eighty-five-year-old Ayatollah was not happy about it, however. In a message to the Iranian people, he said: "Happy are those who

AYATOLLAH KHOMEINI
VOTES IN A NATIONAL
REFERENDUM FOR HIS
ISLAMIC CONSTITU-
TION, WHICH WAS
ADOPTED BY IRAN IN
NOVEMBER OF 1979.

have departed through martyrdom…Unhappy am I that I still survive. Taking this decision is more deadly than drinking from a poisoned chalice."

In the end, Khomeini's dream of spreading his brand of radical Islam to Iran failed, nor was he able to overthrow the Baathist regime of Hussein. At the close of the war, Iran was faced with a massive rebuilding process that necessitated a certain amount of cooperation with foreign powers. Thus more secular, more pragmatic voices in the Iranian government came to be heard, although the clerics wielded, and still wield, power. But Khomeini would not live to see this. He died in June 1989, a year after the end of the war. Two million Iranians attended his funeral.

The Iranian Soldier

Up until 1979, the Iranian army was one of the finest in the region, with sophisticated weapons and well-trained officers. The bulk of military aid to Iran had come from its ally the United States, whose advisors maintained close relationships with Iranian forces, helping them hold field training exercises and providing them with sophisticated computers and weapons systems.

All that changed when the revolutionary forces of the Ayatollah Khomeini swept into power, forcing the Shah into exile in Egypt (where he died in 1980) and capturing and holding U.S. diplomatic hostages. Aid to the Iranian army stopped immediately, while most of the officers trained by the Americans were shot or sent to prison by the mullahs. Thus, when Saddam Hussein attacked, he faced a large army (about 150,000 troops) but an inexperienced one. Khomeini's purges had killed or jailed half of the army's senior officers (from the rank of major to colonel), some 12,000 men. The new army was made up of the Pasdaran, or Revolutionary Guard, along with 100,000 volunteers recruited in the midst of patriotic war fever in Iran after Hussein's invasion.

At first the army was well-equipped with U.S. weapons, but it soon ran out of spare parts. Not only that, but the inexperienced Iranian commanders did not know how to use the computerized weapons systems they had (e.g., they often simply dug tanks into the ground and used them

as artillery pieces) and thus rendered the weaponry almost useless. They preferred, instead, World War I–style massive frontal attacks against entrenched Iraqi positions, sometimes using young boys (see "Boy Soldiers of Iran," p. 406) to clear minefields and act as human shields.

While some Iranian soldiers fought with extreme bravery, they were also hindered by a power struggle between the ideologically motivated Pasdaran and those regular army officers who remained, which resulted in a lack of coordinated command and consistent strategic thinking, as well as supply deficiencies. The two bright spots in the Iranian armed forces were its navy, which

was consistently superior to that of Iraq, and its air force, whose U.S. F-4 Phantom fighter jets and attack helicopters were used with expertise and bravery by Iranian pilots—many of whom had been released from jail by Iranian religious authorities, despite the fact that they were suspected of being loyal to the previous regime, simply because their experience was desperately needed.

IRANIAN SOLDIERS WERE OFTEN BRAVE, BUT, WITH MOST OF THEIR OFFICERS IN JAIL FOR POLITICAL REASONS, WERE POORLY LED AND DIED BY THE THOUSANDS.

Associated Press

The Iraqi Soldier

When Saddam Hussein's forces invaded Iran in September 1980, they numbered about 200,000 and were a more coherent and organized military force than that of the Iranians. But after their initial advances in the first month of the war, they were steadily pushed back by the less-experienced Iranian troops. Part of the reason for this was that many of the Iraqi soldiers, especially the Shi'ites, did not feel any particular loyalty to the Sunni regime of Hussein and sometimes deserted or even turned their guns on their officers.

Another reason, however, was that Hussein, after his initial invasion, decided that he wanted the war to stop before he absorbed more casualties than his people would stand for. Therefore, to the frustration of his generals, he fought a cautious, defensive war and stopped his advance into Iraq too soon. After 1981, the war became one of attrition. If the Iranians had been a more skilled and sophisticated force, they might have destroyed the Iraqi army. As it was, they skillfully stirred up Kurdish rebels in northern Iraq, creating a major headache for Hussein's regime behind his own front lines, while at the same time hammering attack after attack home against the Iraqi army.

However, the Iraqis soon learned—with the help of Soviet advisors—how to create extremely well-constructed defensive positions around major Iranian attack points such as the city of Basra. These deep bunkers, bristling with machine guns and artillery, commanded what were

known as "killing zones." As the Iranian army, Pasdaran, and boy soldiers attacked, the Iraqis blew them away.

Finally, in 1987, Hussein's generals convinced him to go on the offensive again. The Iraqi army, now vastly improved, with a massive influx of Soviet war materiel—as well as the use of mustard gas and sarin nerve gas—made rapid gains against the Iranians, helping precipitate the end of the war.

MANY OF THE IRAQI SHI'ITE SOLDIERS FELT NO LOYALTY TO SADDAM HUSSEIN AND HIS SUNNI REGIME, SOMETIMES DESERTING OR TURNING GUNS ON THEIR OFFICERS.

The Sunni-Shi'ite Split

One of the things that perpetually worried Hussein was the way in which Ayatollah Khomeini and his mullahs attempted to stir up the Shi'ite population within Iraq, which was ruled by the Sunnis, who represented a far smaller proportion of the citizenry.

The division of the Muslim faithful into these two religious sects occurred in the seventh century AD, not long after Mohammed's death. Mohammed had named as his first successor, or caliph, Abu Bakr, who died and was replaced by a man named Umar ibn al-Khattab, who was murdered in 644. After his death yet another caliph, named

Uthman ibn Affan, was picked. But he, too, was murdered, and in 656, a man named Ali ibn Abu Talib replaced him.

Ali was a controversial choice. He was a first cousin of Mohammed's and there were those who said that Mohammed had actually picked him as the first caliph, but that the position had been stolen from him by other of Mohammed's former companions. But there was also a sizeable group of Muslims who thought Ali was a fraud and had even had something to do with the murder of Uthman. One of these was the governor of Damascus, a man named Mu'awiyah, cousin of Uthman. His forces and

those of Ali battled inconclusively, but shortly thereafter Ali was murdered, and Mu'awiyah took over his position as caliph.

This factional infighting created the division that exists to this day. Supporters of Ali and his descendants became known as the "party of Ali," or *shi'a Ali,* or Shia, while those who supported the succession of the first four caliphs were termed as having followed the *sunnah,* or "path followed by Mohammed." Centuries later, the Sunnis and Shi'ites were still deeply divided, which was something Khomeini sought to take advantage of when undermining Hussein's regime.

The War of the Cities: Missiles Raining from the Sky

In the spring of 1985, Iraq bombed a steel factory in one Iranian town and an unfinished nuclear plant in another. These were legitimate military targets, which, however, involved Iranian civilian deaths. In retaliation, the Iranians shelled Basra with their heavy artillery. Iraq, in turn bombed seven Iranian towns and cities, without even making a pretext of seeking military targets in them. When Iran retaliated by bombing a suburb of Baghdad, the so-called "war of the cities" was on.

Iraq began high altitude, indiscriminate bombing of Tehran twice a day, eventually boasting of

more than 180 missions against the Iranian capital. Their purpose, said a high-ranking Iraqi officer, was to "bring the Iranian people into the front lines of the war" and get them to rebel against their leaders. Iraq responded to this by firing Scud missiles—tactical ballistic missiles developed by the Soviet Union and widely exported—at Baghdad. But Iraq had the edge in surface-to-air missiles due to being directly supplied by the Soviet Union. From 1985 to 1988, Iraq fired 361 Scuds at Tehran. In contrast, Iran could muster only 60 Scuds launched against Baghdad.

In 1988, intensifying its war against Iranian cities, Iraq launched 191 Al-Hussein Scuds, a new variety with longer range and accuracy, at Tehran. These caused relatively little damage, although 2,000 people were killed, but they had a powerful psychological effect on the Tehran population, because the Al-Husseins were capable of carrying chemical warheads. Nearly 30 percent of the population of Tehran fled the city, having lost faith in their leaders' ability to protect them. It was this defection, as much as anything else, that caused Khomeini and his clerics to accept a truce.

Boy Soldiers of Iran: "They Chant Allahu Akbar"

The Iraq-Iran War was one of the most vicious of modern times. Chemical agents were used to kill (mainly Iranian) soldiers, civilian populations were targeted for missile attacks, and huge electrodes were placed in channels leading into the Shatt al-Arab waterway, to electrocute fleeing Iranian soldiers who might dive into the waterway. But one of the more horrifying sights of the war was Iran's use of the troops who became known as "boy soldiers."

These youngsters could range in age from nine years old to twelve. They came from devout Shi'ite families in Iran, mainly poor, rural ones. Some of the boys were volunteered by their families, while others had run away to join the Pasdaran themselves, swayed by patriotic fervor. Some, however, especially in the latter part of the war, were coerced and had to be roped together as they went to the front. The boy soldiers wore red headbands of martyrdom, white cloth pinned to their uniforms (which was meant to symbolize their shrouds), and tiny plastic keys around their necks, which signified the keys to the kingdom of heaven, which their martyrdom would attain for them.

The boy soldiers were poorly armed, if at all. Their main job was to move ahead of the regular army or Pasdaran to act as human minefield

sweepers. One Iraqi officer watched them, almost in awe. "They come on by the hundreds, often walking straight across the minefields, triggering them with their feet, as they are supposed to do. They chant 'Allahu Akbar' [God is great!] and they keep coming and we keep shooting, sweeping our fifty millimeter machine guns around like sickles."

After almost every major battle in the Iran-Iraq War, the battlefield was littered with the bodies of these children, thousands of whom died in the war.

BOY SOLDIERS BEING LED INTO BATTLE BY MULLAHS. THE BOYS ARE WEARING THE SYMBOLIC WHITE ROBES OF MARTYRDOM.

Getty Images

The Tanker War

Aside from the War of the Cities, another distinct area of fighting in the Iran-Iraq War was called the "tanker war," which Hussein launched in 1984. Previous Iraqi attacks had taken place against Iran's civilian shipping, but these new attacks, carried out with missiles and jet fighters, were aimed at something else entirely: the international community. Hussein wanted to draw western powers such as the United States directly into the war in the hopes that they might intervene and break the stalemate that existed in the ground war, which was currently grinding on into its fourth year.

Hussein also hoped that stepping up his attacks on shipping might cause Iran to do something rash that would force the United States into intervening. So, beginning in February 1984, Iraq attacked tankers of any nationality sailing in or out of the Iranian oil facilities at Kharg Island. Iraq began to average four such attacks per month. But the Iranian government understood what Iraq was trying to do and refused to be provoked, limiting its naval attacks to those against ships from Kuwait and Saudi Arabia, allies of Iraq.

However, Iraq's sustained attacks against shipping cut Iranian oil exports by 50 percent, doing serious economic damage to the country and slowing the flow of oil to the rest of the world. The UN stepped in and got both sides to agree to a moratorium on attacks against shipping, but Iraq shortly began ignoring the agreement and continued its attacks against shipping bound for Iran. When, in return, Tehran stepped up its attacks against Kuwaiti oil tankers, the Kuwaitis approached the United States for protection. The United States responded by "reflagging" eleven Kuwaiti tankers as American and escorting them through the gulf. The Soviet Union, too, began to protect Kuwaiti shipping, with the result that by the end of 1987, two major navies and any number of smaller ones were patrolling a very crowded theater of operations in the gulf. Hussein had gotten his wish: Iran and its navy were being contained.

A TANKER ON FIRE IN THE ORMUZ STRAITS AFTER ATTACK BY THE IRANIANS. PICTURES LIKE THESE, SEEN AROUND THE WORLD, DEEPLY CONCERNED WESTERN OIL INTERESTS.

Image Works

Chemical Weapons: The Horror of Halabja

Almost as a matter of course, Iraqis used chemical weapons—chiefly mustard gas, but also cyanide, and sarin and tabun nerve gases. These were delivered in any number of ways—shot in artillery shells, dropped in 250- and 500-kilogram bombs, and placed in the warheads of Scud missiles. The Iraqis even installed spray tanks on helicopters that flew low over the enemy, spraying them as if they were insects. In fact, one prominent Iraqi general said as much: "If you gave me a pesticide to throw at these swarms of insects to make them breathe and become exterminated, I would use it."

Chemical weapons, which could kill in anywhere from a few seconds to three hours, were especially useful in breaking up the large, lightly armed concentrations of Pasdaran fighters and militia that attempted to swarm the Iraqi lines. But the Iraqis also used chemical weapons for another purpose: the destruction of the Kurds. The Kurds' battle for independence for their northern Iraqi region of Kurdistan had long plagued the Iraqi government, especially because many Kurdish fighters had allied themselves with the Iranians. As the war turned in Iraqi favor in 1987 and 1988, Hussein decided to settle the Kurdish problem once and for all. In May 1987, twenty Kurdish villages were attacked by

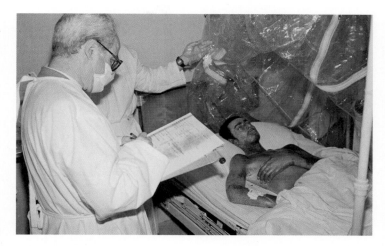

helicopters spraying mustard and nerve gases, killing one hundred people and injuring many more.

But the worst attack came against the Kurdish town of Halabja, population about 70,000, 15 miles (24 km) inside Iraq. In early March 1988, Iranian forces had attacked and seized Halabja. On the early evening of March 16, Iraqi airplanes appeared in the sky overhead and began dropping chemical bombs that caused clouds of white, black, and yellow "smoke" to rise 150 feet (46 m) into the air. This smoke was in fact the chemical agents—certainly mustard gas, but also probably sarin and tabun nerve agents, as well as cyanide gas. Some people dropped dead immediately; others spewed green vomit and lived

for a few minutes. Five thousand people died in a single day—men, women, and children—while 10,000 were injured, some of them disabled for life.

Hussein blamed Iran for the attack; even the United States believed this, for a time. But eventually the truth came out, and the attack on Halabja was widely branded as an act of genocide.

AN IRANIAN SOLDIER, ABOVE, RECOVERS FROM A CHEMICAL ATTACK DURING THE WAR. A CHEMICAL ATTACK IN THE KURD- ISH TOWN OF HALABJA IN 1988 KILLLED 5,000 PEOPLE IN ONE DAY.
Associated Press

ACKNOWLEDGMENTS

Once again, I'd like to thank Fair Winds Press publisher Will Kiester for his help and encouragement on *The War Chronicles*, Vols. 1 & 2. Additional thanks should go to Cara Connors, whose able editing enhanced the book considerably. Jennifer Bright Reich's careful copyedits sharpened the focus of the final draft, while the photos and artwork gathered by Anne Burns make a great accompaniment to the text.

Thanks also to Tiffany Hill, Daria Perreault, Rosalind Wanke, and Megan Cooney.

1

THE FRENCH REVOLUTIONARY WARS

Furet, Francois and Richet, Denis. *The French Revolution.* New York: The MacMillan Company, 1965.

Hibbert, Christopher. *The Days of the French Revolution.* New York: William Morrow & Co., 1980.

Schama, Simon. *Citizens: A Chronicle of the French Revolution.* New York: Alfred A. Knopf, 1989.

2

THE NAPOLEONIC WARS

Rothenberg, Gunther E. *The Napoleonic Wars.* New York: Smithsonian Books, 1999.

Schom, Alan. *Napoleon Bonaparte.* New York: HarperCollins, 1997.

Schom, Alan. *One Hundred Days: Napoleon's Road to Waterloo.* New York: Atheneum, 1992.

3

THE WAR OF GREEK INDEPENDENCE

Brewer, David. *The Greek War of Independence.* Woodstock, New York: Overlook Press, 2001.

4

THE MEXICAN-AMERICAN WAR

Chidsey, Donald Barr. *The War with Mexico.* New York: Crown Publishers, 1968.

Johannsen, Robert W. *To the Halls of Montezuma: The Mexican War in the American Imagination.* New York; Oxford University Press, 1985.

Nichols, Edward J. *Zach Taylor's Little Army.* New York: Doubleday & Co., 1963.

5

THE TAIPING REBELLION

Pelissier, Roger. *The Awakening of China, 1793–1949.* New York: G.P. Putnan's Sons, 1963.

Spence, Jonathan D. *God's Chinese Son: The Taiping Heavenly Kingdom of Hong Xiuquan.* New York: W.W. Norton & Co., 1996.

6

THE CRIMEAN WAR

Royle, Trevor. *Crimea: The Great Crimean War: 1854–1856.* New York: Palgrave MacMillan, 2000.

Woodham-Smith, Cecil. *The Reason Why.* New York: McGraw-Hill, Inc., 1954.

7

THE U.S. CIVIL WAR

Linderman, Gerald F. *Embattled Courage: The Experience of Combat in the American Civil War.* New York: The Free Press, 1988.

McPherson, James M. *Battle Cry of Freedom: The Civil War Era.* New York: Oxford University Press, 1988.

Mitchell, Lt. Col. Joseph B. *Decisive Battles of the Civil War.* New York: Fawcett Books, 1955.

8

THE FRANCO-PRUSSIAN WAR

Howard, Michael. *The Franco-Prussian War: The German Invasion of France, 1870–1871.* London: Routledge, 2001

Wawro, Geoffrey. *The Franco-Prussian War: The German Conquest of France in 1870–1871.* New York: Cambridge University Press, 2003.

9

THE ANGLO-ZULU WAR

Greaves, Adrian. *Crossing the Buffalo: The Zulu War of 1879.* London: Cassell, 2006.

Morris, Donald R. *The Washing of the Spears: The Rise and Fall of the Zulu Nation.* New York: Touchstone Books, 1965.

10

THE SPANISH-AMERICAN WAR

O'Toole, G.J.A. *The Spanish War: An American Epic-1898.* New York: W.W. Norton & Co., 1984.

Trask, David R. *The War with Spain in 1898.* Lincoln, Nebraska: University of Nebraska Press, 1996.

11

THE RUSSO-JAPANESE WAR

Connaughton, R.M. *The War of the Rising Sun and the Tumbling Bear: A Military History of the Russo-Japanese War, 1904–5.* London: Routledge Press, 1988.

Jukes, Geoffrey. *The Russo-Japanese War 1904–1905.* Oxford, England: Osprey Publishing, 2002.

12

THE MEXICAN REVOLUTION

McLynn, Frank. *Villa and Zapata: A History of the Mexican Revolution.* New York: Carroll & Graf, 2000.

13
WORLD WAR I

Fussell, Paul. *The Great War and Modern Memory*. New York: Oxford University Press, 1975.

Hart, B.H. Liddell. *The Real War: 1914–1918*. Boston: Little, Brown and Company, 1930.

Keegan, John. *The First World War*. New York: Alfred A. Knopf, 1999.

Kiester, Edwin, Jr. *An Incomplete History of World War I*. Sydney, Australia: Murdoch Books, 2007.

Vaughn, Edwin Campion. *Some Desperate Glory: The World War I Diary of a British Officer, 1917*. New York: Henry Holt & Co., 1981.

14
THE RUSSIAN CIVIL WAR

Crankshaw, Edward. *The Shadow of the Winter Palace: Russia's Drift to Revolution 1825–1917*. New York: Viking Press, 1976.

Lincoln, W. Bruce. *Red Victory: A History of the Russian Civil War*. New York: Simon & Schuster, 1989.

Trotsky, Leon. *Stalin*. New York: Stein & Day, 1967.

Volkogonov, Dmitri. *Trotsky: The Eternal Revolutionary*. New York: The Free Press, 1996.

15
THE CHINESE CIVIL WAR

Pelissier, Roger. *The Awakening of China, 1793–1949*. New York: G.P. Putnan's Sons, 1963.

Spence, Jonathan D. *The Gate of Heavenly Peace: The Chinese and Their Revolution, 1895–1980*. New York: The Viking Press, 1981.

16
THE SPANISH CIVIL WAR

Jackson, Gabriel. *A Concise History of the Spanish Civil War*. New York: John Day Company, 1974.

Thomas, Hugh. *The Spanish Civil War*. New York: Harper & Row, 1977.

17
WORLD WAR II

Ambrose, Stephen E. *D-Day: June 6, 1944: The Climactic Battle of World War II*. New York: Simon & Schuster, 1994.

Keegan, John. *The Second World War*. New York: Penguin Book, 1989.

Toland, John. *Infamy: Pearl Harbor and Its Aftermath*. New York: Doubleday & Co., 1982.

18
THE ARAB-ISRAELI WAR

Karsh, Efraim. *The Arab–Israeli Conflict: The Palestine War, 1948*. London: Osprey Publishing, 2002.

Morris, Benny. *1948: The First Arab-Israeli War*. New Haven: Yale University Press, 2008.

19
THE VIETNAM WAR

Karnow, Stanley. *Vietnam: A History*. New York: The Viking Press, 1983.

Langguth, A.G. *Our Vietnam: The War 1954–1975*. New York: Simon & Schuster, 2000.

20
THE SOVIET-AFGHAN WAR

Kakar, M. Hassan. *Afghanistan: The Soviet Invasion and the Afghan Response, 1979–1982*. Berkeley, California: University of California Press, 1995.

21
THE IRAN-IRAQ WAR

Hiro, Dilip. *The Longest War: The Iran-Iraq Military Conflict*. New York: Routledge Press, 1991.

Karsh, Efraim. *The Iran-Iraq War: 1980–1988*. London: Osprey Publishing, 2002.

GENERAL REFERENCE

Black, Jeremy. *The Seventy Great Battles in History*. London: Thames & Hudson. Ltd., 2005.

Cowley, Robert, and Geoffrey Parker. *The Reader's Companion to Military History*. Boston: Houghton, Mifflin & Co., 1995.

Cummins, Joseph. *Great Rivals in History*. Sydney: Pier 9, 2008.

Cummins, Joseph. *History's Greatest Hits*. Sydney: Murdoch Books, 2007.

Cummins, Joseph. *Turn Around and Run like Hell*. Sydney: Murdoch Books, 2007.

Daniels, Patricia S., and Stephen G. Hyslop. *The National Geographic Almanac of World History*. Washington, D.C., 2003.

Kohn, George Childs. *Dictionary of Wars, Third Edition*. New York: Checkmark Books, 2007.